POCKET
CROSSWORD
DICTIONARY

POCKET
CROSSWORD
DICTIONARY

B. J. Holmes

A & C Black • London

www.acblack.com

Crossword Clues and Extracts

Throughout this book we have used parts of clues and clues to illustrate a particular style of puzzle and how to solve the clue. It would have been difficult and confusing to include the source of each clue in the main layout of the book. Instead, we have credited the sources below. The clues we have used have come from a range of newspapers and magazines – we are indebted to the crossword setters for making the puzzles interesting, challenging and enjoyable to solve!

The publications used as sources include: *Daily Express, Daily Mail, Daily Mirror, The Daily Record, Daily Telegraph, Financial Times, The Guardian, Independent, Independent on Sunday, The Observer, Radio Times, The Sun, Sunday Telegraph, Sunday Times, The Times*

First published in Great Britain 2001
Reprinted 2003
This second edition published 2005

A & C Black Publishers Ltd
37 Soho Square, London W1D 3QZ

A CIP record for this book is available from the British Library.

ISBN-10: 0-7136-7503-9
ISBN-13: 978-0-7136-7503-0

1 3 5 7 9 8 6 4 2

A & C Black uses paper produced with elemental chlorine-free pulp, harvested from managed sustainable forests.

Text processed and typeset by A & C Black
Printed in Great Britain by Clays Ltd, St Ives plc

INTRODUCTION

Crosswords are a waste of time. There's always something more useful to do. Like pursuing a career, raising kids, wallpapering, walking the dog, writing a novel. At least, that's the way I saw it for many years.

That is until I found myself flat on my back with a chronic illness. In that situation even the delights of TV, radio and records began to pall and, in frustration, I turned my attention to the cryptic puzzle in my daily paper. Up till then I had never given the wretched, impenetrable thing more than a glance. At first I had little success, managing maybe a couple of answers if I was lucky before throwing it aside in frustration. However, in time and using assorted reference books, I eventually completed my first grid – to my surprise and immense satisfaction. From then I was hooked, and was soon sampling all the broadsheet and tabloid papers – buying, begging, borrowing or stealing.

And, in time, I was picking up prizes from national newspapers such as the *Financial Times* and the *Independent*.

Looking back, I can see that my interest in cryptics was kick-started when it dawned on me that there was some regularity in the tricks that compilers got up to. As I couldn't keep all their little dodges in my head I began writing them down, solely for my own reference. In time the notes became a thick file by the side of my bed.

Although I use assorted dictionaries, thesauruses, reference books and so on – it was when I realised my own file had become not only my **first** means of attack when facing a virgin grid, but also my **most-used** source, it occurred to me there was a book in it that could be useful to others. And you hold the results in your hand.

BACKGROUND

The story goes that the first crossword appeared in an American newspaper (the Sunday edition of the *New York World*) at the beginning of the last century. Since then crossword puzzles have spread to most cultures and have taken a variety of forms – from the original straightforward definitional type requiring factual answers to the more abstruse cryptic kind characterised by the use of convoluted clues, using puns and the playing of language games (*see next page*). Today's grids can be square, rectangular or odd-shaped and can have either black squares or thick lines to separate the answers.

WHAT'S THE POINT?

For a start cryptic crosswords must be enjoyed by a large number of the population because virtually every British newspaper, national and local, carries one. And there have been many famous addicts, notably film star Richard Burton, who we are told, had to have daily access to British cryptics no matter to what part of the world his job or wealth had taken him.

Moreover, there is mounting medical opinion that they are downright healthy! Regular mental exercise is just as important as daily physical exercise and several prominent doctors have extolled the virtues of the crossword habit in staving off the ravages of age on the brain.

THE NATURE OF CRYPTICS

Crosswords can be classified broadly into two groups. Firstly there is what is called the definitional type. They are easily recognized because their clues are usually short and their solution calls for knowledge rather than language manipulation. They appear under various titles such as Quickie, Coffee-break and Concise. They have two main sub-categories: the general knowledge type and the specialised, the latter appearing in magazines and drawing on the specialist knowledge of their particular readership from pop music and golf to train-spotting.

Then there is the cryptic which has less the nature of a knowledge test and more the character of a game – a naked battle of wits between the compiler and the punter. And, like a game, it has its rules and conventions. An understanding of these is necessary and that is one of the purposes of this book.

CRYPTICS – CRACKING THE CODE

In order to solve cryptics it is useful to look at the exercise from the point of view of the compiler. The setter of a crossword is actually on a par with a conjuror. In both activities the name of the game is deception. Deception has two forms. Firstly, **disguise**. A conjuror will disguise the trappings of his trade: what seems like a solid box, can be hollow. Similarly, through the clever use of words a crossword compiler will draw a veil over his actual intent. For example,

        'Serve held by the Italian superstar' (4)

embodies a couple of disguises. 'Serve' is dressed up in the clue as a **noun**, whereas the underlying intention is that it should be equated with the **verb** 'to DO' (i.e. as a charlady). On the other hand, 'Italian' is disguised as an adjective relating to 'superstar', yet its role lies in the **two** words 'the

Italian' (i.e. Italian for 'the') which is IL. Finally, DO 'held by' IL yields the solution IDOL, a term which can be applied to a superstar.

Conversely a noun can be dressed up as a verb to throw you off the scent. Take

```
'Hide article held by Goneril's father' (7)
```

Sitting at the front 'Hide' looks for all the world like a verb and you probably wouldn't realise it isn't until you start putting the thing together from the clue's other parts. Goneril's father is LEAR – don't worry if you didn't know this, it's the kind of thing we have in our glossary. Then, LEAR goes around THE (article) to produce the answer LEATHER, a noun synonymous with hide.

The second form of deception is **misdirection**. The astute observer knows that whenever a conjuror says 'Look, nothing in my hand', the real business is likely to be taking place somewhere else, like the magician's other hand. And so too, with the crossword. One must fight the temptation to look where the compiler is directing our attention.

Example:

```
'Set meal' (2,6)
```

This is a familiar phrase describing restaurant fare. Once we are on our guard that we might be being misdirected, the **last** thing we should think of is a restaurant! So, what else can the word 'set' imply? A radio set? A television set? Bells might ring at that point, leading to the notion that, in that context, a 'set meal' is in fact a TV DINNER.

Remember, the crossword clue has to be synonymous with the solution (or at least be strongly suggestive of the answer) so the compiler will be very wily in using the only tools available to the craft: **disguise** or **misdirection**, usually both at the same time.

EQUIPMENT FOR THE JOB

The beginner really needs to have a handful of reference books handy. Now, there is a feeling amongst many solvers that the use of books, etc. is in some way cheating. I have no such qualms. Of course, there will be expert solvers who will pride themselves on finishing a broadsheet cryptic with no use of aids, but these lucky people must be a minority, an enviable elite. My attitude has always been that the compiler has many books and aids at his disposal so why should the common-or-garden solver (like me and most of the readers of this book) be at a disadvantage?

So you need:

1 a standard **dictionary**, the bigger and the more up to date the better. Obviously you can only use a dictionary if you already know what you are looking for, so the main function of your dictionary will be for confirming spelling. However it can also be used for checking the existence of a word you've never heard of.

As an example, the word 'barathea' may mean nothing to you – as it meant nothing to me when I tackled the following clue:

```
'Arab returns holding two articles made from a
            fine woollen cloth' (7)
```

However, 'Arab returns' gives you BARA, while THE and A are 'two articles'. Putting the articles into BARA leads you to BAR-A-THE-A. Never heard of it, we say. But you look it up in your regular dictionary and discover (again, as I did) that BARATHEA is some kind of fabric.

Another valuable use for dictionaries is to search for some combination or phrase, provided you know the first word. Say you are faced with

```
'Tossed aside?' (9,6)
```

and the letters you already have suggest that the first word might be 'throwaway' but you have a mental block over 'aside' (mental blocks do happen). Looking through a dictionary can reveal the expression THROWAWAY REMARK – and you're there.

2 a **thesaurus**, which will provide synonyms. The original thesaurus (Roget) now has several versions on the market.

3 an **atlas**. One of the side benefits of crossword puzzles for me is that I am pushed into brushing up my geography.

4 a **UK Gazetteer** (for example, an AA book) as almost any town and village in the UK is fair game. Also be warned: a knowledge of London landmarks and suburbs, not to mention Underground stations and lines, is assumed. If you live out in the sticks like me you will need some kind of map of the capital.

In addition you will find useful

5 **Brewer's Dictionary of Phrase and Fable**. I had never heard of this wonderful tome until someone bought me one as a present. It is invaluable as a reference work on Classical Mythology and a whole range of literary and linguistic material.

6 a **book of quotations**. Not essential but you will get the occasional quotation thrown at you. But don't be too worried because the quotes will be well-known ones.

7   anything with **elementary** French, German, Spanish, etc. (say, a tourist phrase book) as compilers are prone to include basic words from the major languages when they have a mind to. However, the most common borrowings from foreign tongues that are used in solution construction will be found in our glossary.

8   a **book of lists**, usually with Crossword in the title. Such a book not only gives all kinds of lists (flowers, mountains, etc.) but does so very helpfully in order of word-length. For example, *Crossword Lists*, published by A & C Black. (In the present book we do incorporate lists but we restrict ourselves to the short words amenable to being used as components.)

Also, some of these books (and some dictionaries) list **abbreviations**, which figure constantly in cryptics. The present book does not aim for comprehensiveness in the provision of abbreviations, but most common ones have been included in the glossary along the way.

9   finally, the kind of books that you might find on the family bookshelf – **the Bible, history books, general knowledge books, the works of Shakespeare** and so on – will not come amiss. The characters created by Messrs Shakespeare and Dickens are regular cast members on the crossword stage. See *Exit, pursued by a bear*, also published by A & C Black.

Incidentally, don't be put off by the length of the above list. One or two books you probably have already and you can pick up the others piecemeal. I found that once people close to me knew of my new pastime, I began receiving appropriate books as presents.

A daily dose of cryptic puzzle solving not only keeps the mind active – and you'll be surprised how many people you meet (strangers included) who share your pastime once you get into the swing of it – it is also an ongoing educational experience. That is why it is no sin to use the back-up of reference books – indeed, even a pocket crossword machine. I received one of the latter as a present and am not ashamed to include it in my armoury.

My technique is to tackle a puzzle in three stages:

1   I go through and see what I can do unaided;

2   then use books (starting with this one), and finally

3   take recourse to my little battery-operated friend, when there are any obstinate holes left in the grid, as there usually are. Again, this isn't 'cheating'. Professional compilers use them, so why shouldn't we?

Interestingly, it is one of the constant pleasures of crossword solving that, after hitting a brick wall with a particular grid and putting the thing aside for a while, a critical answer can come easily when one returns to it. As in other areas of activity, the value to the mind of a break is a mysterious but real phenomenon. (Hey, phenomenon – that's a word I can now spell, thanks to crosswords.) Still a mystery to psychologists as to its exact workings, the phenomenon seems to come about either because a break allows the brain to come at a problem from a different angle, or during the break the subconscious still works on the problem in some mysterious way.

Finally, there is a clear pecking order in terms of difficulty with regard to the different national newspapers. Generally, the more popular the paper, the easier is the paper's cryptic. So, the beginner may choose to start with a tabloid. However, test runs have shown that using this book, the novice can actually start with one of the broadsheets – the 'Ivy League' of crosswords – if so choosing.

Before we go any further let's get some technical words out of the way.

CROSSWORD TERMS

Definition: It is one of the basic rules of the game that the compiler includes a word or phrase which defines the answer in some way. It will be in the form of a definition or an example. If the answer is MARSUPIAL the clue will include either a definition of marsupial or an example (for instance 'kangaroo' or 'jumper'), the latter usually prefixed by 'say' indicating it is an example.

Synonym: A word or phrase that has the same meaning as another (dog, cur, canine and so on). Because compilers will not usually give precise dictionary definitions of what they are after, the term 'definition' and 'synonym' themselves have the same meaning for our purposes.

Component: The most common form of cryptic clue is the compound type where one is required to build up the solution from given bits. These bits are letters, groups of letters or complete words, and throughout this book we call them components or elements. They can be used as they stand or require adaptation (shortening, reversing etc.) as signalled by indicators.

Indicator: We use the term indicator to describe a coded instruction about handling components. For instance, anagrams (mixing up letters) are one of the commonest devices and are signalled by indicators such as 'mixed up', 'changed', etc.

GUIDELINES AND CROSSWORD TRICKS

A SIMPLE STARTING POINT

About 80% of cryptic clues will contain the vital synonym either at the beginning or the end of the clue. Effectively this reduces the cryptic, at least in part, to an easier 'concise' puzzle. So one can make a start by limiting one's attention to the beginning of a clue, and if this doesn't throw up anything useful, concentrate for an equal amount of time on the end. Consider the following clue:

'Move quickly to squeeze Conservative out' (4)

In this example the synonym lies at the **beginning**. Hence we need a synonym for 'Move quickly'. Well, we take CRUSH (i.e. squeeze) from which we omit or 'out' C for Conservative, leaving us with the answer – RUSH.

On the other hand, the synonym lies at the **end** of

'Beat veteran to the starting place' (9)

Some kind of 'starting place' is what we require and THRESH (beat) + OLD (veteran) leads to THRESHOLD.

So remember, about 40% of the time the definition of your answer is the first word or words of the clue, and about 40% it is the last word or words.

Which leads us to another tip: if you can't solve a clue straight away but notice the first and last words end in S, then there's a good chance the answer ends in S. But use a pencil when you put it in, just in case.

LITTLE WORDS MEAN A LOT...

(...AND MAY NOT BE AS INNOCENT AS THEY LOOK)

Often the definite and indefinite articles (a, an, the) and other parts of speech are openly used in the clue to build the answer itself. For example,

'The gilt-edged alternative' (5)

is deliberately written in a way that encourages you to overlook 'The'. Yet its very letters are the bulk of the answer! THE edged with OR (i.e. gilt) is needed to construct O(THE)R which we run together to give the answer OTHER, the required synonym for 'alternative'.

The trick is a little more abstruse when we not only have to focus on a small word that our eye may skim over, but then be required to use only part of it. Consider the following cleverly constructed clue:

'Split half of capital' (5)

On the face of it, this looks like we are seeking a word synonymous with 'Split' which consists of half the letters of some capital city. If we think this then we have been successfully misdirected because, in fact, the 'half' applies to 'of'. Then, with QUIT for 'split' and adding the O from 'of', we get QUITO, the capital of Ecuador. So keep an eye on the little words!

WORDS PUT INTO THE 'WRONG' CONTEXT

The compiler will try to nudge your brain in the wrong direction by deliberately confusing parts of speech (using nouns as verbs, adjectives as nouns etc.) as in the following.

```
'Not the main sort of crustacean' (4-4)
```

'Main' is made to look like an adjective in the sense of 'principal' or 'chief'. In fact it needs to be seen as a **noun** meaning 'sea'. Thus, a crustacean **not of the sea** leads to the answer LAND-CRAB. (Incidentally, the compiler's use of a noun as an adjective is not cheating in the sense of being grammatically illegal. Unlike many other languages which severely restrict parts of speech, English positively thrives on its looseness.)

SPOONERISMS

If you didn't already know it, The Rev. W.A.Spooner of Oxford is credited (or discredited) with the slip in speech where initial sounds of words are transposed so as to form some ludicrous combination, such as 'The Lord is a shoving leopard' (for 'loving shepherd'). As a result the so-called spoonerism makes an occasional appearance in crosswords. A convoluted example is demonstrated by

```
'Not served by Hatter, one at tea-party put to
sleep (as the eccentric Oxford don had it!)' (10)
```

Ready? Then here we go: 'One at tea party' = HARE (remember the March Hare from 'Alice in Wonderland'?). 'Put to sleep' = BEDDED. This gives us HARE-BEDDED which is then **spoonerised** to provide the answer BARE-HEADED (i.e. not served by hatter – or more plainly, without a hat). Phew!

WORDS DO NOT HAVE SACROSANCT BOUNDARIES

A component word can be used to cross from one word to another in the answer. For example:

    'City porter's to carry on to the end' (4,3)

The 'City' is LA (i.e. the American city) and the required synonym for porter (i.e. the drink) is STOUT. This gives us LASTOUT – which we have then to split appropriately to give us LAST OUT i.e. to carry on to the end,

MISDIRECTION

As we have said, misdirection is a standard ploy. For instance, the compiler can give a string of elements which automatically suggest a certain group or idea. In the following clever example one has difficulty avoiding the notion of publications when, in fact, the compiler has a completely different grouping in mind:

    'Common feature of The Times and The Guardian –
                    but not Punch' (7, 7)

The important classification is not 'publications' but 'parts of speech', thus what is common to the first two titles but not the last is 'The'. From this example, the answer: LEADING ARTICLE.

IGNORE PUNCTUATION!

Beware of punctuation. While used to make some kind of sense to the clue, punctuation will also be used to misdirect the solver. Consider:

    'Improvise after trade gets into difficulty, in
                    a way' (7,3)

'In a way' looks separate from the rest, being split off with a comma. However, we should ignore the comma and read the last four words as a whole – because we need to look for something synonymous with 'difficulty in a way'.

Thus, 'Improvise' (JAM from jazz) placed **after** 'trade' (TRAFFIC) gives a 'difficulty in a way': TRAFFIC JAM, the answer. Note how the compiler has naughtily thrown in the comma to break up the synonym and put the solver off the track – as 'difficulty in a way' should be read as a whole without a break.

THE SENTENCE ITSELF

One of the aspects of playing with words is to refer to the sentence itself while misdirecting attention or simply aiming to confuse.

Consider:

```
'This would define it where you have to get it'
                        (6,6)
```

This could send your brain off in search of some form of shop. Following this train of thought you might come up with something like RETAIL OUTLET which has the requisite number of letters. But you should be uneasy with this, as it is only partially satisfactory. Further consideration might suggest that 'it' is actually the definition and we come up with the answer, DIRECT OBJECT, which is the grammatical function of 'it' in the sentence that makes up the clue.

THE DREADED PUN – WHERE BOOKS AREN'T USEFUL

A small number of clues are not based on synonyms and therefore are not amenable to book research. These are usually pun-based or otherwise tongue-in-cheek. With these cases there is nothing for it but to put on the old thinking cap. For instance:

```
'Might one be worn by a feller?' (6-6)
```

A question mark often indicates that some extra trickery is going on. Here, the compiler is playing with the word 'feller', suggesting it is a casual way of spelling 'fellow' where in fact a **feller of trees** is the base reference, which directs us to the answer: LUMBER-JACKET.

OLD WORKHORSES

These are the clichés of the game that are frequently used ('feller' in the above example is one of them), confounding beginners – and arousing an amused 'Oh not again' response from veterans. If you're a beginner you'll soon join the ranks of the groaners. For the record, amongst the commonest are 'flower' to denote a river and 'number' to denote some kind of painkiller. Another one, which we might call **The Hidden 'And'**, requires AND to be inserted, without a direct reference to it in the clue. An easy example is:

```
'Measurement of horse's extremities?' (5)
```

The extremities of the word 'horse's' are the letters H and S. Inserting the implied AND we get H AND S, giving HANDS. Do I hear a groan already?

PLAYING THE GAME

We have likened the crossword compiler to a conjuror. However, the analogy is not total because, unlike a conjuror, the compiler is not supposed to cheat. While a conjuror can tell us downright lies, a compiler is obliged to tell us the truth – albeit in a convoluted form. In this sense he is playing a game and like all games there are rules.

One of these is that all words must count. No words must be thrown in just to make the clue look better. The implication of this is that the solver should consider every word. If you're stuck, a useful tactic is to go through the clue again looking at each word **separately**. Having said that, there is some bending of this convention with little words. For instance, some setters do use definite and indefinite articles which are not strictly necessary for the definition.

Another rule is that each clue must contain at least one definition of, or synonym for, the answer. What you are looking for – either as a word or phrase – is in there somewhere! In addition, the definition is supposed to be a good match with the solution. Again a reservation, as opinions do differ on this one with regard to particular cases. For example, *The Times* team are not allowed to equate CAN and ABLE. But the entries in this book are geared to what appears in a wide spread of puzzles and as other setters regularly use this specific pair they are included. I have to say that quite a few times I have quibbled with an example that I have come across – maybe it was a little unfair, clumsy or even non-PC – but my rule in compiling the glossary is that if it has appeared in practice it merits inclusion.

FORMS OF CLUE

Usually the clues in a cryptic crossword fall into one of four categories: the compound, single definition, double definition and one that, for want of a better term, I call the whimsical clue.

The Compound Type

This is the most common form. Here the compiler provides components with instructions on how to put the solution together like a set of Lego bricks. The instructions are largely in the form of indicators (described later). This type has also been compared to Charades, being similar to the parlour game where hand signals are the coded instructions and mimes supply the components to make up the answer.

Compound clues can be short and straightforward as:

'Stupid person departs with tear' (4)

D (for departs) along with RIP (for tear) gives DRIP, a stupid person.

The following is much longer but still straightforward:

> 'Not generating a profit, one French company has
> no managing leader in charge' (10)

UNE (one French) + CO (company) + NO + M (managing leader) + IC (in charge) adds up to UNECONOMIC, not generating a profit.

Some help on the compound type comes later when we look at indicators.

Single Definition

Masquerading as a clue from an 'easy' or 'quick' crossword this type gives what appears to be a straightforward definition, usually two words. However, for it to justify its position in a cryptic there must be a twist. Example:

> 'English flower' (5)

The uninitiated might immediately start trawling a book of lists for a flower (i.e. a bloom) of five letters. However one should realise that the word 'English' is in there for a reason, denoting some kind of twist, The problem with these apparently simple ones is that even a seasoned solver cannot be sure of the answer until he has a few letters in. Say we have T-E-T and we are still having trouble finding a flower that fits. With experience we come to realise that 'flower' is an old standby for river (mentioned earlier), and we get TRENT.

Double Definition

This consists of two words (or phrases) that are synonymous with each other. Again, no indicators are used leaving the solver to rely entirely on his knowledge of words (or the books beside him). Example:

> 'Medium number' (5)

The 'medium' that was assumed in former days to permeate space is ETHER, and it is also a 'number' (with a silent 'b'), one of the old workhorses we have mentioned.

Whimsical Clues

The clues for these (and their answers) are usually longer than normal. A phrase or sentence is given very often with a question mark signalling that the answer is related to it in some quirky or humorous way. Of the four types of clue this is the one where reference books are of the least use because, with no indicators or other conventional help, the field is so open. Example:

> 'Not the monarch at Bannockburn?' (6,3,5)

You can look up monarch and get a whole list of kings and queens. You can look up Bannockburn, with little effect, apart from maybe suggesting a

Scottish king, say Robert the Bruce – another red herring. Then it might occur to you to split up the last word and look up 'bannock' separately. That gives you 'Scottish bread or cake'. Still no sense. Eventually, hopefully, you might relate 'cake' to 'burn' and, bingo, you come up with ALFRED THE GREAT.

This type of clue can be quite a stumbling block in the completion of a grid and is thankfully restricted in use, although they do provide satisfaction and maybe a chuckle when cracked.

Now, back to the most common type of clue, the **compound**.

INDICATORS

The compiler will get up to all kinds of tricks to misguide the solver in building up the compound solution but the rules of the game require that he plays fair. Namely, he needs to specify what kind of legerdemain he is up to and he does this by using a set of codes that we have called indicators.

A large number of such indicators has been built up and the most common ones will be found in this book. However, such a list can never be complete because adventurous setters are continually designing new ones. For our purposes indicators consist of the following groups.

Anagram indicators

Examples: mixed up, replaced, gusty, fixing, clumsy

An anagram is a word of phrase formed from transposed letters of another word or set of words, e.g. LAIR and RAIL. Where the answer requires the construction of an anagram, an appropriate indicator will be given. Anagram indicators are many and varied but they all have in common the notion of something being **wrong** (e.g. broken, off) or **changed** (e.g. altered, redistributed) or **worked on** (e.g. hammered, sorted), that kind of thing.

In the simplest form, the letters to be reworked will be contained in a single word as in the following example:

```
'Exceptionally good purse distributed' (5)
```

Here the anagram indicator is 'distributed' telling us we have to shuffle some letters. The indicator is usually adjacent to the word (or words) to be operated on and in this case the target word is PURSE. The definition is 'exceptionally good' and, juggling the letters of PURSE leads us to the answer SUPER. A little more difficult is when we have several words or components to work on, as in:

```
'Draw entailed clashing with European' (9)
```

The word 'clashing' signals an anagram. However, there are not enough letters in 'entailed' and we have to throw E (signalled by European) into the mix. Our task then is to rearrange ENTAILED along with E to get a synonym for 'draw' – DELINEATE.

Omission indicators

Examples: drop, leave, quit

Here target letters, words or components have to be omitted in order to help construct the answer. This requirement is signalled by such words as 'out', 'not entirely' and so on.

Example:

```
'Out east, sell vehicle for writer' (4,5)
```

'Out east' suggests we should drop E (for east) from 'sell' or a word meaning the same. Thinking about it leads hopefully to MARKET which, with the E 'outed', becomes MARKT. 'Vehicle' clues WAIN while 'writer' is the definition, telling us a writer's name is required. Putting MARKT and WAIN together, then splitting them appropriately we get the answer, the novelist MARK TWAIN.

Reversal indicators

Examples: return, rising, northern

These make an appearance in the form of straightforward words like 'back', 'over', or more subtlely in words like 'retiring'.

Once we suspect a reversal we have to decide whether it requires us to reverse **letters** or **whole components**. In the following example, 'retiring' is the reversal indicator and it is the **letters** that have to be reversed:

```
'Papal diadem represented by retiring Italian
                painter' (5).
```

IT (for Italian) is reversed, followed by ARA (i.e. an Associate of the Royal Academy) to give the Papal diadem: TI + ARA, that is TIARA.

On the other hand, letter-order is to remain the same but the order of **components** is to be reversed in:

```
        'Cheerful mug? Just the reverse' (6).
```

'Mug' clues BEAT UP, then the two **words** are put in reverse order to give 'cheerful': UPBEAT.

In this second form, the reversal indicator can also be thought of as an ordering indicator – see later.

Nesting indicators

Examples: accepted, accomodation, nursing

Here one component is to be nested or embedded **within** another. The instruction can be in one of two forms. Firstly there is the notion of one component going **into** another (penned in, engaged in etc.) as in:

```
'First (first of Romans) engaged in building
                    empire' (7)
```

'First' gives us the synonym for the word we are looking for, while 'first of Romans' gives us 'R'. 'Building' is an anagram indicator signalling that 'empire' is an anagram. Fiddling around with the letters we get PEMIER. Into this we have to 'engage' or nest R to get PREMIER (i.e. first).

Secondly, the indicator can focus on one component **going round** the other (examples: penning, restricting, absorbing, circling, choking etc.) as in:

```
'Rank ivy choking short bough's vitality' (8)
```

'Rank' indicates that 'ivy' is an anagram (VIY). 'Short' indicates that a synonym for 'bough' (BRANCH) should be shortened, specifically BRANC. Then 'choking' signifies that VIY should encircle BRANC to give 'vitality', namely VIBRANCY.

Homophone indicators

Example: audition, spoken, we hear

A homophone is simply a component or word that sounds like another but has a different meaning, such as HEIR and AIR, and is a common device in crosswords. That such a target is sought is signalled by such words as 'soundly', 'sounding', 'broadcast', and by phrases like 'on the radio' etc. as in:

```
'Facilitate the sounding of notes' (4)
```

Firstly, the word 'sounding' can be a homophone indicator, so we might be looking for sound-alikes. The notes required are EEs which is a homophone for EASE, the answer, i.e. 'facilitate'.

Another way the homophone game is played is to misguide us by the use of capital letters which are **appropriate** for the sense of the clue but **inappropriate** for getting the answer. For example:

```
'Popular accommodation inside Hull, we hear' (7)
```

'We hear' is a popular homophone indicator and its role in this clue is to suggest to us that we go by the **sound** of 'Hull'. So we should read it, not as the town with a capital H, but as the common noun 'hull'. In other words we are looking for something indicative of the interior of a boat. 'Popular' clues IN, 'accommodation' clues BOARD and we have the answer: INBOARD.

Run indicators

Examples: run, piece of, outburst, occurring in

In this case the setter is signalling that the answer (or required component) is embedded in the clue itself as a run or series of consecutive letters, usually crossing from one word to another.

Common run indicators: 'part of', 'not all', 'sampled in', 'section'. The beauty of this type is that once we have identified it as a straight 'run' clue it is the easiest to solve because the answer is staring us in the face as in the following:

```
'Oriental city with a noisy section' (5)
```

'Section' is cluing that we should look for a run, which inspection reveals to be within the phrase 'with a noisy' – HANOI which is the Oriental city of the answer.

Strictly, 'Hanoi' requires a capital letter but another lesson that might be learned from the above example is that the normal rules about the use of capital letters are invariably ignored. So you may have to **imagine** the capital letter, as in the above. On the other hand, as in our Hull example, you might have to **discount** a capital letter to get to the answer. Here's another one:

```
'Specific humidity as sampled in Cape' (5)
```

'Sampled' suggests that the answer lies in a run, and it does, But we are misdirected by the capital letter to Cape which suggests the answer is geographic. However, the answer is FICHU, which appears as a clear run of letters within the clue. And a fichu, our dictionary shows us, is a cape, an item of women's clothing.

As this type is one of the easiest to solve, there is rarely more than one within a crossword. But to confuse the issue, such a run may be in reverse or consist of alternate letters, the sequence of which can be signalled by odd, even, etc. as in

```
'Sway, creeping in at regular intervals' (5)
```

Here, 'Sway' is the definition and the answer is REIGN, indicated by the even-numbered letters (i.e. at regular intervals) in the sequence 'creeping in'.

Whimsy indicators

Examples: ?, " ", !

When the compiler takes a flight of fancy, pursues some caprice, uses poetic licence, stretches a point or otherwise breaks the rules, usually with humorous intent, there will be some indication by what we may call a whimsy indicator. The most common such indicator is the use of a question mark. Also beware of an exclamation mark or quotation marks.

Example:

```
'A "silly" place for flowers' (6,3)
```

The answer is WINDOW BOX – the logic being that a window box is on a sill and therefore may be described as "silly". Do I hear another groan?

The remaining indicators require little explanation.

Abbreviation indicators

Examples: short, little, small

Abbreviations are probably the most common device of all in cryptics and can be cued by words such as 'briefly'. However, that an abbreviation is required is not always signalled, presumably because they are seen as a part of everyday speech. They fall into two types.

Firstly, acronyms like RAF. Ideally the solver should have a separate abbreviations reference list but the present book includes most of the common examples and you'll soon get used to the popular ones anyway, such as 'artist' calling for RA or ARA; 'defence body' for NATO, 'accountant' for CA and so on. Of course, computer acronyms are becoming increasingly common – DOS, RAM, ROM etc.

The second kind are common shortenings and diminutives, and these are often signalled by 'little' for example. 'Boy' and 'little boy' call for a shortened first name (RON etc.). The same applies to 'little girl' with DI coming near if not at the top of the list. She makes one of her many appearances in this one:

```
'Absent-minded little girl with crazy artist' (8)
```

which emerges as DISTRAIT (DI + an anagram of ARTIST)

Colloquialism indicators

Example: commonly, Cockney

Apart from a small number (such as AINT) these are not very frequent and call for slang or other informal speech. If regional dialect is called for it will usually be signalled e.g. GANG requires 'Scottish' in the clue, NOUT and OUT (for nothing and something) requires 'Northern' or 'Yorkshire', and so on.

Probably the most widespread use of colloquialism is the dropping of initial H signified by an apostrophe (') as in

```
'Courageous London coppers start to take over the
                French 'abitation' (10)
```

where the last word clues OME (i.e. 'ome). Result: MET + T + LES + OME = METTLESOME.

Repetition indicators

Examples: again, repeatedly

Just as it says, some letter or component (or its synonym) has to be repeated to complete the answer.

Initial letter indicator

Examples: leader of, hint of, pointer

The signal that you are to use only the first letter of a word usually comes in the form of straightforward words like 'front', 'beginning' or 'start', as 'start of hostilities' cues H.

However, the compiler may use a more abstruse word such as 'top' as where 'top-sail' clues S. Even more abstruse is the use of a synonym for 'top' that fits the character of the clue. Consider:

```
'Old boat's load seen with hatch removed' (4)
```

The initial letter indicator is 'hatch' (i.e. top). Removing the initial letter from CARGO (load) we get ARGO, an 'old boat', the vessel of Jason and his Argonauts.

Other specific letter indicators

Examples: last, finally, middle

Apart from the initial letter indicator, indicators can call for the last or central letters of words to be used. Occasionally, a **numbered** letter may be stipulated. For example 'the fourth of July' identifies Y. With me being an avid classics fan, it took a long time to sink in that, in the context of cryptics, Beethoven's Fifth has got nothing to do with old Ludwig at all.

Ordering indicators

These specify the order in which components are to be set and are usually self-explanatory in the form of 'first', 'last', 'before' and so on. In the following, 'chases' is an ordering indicator:

```
'Wild lady chases thousand in a crazy manner' (5)
```

Its function is to tell you that 'wild lady' (an anagram of LADY) follows M (for thousand) – giving MADLY.

Palindrome indicators

A palindrome is a word which is spelled the same whichever way you read it e.g. LEVEL, ANNA and their use is indicated by phrases such as 'in both directions'. In the following 'whichever way you look at it' plays the role of a palindrome indicator:

```
'It's to be done whichever way you look at it'
                        (4)
```

which is satisfied by DEED. Such words do crop up but, just as they are rare in reality, they are rare in crosswords too.

Combinations

Most compound clues will contain a combination of indicators, usually two but three or more are possible. For example,

```
'Singer pockets rearward ball, then another, in
                    pool' (9)
```

incorporates three:

> 'pockets' is a nesting indicator
>
> 'rearward' is a reversal indicator
>
> 'another' is a repetition indicator

Here we go. 'Ball' is **reversed** – LLAB, to be followed by **another** ball (i.e. O) to give LLABO. This is then **nested** within the singer BING (the compiler assumes you remember him) yielding BI-LLABO-NG, i.e. BILLABONG, an Australian word for pool!

SUMMARY

1   Remember that in the majority of cases the synonym for the answer is the **first** or **last** part of the clue.

2   Ignore the obvious. Remember that the setter is trying to trap you with the obvious, so look for a **less** obvious meaning.

3   Consider each word **separately**, especially when the words have been made to look as if they go together.

4   Be on the lookout for the code words and phrases that serve as indicators.

5   When you reach an impasse with a particular grid, don't lose your cool and give up. Just put it aside for a while, do something else and return to it at another convenient time. Remember, these things are supposed to be fun.

A LAST WORD

Finally, it has to be said that a book such as this can never be complete. New words are being coined everyday and old words are taking on new meanings, so even an imposing authoritative dictionary can never be up-to-date.

Bearing that in mind, the entries in this book can be seen as being of two kinds. Firstly there is the core of standard indicators and components that are a part of the compiler's armoury. While we hope that most of them are contained here, it must be borne in mind that compilers are an ingenious lot and are forever devising new tricks with which to challenge us.

The glossary's other entries may be seen as peripheral in the sense that they surround this core and are themselves at the edge of the vast lexicon that is the evolving and expanding English language. This is where your dictionaries and other reference books come in.

Therefore, if you are a beginner and are prepared to persevere, this book should certainly help you to make some inroads into a grid. And, if it does that for you, it's done its job.

As implied at the beginning, I now have a modicum of experience at puzzling, but the following glossary is still my main source of reference – so I'm sure even case-hardened veterans will find it of use.

OK, keep your wits about you, be alert to the continual flood of new words and, if this is your copy, don't be afraid to write your own discoveries in the margins – that's what they're there for.

Lastly, to beginners and veterans alike – happy puzzling!

PREFACE TO THE SECOND EDITION

As with the first edition, the aim continues to be the provision of a handy reference for the codes and words used for building solutions to cryptic crosswords. Apart from considerable increase in content, some minor changes have been incorporated. Where a headword is accompanied by a long list, the entries are now divided into two. As an aid to the solver's task, abbreviations, components and *the most common words* are provided first. Then, following the ■ symbol, longer and less common words are given. Although it is not the intention to provide a comprehensive thesaurus, these longer entries, being complete words, are more likely to be full answers in themselves. In the choice of these particular words, some priority has been given to those which, it is thought, may not occur readily to the solver.

Also, technical terms used in the discussion of crosswords are now included and these are positioned alphabetically in the text preceded by the symbol ★. As they have already been explained in the introduction, they are provided in the text more as reminders for the reader to stumble upon but they can be looked up specifically to help one's understanding as they provide extra examples and may give a different slant.

FORMAT OF ENTRIES

Entries are usually made up in the following way:

(1) Listed first in alphabetical order are possible components that are often used in the construction of words. Then, following a black square (■) as explained above, complete words are shown that are longer and likely to be full answers in themselves. When lists are extensive, this lay-out has the added advantage of splitting up the items into the more common, then the less common, which should make the reader's task a little easier.

(2) Next come comments on the entry with regard to its use as a coded instruction i.e. anagram indicator, homophone indicator etc.

(3) Finally, in squared brackets marked ◊, some words are offered which are commonly associated with the entry. For example, the **sausage** entry will give BANGER and so on, but will round off with [◊ DOG].

CROSS-REFERENCING

Two kinds of cross-referencing are used. Where a word is in the entry as a useful component in itself but can further expand the synonyms that the solver may be looking for, it is marked by (qv) so that it can be referred to as a headword in its own right. Where it may be to advantage to look up a word that is *not* in the entry list, the reader's attention will be drawn to it at the end of the relevant list preceded by the instruction '*see …*'

ABBREVIATIONS USED IN THIS BOOK

AC	Across clue
A.S.	Anglo-Saxon
abbr.	abbreviation
adj.	adjective
Afr.	African
alt.	alternative
anag.	anagram
anat.	anatomical
ans.	answer
arch.	archaic
Aus.	Australian
bot.	Botanical
Chin.	Chinese
colloq.	colloquialism
cric.	Cricket
DC	Down clue
East.	Eastern
eng.	engineering
esp.	especially
excl.	exclamation
Gael.	Gaelic
hom.	homophone
imper.	imperative
Ital.	Italian
Lat.	Latin
mus.	music
myth.	mythology

naut.	nautical
physio.	physiology
pr.	printing
(qv)	indicates a word that is a headword in itself
rev.	reverse, reversal
Scand.	Scandinavian
Scot.	Scottish
Shak.	Shakespearean
sp.	spelling
Sp.	Spanish
univ.	university
U.S.	United States
v.	verb
with cap	with a capital letter
Yid.	Yiddish

SYMBOLS USED IN THIS BOOK

◊	associated word or words
→	leads to, gives the following answer
(!)	the exclamation mark is used to emphasise that a device may need thinking about or has an element of wit
■	used as a divider between more common and less common words and components in entry lists
★	denotes a technical term used in crosswords
*	denotes that what is given in the clue is not the definition but an example of the definition. So, in our book the headword trade will give DEAL, SWAP etc. which are 'definitions'. However, the headword trade* covers cases such as 'trade for example', 'trade for instance', 'trade, say' against which you will find WIND to suggest to you that the unstated reference might be trade wind

Aa

a, A ONE; PER; TOP; UPPER; be wary that 'a' is often used in the guise of being part of the grammar of the clue sentence when it is in fact a component to be used in constructing the answer

a change of air ARIA

a follower B

a foreign EIN; UNE; UNE

A4 SHEET

a French UN; UNE

a German EIN

a head EACH; PER

a Parisian UN; UNE

a second AS

a university's AUS

AA can indicate something to do with (i) Alcoholics Anonymous, (ii) Automobile Association, or (iii) author A. A. Milne, creator of Winnie the Pooh

Aaron's brother MOSES

AB RATING; TAR; can indicate something to do with sailors, boats, navy etc.

abacus COUNTER

abandon CEDE; CUT; DITCH; DROP; DUMP; FREE; JILT; LEAVE; QUIT; SCRAP; SHED; SLOUGH; STRAND; YIELD; ■ AXE; CHANGE; DESERT; SHELVE; omission indicator, as "seen to abandon extremes" → EE

abandon, with anagram indicator

abandoned EX; FREE; LEFT; LOOSE; LORN; OFF; QUIT; SHED; anagram indicator; omission indicator

abandoned item RELIC

abandoning anagram indicator

abandonment CESSION

abash SHAME

abase LOWER

abate FALL

abated FELL

★ **abbreviations** being short groups of letters (or even a single letter), abbreviations are a common staple of cryptics in which they are used as building blocks to form answers. For example, "doctor" (qv) can require the use of DR, MO etc., while "say" or "for example" can be code for the use of EG (an abbreviation of the Latin *exempli gratia* in the form of e.g.) and so on

abdicate RESIGN

abdominal pain COLIC

Abel's murderer CAIN

abet AID; *see* HELP

abhor DETEST

abhorrent ODIOUS

abide BEAR; BROOK; DWELL; LIVE; STAND; STAY

Abigail MAID

ability ART; FLAIR; POWER; SENSE; SKILL; TALENT

ability, natural APTITUDE

able ACUTE; BRAINY; BRIGHT; CLEVER; DEFT; FIT; GOOD; HANDY; QUICK; SHARP; SLICK; ■ ACTIVE; ADEPT; with a capital letter, can signify a sailor

able, be, is CAN

ablution BATH

ably WELL

abnormal ODD (qv); anagram indicator

abnormal form SPORT; ■ MUTATION

abnormality WARP

aboard ON; run indicator; nesting indicator which is usually disguised in a seafaring context as "Family aboard tanker" → OILSKINS (i.e. KIN is nested within OIL S.S.)

aboard ship can indicate that a component is to be nested within SS

abode PAD; *see* DWELLING

abode, poor HOVEL

abolish SCRUB; *see* BAN

abolished omission indicator; can indicate a word (or phrase) beginning with NO (as "Service abolished? That's fate" → NORN)

abominable anagram indicator

abominable snowman YETI

aborted anagram indicator

abound SWARM; TEEM

about A; AROUND; ASTIR; AT; (i.e. circa); CA; OF; ON; OVER; RE; UP; anagram indicator; reversal indicator; nesting indicator

about noon requires N to be nested within a component

about now anagram of NOW; NOW or a synonym (e.g. AD) to be nested within a component

about time CAGE (i.e. c + age); CT; RET; T to be nested within a component; a synonym for time (e.g. AGE) to be nested within a component – *see* TIME for synonyms

about to dock ROOM

about to drop ALLIN (i.e. all in)

about to go READY; SET; indicator for C to be omitted

about to break into RE to be nested within a word or component

about to leave can indicate that a synonym of "about" (e.g. C, RE, *see* ABOUT) is to be omitted

above OVER

above all a component to be placed in front of ALL, SUM etc

above all others BEST; CREAM; TOP

Abraham's nephew LOT

Abraham's place/of birth UR

abrasion SCRAPE

abreast LEVEL

abridge *see* CUT

abridged omission indicator (as "abridged edition" → ED); can call for some abbreviation

abroad AWAY; GONE; OFF; OUT; ■ ABSENT; can indicate the foreign version of a word as "abroad she" → ELLE; anagram indicator

abrupt (very) CURT; RUDE; TERSE

abscond BOLT; DESERT; ELOPE; FLEE; RAT; *see* RUN

absence BLANK; LACK; NEED; WANT

absence of NO; ■ WITHOUT; omission indicator (as "absence of oxygen" calls for O to be omitted)

absent AWAY; GONE; OFF; OUT; ■ ABROAD; MISSING; omission indicator

absent-minded SCATTY; ■ DISTRAIT

absent oneself GO

absolute SHEER; UTTER

absolutely QUITE; YES

absolve CLEAR

absorb EAT; nesting indicator

absorbed by nesting indicator

absorbing nesting indicator

abstain FAST; ■ DESIST

abstainer TT

abstainers AA

abstaining anagram indicator

abstemious TT

abstemious, time to be LENT

abstentionist DRY

abstinence, period of/time of FAST; LENT

abstract DIGEST; PRECIS; RESUME; anagram indicator

abstract painting OPART (i.e. OP ART)

absurd DAFT; SILLY; WILD; anagram indicator

absurdly anagram indicator

abundance, be in TEEM

abundant RICH

abuse CHEEK; CURSE; FLAK; HARM; ILL; LIP; MUD; RAIL; RAILING; RATE; anagram indicator; ■ INSULT; REVILE; TIRADE VERBAL

abused HURT; anagram indicator

abusing anagram indicator

abusive, be *see* ABUSE

abysmal BAD; POOR; ■ CHASMIC

abysmally anagram indicator

abyss DEEP; HELL; HOLE; PIT

acacia WATTLE

academic BA; DON; FELLOW; LECTOR; MA; PROF; *see* DEGREE; ■ GRADUATE; PROFESSOR; READER

academic achievement BA; MA; *see* DEGREE

academic appointment CHAIR

academic award GRANT

academic establishment LSE; MIT; SCHOOL; U; UNI; *see* COLLEGE, UNIVERSITY

academic position CHAIR

academic stream CAM; ISIS

academic terms SESSION

academician ARA; RA

academy A

accent ACUTE; BEAT; BROGUE; BURR; GRAVE; MARK; PITCH; SOUND; STRESS; TONE; TWANG

accent, "correct" RP

accept PASS; TAKE; WEAR; nesting or run indicator

accept without questioning SWALLOW

acceptable DONE; GOOD; LICIT; MEET; NICE; ON; OK; U; WORTHY; nesting indicator as "an acceptable" requires AN to be nested

acceptable, socially DONE; IN; U

acceptance from France OUI

accepted IN; TOOK; U; nesting indicator

accepting nesting indicator

access DOOR; ENTREE; ENTRY; GATE; nesting indicator

access, gain HACK

accessory EXTRA; TIE

accident BUMP; CHANCE; CRASH; FLUKE; SMASH; SPILL; anagram indicator

accident, by FLUKEY; FLUKY

accident, have an SLIP

accident, minor SHUNT

accident, narrowly avoided MISS

accident, no MEANT

accidental FLAT (mus.); HAP

accidentally anagram indicator

acclaim PRAISE

accommodate ADAPT; BOARD; HOUSE; nesting indicator

accommodated by nesting indicator

accommodates nesting indicator

accommodating KIND; nesting indicator; run indicator

accommodation BB; BOARD; DIGS; FLAT; HOME; HOUSE; MESS; MOTEL; NEST; PAD; ROOM; SPACE; VILLA; ■ CAMP; HUTCH; LODGING; MANSE; QUARTERS; SHELTER; STABLE; nesting indicator; anagram indicator; *see* BUILDING

accommodation, more ANNEXE

accommodation, temporary CAMP; TENT

accommodation to, affording/ giving nesting indicator

accommodation for nesting indicator

accommodation for animals CORRAL; DEN; LAIR; PEN; POUND; STY; ZOO

accommodation, give HOUSE

accommodation, one renting TENANT

accompanied ACC

accompanied by WITH

accompanied by Cockney WIV

accompaniment BACKING; can signify a phrase beginning with WHILE

accompany BACK

accompanying AND; WITH; can simply mean that one component is to follow another

accomplished ABLE; DID; DONE; OVER; *see* ABLE

accomplishment FEAT; SKILL

accord COMPLY

according to AFTER; PER

accordingly SO; THUS

accost STOP; ■ MOLEST

account AC; ACC; BILL; FUND; RESUME; SCORE; STORY; TALE; TALLY; VERSION; SCORE; TALLY; ■ RECORD;

RELATION; REPORT; can indicate something to do with a novel

account, brief AC; ACC; NOTE

account, long EPIC

accountant ACC; CA; CLERK; ■ AUDITOR; [◊ AUDIT; BALANCE]

accountants CACA; CAS

accumulate AMASS; KEEP

accuracy TRUTH

accurate EXACT; RIGHT; ■ PRECISE

accurate, not OUT

accusation CHARGE; SLUR

accusation, bring an LODGE

accusation, response to PLEA

accuse BLAME; BOOK; BRAND; CHARGE; INDICT; NAME; SMEAR; SUE; TAX

accustomed USED; ■ INURED

ace A; BEST; CARD; CRACK; ONE; SERVE; STAR; STROKE; SUPER; TOP; ■ EXPERT; PRIME; WINNER

ace, flying BADER

acerbic BITTER; SHARP; SOUR; TART

acetic SHARP

ache LONG; SMART; YEARN

ache, slight TWINGE

achieve DO; GET; HIT; MEET; PASS; WIN

achieved DONE; GOT; HIT; MET

achieved, isn't quite last letter(s) to be omitted

achievement FEAT; SLAM (i.e. at cards)

acid BITTER; SOUR; TART; URIC; ■ PHENOL

acid* JAZZ

acid, measure of PH

acid, type of FOLIC

acidity level PH

acidity, soil PH

acknowledge ACK; ALLOW; KNOW; NOD; OWN; WAVE; ■ ADMIT

acknowledged ACK; KNEW

acknowledgement LETTER; NOD; ROGER; WAVE; can indicate a specific greeting e.g. HI

acknowledgement of mistake OOPS

Ackroyd ROGER

acme PEAK; TOP (qv)

acne SPOTS

acorn SEED; ■ ANCESTOR; FRUIT; [◊ OAK]

acquiesce RESIGN; ■ AGREE

acquire BAG; CATCH; EARN; FIND; GAIN; GET; LAND; NET; TAKE; WIN

acquire unfairly see STEAL

acquired BOUGHT; FOUND; GOT

acquiring nesting indicator

acquisition BUY

acquit BEAR; CLEAR; FREE; ■ ABSOLVE; RELEASE

acre AREA; FIELD

acreage STRETCH

acrid BITTER; SHARP

acrobat TUMBLER

acrobatic FLEET; anagram indicator

acrobatically anagram indicator

acronym first letters indicator; can indicate a standard acronym (UN, RA, RAF etc)

across AX; OVER; ■ ATHWART

act BILL; BLUFF; DEED; DO; LAW; MOVE; PLAY; POSE; SHAM; SHOW; STUNT; TURN; ■ PERFORM

act badly HAM

act foolishly TRIFLE

act in exaggerated fashion HAM

act indecisively DITHER; WAVER

act out PLAY; anagram of ACT

act partly SCENE

act, reversal of REPEAL

act uneasily anagram of ACT

act, unkind CUT

act vigorously GOIT (i.e. go it)

acted DID

acting anagram indicator

acting, system of METHOD

action CASE; DEED; FIGHT; PLAY; SUIT; WAR; ■ BATTLE;

DOING; STEP; STRIKE; anagram indicator; [◊ FORCE]

action, in anagram indicator

action, person taking DOER

action, prepare for ARM

action, start SUE

action, started SUED

activate BOOST; CHEER; HEAT; MOVE; ROUSE; START; STIR; WAKE

activated, activating anagram indicator

active ABLE; ABOUT; BUSY; SPRY; UP; anagram indicator

active, be DO

actively anagram indicator

activity FEVER; HUM; RUSH; ■ BUSTLE; DOING; FERMENT; HUSTLE; anagram indicator

activity, corrupt VICE

activity, non serious PLAY

actor AGENT; EXTRA; GABLE; HAM; LOM; PLAYER; TREE; ■ DOER; OLIVIER; PECK; [◊ LINES; SCRIPT; STAGE]

actor, bad, poor HAM

actor, big-name STAR

actor, clumsy HAM

actor, leading STAR

actor, old TREE

actor's words LINES

actors CAST; ■ TROUPE; can indicate something to do with acting, role, part, stage

actors' union EQUITY

actress LEIGH

actress, famous TERRY

actress, old GISH

acts can indicate something to do with Acts, the Biblical book

actual REAL; TRUE; VERY

acute KEEN; SHARP

ad see ADVERTISEMENT

ad hoc anagram indicator

adage SAW

Adam's ale HYDRO; WATER

adapt ADJUST (qv); FIT; ■ CHANGE; IMPROVE; anagram indicator

adaptable, adapted, adapting, adaptation anagram indicator

ADC AIDE

add PUT; SUM; TOT; TOTAL; ■ APPEND; CAST (arch.)

add alcohol LACE

add secret ingredient LACE

add up MUS; see ADD

added ON; PLUS

added item PS

added to a component is to be placed alongside another; nesting indicator

adder SNAKE; SUMMER; can indicate something to do with an accountant, calculator etc

addict USER; ■ FIEND

addict's treatment DETOX

addicted HOOKED

addition EXTRA; MORE; ON; PS; SUM; ■ ANNEX

addition, in AND; PLUS; TOO; ■ ALSO

addition to, in ON

additional EXTRA; MORE; NEW; OTHER; OVER; PLUS; SECOND

additional item MORE; PS

additional material/words PS

addled BAD

addling ROTTING

address DIRECT; FACE; HOME; PAD; PLACE; ORATION; SPEAK; TALK; ■ LOCATION; NUMBER; SPEECH; TITLE

address, give ORATE; SPEAK; see ADDRESS

address, in homophone indicator

addressed SENT

adept HANDY; PRO; see ABLE, CLEVER

adequate AMPLE; ENOUGH; OK

adequate, are SERVE

adequate, barely SCANT

adequate, be PASS

adequately OK

adhere CLEAVE; CLING; STICK

adherent FAN; BUFF; can indicate a word ending in IST (e.g. impressionist)

adherents CAMP

adhesive GLUE; GUM; PASTE; STICKY

adjacent BESIDE; CLOSE; NEAR; NEXT; ordering indicator

adjourned ROSE

adjournment BREAK; RECESS

adjudication JURY

adjust ALIGN; ALTER; ARRANGE; FIT; ORDER; SET; TUNE; ▪ CHANGE

adjustable, adjusted anagram indicator

adjusting anagram indicator

adjustment anagram indicator

adjustment, make TWEAK

adjustment, needing anagram indicator

administer APPLY; DIRECT; RUN

administered RAN; anagram indicator

administration anagram indicator

administrative district WARD

administrative division PARISH; REGION

administrator HEAD; REGENT; *see* CHIEF

admirable person BRICK; HERO; ST; TRUMP

admiral ADM; DRAKE; HOOD; ▪ BLIGH; NELSON

admire LIKE; REVERE

admired man HERO

admirer BEAU; FAN; LOVER; SUITOR

admission ENTRY; IM (i.e. I'M); nesting indicator

admission card TICKET

admission, giving nesting indicator

admission office RECEPTION

admission, publicise OUT

admit ALLOW; ENTER; GRANT; OWN; LET; ▪ ACCEPT; can require I followed by a AM or DO etc as "Heathen admits to being a procrastinator" → IDOLATOR

admit superiority CEDE; YIELD

admits nesting indicator; can require I followed by a AM or DO etc, *see* ADMIT

admittance, seek KNOCK

admitted IN; OWNED; nesting indicator

admitted (to secrets) PRIVY

admonish CHIDE; WARN

ado TROUBLE (qv); anagram indicator

adopt AFFECT; TAKE

adopted nesting indicator

adopted by nesting indicator

adolescence YOUTH

adolescent TEEN; YOUTH

adore LOVE

adorn DECK; ▪ BEDECK; DECORATE

adornment *see* GEM, JEWELLERY, STONE

adornment, with little BALD; PLAIN

adrenalin, source of GLAND

adrift FREE; LOOSE; OFF; OUT; anagram indicator

adroit CLEVER

adult A; BLUE; MAN

adult males MEN

adulterate FIX; ▪ DOCTOR

adulterated MIXED; anagram indicator

advance COME; CLIMB; GAIN; LEAD; LEND; LOAN; MOVE; OFFER; ON; PRE; PREFER; RAISE; RISE; STEP; SUB; ▪ NEAR; PROGRESS

advance, amorous PASS

advance cautiously INCH; NOSE

advance, in can indicate a word beginning with PRE

advance, made LENT

advance, make LEND; LOAN

advance of funds IMPREST

advance payment ANTE; SUB

advance stealthily CRAWL; CREEP; EDGE; INCH

advanced AHEAD; EARLY; LENT; NEW; ▪ FORWARD

advanced in years AGED; OLD

advanced, is can indicate that a letter in a word is brought forward (usually by one place) as "Man: leading intelligence in brain is advanced" → BRIAN

Advanced Passenger Train APT
advances, made LENT
advancing COMING; RISING;
   one letter to be moved to beginning of word
advantage ASSET; BOON;
   EDGE; GAIN; GOOD; PLUS;
   PRO; START; VAN; ■
   BENEFIT; PROFIT; [◊ CAP]
advantage of, take USE
advantage of, taken USED
advantage, take AVAIL; MILK;
   USE
advent COMING
advert see ADVERTISEMENT
advertise PLUG; PUFF; PUSH; ■
   PROMOTE
advertised, effectively SOLD
advertisement AD; HYPE;
   NOTICE; PLUG; POSTER;
   PUFF
advertiser's broadcast message
   BY
advertiser's message BUY
advertising PROMO; see
   ADVERTISING
advertising firm HOUSE
advice CLUE; HELP; HINT; TIP;
   ■ COUNSEL
advice, former/old REDE
advisable WELL
advisable, more BETTER
advise CAUTION; GUIDE;
   INFORM
advise, strongly URGE
advisor MENTOR
advocacy, exaggerated HYPE
advocate PLEAD; URGE
advocate in court PLEAD
advocates BAR
aerial UP
aerobatic manoeuvre LOOP
aeroplane BUS; CRATE
aeroplane, part of CABIN;
   WING
aesthete, like an ARTY
aesthetic ARTY
affair AMOUR; DO; FLING;
   MATTER ■ CONCERN;
   INTRIGUE

affect MOVE; ■ CONCERN;
   IMPRESS; TOUCH
affect, badly DENT
affect slightly TINGE
affectation POSE; anagram indicator
affected ARCH; ARTY; CAMP;
   anagram indicator
affected attitude AIRS
affected by drink/drug ⎯
   SMASHED
affected, one FOP
affecting anagram indicator
affection LOVE
**affection, demonstration / show /
   sign of** CARESS; HUG; KISS
affection, sign of KISS
affection, token of RING
affectionate FOND; TENDER; ■
   LOVING
affiliation LINK; TIE
affirm AVER; OK; STATE;
   SWEAR
affirmative AY; AYE; OK; YES
affirmative yore AY
affirmed SWORN
affixed STUCK
afflicted LAME; ■ STRICKEN;
   anagram indicator
affliction ACHE; TRIAL; anagram
   indicator; see ILLNESS, PAIN
affluence EASE
affluent RICH
affray MELEE
affront INSULT; SLIGHT (qv)
Afghan DOG
aficionado FAN
afield ABROAD; AWAY; OUT
aflame ALIGHT; BURNING; LIT
aforesaid DITTO
afraid LEERY; SCARED; WINDY;
   ■ CHICKEN; DREADING;
   FEARFUL; YELLOW
afresh RE; anagram indicator
Africa, part of NATAL; ■ BENIN
African MOOR; RIFF
African chief OBA
African city TUNIS
African country BENIN
African party ANC
African port ORAN

African prince RAS
African province NATAL
Afro-Caribbean BLACK
aft BACK
after LATER; PAST; POST; SINCE; ■ SEEKING; ordering indicator
after a time LATE; a component to follow AT
after hours LATE
after midnight AM
after-school activity FISHING(!)
after speaking LATOR (hom.)
after that time SINCE
after tax NETT
after time LATE
after you were meant to LATE
afternoon PM
afternoon, early in the ATI (i.e. at one)
afterthought PS
afterwards LATER; THEN
again ANEW; BACK; BIS (mus.); MORE; OVER; RE; can indicate an element is to be repeated; anagram indicator
again, perform REDO
against AGIN; ANTI; AVERSE; CON; CONTRA; V; ■ COUNTER; one component is to be placed alongside another
against, be OPPOSE
against it, to be up ABUT
age CYCLE; ERA; EON; TIME; PERIOD; YEAR; ■ AEON
age, at a young EARLY
age, show evidence of DATE; YELLOW
ageing GREY; OLD
agencies MEDIA
agency CIA; HAND; MEANS; ■ BUREAU; OFFICE
agency girl TEMP
agency, intelligence CIA
agency, news TASS
agency worker TEMP
agent BOND; FACTOR; FED; REP; SPY; TOOL; ■ BROKER; BUYER; DELEGATE; IMPLEMENT; SLEEPER; can indicate a specific tool (as "bor-

ing agent" cues AWL); can indicate any thing that produces a result, thus "press agent" can lead to FLATIRON
agent, business FACTOR
agent, insurance BROKER
agents CIA; MI; SPIES
ages YONKS; *see* AGE
aggravate IRK; NETTLE; PRY
aggravated, aggravating anagram indicator
aggregate, mineral ORE
aggressive HARD; ■ FIERCE; MACHO
aggressive person BULL; BULLY
aggressively masculine BUTCH
aggrieved SORE; anagram indicator
aggro TROUBLE
agile SPRY; ■ NIMBLE
aging OLD
aging, show signs of YELLOW
agio COST
agitate IRK; SHAKE; STIR; ■ CHURN; FLUSTER; NEEDLE
agitated SHOOK; ■ TWITCHY; anagram indicator
agitated, be FLAP; SHAKE; SIMMER
agitating anagram indicator
agitation LATHER; anagram indicator
agitator REBEL; ■ CHARTIST; anagram indicator
agonise BROOD
agony HELL; PAIN; ■ THROES; TORMENT
agony, in anagram indicator
agony, cause RACK
agree CHIME; GRANT; MATCH; NOD; OK; SETTLE; SQUARE; SUIT; TALLY; UNITE; ■ ASSENT; COMPROMISE; CONTRACT; CORRESPOND; EQUATE; OKAY; ROGER; STRIKE; YIELD
agree, don't DEMUR; OBJECT
agree to do business CONTRACT
agreeable FINE; GOOD; NICE; OK; SWEET; ■ PLEASANT

agreeable, be NOD; ■ COMPLY

agreeable situation, in a a component to be nested within NICE, OK etc

agreeably WELL

agreed DONE; OK; OKED (i.e. okayed); ON; ■ ATONE (i.e. at one); SURE; TALLIED

agreement AY; AYE; BOND; DEAL; NOD; OK; PACT; SYNC; UNION; YEA; YES; ■ ACCORD; ASSENT; COMPACT; CONTRACT; SAYSO; TREATY; TRUCE

agreement, acknowledgement of OK; SURE; YES; *see* AGREEMENT

agreement, announce ASCENT

agreement in Germany JA

agreement, old, traditional YEA

agreement, show NOD; SIDE

agreement, sign of NOD

agricultural building BARN; FARM

agricultural business FARM; HOLDING; RANCH

agricultural machinery TRACTOR

agriculture FARMING

aground ASHORE

ague FEVER; FIT

ah O

ahead A; ON (as in "get on"); UP; ■ FORWARD; LEADING; WINNING; one component to precede another

ahead, go LEAD

ahead, went LED

aid ABET; CRIB; HELP; RELIEF

aide ADC; [◊ DECAMP]; *see* ASSISTANT

ail TROUBLE

aileron FLAP

ailing ILL; SICK; ■ HURT; anagram indicator;

ailment, minor COLD

ailments, disposed to frequent WEAK

aim END; GOAL; MEAN; PLAN; POINT; TRAIN; TRY; ■ DESIGN; DIRECT; INTEND;

INTENT; LEVEL; MISSION; OBJECT; TARGET; TELOS

aim high LOB

aim of sportsmen GAME

aim to score goal SHOOT

aimed MEANT

aimlessly anagram indicator

aimlessly, move DRIFT; MILL

air AURA; GAS; PORT (Gael.); SIDE; SONG; STRAIN; TED; TUNE; WARM; WIND; ■ BEARING; DISPLAY; MANNER; MIEN; OZONE; PARADE

air current WIND

air defence AD

air, foul SMOG

air, go by FLY

air, in the UP; anagram indicator

air-intake VENT

air, passage through FLIGHT

air speed , high MACHI (i.e. mach 1)

air-trip HOP; anagram of AIR

air trooper PARA

airborne, become/get FLY; RISE

airborne soldier PARA

aircraft CRATE; JET; MIG; PLANE

aircraft company LINE

aircraft compartment BAY

aircraft control FLAP

aircraft, part of WING

aircraft staff CREW

aircraftman AC

aircraftsman ERK

airhole VENT

airline, old BEA

airman AC; FLIER; LAC; PO; ■ PILOT

airmen RAF

airplane CRAFT; *see* AIRCRAFT

airport LUTON; [◊ STRIP; TERMINAL]

airport, move around TAXI

airy LIGHT

ait ISLE

ajar OPEN

Alabama AL

alarm APPAL; BELL; DREAD; FEAR; RATTLE; ROCK;

SCARE; SHOCK; WORRY; ■
ALERT; HOOTER; PANIC;
SIREN; WARNING

alarm, cause ROCK ■ AFRIGHT;
FRIGHT; FRIGHTEN; *see*
ALARM

alarm, cry of O; OH

alarm, noise of BLEEP

alarm, show sudden START

alarm system GUARD

alarmingly anagram indicator

alas ALACK; SHAME

Albania AL

albeit THOUGH

albeit briefly THO

Albert AL; WATCH

Albert Hall event PROM

album BOOK; DISC; LP;
TRACKS

albumen GLAIR

alcohol BEER; CIDER; DRINK
(qv); GIN; KIR

alcohol, add extra LACE

alcohol free DRY; TT

alcohol, not having DRY; TT

alcohol, not having much LITE

alcohol of, large quantity CASE;
see BARREL

alcohol supplier of BAR; PUB
(qv)

alcohol, take TIPPLE

alcoholic *see* DRUNKARD

alcoholic refreshment MEAD;
see ALCOHOL

ale BEER; DRINK (qv); [◊ BREW]

ale, long drink of YARD

alert AWAKE; QUICK; WARN

alert mind, of ABLE

Alfred ALF; [◊ GREAT]

alfresco OUT

Algerian music RAI

Algerian port ORAN

Ali CLAY

alias AKA; anagram indicator

alien ET; ■ STRANGE;
STRANGER; anagram indicator,
as "alien race" → an anagram of
RACE

alienating anagram indicator

Alighieri DANTE (i.e. the poet's
first name)

alight IN; LAND; ■ BLAZING

alight, set FIRE; ■ BLAZE

align DRESS; ■ ARRANGE

alive QUICK

all FULL; FULLY; LOT; PER;
QUITE; SUM; TOTAL; TOUT;
U; WHOLE

all about anagram indicator

all but one letter to be omitted, usually the last

all but the first initial letter to be
omitted

all in French TOUT

all in Paris TOUT

all of France TOUT

all of us UN

all one has SUM (qv)

all over can act as simple reverse
indicator (as **over**) but more often
it signifies that *all* components
referred to are to be reversed

all over the place anagram indicator

all points NEWS

all right APT; FAIR; FINE; FIT;
GOOD; OK

all round nesting indicator; a component to be nested within ALL
(or a synonym such as SUM)

all-round RING

all-rounder BALL; SASH;
SPHERE

All Saints' Day NOVI (i.e. November 1st)

all the time EER; EVER

all through OVER

all-time EVER

all times EVER

all to see, for U (i.e. film category)

all wrong LAL; LLA

allay CALM; LULL

allegation CHARGE; CLAIM

allegation, damaging MUD

allegations, make CHARGE;
CLAIM; ■ CONTEND

allege CONTEND

allegiance, showing LOYAL

allegiance, transfer DEFECT;
RAT

allegory PARABLE

allegro FAST

alleviation RELIEF

alley LANE; PATH; ■ MARBLE

alliance AXIS; BLOC; MATCH; NATO; UNION; ■ LEAGUE

alliance, of/in anagram indicator

allies BLOC

allocate ASSIGN

allocate resources BUDGET

allocated anagram indicator

allocation QUOTA; RATION; SHARE; anagram indicator

allot ASSIGN; GRANT; SHARE

allotment BEDS; GRANT; PART; PLOT; SHARE; RATION; ■ GARDEN

allow CLEAR; ENABLE; GRANT; LET; OK; PASS; ■ OKAY

allow access ADMIT

allow, don't BAN; BAR

allow, not BAN; BAR; STUNT

allow use of LEASE

allowance GRANT; QUOTA; RATION; ■ BUDGET

allowed LET; LICIT; ON; ■ LEGIT

allowed back TEL

allowed, is MAY

allowed, not BANNED; OUT

allowed, what's RATION

alloy BRASS

allude REFER

allure CHARM

allusion to, make REFER

alluvial area DELTA

ally PAL; *see* FRIEND

Almighty GOD

almost NEAR; NEARLY; NIGH; omission indicator, usually one letter from the end of a word (note that the omission can be of an implied word, as "almost everyone" → AL)

almost all AL; MOST

almost at once SOON

almost certainly SUR

almost everything AL

almost fail DI

almost give up VIG

almost nobody NOON

almost time NIGHT (i.e. nigh-t)

aloft HIGH; UP

alone SOLE; SOLO; ■ ONLY

along BY

along with AND

alongside BY; CLOSE; NEAR

aloof COLD; ICY

aloud homophone indicator

Alp MOUNT; PEAK

alphabet ROMAN

alphabet, half the ATOM (i.e. A to M)

already arranged PRIOR

also AND; TOO

also go back OOT

also in France (Paris etc) ET

also known as AKA

also once ITEM (arch.)

alter AMEND; COOK (as in cook the books); CHANGE; REFORM

alter ego HYDE; anagram indicator

altercation ROW (qv); anagram indicator

alteration CHANGE; anagram indicator

alteration to end of last letter to be changed

alterations, without any ASIS

altered anagram indicator

altered state TRANCE

alternate can indicate the use of alternate letters as "Theorize air's iamb as showing alternate rhyme scheme" gives TERZA RIMA

alternative ALT; OR; OPTION; OTHER; ■ STEAD; anagram indicator

alternative case OTHER

alternative expression AWE (hom.)

alternative quarters OR to be placed between two compass points to give NORW, SORE, EROS etc

alternatively OR; anagram indicator

alternatively named AKA

altitude HEIGHT

altogether NUDE

aluminium AL

alumnus OB

always AY (Middle English); EER; EVER; ■ ETERNAL

always returned REE; REVE

am unable CANT

amalgamate MERGE; anagram indicator

amass GATHER; HOARD; SAVE

amateur A; AM; LAY; LOVER

amateur, not PRO

amaze STUN; ■ STAGGER

amazement AWE; WONDER

amazement, struck with AWED; DUMB

amazing, amazingly anagram indicator

Amazon can indicate something exclusive of men

ambassador HE (abbr. for His Excellency)

ambiguous anagram indicator

ambit RANGE; SCOPE

ambition DREAM; END; GOAL; GRAIL

ambitious type PUSHER

amble STROLL

amend ALTER; FIX; anagram indicator

amended anagram indicator

amending, needs anagram indicator

amendment CHANGE; FIFTH; anagram indicator

amends, make ATONE; REQUITE

amenities NT

America AM; STATES; UNION; USA US

America, change in DIME

America, from can indicate American spelling as in "Letter from America" → REALTOR

America, in can indicate American spelling as "beauty in America" clues LUSTER

America, part of STATE

America, people from MAYA

America's cut AX

America, small profit in BUCK

American A; AM; GI; INCAN; US; YANK; *see* AMERICAN INDIAN; can indicate the American spelling of a word (color, pretense, thru etc)

American associate BUD; PARD

American band TIRE

American bill CHECK; TAB

American bonnet HOOD

American car LIMO; SEDAN; [◊ HOOD; SHIFT; TRUNK]

American chap BO

American college *see* AMERICAN UNIVERSITY

American colony, founder of PENN

American cutter AX

American, defective TRICK (i.e. adj. in US)

American, dull GRAY

American exclamation GEE

American firm INC

American flag COLOR

American fool SHMO

American friend BUD

American fuel GAS

American girl BROAD; DOLL; GAL

American guy MAC; ■ BUSTER

American hack AX

American heart CENTER; RI

American heartland CENTER

American hero REVERE

American Indian BRAVE; CREE; CREEK; CROW; FOX; HOPI; OSAGE; UTE; ■ APACHE; CARIB; INCAN

American kid BUB

American lawyer DA

American letter ZEE

American litigant, typical DOE

American magazine LIFE

American money BUCK; CENT; DIME; FOLD; QUARTER; ROLL

American novel, hero of FINN

American nuts NOODLES

American, ordinary JOE

American people CREE; HOPI; UTE; *see* AMERICAN INDIAN

American poker STUD

American prosecutor DA

American, serving GI

American ship *see* AMERICAN VESSEL

American side ENGLISH

American's blue, perhaps COLOR

American's finished off THRU

American's mood COLOR

American, serving GI

American soldier GI; GRUNT

American state AL; ALA; ALAS; ARK; AZ; CAL; COL; COLO; CONN; DAK; DEL; GA; I; IA; ID; ILL; IND; KANS; KS; KY; LA; MA; MAINE; MASS; ME; MICH; MINN; MISS; MO; MONT; ND; NEB; NEV; NH; NJ; NY; OK; OR; ORE; PENN; RI; SC; SD; TENN; TEX; TX; UT; VA; VT; WASH; WIS; WYO

American suits DECK

American tone COLOR

American uncle SAM

American university MIT; YALE

American vessel US; USS

American volume LITER

American waistcoat VEST

American warrior *see* AMERICAN INDIAN

American wood LUMBER

American woman, vulgar BROAD; DAME

American writer POE; ■ EMERSON

Americans GIS

Americans, a quantity of LITER

Americans' ready BUCK; *see* AMERICAN MONEY

Amerindian CREE; HOPI; UTE; *see* AMERICAN INDIAN

amicable KIND

amid AMONG; nesting indicator

amid confusion anagram of AMID

amidships a component to be nested within SS or another synonym for ship (qv)

ammo, old GRAPE

ammunition BALL; BULLET; ROUND; SHOT

amok WILD; anagram indicator

among AMID; IN; MID; nesting indicator; run indicator

amorous FRESH; LOVING

amorous, be BILL; COO; SPOON

amorous type LOVER

amorously, behave NECK; *see* AMOROUS, BE

amount DROP; LOT; SOME; STAKE; SUM; TON; ■ EXTENT; SUPPLY; TOTAL

amount, large TON; ■ PECK

amount, least WHIT

amount of nesting or run indicator

amount owed BILL

amount, say can refer to a mountain (where 'say' is acting as a homophone indicator)

amount, small DAB; DOT; DRIB; SPOT; TOT; TRACE ■ MICRON; OUNCE; WHIT

amount to BE; TOTAL

amount, unspecified SOME

amour BEAU; LOVER

amphetamine SPEED

amphibian CROC; EFT; FROG; NEWT; TOAD

amplify BOOST

amplitude RANGE

ample RICH; ■ ENOUGH

amply WELL

amulet CHARM

amuse TICKLE; ■ DIVERT

amuse greatly KILL

amusement FUN; ■ LAUGHTER; can indicate any pastime (game, skipping etc.)

amusement, shout of HA

amusement, show SMILE; *see* SMILE

amusing DROLL; FUN; FUNNY; ■ WITTY

amusing character/person CARD; CAUTION; WAG; WIT

amusing item/thing TOY

an remember that AN itself can be part of the solution

anaemic-looking PALE

anaesthetic ETHER; LOCAL; NUMBER

anaesthetise FREEZE; GAS

anaesthetised NUMB

★ **anagram** in normal use, an anagram is a word of phrase which is formed by the letters of another in a different order. It is probably the most common device in cryptics, for example: "For Ed, a fancy hat" → FEDORA. However, it can be extended to the manipulation of *part* words (as "anti-coagulant" can require you to form AINT, for example in building up the answer FAINT or TAINT)

★ **anagram indicators** these are the coded words in the clue which tell us we have to solve an anagram. For example, the role of "fancy", "involved", "new", "reordered" etc in a clue is usually that of an anagram indicator

analgesic NUMBER

analyse TEST; ■ PARSE

analyse sentences PARSE

analysis anagram indicator

analysis, brief CRIT

analyzing anagram indicator

anarchic LAWLESS; anagram indicator

anarchy anagram indicator

Anatole FRANCE

ancestor can indicate the beginnings of anything living, so "ancestor of tree" → ACORN

ancestors LINE; TREE

ancestry LINE; RACE

anchor CAT; KEDGE; MOOR; ■ WEIGHT

anchor, part of FLUKE

anchor, raise WEIGH

anchor, raised AWEIGH

anchorage ROADS

ancient AGED; ELDER; FLAG; O; OLD; OLDEN; SAGE; ■ ENSIGN; can indicate a person in a senior position; with a cap it is likely to refer to IAGO (Shakespearean character), *see* OTHELLO

Ancient Briton PICT

ancient city ROME; TROY; UR; ■ ILIUM; THEBES

ancient custom RELIC

ancient letter RUNE

Ancient Mariner, The SALT

ancient, more OLDER

ancient oath ODS

ancient, the YE

ancient times BC

ancient tongue LATIN

ancient vessel ARGO

and PLUS; THEN; WITH; note that AND itself can be part of the solution; also beware that it can represent the three letters to be omitted as in "...and gets thrown out" → AND is to be omitted

and* JOINER

and French ET

and German UND

and in French ET

and in German UND

★ **& Lit** refers to the type of clue which is written in such a way that it simultaneously provides the definition of the solution *and* the instructions for solving it, so that it has to be read through twice. Example: "Some male – cocksure?" (4). Here, the definition is a "male – cocksure" (better understood as a "cocksure male"), while "Some" is hinting that the answer is a run of letters within the clue, leading to ALEC i.e. as in smart Alec

and not NOR

and others ETAL (i.e. et al); ETC

and so on ETC

anecdotes ANA

Andes* RANGE

anew AGAIN; anagram indicator

angel BACKER; BRICK; ■ DARLING; SERAPH

angel* COIN; can refer to a specific angel e.g. Gabriel

angelic fashion WINGS

anger BILE; FIRE; FURY; GALL; HEAT; IRE; IRK; RAGE; RILE; ■ ANNOY; TEMPER; WRATH

anger, fit of HUFF

anger, show STAMP

anger, showing CROSS; MAD

angered GALLED; HEATED; HOT; IRKED; RAGED; RILED

angle BEND; CAST; CORNER; FISH; LINE; SLANT; TURN; VIEW

angle, set at an RAKE

angler WALTON; [◊ LINE]

angler, cast by LINE

angler's equipment CREEL; NET; REEL; ROD

Anglican CE

Anglican cleric VEN

Anglicans CE

angrily anagram indicator

angry BLACK; CROSS; HOT; IRATE; RED; SORE; SPARE; WILD; ■ HEATED; HET(UP); HOPPING; SEETHING; *see* ANGERED; anagram indicator

angry, be FUME; RAGE; RANT; ■ SEERED (i.e. see red); SEETHE; STORM; *see* ANGER

angry display PADDY

angry feeling IRE

angry, get FUME; SIMMER

angry looking BLACK; RED; ■ GLARY

angry, visibly BLACK; RED

anguish WOE

angular BONY

animal APE; ASS; BEAST; BOAR; CAMEL; CAT; CONY; DEER; DOG; HARE; KID; LION; MOOSE; PET; RAM; RAT; SABLE; SLOTH; SOW; STAG; YAK; ■ BISON; BRUTE; COATI; ELAND; HOG; MONKEY; RABBIT; STEER; WEASEL

animal, arboreal MARTEN

animal, badger-like RATEL

animal call NEIGH

animal controller LEAD; LEASH

Animal Farm can indicate something to do with one of the characters in Orwell's book e.g. Major, Napoleon

animal enclosure CAGE; FOLD; PEN; STY; can indicate that an animal is to be nested

animal fat TALLOW

animal flesh MEAT

animal fodder STRAW

animal housing STY

animal's call BRAY

animal sanctuary ARK; PEN; RESERVE

animal shelter COTE; ZOO

animal, small ROO

animal, smallest RUNT

animal sound BAA; BARK; GROWL; GRUNT; LOW; MEW; MOO; PURR; YAP

animal specialist VET

animal that might fly PIG

animal transport ARK

animal, wild BOAR; STRAY; *see* ANIMAL

animals ASSES; FLOCK; HERD; MICE; NEAT; PACK; STOCK; SWINE; ZOO; *see* ANIMAL

animals, farm STOCK

animals, inferior CULL; CULLS

animals, lots of ZOO

animate JOLT; MOVE; STIR; ■ EXCITE

animated LIT; anagram indicator

animation shot CEL

animosity FRICTION; PIQUE; SPITE

Anita LOOS

annal RECORD

annex APPEND

annexe GRAB

announce CALL; SAY; STATE; USHER

announced, announcing homophone indicator

announcement AD; BILLING; homophone indicator

announces, he SAYER

annoy ANGER; BUG; GALL; GRATE; IRK; MIFF; NARK; RIDE; TEASE; TRY; VEX; ■ BOTHER; HACKLE; HASSLE; NETTLE; PEEVE; PESTER; RATTLE; TROUBLE

annoyance ANGER; PIQUE

annoyance, cause BUG; ■ AGGRIEVE; RANKLE; *see* ANNOY

annoyance, express SWEAR; TUT

annoyed ATE; CROSS; RODE; SORE; ■ RATTY; SHIRTY; TRIED; *see* ANGRY

annoyed exclamation RATS

annoyed, get RILE

annoying person BLIGHTER; PEST

annoying young person BRAT

annual* BOOK

annual return AR

annul CANCEL

annulment, to effect an CANCEL

anode POLE

anoint ANELE (archaic)

anointing UNCTION

anon SOON

anonymous ANON; GREY

anonymously usually a signal that N is to be omitted from indicated word

anorak GEEK; NERD

another SECOND; SOME; anagram indicator; when used with a verb can indicate use of prefix RE-; [◊ DOUBLE]

another way, in anagram indicator

answer A; ANS; FIT; RETORT; RETURN; ■ REPLY; RESPOND; RESPONSE; SERVE; SOLUTION; [◊ QUESTION]

answer, fail to PASS

answer, find the CRACK; SOLVE

answer, have the SOLVE

answer, near to WARM

answer, provide an REACT

answer, sharp RETORT

answer, short A; ANS

answers, set of KEY

antagonism OPPOSITION

★ **antagonym** a term recently coined to describe a word that has two contradictory meanings. As the meanings of such words depend on context they can be the source of confusion in everyday use and therefore make regular appearances in crosswords so it pays to be aware of them. For example, " cleave" means "stick together" or "split apart" depending on its context. Such words can come about through natural evolution of the language, as "bound" can

mean "moving" in a clause like "the coach is bound for the capital" but can signify "unmoving" when it is used to mean "tied". However, some words are given contrary meanings deliberately, usually as a code within a closed group. In recent years young people have borrowed "wicked" from the jazz world where for generations it has been used to mean "good". Likewise the jazzman's use of "cool" to mean "good" has now become widespread amongst the young, its newer positive meaning contrasting with the word's negative sense in contexts such as "his idea met with a cool response"

Antarctic POLE

Antarctic dependency ROSS

ante BEFORE; STAKE; *see* BET; [◊ POST]

antelope ELAND; GNU; SABLE; TOPI; ■ NAGOR

anthropoid HUMAN; *see* APE

anti AGAINST; AGIN; CON; NO

anti aircraft AA

anti-aircraft fire FLAK

anti smoking group ASH

anti-union place RENO

antic CAPER; GAME; PRANK

anticipation HOPE

anticlimax BATHOS

anticoagulant can indicate an anagram of ANTI

anticyclone HIGH

Antipodean AUSSIE; MAORI

antiquated OLD

antique OLD; PERIOD; ■ AGE (qv)

antique coin DUCAT

antique, more OLDER

Antony MARK

★ **antonym** a word (or phrase) that has a meaning opposite to another (TALL/SHORT, CLEAN/DIRTY etc); antonyms are commonly used in cryptics as "Note the advertisement is no good" (3) → BAD

anvil can indicate something to do with the inner ear

anxiety CARE; STRESS; WORRY; ■ ANGST; CONCERN; PANIC

anxiety cause SCARE; ■ ALARM; *see* ANXIETY

anxiety, causing FRAUGHT

anxious KEEN; TENSE; anagram indicator

anxious, highly [◊ ACRO-PHOBIA; VERTIGO]

anxious, be CARE; FRET; WORRY

anxious, was CARED

anxiously anagram indicator

any SOME

any more AGAIN

any number N

anything but NOT

anybody ONE

anyhow anagram indicator

anything AUGHT; OUT; OWT

anyway anagram indicator; can indicate a palindrome (as "Appeal, anyway" leads to REFER)

apart ASIDE; ASUNDER; AWAY; anagram indicator

apart from SAVE

apartment APT; FLAT; PAD; ROOM

apathetic COOL

apathetic, be MOPE

ape COPY; CHIMP; GIBBON; MIMIC; ORANG; ■ ECHO; SIMULATE

aperture GAP; *see* HOLE

apex PEAK; TOP

aphrodisiac PHILTRE; PHILTER (thus "aphrodisiac said" → FILTER)

Aphrodite, son of EROS

Apocryphal book TOBIT

apologetic SORRY

apostle PETER; SPOON; ■ PAUL

apostrophe (') when an apostrophe is placed *before* a word it usually signals the omission of the initial 'h' which in turn indicates that 'h' is to be dropped from the beginning of the target word to provide the solution;

when an apostrophe appears at the *end* of a word it usually signals the omission of the 'g' in 'ing' which in turn indicates the omission of the final 'g' in the target word

appal SHOCK

appalling DIRE; ■ CHRONIC; anagram indicator

appallingly anagram indicator

apparatus RIG

apparel DRESS; *see* CLOTHING

apparent CLEAR; OVERT; PLAIN

apparent in run indicator

apparently AP

appeal ASK; BEG; CHARM; CRY; IT; O (e.g. as in 'O Jerusalem'); PLEA; PLEAD; REFER; SA (i.e. sex appeal); SUE; UMP (verbal cricket appeal) appeal; may mean that the answer is in the form of a question

appeal, make an PLEAD

appeal, earnest PLEADING

appealing CUTE; FETCHING

appealing, not very PLAIN

appear BE; COME; EMERGE; LOOK; LOOM; SEEM; SHOW; anagram indicator as "idols appear" → SOLID

appear as anagram indicator

appear, it may anagram indicator

appear to do ACT

appearance AIR; CAST; ENTRY; FACE; FRONT; GUISE; LOOK; LOOKS; ■ ASPECT; ENTRANCE; MIEN; ONSET

appearance, deceptive FRONT

appearance, first DEBUT

appearance, put in an ATTEND

appeared CAME

appearing ON; anagram indicator

appearing unusual anagram indicator

appears can indicate that the definition precedes

appease CALM

appellation NAME

append ADD; ANNEX

appended ON; something to be appended to a component

appendix END; can indicate a noted appendix e.g. the Apocrypha

appetite HUNGER; TASTE

appetite, abnormal PICA

applaud CHEER; CLAP; PRAISE; ■ ACCLAIM; EXALT

applause CHEER; CHEERS; HAND; ■ ACCLAIM; CLAPPING; OVATION

applause, acknowledge BOW

applause, round of HAND

apple COX; CRAB; EATER; ■ RUSSET

appliance anagram indicator; *see* TOOL

application APP; COAT; USE; ■ PLASTER; REQUEST; anagram indicator

application document FORM

application for cut PLASTER

applied ON; anagram indicator

applied to ON

apply BEAR; USE; ■ EXERT

apply light touch DAB

apply lubricant OIL

applying care TEND; ■ NURSE

appoint ASSIGN; ■ ORDAIN

appointment DATE; POST; JOB

appointment, make an DATE

apportion ALLOT

apportioned anagram indicator

appraisal anagram indicator; ■ REVIEW

appreciate DIG; GROW; KNOW; LIKE

appreciate, do not RESENT

appreciation GAIN

appreciation, show CLAP

apprehend ARREST; FEAR; DREAD; GRASP; *see* CATCH

apprehended CAUGHT; *see* CATCH

apprehension DREAD; FEAR

apprehensive WINDY; ■ DREADING

apprehensive, be DREAD; FEAR

apprentice BOY; CUB; L; ■ LEARNER; TRAINEE; TYRO

approach ANGLE; CLOSE; COME; DRIVE; LINE; NEAR; RULE; TAKE; WAY; ■ ACCESS; COMING

approach, method DOOR; GATE

approach threateningly LOOM

approaching ALMOST; NEAR; TO; one element to precede another

approbation can indicate some expression of approval such as "Well done"

appropriate APT; DUE; FIT; JUST; RIGHT; ROB; STEAL; TAKE; WHIP; ■ ASSUME; COLLAR; FITTING; PILFER; PIRATE; POCKET; PROPER

appropriate backing MEET; *see* APPROPRIATE

appropriate to FOR

appropriately WELL

approval AMEN; FAVOUR; NOD; OK; YES; ■ ASSENT; *see* APPROVE

approval, cry of BRAVO

approval from France OUI

approval from Germany JA

approval, mark, sign of TICK

approval, seal of OKAY

approval, word of AMEN; YES

approve ALLOW; GRANT; LIKE; NOD; OK; PASS; TICK; ■ ADOPT; COMMEND

approve of LIKE

approve, those who CLAPPERS

approved OK

approved, was OKED (i.e. okayed)

approving FOR

approximate NEAR; ROUGH; anagram indicator

approximately ORSO (i.e. or so); ROUGH (as "Food, approximately how old?" → ROUGHAGE); anagram indicator

apt ABLE; FIT; FITTING; MEET; PRONE; RIGHT; ■ APPROPRIATE; LIABLE; LIKELY

apt, are/be TEND

apt, increasingly FITTER

aptitude BENT; FLAIR; TALENT

aquatic beast HIPPO; ■ WHALE

aquatic bird GULL; LOON; *see* BIRD

aquatic creature OTTER; WHALE; ■ FISH; MINKE

aquatic mammal SEAL

Ar ARGON

Arab AR; HORSE; ■ OMANI

Arab chief SHEIK

Arab country OMAN

Arab territory once UAR

Arabia AR

Arabia, part of OMAN

Arabian AR

Arabic pot KIF

arbiter REF

arbitrary anagram indicator

arbitrator REF

arbour BOWER

arc BEND; BOW; ■ CURVE

arcade CLOISTER

arch BAND; BEND; BOW; BRIDGE; CHIEF; SLY; TOP; ■ CUNNING; SKEW; VAULT; anagram indicator

arch, sort of SKEW

archaeological site (*etc*) DIG

archaeologist DIGGER [◊ DIG]

Archbishop LANG; ■ RUNCIE; TUTU

archdeacon VEN

archer HOOD; TELL

architect NASH; SPENCE; WREN; ■ ADAM

architects RIBA

architecture, style/type of ADAM; ORDER; ■ IONIC; NORMAN

Arctic POLE

Arctic, in the/of the POLAR

'ard ARSH

ardent AVID; KEEN; ■ ZEALOUS

ardour ZEAL

arduous HARD

arduous, not very EASY; LIGHT; SIMPLE

are A; EXIST; with a homophone indicator can mean R

are confused AER; EAR; ERA; RAE; REA

are French ES

are in nesting indicator; ARE to be nested within a component

are not ARNT

Are you French? ESTU (i.e. es tu?)

Are you hearing right? RUR

Are you talking? RU

area A; ACRE; AREA; DEPT; FIELD; LAND; PLACE; RANGE; REGION; ROOD; ROOM; SITE; SPACE; TRACT; ■ EXTENT; LOCUS; PART; ZONE

area, copper's MANOR

area, extended TRACT

area for playing COURT; GROUND

area, in the immediate BY

area, military SECTOR; ZONE

area of land ACRE; HIDE (arch.); ROOD

area, of the LOCAL

area, playing COURT; FIELD

area, protected RESERVE

area, specialised DEPT

arena LISTS; RING; ■ GROUND

arête RIDGE

argon AR

Argonaut captain JASON

argot CANT

argue PLEAD; REASON; ROW; SPAR; ■ BICKER; DEBATE

argue about, something MOTION

argue for PROPOUND

argument CON; DO; ISSUE; PLEA; RIFT; ROW; SPAR; SPAT; TIFF; WORDS; ■ BARNEY; DEBATE; SETTO (i.e. set-to); TODO (i.e. to-do); anagram indicator

argument against CON

argument, have a ROW; SPAR; *see* ARGUE

argument in favour/support PRO

argument over a synonym for "argument" to be reversed e.g. WOR, TAPS, *see* ARGUMENT

argument, typical of ERISTIC
arguments, heard ROUSE
argumentative ROWING
argumentative, be CARP; ROW
arguments in favour/support
PROS
argy-bargy *see* ARGUMENT,
FIGHT
arise EMERGE
arising reversal indicator
aristocracy GENTRY
aristocrat COUNT; EARL;
LORD; NOB; NOBLE; PEER;
TOFF; ■ COUNTESS; DUKE
aristocrat, old THANE
aristocratic NOBLE; U
aristocratic young man BUCK
arithmetic R (as in the thee R's)
Arizona AZ
ark BOX (arch.)
Arkansas AR
'arken EAR (i.e. 'ear)
'arkened EARD (i.e. 'eard)
Arkwright NOAH
arm GAT; GUN; LIMB; RIFLE;
WING; ■ BRANCH; MEMBER;
ROTOR; *see* WEAPON
arm, end of CUFF; HAND; M
armada FLEET
armchair [◊ CRITIC]
armed assailant GUNMAN
armed conflict ACTION;
BATTLE; WAR
armed men POSSE
armed services FORCES
armlet BAND
armour MAIL; ■ GREAVE
armour, piece of VISOR
armoured vehicle TANK
armoury TANKS
army A; FORCE; HORDE; HOST;
MEN; TA
army branch, corps, part of RA;
RE; REME; RI; UNIT
army chief/supremo OC; ■
GENERAL
army corps *see* ARMY BRANCH
army craftsmen REME
army depot CAMP
army doctors RAMC
army drill BULL

army man SM; *see* OFFICER,
SOLDIER
army medic MO
army, part (unit, part of) CORPS;
■ CADRE; DIVISION; *see*
ARMY BRANCH
army vehicle JEEP; TANK
Arnold, Dr HEAD
aroma REEK; SCENT
aromatic ingredient SPICE
around C; CA; RE; anagram indicator; reversal indicator; nesting
indicator, for example "around
midnight" indicates that G (i.e.
the middle of "night") is to be
nested within a component or between components; ■ CIRCUM
around, for instance GE (i.e. e.g.
reversed)
around us HERE; US to be nested
arouse STIR
aroused, arousing anagram indicator
arrange ALIGN; DO; DRESS;
EDIT; FIX; ORDER; PLAN;
POSE; RIG; SCORE; SORT;
STAGE; ■ COMB; LAY;
MARSHAL; SETTLE; anagram
indicator
arrange appointment DATE
arrange to meet DATE
arranged LAID; SET; anagram indicator
arrangement DEAL; ORDER;
PACT; PLAN; anagram indicator;
■ CONTRACT; SET-UP;
SYSTEM
arrangement of sails RIG
arranging ORDERING; anagram
indicator
arrant UTTER
array ORDER; ROW
arrayed anagram indicator
arrears DEBT; IOUS
arrears, in (financial) OWING;
SHORT; SHY
arrest BOOK; BUST; CATCH;
CHECK; COLLAR; COP;
GRAB; NAB; STEM; STOP;
STUNT; ■ LIFT (slang); NICK;
PULL; PULLIN (i.e. pull in);

RESTRAIN; RUNIN (i.e. run in); nesting indicator

arrested nesting indicator

arresting nesting indicator

arrival ADVENT; ARR; COMER; COMING; ■ LANDER; REACHER

arrival, expected time of ETA

arrive ARE; ARR; COME; LAND; REACH

arrive at ATTAIN; HIT; REACH

arrive noisily CUM

arrived ALONG; ARR; CAME; GOT; HERE; IN

arrives ARR; *see* ARRIVE

arriving ALONG

arriving, someone COMER

arrogance SIDE

arrogant COCKY; HIGH

arrogant person SNOB

arrow DART; ■ BOLT; MARKER; POINTER; SIGN

arsenic AS

'arsh ARD

arsonist LIGHTER

art CRAFT; PIC; SKILL; ■ CUNNING; TECHNIQUE

Art TATUM

art, classical ARS

art equipment BRUSH; EASEL

art form DADA

art, French ES (i.e. French verb)

art school SLADE

art, style of DECO

art work anagram of ART

art, work of BUST; MURAL; OIL; ■ ABSTRACT; PAINTING

artery ROAD

artfully anagram indicator

Arthur ART

artic LORRY

article A; AN; DER; DIE; EL; IL; IT; ITEM; LA; LE; LES; LOS; PAPER; PIECE; THE; THING; UN; UNE; ■ CLAUSE; COLUMN; LEADER; OBJECT

article, definite THE

article, indefinite A; AN

article, newspaper STORY; ■ ITEM

article, old YE

article, useless LEMON

articles WARE; can indicate that definite or indefinite articles (*see* ARTICLE *above*) are to be linked in some kind of combination e.g. ANTHE (e.g. to construct "panther"); the last example uses English articles but if the clue has some non-English reference then articles from foreign languages might be needed as ILDER (e.g. to construct "wilder")

articulate FLUENT; UTTER; VERBAL

artificial FAKE; MOCK; SHAM; anagram indicator

artillery RA

artist ETTY; HALS; HUNT; MUNCH; RA; TITIAN; TURNER; ■ DALI; DURER; LEGER; LELY; MATISSE; MANET; MIRO; MONET; PAINTER

artist's model FIGURE

artist's piecework COLLAGE

artist's stand/support/tripod EASEL

artist, sit for POSE

artistic man RA

artistic set RAS; RSA

artistic society RSA

artistic technique OIL

artistic work ICON; *see* ART

artistry CRAFT; SKILL

artless SIMPLE; ■ NAIF

as LIKE; QUA; SINCE; SO

as before DO (abbr. of ditto); SAME

as far as TO

as I see it TOME (i.e. to me)

as if anagram indicator

as it happens LIVE

as it were QUASI

as new anagram indicator

as regards RE

as soon as ONCE

as usual PAR

as well AND; TOO

as you might say homophone indicator

ascend CLIMB; MOUNT; RISE; SCALE; reversal indicator

ascended ROSE

ascent CLIMB; RISE

ascetic FAKIR; YOGI; ■ ESSENE

ashamed RED

ashen PALE; PALING

ashes EMBERS

ashore AGROUND; LANDED

Asia EAST

Asian INDIAN; PATEL; THAI

Asian dish, food BALTI

aside APART

ask BEG; BID; DEMAND; PLEAD; POSE; ■ APPEAL; CHARGE; ENTREAT; QUIZ; REQUEST

ask advice CONSULT

ask for CLAIM; SEEK

ask for help CONSULT

ask question again REPOSE

ask questions PRY

ask piteously BEG

asked BADE

askew anagram indicator

asking ROGATION

asleep ABED; OUT

aspect ANGLE; FACE; FACET; HUE; SIDE; TONE; VIEW

aspersion SLUR; SMEAR

aspersions, cast SMEAR

asphyxiate SMOTHER; ■ STRANGLE

aspiration AITCH; DREAM; H; HOPE

aspiration, without H to be omitted

aspire HOPE; LONG; YEARN

aspiring, one HOPER

ass DOPE; FOOL; MOKE

ass, sound like an BRAY

assail ATTACK

assailant RAPIST

assassin BOOTH; KILLER; ■ CUT-THROAT

assassinated, assassination anagram indicator

assault HIT; RAID; RUSH; ■ CHARGE; STORM; STORMING

assault, serious RAPE

assay TEST; TRY

assemble BUILD; EDIT; GATHER; HOARD; MAKE; MEET; MUSTER; SIT; ■ COLLECT; anagram indicator

assembled MET; SAT; anagram indicator

assembly DIET; MEET; MEETING; RALLY; SITTING; ■ TURNOUT; anagram indicator

assent OK; YES

assert CLAIM; STATE; SWEAR

assertion, make AVER; CLAIM; STATE

assertiveness PUSH

assess CHECK; GAUGE; GRADE; MARK; RATE; TEST

assessment GRADE; MARK; RATING; SCORE; TEST; TRIAL

asset PLUS; ■ BENEFIT; RESOURCE

assets ESTATE ■ CAPITAL

assign GRANT; PIN; POST; ■ APPOINT; DETAIL

assignation DATE

assignment JOB; MISSION; TASK

assimilate DIGEST; nesting indicator

assimilates nesting indicator

assist ABET; AID; BACK; HELP; SERVE

assist in negotiation MEDIATE

assistance AID; HAND; HELP; ■ RELIEF; SERVICE

assistance, financial BACKING; GRANT; RELIEF

assistance, without ALONE

assistant ADC; AIDE; AIDER; DRESSER; MATE; PA; ■ ABETTER; HELPER; SECOND; can be stretched to include *anything* which assists, thus "swimmer's assistant" → FIN

assisted AIDED

associate ALLY; MATE; PAL; ■ COLLEAGUE; MEMBER; RELATE

association BOND; CLUB; GUILD; RING; TIE; UNION

Association member GUIDE

association, old trade GUILD

assorted, assortment anagram indicator

assuage ALLAY; SLAKE

assume DON; GUESS; ■ ADOPT; POSIT; PUTON (i.e. put on); SEIZE

assumed TACIT

assuming nesting indicator (as "assuming a" could require A to be nested)

assumption can indicate an item of clothing

assurance NERVE

astern AFT; BACK; ■ BEHIND

astonish SHOCK; STAGGER

astonishing anagram indicator

astonishing, that's COR

astonishment AWE; SHOCK; WONDER

astonishment, cause *see* ASTONISH

astray LOST; anagram indicator

astray, go ERR; SIN; WANDER

astride ON; UP; nesting indicator

astronomer HALLEY; HUBBLE

astronomical unit EPACT

astute ABLE; CLEVER (qv); QUICK; SHREWD; WISE

asylum RETREAT

asymmetric, make SKEW

at IN

At chemical symbol for astatine

at all EVER

at all times EER; EVER

at any time EER; EVER

at church ATCH

at first ERST; IST (i.e. 1st); initial letter indicator as "Honour kept us doing our shoes at first" clues KUDOS

at heart insertion indicator; can indicate that middle letter(s) are to be used, as 'liberal at heart' clues E or BER

at home IN

at last last letter indicator, usually applicable to one word but can apply to the last letters of several words in the clue

at liberty FREE; LOOSE

at no time NEVER

at once NOW

at one time EX; ONCE; ■ FORMER

at sea ADRIFT; SAILING; anagram indicator as "lost at sea" → anagram of LOST

at that time THEN

at the moment NOW

at the present time NOW; can indicate something associated with Christmas (i.e. time for presents)

at this point HERE; NOW

at work anagram indicator

ate BIT; CHEWED; DINED

Athenian ATTIC; TIMON

Athenian character TIMON; can indicate a Greek letter needs to be used as a component (*see* GREEK CHARACTER)

Athens, in can indicate the use of a Greek letter (*see* GREEK CHARACTER)

athlete BLUE; RUNNER

athletic FIT

athletic event HEAT; JUMP; MILE; RACE; RELAY; RUN; SHOT; ■ DISCUS

athletic type BLUE; RUNNER

athwart ACROSS; SLANT

atlas CHARTS; ■ MAPS

atmosphere AIR; AURA; FUG; ■ AMBIENCE; SPIRIT

atmosphere, heavy/unpleasant FUG

atomic particle ION

atomic pile REACTOR

atone PAY

atop UPON

atrium COURT; HALL

atrocious DIRE; anagram indicator

atrociously anagram indicator

attach FIX; PIN; STICK

attached ON

attachment BOND; LINK; LOVE; TAG; TIE

attack ASSAIL; BOMB; CHECK (i.e. in chess); CLUB; FIT; GOAT (i.e. go at); HIT; PUSH; RAID; SHELL; SORTIE; TILT ■ GO FOR; KICK; POUNCE;

SNIPE; STORM; STRIKE; anagram indicator; *see* UNDER ATTACK

attack, continuous FIRE

attack, pointed STAB

attack, sudden FORAY

attack with club COSH

attack with explosives SHELL

attacked BIT; HIT; ■ SETON (i.e. set on)

attacker RAIDER

attain REACH

attar OIL

attempt AIM; BID; CRACK; GO; SHOT; SHY; STAB; TACKLE; TRY; ■ FLING; GOAT (i.e. go at); TRIAL

attempt at goal SHOT

attempt to win COURT

attempts TRIES

attend APPEAR; BEAT (i.e. be at); GRACE; HEAR; HEED; MAKE (as in "make it"); SHOW; WAIT

attend carefully to NURSE

attendance GATE; TURNOUT

attendance, in PRESENT

attendant BUTLER; CARER; GROOM; MAN; NURSE; PAGE; USHER; ■ COURTIER; KEEPER; WAITER

attendant, theatre USHER

attendants TRAIN; ■ PAGES; RETINUE

attendants, royal COURT

attending AT; HERE; IN; PRESENT

attending, lot/number/those GATE

attention CARE; EAR; HARK; HEED; NOTE; ■ INTEREST

attention! SHUN

attention, call for HO

attention, give/pay CARE; HARK; HEED; NOTE

attention, pay no DISCOUNT; ■ IGNORE

attention, requiring TODO (i.e. to do)

attention, this draws AHEM

attest SWEAR

attic GARRET; LOFT; with a capital letter can indicate something to do with Greece, e.g. the country, alphabet, mythology

attire DRESS; FROCK; GOWN; RIG; SHIRT; SKIRT

attire, item of TIE; *see* ATTIRE

attitude AIR; LINE; MANNER; POSE; STAND; TONE; ■ POSITION; POSTURE; STANCE

attitudinise POSE

attorney ATT; DA; *see* LAWYER

attract DRAW; ENGAGE; LURE; PULL; TEMPT; ■ ENTICE

attract attention STAR; *see* ATTRACT

attracted DREW

attracted to the components on either side of the phrase to run consecutively

attraction BAIT; DRAW; IT; LURE; PULL; RIDE

attractive CATCHY; CUTE; DISHY; FAIR; GLAM; NICE; PLUM; PRETTY; TAKING; TASTY; ■ BECOMING; DRAWING; FETCHING; WINNING

attractive, be DRAW

attractive female, girl, woman BELLE; DOLL; DISH; LOOKER

attractive, notedly CATCHY

attractive one CUTIE; *see* ATTRACTIVE FEMALE

attractive person CRACKER

attractive, something DRAW; LURE; ■ HONEYPOT; MAGNET

attractive, was DREW; LURED

attractive, what's *see* ATTRACTIVE, SOMETHING

attractive woman BELLE

attractiveness, superficial GLOSS

attribute ASCRIBE; CREDIT; ■ ATTACH

attribute of run indicator

atypical RARE; STRANGE

Au GOLD

auction SALE

auction item LOT

auctioneer, equipment for GAVEL

audacious BRAVE; COOL; FORWARD; LIPPY; RASH

audacity BOTTLE; CHEEK; GUTS; NECK; NERVE

audible homophone indicator

audible disapproval BOO; HISS

audibly ALOUD; homophone indicator

audience EAR; HOUSE; PUBLIC; ■ HEARING; READERS

audience, appreciative CLAPPERS

audio homophone indicator

audio equipment EAR

audio-visual AV

audit CHECK; ■ INSPECT

audition HEARING; TRIAL; homophone indicator; [◊ EAR(S)]

auditioning homophone indicator

auditor EAR

auditor, for the homophone indicator

auditor, to homophone indicator

auditory equipment, to do with OTIC

augur SEER

August AUG; GREAT; ■ IMPERIAL

Augustus GUS

Aunt Sally BUTT

aura CHARM

aureole HALO

Aurora DAWN

auspicious LUCKY

Aussie fellow SPORT

Aussie party DING

Austen heroine EMMA

austere DOUR; HARSH; SEVERE; ■ BRUTAL; SPARTAN; STRICT

Australia AUS; OZ

Australia, water in DARLING

Australian AUS; OZ; STRINE

Australian, coarse OCKER

Australian fool DILL

Australian friend COBBER

Australian lake EYRE

Australian man BRUCE

Australian, red-haired BLUE

Australian runner EMU

Australian sheep shearer RINGER

Australian truck UTE

Australian utility, fire UTE

Austria A

Austrian architect LOOS

Austrian, old ALT

Austrian scientist MACH

authentic GEN; REAL; TRUE; ■ ECHT; see GENUINE, REAL

authenticate SIGN

author BARRIE; ECO; ELIA; HOPE; LEWIS; ME; PARENT; PEN; POTTER; READE; SAND; SNOW; TWAIN; WELLS; YEATS; ■ CAMUS; ELIOT; JEROME; LAMB; ORWELL; PROUST; SCRIBE; SETTER; URIS; VERNE; WRITER; see NOVELIST, WRITER

author, German MANN

author, humorous JEROME

authorisation OK; ■ SANCTION

authorisation, give see AUTHORISE

authorise OK; ORDER; SIGN

authoritative instruction ORDINANCE (useful for making ORDNANCE)

authority ARM (as in "arm of the law"); CLOUT; EXPERT; MIGHT; OK; POWER; RIGHT; RULE; SAGE; SAY; SWAY; ■ SAY-SO

Authority BOARD

authority, position of CHAIR

autobiography LIFE; [◊ BY]

autograph SIGN

automatic reaction TIC

autumn FALL

autumn, part of OCT

avail SERVE; USE

avail, to no IDLY

available AROUND; FREE; IN; ON; OPEN; OUT; TAP; anagram indicator

available in nesting indicator

available, not OFF; OUT

available, people (or resources etc) POOL

available, readily HANDY

available, what is RANGE

availing USING

avant-garde VAN; anagram indicator

avarice GREED

avenue AVE; DRIVE; MALL; WAY

aver AFFIRM; STATE

average AV; AVE; MEAN; MEDIUM; NORM; PAR; SOSO (i.e. so-so); ■ MEDIAL

average, above HIGH

average, less than LOW

aviation FLYING; [◊ FLIGHT]

aviator PILOT

avocado PEAR

avoid DUCK; ELUDE; FLEE; MISS; SHUN; WARE; ■ ABSTAIN; DODGE; ESCAPE; ESCHEW; EVADE

avoid being decisive HEDGE

avoid commitment HEDGE

avoid one's duty SKIVE

avoid offending RESPECT

avoid reading SKIP

avoid straight answers FENCE

avoiding omission indicator, as "avoiding greeting" → HI to be omitted

Avon can indicate something to do with Shakespeare

avow SWEAR

aw GEE; *see* EXPRESSION OF SURPRISE

Aw! SHAME

await BIDE

awaiting payment OWING

awake AWAKE; UP

awaken ROUSE

award BAY (i.e. laurel wreath); CUP; EMMY; GOLD; GRANT; MM; OM; PALM; POT; PRIZE; TONY; ■ OSCAR; TROPHY; *see* HONOUR, MEDAL

award points to can indicate some combination of the points of the compass (N, S, E, W) to be included in the solution e.g. EN

award, public service BEM

award, sporting CAP

award, theatre TONY

aware AWARE; HIP; ONTO

aware, are KNOW

aware of INTO

aware of trends HIP

awareness SENSE

away ABROAD; AFIELD; GONE; HENCE; OFF; ■ APART; anagram indicator; omission indicator, such as initial or final letter

away from OFF; OUT OF

away from home ABROAD; AFIELD

away, put DINE; EAT

awe DREAD; FEAR; WONDER

awful BAD; LOUSY; ■ CHRONIC; FRIGHTFUL; NASTY; VILE; anagram indicator

awfully anagram indicator

awfully good PIOUS

awkward BAD; STICKY; ■ NAFF; anagram indicator

awkward position (situation) CORNER; FIX; HOLE; JAM; PICKLE; SPOT

awn BEARD

awning SHADE

awkwardly anagram indicator

axe CHOP; CUT; FIRE; HEW; SACK; ■ CHOPPER; HATCHET; as a term in jazz, can refer to a musical instrument (e.g. saxophone); in more recent years has been borrowed by rock music to refer specifically to a guitar

axed CUT; HEWN; first letter to be omitted; *see* CUT

axeman CHOPPER; HEWER

axing first letter to be omitted; *see* CUT

axis LEAGUE; PIN

Ayrshire COW

Bb

B KEY
babble PRATE; PRATTLE
babbling homophone indicator
Babe RUTH
baby CHICK; CHILD; CUB; KID; KITTEN; PUP; SMALL; [◊ QUILT]
baby-carrier PRAM; STORK
baby food RUSK
baby, look after SIT
baby-sitter MINDER
babywear NAPPY
Bach [◊ G]
Bach's works, like some of FUGAL
bachelor B; BA; SINGLE
bachelor's home PAD
back AFT; AGAIN; BET; END; HIND; HOME; REAR; SECOND; SPINE; STERN; TAIL; ■ CHAMPION; ENCOURAGE; HELP; RATIFY; SWEEPER; reversal indicator; can indicate an adjective or verb beginning with RE-
back at sea AFT
back door POSTERN
back entrance ROOD (rev.)
back, not TON
back-numbers SON
back of last letter indicator (as "back of store" clues E)
back on see BACK OF
back pain YNOGA (a reversal which is useful because losing the N gives YOGA)
back-pay YAP; ■ DRAWER i.e. reversal of "reward"
back-room DRAW; MOOR
back row WOR
back-street a synonym for "street" to be reversed, thus ENAL, TS etc
back street in Paris EUR
back to OT

back to the East OTE
back up PU (i.e. "up" reversed); a synonym of "back" to be reversed e.g. TEB; for synonyms see BACK, SUPPORT
back-up RESERVE; anagram indicator
backbone CHINE; SPINE
backchat LIP
backed reversal indicator
backed by YB; joint run and reversal indicator as "Statesman backed by Labour henchman" → NEHRU; can indicate a component is to come last in the solution
backer ANGEL; ■ SECOND; SPONSOR
backfired reversal indicator
background PAST; REAR; STORY; ■ AMBIENCE
background music, supply PIPE
backhander BUNG
backing AID; reversal indicator; element to be placed at end of word
backing, given reverse indicator
backslapping HEARTY
backstreet ALLEY; TS (i.e. reversal of ST)
backtracking reverse indicator
backward DRAW; HIND; reversal indicator
backwards AFT; reversal indicator
bacon RASHER
bacon, cut of BACK; GAMMON; see BACON
bacon, feature of STREAK
bacteria CULTURE
bad CROOK; DIRE; EVIL; HARD; HIGH; ILL; OFF; POOR; ROTTEN; ■ ADDLED; MAL; SEVERE; WICKED; anagram indicator; can indicate a word beginning with MIS-
bad actor HAM
bad acting HAM
bad back ROOP (i.e. rev.)
bad, become ROT
bad behaviour CRIME; SIN
bad conditions RAIN
bad end D

bad feeling HATE; SPITE; ■ MALICE; ODIUM

bad for Americans BUM

bad French MAL

bad habit VICE

bad hat CAD; ROTTER

bad, is not as EASES

bad language CUSS; OATH

bad lot ROTTER

bad manners, one with BOOR

bad name MUD

bad name, give a BRAND

bad odour *see* BAD SMELL

bad return LIVE (i.e. rev.)

bad service FAULT

bad situation PASS; *see* SPOT

bad smell BO; PONG

bad taste, in TACKY

bad tempered CROSS; MEAN; TESTY; ■ CRABBY

bad thing CRIME; SIN

bad time SLUMP

bad turn LLI (i.e. rev.)

bad, turn ADDLE

bad, very CHRONIC; EVIL

bad visibility FOG

bad weather FOG; HAIL; RAIN; SNOW

badge MARK; SIGN; TAG

badge of rank STRIPE

badger BROCK; NAG; RIDE; ■ HARRY; HOUND; PESTER;

badger's hole, home EARTH; SETT

badgered anagram indicator

badinage CHAFF

badly ILL; anagram indicator

badly, behave SIN

badly-built anagram indicator

badly-cooked anagram indicator

badly formed anagram indicator

badly lit DARK; DIM; anagram of LIT

badly made TRASHY; anagram indicator

badly written anagram indicator

baffle STUMP

baffling anagram indicator

bag CASE; CATCH; CLAIM; GRIP; LAND; NAIL; NET; POKE; PURSE; SAC; SACK; ■ CARRIER; RESERVE; SACHET; SATCHEL; STEAL; nesting indicator

bag, in the PACKED; STOWED; can indicate that a component is nested within a synonym of "bag" (*see* BAG)

bag, large SACK

bag reportedly, in the PACT

bagel ROLL

baggage CASE; GEAR; GRIP; SLUT; TART; ■ SLATTERN; TROLLOP

baggage handler/man PORTER

bagged GOT

bagging nesting indicator

Baggins BILBO

baggy, get STRETCH

bagpipe, part of CHANTER

bags LOTS; OODLES; can indicate something to do with trousers, plus-fours, trews etc; nesting indicator

bail BAR; SCOOP

bailiff REEVE

bait KID; LURE; RIB; TEASE; ■ GENTLE (fishing); SPRAT (i.e. to catch a mackerel)

bait, accept the BITE; RISE

bake COOK; FIRE; TAN; can indicate something to do with sun-bathing

baked anagram indicator; [◊ BEAN]

baker COOKER

baking HOT

baking, some CAKE; PIE; TART

balance POISE; REST; SCALES; WEIGH; ■ CREDIT; EVEN

balanced EVEN; LEVEL; SANE; ■ RATIONAL; SQUARE

bald BARE; PLAIN; STARK

bale PAIN

baleful SULKY; SULLEN

Balkan SERB; TURK

Balkan town SPLIT

ball BLACK (i.e. colour in snooker); BLUE; BROWN; DANCE; GREEN; JACK; LOB; O; ORB; PILL; PINK; RED; SHOT; SLUG; ■ BUMPER; DELIVERY; MARBLE; PARTY;

PELLET; POMPOM; TICE;
YELLOW; YORKER

ball, fetch FIELD

ball, go to FIELD

ball, high LOB; SKYER

ball in the net GOAL

ball of yarn SKEIN

ball shot CANNON

ballad AIR; LAY; POEM; SONG

ballet exercise support BARRE

ballet leap JETE

balloon O; GLASS; SWELL

ballot POLL; VOTE

balls OO; OVER

bally BLOODY; WRETCHED

Balmoral HAT

Baltic port RIGA

balustrade FENCE; RAILING

ban BAR; BLACK; DEBAR; OUT;
STOP; VETO

ban on spirits usually refers to exorcism

banal DULL; FLAT; TRIPE;
TRITE

bananas BATS; HAND; HANDS;
MAD; NUTS; ■ NUTTY;
CRACKERS; anagram indicator

band ARCH; BAR; BELT;
CIRCLE; FESS; GANG; GIRD;
GROUP; HOOP; LINE; LOOP;
O; RANGE; RING; SASH;
SHOE; STRAP; STREAK;
STRIP; STRIPE; TEAM; TIE;
TRACK (as on a record); WAVE
(i.e. radio); ZONE; ■ BANGLE;
COLLAR; COMBO; ELASTIC;
ROUT (archaic); TROOP; can in-
dicate something to do with
Robin Hood or one of the
well-known members of his band

band for arrows, narrow
DOUBLE; TREBLE

band, decorated FRIEZE

band leader B

band, member of PLAYER; can
indicate a specific instrument e.g.
TUBA

band, metal SHOE

band performance GIG

band, record TRACK

bandage DRESS; SWADDLE;
SWATHE

bandit BRIGAND

bandleader B

bandsman LOSS; MILLER

bang BLOW; CLAP; KNOCK;
REPORT; SLAM; STRIKE;
WHAM

bang down feet STAMP

banged out anagram indicator

banged up INSIDE

banger CAR; CRATE; GUN;
HEAP; can indicate something to
do with explosive, chemical constituents of, etc; or sausage,
chipolata etc

Bangkok, cash in TICAL

bangle BAND

banish OUST

banished anagram indicator

bank BAR; BLUFF; CAY; HEAP;
LEAN; REEF; RELY; ROW;
SCARF; SHELF; SIDE;
SHORE; SLOPE; STOCK;
TIER; ■ BRAE; CAMBER;
LENDER; LIAN; LIST; MASS;
STORE

bank employee/worker TELLER

bank of river BAR

Bank of Scotland BRAE

bank robbery HEIST

bank, sort of GIRO

bank transfers can indicate something to do with ferryman e.g.
Charon

banker CAMBER; LENDER; a favourite with compilers, indicating
a river (in the form of banked, between banks etc); *see* RIVER

banker, popular GIRO

banking CAMBER

banking facility/system GIRO

banknote BILL; FIVER; TENNER

banknotes ROLL; WAD

bankroll WAD

bankrupt BROKE; BUST; ■
INSOLVENT

bankrupt, go CRASH; FOLD

bankruptcy RUIN

banks indicates first and last letters
to be used

banned OUT; TABU

banned reportedly BARD

banner FLAG; ■ HEADLINE;
PROHIBITIONIST;
STANDARD

bannock BREAD; CAKE; LOAF

banquet FEAST

banter CHAFF; JEST; RALLY

bap BREAD; ROLL

baptism DIP

baptism, place for FONT

bar BAIL; BAN; BAND; BANK;
BILLET; BLACK; BOLT; BUT;
COUNTER; EXCEPT; FRET;
GATE; INN; LATCH; LEVER;
LINE; LOCAL; PUB; RACK;
RAIL; RAY; ROD; RUNG;
SAVE; SHELF; SHOAL; SPAR;
STOP; STREAK; STRIP;
STRIPE; ■ CLOSE; ESTOP;
PIG; PREVENT; PUBLIC;
SALOON; SAVING; TAVERN;
VETO; often indicates something
to do with the legal profession; in
the singular or plural can indicate
something to do with music or a
composer; can indicate some-
thing to do with a pub or the
high-jump; [◊ CODE; SOAP]

bar, disreputable DIVE

bar group COUNSEL

bar parlour SNUG

bar, seedy DIVE

bar, sleazy DIVE

bar, type of PUBLIC

bar-work GRILL

barb ARROW; DIG; HOOK

Barbara MAJOR (title of Shaw
play)

Barbarian GOTH; HUN; ■
SAVAGE

barbaric person BRUTE; *see*
BARBARIAN

barbarism TERROR

Barbie DOLL

Barcelona NUT

bard POET

Bard WILL

bare BALD; PLAIN; ■ LACKING;
NAKED; NUDE; SIMPLE; [◊
BUFF]

bare teeth GRIN

barely JUST

barely adequate/sufficient
SCANT

barely visible FAINT; *see* FAINT;
can indicate something to do with
striptease (strip club, strip show,
etc)

bargain DEAL; HAGGLE; SNIP;
TRADE

bargain, where one gets a SALE

barge BOAT; BUMP; LIGHTER;
SCOWL

barge through tunnel, propel
LEG

bark BAY; GRAZE; SCRAP;
SNAP; SHIP; TAN (i.e. leather);
YAP; ■ SHOUT; *see* BOAT; [◊
SHIN]

barked, one can indicate a tree

barker DOG; can refer to a specific
breed of dog; *see* DOG

barking MAD; YELP; anagram indicator; [◊ SHIN]

barley GRAIN; MALT; [◊ AWN]

barmy NUTS (qv); SILLY; anagram indicator

barn-dance anagram of BARN
e.g. BRAN

Barnaby RUDGE

barney *see* ARGUMENT

barometer GLASS

baron B; LORD; PEER

baron, Scottish HOME

baronet BART; BT

baroque FANCY; anagram indicator

barrack BOO; ■ HECKLE

barracks CAMP; ■ QUARTERS

barrage balloon BLIMP

barred can indicate the site of a
drinking establishment such as
the "nineteenth hole" at a golf
course

barrel B; BIN; BL; BUTT; CASK;
DRUM; KEG; PIN; TUN; *see*
CASK

barrel part STAVE

barren BLEAK; DULL; DRY;
STARK

barren area/terrain DESERT;
HEATH; WASTE

barricade FENCE; WALL

Barrie can indicate something to do with Peter Pan, Hook, Wendy, Lost Boys etc
Barrie's dog NANA
barrier BLOCK; BOOM; DAM; FENCE; GATE; HEDGE; PALE; PLUG; RAIL; RAILING; WALL; ■ CORDON; RAILING
barrister BRIEF; SILK; ■ COUNSEL; LAWYER; TEMPLAR; [◊ BAR]
barrister's requirement WIG
barrow CART; GRAVE
bars CAGE; GRATING; GRILL; RAILING; *see* PRISON
bartender [◊ COUNTER]
barter TRADE; TRUCK
base BAD; BED; CHEAP; EVIL; FOOT; FOUND; HOME; LOW; MEAN; MOUNT; REST; ROOT; SEAT; VILE; ■ BOTTOM; DEPOT; FLOOR; STATION
base, firm ROCK
base of final latter indicator
baseball game INNING
baseball player CATCHER; PITCHER
bash BEAT; BUMP; CLUB; DO; GO; HIT (qv); PARTY; RAM; THUMP; TURN; ■ BATTER; BUFFET; CLOBBER; PUNCH; *see* HIT
bashed anagram indicator
bashful COY; SHY
basic CRUDE; RAW; RUDE; ■ SPARTAN; STAPLE
basic instinct ID
basil HERB
basin BOWL; DOCK; SINK; STOOP (for holy water)
basis STAPLE
basket CREEL; FRAIL (for figs); HAMPER; LEAP; TRUG; ■ DILLY; SKEP e.g. of wickerwork); TROLLEY
basket, type of MOSES
bass DEEP; FISH; LOW; SINGER
bastard SHAM
baste SEW; TACK
bat BLINK; CLUB; HIT; RAP; STICK; ■ RACKET; STRIKE; WILLOW

batch SET
bate RAGE
bath DIP; POOL; TUB; ■ SALINA (Sp.); [◊ SOAP]
Bath can refer to some aspect of the city
bath, lie in the SOAK
bath towel WIPER
bathe LAVE; STEEP; WASH
bathing, go DIP
bathroom LAV; LOO; PRIVY; *see* TOILET
bathroom accessory TOWEL
bathroom feature SINK
baton ROD; STICK; can indicate something to do with relay race, conducting
bats DAFT; MENTAL; anagram indicator; *see* BAT, NUTS
bats, getting anagram indicator
batsman OPENER; STRIKER
batsman's hit STROKE
batsman, leading OPENER
batsman's position CREASE
batsman's spell KNOCK
batsman's turn INNINGS
batsmen, late TAIL
batten down NAIL
batter BASH; COAT; RAM; STRIKE; ■ CRICKETER; POUND; *see* HIT
batter, piece of FRITTER
battered anagram indicator
battering anagram indicator; nesting indicator
battery GUNS; [◊ CELL]
battery, not FREE (i.e. free-range with regard to chickens)
battery, part of CELL
batting IN
batting first word to begin with IN
batting session INNING(S)
battle ACTION; CLASH; FIGHT; FRAY; SCRAP; WAR; can refer to a specific battle e.g. ALMA, CRECY, LOOS, MARNE, MONS, SEDAN: SOMME
battle-axe CROSS
battle, do FIGHT; WAR
battle, in the midst of a component to be nested within TT

battle line FRONT
battle with ENGAGE; FIGHT
battle zone FRONT
battles anagram indicator
battles, series of WAR
battleship RAM
batty anagram indicator
bawdy BLUE; CRUDE; EARTHY
bawl CRY
bawl out RATE
bay BARK; BIGHT; BROWN;
  COVE; CRY; HORSE; HOWL;
  ROAD; ROAN; SPACE; ■
  BELLOW; NICHE; can indicate
  something to do with a house or
  window
bayed can indicate something to do
  with being honoured as a laureate
Bayeux can indicate something to
  do with sew, sewing
bazaar FAIR; FETE; SALE; anagram indicator
BB with a homophone indicator can
  call for BEES
BBC AUNTIE
be EXIST; LIVE
be able CAN
be against OPPOSE
be angry RANT; *see* ANGRY
be back EB; RETURN
be careful! EASY; OOPS
be clearly SHOW (as "be clearly
  worried" gives SHOW FEAR)
be down OWE
be first LEAD; WIN
be given GET
be likely TEND
be paid EARN; GET
be roused WAKE
**be, to (with some indication of
France)** ETRE
be told HEAR
be unwell AIL
be upset CRY
beach COAST; LIDO; SAND;
  SHORE; STRAND; ■ SHINGLE
beach area SAND; *see* BEACH
beachwear THONG
bead DROP; [◊ DRAW]
beak BILL; HOOTER; NEB
  (Scot.); NOSE; RAM

beam BAR; GLOW; LIGHT; RAY;
  SHAFT; SHORE; SMILE; ■
  LASER; RAFTER; TRAVE (on a
  cart)
beam, type of LASER
bean HEAD; PULSE; SEED
beano *see* PARTY
bear ABIDE; BROOK; CARRY;
  SELLER; SHOW; STAND;
  TOTE; ■ ACQUIT; BALOO;
  BRUIN; ENDURE; GRIZZLY;
  KODIAK: POOH; SHOULDER;
  THOLE; TOLERATE; WINNIE;
  YIELD
bear in America TOTE
bear witness VOUCH
beard AWN; FACE; ■ GOATEE;
  IMPERIAL
bearded fellow AARON
bearing AIR; E; EAST; N; NE;
  NORTH; NW; POSE; S; SE;
  SOUTH; SW; W; WEST; ■
  MANNER; MIEN; PRESENCE;
  nesting indicator
bearing weapons ARMED
bearings *see* BEARING
bearskin, we hear homophone indicator for BARE or a synonym,
  see NUDE
beast ASS; BOAR; BRUTE;
  CAMEL; LION; *see* ANIMAL
beast, large ELK
beast of burden ASS; MULE
beast, sound like a LOW; *see*
  BEASTLY SOUND
beastly VILE; anagram indicator
**beastly accommodation, home,
place etc** DEN; LAIR; STY
beastly type *see* ANIMAL
beastly disease BSE
beastly sound GROWL; GRUNT;
  MOO; ROAR
beasts STOCK
beat BASH; BEST; CAP; CANE;
  CLOCK; CLUB; COSH; DRUB;
  DRUM; FLOG; FOIL; LACE;
  LAM; LASH; LICK; PASTE;
  PIP; POUND; PULSE; RAP;
  ROUT; SCOOP; SLAM; SLAP;
  STRIKE; SWITCH; TAN;
  THRASH; THRESH; THROB;
  TICK; TOP; WHIP; ■ ALLIN

(i.e. all in); BETTER; CREAM; CUFF; LEATHER; MASTER; ORBIT; ROUND; SCOURGE; TROUNCE; WALLOP; WELT; WHISK; can indicate a word beginning with out (outrun, outplay, outstrip etc) [◊ HEART]

beat everything else TOP

beat on board MATE

beat soundly CAINE; KANE

beat up BASH

beaten CANED; ROUTED; anagram indicator

beaten, be, get LOSE

beaten up anagram indicator

beatified ST to precede a name, as "beatified Fitzgerald" → STELLA

beating HIDING; LASH; PULSE; anagram indicator

beating, administer a CANE; LACE; *see* BEAT

beating retreat reversal indicator

beau DANDY; LOVER; *see* BOYFRIEND

Beau NASH

beautiful FAIR

beautiful creature PERI

beautiful girl PERI; ■ NYMPH

beautiful Italian BELLA

beautiful lady, woman BELLE; VENUS

beautiful thing GEM

beauty BELLE; DISH; GEM; GLAM; LOOKS; PERI; ■ GLAMOUR; can indicate something to do with sleep

beauty competition, entrant in MISS

beauty in America LUSTER

beauty queen MISS

beauty spot EDEN; MOLE

became anagram indicator

because AS; FOR; SINCE

because of FOR; FROM

beck STREAM

beckon MOTION

Becky SHARP

become FIT; GET; SUIT; TAKE (as in "take ill"); TURN; anagram indicator

become less ABATE; ■ SHRINK

become tired FLAG; WANE

becoming APT; FIT; PROPER; *see* ATTRACTIVE

bed BUNK; COT; COUCH; CRIB; DIVAN; FORM; KIP; LITTER; PATCH; PLOT; REST; SACK (as in "hit the sack"); ■ BERTH; GARDEN; LAYER; LITTER; PALLET; can indicate something to do with flowers, gardening (as exemplified by "skill in bed" → GREEN FINGERS(!)) or the sea-bed; [◊ COVER; DORM; DREAM; PROCRUSTES; QUILT; SHEET; SLEEP]

bed cover QUILT; SHEET

bed, didn't stay in ROSE

bed, French LIT

bed, get out of RISE

bed, go to RETIRE

bed, got out of ROSE

bed, in NOT UP (which conveniently reverses to get PUT ON); a component to be nested within BED or COT

bed, one in usually refers to a garden flower, *see* FLOWER

bed, out of ASTIR; UP

bed, ready for TIRED

bedaub SPLODGE; *see* DAUB

bedding LITTER

bedding LITTER

bedding, Japanese FUTON

Bedouin ARAB

bedroom DORM

beds GARDEN

bedsitter FLAT; PAD

bedspread QUILT

bee note that, apart from an insect, a bee is also a form of social gathering

beef BARON; BRAWN; BULLY; GRIPE; GROAN; GROUSE; MEAT; MIGHT; OX; ROAST; STEER; WHINE; ■ COMPLAIN; GRIEVANCE; GRUMBLE; MUSCLE; can indicate a cut of beef e.g. FILET, RUMP, TOPSIDE; CARP

beef, cut of SIDE

beef producer COW

beef, producing CALVING

beehive SKEP

Beelzebub DEVIL

been out, having anagram of BEEN

beer ALE; BREW; HALF; KEG; LAGER; MILD; PILS; PINT; ■ BITTER; DRAUGHT; PORTER; SWIPE(S); WALLOP

beer-barrel TUN; *see* BARREL

beer froth HEAD

beer, glass of HALF; JAR; PINT

beer, ingredient of (for) HOP

beer mug STEIN

beer, small HALF

beer, something in HOP(S)

bees sounding like B's this word can, with a homophone indicator, refer to BB

beet MANGEL

Beethoven, like DEAF

beetle DOR

before ANTE; ERE; PRE; preceding indicator; can indicate a preceding number, hence "before five" can cue FOUR or IV, "before eleven" TEN or X and so on

before, as DO

before long ANON; SOON

before magistrate UP

before mid-day AM

before noon AM

before now AGO; ALREADY

before time EARLY

befuddled anagram indicator

beg ASK; PLEAD; PRAY; SUE ■ APPEAL; ENTREAT

began AROSE

begged ASKED; PLED

begin ARISE; OPEN; SETTO (i.e. set to); START; ■ BROACH; FOUND; *see* START; with a capital letter can refer to the Israeli statesman

begin again RENEW

beginner L; SEED; TIRO; TYRO; ■ FOUNDER; LEARNER; TRAINEE; initial letter indicator

beginning A; ALPHA; BIRTH; DAWN; SEED; START; initial letter indicator; [◊ NEW]

beginning, near EARLY

beginning of life EGG

beginning of new era OAD (i.e. zero AD)

beginning to be BECOMING

beginning to end, from THROUGH

beginning to learn L

beguile CHARM; ENCHANT

begun STARTED

behalf INTEREST; PART

behalf of, on FOR; PRO

behave ACT

behave badly SIN

behaviour ACTION; PLAY; ■ CONDUCT; MANNER

behaviour, silly ANTIC; CAPER; PRANK

behaviourist SKINNER

behead TOP; *see* BEHEADED

beheaded TOPPED; indicator that the first letter is to be omitted

beheaded king CR

behind AFT; AFTER; BACK; DOWN; DUE; END; LATE; PAST; REAR; RUMP; STERN; TAIL; ■ ASTERN; TARDY; TRAILING; can also indicate the last letter or letters of the answer

behind bars INSIDE; can indicate something to do with drinks or the serving of drinks e.g. bottle, cocktail shaker

behind, be TRAIL

behind in points DOWN

behind schedule LATE

behind, show MOON

behind the ship ASTERN

behind time LATE

behindhand DUE; LATE; TARDY

behold LA; LO; OBSERVE; SEE; ■ ECCO; HERES (i.e. here is)

beige BUFF

Beijing reported PEAKING

being AS; PERSON; LIVER; MAN; SELF; SOUL

being performed ON

being shown ON

being simple DILL; *see* FOOL

being staged ON

being very big TITAN; ■ GIANT

beleaguer CRAMP
belfry [◊ BATS]
Belgian FLEMING; ■ LEIGE
Belgian province NAMUR
Belgian singer BREL
Belgium, town in MONS; SPA
belief CREDIT; CREED; FAITH; ISM; TENET
belief in God DEISM
believe CREDIT; FEEL; HOLD; ■ SWALLOW
believe, hard to TALL
believer DEIST; RC
believer in God DEIST
believing, someone DEIST
belittle DECRY; KNOCK; REDUCE; ■ LESSEN
bell TOLL; ■ ALARM; CHIME
bell-boy PAGE
bell, part of CLAPPER
bell, ring TING
bell sound CHIME; CLANG; DING; RING; TING; TOLL
bellicose VIOLENT
Bellini heroine NORMA
Bellini's work NORMA
bellow BAWL; BAY; BLARE; ROAR
bellows mender FLUTE (character from *Midsummer Night's Dream*)
bells PEAL
belly GUT; PAUNCH; POT; TUM; TUMMY
bellyache CARP; MOAN; GRIPE; WHINE
belong to run indicator
belonging to IN; OF; run indicator; can indicate a word ending in S (i.e. 's)
belonging to us OUR
beloved DEAR; ■ INAMORATA
beloved Parisian CHER
below DOWN; INFRA; UNDER
belt BAND; FLOG; HIT; HURRY; KNOCK; SWIPE; ■ POUND; ZONE; *see* RUN; [◊ GARTER]
bemused MAD; anagram indicator
Ben HUR
bench FORM; PEW; SEAT; SETTLE

bench, one on the SUB
bend ARC; ARCH; BIGHT; BOW; FOLD; HOOK; KNOT; LEAN; PLY; S; SAG; TURN; U; Z ■ CORNER; CROOK; CURVE; STOOP; WARP; anagram indicator
bend, go round the CORNER; TURN
bend over HEEL
bender KNEE
beneath BELOW; LOW; UNDER; ■ INFERIOR
Benedictine DOM; NUN
benediction, give BLESS
beneficial to FOR
beneficiary HEIR
benefit AID; ASSET; AVAIL; BOON; DOLE; GAIN; GOOD; HELP; PERK; RIGHT; USE; ■ CREDIT
benefit, sort of FRINGE
benefit, unexpected MANNA; ■ WINDFALL
benevolent KIND
Bengal [◊ LANCERS; TIGER]
benign GOOD
bent ASKEW; CROOK; CROOKED; HABIT; LEANT; ■ BOWED; LEANING; TALENT; anagram indicator
bent forward BOWED
bent one CROOK; LIAR
berate SCOLD
berated anagram indicator
Berkshire PIG
Berlin, one in EIN
berserk anagram indicator
berth BUNK; DOCK; PLACE; POSITION
beseech ENTREAT
besieged by anagram indicator
beside ON; NEAR
besmirch SMEAR
besmirching STAIN
besom BROOM
besotted anagram indicator
bespattered anagram indicator
Bess's man PORGY
best BEAT; CAP; CREAM; ELITE; FINEST; FIRST;

FLOWER; IDEAL; PASTE; PEAK; PICK; PLUM; NOI (i.e. No.1); STAR; TOP; TOPS; ■ DEFEAT; THRASH; WORST

best China MING

best, do your TRY

best man TOASTER

best quality AI; TOP; *see* BEST

best part CREAM

best-seller HIT

bestow AWARD; GRANT

bet ANTE; BACK; GAMBLE; LAID; LAY; NAP; PUNT; RISK; STAKE; WAGER; ■ FLUTTER; TREBLE; [◊ CHANCE; RACE]

bet, good CERT; EVENS

bet on BACK

betimes EARLY; SOON

betray DESERT; RAT; SELL; SHOP; RATON (i.e. rat on)

betrayal TREASON

betrayed SOLD

better ABLER; BACKER; BEAT; CAP; EXCEL; FINER; FITTER; LAYER; MASTER; PUNTER; TOP; ■ IMPROVE; MEND; SUPERIOR; can indicate something to do with betting e.g. TOTE; in conjunction with a verb can indicate the use of OUT, as "be a better pilot" → OUTFLY, for example

better, get EASE; IMPROVE

better, got EASED; IMPROVED

better half BET; MATE; TER

better, make CURE; ENHANCE; HEAL; IMPROVE

better qualified FITTER

better state, bring to a CURE; IMPROVE

better, take a turn for RALLY

better, to get CAP; RALLY; RISE; ■ IMPROVE

betting SP; STAKING

betting-machine TOTE

betting record BOOK

betting system TOTE

between INTER; ■ AMONG

between poles a component to be nested between some combination of N, E, W or S

between sides a component to be nested between R and L, or L and R

bevel CANT

beverage CUP; DRINK (qv)

bewail KEEN; LAMENT

bewilder CONFUSE (qv); DAZE

bewildered anagram indicator

bewitch ENCHANT

beyond OVER; PAST

bias SKEW; SPIN; anagram indicator

bias, without FAIR

biased ASKEW; ■ PARTIAL; anagram indicator

bib POUT

Bible AV; RV

Bible class RI

Bible, part of HEB; NT; NUM; OT; VERSE; *see* BIBLE, BOOK

Bible, short passage from TEXT

Bible story PARABLE

Biblical character EVE; JOB; LOT; MARK; SAUL

Biblical king OG

Biblical mountain SION

Biblical twin ESAU

biblical version RV

Biblical writer LUKE; MARK

bicycle BIKE; [◊ SPOKE]

bid CALL; CHARGE; OFFER; ORDER; TENDER; ■ DOUBLE (i.e. in bridge); INVITE

bid, ambitious SLAM

biddable TAME

bide STAY

biff BLOW

big GREAT; HUGE; LARGE; OS; TALL; ■ HIGH; HOT; MAJOR; GRAND; VAST

Big Apple NY

big band music SWING

Big Ben CLOCK; [◊ FACE]

big car LIMO

big cat CHEETAH; *see* CAT

big cheese VIP

big effort HEAVE

big end G

big-headed B

big hit SIX

big house GRANGE; MANOR
big name STAR; VIP; ■ CELEBRITY
big-name actor STAR
big noise VIP
big one WHOPPER
big part, play a STAR
big, really MEGA
big shot VIP; WORTHY
big top B; TENT; ■ MARQUEE
bigger than average OS; TALL
biggest TOP; ■ RECORD
bighead B
bigheaded B
bight BAY; BEND; COVE; LOOP
bigness SIZE
bigwig CHEESE; NOB; VIP
bike CYCLE; MOPED; [◊ RIDE]
bike out, take the CYCLE
bikini TANGA
Bikini ATOLL
bile SPLEEN
bill AC; ACT; AD; BEAK; NOSE; NOTE; POSTER; TAB; ■ ADVERT; CAST (i.e. in theatre); CHARGE; COST; INVOICE; can indicate something to do with a bird; [◊ LAW]
Bill W
bill in U.S. CHECK; NOTE; TAB
Bill's partner COO
bill to pay CHIT; [◊ DEBT; IOU]
billet BAR; JOB; LOG (as fuel); NOTE; TASK; ■ QUARTERS
billiards, start playing BREAK
billion B; BN
billions B
billow SWELL
billowing anagram indicator
Billy BUDD; GOAT; KID; can indicate something to do with having a beak
billy goat GRUFF
bin DROP; STORE; *see* DISPENSE WITH
binary digits IO; OI
bind FASTEN; GEL; HOLD; HOLE; JAM; PEST; STRAP; TAPE; TIE
bind, to anagram indicator
binder together CEMENT

binder COIL; CORD; FOLDER; ROPE; ■ STRING
binding CORD; TIE; ■ CEMENT; VALID
binge BLIND
bingo LOTTO
biography LIFE; [◊ BOSWELL]
biology group GENUS
birch CANE
bird CAPON; CHAT; COCK; COOT; CRANE; CROW; DAW; DIVER; DRAKE; DUCK; EAGLE; EGRET; EMU; FINCH; FOWL; GULL; HAWK; HEN; HOBBY; JAY; KITE; KNOT; LARK; LIFE; LOON; LORY; MINA; MOA; PEN; PIE; RAIL; RAVEN; REE; ROLLER; ROOK; RUFF; SAKER; SCOTER; SMEW; SWAN; TEAL; TERN; THRUSH; TIME; TIT; WREN; ■ BUDGIE; CHOUGH; CUCKOO; DIPPER; GANNET; GOOSE; GREBE; GROUSE; HARRIER; IBIS; NODDY; OUSEL; PHEASANT; RHEA; ROBIN; ROOSTER; SARU; SHRIKE; SNIPE; SPARROW; STORK; SWALLOW; TUI; [◊ ROOST; WING]
bird, bright TOUCAN
bird, dead MOA; ■ DODO
bird disease GAPES; ROUP
bird, early LARK
bird, extinct MOA
bird, fabulous, legendary, myth-ological ROC
bird, flightless EMU; RHEA; ■ MOA; PENGUIN; OSTRICH
bird, large ERNE
bird, male COCK; DRAKE
bird no longer DODO; MOA
bird, nocturnal OWL
bird, noisy STARLING
bird, old DODO; MOA
bird, royal SWAN
bird's nest [◊ CLUTCH]
bird sanctuary NEST
bird song TRILL; TWEET
bird sound CHEEP; CLUCK; COO; TWEET

bird, voracious RAVEN
bird, wise HOOTER; OWL
birds, a lot of FLOCK
birds, of/to do with AVIAN
birdwatchers'retreat HIDE
Birmingham BRUM; note, can refer to Alabama or the American South as well as the English Midlands city
Birmingham, part of ASTON
Birmingham venue NEC
birth ORIGIN
birth date AGE
birth, of NATAL
birthplace MANGER
birthstone GARNET
biscuit NUT; RUSK; SNAP; ■ CRACKER; WAFER
bisect SPLIT; ■ HALVE
bish ERROR (qv); ■ BLOOMER
bishop B; MAN; PIECE; RR
bishop's domain/office/place SEE
bishop's responsibility SEE
bishop's staff VERGE
bishopric ELY; SEE
Bismarck OTTO
bistro CAFE
bit CRUMB; DROP; GRAIN; JOT; LITTLE; LUMP; NIPPED (i.e. verb); ORT; PART; PIECE; PINCH; RAG; SCRAP; SHRED; SPOT; TAD; TASTE; TRACE; ■ IOTA; MORSEL; PARTICLE; PORTION; SECTION; SNAFFLE; run indicator
bit, for a run indicator
bit, little WHIT
bit of SOME; run indicator; can indicate one or two letters to be used from the word that follows usually from the beginning
bit of, a SHORT
bit of fun LARK; LAUGH; SPREE; ■ JOKE (qv)
bit part CAMEO; EXTRA
bit, tiny DRIB
bite CHAMP; CUT; EDGE; GNAW; GRIP; NIP; SNACK; SNAP; STING; TANG

biter GNAT; NIPPER; SNAPPER; TOOTH; *see* TOOTH
biting RAW; TART; nesting indicator
★ **bits and pieces** a term often used for the selected letters or abbreviations used to build a solution (most of the common abbreviations and letter indicators will be found in the present book); also refers to the type of clue which is made up entirely of them, otherwise known as the charade clue (qv)
bitten NIPPED
bitter ACID; ACRID; ALE; BEER; ICY; SHARP; SOUR; ■ KEEN; SARKY
bitter plant ALOE
bitterness GALL; WARP
bitterness, feel RESENT
bivouac CAMP
bizarre ANTIC; MAD; RUM; WEIRD; ■ OUTRE; anagram indicator
blab CRY
black B; BAN; BAR; BL; INKY; JET; NIGHT; SABLE; ■ CARBON; EBONY; NOIR; RAVEN; TARRY
black coat TAR
black eye MOUSE; SHINER
Black Hills state SD
Black Horse BESS
black, looking GRIM; TARRY
black magic BART (i.e. black art)
black marketeer TOUT
black rock COAL
black, something CLUB; NIGHT; SPADE
black stuff JET; SOOT; TAR
black, turn CHAR
black, very BB
blackberry bush BRAMBLE
blacken INK; SLANDER
blackguard CAD; KNAVE; RAFF
blackleg RAT; SCAB
blade EDGE; OAR; SHARE; SWORD; VANE; ■ CUTTER
Blair ERIC
blame RAP; SLUR
blame, it's said WRAP

bland DULL; MILD
Blandings, Empress of PIG
blandish FLATTER
blank NOTHING; VOID
blanket SHEET
blast BLOW; RAIL; ROAST; TRUMP; WIND; ■ DAMN; REPORT
blasted anagram indicator
blasted place HEATH
blatant GLARING; LOUD
blaze FLARE; MARK
blazer COAT; FIRE; SUN; STAR; ■ JACKET; can refer to something involving fire as "Blazer at the present time" → YULE-LOG
blazing, are BURN
bleak FISH; POOR; SPARE; *see* DRAB
blear DIM; FOG; ■ DREARY
bleeding heart ED
blemish DEFACE; FLAW; MARK; SCAR; SMEAR; STAIN; TAINT; WART
blend MINGLE; MIX
blend of anagram indicator
blending anagram indicator
bless HALLOW
blessed HAPPY; HOLY
blessing ASSET; BOON; GRACE
blight BANE; DASH; MAR; RUST
blighted anagram indicator
blighter CAD; IMP
blimey COO; COR
Blimp COL
blind BINGE; DAZZLE; SCREEN
blind man PEW
blink BAT
blinking BALLY; DANG
bliss DELIGHT; HEAVEN; JOY
bliss, create DELIGHT; ELATE
blithe HAPPY
blob BLOT; O
bloat SWELL; *see* ENLARGE
block BAR; BARRIER; BRICK; CHECK; CLOSE; CONDO; CUBE; DAM; DIE; LET; PAD; SET; SETT; STEM; STONE; STOP; VETO; WEDGE; ■ THWART
block between banks DAM

block of paper PAD
block of seats TIERS
block off road CONE
blockage DAM
blockage, cause a DAM; IMPEDE
blockbuster EPIC
blocked run indicator
bloke BOD; CHAP; COVE; GENT; LAD; SID; *see* MAN
blokes MEN
blonde FAIR
blood CLOT; GORE; RACE; RED; STOCK; STRAIN; ■ DANDY
blood group A; AB; B; O
blood, involving much GORY
blood, lost BLED
blood sport HUNTING
blood-vessel VEIN
bloodshed GORE
bloodshed, involving much GORY
bloodsucker FLEA; GNAT; LOUSE
bloodsuckers FLEAS; LICE
bloodthirsty GORY
bloody RARE; RED; GORY; ■ BALLY
bloom BLUSH; FLUSH; FLOWER; can refer to steel making; *see* FLOWER
bloomer BISH; BLOOM; BLUSH; BOOB; BREAD; ERROR; FLOWER; LOAF; SLIP; can refer to a flower e.g. ASTER, *see* FLOWER
bloomer, bit of a *see* FLOWER-PART
blooming OUT; ■ BALLY; FLORAL; HEALTHY; RUDDY
blossom MAY; ■ BLOOM; FLOWER
blot SMUDGE; SPLODGE; SPOT
blotchy anagram indicator
blouse TOP
blow BIFF; BLAST; CLIP; CUFF; GALE; GUST; HIT; JAB; PUFF; PUNCH; SHOCK; SLUG; SMACK; SOCK; SPEND; STRIKE; STRIPE; STROKE; TAP; THUMP; TOOT; WAFT; WIND; ■ BUFFET; BUMP; can

indicate something to do with
sneeze

blow a fuse RAGE; RANT

blow briefly TOOT

blow, deliver HIT; *see* BLOW

blow, final COUP; OK

blow, force of BRUNT

blow, heavy ONER; *see* BLOW

blow horn HOOT

blow, light CLIP; SMACK; TAP

blow-out FEAST; a component to
be nested within a synonym of
blow such as GALE

blow, sharp JAB

Blow this! can signify a wind instrument

blow to the French COUP

blow up BLAST; ENLARGE; ■
BOMB; EXPLODE; anagram indicator

blower PHONE; can indicate a specific wind e.g. north-easter, si-
rocco, *see* WIND

blowing anagram indicator

blown SPENT

blown up anagram indicator

blows can indicate something to do
with wind e.g. weather-cock,
vane, storm-cone

blows his top first letter to be
omitted

blows up anagram indicator

blub CRY; SOB; WEEP

blubber *see* CRY

bludgeon CLUB

blue ADULT; AZURE; BLOW
(slang for 'squander'); CAM (i.e.
university colour); DOWN;
LOW; NAVY; RIGHT; ROYAL;
SAD; SEA; SKY; TORY; ■
ANIL; BICE; GLOOMY;
LEWD; PRUSSIAN; RIBALD

blue, be MOPE

blue eyed boy PET

blue material DENIM

blue party CON

blue-pencilled CUT

blue peter being the flag hoisted
before sailing can indicate
SAILING, GOING, LEAVING

blue, shade of LIGHT; NAVY;
ROYAL; SKY; *see* BLUE

Bluebeard usually indicates something to do with having several
wives

bluebottle COP; FLY; *see*
POLICEMAN

Bluegrass state KY

blues, the DEJECTION

bluish-grey PERSE

bluff FRANK; KID; HEARTY; ■
CLIFF; *see* DECEIVE

blunder BISH; BOOB; BONER;
ERR; ERROR; GAFFE; TRIP; ■
FAULT; HOWLER; *see* ERROR

blundering anagram indicator

blunt CRUDE; DULL; PLAIN;
RUDE; STARK; ■ POINTLESS

blur FUZZ; SMUDGE

blurb AD; HYPE; PUFF

blurred VAGUE; ■ FUZZY; anagram indicator

blush BLOOM; GLOW;
REDDEN; ROUGE

blushing PINK; RED

blustery anagram indicator

boa FUR; STOLE

boar PIG; SWINE

board DEAL; DECK; FOOD;
PLANK; TABLE; ■ COUNTER;
DIRECTORS; EMBARK;
PANEL; PENSION; TIMBER;
also can refer to material used in
boards e.g. DEAL; can indicate
something to do with chessboard
(commonly MAN, MATE); can
indicate something to do with
dartboard (commonly BULL,
INNER, OCHE, OUTER); can
indicate something to do with
food; can indicate something to
do with cheese; [◊ CHALK;
FILE; IRONING; RANK; SURF]

board game GO

board, go on EMBARK

board meeting can indicate a formal meal (as "Main board meeting" → DINNER)

board member EXEC

board, on often indicates that an
element is to be inserted between
the letters SS (i.e. for Steamship)
as "is not on board" → SAINTS;
a little less often can require a

component to be nested within TABLE

board ship EMBARK

board, sweep the WIN

board, taken by can indicate that a component is to be nested within TABLE

boarded nesting indicator

boarding PENSION; can indicate something to do with the timber industry as "Boarding establishment" → SAWMILL; nesting indicator

boarding house PENSION

boards can indicate something to do with the stage or chess

boards, the STAGE

boards, he treads ACTOR; ■ HAM

boast BRAG; CROW; VAUNT

boasted CREW

boastful manner SIDE

boastful, was CREW

boasting, idle BLUSTER

boat ARGO; ARK; BARGE; BARK; CAT; CRAFT; EIGHT; GALLEY; GIG; HOY; KETCH; PRAM; PUNT; RAFT; REEFER; SCOW; SHELL; SHIP; SMACK; SS; STEAMER; SUB; TRAMP; TUB; TUG; ■ BARQUE; CUTTER; DHOW; FISHER; LAUNCH; LIGHTER; PACKET; PROA; SKETCH; SKIFF; YACHT; *see* SHIP; can indicate something to do with Jerome K. Jerome's *Three Men in a Boat*, characters etc. e.g. Harris; [◊ OAR]

boat, Arab DHOW

boat, fishing PROA; SMACK

boat, front of BOW; PROW

boat, on ABOARD

boat out, push the LAUNCH

boat, second man in a HARRIS (character from Jerome's book)

boat trip ROW; SAIL; ■ CRUISE

boat, use ROW; SAIL

boater HAT; can indicate something to do with a sailor

boating team EIGHT

boatman COX; NOAH; OAR; RATTY; *see* SAILOR

boatmen CREW; EIGHT

Boaz can indicate something to do with RUTH (Bible)

bob BOW; CUT; DIP; ■ DUCK; S (i.e. shilling); TRIM; ■ CHIME; FLOAT; JIG; PEAL; RING; can indicate something to do with haircut

Bob UNCLE

Bob, Old S

bobbin REEL; SPOOL

Boche HUN

body MASS; MUMMY; SECT; SOMA; STIFF; ■ CORPSE; GROUP; VOLUME

body, as a ALL

body builder STEROID

body condition, good TONE

body of work CORPUS

body, part of ARM; BACK; CHEST; EAR; FOOT; HAND; HEAD; HEART; HIP; LEG; LIMB; LIVER; NAIL; SHIN; SPINE; ■ ANKLE; CHIN; FINGER; ORGAN; TOE

body snatcher HARE

bodyguard HEAVY; MINDER; ■ AIR BAG

bog FEN; MARSH; MIRE; SWAMP; ■ QUAG; SLOUGH; *see* TOILET

bog fuel PEAT

bog plant MOSS

bog product PEAT

bogged down can indicate a component is nested within MUD

boggy area FEN

bogus FAKE; SHAM; anagram indicator; *see* FAKE

Bohemian ARTY

Bohemian girl MIMI

boil HEAT; ■ FUME; SIMMER

boil over anagram of BOIL

boiler HEATER; RANGE

boiling anagram indicator

boisterous ROUGH; anagram indicator

bold BRASH; BRAVE; DARING; ■ IMPUDENT; INTREPID

boldness NERVE

Bolshevik LENIN

bolt ARROW; BAR; DASH; EAT; ELOPE; FLEE; LOCK; PIN; RIVET; RUN; STUD; TEAR; WOLF; ■ GORGE; LEVANT (old slang); SHOOT

bolted ATE; *see* BOLT

bolting anagram indicator

bomb A; ATOM; ATTACK; DUD; EGG; FALL: FLOP; H; VI

bomb attack PRANG

bombard SHELL

bombast RANT

bombastic speech RANT

bombed anagram indicator

bombshell BLONDE

bon mot QUIP

bona-fide REAL

bond KNOT; LINK; TIE; ■ MANACLE; RELATION; SHACKLE

Bond perhaps AGENT; JAMES; SPY

Bond perhaps briefly JAS

bonds, in TIED

bone AITCH; RIB; SHIN; STEAL; ■ FILLET; ILIUM; INCUS; STERNUM

bone cavities ANTRA

bonehead B; *see* FOOL

bones DICE; ILIA; SACRA; TARSI

bonfire BLAZE

bong PIPE

bonnet CAP; HAT; HOOD; POKE

bonnet, American HOOD

bonus BOON; EXTRA; PERK; PLUS

bonus, unexpected ICING

bony LEAN; SPARE; THIN

boo JEER

boob ERROR (qv); ■ BLOOMER

booby TRAP

book ACTS; AMOS; AV (for authorised version); B; DAN (for Daniel); EDITION; EPH; EX; HEB; HOLD; HOS; JER; JOB; KIM; KINGS; LIB; LOG; MAL; MARK; MATT; NT (for New Testament); NUM; NUMB; OT (for Old Testament); PRIMER; READ (as in "a good read");

RESERVE; RUTH; SHE; TIM; TITLE; TOME; VOL; ■ ALBUM; ANNUAL; CHARGE; ENGAGE; FOLIO; JOSH; JUDGES; LEDGER; PSALMS; QUARTO; SUTRA; *see* BIBLE

book, basic PRIMER

book, brief contribution to CHAP

book, change EDIT

book division CHAPTER

book end FINIS; K

book, finish BIND

book, finished BOUND

book, French ROMAN

book, good JUDGES; *see* BIBLE, BOOK

book illustration PLATE

book, last K; REV

book, OT NUMB; *see* BIBLE, BOOK

book, part/section of LEAF; PAGE; ■ CHAPTER

book, short can indicate an abbreviation of either a synonym of "book" e.g. VOL or of a specific title, usually from the Bible e.g. TIM for Timothy, NUM for Numbers

book-work STUDY

booked can allude to a novel or fictional character as "Singer booked by Fielding?" → TOM JONES

bookmaker BINDER; WRITER; can allude to a novelist; can indicate a person's name used as the title of a Biblical book e.g. JOHN, MARK

bookmaker, work for a BINDING

books AV; NT; OT; *see* BOOK

bookworm READER

boom BANG; SPAR; POLE; ■ REPORT; RESOUND

boomer ROO

boomer, baby JOEY

boomeranged reversal indicator

booming RACKET

boors SWINE

boor LOUT; ■ YAHOO

boost KICK; RAISE

boost, given a reversal indicator
boot KICK; SACK; SHOE
boot out BOUNCE
boot, to TOO
bootblack SHINE
booted character PUSS
booth STALL; STAND; TENT
booty LOOT; SPOILS
booze ALE; BEER; DRINK (qv);
    TIPPLE
boozer BAR; PUB; TOPER; *see*
    DRUNKARD, PUB
boozy session BENDER
bop DANCE
Bordeaux CLARET; PORT; as the
    name belongs to a place as well
    as a wine it can be used merely to
    signify something French
border ABUT; BOUND; EDGE;
    EDGING; FRINGE; HEM;
    LIMIT; LINE; LIST (i.e. in joust-
    ing); MARCH; MARGE (old
    word); METE; ORLE (heraldry);
    RIM; SIDE; TRIM; VERGE
border control CUSTOMS
border flower TWEED
border, reinforced WELT
borderline HEM; *see* BORDER
borders can indicate first and last
    letters as "borders of Europe" →
    EE
bore BIND; BRED; DRAG;
    DRILL; DRIP; EAGRE; FAG;
    IRK; PAIN; PALL; PEST;
    PIERCE; REAM; WELL; ■
    CARRIED; MUZZLE; TIRE;
    WAVE; YIELDED
bored BLASE
boring ARID; DEAD; DRY;
    DULL; FLAT; SLOW; VAPID; ■
    STODGY; can indicate some
    cognate of NUMB; [◊ YAWN]
boring, become PALL
boring bit BROACH
boring into nesting indicator
boring item AWL
boring job/task CHORE; WELL
boring place WELL
boring, something AWL
boring tool AWL
boring type NERD
born B; NEE

borne CARRIED; nesting indicator
borne by ON
Bosche HUN
bosom HEART
boss ED (i.e. newspaper); HEAD;
    LORD; ORDER; RUN (i.e.
    verb); STUD; SUPER; ■ CHIEF;
    GAFFER; LEADER; MASTER
bosses BOARD
Boston institute MIT
botch BUNGLE; GOOF
both TWAIN
bother BANE; CARE; DO; DRAT;
    EAT; FUSS; HECK; HINDER;
    NARK; PEST; RATS(!); RILE;
    ROW; TIFF; WORRY; ■
    BRAWL; HINDER; PESTER;
    TROUBLE; anagram indicator
both flanks LR; RL
both hands, in a component to be
    nested within LR or RL
both of us WE
both sides ALL; LR; RL
bother MIND; ■ FLUSTER;
    TROUBLE (qv); WORRY
bothered ATE; CROSS; anagram
    indicator
bothering anagram indicator
bothering person *see*
    NUISANCE
bottle NERVE; ■ FLAGON;
    PHIAL; can indicate the contents
    of a bottle (ale, port etc); [◊
    WEAN]
bottle-opener B
bottle top B; CORK; TEAT
bottle, with extra BRAVER
bottled anagram indicator
bottles anagram indicator; nesting
    indicator
bottom BASE; BED; BUM;
    FOOT; KEEL; LAST; LUG;
    RUMP; SEAT; STERN; ■ HIPS;
    PRAT; last letter indicator as
    "bottom of pile" → E
bottom pinched, getting last let-
    ter to be omitted
bottom, river/sea BED
bottomless last letter to be omit-
    ted, as "bottomless lake" →
    MER

bottle GRIT; NERVE; ■ FLAGON; GUTS; MAGNUM; PHIAL; VIAL; *see* AUDACITY; [◊ CORK]

bough BRANCH

bought it something to do with having died

boulder ROCK

bounce BOB; BUMP; EJECT; GO; ■ SPRING

bounced anagram indicator

bouncer BALL

bouncy anagram indicator

bound END; HOP; JUMP; LEAP; LIABLE; LOPE; READY; SPRING; SURE; TAPED; TIED; ■ BORDER; CAPER; CORDED; HEADED; INTENT; LOLLOP; STRAPPED; nesting indicator, as "duty-bound" might require a component to be nested within EXCISE or TAX [◊ BOOK]

bound over CLEAR

bound, say TIDE

bound, we hear PACT; TIDE; TRUST

boundaries first and last letters of associated word to be used as "city boundaries" signifies CY; *see* BOUNDARY

boundaries of first and last letters of the word following to be used (as "boundaries of Durham" signifies DM)

boundary BORDER; EDGE; END; FENCE; FOUR; HEDGE; IV; LIST (i.e. in jousting); METE (boundary stone); RIM; SIX; VI; RUNS; WALL; ■ LIMIT

bounder CAD; FENCE; HEEL; ROO; ■ KNAVE; ROTTER

bouquet AROMA; AURA; NOSE; POSY; SCENT

bout FIT; JAG; SPELL; ■ MATCH

bout, short FIT

bovine OX; STOLID

bovver boy SKIN

bow ARC; ARCH; BEND; BOB; FRONT; HEAD; KNOT; PROW; STEM; STOOP; YIELD; can refer to something to do with a violin, viola, violinist or a ship; first

letter indicator as "vessel's bow" → V

bow, at the FORE

Bow, in can indicate the dropping of an initial H

bow tie PAINTER(!)

bower ARBOUR

bowl DISH; FONT; PAN; PLATE; SPEED; WOOD; YORK; ■ JACK; HOLLOW; STUMP (cric.)

bowl over WOW

bowl, shallow PLATE

bowl, sort of FINGER

bowled B; OUT

bowled over reversal indicator

bowler DERBY; DRAKE; HAT; TILE; ■ SPINNER; [◊ BALL; JACK; OVER]

bowler, type of SPIN

bowling ON; OVER; SPEEDING; anagram indicator

bowling lane ALLEY

bowling, sort of SPIN

bowling, spell of OVER

bowling success STRIKE

bowling venue GREEN

bowls target JACK

bowman ARCHER; HOOD; TELL

box ARK; BIN; CASE; CASKET; CHEST; COFFER; CRATE; CUFF; FIGHT; LOGE; PACK; SPAR; TIN; TREE; TUBE; TV; ■ CARTON; INRO; TELLY; [◊ PUNCH]

box, Japanese INRO

box of cards SHOE

box, private LOGE

box, put in CRATED

box, pill INRO

box, sort of ICE

boxed CASED; CRATED

boxed, something COMPASS

boxer ALI; DOG; PUG; ■ CRATER(!)

Boxer as the name of the horse in Orwell's *Animal Farm* can indicate something to do with the horse, the book or Orwell

boxes TELLIES; *see* BOX

boxing nesting indicator; [◊ BOUT; RING]

boxing match ROUNDS

boy LAD; PAGE; SON; SONNY ; can signal a male proper name e.g. MILES, PETER but very often the use of "boy" calls for the diminutive of a proper name e.g. AL, ART, NED, PHIL – for other male first names *see* MAN'S NAME

boy, armed CUPID

boy, chubby PUTTO (art)

boy, expectant PIP

boy king TUT

boy of fifties TED

boy standing up DAL

boycott, boycotted BLACK

boyfriend BEAU; DATE; FLAME; STEADY; LOVER

boys, little PUTTI (art)

brace COUPLE; PAIR; STEEL; STRUT; TENSE; TWO

bracing BRISK

bract LEAF

brad NAIL

brag BOAST; CROW; ■ BROADCAST

braid JOIN; LACE; TAPE

brain HEAD; HIT; (remember, the giraffe has the most superior brain!)

brain, of little DENSE; THICK

brainless DENSE; THICK

brains WIT; ■ NOUS

brains, bit of LOBE

brains, without *see* BRAINLESS

brainwave IDEA; anagram of BRAIN

brainy ABLE; BRIGHT; CLEVER

brainy, not THICK

brake CATCH; COPSE; FERN; GROVE; REIN; SLOW; STOP; THICKET; [◊ DISC]

brake, part of SHOE

branch ARM; BOUGH; FORK; LIMB; LOG; SPRAY; SPUR; STICK; SUB (as in sub office); TINE; TWIG

branch line SPUR

branch out FORK; ■ EXPAND

branch, tiny end of TWIG

branching out FORK

brand CLASS; LINE; LABEL; MAKE; MARK; MARQUE; NAME; SEAR; SORT; TYPE

brandish SHAKE; WAVE; WIELD

brandishing anagram indicator

brandy FINE; MARC; PEG

brash FLASHY

brash child BRAT

brass BUGLE; CASH; CHEEK; HORN; HORNS; NECK; NERVE; LIP; TUBA; ■ MONEY; RHINO; SAUCE; *see* MONEY

brasserie BAR

brassie CLUB

brassy CHEEK; FRESH; LOUD

brat IMP

brave BOLD; CREE; DARING; DEFY; DOUGHTY; FACE; GOOD; GRITTY; INDIAN; STOUT; *see* AMERICAN INDIAN

brave device HATCHET

brave man HERO; *see* AMERICAN INDIAN

brave partner SQUAW

brave person, type LION

bravery GUTS; *see* NERVE

bravo BULLY; OLE

brawl ROW; SCRAP; SETTO (i.e. set to); ■ DISPUTE; MELEE

brawn BEEF; JELLY

brazen BOLD

Brazil BR; [◊ NUT]

Brazilian state ACRE; PARA

breach GAP; RENT; RIFT; SPLIT; ■ CRACK; FOUL; RUPTURE SCHISM

breach of duty TORT

bread BRASS; CASH; COB; DIME; FARE; LOAF; NAN; PITA; ROLL; ■ BAP; NAAN; TOAST; *see* MONEY; [◊ CRUST]

bread, chunk of ROLL

bread, dry CRUST

bread, Indian NAAN; NAN

bread, loaf of TIN

break BUST; CRACK; GAP; LAPSE; PART; PAUSE; REND; RENT; REST; RIFT; SHEAR; SMASH; SNAP; SPLIT; STAVE; STOP; TRASH ■ CRUMBLE; FLOUT; DETACH; HOLS (i.e. holidays); RECESS; RESPITE; RUIN; SHATTER; SPLINTER; anagram indicator;

break around PANS

break down FAIL; STOP; anagram indicator; anagram of DOWN

break head BRAIN

break-in RAID; nesting indicator

break in electricity OUTAGE

break into song SING

break new ground DIG

break off SNAP

break out ESCAPE

break out violently RIP

break rule INFRINGE

break, short COMMA

break, sort of TIE

break up LAUGH; REND; SCRAP; anagram indicator; nesting indicator

break-up, part of SHARE

breakable anagram indicator

breakdown BREACH; anagram indicator

breaker ROLLER; WAVE

breakfast can indicate some kind of cereal

breakfast, bit of *see* BREAKFAST FOOD

breakfast food EGG; KIPPER; ROLL; TOAST; *see* CEREAL

breaking anagram indicator

breaking out in anagram indicator

breaking up anagram indicator

breaks anagram indicator; nesting indicator

breaks down anagram indicator

breakthrough nesting indicator

breakwater MOLE

breath GASP; HINT

breath, catch one's GASP

breath, deep SIGH

breath, out of WINDED

breathe quickly PANT

breather BREAK; GILL; LUNG; PAUSE; REST

breathing equipment NOSE

breathless, be GASP

bred RAISED

breed KIND; RACE; RAISE; REAR; STRAIN

breeding establishment STUD

breeze WIND

breeze, be borne on WAFT

breeze, cold DRAUGHT

breezing around anagram indicator

breezy AIRY

Bren GUN

Brent GOOSE

brew BEER; MASH; PLAN; anagram indicator; [◊ ALE; BITTER; TEA]

brew tea anagram of TEA

brewed anagram indicator

brewing AFOOT; anagram indicator

briar ROSE

bribable VENAL

bribe BUNG; OIL; SOP ■ NOBBLE; SQUARE

bribery, open to VENAL

brick BLOCK; STRETCHER

brick box HOD

brick waste GROG

bricklayer, something used by HOD

bricks, pile/stack of CLAMP

bride WIFE; [◊ GROOM]

bridegroom say, what did the IDO

bridge ARCH; CROSS; GAME; LINK; SPAN; TOWER; SPANNER; [◊ RUBBER]; can refer to the nose or some aspect of it

bridge bid NT

bridge games RUBBER

bridge players/opponents etc. usually refers to various combinations of N, S, E, W

bridgework DENTURE

brief CURT; LETTER; MINI; NOTE; PRIME; SHORT; SPEC;

TASK; TERSE; ■ COMPACT; REMIT; SILK (i.e. law); TINY; can indicate that something is of short duration, or concise in expression; abbreviation indicator; *see* SHORT

brief, not LONG
brief note MEMO
brief shower SPAT
briefs maker SILK
brier HEATH
brigand BANDIT; RAIDER
bright BRAINY; CLEVER; FAIR; LIGHT; LIT; LOUD; SHINY; SUNNY; ■ GLAD; GOLDEN; *see* CLEVER
bright light SUN
bright, not UNLIT; *see* DULL
bright, was GLARED; GLOWED; SHONE
brighten CLEAR; LIGHT
brighten up CLEAR
brightened LIT
brightened up LIT
brightly coloured RED
brightness SUN; SHEEN
brightness, measure of IQ
brill TOPPING
brilliance FLAIR
brilliant STAR; SUPER; ■ MEGA
brilliant, be SHINE
brilliant effect ECLAT
brim EDGE
bring FETCH
bring about CAUSE; EFFECT
bring ashore LAND
bring down LAND; RASE; RAZE
bring forth BEAR; BREED
bring home EARN; STRESS
bring in EARN; IMPORT; NET
bring on INCUR
bring out EDUCE
bring to bear EXERT
bring to light EXPOSE; OUT
bring together (troops) MUSTER
bring up BROACH; REAR; RAISE; reversal indicator
brink EDGE; RIM; VERGE; ■ LIMIT
briny MAIN

brio GUSTO
brisk LIVELY; SMART; SPRY; ■ BRACING; QUICK
bristle AWN; TEEM
bristles BEARD; ■ SETAE (botany); STUBBLE
Brit POM
Britain, most crowded area of SE
British B; BR; UK
British administration RAJ
British Columbia BC
British control, rule RAJ
British Isles BRIS
British rugby player LION
Briton, early PICT
Briton, North PICT; SCOT
Briton in Australia POM
Britten, character of BUDD
broach BEGIN; OPEN; SPIT; TAP
broaching anagram indicator
broad LARGE; WIDE
broad and slow, musically LARGO
broad-minded OPEN
broadcast AIR; BEAM; BRAG; EMIT; ISSUE; RELAY; OB; SEND; SENT; SHOW; SOW; SOWN; SPREAD; STREWN; ■ SCATTER; anagram indicator; homophone indicator
broadcast, outside OB
broadcaster RADIO; SOWER; ■ AIRER
broadcasters CHANNEL
broadcasting AIRING; ON; anagram indicator
brochure TRACT; ■ PROSPECTUS
broke BUST; SKINT; SPLIT; STUCK; ■ SMASHED; STONY; STRAPPED; TRASHED; anagram indicator; nesting indicator
broke, almost BUS; SKIN
broken BUST; anagram indicator
broken down anagram indicator
broken heart ATHER
broken leg, with word to end in GLE
broker AGENT; FACTOR
bronze TAN; THIRD

brooch CAMEO; PIN

brood ISSUE; LITTER; NEST; SIT; STEW; SULK

brooded SAT

brook ABIDE; B; BEAR; BURN; RILL; STAND; STREAM

broom BRUSH; SHRUB

broth DISH

brother BR; BRO; FR; MONK; PAL; SIB; ■ BRER

brotherhood COWL

brothers BROS; GRIMM; ORDER

brought GOT; LED

brought about anagram or run indicator

brought back reversal indicator

brought forth BRED

brought in nesting indicator

brought to light BORN; EXPOSED; OUT

brought round nesting indicator

brought up BRED; reversal indicator

brow EDGE; HILL; RIDGE; TOP

browbeat BULLY; COW

brown BAY; BREAD; DUN; RUST; RUSTY; TAN; UMBER; ■ BEIGE; BICE; DARK; SIENNA

brown bread TOAST

brown, dark UMBER

brown, light FAWN

brown, purplish PUCE

browned off, get TAN

brownie IMP

browning TAN

Browning GUN

Browning, with ARMED

Brownish SEPIA

brownish-grey TAUPE

brownish-yellow AMBER

browse EAT; NIBBLE; READ

Bruckner ANTON

bruise MARK; WELT

bruised anagram indicator

Brunel [◊ BRIDGE]

brunette, not FAIR

brush BROOM; BUFF; SCRUB; SCUFF; SPAT; SWEEP; TAIL; TIFF; TOUCH; ■ CLEANER]

brusque BRIEF

Brussels EU

brutal CRUEL; FERAL

brutal person BEAST; FIEND

brute BEAST

Brutus ROMAN

bubble BOIL; SEETHE; SIMMER

bubbly ASTI; FIZZY; anagram indicator

buccaneer PIRATE; see PIRATE

buck DEER; HIND; JUMP; KICK; [◊ DOE]

buck up CHEER; REAR

bucked anagram indicator

bucket PAIL

bucking anagram indicator

Buckingham, for example PALACE

buckle BEND; CLASP; FASTEN; SHIELD; WARP

buckler SHIELD

bucks can indicate something to do with rabbits

Bucks town IVER

bud GERM; PAL; SHOOT; see FRIEND

Buddhism ZEN

Buddhism, practise DOZEN (i.e. do Zen)

Buddhist ZEN

Buddhist monk LAMA

buddy PAL; see FRIEND

Buddy HOLLY

budge MOVE

budgy PET; ■ BIRD

buff FAN; NUT; POLISH

buff, in the see NAKED

Buffalo Bill CODY

buffer can indicate someone who polishes e.g. shoeblack

buffet BAR; BASH; BEAT; BLOW; STRIKE

buffoon see FOOL

bug ANT; GERM; LOUSE; PEST; ■ INSECT; MIDGE; see ANNOY, INSECT, IRRITATE

bugging device TAP

bugle BRASS; PLANT; WIND

build FORM; FOUND; MOUNT; ■ ERECT

builder anagram indicator

builder's carrier HOD

building B; BLOCK; DOME; HALL; HOUSE; HUT; PILE; SHACK; SHED; TOWER; VILLA; anagram indicator

building block BRICK

building for storage BARN

building, imposing PALACE

building material BRICK; CEMENT

building, part of large WING

building, sacred CHAPEL; CHURCH; TEMPLE; ■ CATHEDRAL; MINSTER; MOSQUE

building, side of WALL

building, tall TOWER

buildings, collection of COMPLEX; ESTATE

built of anagram indicator

built-up anagram indicator; reversal indicator

built-up area CITY; ESTATE; TOWN

bulb CLOVE; LAMP

bulb, garlic CLOVE

bulge SAG

bulk see MASS

bull CENTRE; NEAT; OX; ROT; see RUBBISH; can indicate something to do with darts (e.g. inner, outer, board)

bull's eye GOLD

bullet ROUND; SHELL; SHOT; SLUG; TRACER; [◊ BARREL; CHAMBER]

bullet, sound of PING

bulletin NEWS

bullets AMMO; ROUNDS; see BULLET

bullock STEER; ■ STOT

bully BEEF; BRAVO; HECTOR; ■ BOSS; BROWBEAT; COWER; OPPRESS; TYRANT; anagram indicator

Bulwer-Lytton hero ARAM

bum RUMP; TRAMP; anagram indicator

bump BARGE; BLOW; CRASH; ■ COLLIDE; STRIKE

bumped into MET; nesting indicator

bumper GLASS

bumpkin CLOD; HICK; LOUT; OAF; RUBE (U.S.); YOKEL

bumpy anagram indicator

bun MOP; WAD (slang)

bunch CLUSTER; FLOCK; GANG; LOT; POSY; SET; WAD; see GROUP

bunch of documents FILE; WAD

bunch of girls BEVY

bunch of keys some combination of A, B, C, D, E, F, G

bundle BALE; PACK; STACK; WAD

bundled anagram indicator

bundles, in anagram indicator

bung BRIBE; PLUG; SOP; STOP; STOPPER

bungle GOOF; MASH; MUFF; ■ BOTCH; MUDDLE

bungled anagram indicator

bunk BED; BERTH; COT; ROT; see RUBBISH

bunk off can be a general omission indicator or can mean that a synonym (e.g. bed, cot) is to be omitted

bunker SAND

bunting FLAGS

buoy FLOAT

buoyancy CHEER

buoyant, be FLOAT

bur STICKER

burden CROSS; HEAVY; LADE; LOAD; LUMBER; ONUS; PACK; TAX; WEIGHT; ■ CUMBER; SADDLE

burden, carry SHOULDER

burdened LADEN; TAXED

bureau AGENCY

burgeon SPROUT

burgle ROB

burgundy RED; WINE; ■ MAROON

burial place GRAVE; TOMB; ■ CHAMBER

burial mound BARROW; TUMULUS (useful to get CUMULUS)

buried HID; UNDER; nesting indicator

buried in run indicator; nesting indicator

Burlington House RA

burn BROOK; CHAR; FIRE; FLARE; ITCH; RILL; SCALD; SEAR; SINGE; WATER; ■ CREMATE; IGNITE; SIZZLE; STREAM

burn, lightly SINGE

burn slowly SMOULDER

burn-up CREMATION

burn with a strong flame BLAZE

burning AFIRE; ABLAZE; AFLAME; ALIGHT; HOT; LIT; LIVE; ON; ■ ITCHING; KEEN; anagram indicator

burnish RUB; SHINE

Burns POET; can indicate something to do with rye

burp BELCH; [◊ WINDY]

burrow HOLE; SETT

burst POP; SPLIT; anagram indicator

burst of activity FIT

bursting anagram indicator

burton TACKLE

Burton, gone for a anagram indicator

bury HIDE; INTER

bus COACH; [◊ STOP]

bus garage DEPOT

bus, on ABOARD

bush PLANT; see PLANT; ■ INN SIGN

busiest PEAK

business ADO; AGENCY; BIZ; CO; DEAL; DO; FIRM; HOUSE; LINE; SHOP; TRADE; ■ AFFAIR; COMMERCE; CONCERN; OPERATION; PIGEON; see COMPANY, TRADE

business, agricultural FARM; HOLDING

business centre CITY

business community CITY

business deal SALE

business, do DEAL; TRADE

business graduate MBA

business qualification MBA

business transaction, bit of DEAL; SALE

businessman EXEC; TYCOON

businessman, top CEO

busk [◊ AD LIB; PLAY; STREET]

buss KISS

bust ARREST; BREAK (qv); BROKE; CHEST; PARTY; RAID; SMASHED; ■ FIGUREHEAD; see BREAK; anagram indicator

busted anagram indicator

bustle ADO; FLAP; HUM; STIR

bustling ASTIR; anagram indicator

busy ACTIVE; ENGAGED; PEAK; anagram indicator

busy character BEE

busy, get WORK

busy person/type BEE

busy worker ANT; BEE

busybody PRY

but SAVE; ■ EXCEPT; ONLY; may call for the *opposite* – as "right angle" could be clued by "But one could turn left at the corner ..."

but in Latin SED

but not EXCEPT

but not a A to be omitted

butcher KILL; MANGLE; SLAY

butcher-bird SHRIKE

butcher's LOOK

butchered anagram indicator

butchers LOOK; ■ DEKKO

butler SERVANT; [◊ PANTRY]

Butler RAB

butt CASK; END; FISH; STUMP; ■ STOOGE; TARGET; can indicate something to do with shooting practice; last letter indicator

Butt CLARA

butter FAT; GOAT; RAM; ■ GHEE

butter, portion of PAT

butterflies anagram of BUTTER

butterfly COMMA; STROKE; ■ ADMIRAL; IMAGO; SKIPPER; with a capital letter can refer to something to do with the opera 'Madam Butterfly'

button KNOB; [◊ PANIC, PUSH]

buttonhole ACCOST; COLLAR; nesting indicator
buttonholed nesting indicator
Buttons PAGE
buttress PIER; PROP
buy GET; SHOP; STAND
buy it DIE
buyer BULL
buyer's option BO
buzz HUM; KICK; RING; can indicate something to do with bee e.g. drone; ■ THRILL
buzzer BEE; BELL; WASP
buzzing HUM; anagram indicator
by AT; IN; NEAR; OVER; PER; THRO; VIA; X; ■ ALONG; THROUGH
by all means DO
by climbing REP (i.e. reversal)
by, French DE; DES
By God! EGAD
by hiding nothing BOY
by means, or by way of PER; VIA
by mouth ORAL
by oneself ALONE; LONE; SOLE; SOLO
by stopping sin BERRY (i.e. b-err-y)
by the way can indicate something located at the roadside (e.g. kerb, gutter) or street furniture (e.g. streetlamp, post-box)
by virtue of being QUA
by way of IN; VIA
by-law RULE
bye RUN
bygone OLD; OLDEN; PAST
bypass DODGE
byre SHED
byway LANE

Cc

cab TAXI
Cabaret **performer** BOWLES
cabbage COLE; KALE; LODGE

cabbage, some HEART
cabin CHALET; CRIB; HUT; SHACK
cabinet CLOSET
cable CORD; LINE; ROPE; WIRE; ■ FLEX
cache HIDE; HOARD; STORE
cackle CHATTER; GAS
cacophony DIN; ROW
cad BOUNDER; CREEP; HEEL; ROTTER
cadence CLOSE; FALL
caddis FLY; YARN
cadet L; SCION; ■ TRAINEE
Cadmus, daughter of AGAVE
cadre GROUP; UNIT
Caesar's fateful day IDES
Caesar's last question ETTU (i.e. et tu)
cafe DINER
cage COOP; PEN; POUND
cake BUN; PUFF; ROCK; ROLL; SCONE; SET; SOAP; WAD; ■ ANGEL; CLOT; PASTRY; PAT; SPONGE; TORTE
cake ingredient CURRANT
cake mixture BATTER
cake, piece of EASY
caked SET
cakes BAKING
calamitous FATAL; anagram indicator
calculate ADD; INTEND
calculation SUM; anagram indicator
calculator ADDER
Caledonian PICT; SCOT
calf LEATHER
calibre BORE
California CAL
Caligula ROMAN
call BID; CITE; CLAIM; CRY; DIAL; DUB; HAIL; HEADS; HI; HOOT; LET (i.e. in tennis); NAME; NEED; O; PAGE; PHONE; PLEA; RING; TAILS; TERM; TIME(!); TITLE; ■ DEMAND; EXCLAIM; HOLLER; SHOUT; TITLE; YODEL
call attracting attention AHEM

call back ETIC

call for NEED; USE; WANT

call for help SOS

call names SLAG

call out man's name HUGH

call to attract attention HO

call up ETIC (i.e. cite reversed); EVOKE; RING

call-up EMAN (i.e. name reversed); *see* CALL UP

Callas MARIA

called CRIED; RANG; RUNG

called in French DIT

caller GUEST

calling CAREER; VOCATION

Calliope MUSE

calls for homophone indicator

calm COOL; EASE; EVEN; LULL; PEACE; STILL; ■ ALLAY; APPEASE; PLACATE; QUELL; QUIET; SEDATE; SERENE; SOOTHE

calmer SOP

calmness POISE

calorie allowance DIET

calumniate *see* CALUMNY

calumny SLANDER; SMEAR

camber BANK

Cambridge University CU; MIT

came across FOUND; MET; READ

came down RAINED

came first LED; WON

came to AWOKE

came up AROSE; ROSE

camp BASE; GAY; PARTY (qv); TENT

campaign ACTION; DRIVE; FIGHT; WAR

campanologist RINGER

can BILLY; GAOL; KEN; KNOW; LOO; MAY; STIR; TIN; ■ JOHN; PICKLE; PRESERVE; *see* PRISON

can be anagram indicator

can be bought VENAL

can containing nothing TION

can get can indicate that the synonym for the answer follows

can lead to anagram indicator

can work out anagram indicator

Canada CAN; in a phrase such as "in parts of Canada" can indicate a French word, *see* FRANCE, FRENCH

canal CUT; GUT; GUTTER; can indicate a specific canal e.g. Panama, Suez

canal boat BARGE

canal constructor NAVVY

canal, stretch of LOCK

canap SNACK

canary FINCH

cancel CUT; ERASE; REVOKE; SCRUB; ■ ANNUL; BIN; DELETE; DROP; DUMP; SCRAP; TRASH; UNDO; omission indicator

cancellation OFF

cancelled OFF; omission indicator, as "one is cancelled" requires I to be omitted

candid FRANK; OPEN; PLAIN

candidates FIELD

candle LIGHT; TAPER; [◊ WICKED]

cane BEAT; GRASS; REED; ROD; STAFF; STEM; STICK; THRASH; ■ BIRCH

canine FANG; TOOTH; note, can refer to a dog, usually a specific breed

canker ROT

cannabis HEMP; JOINT; POT

canned nesting indicator; particularly it can call for a component to be nested within TIN as "Poison derived from canned meat" → TOXIN (i.e. T-OX-IN)

cannon ORDNANCE (useful to make ORDINANCE)

canny CLEVER; CUTE; SHREWD; WISE

canoe racing ROWING

canon LAW; ROUND; RULE; TEST

canons CHAPTER

canopy TESTER

canopy of sky DOME

cant HEEL; LIST; SLANG; SLOPE; ■ ARGOT; BEVEL

Canterbury LAMB; SEE

cantilever BEAM

canvas SAIL; TENT; can indicate something to do with circus or circus artistes

canvas shoe SNEAKER

cap BEAT; COVER; CROWN; HAT; LID; TAM; TOP; ■ BETTER; BONNET; FINIAL (arch.); TIP

cap decoration HACKLE

cap off/removed first letter to be omitted

capable FIT

capable of anagram indicator

capacity G; GAL; JOB; ROOM; VOL; ■ ABILITY; CONTENT; GALLON

capacity of, in the QUA

cape C; CLOAK; HORN; NESS; ■ TIPPET (clothing)

cape, American SABLE

caper ANTIC; LARK; LEAP; PRANK; SKIP; ■ BOUND; FROLIC; CRIME; TARTAR SAUCE (i.e. an ingredient in); SCAM; anagram indicator

capering anagram indicator

capital AI; CAP; CITY; GOOD; GREAT; HEAD; SUPER; TOP; ■ BACKING; FUNDS; HAVANA; LEADING; MONEY; RESOURCES; WHEREWITHAL; initial letter indicator; can refer to a capital city, popular examples: ADEN, CAIRO, LIMA, PARIS, RIGA, ROME; SOFIA; can indicate something to do with head, brain or hair

capital, island PALMA

capital, provide FUND

capitulate CEDE; YIELD

Capone AL; ■ SCARFACE

capricious anagram indicator

capsized anagram indicator; reversal indicator

captain BLIGH; CAP; CAPT; HARDY; HOOD; KIDD; PILOT; SKIP; ■ FLINT; MORGAN; NEMO; SKIPPER

captivate CHARM; nesting indicator

captivated, captivating nesting indicator

captive POW

captives nesting indicator, as "ten captives" requires TEN to be nested

capture BAG; LAND; TAKE; TRAP; ■ CATCH; SNARE

captured TAKEN; TOOK; nesting indicator

capturing nesting indicator

car AUTO; COUPE; ESTATE; GT; LIMO; TRAM; ■ HEARSE; can refer to a specific make or model: ETYPE; FORD; JAG; MAXI; MINI; POLO; ROLLS; ROVER; UNO

car control BRAKE; CLUTCH

car, dilapidated HEAP

car, fast GT

car, go by DRIVE

car, leave PARK

car, old CRATE; HEAP; ■ BANGER; MORRIS

car, smart RR

car, US DODGE

car, went by DROVE

carapace SHELL

carbonaceous rock COAL

card A; ACE; CLUB; COMB; COVE; HEART; J; JACK; K; KING; Q; TREY; WAG; WIT; ■ CAUTION; CHARACTER; DEUCE; DIAMOND; QUEEN; SPADE; TAROT

card game BRAG; BRIDGE; LOO; NAP; POKER; SNAP; STUD; ■ BANKER; OMBRE; PIQUET; SKAT; RUMMY; WHIST; [◊ DEAL; HAND; TENACE; TRUMP]

card player B; EAST; N; NORTH; S; SOUTH; W; WEST

card session DEAL; HAND; RUBBER

cardinal CHIEF; HE; MAIN; RED; STRESS; WINE; ■ RED HAT; can refer to the cardinal points of the compass: N, E, W, S; can indicate a cardinal number ONE, TWO, etc including foreign cardinal numbers as "first French cardinal" clues UN etc

cards DECK; HAND; HANDS; PACK; PAIR

cardsharp ROGUE

care CHARGE; MIND; RECK (archaic word but still retained in reckless); TEND

care of CO

care of, take MIND

career DASH; JOB; LINE; RACE; RUN; RUSH; SPEED; TEAR; WORK; ■ CALLING

career golfer PRO

carefree GAY

careful MIND

carefully anagram indicator

careless LAX; SLACK; ■ REMISS; SLOPPY; anagram indicator

caress BILL; NECK; PET; STROKE

cargo LADING; LOAD; ■ FREIGHT

cargo on, put LADE; LOAD

cargo space HOLD

Caribbean SEA

Caribbean island CUBA

caricature GUY

carnival site/venue RIO

carnivore, small MINK; STOAT; WEASEL

carol SING; SONG; WASSAIL

carol singers WAIT

carol singing WASSAIL

carousel can indicate something to do with luggage e.g. cases

carp BEEF; CAVIL; FISH; NAG

carpenter CHIPPY; CHIPS; ■ QUINCE

carpenter's appliance VICE

carpet LAYER; MAT; RAP; RATE; ROAST; RUG

carriage BRAKE; CAB; COACH; FLY; GAIT; GIG; PORT; PRAM; SET; STAGE; TRAP; ■ BEARING; CHAISE; HACKNEY; MIEN; POSTURE; SURREY

Caribbean WI

carried BORNE

carried away RAPT; SENT

carried by run indicator

carrier BAG; CARTER; HOD; SACK; SHIP; TRAY; TRAIN; ■ MULE; PORTER

carries nesting indicator; run indicator; *see* CARRY

carries on ON to be nested

carrot BAIT; LURE; VEG; ■ BRIBE; UMBELLIFER

carry BEAR; CART; HOLD; LUG; TOTE; ■ ENDURE; HANDLE; STOCK; TAKE; nesting indicator

carry away SEND; TAKE

carry on FLIRT; LAST; RAGE; WAGE

carry out DO; EFFECT; RENDER

carrying BEARING; TOTING; anagram indicator; nesting indicator

cart BARROW; DRAY; GIG; TRAP; ■ CARRY; DILLY; WAGON; WAIN

carte MENU

cartoon STRIP

cartoon hero BATMAN

carve CUT (qv); ETCH; FORM; HEW; SHAPE; SLICE; [◊ JOINT]

carved CUT; ETCHED; GRAVEN; HEWN; insertion indicator; anagram indicator

Casanova LOVER; ■ ROUE

case ACTION; APPEAL; BAG; BOX; COVER; CRATE; FILE; FRAME; GRIP; NUT; POD; SHELL; SUIT; TRIAL; ■ COMPACT; ETUI; EXAMPLE; HOLSTER; INSTANCE; PATIENT; SHEATH; SHEATHE; VALISE; WALLET; nesting indicator; can refer to a grammatical case such as DATIVE, VOCATIVE or in abbreviated form – DAT, VOC, ACC, GEN, ABL; can refer to something to do with patient, illness, hospital etc; can indicate something to do with the difference in letter case, i.e. between upper and lower case, such as to express 'I' in

lower case (i) requires a DOT;
can indicate something to do with
luggage e.g. bellhop; can indicate
first and last letters as "case to
try" → TY

case for can indicate that the item
that follows is to be nested, for
example "case for Oriental" can
mean that E is to be nested

case, in LEST

cases can refer to the outer letters
of a word (so that "brief missing
cases" → RIE)

cash CHANGE; COIN; NOTE;
PENNY; PROP (i.e. property);
READY; TIN; ■ LUCRE;
MONEY; TENDER can signify a
specific currency e.g. ANNA,
DIME, QUARTER etc; *see*
CURRENCY, MONEY

cash for the day, a bit of FLOAT

cash drawer TILL; ■ REGISTER

cash, hard COIN

cashier FIRE; TELLER

casing COVER; RIND; SHELL;
first and last letter indicator; nesting indicator

casing, tough RIND; SHELL

cask BUTT; KEG; PIN; PIPE;
TUN

cassette TAPE

cast ANGLE; BUNG; DASH; DIE;
FLING; FORM; FOUND;
HEAVE; PITCH; SET; SHAPE;
SHED; SHIED; SHY; SLING;
THREW; THROW; ■ CHUCK;
COMPANY; PLAYERS;
TROUPE; anagram indicator

cast down LOWER

cast light LIT

cast out EVICT; EXILE

caste CLASS

castigated anagram indicator

Castilian, the EL

castle C; FORT; KEEP; PIECE;
ROOK; ■ FASTNESS

castle, Englishman's HOME

castle, old* RUIN

casual EASY; LAX; ODD; anagram indicator

casual shirt T

casual worker TEMP

casual workers LUMP

casually DOWN (as in dress
down); anagram indicator

casually turn over RIFFLE

casualties DEAD

cat FAN; FLOG; KIT; LASH;
LION; OUNCE; PET; PUSS;
ROPE; TOM; WHIP; ■ FELINE;
GENET; KITTY; MOGGY;
MOUSER; PANTHER; PUSSY;
QUEEN; SCOURGE; TABBY;
TIGER; can indicate something
to do with jazz, New Orleans etc;
[◊ FUR; FURRY; MEW; PURR]

cat's paw PAWN; TOOL

cat, theatre GUS

cataclysm anagram indicator

catalogue LIST; anagram indicator

catapult SLING

catastrophe RUIN

catcall BOO; JEER; MEW

catch ARREST; BAG; BOLT;
BRAKE; COP; GET; GRAB;
HEAR; HOOK; LAND; NAB;
NAIL; NET; NIP; SEE; SNAG;
TAG; TAKE; TRAP; TRICK;
TRIP; ■ CLASP; CLOSER;
COLLAR; CORNER; DETENT;
ENTRAP; FASTENER; HOLD;
LASSO; POT; SNARE; SNIB
(small bolt); nesting indicator;
can indicate something to do with
angling, fish, fishing industry,
fishing boats etc.

catch fish TROLL; *see* FISH

catch sight of ESPY; SPOT; ■
NOTICE

catch up TEN

cater FEED

catering for anagram indicator

caterpillar LOOPER

cathedral CHESTER; DOM; ELY;
MINSTER

cathedral city CHESTER; ELY

cathedral precinct CLOSE

catholic BROAD

Catholic RC

Catholic dignitary DOM;
DOMINEE

cats PRIDE

cats and dogs RAIN ■
BUCKETS

cattle BEEF; COWS; HERD; KINE; NEAT; STEER(S); STOCK

cattle disease BSE

cattle food CUD; MANGEL

cattle pen CORRAL

catwalk [◊ MODEL]

caucus CELL

caught C; CT; OUT; ■ NIPPED; SNARED; *see* CATCH; anagram indicator; nesting indicator

caught by nesting indicator

caught in C to be included; run indicator; nesting indicator

caught out C to be omitted

cause DO; GROUND; LET; MAKE; RAISE; REASON; ■ PROMPT; anagram indicator

cause amazement AWE; STUN

cause friction RUB

cause of ferment YEAST

cause of irritation RANKLE

cause stress STRAIN; WORRY

caused by usually indicates that what follows are components of the solution

caustic anagram indicator

caustic comment DIG

caution CARD; CARE; HEED; WARN; ■ AMBER; SCREAM; WARINESS

caution, move with EDGE; INCH

cautionary light AMBER

cautious CHARY; LEERY; WARY

cavalry GREY; HORSE

cavalry man LANCER; RIDER

cave GROT; HOLE; ■ ANTRE (poet.); GROTTO; WARNING (i.e. Latin)

cave-dweller TROG

caved in GAVE

caviar, caviare ROE

cavities ANTRA; *see* CAVITY

cavity CRATER; DENT; GAP; HOLE; SAC

cavort, cavorted, cavorting anagram indicator

CC with a homophone indicator can call for SEAS

CD, item on a TRACK

cease DIE; DROP; HALT; REST; STOP; ■ ABSTAIN; DESIST

cease attending LEAVE

cease employ DROP; SACK (qv); SCRAP

cease to have LOSE

ceded omission indicator

ceiling TOP

celebrate FEAST; FETE; PARTY; SING

celebrated NOTED; SUNG

celebration DO; FAIR; GALA; MASS; PARTY; ■ CARNIVAL; REVEL

celebration in college GAUDY

celebratory FESTIVE; JOLLY

celebrities ALIST (i.e. the A list)

celebrity FAME; HERO; NAME; NOTE; STAR; VIP; ■ LEGEND; LION

celerity SPEED

cell EGG; GROUP

cells TISSUE

Celtic IRISH

cement BOND; FIX; ■ POINTING

cementing nesting indicator

censor BAN; BANNER; CATO; EDIT; GAG; STOP

censorship BAN; GAG

censorship of anagram indicator

censure PAN; RAP; RAIL; RATE; STICK; *see* REPRIMAND

centaur HORSE

central CHIEF; KEY; MAIN; MID; ■ LEADING; MIDDLE; use middle letter(s) of associated word; run indicator

central heating CH

Central London ND (think about it!)

centre BULL; CORE; HEART; HUB; MID; NUB; PITH; WAIST; ■ DEPOT; FOCUS; MIDDLE; use the middle letter(s) of associated word

centre, business CITY

centre-forward W

centre for intelligence BRAIN

centre, in the AMID

centre of population CITY; LA (which can be ingeniously used to get the answer LOS ANGELES!); TOWN

centrepiece middle letter(s) of a word

century C; TON; ■ TRECENTO

century, half L

century, one short of OO (i.e. first digit from 100)

ceramic POT; TILE

ceramic material CLAY

cereal BRAN; CORN; CROP; GRASS; OAT; OATS; RICE; WHEAT; SAGO; ■ BARLEY; MILLET

cereal, bit of EAR

cereal head EAR

ceremonial POMP

ceremony FORM; MASS; POMP; RITE

cert CINCH; NAP

certain ACTUAL; BOUND; SURE

certain, a ONE; SOME; SURE

certain amount SOME

certain French SUR

certain, make ENSURE

certain, not MAY

certain number SOME

certain people SOME

certain quantity RATION

certainly AY; AYE; OK; SURE; YEA; YES; ■ CERTES; INDEED; REALLY

certainty NAP

certificate DEED; SCRIP; TICKET; ■ DIPLOMA

cessation of hostilities TRUCE

cha TEA

chafe FRAY; FRET; RUB; ■ RANKLE

chaff AWN; BANTER; REFUSE; RIB; TEASE; ■ HUSKS

chain BOND; CABLE; LINKS; RANGE; SHACKLE; TIE

chair HEAD; POST; ROCKER; RUN; SEAT; SEDAN; SITTER

chair meeting PRESIDE

chair, took SAT

chairman PROF; PROFESSOR; [◊ BOARD]

Chairman MAO

chairman, act as HEAD

chairs SEATING

challenge CLAIM; DARE; DEFY; TACKLE

challenge for ball TACKLE

chamber PO; POT; ROOM (qv); SOLAR; [◊ BULLETS; STAR]

chamber group TRIO

chamber room VAULT

Chamberlain JOE

champ BITE; CHEW; EAT; MUNCH; *see* CHAMPION; [◊ TEETH]

champagne BRUT; WIDOW (brand name; ■ MAGNUM)

champion ACE; BACK; BEST; CHAMP; KNIGHT; STAR; TOP; VICTOR; ■ ESPOUSE; VICTOR; WINNER

champion, former ALI; LAVER

championship TITLE

chance BET; FALL; FLUKE; HAP; LOT; LUCK; RISK; SHOT; STAKE; THROW; WAGER; ■ GAMBLE; HAPPEN; PROSPECT; RANDOM

chance, take a DICE; RISK; ■ GAMBLE

Chancellor CE

chances ODDS; *see* CHANCE

chancy DICY

change ALTER; AMEND; CASH; EDIT; EMEND; FIX; P; SHIFT; SWAP; SWITCH; TURN; VARY; ■ COPPERS; FLOAT; FLUX; MONEY; MUTATE; SILVER; anagram indicator, as "change of gear" → GREA); can signify money (COIN) especially small coins; can indicate a verb form beginning with RE; [◊ NEW]

change angle TURN

change book EDIT

change course SHEER; TACK

change of NEW, as "change of players" can clue NEWCAST (in order to construct NEWCASTLE for example)

change of course TACK

change opinion SWING

change over a synonym of "change" to be reversed (e.g. PAWS)

change position STIR

change sides DEFECT; within the target word R is to replace L or vice versa

change, small P

change, sudden VEER

change with age YELLOW; ■ MATURE; RIPEN

changed NEW; anagram indicator; replacement indicator (e.g. one letter for another)

changed direction reversal indicator

changes PEAL; VARIES; anagram indicator

changing anagram indicator

changing places change-in-order indicator

changing sides within the target word R is to replace L or vice versa

changing sex substituting F for M or vice versa

changing sides within target word R to replace L or vice versa

channel DITCH; DRAIN; DUCT; MOAT; RIVER; SEWER; SIDE (i.e. TV channel); SOUND; TRENCH; TROUGH; TUBE; ■ COURSE; DIRECT; GUTTER; LANE; SINUS; SOLENT

Channel Island HERM

Channel Islands CI

Channel port DOVER

chant MANTRA; SING; SLOGAN ★

chanted SANG

chaos MESS; PIE (from printing); ■ HAVOC; anagram indicator

chaos, in anagram indicator

chaotic, chaotically anagram indicator

chap BOD; COVE; CRACK; GENT; GUY; HE; MAN (qv); SORE; ■ FELLOW (qv); MISTER; a man's name (usually shortened) e.g. AL, ALF, BILL, DAN, DON, HERB, IAN, JOE, LEN, PHIL, REG, RON, SID,

STAN, TIN, TOM, TONY; *for further names see* MAN'S NAME, FELLOW

chap, greedy PIG

chap, old COVE

chap's HIS

chaps MEN

chaps, you say GUISE

chapter C; PHASE; [◊ VERSE]

chapter, part of CANON

char BURN; CHAR; DAILY; FISH; SINGE; TEA; ■ CLEANER

character AIR; CARD; GIST; KIDNEY; LETTER; MAN; PART; ROLE; RUNE; THORN (runic); TONE; TYPE; ■ ETHOS; DISPOSITION; NATURE; can refer to a specific letter either at face value e.g. A, B, C or as a homophonic 'word' e.g. BEE, DEE, GEE, ESS etc; can refer to a Greek character. alpha etc

character-forming can indicate something to do with writing or graphology

characteristic TRAIT; ■ IDIOMATIC; PROPERTY

characters CASE (i.e printing); CODE; *see* CHARACTER; anagram indicator; run indicator

characters, in anagram indicator; run indicator

characters' limits AZ

characters lined up TYPE

characters, relating to old RUNIC

charades refers to the type of clue where the answer is wholly built up using bits and pieces, in the manner of the well-known parlour game. Example: "Attack American president" (6) Answer: AMBUSH

charge AC; ACC; ASK; BILL; BOOK; C; CARE; CH; COST; DEBT; DUE; FEE; FILL; HOLD; ION; LOAD; LUNGE; PRIME; ORDER; PRICE; RAM; RAP; RATE; RENT; RUN; RUSH; SUE; TAX; TOLL;

WARD; ■ ACCUSE; ATTACK;
CANTON (heraldry);
COMMAND; DEVICE (her-
aldry); FREIGHT; INDICT;
INVOICE; LEVY; POSTAGE;
RETAINER; TITHE; TRUST;
can signify something to do with
electricity, neutron, etc; can indicate something to do with heraldry

charge, criminal RAP
charge, in IC; OVER
charge, not at a FREE
charge of, in IC; OVER
charge of, take BOSS; RUN; ■
MANAGE
charge, sort of DEPTH
charge, was in LED
charge, without FREE
charged HADUP (i.e. had up);
LIVE
charged, not FREE
charged one ION
charges DUES; TERMS
chariot CART
charioteer HUR
charitable organisation LIONS
charity AID; ALMS; CAUSE;
RAG
charity event FETE; RAG; ■
RAFFLE
charlady CLEANER; DAILY
Charles CHAS; CHUCK
Charlie ASS; MUG; can signify a
celebrity of that name e.g. Chaplin, Parker; can indicate something to do with cocaine; *see*
FOOL
charm AURA; ENGAGE; OBI;
SPELL; TAKE; ■ APPEAL;
ENAMOUR; ENCHANT;
SMOOTH; TALISMAN;
UNCTION
charmer WITCH
charming CUTE; SWEET; ■
ENTHRAL; can indicate something to do with casting a spell
chart GRAPH; LIST; MAP;
PLAN; PLOT; TABLE; ■
SURVEY
charter CONTRACT
charts ATLAS; MAPS

chary WARY
chase HUNT; ETCH; FOLLOW;
FRAME; HARE; RUN; TAIL; ■
ENGRAVE; PURSUE
chased RAN; *see* CHASE
chasm GORGE; RENT; SPLIT
chaste MODEST
chat PATTER; RAP; SPEAK;
TALK; *see* TALK
chat inconsequentially
PRATTLE
chatter GAB; GAS; PRATE;
RABBIT; TALK; ■ NATTER
chatting homophone indicator
chauffeur DRIVER
chauffeur, be a DRIVE
cheap LOW; BASE; PALTRY
cheap stuff TAT
cheaper DOWN
cheat CLIP; CON; DO; DUPE;
RIP; ROOK; RUSH (colloq.);
SCREW; SHARP; STING;
TRICK; TWIST; GYP; ■
COZEN; DIDDLE; DUPER;
FIDDLE; FLEECE; KNAVE;
SWINDLE (qv)
cheated DID; ROOKED;
TRICKED
cheater CON; DUPER; FIDDLER
cheating, no FAIR
check AUDIT; BLOCK; CH;
CURB; DAM; DETER; EDIT;
FOIL; LEASH; MARK; PLAID;
RATE; REIN; STAY; STEM;
STOP; TEST; TRY; VET; ■
ARREST; BALK; BAULK;
INSPECT; LIMIT; REBUT;
REPRESS; RESTRAIN;
SCREEN; STAUNCH; STUNT;
THWART; can indicate something to do with chess
check, final MATE
check out VET; *see* CHECK
check-up TEST; can indicate the
reversal of a "check" synonym
e.g. METS, POTS
★ **checked letter** the technical term
for a letter which forms part of
the answer to both an Across and
a Down clue. Checked letters are
the essence of crosswords and are

obviously helpful where an answer is difficult

checked stuff PLAID

checking nesting indicator; *see* CHECK

checkout TILL

Cheddar CHEESE; GORGE

cheek BRASS; CHAP; GALL; LIP; MOUTH; NECK; NERVE; SAUCE; ■ JOWL

cheek in America SASS

cheeky BRASH; PERT; FRESH; INSOLENT; *see* IMPERTINENT

cheer CLAP; ELATE; LIVEN; OLE; PERK; PLEASE; RAH; ROOT; SHOUT; ■ BRAVO; ENCOURAGE

cheer, give a ROAR

cheer up ELATE; LIVEN; PLEASE

cheerful BRIGHT; GLAD; HAPPY; HIGH; JAUNTY; PERKY; ■ CHIPPER; SUNNY; UPBEAT

cheerful, not *see* CHEERLESS

cheerless DISMAL; DOUR; DREAR; DRAB; SAD; ■ DREARY

cheers TA; TATA

cheese BRIE; EDAM; FETA; ■ CHEVRE; TRUCKLE

cheese, different from CHALK

cheese, French BRIE

cheesecake PIN UP

chef COOK

Chelsea BUN

chemical CH; ESTER; OXIDE; TIN; *see* CHEMICAL ELEMENT

chemical element when a chemical element is specified to be used as a component it usually signifies that the technical symbol for the element is to be used, such as AS for arsenic, etc.

chemical firm ICI

chemical happening REACTION

chemise SHIFT

chemist CURIE; DAVY; HENRY

cherish HUG; LOVE

Cheshire CHEESE; [◊ CAT]

Cheshire town CREWE

chess, constricted position in PIN

chess opponents BW; WB

chess player BLACK; WHITE

chess player, very good MASTER

chessman B; K; KING; KNIGHT; KT; N; P; PAWN; PIECE; Q; QUEEN; R; ROOK

chest ARK; BOX; BUST; COFFER; ■ BREAST; BUREAU; THORAX

Chester DEVA

Chesterton GK

chestnut GAG; SAW

chesty noise RALE

chevron STRIPE

chew CHAMP; CHOMP; EAT; MUNCH; NIBBLE; [◊ CUD]

chew, something to GUM; QUID

chewed BIT; GROUND; anagram indicator

chic SMART

chicken BROILER; FOWL; HEN; SCARED; WINDY; YELLOW ■ COWARD

chicken cage COOP

Chicago, train in EL

chide SCOLD (qv)

chief AGA; ARCH; BOSS; C; CAPO; CH; CINC (i.e. C in C); FIRST; HEAD; KEY; KING; LEAD; MAIN; PRIME; TOP; ■ EMIR; LEADER; PRIMARY; RULER; STAPLE; THANE; initial letter indicator

Chief Education Officer CEO

chief executive CHAIR; DG; CE

child BABE; BAIRN; BOY; CH; ELF; IMP; INFANT; ISSUE; KID; LAD; MITE; SON; TOT; ■ CUB; NIPPER

child in street GAMIN

child minder NANNY

child, mischievous ELF; SCAMP

child, naughty/precocious BRAT; IMP; ■ BLIGHTER; PICKLE; TERROR; URCHIN

child of five QUIN

child, Scottish BAIRN; WEAN

child, small CH; *see* CHILD

child's fare HALF

child, troublesome *see* CHILD, NAUGHTY

child worker PAGE

childless D (for daughter) or SON to be omitted

children ISSUE; KIDS; SEED; *see* CHILD

children's writer MILNE

chill COLD; COOL; ICE; ICED

chilled COLD; ICY

chilling ICY; RAW

chilly COLD; ICY; PARKY

chime PEAL; RING; ■ AGREE; BELL; STRIKE

chimney CLEFT (in climbing); FLUE; FUNNEL; LUM; STACK

china CH; CHUM; COBBER; CUP; FRIEND; MATE; MING; PAL; POT; ■ AMIGO; CROCKERY; MINTON; SAUCER; *see* FRIEND

China CATHAY

China, right in, (proper in) TAO

chine JOINTS; RIDGE; SPINE

Chinese criminals, criminal society TONG

Chinese detective CHAN

Chinese dish RICE

Chinese dynasty HAN; MING; SUNG; TANG

Chinese gang TONG

Chinese leader C; MAO

Chinese life force CHI; QI

Chinese measure LI

Chinese port CANTON

Chinese vase MING

Chinese vessel JUNK

chink CRANNY; GAP; RIFT

chinwag CHAT

chip BIT; CUT; LOFT; SILICON; SLICE; SLIVER; in its meaning as a golf stroke can indicate something to do with the game

chips STAKE; can indicate something to do with sculpting, sculptor etc; [◊ FISH; SALT]

chiropodist [◊ FOOT]

chisel CARVE; CHEAT; CUT; FIDDLE; GOUGE; TOOL; TRICK

chit DOCKET; NOTE

Chlorine CL

choc a block FULL

chock WEDGE

chocolate, some BAR

choice CREAM; EITHER; ELITE; FINE; GOOD; OPTION; PICK; PLUM; RARE; TOP; ■ PICKED; SELECT; SELECTION; can indicate something to do with voting; can indicate that OR (i.e. signifying an alternative) is to be inserted between two components as "Girl has choice of dress arrangement initially" → DORA; [◊ MENU]

choice, make a *see* CHOOSE

choice product FLOWER

choir SINGERS

choir member SINGER

choirboy TREBLE

choke GLUT; ■ STRANGLE; THROTTLE

choking nesting indicator

choleric CROSS

choose DRAW; ELECT; LIST; OPT; PICK; SELECT

choosing OPTION

chop AXE; CRACK; CUT; DICE; HACK; HEW; LOP; MINCE; SACK

Chopin's friend SAND

chopped CLOVE; CUT; HEWN; last letter to be omitted; anagram indicator

chopped up CUT; HEWN; anagram indicator

chopper, US AX

choppers TEETH

choppy anagram indicator

chore FAG; JOB; TASK; WORK

chorus SING

chosen DRAWN; ELECT; GOOD; PICK; OPTION; RARE; TOP; ■ ELECTED; ELITE; NAPPED; PICKED; SELECTED

chosen people/person ELECT

christen DUB; NAME

Christian COPT; ■ COPTIC; can indicate something to do with Fletcher Christian, Bounty, mutiny, Hans Christian Andersen

Christian sayings LOGIA

Christine TINA
Christmas NOEL; YULE; [◊ CRACKER: HOLLY; PRESENT; SANTA; WISHBONE]
Christmas, around CED (i.e. rev. of December); DEC
Christmas decoration HOLLY
Christmas dinner TURKEY
Christmas offering CARD
Christmastime DEC
chromium CR
chromosome X; Y
chromosome, man's XY
chronicle ANNAL; RECORD
chuck CAST; FLING; THROW; anagram indicator
chuck out DUMP (qv)
chucked CAST; FLUNG
chucked in nesting indicator
chuffed GLAD
chum BUD; PAL; MATE
chump FOOL (qv)
chunk LUMP
chunter GRUMBLE
church ABBEY; CE; CH; CLOTH; MISSION; RC; ■ FOLD; KIRK; MINSTER; ORATORY; ROME; SION; [◊ ALTAR, APSE, CHANCEL; NAVE; ROOD]
church dignitary CANON; VEN
church feature ALTAR; APSE; CHANCEL; NAVE; ROOD; SPIRE; ■ AISLE; STEEPLE
church land GLEBE
church liturgy USE
church office NONES
church official ELDER; USHER; VERGER
church, part of *see* CHURCH FEATURE
church response GRADUAL
church roof LEAD
church, Scots KIRK
church season ADVENT
church service MASS; RITE
church service, part of PROPER
church, underground CRYPT
Churchill WINNIE
churchman CANNON; CLERIC; CURATE; ELDER; REV; VERGER; VICAR

churchwarden PIPE
churned up anagram indicator
chute SLIDE; TROUGH
cicatrice SCAR
CID man DI; *see* POLICEMAN
cigarette FAG; GASPER; REEFER
cinch CERT; ■ HOLD
circle BALL; BAND; BELT; HOOP; LOOP; O; RING; ROUND; ■ ORBIT; WHEEL; WHIRL; anagram indicator; can indicate something which is characteristically circular e.g. tonsure
circle line OL; ORY
circles OO; OS; nesting indicator
circling anagram indicator; nesting indicator
circuit LAP; RING; ROUND; WAY; can indicate something to do with motor racing
circuitous INDIRECT
circular O; ROUND; anagram indicator ■ ROUNDED
circular stone DISCUS
circulate FLOW; ISSUE; UTTER; ■ ORBIT; anagram indicator; *see* PUBLISH
circulated ROUND; anagram indicator
circulating anagram indicator; reversal indicator
circulation anagram indicator; can indicate a palindrome as "Old foreign coin retained in circulation" → ANNA (i.e. a foreign coin which reads the same both ways)
circulator FAN
circumnavigator FOGG
circumscribed nesting indicator
circumstance CASE; STATE
circumstances can act as a nesting indicator (as "in rare circumstances" could indicate a component is to be nested in RARE)
circumstances, existing ASIS (i.e. as is)
circumstances, in the a component to be nested within THE

circus RING; note, as well as the 'big top' this includes the Roman circus and its associations e.g. gladiators

cistern TANK

cite NAME; QUOTE

citizen BURGER

citrus LIME

city TOWN; URB; WEN; specific city names are often used as components to build up solutions and popular British ones include BATH, DERBY, DERRY, ELY, HULL, STOKE, TRURO, YORK; common foreign ones used in word construction include ADEN, BONN, EC (abbreviation for Empire City, one of New York's nicknames), LA (i.e. Los Angeles), NANCY, NY (New York), PARIS, RIO, ROME, SALEM, TURIN, UR (ancient city); *see* CAPITALS; [◊ URBAN]

City SMOKE; WEN

city, ancient (old) ROME; TROY; TYRE; UR; ■ ILIUM

City area/district usually indicates a London postcode, EC1, N1, SE, EC, etc

circle, biblical UR

city, going to UP

city in Kansas DODGE

city limits CY

city of the Angels LA

city outskirts CY

city reportedly SITY

City Road pub EAGLE

city, way to UP

civil LAY; ■ POLITE

civil disorder RIOT

civil engineer CE

civil, less RUDER

civil, not RUDE

civil servants IRS

Civil Service CS

civil wrong TORT

civilisation CULTURE

clad CLOTHE; ■ ENROBE

clad in nesting or run indicator

claim ACTION; ASSERT; AVER; AVOW; BAG; CALL; DEMAND; GET; HOLD; PLEAD; RIGHT; TITLE; ■ ALLEGE; CAUSE; DROIT; MAINTAIN; PROFESS; can indicate a word beginning with IM (i.e. I'm) as "Tense claim by paragon" → IMPERFECT (i.e. I'm perfect); similarly can indicate a phrase beginning with AM, as "Claim to be myself" → AMME (i.e. am me) to build up "rammed" for example

claim, justified RIGHT

clairvoyant FEY

clamber CLIMB

clamour BRUIT; CRY; DIN

clan SEPT (Irish); TRIBE

clanger BELL; ERROR; GAFFE

clap CRACK

claptrap CANT; ROT

claret RED

clarify REFINE; RENDER

clash FIGHT; JAR; SCRAP; WAR

clasp CATCH; GRIP; HOLD; LOCK; ■ TACHE (from Bible)

class BRAND; CL; CASTE; FORM; KIND; LINE; ORDER; RANK; RATE; RATING; SECT; SET; SORT; TABLE; TERM; TYPE; ■ GENRE; GENUS; GRADE; GROUP; LEAGUE; LESSON; POLISH; REMOVE; STREAM; TEACHING

Class A UPPER

class, one of MEMBER

class system CASTE

classic DERBY; OAKS; can indicate word or phrase taken directly from Latin and usually unaltered in its modern use; *see* CLASSICAL

classical TRAD; ■ GREEK; LATIN; OLD; ROMAN; can indicate that a common Latin term is required as "this classical" calls for HIC

classical art ARS

classical character *see* GREEK LETTER

classical style ATTIC; DORIC; IONIC

classical theatre ODEON

classification RANK; RANKING;
STATUS

classification, requiring anagram
indicator

classify GRADE; RATE; SORT; ■
CODE

classmates FORM; STREAM

classy U

clatter RATTLE

claw NAIL; TALON

clay LUTE; TILL; not that if beginning with a capital letter this can
denote ALI

clean BATHE; BRUSH; CHAR;
DUST; FAIR; GROOM; LAVE;
MOP; PURE; SCRUB; SWEEP;
WASH; ■ LAUNDER; PREEN;
WIPE

clean cut NEAT; TRIM

clean, thoroughly PURGE;
SCRUB; ■ SCOUR

clean out an anagram of CLEAN

clean up HOOVER; MOP;
SWEEP; WIN

cleaned SWEPT

cleaner BRUSH; CHAR; DAILY;
MOP; SWEEP; ■ MOPPER;
SCRUBBER

cleanse WASH; ■ SOAP

clear ALLOW; FAIR; FREE; NET;
NETT; OPEN; OVERT;
PATENT; PLAIN; PURE;
PURGE; RID; SHEER; STARK;
WIPE; ■ ABSOLVE; ACQUIT;
DISTINCT; JUMP; LIMPID;
LUCID; SURE; VAULT; ana-
gram indicator

clear-headed C

clear, make RID

cleared out DECLARE (i.e. an
anagram)

cleared up anagram indicator

clearing GLADE; omission indicator

clearly PLAIN; WELL

cleave PIERCE; SPLIT; STICK;
SUNDER; ■ ADHERE

clef KEY

cleft GAP; SPLIT; ■ CHIMNEY
i.e. in climbing

clement MILD

clergy CLOTH

clergyman ABBE; CANON;
CURE; DEAN; PARSON;
PASTOR; RECTOR; REV;
REVD; ■ CURATE; DEACON;
MINISTER; PRIEST; VICAR;
see CLERIC

clergymen CLOTH

cleric CANON; DD; DEAN;
MINISTER; PARSON; REV;
VEN; ■ RECTOR; *see*
CLERGYMAN

clerical garment ALB

clerical worker TEMP

clerics CLOTH; CHAPTER

clever ABLE; BRAINY; BRIGHT;
CUTE; FLY; HANDY; SHARP;
SMART; ■ CANNY; DEFT;
NIFTY; WITTY; anagram indica-
tor

clever chap MA

cleverly anagram indicator

cleverness GUILE

clich CORN

cliff BLUFF; CRAG; SCAR;
SCREE

climax HEAD; TOP

climb MOUNT; RISE; SCALE;
SHIN; ■ ASCEND; ASCENT;
CLAMBER; reversal indicator;
can indicate a verb followed by
UP

climbed ROSE

climber IVY; PEA; VINE; ■
LIANA

climbing reversal indicator

cling CLEAVE; HOLD; STICK

clinic SAN; ■ HOSPITAL

Clio MUSE

clip BLOW; CHEAT; CLOUT;
CUT; HIT; PACE; PEG; PIN;
SHEAR ■ PRUNE; STAPLE;
STRIKE; anagram indicator;

clipped CUT; SHORN; indicator
for first and last letters of associated word to be omitted

clippers SHEARS

clique RING; SECT

Clive can indicate something to do
with India, Empire etc

Cliveden, former occupant of
ASTOR

cloak CAPE; COPE; HIDE;
TOGA; ■ DOMINO; MANTLE

clobber BASH; CLUB; DRESS;
GEAR; ■ CLOTHES

cloche HAT

clock DIAL; FACE; HIT; MUG;
SEE; TIME; TIMER; ■ STRIKE;
WINDER

clod FOOL (qv); LUMP

clone COPY

close BAR; BLOCK; BOLT;
DEAR; END; ENDING; FOLD;
HANDY; LOCK; MEAN;
NEAR; NIGH; ON; STOP;
SEAL; SHUT; STICKY; TIGHT;
WARM; ■ CORK; HUMID;
LOOMING; NARROW;
STUFFY; can indicate the last
letter of an adjacent word; [◊
LAST]

close, come LOOM; NEAR

close fitting TIGHT

close to BY; NEAR; last letter indicator

close up PURSE

closed can indicate a word beginning with NO as "Negative con-
sequences of gym being closed"
(4) → NOPE (i.e. no PE)

closely follow DOG

closer CATCH

closet PRESS

closing END; LAST; NET

closing date E; END

clot ASS; DOPE; SET

cloth FELT; LAWN; PLAID; RAG;
REP; RIG; SATIN; SERGE;
TOWEL; TWEED; ■ LINEN;
LUNGI; REPP; TERRY;
WORSTED

cloth, man of the DRAPER

cloth sample SWATCH

clothe CLAD; ■ DRESS;
ENROBE

clothes DUDS; GARB; GEAR;
KIT; SLOPS; SUIT; WEAR; ■
CLADS; CLOBBER; [◊ HORSE]

clothing ATTIRE; BELT; COAT;
DRESS; GARB; GEAR; HABIT;
KIT; POLO; SHIFT; SUIT; TIE;
VEST; ■ CLOBBER; JACKET;
RAIMENT; REEFER;
SPENCER; TOGS; *see*
GARMENT; nesting indicator

clothing, item/piece of SCARF;
see CLOTHING

cloud RACK; ■ CUMULUS (useful to get TUMULUS); NIMBUS

cloudiness GLOOM

cloudy DIM; DULL

clout CLIP; HIT; MIGHT;
POWER; PULL; ■ CUFF; NAIL;
STRIKE

clove CUT (qv); ■ SPICE

clown ANTIC; COCO; FOOL;
TWIT; ■ AUGUSTE; COMIC;
FESTE (Shak.); IDIOT; JESTER;
PIERROT; *see* FOOL

club BAT; BASH; C; CARD;
DISCO; DRIVER; HIT; MACE;
PASTE; SIDE; TEAM; ■ COSH;
GROUP; IRON; MALLET;
PRIEST; PUTTER; RAC;
SOCIETY; STAFF; STRIKE; [◊
GLEE; GROUP; ROTARY]; can
refer to pregnancy; or a specific
football club e.g. SPURS; *see*
GOLF CLUB

club, someone in the MEMBER

clubman MEMBER

clubs* SUIT

clue HINT; KEY; LIGHT (i.e. the
technical term for a crossword
clue); POINTER SIGN; TIP

clue for... (sometimes followed by
?) reverses the role of solver and
setter, requiring the solver to produce an appropriate clue for the
word or phrase given. Examples:
'...clue for pore...' (8-4) gives
SKIPPING-ROPE, '...clue for Fi-
del...' (7-5) gives
PLAYING-FIELD

clue, this ACROSS; DOWN (i.e.
the direction of the clue itself in
the grid}

clumsy, clumsily anagram indicator

clumsy person APE; OAF

cluster BUNCH; CLUMP;
SWARM; anagram indicator

clutch BROOD; GRAB; GRASP;
HOLD; SITTING; ■ PEDAL;
SEIZE; STICK [◊ EGG]

clutch, part of EGG
clutching nesting indicator
coach BUS; FLY; SCHOOL; STAGE; TEACH; TRAIN; ■ CARRIAGE; TRAINER; TUTOR
coaches TRAIN; TRAINS
coagulate CLOT
coal EMBER; SLACK; [◊ PIT; MINE; SEAM]
coal-scuttle HOD
coal supplier MINE; PIT
coalesce FUSE; MERGE
coarse CRUDE; EARTHY; ROUGH; RUDE; THICK; ■ RABELAISIAN
coarse person LOUT; OAF; SLOB
Coast, East/West note, the term can refer to countries other than UK, usually US
coast, part of BEACH; CAPE; SHORE
coast, not near INLAND
coastal area, region BAY; COVE
coat COVER; FILM; FUR; HIDE; LAYER; MAC; MAXI; PLATE; SPRAY; TAILS; ■ BATTER; FLEECE; JACKET; MIDI; PLASTER; REEFER; VARNISH
coat, expensive FUR
coat, kind of ARMS
coat of arms *see* HERALDRY
coat, part of TAIL; ■ LAPEL; SLEEVE
coated inside LINED
coating COVER; FILM; LAYER; ■ FLAMBE; LINING
cobbled anagram indicator
cobbler can indicate something to with 'last' i.e. cobbler's tool
cobblers NUTS; ROT
cocaine C
cocaine abuse OCEANIC
cocaine, dose of LINE
cocked READY; SET; anagram indicator; reversal indicator
cockfight MAIN
cockney usually the cue to drop initial H from a word, as "tough Cockney" clues ARD; can indicate the use of cockney rhyming

slang (example: "Cockney charlady" → ROSIE LEE)
cockney chief EAD (i.e. 'ead)
cockney lady ER (i.e. 'er)
cockney man IM (i.e. 'im)
cockney pal CHINA
cocktail anagram indicator; ■ GIMLET
coconut PATE; *see* HEAD
cod FOOL
coda ENDING
code LAW; MORSE; [◊ BAR (i.e. as in barcode)]
coded anagram indicator
coerce FORCE; ■ COMPEL; DRAGOON; IMPEL
coercive measures, use FORCE; *see* COERCE
coffee MOCHA
coffee* BLACK; FILTER
coffee, style of French NOIR
coffer ARK; BOX; CHEST
coffin KIST (Scot.)
coffin nails usually indicates something to do with cigarettes, smoking etc
cogitate MUSE; ■ DEBATE; PONDER; THINK
cohere GEL
coil BIND; HANK; RING; SPRING; TWINE; WIND
coin BIT; CASH; CENT; CROWN; CHANGE; DIME; ECU; MARK; ORE; P; PENNY; STAMP; ■ ANGEL; DINAR; NICKEL; RIAL; TENDER
coin in America BIT; *see* COIN
coin, old AS; BIT; CROWN; D; GROAT; S; SOU; TANNER; ■ DUCAT; FLORIN; JOEY; SHILLING
coinage CASH; *see* CURRENCY; [NEW WORD]
★ **coinage** a word which is invented. Compilers have a penchant for inventing their own words that make sense but are not in normal usage. An old warhorse that appears in the grids is "de-tail" in the sense of cutting off the tail. For example "Removes the E from 'minutiae'?" has the answer

DETAILS, a word that you are unlikely to find in a dictionary. Similarly, "The tight-lipped ship's officer?" is solved by PURSER, another word which, in the sense of a person who is tight-lipped, exists only in cross-words

coined word *see* COINAGE

coins CHANGE; PENCE; SPECIE

coins, make MINT

cold C; CHILL; CHILLY; DANK; DEAD; ICY; NIPPY; OUT; SNIFF; ZERO; ■ ALOOF; DISTANT; FRIGID; can indicate something to do with charity

cold cabinet FRIDGE; ■ ICE-BOX; FREEZER

cold shoulder SHUN; ■ REBUFF

cold spell SNAP

cold stuff FROST; ICE; SNOW

colic PAIN; WIND

collaborator ALLY

collaborationist LAVAL

collapse BANG; BUMP; DROP; END; FAIL; FALL; FOLD; GO; RUIN; SAG; SLUMP; ■ BUCKLE; anagram indicator

collapsed FELL; FLAT; anagram indicator

collapses, collapsing anagram indicator

collar BAND; CATCH; COP; NAB; PINCH; RING; RUFF; ■ ARREST; NICK

collar-fixer STUD

collared by nesting indicator

colleague ALLY; MATE; OPPO; PARTNER; ■ ASSOCIATE

collect AMASS; GATHER; GLEAN; HOARD; MASS; REAP; ■ HARVEST; PRAYER; nesting indicator

collected anagram indicator; nesting indicator

collection BUNCH; FILE; LIST; LOT; PACK; SET; ■ BUNDLE; RANGE; anagram indicator; can signify amalgamation of elements to achieve solution

collection, large RAFT

collection of books NT; OT

collection of papers FILE; REAM; SHEAF

collection of stories ANA

collection of suits DECK; PACK

collective wisdom LORE

collector's item CURIO

college C; ETON; HALL; KINGS; LSE; MIT; POLY; TECH; ■ DOWNING; INSTITUTE; ORIEL

college, at UP

college celebration RAG

college once POLY

college servant SCOUT (Oxford)

college term SESSION

college, time at CLASS; COURSE; TERM; SESSION

collide CLASH; CRASH

colliery PIT

collision BUMP; CRASH; HIT

★ **colloquialisms** are expressions used in speech rather than in print and are very common in cross-words e.g. IM for "I am", S for "is" as in "he's", etc; then there is HI (signalled by "greeting") and EH which is the sound we might make to emphasise a question and is signalled by words such as "questionable", and so on

colonel CO; COL

colonialist RHODES

colonise SETTLE

colonist ANT; PENN; SETTLER

colonists, new SWARM

colonnade STOA

colony GIB; HIVE

colony, former/old ADEN

colony, found SETTLE

colophony RESIN

Colorado CO

colour AMBER; AQUA; BLUE; DYE; FLAG; FLAME; GREEN; HUE; ORANGE; PAINT; RED; SHADE; STAIN; TAN; TEAM; TINGE; TINT; TONE; ■ CYAN; IRIS; LAKE; LAVENDER; OCHRE; PASTEL; PIGMENT; PINK; PUCE; SILVER; TAINT; YELLOW

colour, add DYE; PAINT; SHADE TINGE; TINT

colour, light ECRU
colour, lose FADE; PALE
colour, with less ASHIER; PALER
colourful can indicate any colour (*see* COLOUR) usually to be used as an adjective, as "colourful digits" → GREEN FINGERS
colourless ASHEN; GREY; PALE; WAN; WHITE; can indicate that a colour is to be omitted, usually RED
colours FLAG (qv); ■ STANDARD; *see* COLOUR
column FILE; LINE; LIST; POST; SPINE; SPIRE; ■ ARTICLE; PILLAR; [◊ CAPITAL]
comb CARD; CREST; CURRY; SEARCH
combat FIGHT
combat/fight, scene of ARENA; LIST; LISTS
combination FUSION; UNION; anagram indicator
combination, in anagram indicator
combine MERGE; POOL; SPLICE
come ENSUE
come after TRAIL; ■ ENSUE; FOLLOW
come ashore LAND
come down DIP; DROP; LAND; LIGHT; RAIN; SNOW; *see* FALL
come-down *see* COME DOWN
come down on WHAM
come first LEAD; WIN
come from anagram indicator
come in ENTER; LAND
come out FLOWER
come round AWAKE; ROUSE; TURN; WAKE; WAKEN; nesting indicator; a component to be nested within COME; reversal indicator
come through WEATHER
come to AWAKE; ROUSE; TOTAL; WAKE
come to rest HALT; STOP
come up ARISE; RISE
come upon FIND

comeback RETURN; reversal indicator
comedian CARD; DODD; JOKER; SCAMP; TATI; WAG; WIT; ■ GAGSTER; SCREAM; *see* COMIC
comedian Will HAY
comes back reversal indicator
comes round nesting indicator; reversal indicator
comes from anagram indicator
comes to grief anagram indicator
comes up reversal indicator
comeuppance reversal indicator
comfort CHEER; EASE; RELIEF; ■ SOLACE; SOOTHE
comfortable COSY; EASY; NICE; SNUG; WELL
comfortable, get NESTLE
comfortable, more COSIER
comfortable place/position BED; NICHE
comforter DUMMY; SCARF
comfortless BLEAK
comic DANDY; DROLL; FOOL; SCAMP; WAG; ■ CHAPLIN; CLOWN; GAGSTER; TICKLER; anagram indicator; *see* COMEDIAN
comical DROLL; FUNNY; RICH
coming ADVENT
coming back reversal indicator
coming from EX; OF; what follows to be used as the basis for an anagram
coming in nesting indicator
coming out anagram indicator
coming round nesting indicator; reversal indicator
coming up RISING; reversal indicator
comma STOP; can indicate something to do with insect, butterfly
command BID; CHARGE; DIRECT; EDICT; FIAT; MUSH; ORDER; ■ BIDDING; DECREE; ENJOIN; GOVERN; RULE; [◊ TOP]
command to accelerate GEE
command to dog SIT
commanded BADE; BID

commander AGA; CINC (i.e. C in C); CO; COM; HEAD; OC; ■ CBE; CHIEF; EMIR; HEAD; SHOGUN; SUPREMO

commendation PRAISE; TRIBUTE

commandment RULE; *see* COMMAND

commandments, all the/ number of TEN

commence START

commences first letter indicator

commend LAUD; PRAISE

commendation PRAISE

comment NOTE; OPINE; REMARK; RIDER; SAY; ■ MAXIM; SHOT; can indicate the noise of some animal as "setter's comment" → BARK

comment, witty SALLY

commented SAID

commerce TRADE

commercial AD; ADVERT

commercial venture SPEC

commission CHARGE; CHARTER; CUT; ORDER; TASK; ■ APPOINT; ERRAND; RETAIN

commitment DEVOTION

committed LIABLE

committee BOARD; COM

committee boss CHAIR

common BANAL; C; GREEN (as in 'village green'); RIFE; STOCK; TRITE; ■ GENERAL; NORMAL; can indicate a colloquialism or slang (so-called 'common' speech) such as the dropping of aitches from the beginning of a word (thus "common border" leads to EM i.e. 'em); *see* WIDESPREAD

Common Market EC

common name SMITH

common sense NOUS

commonly colloquialism indicator, e.g. "friend commonly" → MATE, "isn't commonly" → AINT; indicator for dropping initial 'h'

commonplace BANAL; LOW; TRITE; TRUISM; ■ PLATITUDE

Commons CHAMBER

commonsense NOUS

commotion ROW; STIR; STORM; ■ NOISE; anagram indicator

commotion, cause a STIR

communicate PHONE; REPORT; STATE (qv); TALK; WIRE; ■ CONVERSE; EXPRESS; IMPART; RESPOND; SIGNAL

communicate non-verbally SIGN

communication FAX; LETTER; LINK; MAIL; MEMO; NOTE; POST; SIGNAL; ■ CONTACT; MESSAGE

communication, intuitive ESP

communication, means of BLOWER; MORSE; PHONE; *see* COMMUNICATION

communist COM; COMM; MAO; RED; TROT

communist leader C; MAO

community CITY; GROUP; NATION; PUBLIC; STATE; TOWN; VILLAGE; ■ ABBEY; can indicate the name of a specific town or city;

Community EC

community, business CITY

commute CUT; anagram indicator; omission indicator

compact BRIEF; CASE; DENSE; SNUG; TIGHT; TRIM; [◊ POWDER]

compact disc CD

companies, amalgamation of MERGER

companion CH; DATE; MATE; PAL

companion, honoured CH

company ACTORS; BAND; CAST; CO; COY; CREW; FIRM; GUEST; GROUP; HOST; ICI; MEN; PLC; REP (i.e. stage company); THREE; TROOP; TWO (i.e. as in "two's company"); ■ CONCERN; HOUSE; ENTOURAGE; [◊ ALONG; AMONG]; *see* BUSINESS

company, large ICI
company, theatre REP
comparatively can indicate a comparative adjective (i.e. ending in ER)
comparatively little LESS
compare LIKEN; MATCH
compartment BAY; CAR; HOLE; PLACE; SPACE
compass RANGE; ROOM
compassion PITY; RUTH
compel DRIVE; FORCE; MAKE
compensate ATONE; EXPIATE
compere FRONT; HOST; ■ PRESENT; PRESENTER
compere, act as see COMPERE
compete BID; RACE; VIE
compete for possession TACKLE
competent ABLE; FIT; PRO; ■ CAPABLE
competent person PRO
competent way, in a ABLY
competition COMP; CUP; EVENT; HEAT; OPEN; RACE; RALLY; TIE; ■ CONTEST; STRIFE; TRIAL
competition, be in RUN; VIE
competition, early stages of HEAT
competition, was in RAN; VIED
competitive activity SPORT
competitor PLAYER; ■ ENTRANT; ENTRY; RIVAL
competitors ENTRY; FIELD
compile LIST
compiled anagram indicator
compiler I; ME; SETTER
compiler, this ME
compiling anagram indicator
complacent SMUG
complain BEEF; BIND; BITCH; BLEAT; CARP; GRIPE; MOAN; NAG; OBJECT; RAIL; WHINE; WHINGE; ■ GROUSE; GRUMBLE; LAMENT
complainant CARPER; GRIPER
complaint BEEF; BENDS; BLEAT; COLD; FLU; GOUT; GRIPE; GROUSE; MOAN; NAG; RASH; STRESS; STYE;

TB; WHINE; ■ AGUE; MALADY; WHINGE; YAMMER
complaint, French MAL
complaints ILLS
complement CREW
complete ALL; CLEAN; DEAD; ENTIRE; END; FILL; FULL; OVER; RANK; READY; ROUND; SHEER; TOP; UP; UTTER; WHOLE; ■ ARRANT; GENERAL; INTACT; THOROUGH
completed ENDED; OVER; DONE; OUT; THRO; UP; WHOLE; ■ THROUGH
completely ALL; CLEAN; FULLY; QUITE; SHEER; UP
complex PHOBIA; ■ INTRICATE; anagram indicator
complex, not EASY; SIMPLE
complexion HUE
compliant EASY; YIELDING
complicate MUDDLE; RAVEL; TANGLE
complicated MUDDLED; TANGLED; can signify a word beginning with OVER (e.g. over-elaborate); anagram indicator
complicated system MAZE
complication HITCH; SNAG; TANGLE; anagram indicator
complimentary FREE
comply ACCORD; OBEY
comply with OBSERVE
component BIT; PART; UNIT
components anagram indicator
compose PEN; SCORE; SETTLE; WRITE; anagram indicator
composed CALM; COOL; SERENE; STILL; STILLED; anagram indicator
composer ARNE; BACH; BERG; BLISS; BRIDGE; CAGE; FIELD; GLUCK; HOLST; PARRY; RAVEL; ■ BYRD; CHOPIN; DELIUS; DOWLAND; FALLA; FRANCK; HANDEL; LEHAR; IVES; LISZT; LULLY; ORFF; SATIE; STAINER; SUPPE;

TIPPETT; VERDI; WAGNER; WALTON; WEILL

composite, not SIMPLE

composition DUET; ESSAY; NUMBER; PIECE; TRIO; TUNE; ■ NONET; SONNET; anagram indicator

composure anagram indicator

compound ALUM; AMINE; PEN; can indicate some chemical e.g. chrome, ester, oxide; anagram indicator; nesting indicator; can indicate the compound type of clue

comprehends nesting indicator

comprehensible CLEAR; PLAIN

comprehensive FULL; GENERAL

comprehensive coverage BLANKET

comprehensively ALL

compromised anagram indicator

compromises HAS

compunction REGRET

computer APPLE; ERNIE; MAC; SUMMER; [◊ DOS; GOPHER; ICON; MOUSE; SCROLL; SCREEN]

computer accessory, equipment MOUSE

computer class IT

computer facility SERVER

computer group BYTE

computer industry IT

computer key ESC

computer memory units RAM

computer part BUS; DRIVER

computer program DOS; LOADER

computer program text CODE

computer science IT

computer store ROM

computer studies IT

computer system DOS

computer system, access HACK

computer tool MOUSE

computerised tool ROBOT

computers IT

computers installed, having no ITLESS (i.e. IT-less); can indicate IT to be omitted

comrade ALLY; *see* FRIEND

con AGAINST (qv); CAN; CHEAT; DO; FOOL; HAVE; KEN; KNOW; LAG; LIFER; NAY; ROOK; SCAM; STEER; ■ FIDDLE; STING; SWINDLE

con man CHEAT; *see* CHEATER

conceal BURY; HIDE; PALM; SCREEN; VEIL; ■ ECLIPSE

concealed BLIND; HID; HIDDEN; LATENT; run indicator

concealed by nesting indicator; run indicator

concealed at first initial letter to be omitted

concealing HIDING; nesting indicator; omission indicator e.g. "boat concealing bottom" clues PUN where 'bottom' refers to the last letter of 'punt'; run indicator

concealment COVER

conceals, it COVER; SCREEN

concede ADMIT; ALLOW; CEDE; GRANT; OWN; YIELD

conceited VAIN

conceited fellow TOAD

conceited young man PUP

conceivably can indicate the compiler is stretching a point, so expect something especially tricky

concentrate MASS

concentrated INTENT; STRONG; THICK

concept IDEA; NOTION; THOUGHT; ■ THEORY

conception *see* CONCEPT

concern CARE; FIRM; MATTER; WORRY; ■ AFFAIR; BOTHER; BUSINESS; COMPANY; INTEREST; PIGEON

concern, excessive FUSS

concern, show CARE; RECK

concerned CARING

concerned, be CARE

concerned with ABOUT; IN; ON; RE

concerning ABOUT; ASTO (i.e. as to); OVER; RE; ON

concert GIG; PROM; UNITY; UNISON

concession SOP

concise BRIEF; TERSE
condiments, add SEASON
condition, make LIMIT
conscious SENTIENT
conclude END; CLOSE; INFER; ■ DEDUCE; REASON
conclusion END; TAIL; Z; ■ CODA; ENDING; FINDING; OMEGA; POINT; can indicate that the last letter(s) of a word should be used
conclusion of game E; MATE
concoct HATCH
concocted, concoction anagram indicator
concupiscent RANDY
condemn DOOM
condemnation, condemned anagram indicator
condescend DEIGN; STOOP
condescension, show DEIGN
condition COMA; IF; NICK; STATE; TEACH; TRAIN; ■ FETTLE; RIDER; TONE
condition, hopeless DESPAIR
conditioned anagram indicator
conditions STATES etc; anagram indicator
conduct LEAD; RUN; TAKE; USHER
conductor COPPER; EARTH; WOOD (i.e. Sir Henry); ■ BEECHAM; [◊ BATON; TIME]; can indicate any kind of leader, for example "Neat conductor" → DROVER or HERDSMAN
conduit GUTTER
confab CHAT; TALK; WORDS
confection anagram indicator; *see* CONFECTIONERY
confectionery CAKE; SWEET; TRUFFLE
Confederacy SOUTH
confederate ALLY; with a capital letter can indicate something to do with that aspect of American history e.g. LEE
confer AWARD; GRANT; ■ BESTOW; DISCUSS
conference SESSION; with a capital latter can indicate PEAR; ■ MEETING

confess ALLOW; OWN; SING; ■ ADMIT
confession IAM (i.e. I am)
confidence BOTTLE; SECRET; TRUST
confidence, lack DOUBT
confidence trick SCAM
confident SURE
confident expectation TRUST
confidential CLOSED; SECRET
confidential, not OPEN
confine GATE; HOLD; PEN; GATE; INTERN; ■ CHAIN
confined IN; PENT; anagram indicator; nesting indicator
confined space COOP
confined to quarters can indicate that a component is to be nested within two points of the compass as where "always confined to quarters" → SEVERE (i.e. EVER within SE)
confirm OK; PROVE; RATIFY; ■ ATTEST
conflab *see* CONFAB
conflict ACTION; CLASH; FRAY; JAR; STRIFE; WAR; ■ ENCOUNTER
conflict, in anagram indicator
conflict, prepare for ARM
conform FIT; SUIT
confound it anagram indicator
confounded BEAT; anagram indicator
confront BEARD; FACE; MEET; TACKLE
confronted MET
Confucian way TAO
confuse ADDLE; DAZE; FOX; ■ BAFFLE; BEWILDER; RAVEL; SCRAMBLE
confused ADDLED; anagram indicator
confused, get *see* CONFUSE
confused matter/state *see* CONFUSION
confused with anagram indicator
confusing anagram indicator
confusion BABEL; BOTHER; DAZE; DUST; FOG; MESS; ■ CLUTTER; MUDDLE; SNAFU; TANGLE

confusion, in anagram indicator

congealed SET

congregate GATHER; MASS; MEET; RALLY; SWARM anagram indicator

congregation FOLD

conifer FIR; PINE; YEW

conjecture GUESS

conjunction AND; BUT; NOR; UNION

conjured up anagram indicator

conk BEAK; HEAD (qv); HOOTER; NOSE

connect BRIDGE; LINK; MEET; TIE

connected TIED

connected to RE

Connecticut CT

connection BOND; BRIDGE: EARTH; LINE; LINK; TIE; ■ JOINT; RELATION

connection, make BOND; JOIN; RELATE

conned DID; HAD; READ

conniving anagram indicator

connoisseur EXPERT; PRO; ■ FANCIER

conquer BEAT; ROUT; TOP

conqueror NORMAN

conscious AWAKE; AWARE; ■ SENTIENT

consciousness EGO; HEAD

consecrate BLESS

consecrated BLEST

consecutive letters can refer to the use of consecutive letters in the alphabet, e.g. FGH; run indicator

consent OK

consequence EFFECT; END

consequently ERGO; SO

conservation body, conservationists NT

conservative C; CON; RIGHT; SAFE; SQUARE; TORY; ■ HIDE-BOUND

conservative, moderate WET

conserve SAVE

conserve energy E to be nested

consider CASE; COUNT; DEEM; FEEL; JUDGE; MULL; PONDER; RATE; SCAN; SEE; THINK; WEIGH; ■ DEBATE; FIND; REGARD; VIEW

consider carefully NB; WEIGH

considerable BIG; HUGE; TIDY

consideration CARE

considered FOUND; RATED; SAW; THOUGHT; anagram indicator

consign SHIP

consigning nesting indicator

consistent EVEN; ■ REGULAR; UNIFORM

consolidate PUN

conspicuous, be SHINE

conspiracy CABAL; PLOT; ■ INTRIGUE

conspirator BRUTUS; ■ CASCA; CINNA; FAWKES; [◊ PLOT]

conspirators CELL

conspire PLOT

constable COP; PC; SPECIAL; *see* POLICEMAN; [◊ BEAT]

constant C; K; PI; STILL; ■ STATIC

Constantine's mother HELEN

constantly EVER

constellation LEO

constituency SEAT

constituent FRACTION; PART

constituents (in) anagram indicator; run indicator

constitution CHARTER; ■ NATURE; anagram indicator

constrain URGE

constraint LET

constricted NARROW

construct BUILD; MAKE; WEAVE; ■ ASSEMBLE

constructed, constructing anagram indicator

construction ART; MAKE; READING; anagram indicator

construction worker RIGGER

construed anagram indicator

consume DRINK; EAT; SCOFF; SWALLOW; TAKE; USE

consumed ATE; DRUNK; EATEN; anagram indicator; nesting indicator

consumer DINER; EATER; SCOFFER

consumerism, end of FAST

consumption, not ready for GREEN; RATHE; RAW; ■ UNCOOKED

contact MEET; RING; TOUCH; ■ TACTION

container BAG; BASKET; BIN; BOWL; BOX; CAGE; CAN; CASE; CASK; CHEST; COFFER; CRATE; CUP; DISH; DRAM; DRUM; EWER; HOD; JAR; PAIL; PAN; PEN; POD; POT; PURSE; SACK; SKIP; TIN; TRAY; TUB; TUN; URN; VASE; VAT; ■ BOTTLE; CANISTER; DRAWER; HOPPER; OLLA; PACKET; SKEP (straw basket); STEIN; TANK; *see* VESSEL; note: can indicate a body part that *contains* e.g. ribcage

★ **container** refers to the device whereby a component is embedded in another, elsewhere called nesting. Example: "Principal university lecturer keeping ring for evidence" (5) Answer: PROOF (i.e. O for ring is nested within PROF for professor)

container, water BATH; TANK; WELL; *see* CONTAINER

containing nesting indicator; run indicator

contaminant TAINT

contaminated anagram indicator

contemplate MUSE; PONDER; THINK

contemporary IN; MOD; NEW

contempt SCORN

contempt, show HISS

contempt, shout of BOO

contemptible BASE; LOW; SHABBY; ■ PISH; SCURVY

contemptible person CAD; CUR; HEEL; LOUSE; RAT; TOAD; ■ INSECT

contemptuous expression ROT

contend HOLD; VIE; ■ CHALLENGE; COMPETE

contending VYING

content HAPPY; PLEASE; PLEASED; ■ MATERIAL; run indicator; can indicate something that fills (in this way "less content" → EMPTIER)

contented noise PURR

contention WAR

contention, in VYING

contents INDEX; nesting or run indicator

contents must be nesting indicator, as "contents must be fair" can require JUST to be nested (to get ADJUSTS, for example)

contents of use middle letters of the word that follows; with longer words this can indicate that all but the first and last letters of following words to be used; can indicate a synonym for the word that follows is trimmed of first and last letter (as "contents of epistle" → ETTE)

contest BATTLE; BOUT; CUP; DUEL; EVENT; FIGHT; GAME; HEAT; MATCH; PLAY; RACE; ROUND; SCRAP; TRIAL; WAR; ■ LISTS; STRIFE; TENSON; VIE

contest between troubadours TENSON

contest, part of BOUT; ROUND; *see* CONTEST

continent ASIA; CHASTE; NA

Continental FRENCH

continental, a EIN; EINE; UN; UNE

Continental, that QUE

Continental, the DER; EL; IL; LE; LA; LES

continue KEEP; LAST; RESUME; STAY; can indicate that a verb is required which is followed by ON to make another word or component e.g. ACT/ON, BAT/ON, GO/ON, FLAG/ON. (Example: "Continue to desire a hussy" → WANTON}

continue to restrict KEEP

continued CONT

contract CATCH; CRAMP; DEAL; DEED; GET; KNIT;

LEASE; MAKE; NARROW; PACT; PURSE; TREATY; TUCK; ■ CHARTER; DECLINE; DRAWIN (i.e. draw in); ENGAGE; GATHER; LESSON; SHRINK; can indicate something to do with bridge, e.g. trick, north, south etc

contracted TAUT; TENSE; nesting indicator

contradictory PERVERSE

contradictory response NO

contrary ADVERSE; anagram indicator; can indicate a meaning opposite to the immediately preceding idea. Example: "Series with city setting? On the contrary" uses RUN (series) and NY (city) to provide the answer RUNNY i.e. the opposite of setting

contrary, on the NO; reverse indicator

contrary gardener MARY

contribute ADD; GIVE; OFFER

contributing to component to be included; run indicator

contribution FACTOR; INPUT; SUB; WHACK; ■ POINT

contrive FRAME; PLAN; anagram indicator

contrived, contriving anagram indicator

control DAM; HAND (i.e. as "in hand"); HEAD; HELM, HOLD; LEAD; LEASH; LEVER; MASTER; POWER; REIN; RIDE; RULE; RUN; STEER; ■ BUTTON; CLUTCH; DIAL; DOMINION; POLICE; REIGN; anagram indicator

control horse REIN

control intake DIET

control, lose SKID

controlled RAN; anagram indicator

controller of players BATON; ■ CONDUCTOR

controller, traffic LIGHT

controlling anagram indicator

controls, man/person/woman at the DRIVER; PILOT

controversial/ly anagram indicator

convalesce HEAL; REST

convenience FAST (i.e. food); LAV; LOO; WC; *see* TOILET

convenient APT; HANDY; LUCKY; ■ OPPORTUNE

convention RULE; ■ HABIT; MEETING

conventional SQUARE; STAID

conversation CHAT; TALK; ■ CHATTER; PATTER; TALKING; homophone indicator

conversation, superficial PATTER

conversion anagram indicator

convert ALTER; TURN; ■ CHANGE (qv); PAUL; anagram indicator

converted anagram indicator

converted at last last letter to be changed

convertible anagram indicator

converts anagram indicator

convey BEAR; CARRY; FERRY; LEAD; PASS; PUT; TOTE; TRUCK; ■ TRANSPORT

conveyance BUS; CAB; TAXI; TRAIN; ■ CARRIAGE; *see* VEHICLE

conveyed LED; when in the context of something like 'what is conveyed by' can indicate the answer consists of consecutive letters in the rest of the clue i.e. working as a run indicator

conveyed by IN; run indicator

convict CON; LAG; LIFER; ■ CONDEMN; FELON; INMATE; [◊ INSIDE]

convict, dangerous LIFER

conviction BELIEF

convinced SURE

convincing CREDIBLE

convoluted anagram indicator

convulsion TIC

cook ALTER (as in cook the books); BAKE; BOIL; BRAISE; BROIL; CHEF; DEVIL; DO; FRY; GRILL; POACH; RIG; ROAST; SIMMER; STEAM; STEW; ■ SAUTE; SILVER (i.e. Long John); anagram indicator

cook, place to HUB; *see* COOKER

cooked DONE; FRIED; ROASTED; STEWED; anagram indicator (so beware that "cooked meal" could call for an anagram of MEAL, "cooked pie" → anagram of PIE and so on)

cooked lightly RARE

cooked, previously COLD

cooker AGA; APPLE; HUB; OVEN; POT; RANGE; STOVE; ■ BAKER; CHEF

cooking ON; ■ BOILING; STEAMING; anagram indicator

cooking pot WOK

cooking surface HOB

cooks FRIES; *see* COOK

cool AIR; CALM; CHILL; FAN; HIP; ICE; ICY; OK; ■ COMPOSED; DISTANT; FINE; PLACID; TEPID; can indicate something to do with a cucumber; [◊ SHADE]

cool down CHILL

cool guy CAT

cool sounding PHAN

cooler CAN; FAN; ICER; PEN; STIR; *see* PRISON

coolness CHILL; NERVE

coop PEN; ■ HENNERY i.e. hen coop

cooperate PLAY

cooperative UNION

coordinate DESIGN; PLAN; X; Y

cop CATCH; NAB; NICK; *see* POLICEMAN

cope DEAL; DO; HANDLE; RUN

cope with STAND

copper CENT; COIN; CU; D (i.e. old penny); P; PEELER; PENNY; PC; S; *see* POLICEMAN

copper once D

copper's CUS

coppers CUS; P; PP; PS; *see* POLICEMEN

coppers, collection of CID; *see* COPPERS

coppice THICKET

copse BRAKE; WOOD

copy APE; C; CLONE; CRIB; FAKE; FORGE; PRINT; REPRO; TEXT; TRACE; ■ EDITION

copyist APER; SCRIBE

cor HOMER (measure)

coral PINK

coral ridge REEF

cord CABLE; FLEX; LINE; ROPE; STRING; TWINE

cordial WARM; ■ GENIAL; TONIC

core HEART; WICK

cork BUNG; PLUG; STOPPER; ■ CLOSE; [◊ BOTTLE]

corn CHAFF; EAR; can indicate something to do with foot; [◊ GRIST]

corn, some EAR; EARS

corner ANGLE; BEND; CATCH; HOG; NICHE; NOOK; TRAP; TURN; can refer to a "corner" of the world e.g. SE

cornered nesting indicator

cornet CORN; HORN

Cornish SW

Cornish resort BUDE; LOOE

Cornwall's wife REGAN

corolla, flower's BELL

corporal NYM (Shak. character)

corporal punishment CANE; ■ BEATING; LASHING

corporal punishment, giver of BEATER; CANER; LASHER

corporation POT; TUM; can indicate something to do with stomach, waistline etc

corps CADRE; GROUP; UNIT

corpulent BIG; FAT; GROSS

corral PEN

correct AMEND; DUE; EDIT; EMEND; IMPROVE; MARK; OK; REVISE; RIGHT; ■ PROPER; REDRESS; anagram indicator

correct text EDIT

corrected anagram indicator

correction anagram indicator

correctly RIGHT; anagram indicator

correspond AGREE; RELATE; SUIT; TALLY; WRITE

correspondence MAIL; MATCH; POST; RATIO; ■ IDENTITY; LETTER; LETTERS

corrode RUST

corroded RUSTY

corroding anagram indicator

corrosion RUST

corrupt ABASE; BAD; BASE; ERRING; ROT; SINNING; SPOIL; ■ ROTTEN; TAINT; anagram indicator

corrupt activity VICE

corrupted anagram indicator

corruption ROT; anagram indicator; ■ GANGRENE

corsage SPRAY; ■ BODICE

corset STAY

cosh SAP

cosmetic LINER; TONER

cosset CRADLE; PAMPER

cost BILL; FEE; LOSS; PRICE; RATE; TOLL; ■ AGIO; CESS; CHARGE; OUTLAY

cost, at a cost of FOR

cost, at a great DEAR

cost, high, large BOMB

costly DEAR; HIGH

costume GOWN; HABIT; SUIT WEAR; ■ CLOAK; CLOTHING; DRESS; GET-UP; ROBE

cosy SNUG; WARM

cot BED; CRIB

coterie RING

cottage, small COT

cotter PIN

cotton CHINO

cotton thread LISLE

couch BED; DIVAN; SOFA

couched in nesting indicator

cough CROUP; HEM

could MAY; MIGHT

could be anagram indicator; can also indicate that the idea that immediately follows is an example of the word (or words) required as the solution. Example: "Copper's weapon could be bloody" (4,4) which clues CUSS WORD (i.e. CU's sword)

could have, make anagram indicator

council BOARD; DIET

counsel ADVICE

counsel, old/once REDE

count ADD; NOBLE; POLL; RATE; SCORE; SUM; TALLY; TELL; TITLE; ■ CENSUS; MATTER; NUMBER

count, start of ONE

counter BAR; BOARD; CHIP; DISC; FISH; MEET; TABLE; ■ AGAINST; OPPOSE; REPLY; TOKEN; reversal indicator; can indicate something to do with accountant, adding machine, abacus, shop, shopkeeper

counterfeit BASE; DUD; FAKE; FEIGN; FORGE; MOCK; SHAM; anagram indicator

counterfoil STUB

counterpart TWIN

countries, cooperating ALLIES

country CLIME; LAND; NATION; REALM; STATE; short named countries are often used as components e.g. CHILE, EIRE, LAOS; MALI, OMAN, WALES, and abbreviations especially e.g. GB, UK, US, USA

country, another ABROAD

country, cooperating ALLY

country estate SEAT

country, fabulous UTOPIA

country house GRANGE; HALL; MANOR; SEAT; VILLA

country man PEASANT

country, old RUS

country, open HEATH; MOOR

country, part of TRACT; ■ REGION

country person PEASANT; ■ FARMER

country property FARM; *see* COUNTRY HOUSE

country pursuit HUNT; HUNTING; RAMBLE

country seat ESTATE

country walk RAMBLE

countrywoman can indicate a nation personified as female e.g. BRITANNIA

county AVON; BEDS; BUCKS; CLARE; CO; DOWN; GLAM; HUNTS; KENT; MAYO; MEATH; SHIRE; SOM; STAFFS; ■ DERBY; DORSET; KERRY; NOTTS; SURREY; YORKS

coup anagram indicator

couple BRACE; DUO; HITCH; II; ITEM; LINK; LOVERS; PAIR; TIE; TWO; UNITE; WED; YOKE; ■ CONNECT; DOUBLE; JOIN; TWAIN; can indicate two words (or components) joined by AND as "couple for a Cockney chap" clues ME AND ER i.e. meander; [◊ DUAL]

couple of first two letters of the succeeding word to be used

couples beginning (starting etc) can require either the first two letters of the succeeding word – or the first letters of the two succeeding words – to be used

courage BOTTLE; DARING; GRIT; GUTS; HEART; NERVE; PLUCK; RESOLVE; ■ BRAVERY; SPIRIT; [◊ DUTCH]

courage, having see COURAGEOUS

courageous BOLD; BRAVE; DARING; HARDY; PLUCKY

courier MULE

course DISH; FISH; HUNT; LAP; LAYER; LINE; LINKS; MEAL; MEAT; PATH; PLATE; PPE; RACE; RAN; RIVER; ROAST; ROUTE; RUN; STUDY; TACK; TRACK; TREND; WAY; ■ CURRENT; DESSERT; ENTRE; PUDDING; SOUP; STARTER; STREAM; SWEET; TENOR; can refer to something to do with a meal (e.g. TABLE) or eating, for example "takes courses" → EATS; anagram indicator; can indicate something to do with golf; can mean a flow of water, in this regard see RIVER, CURRENT; can indicate a racecourse feature as "course enclosure" clues RING; can refer to a specific race

course e.g. AINTREE, ASCOT, EPSOM; [◊ TOTE]

course (as 'in course of') nesting indicator

course at Oxford see OXFORD COURSE

course, change of TACK

course, in due SO

course, main LIVER; ROAST

course, of NATCH (i.e. colloq. for 'naturally')

course of action LINE; PATH; TACK; TRACK

course of, during the nesting indicator

course of treatment CURE

course, part of BRICK; CLASS; LEG; STAGE; TEE

course, particular ROUTE; see COURSE

course, second PUD; SWEET; ■ DESSERT

course, state of GOING

course, take TRAIN

courses MEAL; MENU; TABLE

court CT; DATE; QUAD; ROTA; SEE (i.e. Papal See); SEEK; WOO; YARD; ■ ATRIUM; CHANCERY; CURIA; can signal something to do with tennis

court case SUIT; TRIAL

court, go to SUE

court, in TRIED; UP; a component to be nested within CT

court official MACER; USHER

court order DECREE; WRIT

court, person in SUER

court, take to SUE

courtesy, without RUDE

courts ATRIA; see COURT

courtyard GARTH

couturier DIOR

cove BIGHT; BAY; CHAP; ■ INLET

cover BURY; CAP; CAPE; CASE; COAT; DRESS; FILM; FUR; HAT; GAMP; HIDE; HOOD; INTER; LAG; LID; MAC; MASK; PALL; ROOF; RUG; SHEATH; SHELL; SKIN; SPAN; TILE; TOP; WRAP; ■ CASING; DOME; DUVET;

GRATING; INSURE; QUILT;
REPORT; SHADE; SHEET;
SHELTER; SHUTTER;
SLEEVE; STALL; VEIL;
WRAPPER; first letter indicator
(as "insurance cover" → C)

cover for nut HAT (qv)

cover, temporary TENT

cover, took HID

cover up RUG; SHEET; *see*
COVER; can indicate an item of
clothing

coverage of nesting indicator

covered can indicate the use of a
first letter (as "having yard covered" is a cue for the solution to
begin with Y)

covered by IN; nesting indicator;
can indicate that the word or
component that follows is to be
placed at the front

covered in, with nesting indicator

covering BARK; CAP; CAPE;
CASE (qv); COAT; COWL;
CRUST; FOIL; FUR; HAIR;
HAT; HOOD; LID; MAT; ON;
OVER; ROUND; SKIN; ■ BIB;
LINO; MANTLE; TYRE; nest-
ing indicator; can indicate that an
anagram is following; *see*
COVER

cow AWE; LOWER; NEAT;
STEER; ■ FRIGHTEN;
INTIMIDATE; JERSEY; [◊
CUD]

cow-slip KECK

cow, young CALF

coward MOUSE; SOOK (Aus.)

cowardly CRAVEN; YELLOW

cowards MICE

cowboy, film WESTERN

cower BULLY; CRINGE

cowgirl IO (myth.)

cowl HOOD

cows HERD; LOWERS; STOCK;
■ KINE

cowshed BYRE

coy PRIM; SHY; ■ DEMURE

crabstyle, move EDGE; SIDLE

crack ACE; BREAK; CHAP;
CLAP; CHOP; DIG; DRUG;
GIBE; GO; JEST; QUIP; RAP;

RIFT; RENT; SEAM; SHOT;
SOLVE; STAB; TOP; TRY;
TURN; WHIP; ■ BREACH;
CRANNY; EXPERT; REPORT;
SPLINTER; anagram indicator

crack, to anagram indicator

crack troops SAS

crack up PRAISE (qv)

cracked CLEFT; MENTAL;
RIVEN; ■ CRAZY; *see* MAD;
anagram indicator

cracked, become CHAP

cracker WHIP

crackers BARMY; DAFT; MAD;
NUTS; anagram indicator

cracking SPLIT; anagram indicator

crackpot NUT

cracksman, amateur RAFFLES

cradle BED; [◊ ROCK]

cradle-song, use LULL

craft ARK; ART; BARGE; BOAT;
JET; PLANE; PUNT; SHIP;
SKILL; SS; TRADE; WORK;
can indicate a word ending in
"ship" denoting some kind of
skill (e.g. gamesmanship) or
quality (e.g. sportsmanship); *see*
BOAT, SHIP, VESSEL

craft, old ARGO

craft, simple RAFT

craftsman ARTISAN; COOPER;
MASON; POTTER; SMITH;
WRIGHT

crafty ARCH; FOXY; SLY; WISE;
anagram indicator

crafty group GUILD

crag ROCK

cram JAM; STOW; STUFF; SWOT

cramp STUNT

crank HANDLE; LEVER; LOON;
WINCH; *see* ECCENTRIC

cranny CRACK

crash BANG; PRANG; RAM;
RUIN; SLAM; ■ FAILING; anagram indicator

crash into HIT

crashed, crashing anagram indicator

crass CRUDE

crate BOX; CAGE; CASE; HEAP

crater HOLE; ■ BOXER(!)

crawl CREEP; GROVEL; STROKE; can indicate something to do with swimming

crawler can indicate an insect or snake

craze FAD; MANIA; RAGE; WHIM

crazy BARMY; BATS; GAGA; LOCO; MAD; NUT(S); RAVING; SICK; WHACKY; WILD; ■ MENTAL; NUTTY; WACKY; anagram indicator

cream BEAT; BEST; ELITE; PLUM; SKIM

creamy RICH; THICK

crease FOLD; LINE; RUCK; ■ PLEAT; WRINKLE

create FORM; FOUND; MAKE; RANT; ■ COMPOSE

create difficulty STIR

created MADE

creation anagram indicator

creative anagram indicator

creative work ART

Creator GOD

creature EFT; MOLE; STOAT; ■ BEING; see ANIMAL, BIRD, FISH

creature, arboreal SLOTH

creature irresponsibly passed BUCK

creature, miserable WORM

creature, nocturnal BAT; BADGER

creature, stubborn MULE

creature, thick-skinned HIPPO

creature, troublesome MIDGE

creatures, lot of ZOO

credible REAL

credit CR; TICK; ■ ASCRIBE; BELIEF; BELIEVE; HONOUR; MERIT; TRUST

credit card VISA; ■ PLASTIC

credit notes IOUS

creditor CR

credulous NAIVE

creek COVE

creep CAD; EDGE; FAWN; SNEAK; TOADY

cremate BURN

crest COMB; RIDGE; TOP

crevice CRACK; NOOK; SLIT

crew BAND; CUT (i.e. hairstyle); FOUR; EIGHT; HANDS; ISIS; MAN; MEN; SQUAD; STAFF; TEAM; [◊ SHIP]

crewman/crew member AB; HAND; TAR; see SAILOR

crib BED; COT; KEY; MODEL; ■ CABIN; COPY

cricket GRIG (insect); cricketing terms are very popular among compilers so there are many associated words, e.g. BAT; BAIL; IN; LEG; OFF; ON; OUT; OVER; POINT; TEST

cricket* HOPPER

cricket, a little OVER

cricket ball BEAMER; BOUNCER; YORKER

cricket ground LORDS; OVAL; PITCH

cricket kit BAT; PAD(S)

cricket match TEST

cricket pitch GROUND; LORDS; OVAL; [◊ CREASE; STUMPS; WICKET]

cricket season SUMMER

cricket side LEG; OFF; ON

cricketer BAT; GRACE; POINT; SLIP; ■ BOWLER; FIELDER; KEEPER

cricketer, old GRACE

cricketer's position CREASE

cricketer's protection BOX; PAD

cricketers CC; MCC

cried WEPT; see CRY

crikey COR; MY

crime ARSON; EVIL; JOB; SCAM; SIN; THEFT; TREASON; VICE; ■ CAPER; HEIST; OFFENCE; PIRACY

crime squad CID

crime wave MERCI (i.e. anagram)

criminal BAD; BENT; CON; CROOK; FELON; FENCE; FORGER; HOOD; LAG; THUG; ■ COINER; MOBSTER; PIRATE; anagram indicator

criminal activity RACKET; SCAM; ■ PIRACY

criminal charge RAP

criminal group TRIAD

criminal, possible SUS
criminals TONG
crimson LAKE; RED
crimson clad component to be nested within RED
cringe COWER
crippled LAME
crisis DANGER; HEAD
crisp NEW
critical GRAVE; SEVERE; VITAL
critical, be KNOCK
critical remark BARB; DIG
criticise CARP; CHIDE; FLAY; PAN; RAP; RATE; ROAST; SLAG; SLAM; SLATE; SNIPE; ■ ATTACK; BERATE; KNOCK; REVIEW; RUBBISH
criticism FLAK; PAN; PANNING; SLATE; STICK; SLIGHT; ■ REPROACH; REVUE; ROASTING; ROCKET
croak DIE
croaker FROG
Croatia [◊ SPLIT]
crockery CUP; PLATE
crocodile* CLIP
croft FARM
crony see PAL
crook BAD; BEND; CON; STAFF; STICK; can indicate something to do with shepherd; anagram indicator; see ROGUE
crooked AWRY; BENT; SKEW; anagram indicator
crooks anagram indicator
crooned, one who BING
crooner BING
crop CORN; CRAW; CUT; FOOD; GORGE; GRAIN; HAY; OATS; REAP; RICE; RYE; TRIM; YIELD; ■ ETON; MAIZE; MILLET; WHIP; anagram indicator; can indicate a hairstyle e.g. crewcut, tonsure
crop, part of STOCK
crop up ARISE; ■ EMERGE
cropped up AROSE
crops FOOD; SEED; see CROP
Crosby BING
cross BRIDGE; FORD; IRATE; MAD; MULE; PASS; PLUS; ROOD; SORE; SPAN; STERN; TAU; TESTY; TREE; X; ■ FLAMING; IRACUND; KISS; SHIRTY; SNAPPY; TRAVERSE; can indicate something to do with voting, electioneering, St George, Maltese, Eleanor (Queen)
cross, make ANGER; MARK
cross over DOOR
crossed anagram indicator
crossing BRIDGE; FORD; PASS; ■ PASSAGE nesting indicator
crossing point STILE
crossing river R to be nested within a component
crossword BLAST; DAMN (i.e. a cross word); can indicate a feature of a crossword e.g. grid, clue, across, down, or a technical word associated with crosswords e.g. light, checked letter
crossword, do/tackle SOLVE
★ **crossword warhorses** these are the devices that have been used so much by compilers over the years that they have become crossword clichés. Still with us are warhorses like "flower", "banker" and "runner" to denote a river, and "number" to denote a pain-killer – but used cleverly they can still momentarily throw seasoned solvers
crosswords anagram of WORDS
crowd ALL; CRAM; DROVE; FLOCK; GANG; GATE; HERD; HOST; HOUSE; JAM; LOT; MASS; MOB; PACK; PARTY; PRESS; RUCK; SET; SWARM; THREE; ■ HORDE; HUDDLE; RABBLE; SCRUM; THRONG
crowd, milling SCRUM
crowds MANY
crown CAP; CR; DOME; ER; HEAD; NUT; PEAK; TOP
crows, lots of MURDER
crucial GRAVE; KEY
crucial point see CRUX
crucial, said to be QUAY (hom.)
crucible POT
crucifix ROOD

crude BASE; OIL; RAW; ROUGH; ■ COARSE; EARTHY; GROSS; anagram indicator

crudely anagram indicator

crudely formed ROUGH

cruel HARD; ILL; ■ HARSH; ROTTEN; SAVAGE; anagram indicator

cruel emperor NERO

cruise TRIP

Cruise TOM

crumble, crumbled, crumbling, crumbly anagram indicator

crumpled anagram indicator

crush BREAK; GRIND; ROUT; SMASH; STAMP; STAVE; SWAT; ■ SCOTCH; SQUASH; TRAMPLE; anagram indicator

crushed GROUND; anagram indicator

crushed by nesting indicator

crust BREAD; LAYER; PASTRY; SCAB; can indicate that first and last letters are to be used as "crust of bread" → BD

crustacean CRAB; SHRIMP

crutch FORK

crux GIST; KEY; NUB

cry BAWL; BAY; BRAY; CALL; CAW; HOWL; KEEN; MEW; OH; OW; SCREAM; SOB; WAIL; WEEP; YELL; YELP; ■ BLUB; BLUBBER; HAWK; NEIGH; PULE; SHRIEK; YAP; *see* CRY OF ALARM *etc*, EXPRESSION OF JOY, PAIN, *etc*

cry, a brief CALL

cry for help SOS; ■ MAYDAY

cry of alarm O; OH

cry of excitement WHOOP

cry of exultation HO; WHOOP

cry of pain OH; OUCH; OW

cry of surprise COR; HELLO; OH; OO; ■ GOSH

cry of triumph AHA

cry over a synonym for "cry" to be reversed hence BOS, BULB, PAY

crypt VAULT

cryptic the use of this word often requires you to write the clue to

get the solution! Example: "Dare in cryptic way to get info from PC" → READ-OUT where the solution is the cryptic clue to get the implied answer "Dare"

cryptic clue anagram of CLUE

★ **cryptic definition** a clue that contains only a definition and nothing else, the definition being based on some kind of pun – for example "Drop a little lower" (5) for which the answer is CALVE

crystal [◊ GLASS]

Cuba C; can indicate something to do with cigars

Cuban export CIGAR

cube BLOCK; DICE; DIE; EIGHT; SOLID

cube shape DICE

cubist LEGER

cubs LITTER; PACK

cuckoo DAFT

cuckoo pint ARUM

cuddle HUG; PET

cudgel CLUB; RACK (one's brains)

cue TIP; ■ ROD; SIGNAL

cue-ball WHITE

cuff BEAT; BLOW; CLIP; END (of sleeve); HIT; SMACK; ■ CLOUT; STRIKE; MANACLE

cull SELECT

cult FAD; SECT

cultivate COURT; CROP; FARM; GROW; TILL; anagram indicator

cultivated REFINED; TILLED; ■ GENTEEL; anagram indicator

cultivated land GARDEN

cultivated, poorly RUDE

cultivating TILLING; anagram indicator

cultivation TILTH; anagram indicator

culture ART; TASTE

cultured ARTY

cummerbund SASH

cumulus* CLOUD

cunning ARCH; ART; CRAFT; FLY; FOXY; GUILE; SHREWD; SLEIGHT; SLY; TRICKY; WILE; WILY; ■ SNEAKY; anagram indicator

cunningly anagram indicator

cup GRAIL; MUG; POT; TEE; ■ CHINA; TASSE; TROPHY

cupboard ARK; CLOSET; PRESS; ■ DRESSER; LARDER; PANTRY

cupholder SAUCER

cupola DOME

curative waters SPA

curb BIT; CHECK; REIN; STOP; ■ RESTRAIN

cure HEAL; JERK; PRESERVE; SALT; SMOKE; TAN; TREAT; ■ KIPPER; RESTORE; SPECIFIC

cured BETTER; anagram indicator

curia COURT

curious NOSEY; ODD; RUM; ■ FUNNY; NOSY; QUAINT; STRANGE; anagram indicator

curious, be NOSE; PRY

curious, too NOSY

curiosity RARITY; ■ INTEREST

curiosity, show *see* CURIOUS, BE

curiously anagram indicator; can indicate some kind of paradox or opposite (as "As defendant does when court is sitting, curiously" → STAND TRIAL)

curl COIL; TWINE; ■ KINK; WREATHE

curlers can indicate something to do with the sport of curling e.g. SKIP (captain); [◊ HAIR; WAVES]

curling-iron WAVER

curly anagram indicator

currency COIN; EURO; TENDER; *see* CASH, MONEY, FOREIGN CURRENCY; can refer to a river (as "Ireland's capital currency" → LIFFEY)

currency, Asian BAHT

currency charge AGIO

currency, foreign CENT; DM; ECU; EMU; EURO; FRANC; MARK; ORE; RAND; ROUBLE; SOU; YEN ■ ANNA; DOLLAR; KRONA; LIRA; TICAL; YUAN

currency, old/outdated as well as an historically old currency (such as ducat, groat, etc) can refer to the former monetary unit of a country now using the euro, hence it can call for mark, franc etc.

current AC; AMP; AMPS; DC; DRIFT; EDDY; FLOW; I; IN; LIVE; NOW; PRESENT; RACE; RIFE; RIP; RIVER; STREAM; TIDE; TOPICAL; TOW; ■ GOING; RECENT; THERMAL; an old standby to indicate the name of a river, *see* RIVER; or otherwise indicative of running water, sea etc

current form, in its ASIS

current measure AMP

current round EDDY

currently NOW; can indicate something to do with a river or the sea

currently fashionable IN

curry BALTI; COMB; DRESS; GROOM; anagram indicator; can denote something to do with horse grooming e.g. comb, ostler

curse BANE; BLIGHT; CUSS; DAMN; DRAT; HANG; HEX; OATH; SWEAR; can indicate a traditional oath as "The curse of piracy" clues SHIVER MY TIMBERS; ■ ABUSE

cursorily anagram indicator

curt SHORT

curtailed, curtailing last letter to be omitted

curtain DRAPE; NET; VEIL

curtains DEATH; END; FATAL

curtsey BOB

curvaceous anagram indicator

curve ARC; ARCH; BEND; CAMBER

curve downward SAG

curve inshore BAY; BIGHT

curved BENT; BOW; BOWED

curvy figure/shape S

cushion EASE; PAD

cushy JAMMY

custody officer JAILER

custom HABIT; USE; USAGE; WAY; WONT; ■ MANNER; PRACTICE

customary STOCK; TRAD
customer PATRON; SHOPPER; ■ BUYER; REGULAR
customers TRADE
customised anagram indicator
customs MORES
cut AXE; AXED; BARON; BIT; BOB; CHASE; CHIP; CHOP; CHUNK; CLIP; CLOVE; CROP; DICE; DOCK; ELIDE; GASH; HACK; HEW; HEWN; LANCE; LOP; LOPPED; LOWER; MILL; MINCE; MOW; MOWED; MOWN; NICK; PARE; PARED; POLL; PRUNE; REAP; SAW; SAWN; SCORE; SEVER; SHAPE; SHARE; SHEAR; SHORN; SHORT; SKIP; SLASH; SLICE; SLIGHT; SNIP; STAB; STEAK; TRIM; ■ ABRIDGE; BITE; CARVE; CREW; EXCISE; FAIL; GROOVE; NOTCH; REDUCTION; SECTION; SHRED; SNUB; WHACK; *see* CUT OF MEAT; insertion indicator; anagram indicator; omission indicator; last letter to be omitted
cut-back a synonym of "cut" to be reversed hence EXA, POL etc
cut closely SHAVE
cut down FELL; HEW; PARE; REAP; *see* CUT
cut of meat ROUND; RUMP; SHIN; STEAK; ■ LOIN; TOPSIDE
cut off TRIM; *see* CUT; last letter to be omitted
cut, power OUTAGE
cut round POL (i.e. reversal of LOP); *see* CUT
cut, short BOB; CREW; omission indicator (usually last letter); *see* SHORT CUT
cut, small NICK
cut-throat RAZOR; TOUGH
cut up DICE; in a Down clue can indicate the reversal of "cut" (TUC) or of a synonym (e.g. BATS, EXA, POL, PINS, WAS etc); in the same way "American

cut up" → XA; anagram indicator
cutback *see* CUT-BACK
cute CANNY; SHARP; TAKING; *see* SMART; ■ CHARMING
cutie DISH
cutis SKIN
cutter BLADE; SAW; SWORD; ■ SICKLE
cutting CLIP; KEEN; SHARP; SLIP; TART; nesting indicator
cutting edge BLADE; SWORD
cutting grass short LAW
cutting remark BARB; DIG; JAB
cycle AGE; ERA; MOPED; O; RING; ROUND; SERIES; SPIN; TRIKE; TURN; ■ PEDAL
cycle inventor OTTO
cycling anagram indicator
cynic SCEPTIC
cynical contempt, show SNEER
Cynthia MOON
Cyprus CY
cyst SAC

Dd

D-day can indicate something to do with the introduction of decimal currency
d-drops of water DRAIN
dab EXPERT; ■ TOUCH
dab hand ACE; EXPERT
dabble in TRY
Dad PA; POP; PATER
Dad retired AP
Dad's PAS
daffodil BULB
daffy *see* DAFT
daft BATS; CRACKERS; MAD; SILLY; SIMPLE; *see* NUTS, STUPID etc
dagger BLADE; DIRK; KRIS; ■ CREASE
daily CHAR; HELP; PAPER; *see* NEWSPAPER, PAPER; ■ DOMESTIC; [◊ TREASURE]

dainty TWEE; ■ DELICATE
dairy produce/product BUTTER; MILK; ■ CHEESE (qv); CREAM; ■ YOGHURT
Daisy *see* DAISY
daisy ASTER; FLOWER; WEED
Dakota DAK
dam BLOCK; CHECK; WEIR; ■ MOTHER; PARENT; SMOTHER
dam'd WEIRD (i.e. weir + d)
damage BILL; CHIP; COST; CRACK; DENT; HARM; LAME; LOSS; MAR; PRANG; PRICE; SCAR; SLUR; SPOIL; TEAR; TOLL; ■ HURT; IMPAIR; anagram indicator
damage, slight DENT; SCRAPE; ■ SCRATCH
damage to can indicate an anagram of the word that follows
damaged HARMED; HURT; TORN; anagram indicator
damaging anagram indicator
dame, theatrical TERRY
damn CURSE; DARN; DRAT
damp DANK; MOIST; WET
damper BREAD
damsel *see* GIRL
Dan can refer to a judo belt (black, green etc)
dance BALL; BOP; CAPER; DISCO; FLING; GALOP; HAY; HEY; HOP; JIG; JIVE; LIMBO; PASS (i.e. step); REEL; STEP; STEPS; TANGO; TRIP; TWIST; ■ BALLET; CONGA; LAMBADA; LANCERS; MORRIS; POLKA; STOMP; VOLTA; anagram indicator, as "barn-dance" → BRAN
dance around anagram of DANCE; a component to be nested within a synonym of dance, *see* DANCE
dance club DISCO
dance company BALLET
dance, half of CAN
dance, lively GALOP
dance music SWING
dance orchestra BAND
dance, sort of TAP; *see* DANCE

dancer PRIMA; ■ SALOME
dancing BALL; DISCO; HOP; PAS; TAP; anagram indicator
dander TEMPER
dandy BEAU; BLOOD; BUCK; DUDE; FINE; FOP; OK; SWELL; TOFF; ■ NASH
danger PERIL; RISK; ■ HAZARD; THREAT
danger at sea BERG; REEF
danger, disregarding RASH
danger, out of SAFE
danger, posing no SAFE
danger, put in IMPERIL
danger, sign of RED
danger to aircraft ICING
danger warning ALARM; ALERT
dangerous HAIRY; TIGHT; RISKY ■ DODGY; PARLOUS; anagram indicator
dangerous, electrically LIVE
dangerous exploit STUNT
dangerous situation JAWS
dangerous woman WITCH
dangerously anagram indicator
dangerously equipped ARMED
dangle HANG; SUSPEND
Daniel DAN
dank MOIST
dapper SMART (qv)
dappled SPOTTED
dare DEFY
Dare DAN
daring BOLD; BRAVE; HARDY; NECK; NERVE; RISKY
daring manoeuvre STUNT
dark BLACK; DIM; DUN; GREY; NIGHT; ■ GLOOMY; INKY; MIRK; MURK; SHADOW; UNLIT; [◊ HORSE]
dark, after LATE
dark almost NIGH
dark brown UMBER
dark hue NOIR
dark liquid INK
dark, not FAIR; LIGHT
dark patch SHADOW
dark thoughts DREAMS
darkness BLACK; GLOOM; NIGHT; ■ MIRK (alt. sp.);

MURK; can indicate something
to do with MOON

darling DEAR; LOVE; PET;
SUGAR; ■ HONEY; LOVER;
TOOTSY; *see* DEAR

Darling GRACE

Darling pet NANA

darn DASH; SEW

darned FLAMING; MENDED

dart ARROW; LUNGE; RACE;
SHOOT; TUCK

darts GAME; [◊ BOARD; BULL;
DOUBLE; FLIGHT; TREBLE]

darts, line of fire for OCHE

dash BLIGHT; BOLT; DARN;
DART; ELAN; HARE; HINT;
LINE; RACE; RUN; RUSH;
SPOT; SPRINT; TINGE; TROT
■ BRIO; CAST; CAREER;
GALLOP; HASTEN;
SPLATTER; TOUCH

dash about wildly RAMP

dash off anagram of DASH

dashed RAN; anagram indicator

dashing anagram indicator

dashing figure BLADE

dashing, was RAN

data FILE; GEN; INFO; INPUT;
TABLE

data, set of LIST; TABLE

data transmission DT

date DAY; ERA; IDES; TIME;
YEAR; ■ ENGAGEMENT

date, fateful IDES

date, usual STEADY

dated OBS; OLD

dates, list of CALENDAR

dative CASE

datum FACT

daub COAT; PAINT; SMEAR;
SPLODGE

daughter D; MISS

daughter, treacherous REGAN

David can indicate the French
painter, or one of the biblical
Davids

Davy [◊ LAMP]

dawdle DALLY; POTTER

dawn MORN; START; ■ COCK

day D; DATE; LIGHT; IDES;
PERIOD; day of the week in ab-

breviated form: MON, TUE,
WED, THURS, FRI, SAT, SUN;
where a number precedes it, it
can refer to the name of a month
e.g. "thirty day month" calling
for April, June, September or November and so on; with a capital
letter can indicate DORIS or
something to do with film stars

day before EVE

day, big VE

day-centre A

day, fateful IDES

day in France JOUR

day in Rome DIES (Lat.)

day, last working FRI

day of month IDES

day of victory VE

day off the abbreviation for a day
to be omitted, as "Arthur's day
off" → AR

daybreak D; DAWN; anagram of
DAY

daydream REVERIE

daylight DAWN

days DD; WK (abbreviation of
week)

days, number of LENT; *see*
DAYS

days of fasting EMBER; LENT

days, these AD; LATELY; *see*
NOW

daze STUN

dazzle AWE; BLIND

dazzling display RIOT

dazzling one GLAM

dead DULL; FLAT; GONE; LATE;
NUMB; OUT; OVER; QUIET;
STILL; [◊ BIER]

dead beat anagram of DEAD

dead bird DODO; MOA

dead-line DATE; DL; LIMIT

deadheaded D; first letter to be
omitted

deadly AWFUL; FATAL; ■
LETHAL; MORTAL

deal ALLOT; CONTRACT; COPE;
DATE; HAND; PINE; PLAN;
SALE; SHARE; TRADE;
TREAT; TREATY; WOOD; ■
EXCHANGE; anagram indicator;
can indicate something to do with

playing cards e.g. CARD; can indicate something to do with
plank, carpentry

deal, a good BAGS; LOT; LOTS;
MANY; OODLES

deal effectively COPE

deal incompetently with MUFF

deal with COVER; TREAT; ■
ADDRESS; HANDLE;
SETTLE; TACKLE;

dealer AGENT; TOUT; TRADER;
■ COSTER; PEDDLER; PACK

dealer, crooked FENCE

dealers in collaboration RING

dealing anagram indicator

dealings, have TRADE

dealing with ABOUT; ON; RE;
anagram indicator

dealings TRUCK

dealt anagram indicator

dealt with DID

dean INGE; SWIFT

Dean NELLIE; can indicate something to do with forest; *see*
DEAN

dear CLOSE; DUCK; HONEY;
LAMB; LOVE; PET; PRICEY;
PRICY (alt. sp); SWEET; ■
EXPENSIVE; SWEETIE; *see*
DARLING

dear French CHER

dear in Paris CHER

dear me TUT

dear, my LOVE; PET

dear one *see* DARLING, DEAR

dearth LACK; WANT

death BANE; END; EXPIRY; ■
DEMISE; PASSING; [◊ LAST]

death notice OBIT

deathly PALE

debacle anagram indicator

debar SUSPEND; *see* BAN

debarked ASHORE

debase DEVALUE; LOWER

debatable MOOT

debatable idea MOTION

debate ARGUE; MOOT;
REASON; TALK

debate, place for FORUM

debated, to be MOOT

debauched IMMORAL

debauchery, place of DEN; STY

debilitated TIRED; WEARY; ■
FEEBLE

debilitated, become ROT

debt IOU; RED

debt, be in OWE

debt collector DUN

debt, out of AFLOAT; SQUARE

debt, was in OWED

debtor OWER

debtor, chase DUN

debts IOUS

debut START

decade TEN

decade, half a *see* FIVE YEARS

decamp LEAVE; [◊ AIDE]

decant POUR; anagram indicator

decant wine an anagram of wine
(usually WEIN or WIEN)

decapitated initial letter to be
omitted

decapitation TOPPING

decay ROT; RUST; ■ CARIES;
CRUMBLE; anagram indicator

decay, indication of RUST

decayed BAD; OFF; ROTTED;
ROTTEN; anagram indicator

deceased DEAD; DEC; EX;
GONE; LATE; [◊ ESTATE;
WILL]

deceit FRAUD; LIE; LYING;
SHAM; TRICK

deceitful LYING

deceitful device TRICK

deceive CHEAT; CON; DUPE;
FOX; HAVE; KID; TRICK; ■
BLUFF; SWINDLE

deceived DONE; HAD; SOLD

deceiver CHEAT; FRAUD; LIAR

December 1st D; DECI

decent CLEAN; PROPER;
RIGHT; ■ PASSABLE

deception CHEAT; FRAUD; LIE;
SCAM; STING; TRAP; TRICK;
■ GAMMON; SLEIGHT

deceptive LYING; anagram indicator

deceptive appearance FRONT

decide CHOOSE; RESOLVE;
SETTLE

decide on CHOOSE; PICK; SELECT

decide upon ELECT

decide who will play CAST

decided AGREED; CHOSE

decimal OFTEN (i.e. *of ten*)

deciphered anagram indicator

decision RULING; VOTE; [◊ SNAP]

decisive move MATE

deck ADORN; BOARD; COVER; DRESS; FLOOR; GROUND; PACK; ■ POOP

deck, part of can indicate a card suit

declaration DEC; homophone indicator; can indicate a word beginning with IM (i.e. I'm) as in "Tense declaration of total self-esteem" → IMPERFECT

declare ASSERT; AVER; AVOW; STATE; SWEAR; ■ ALLEGE; CLAIM

declared homophone indicator

declarer, belonging to MY

decline AIL; DIE; DIP; DOWN; DROOP; DROP; EBB; FADE; FALL; FLAG; LAPSE; ROT; SAG; SET; SINK; SLIDE; SLUMP; WANE; ■ CONTRACT; DECREASE; DWINDLE; REFUSE

declined AGED; FELL

declining EBBING; WANING

decommission in the sense of taking out of operation can indicate some word trick such as an anagram, omission or run

decompose ROT

decomposed HIGH; OFF; anagram indicator

decorate ADORN; ICE; PAINT; TRIM; ■ COLOUR

decorated ICED; ORNATE; can indicate that a component is to be nested *within* a synonym for "decorate" or "decoration", *see* DECORATE, DECORATION

decorating, start PRIME

decoration BRAID; FRILL; ICING; OBE; SASH; SEQUIN; TRIM; ■ FINIAL; GARNISH; PICOT; *see* MEDAL, HONOUR

decorative anagram indicator

decorative band SASH

decorative fringes, with LACY

decorative wear SASH

decorous DEMURE; PROPER

decoy LURE

decrease DIP; DOWN; FALL; IRON (i.e. de-crease); *see* CUT, DECLINE

decree ACT; EDICT; FIAT; LAW; ORDER; RULE

decrepit anagram indicator

dedicated SACRED

dedication can indicate TO followed by a name as "dedication for a Scot" clues TOKEN (i.e. to Ken)

deduce GATHER; INFER

deduct, deducted omission indicator

deduction CUT; DISCOUNT; omission indicator

deduction from wages NI

deed ACT; ACTION; FEAT; PAPER; ■ CONTRACT; GEST (i.e. heroic); can indicate something to do with land ownership, mortgage, etc

deem JUDGE; RATE

deep BASS; LOW; MAIN; SEA; ■ DOWN; PROFOUND; RADICAL

deep division can indicate a stretch of water (channel, sea, strait) separating two land masses

deep in trouble anagram, commonly EPED or PEDE

deer BUCK; DOE; ELK; GNU; HART; HIND; RED; ROE; STAG; ■ AXIS; PRICKET; MOOSE; [◊ RUT]

deerstalker HAT

deface SCAR

defamation *see* DEFAME

defamatory statement LIBEL

defame SMEAR; ■ LIBEL; MALIGN; SLANDER; SLUR

defeat BEAT; BEST; FAULT; FLOOR; HAMMER; KO; LICK; LOSS; PIP; ROUT; RUIN;

UNDO; WORST; ■
DRUBBING; LICKING; MATE;
TROUNCE; WATERLOO

defeat, one suffering LOSER

defeated BEAT; LICKED;
LOSER; OUT

defeated, be LOSE

defeated party LOSER

defect ERROR; FAULT; FLAW;
GO; LEAVE; SPOT; STAIN;
VICE; ■ FAILING

defected GONE; LEFT; WENT;
omission indicator, usually of immediately preceding element(s)

defection omission indicator, usually of immediately preceding el-
ement(s)

defective anagram indicator; omission indicator; *see* FAULTY

defective from the start first letter to be changed or omitted

defective, very V to be omitted

defence ALIBI; FORT; KEEP;
WALL; ■ AEGIS; GROYNE;
REDOUBT; SHIELD

defence body MOD

defence of, in FOR; PRO

defenceless NAKED

defendant ACCUSED

defendant, place for DOCK

defender ALLY; BACK

defender of the faith DF;
HENRY

defenders, our MOD

defensive place FORT

defensive system TRENCH

defer DELAY; STAY; YIELD

deficiency GAP; LACK; LOSS;
omission indicator

deficiency disease RICKETS

deficiency of NO

deficient BELOW; SCANT;
SCARCE; SHORT; UNDER;
omission indicator; last letter to
be omitted

deficit LOSS

defile GORGE; PASS; SOIL; ■
SLANDER

definite SURE; ■ CERTAIN;
POSITIVE

definitely SURELY

definition MEANING

★ **definition** that part of the clue
which gives the synonym for the
solution; it is the equivalent that
we have to find. Example: "fighting" is the definition in "Sci-fi
stuff involved fighting" (10)
where we have to come up with
FISTICUFFS ("involved" indicates an anagram of "Sci-fi
stuff")

★ **definition by characteristic** a
clue in which the compiler only
mentions one of the features of
the thing we are looking for. For
example "Ruthless one has an
edge" (3-6) for which the answer
is CUT-THROAT. This is a
straightforward double definition
clue but the secondary definition
(i.e. "a cut-throat razor") is only
signalled to us as something that
"has an edge"

★ **definition by example** a clue in
which the compiler mentions
only an example of the thing we
are looking for, as exemplified by
the rather difficult "Bumped into,
on my returning glass for a drink,
maybe?" (7) where the answer is
METONYM (a bits-and-pieces
type clue built up via
MET-ON-YM – *see*
METONYM). A less demanding
example is given by "Lost, as a
dog may be" (6). This is a dou-
ble-definition type with the answer ASTRAY. "Lost" obviously
equates with "stray", but as far as
a dog is concerned "a stray" is
only one example of a type of
dog

★ **definition by function** this where
a definition is restricted to its
function as in "They try to keep
you from losing your grip" (6).
The answer is PLIERS where the
second definition relates only to
the function of a pair of pliers.
Similarly "It throws light on a
possible bloomer" (4) the solution of which is BULB, another
double definition where one of
the definitions is restricted to its

function i.e. it is a light bulb that "throws light"

deflate POP; PRICK

deflect TURN; reversal indicator

Defoe's creation MOLL; ■ CRUSOE

deform STUNT

deformed anagram indicator

deformation LIBEL

defraud CON; STING

deft ABLE; CLEVER; HANDY; NEAT; NIMBLE; *see* ABLE, NEAT

defunct anagram indicator

defy BRAVE; FACE

degeneracy anagram indicator

degenerate FALL; ROT; SINK; ■ EFFETE; anagram indicator

degeneration ATROPHY

degree BA; BED; C (i.e. Centigrade, Celsius); F (i.e. Fahrenheit); MA; ORDER; PASS; PHD; PPE; RATE; STEP; ■ EXTENT; *see* GRADUATE; [◊ STUDY]

degree course PPE; MBS; *see* DEGREE

degree, inferior PASS

degree, of small SLIGHT

degree of soil acidity PH

degree without honours PASS

degrees ANGLE; BAS; BEADS; HEAT; MAS

degrees, higher HEAT

deity GOD; RA; SOL; ■ ZEUS

dejected LOW; SAD

Delaware DE

delay DALLY; DEFER; HINDER; ICE (as in "put on ice"); KEEP; LAG; PAUSE; STAY; TARRY; WAIT ■ LINGER; LOITER; [◊ LATE; TIME]

delay (in) returning GAL

delay, without DIRECT; FAST

delayed LATE

dele EFFACE

delegate AGENT; ASSIGN; DEPUTE; REP

delegates COMMISSION

delegation MISSION

delete DROP; ERASE; OMIT; STRIKE

deliberate PONDER; ■ CONSIDER

delicate AIRY; NICE; TENDER; ■ DAINTY; ELFIN; FRAGILE; LACY; WEAK

delicate area GROIN

delicate fabric LACE

delicate situation SPOT; *see* DIFFICULTY; ■ FLASHPOINT

delicately pretty DAINTY

delicacy CAKE; ICE; SWEET; TASTE

delicious TASTY; YUMMY

delight ELATE; GLEE; GUSTO; JOY; PLEASE; REVEL; TREAT; ■ ELATION; ENTRANCE; TICKLE; TRANSPORT

delight, give REGALE

delight, show YELL

delighted GLAD; SENT

delightful NICE; PLEASANT

delightful person GAS

delinquent TED

deliver BOWL; CARRY; FREE; HAND; RID; SAVE; SERVE; SHIP; ■ PIPE; RELEASE; SUPPLY; anagram indicator; [◊ SPIN i.e. cricket]

deliver ball BOWL; SERVE

deliverance RELIEF

delivered FREED; IN; RID; SAID; anagram indicator

delivered first D; ELDEST

deliveries BALLS; OVER (i.e. from cricket); *see* DELIVERY

delivery BABY; BALL; DROP; POST; ■ BOUNCER; LABOUR; LETTER; ORATION; YORKER; can indicate something to do with birth (e.g. storks)

delivery charge can refer to something to do with kidnapping, ransom etc

delivery date usually refers to birthday

delivery, make a BOWL; SERVE

delivery route, service ROUND

delivery task ROUND

delivery truck TIPPER

delude CON

deluge FLOOD; ■ DROWN

delve DIG; FORAGE

demand ASK; BID; BILL; CALL; CLAIM; DUN; MARKET; NEED; ORDER; ■ EXACT; EXPECT; REQUEST

demand, huge RUSH

demand, in HOT

demand, make CLAIM

demand payment DUN

demanding HARD; STERN; TOUGH; TRYING; ■ EXACTING

demands, make TRY

demands, make great EXACT

demean HUMBLE; LOWER

demeanour AIR; FRONT

demented MAD; anagram indicator

demise END; ■ DEATH

demo MARCH; TAPE

demoiselle CRANE

demolish RUIN; WRECK

demolished anagram indicator; [◊ CRASH]

demolition anagram indicator

demon DEVIL; FIEND; IMP

demon driver TOAD (character in "Wind in the Willows")

demonstrate MARCH; PROVE; SHOW

demonstrated MARCHED; SATIN (i.e. sat in); ■ PROVED; SHOWN

demonstrating often immediately precedes the synonym for the solution

demonstration MARCH; PROOF; SHOW

demote LOWER; RELEGATE

demoted (in conjunction with a word like "leader") can indicate that the first letter of a word is to be transposed to the end

demur REFUSE

demure COY; OBJECT; PRIM; ■ MODEST

den DIVE; EARTH; LAIR; HOLT; NEST; RETREAT; ROOM; STUDY

denarius D

denial NO; ■ NEGATION

denial, old fashioned NAY

denied omission indicator (as "denied kiss" requires X to be omitted)

denied love O to be omitted

denigrate ABUSE

denomination CLASS

denote MEAN

denounce NAME; SHOP

denouement END; ENDING; can indicate the last letters(s)

dense THICK

dense, not THIN

dent MARK; HOLE; ■ HOLLOW

dental condition/problem PLAQUE

dental decay CARIES

dented anagram indicator

dentures PLATE; SET

denude STRIP

deny DISOWN; REFUSE; ■ NEGATE; *see* DISALLOW

denying omission indicator

depend LEAN; RELY

dependable STAUNCH

depart DIE; GO; LEAVE

departed DEAD; DIED; GONE; LATE; LEFT

departed for Scotland AWA

department AREA; DEPT; FIELD; can also refer to a French administrative district

departs D; *see* DEPART

departure EXIT; GOING; ■ EGRESS

depend HINGE; RELY

dependable TRUSTY; ■ CERTAIN; STOUT

dependent SUBJECT

depleted LOW

deplorable, deplorably anagram indicator

deplore RUE; ■ REGRET

deploy USE

deployed USED; anagram indicator

deployed by anagram indicator; run indicator

deployed in nesting indicator; run indicator

deploying anagram indicator

deployment USE

deportment BEARING

depose OUST; USURP

deposed anagram indicator; omission indicator, as "leader being deposed" calls for the omission of the initial letter

deposit ASH; LAYER; LODE; LODGE; ORE; PARK; PLACE; SET; STORE; SUM

depot BASE; STATION

depravity EVIL; SIN; VICE

depredate LOOT; ROB; RAID

depress LOWER

depressed BLUE; DOWN; GRIM; LOW; LOWER; SUNK

depressed area DELL; GLEN; TROUGH; see DEPRESSION

depressed, be MOPE

depressed by in a Down clue, can indicate that a component is preceded by (i.e. "pushed down by") another as in "Revolutionary man depressed by cold" → CHE

depressed, get SINK

depressed, one's KEY

depressing GREY; SAD; ■ DISMAL; can indicate something to do with typewriting, keyboard etc

depressing event DOWNER

depression COL; COMBE; DALE; DELL; DENT; DIP; GLEN; HOLLOW; LOW; PIT; RECESS; RUT; SAG; TROUGH; VALE; ■ CRATER; DUMPS; VALLEY; in a Down clue can be a reversal indicator;

deprivation LACK; NEED

deprive DENUDE; ROB; see ROB, STEAL

deprive of TAKE; see CUT

deprived BEREFT; NEEDY; anagram or omission indicator; can indicate an adjective beginning with UN or one ending in LESS; omission indicator as "deprived of powers" requires P to be omitted

deprived of can indicate an adjective ending in -LESS

depth MEASURE

depth, ascertain SOUND

depth, be out of one's FLOUNDER

depth of water DRAUGHT

deputy DEP; SUB; ■ LOCUM; PROXY

deputy head D

deputy leader D

deranged MAD; anagram indicator

Derby* CHEESE; CLASSIC; HAT; RACE; SAGE

Derek DEL

derelict TRAMP; anagram indicator

deride JEER; MOCK; TAUNT

derider MOCKER

derision BOO; JEER; SCORN

derision on, heap MOCK (qv)

derisive, be SCOFF

derisive remark JEER

derisive sound BOO; YAH

derivable from the word(s) that follow to be used as the basis of an anagram

derivation ORIGIN

derogatory SNIDE; ■ SLIGHTING

Descartes THINKER ("I think therefore I am")

descend DROP; FALL; SINK; STOOP

descendant SCION

descendant of anagram indicator

descendants LINE; TREE; ■ FAMILY

descent DIVE; RACE; STOOP

describe CALL; DEPICT; DETAIL; DRAW; EXPRESS; PRESENT; RECOUNT; REPRESENT; SKETCH;

describe, can/may anagram indicator

describe vividly PAINT

description SPEC; ■ ACCOUNT

description, detailed SPEC

desecrated SOILED; anagram indicator

desert ARID; DEFECT; DUE LEAVE; QUIT; RAT; SAND; WASTE; ■ BETRAY; DROP; MAROON; REWARD

deserted LEFT; WENT; omission indicator
deserter RAT
deserts DUE
deserve EARN; RATE; ■ MERIT
deserving EARNING; GOOD; JUST; RATING
desiccated DRY
design AIM; ART; END; DECOR; MEAN; PLAN; PLOT; ■ FIX; INTENT; PATTERN; STYLE anagram indicator;
designate NAME; TERM
designation NAME; TITLE
designed MEANT; anagram indicator
designer, fashion DIOR; QUANT
designer, Victorian MORRIS
designing CRAFTY
designing individual ETCHER; PLANNER; *see* ARCHITECT, ARTIST
desirable DES; PLUM
desirable, most BEST
desire CRAVE; DREAM; FANCY; GREED; HOPE; HUNGER; ITCH; LONG; LUST; URGE; WANT; WHIM; WILL; WISH; YEARN; YEN; ■ ENVY; PASSION
desire, strong LUST
desist CEASE; STOP; ■ ABSTAIN; REFRAIN
desk AMBO; TABLE
desolate LORN
desolation RUIN
despatch END; KILL; POST; SEND; *see* DISPATCH
despatched SENT
despatched again RESENT
desperate DIRE; anagram indicator
desperate character DAN
desperate-sounding DIA (i.e. homophone of DIRE)
desperately DIRE; anagram indicator
despicable BASE; CHEAP; LOW; VILE
despicable man/person CUR; HOUND; RAT; SCAB; TOAD

despise CONTEMN
despised person LEPER
despondency DESPAIR
despondent BLUE; DOWN
despot TSAR
despot, rule as DICTATE
despotic IMPERIOUS
dessert AFTERS; APPLE; FLAN; FOOL; FRITTER; ICE; KISS; MOUSSE; PIE; PUD; SPLIT; TART; TRIFLE; WHIP; ■ JELLY; PUDDING; SWEET
destabilised anagram indicator
destined BOUND; FATED; MEANT
destiny FATE; KARMA; LOT
destitute NEEDY
destroy DISH; END; RASE; RAZE; ROUT; RUIN; SLAY; TRASH; UNDO; WRECK; anagram indicator
destroy by fire BURN
destroyed ATE; GONE; anagram indicator
destroyed, gradually ATE
destroyer KILLER
destroying anagram or omission indicator
destruction END; RUIN; WRACK; ■ HAVOC
destructively anagram indicator
desultory, desultorily anagram indicator
detach BREAK; PART; SEVER
detached APART; ■ CLINICAL anagram indicator
detached territory ISLE
detachment UNIT; can indicate that a component is split
detail FACT; ITEM; LIST; PIECE; POINT; RESPECT; SPEC; ■ PARTICULAR; last letter of a word to be omitted (.e. de tail)
detail, lacking SKETCHY
detailed last letter of a word to be omitted (i.e. de-tailed)
detailed description SPEC
detain HOLD; JAIL; KEEP; GATE; nesting indicator
detained HELD; JAILED; nesting indicator

detect CATCH; NOSE; SENSE SPOT; TRACE

detective COP; DI; DICK; DS; EYE; PI; TEC; ■ GMAN; HOLMES; MARPLE; MORSE; can indicate a colloquial term for detective such as busy, gumshoe

Detective Charlie CHAN

Detective Inspector DI

Detective Sergeant CLUFF; DS

detectives CID; PIS; TECS; YARD; ■ GMEN

deter HAMPER; STOP

detergent CLEANSER

deteriorate AGE; ROT; RUST; ■ MOULDER; PERISH

deterioration RUST; anagram indicator

determination WILL

determination, with FIRM

determine FIX; SET; ■ GUESS; RESOLVE

determined DOUR; EARNEST; INTENT; SET; anagram indicator

detest HATE

dethrone OUST; USURP

detonator CAP; FUSE

detour anagram indicator

detrimental HARMFUL; *see* HARMFUL

detrimental, be IMPAIR

detrimental to, be *see* HARM

devalue DEBASE; LOWER; ■ ALLOY

devastated anagram indicator

develop COME; FORM: GROW; ■ APPEAR; EVOLVE; anagram indicator; can indicate something to do with photography e.g. darkroom

develop slowly CREEP

developed EVOLVE; GREW; READY; RIPE; ■ UNFOLD; anagram indicator

developed, not fully can indicate that a large section of word is omitted

developer anagram indicator

developing, development anagram indicator

deviant anagram indicator

deviate ERR; STRAY; SWITCH; WANDER; YAW; ■ SWERVE

deviation SHEER

device CHARGE (heraldry); LASER; LOGO; RUSE; SIGN; THING; TOOL; TRICK; WINCH

device for holding TONGS

devices FANCY; WILL

device, electronic TIMER

devil BOGLE (Sc.); DEMON; DICKENS; DIS; DRUDGE; FIEND; HECK; IMP; NICK; SATAN

devil, little IMP

Devil's hoof, like CLOVEN

devilish EVIL; anagram indicator

devilish character FIEND

devilish group COVEN

devious SHIFTY; anagram indicator

deviously anagram indicator

devise FRAME; RIG; PLAN; SET; ■ GET UP; INVENT

devised SET; anagram indicator

devising anagram indicator

devoid of content only first and last letters to be used

Devon SW

devoted AVID; KEEN; PI

devotee BUFF; FAN; NUT

devotion LOVE; PIETY

devotion, show ADORE; LOVE

devour EAT; GORGE; nesting indicator

devoured ATE; anagram or nesting indicator

devout PIOUS; HOLY

dewy WET

dexterity SLEIGHT

diabolical anagram indicator

diabolically anagram indicator

diacritical mark HACEK

diagram GRAPH

dial CALL; CLOCK; FACE; PAN; RING; ■ LAID-BACK(!)

dialogue EXCHANGE; LINE; TALK

dialogue, informal RAP

diamond D; GEM; STONE; ■ SPARKLER; can refer to a specific diamond e.g. Koh-i-noor; can indicate something to do with baseball

diamond, quality of WATER

diamonds DD; ICE; ROCKS; SUIT

Diana DI; DORS

diaphanous SHEER

diary LOG; PLANNER

diary item ENTRY

diatonic note C

diatribe RANT; TIRADE

dice BONES; CHANCE; CHOP; CUBE; CUT; RISK

dicey TRICKY; in the context of a game can refer to backgammon etc

dick *see* DETECTIVE

Dickens DEVIL; HECK; HELL

Dickensian character (hero, heroine) DODGER; NELL; PIP; OLIVER; RUDGE; TWIST

dicky (Dicky) DODGY; IFFY; ILL; anagram indicator

dictate ORDER

dictated homophone indicator

dictation can indicate something to do with dictation e.g. shorthand

dictator DUCE; FRANCO; IDI; SHOGUN; TITO

dictionary DICT; OED

dictum SAW

did (something) ACTED

did very well SHONE

diddle CHEAT; CON; DO; anagram indicator; *see* SWINDLE

didn't lose WON

didn't stand SAT

didn't win LOST

didn't win or lose DREW

did the same thing APED; COPIED

die BLOCK; CUBE; DROWN; END; EXIT; FADE; FAIL; FALL; GO; LONG; STAMP; STOP; YEARN; ■ CROAK; PERISH; TESSERA

die around one PASSION (i.e. PASS-I-ON)

die is cast, the anagram of DIE

died D; FELL; OB; OBIT (Lat.)

died in prison BRIDG i.e. BRI-D-G (to construct BRIDGE for example)

died out D to be omitted

diesel oil DERV

diet FARE; FAST; REDUCE; SLIM; ■ SLIMMING

Diet HOUSE; can refer to specific seat of government

differ VARY; anagram indicator

difference CHANGE; GAP; SPAT; TIFF; anagram indicator

difference, having OTHER

difference, make a AFFECT; ALTER; AMEND; MATTER; TELL

different APART; CHANGE; ELSE; OTHER; ■ ALIEN; ANOTHER; anagram indicator

different one OTHER

different people OTHERS

different position, put in RESITE

different version to anagram of what follows

different way, find a DIVERT

differently anagram indicator; can indicate a verb beginning with RE

differing anagram indicator

difficult BLACK (as in black spot); HARD; HELL; HOT (as in hot seat); STICKY; STIFF; TIGHT TRICKY; anagram indicator

difficult for, too BEYOND

difficult job/task CHORE; GRIND

difficult, not EASY

difficult position, situation LURCH; STRAIT; *see* DIFFICULTY

difficult to accept BITTER

difficult to believe TALL

difficult to deal with STEEP

difficult to see DARK; DIM

difficulties MIRE; anagram indicator

difficulties, in anagram indicator

difficulty ADO; BIND; CORNER; FIX; HARDNESS; HOLE; JAM; LURCH; MESS; NET; PASS; PLIGHT; RUB; SCRAPE;

SNAG; SPOT; ■ TROUBLE; anagram indicator

difficulty, advance with LIMP

difficulty, create STIR

difficulty getting back BUR

difficulty, in some anagram of SOME

difficulty, minor BUG; GLITCH; KINK

difficulty, walk with LIMP

diffident COY; SHY

dig BARB; CRACK; DELVE; GIBE; GRUB; JAB; JIBE; MINE; NUDGE; POKE; PROD; SEE; SPIT (i.e. with reference to spade); TILL; [◊ INFRA]

dig in ENTRENCH

dig out anagram of DIG

dig up GID

dig with one's feet HEEL

digest ABSTRACT; anagram or nesting indicator; ■ CONSUME; UNDERSTAND

digest, easy to LIGHT

digesting anagram indicator; nesting indicator

digger MINER; SHOVEL; SPADE

digging MINE

digit FIGURE; FINGER; NUMBER; THUMB; TOE

digital equipment FINGER; THUMB; TOE

digital heater MUFF

digital signal can indicate a hand signal e.g. THUMBS UP

dignified SEDATE

dignitary LION; VIP

dignity FACE; PRIDE

digress RAMBLE; STRAY

digs, something for SHOVEL; SPADE

dilapidated SHABBY; TATTY; anagram indicator

dilapidated castle/house RUIN

dilatory LATE; SLOW; TARDY

dilapidated car BANGER; CRATE; HEAP

dilemma PLIGHT; SCRAPE; *see* DIFFICULT POSITION, DIFFICULTY

dilettante LAY

dilettante interest in, take DABBLE

dilute WATER

diluted WATERY; WEAK

dim BLEAR; DARK; FADE; FAINT; LOWER; MIST; SLOW; THICK (qv); UNLIT.

dim-witted SLOW; THICK (qv)

dimensions, relative SCALE

diminished omission indicator

diminished man GENT; can indicate the diminutive of a male name e.g. TED – *see* MAN

diminutive SHORT; SMALL; TINY; abbreviation indicator; omission indicator

diminutive chap TOM

diminutive person SQUIT

din NOISE; RACKET; ROW

dine EAT; SUP

dine out anagram of OUT

dined ATE; EATEN

diner EATER

dingy DRAB; DULL

dining room HALL; MESS

dining room, feature of TABLE

dinner MEAL; SPREAD

dinner, invitation to GONG

dinner, traditional ROAST

dinosaur TREX (i.e. T. Rex)

dint BLOW; STROKE; ■ EFFORT

diocesan SEE

diocese ELY; SEE; WELLS

diode TUBE

dip BATH; DROP; DUCK; DUNK; SAG; SWIM; RAMP; ■ PADDLE; IMMERSE; SAUCE

diplomacy TACT; [◊ SHUTTLE]

diplomat HE; ■ ATTACHE; ENVOY

diplomatic [◊ TACT]

diplomatic mission LEGATION

dipper SCOOP

dire BAD; EVIL; anagram indicator

direct AIM; CAST; FRANK; LEAD; OPEN; ORDER; POINT; RUN; SHOW; STEER; STRAIGHT; TRAIN; ■ ADDRESS; BLUFF; CHANNEL

direct debit DD

direct steering CON
directed LED; RAN
direction BEARING; COURSE; END; TACK; WAY; a compass bearing in full: EAST; NORTH; SOUTH; WEST, or abbreviated: E; N; NE; NW; S; SE; SW; W; similarly can indicate LEFT, RIGHT or L, R; ■ ACROSS; BEARING; can refer to a stage direction e.g. exeunt
directions two or more compass bearings, usually as letters, WS, NE, SEE etc
directions, going in different word or component to be nested within two letters from N, E, W or S
directions, in both palindrome indicator
directions, in opposite word or component to be nested within two opposite compass points (NS, EW); or within two opposite sides (RL) as "Animal took food in opposite directions" → RATEL
directive DECREE; EDICT; ORDER
directly DUE
director BOSS; DIR; DRIVER; HEAD; SOIL
director, Austrian/German LANG
directorate BOARD
directors BOARD; D
directors, lots of BOARDS
directory INDEX
direly anagram indicator
dirge LAMENT
dirk BLADE; DAGGER
dirt BLUE; FILTH; GRIME; GROT; SCUM
dirt, bit of SMUT
dirty LOW; MEAN; SOILED; ■ BASE; FOUL; SHABBY; STORMY; *see* BASE
dirty look FROWN
dirty stuff SOOT
dirty talk SMUT
dis- can indicate an anagram of the remainder of the word as "dis-

pleases" signals an anagram of PLEASE (e.g. ELAPSE)
disable KO; SCOTCH; ■ NOBBLE
disadvantage CATCH; CON; LOSS; MINUS; SNAG
disagreeable BAD
disagreement RIFT; SPAT; TIFF; ■ BREACH; NEGATION
disallow BAN; NEGATE; REFUSE; ■ ANNUL; CANCEL
disappear GO; MELT; VANISH
disappeared GONE; WENT
disappearing GOING; omission indicator
disappointed, very GUTTED
disappointing OFF; POOR
disappointment SELL ■ MARE'S NEST
disapproval ODIUM
disapprove soundly BOO; TUT
disapproval, audible (express, voice, voiced, etc) BOO; TUT
disapproval loudly, show BARRACK
disarray anagram indicator
disaster DOOM; ROUT; RUIN; ■ HUBRIS; anagram indicator
disastrous DIRE; FATAL; LETHAL; ■ ADVERSE; anagram indicator
disastrously anagram indicator
disbelieving expression BAH
disbursed PAID
disc COUNTER; O; PLATE; RECORD (qv); TOKEN
disc-jockey DJ
discard DUMP; REJECT; SHED; TRASH
discarded SHED; omission indicator
discarding omission indicator
discern SPY
discerning CLEVER
discernment EAR
discharge ARC; EMIT; FIRE; MATTER; PAY; PUS; SACK; SHOT; SHOOT; SPARK; VENT; ■ ABSOLVE; BOOT; EJECTION; QUIETUS; RHEUM; SALVO

discharged SHOT; SACKED; omission indicator

disciple can indicate a specific disciple of Christ e.g. MARK; ■ CHELA; LEARNER

discipline ORDER; ■ CHASTEN; SUBJECT; [◊ WHIP]

discipline, enforcing STERN; STRICT

disciplined CANED; TAUGHT; anagram indicator

disclose REVEAL; STATE; ■ BREAK (as the news)

disclosure LEAK

disco CLUB; DANCE

disco lighting STROBE

discoloration STAIN

discomfort ACHE; PAIN

disconcert ABASH; RATTLE; ■ FLUSTER; THROW

disconcerted THREW; THROWN; anagram indicator

disconnect CUT; SEVER

disconsolate LOW

discontented anagram indicator

discontented reaction RUMBLE

discontinue DROP; END; STAY; STOP

discontinued EX; OFF

discord CLANG

discordant anagram indicator

discordantly anagram indicator

discount CUT; ■ AGIO; REBATE; SAVING; omission indicator

discount, at a pound L to be omitted (similarly **at a two-pound discount** in which LL is to be omitted)

discount, initial omission indicator for initial letter

discourage DASH; DAUNT; DETER; UNMAN

discouraging sign NO

discourse CHAT; ORATE; SPEAK; TALK; ■ CONVERSATION; LECTURE

discourteous RUDE

discourtesy SLIGHT; SNUB

discover FIND; LEARN; RUMBLE; TRACE

discovered FOUND

discovered in anagram indicator; nesting indicator as "discovered nothing in" requires O to be nested

discovery FIND

discreet POLITIC; WISE

discreet, more WISER

discretion TACT; TASTE

discrimination TASTE

discriminatory SEXIST

discuss AIR; CHAT; ■ DISPUTE

discussing ON; can require that ON is used in conjunction with its subject as "doctor discussing" → MOON

discussion AIRING; CHAT; DEBATE; MOOT; PARLEY; TALK; TOPIC; WORD; anagram indicator

discussion about TOOM (i.e. reversal)

discussion, join in CONFER

discussion of homophone indicator

discussion, public AIRING; DEBATE

disdain SCORN; SPURN; ■ CONTEMPT

disdainful, be SNIFF

disease AGUE; GOUT; LURGY; TB; ■ BSE; SCURVY; anagram indicator

disease, baffling ME

disease, bird GAPES

disease, evidence of RASH

disease, flu like ME

disease, put an end to CURE

disease, swelling GOUT

disease, toe-inflammation GOUT

diseased ILL; SICK; anagram indicator

disembark LAND

disfigure MAR; SCAR; SPOIL; anagram indicator

disfigured anagram indicator

disfigurement SCAR

disgorging omission indicator

disgrace BLOT; STAIN; TAINT; ■ SLUR

disgraced BLACKED; FALLEN

disgraceful anagram indicator

disgruntled anagram indicator

disguise ALTER; COVER (qv); HIDE; VEIL; anagram indicator

disguised, disguising anagram indicator

disgust APPAL; REPEL; REVOLT; ■ ODIUM

disgust, sound of UGH; YUCK

disgusted expression UGH

disgusting FOUL; GROSS; ICKY; SICK; ■ FILTHY; anagram indicator

dish ASHET; BOWL; CRUMBLE; FLAN; FOOD; HASH; MEAL; PAN; PEACH; PIE; PLATE; PLATTER; RUIN; STEW; TART; ■ CHARGER; COURSE; CREPE; CUTIE; PLATTER; SCOTCH; can refer to some aspect of a woman; anagram indicator

dish, cold MOUSSE

dish, Italian PASTA

dish out ALLOT; DOLE; SERVE

dish, serving PLATTER

dish, slow-cooked STEW

dish, sort of PETRI

dish up SERVE; DISH, or a synonym for "dish", to be reversed

disharmony FRICTION

dishearten CORE (i.e. take out heart); DAUNT; REJECT; ■ SADDEN

disheartened CORED; omission indicator for middle letter(s) of associated word, as "not disheartened" → NT

disheartened girl GL

disheartening an indicator that the middle letter(s) of an associated word be omitted

dished out anagram indicator

dishevelled anagram indicator

dishonest BENT; CROOK; LYING; SHARP

dishonest, be LIE

dishonest person CROOK; ROGUE

dishonesty LIE; LYING

dishonour SOIL; STAIN

dishonourable man CAD; ROTTER

dishonourably, behaving CADDISH

dishy FAIR

disinclined AVERSE

disinfectant BLEACH

disintegrate CRUMBLE

disintegrating anagram indicator

disjointed BITTY

dislike AVERSION; HATE; ODIUM; RESENT

dislocated RICKED; anagram indicator

dislodged EJECTED; anagram indicator

disloyal FALSE

disloyal, be SHOP

disloyalty TREASON

dismal BLEAK; DREAR; DREARY; POOR; SAD

dismantled anagram indicator

dismay APPAL; DREAD

dismembered anagram indicator

dismiss AXE; BOOT; BOWL; EJECT; FIRE; REJECT; SACK; SHOO; SPURN; STUMP YORK; ■ CASHIER; CATCH; DEMIT; REMOVE; omission indicator

dismiss contemptuously SPURN

dismissal SACK; ■ BULLET; omission indicator

dismissal, accept WALK

dismissed BOWLED; OUT; UP; omission indicator

dismissive remark NO

dismount ALIGHT

Disney [◊ GOOFY; PLUTO]

Disney film while there are many Disney films to pick from, DUMBO and FANTASIA seem to be the most popular in crosswords

disorder FLU; MESS; MUDDLE; ■ CONDITION; ILLNESS; RUMPLE; anagram indicator

disordered MUDDLED; anagram indicator

disorderly ILL; anagram indicator

disorderly character TED

disorderly group GAGGLE; MOB; RABBLE

disorderly scene RAG

disorganised SCATTY; anagram indicator

disoriented anagram indicator

disown CEDE; DENY; YIELD; an anagram of OWN e.g. NOW, WON

disparage BELITTLE; DECRY; SLANDER

disparagement SLUR

disparaging CATTY; DEGRADING; anagram indicator

disparaging words LIBEL; SLANDER

dispassionate COLD

dispatch END; KILL; POST; REMIT; SEND; SLAY; anagram indicator

dispatched KILLED; SENT; SLAIN; SLEW; omission indicator

dispense ISSUE; METE

dispense with BIN; CHUCK; DITCH; DROP; DUMP; WASTE; omission indicator

dispensed anagram indicator

dispersed SPREAD; anagram indicator

dispersing anagram or nesting indicator

dispirited BLUE; LOW

dispiriting can indicate something to do with exorcism

displace OUST

displaced anagram indicator

display AIR; HANG; POMP; SHOW; SPORT; STALL; STAND; ■ ARRAY; PARADE; TABLE; anagram indicator; run indicator; can imply a word beginning with BE followed by an appropriate adjective as "Display humour, producing requisite for retiring camper" → BED ROLL (i.e. be droll)

display, brilliant FLASH

display, lavish RIOT

display of data TABLE

display of watches LED

display strong feeling EMOTE; RAGE; RANT

display, vain POMP

displayed AIRED; HUNG; anagram indicator

displayed in nesting indicator

displaying anagram indicator; nesting indicator

displaying, some nesting indicator

displeasure ANGER

disport PLAY

disposable anagram indicator

disposal SALE; anagram indicator

disposal, at one's USABLE

dispose of DROP; DUMP; EAT; SELL; ■ SETTLE

disposed anagram indicator

disposed, isn't anagram of ISNT

disposed of SOLD

disposes of omission indicator

disposing of anagram indicator

disposition MOOD; TEMPER; ■ NATURE; PENCHANT; anagram indicator

disposition, by anagram indicator

disprove REFUTE

dispute ISSUE; ROW; SPAR; SPAT; TIFF; WAR; WRANGLE; ■ BATTLE; BRAWL; DISCUSS

disqualified OUT; omission indicator

disquiet UNREST

disregard FLOUT; MISS; OMIT; ■ IGNORE; omission indicator

disreputable SEAMY; ■ GRUBBY

disreputable person RIP

disreputable newspaper RAG

disrespectfully to, speak DIS

disrobe BARE

disrupt BREAK; SHATTER; SPOIL; anagram indicator

disrupted TORN; anagram indicator

disrupting anagram indicator

disruption RUFFLE; anagram indicator

disruptions anagram indicator

disruptive anagram indicator

dissatisfaction IRE

dissatisfaction, expression of BOO

dissembling anagram indicator

disseminate, disseminated SPREAD; anagram indicator

disseminating, dissemination anagram indicator

dissent DEMUR; anagram indicator

dissenter REBEL

dissenters, group of FACTION; SECT

dissertation PAPER

dissident anagram indicator

dissipate WASTE; anagram indicator

dissipates, dissipated, dissipating anagram indicator

dissolute LOOSE; ■ RAKISH; anagram indicator

dissolute fellow/type RAKE

dissolving anagram indicator

dissuade DETER

distance CUBIT; GAP; METRE; MILE; STEP; ■ LEAGUE; *see* LENGTH, MEASURE

distance apart GAP

distance, at a/in the AFAR; AFIELD; BACK; FAR; REMOTE

distance, long LEAGUE

distance, short FOOT; FT; IN; INCH; YD

distance, some YARDS

distant AFAR; COLD; COOL; CHILLY; FAR; FARAWAY (i.e. far away); REMOTE; STRANGE

distend STRETCH

distilled, distilling anagram indicator

distinct CLEAR

distinction MARK; SIGN; ■ MERIT; RENOWN

distinction, add GILD

distinctive SPECIAL

distinctive atmosphere AURA

distinctive in style *see* STYLISH

distinguished EMINENT; GREAT

distinguishing feature CACHET

distort BUCKLE; COLOUR; MANGLE; TWIST; anagram indicator

distort signal SCRAMBLE

distorted BENT; anagram indicator

distorting anagram indicator

distortion BUCKLE; anagram indicator

distractedly, distraction anagram indicator

distraught DOWN; LOW; anagram indicator

distress HARROW; IRK; PAIN; REND; ■ AGONY; ANGST; MISERY; RUTH; anagram indicator

distress call SOS

distress, exhibit/show CRY; SOB; WEEP

distress, in anagram indicator

distressed NEEDY; SORRY; anagram indicator; like other words of the root 'distress', can refer to having hair cut, hair restorer etc

distressing BAD; TRAGIC; anagram indicator

distribute ALLOT; DEAL; SHARE; SOW

distributed anagram indicator

distributes cards DEALS

distributing anagram indicator

distribution SHARE; ■ DELIVERY; anagram indicator

distribution of papers ROUND

distribution of power GRID

district AREA; PATCH

District Commissioner DC

distrustful WARY

disturb MOVE; RATTLE; ROCK; SHAKE; STIR; anagram indicator

disturbance RIOT; ROUT; ■ DUST; RACKET; RUCTION; UNREST; UPSET; anagram indicator

disturbances anagram indicator

disturbed MOVED; SHAKEN; anagram indicator

disturbed by the word that follows to be nested

disturbing anagram or nesting indicator

disunited anagram indicator

disunited by nesting indicator

ditch DROP; DUMP; DYKE; MOAT; SCRAP; TRENCH

ditched partner EX

dither HOVER; WAVER

dithering anagram indicator

ditty SONG

diva MELBA

divan COUCH

dive DEN; DUMP; FALL; JOINT; PIKE; PLUNGE SINK; STOOP

dive in ENTER

diver PEARLER; SCUBA; can indicate something to do with a diving bird e.g. grebe

diverge SPLIT

diverging anagram indicator

diverging from centre RADIAL

divers VARIOUS

diversified, diversifying anagram indicator

diversion ANTIC; GAME; PLOY; SPORT; TRICK; ■ DETOUR; anagram indicator

diversion, active SPORT

diversionary ROUNDABOUT

divert AMUSE; TICKLE; anagram indicator

diverted AMUSED; anagram indicator

Dives Latin for rich man, so can indicate something to do with the legendary rich e.g. Midas, Croesus; ■ PLUTOCRAT

divide CLEAVE; CUT; FORK; PART; REND; SHARE; SPLIT

divided APART; RENT; SPLIT; TORN

divided about/by the word that follows to be nested

divider RULER

divine ANGEL; DD; HOLY; SACRED; *see* CRYSTAL-GAZING, PRACTISE

divine being GOD (qv)

divine location, in a component to be nested within RR

divine messenger ANGEL

divine revelation ORACLE

diving attempt HEADER

divinity GOD; *see* GOD, GODDESS

divinity graduate BD

divinity lesson RE

divisible by two EVEN

division ARM; CLASS; CLEFT; SECTION; SPLIT; RENT

division in church AISLE

divorce PART(ING); SPLIT

divorce, centre of RENO

divorce, one involved in EX

divorced APART

divorcee EX; can indicate something to do with Henry VIII

Dixie SOUTH

DIY AUTO

dizzy GIDDY; LIGHT; anagram indicator

DNA, some GENE

do ACT; APE; BASH; CHEAT; CON; COPY; FARE; PARTY; SLAY; STUDY; SUIT; TRICK; TURN; ■ DIDDLE; EXECUTE; FUNCTION; SERVE; TWIST; can signify a specific kind of party as "Do in" → AT-HOME

do at first D

do away with ANNUL; ERASE; KILL (qv)

do badly BOTCH

do battle FIGHT; WAR

do better BEAT; CAP; TOP

do business DEAL; TRADE

do good DOG (i.e. do-G)

do not DONT

do not give away KEEP (qv)

do something ACT

do well WIN; ■ PROSPECT; SUCCEED; THRIVE

do what you're told OBEY

do with, to ON

do without FAST; MISS; SKIP

do wrong ERR; SIN

do you have HAST

docile TAME

dock BERTH; CLIP; CUT; DETAIL (i.e. de-tail); LAND; LOP; PEN; PORT; MOOR; STOP (i.e. from pay); TAIL;

TRIM; WEED; ■ BASIN; HARBOUR; MARINA; SORREL; last letter to be omitted

docked CUT; last letter to be omitted

docket CHIT

doctor ALTER; D; DD; DOC; DR; FAKE; FIX; GP; INTERN; MB; MD; MO; PHD; RIG; TEND; TREAT; VET; WHO; ■ GALEN; FALSIFY; FIDDLE; HEALER; TITLE; anagram indicator; can indicate something to do with a renowned literary or fictional doctor e.g. Jekyll, Doolittle, Who, Strangelove

Dr Arnold HEAD

doctor, evil NO

Dr No MONO (i.e. MO-no)

doctor's charge CASE; PATIENT

doctor's time MOST (i.e. MO's T)

Dr Zhivago's lover LARA

doctors' army RAMC

doctored anagram indicator

doctoring SPIN

doctrine ISM

docudrama FACTION

document DEED; FORM; MS; PAPER; LIST; RECORD; SCREED; SLIP; TICKET; VISA; WILL; WRIT; ■ DIPLOMA (usually to make diplomat); REPORT

documents MSS

dodder REEL; TOTTER

dodderers anagram indicator

doddery AGED; OLD; anagram indicator

dodge AVOID; DUCK; ELUDE; EVADE; PLOY; RUSE; SCAM; SHIFT; TRICK; ■ RACKET

dodging anagram indicator

dodgy ICKY; IFFY; anagram indicator

Dodie SMITH

does ACTS; CHEATS; DEER; can indicate something to do with rabbits

does (old, Shakespearian) DOTH

does wrong ERRS; SINS; anagram of DOES

doesn't start first letter to be omitted

dog BASSET; BEAGLE; BITCH; BITER; CANIS; CHOW; CUR; FOLLOW; HOUND; HUSKY; LAB; MUTT; PET; POM; POODLE; PUG; PUP; SETTER; STRAY; TAG; TAIL; TRACK; TRAIL; ■ BARKER; BOW-WOW; BOXER; CAIRN; COCKER; COLLIE; DINGO; POINTER; POOCH; SHADOW; SPRINGER; YAPPER; can indicate a dog's name, popular examples being Fido, Lassie, Pluto, Rex, Rover, Spot; in the sense of "follow" can mean that one component is to follow another

dog, flea-ridden CUR

dog, hunting SETTER

dog, little D; PUP

dog's name FIDO

dog, oriental CHOW

dog, playful (cinematic, screen) PLUTO

dog, say PEAK; TALE

dog, wild DINGO

dog-wood CORNEL

dogfish NURSE

dogs, going to the anagram indicator

doing ACTION; ■ PLAN; WILL

doing badly anagram of DOING

doing one's own repairs DIY

doing time INSIDE

dole GIRO; METE; RATION; UB

dole money UB

dole out ALLOT; anagram indicator

doleful MOODY; SAD

doll MODEL

dollar BUCK; S

dollar, a ACCENTS (i.e. a hundred cents – A+C+CENTS – where C denotes a hundred)

dollars, lots of G

dollop LUMP

dolly SITTER

dolphins SCHOOL

dolt FOOL (qv); GIT; OAF

domain FIELD; REALM
dome CROWN
domestic DAILY; HOME; MAID; ■ INTERNAL; PRIVATE; *see* SERVANT
domestic animal CAT; DOG; PET
domestic appliance AIRER; IRON
domestic area HEARTH
domestic scene NEST
domesticate TAME
domesticated PET; TAME
dome can indicate something to do with the top of the head
dominant CHIEF; MAIN; SOL (mus.)
domination REIGN
dominate BOSS; RIDE
domineering BOSSY
dominion CONTROL
Domino* FATS
don DRESS; FELLOW; SENOR; WEAR; ■ ASSUME
Don *see* DON QUIXOTE
Don Quixote can indicate something to do with windmills, tilting, Sancho Panza, etc; can indicate the use of a Spanish word, as "Don Quixote's good-bye" → ADIOS
don't agree OBJECT
don't eat FAST
don't ever NEVER
don't follow LEAD
don't give up GOON (i.e. go on)
don't go REMAIN
don't keep ROT
don't let on SH
don't lose WIN
don't take LEAVE
don't take anything FAST
donation GIFT; GRANT; PRESENT
donation, made GAVE
donation, make GIVE
donations ALMS; GIFTS
done OVER; UP; ■ AGREED; TRICKED
done damage to anagram of DONE to be added to the end of a component (for example to

complete a verb in the past tense, as "sport done damage to" → PLAYED ON)
done, not RAW
done wrong ERRED; SINNED; anagram of DONE
donjon KEEP
donkey ASS; FOOL; JENNY; MOKE
donkey's cry BRAY
donor GIVER
dons can indicate something to do with Spaniards, e.g. armada or some other aspect of Spanish history; can indicate a Spanish word
don't go STAY
doodah, all of a anagram indicator
doom DEATH; FATE; RUIN
doomed FATED
door ENTRY; EXIT; GATE; HATCH; ■ ACCESS; POSTERN
door fastening LATCH; LOCK
door, part of HINGE; JAMB
doorkeeper *see* DOORMAN
doorman BOUNCER; USHER
doorpost JAMB
doors ENTRIES
doorway PORTAL; *see* DOOR
doorway, part of JAMB
dope ASS; CLOT; DRUG(S); GEN; GRASS; INFO; POT; SAP; TWIT; WEED; ■ TWERP
dope-taking a synonym such as GEN to be nested – *see* DOPE
dope-usage anagram of DOPE
dopey anagram indicator; *see* FOOLISH
dormant SLEEPING
Dorothy DOT; ■ DOLLY
dorsal BACK
Dorset town POOLE
dosage PILL
dose TREAT
dose of medicine TONIC
dosh *see* MONEY
doss SLEEP
dosser TRAMP
dossier FILE
Dostoevsky (Dostoyevsky) can indicate something to do with

IDIOT, CRIME, PUNISHMENT etc

dot POINT; SPECK; SPOT; ■ MARK; STIPPLE

dote on PET; ■ ADORE

dotty anagram indicator

double BI; DRINK; DUAL; FETCH (naut.); MATCH; SPIT; TWIN; TWICE; TWO; ■ BID (i.e. in bridge); COUPLE; DUPLE; FETCH; RING (i.e. darts); RINGER; can indicate that a letter or component should be repeated

double barrelled can indicate something to do with a hyphen

double bend S; Z

★ **double definition clue** a type of clue which is restricted to two definitions of the solution. Example: "Sit on youngsters" (5) → BROOD

★ **double-duty** some words in a clue have two functions. For example in "Direly enraged" (7), "en-raged" is the material for an ana-gram as indicated by "direly" and is also the synonym for the an-swer angered. Similarly in "Where fires start raging in exits" (ans: GRATES) "start" is part of the clue's definition ("Where fires start") and *also* an initial let-ter indicator requiring R (i.e. start of "raging"); similarly in "The odd grants may be increased by a quarter", the word "odd" serves as an anagram indicator of "grants" and also as the definition of the clue for which the answer is STRANGE

double first AA; II

007 (Double-o-seven)* AGENT

double up CREASE

doubled can indicate double letters

doubled capital can indicate that where L is the initial letter, it is to be replaced by C; similarly M to replace D

doubles can signal the repetition of an element

doublet can indicate double letters

doubt BUT; QUESTION; ■ QUERY

doubt, leave no ENSURE

doubt, little ER; UM

doubt, no CERTAIN; SURE

doubter SCEPTIC

doubtful IFFY; MIGHT; MOOT; ■ UNCLEAR; anagram indicator

doubtless CERTAIN; SURE; SURELY

dough PASTA; PASTE; can indi-cate something to do with money e.g. CASH, BREAD, TENDER

Douglas can indicate something to do with the Isle of Man e.g. Manx, tailless cat

dour GRIM

douse PLUNGE

Dover* PORT

dowdy DRAB

dowel PEG

down BELOW; BLUE; D; DRINK; FELL; FLAT; HILL; LOW; LOWER; NAP; OFF; OVER; OWING; PEAKY; SAD; SINK; UNDER; ■ DEEP; FEATHER(S); SWALLOW; WOLD; anagram indicator; when used with a verb can indicate a word-combination or phrase in-corporating LESS (e.g. "cut down" → DO LESS)

down-and-out TRAMP

down, bring TRIP

down, cast LOWER

down, go DIP; DROP

down-to-earth FALLEN; GROUNDED; REAL

down tools STRIKE

down with French ABAS (i.e. a bas)

downed in omission indicator

downed tools, having OUT

downfall DESCENT; DROP; RAIN; RUIN; anagram indicator

downgrade DEMOTE

downpour RAIN; STORM

downright SHEER

downsized last letter to be omitted

downstairs BELOW

downtown in a Down clue, can in-dicate either the reversal of a

word meaning town etc (e.g.
YTIC) or the reversal of a spe-
cific town/city as "downtown Los
Angeles" → AL

dowry DOT

doze NAP

dozen DOZ

drab DINGY; DOUR; DOWDY;
DULL; ■ TROLLOP; *see*
DREARY

drab surroundings, in a component to be nested within DOUR

Dracula COUNT

draft BILL; MS; PLAN; ROUGH;
SKETCH

drag DRAW; HALE; HAUL;
HEAVE; LINGER; LUG; PUFF;
PULL; TOTE; TOW; TRAIL;
can indicate something to do with
smoking

drag a leg LIMP

drag with force HALE

dragged into nesting indicator

dragon MONSTER

drain DRY; EMPTY; SEWER;
SPEND; SUCK; TAX; TIRE

drain off STRAIN

drainage scheme DITCH

drained ALLIN (i.e. all in); DRY

drake FLY

Drake BOWLER

dram NIP; TOT

drama FUSS; PLAY; NO; NOH; ■
OPERA

dramatic piece SCENE

dramatic, something OPERA;
PLAY

dramatically anagram indicator

dramatis personae CAST

dramatist GAY; PINTER; SHAW;
WILDE; YEATS; *see*
PLAYWRIGHT

draped anagram indicator

drapery CURTAINS

drastically anagram indicator

drat BOTHER; DAMN

draught SLUG; SWIG; TOT;
WIND; can indicate something to
do with a draught animal e.g.
DRAY; ■ MAN (i.e. in board
game); can indicate something to

do with beer as 'draughtsman'
might clue TAPSTER

draught, given a AIRED

draught, take a HUFF

draughthorse DRAY; PUNCH;
SHIRE

draughtsman DRAWER

draw DRAG; ENGAGE; EVEN;
LURE; PULL; SKETCH;
STRETCH; TAKE; TAP; TIE;
TOW; TRAIL; ■ ATTRACT;
DOODLE; ELICIT;
STALEMATE; can indicate
something to do with a cigarette,
smoking etc; [◊ BEAD; MATCH]

draw attention STRESS

draw liquid TAP

draw out anagram of DRAW; ■
EXTEND

draw up FRAME; WARD

drawback SNAG (qv); reverse indicator; especially it can indicate
that "draw" itself should be reversed (to get WARD) or a synonym such as "tie" (to get EIT);
see DISADVANTAGE

drawer PULLER; TILL; TOWER;
can indicate artist, pencil etc

drawer, cash TILL

drawer, top U (i.e. social status)

drawers SHORTS; can indicate
something to do with western
gunfighters; can indicate an item
of furniture with drawers e.g.
TALLBOY

drawing MAP; SKETCH;
TOWING; ■ TRACTION; *see*
ATTRACTIVE, DRAW

drawing in TYING

drawing instrument RULER

drawing, one good at can signify
a draught animal, shire horse etc

drawl SPEAK

drawn PINCHED

drawn up reversal indicator, so "is
drawn up" → SI, "was drawn up"
→ SAW etc

dray CART

dread AWE; FEAR; TERROR

dreaded FEARED

dreadful BAD; DIRE; ■ AWFUL;
SHOCKING; anagram indicator

dreadful (American) BUM
dreadful feeling ANGST
dreadful people SCUM
dreadful, person PILL
dreadful time HELL
dreadfully anagram indicator
dream FANCY; IDEAL;
TRANCE; WISH
dreamer BOTTOM (from 'Midsummer Night's Dream')
Dreamland NOD
dreamy MISTY
drear(y) BLEAK; DRAB; DULL
dreary experience DRAG
dredged up reversal indicator
dregs LEES; ■ GROUNDS
dress COVER; DECK; DON; FIG;
FROCK; GARB; GEAR;
GOWN; GROOM; HABIT;
LINE; ORDER; RIG; ROBE;
SACK; SARI; SHIFT; SKIRT;
SMOCK; SUIT; TOG; WEAR; ■
ALIGN; CLOTHE; GARNISH;
LIVERY; anagram indicator
dress, close fitting SHEATH
dress down BRAG; NOD;
SCOLD; ■ BERATE; PREEN
dress, exotic SARI
dress fussily PRIMP
dress, mean RAG
dress, short MINI; or it can indicate that the last letter of a synonym is to be omitted, hence
FROC, SKIR etc
dress up BRAG (i.e. garb reversed); DECK
dressed CLAD; DECENT;
ROBED; anagram indicator
dressed, badly RAGGED
dressed up anagram indicator
dressing LINT; SALVE; ■
GAUZE; PLASTER; ROBING;
SAUCE; TOPPING; anagram indicator
dressy SMART
drew TIED; TOWED
dribble SLAVER
dried AIRED; ARID
dried flower TEASEL
dried fruit RAISIN
dried grass HAY

dried out AIRED; anagram of
DRIED
dried up SERE
drier OAST; SPINNER; TOWEL;
■ AIRER; HORSE; TEA
CLOTH; TEA TOWEL
drift DUNE; GIST; ROAM;
STRAY; WANDER; YAW; ■
IMPORT; ROLL; TIDE
drill BORE; GYM; PE; PT;
SCHOOL; TEACH; TRAIN; ■
REHEARSAL; *see* EXERCISE
drill, army BULL
drill pioneer TULL
drilling WELL
drink ALE; BEER; BEVVY;
BRANDY; BREW; CAN; CHA;
CHAR; CHASER; CIDER;
COLA; CUP; DOUBLE;
DOWN; DRAM; FLIP; GIN;
GLASS; GROG; HALF; HOCK;
IT; JAR; LAGER; LASSI; LAP;
MAIN; MALT; MEAD; MED;
MILK; NECK (i.e. verb); NIP;
NOG; PEG; PINT; POND;
PORT; PUNCH; ROSE; RUM;
SACK; SAKE; SEA; SHANDY;
SHORT; SIP; SLING; SLUG;
STINGO; STOUT; SUP; SWILL;
TEA; TENT; TIPPLE; TOAST;
TOPE; TOT; WATER; WINE; ■
BOTTLE; CHASER;
CONSUME; CORDIAL; DROP;
KIR; LIQUOR; OCEAN;
PERRY; PORTER; POSSET;
POTION; QUAFF; RAKI;
SHAKE; SHERRY; SHRUB;
SNIFTER; SPIRIT; SQUASH;
TONIC; *see* WHISKY; can indi-
cate the name of a specific sea or
ocean
drink, addition to SODA
drink, after-dinner PORT
drink, amount of GILL; HALF;
PINT; TOT; ■ DOUBLE;
FINGER; TREBLE; *see* DRINK,
LITTLE
drink, ask for ORDER
drink, avoiding DRY; TT
drink, big BUMPER; *see* OCEAN
drink dispenser CUP; OPTIC
drink fast SWILL; ■ GULP

drink fit for the gods NECTAR
drink frequently TOPE
drink, fruit SQUASH
drink, give SERVE; WINE
drink in Japan SAKE
drink, large DOUBLE
drink large amount SWILL
drink, little D; DRAM; DROP; HALF; NIP; PEG; SHORT; TOT
drink, make BREW
drink, make a warming MULL
drink milk SUCKLE
drink, mixed SHRUB
drink, needing a DRY
drink, quick SWIG
drink reportedly AIL; BIER; BROO; SEE; SIDER; WHINE; ■ LICKER; MANE *see* REPORTEDLY
drink, small SIP
drink, soft POP
drink, source of GRAPE
drink, spiced PUNCH
drink, stiff TREBLE
drink to celebrate WET
drink up in a DC, a synonym for "drink" (qv) to be reversed, hence GORG, NIG etc
drinker SOT; TOPER; *see* DRUNKARD
drinking POTATION; nesting indicator
drinking, avoiding/not DRY; TT
drinking bout BENDER; BINGE
drinking den BAR
drinking establishment, place etc BAR; PUB, INN
drinking, fit for POTABLE
drinks for everyone ROUND
drinking session BENDER; BINGE; BOUT
drinks LAPS; ROUND; *see* DRINK
drinks, lots of ROUND; *see* DRINK
drinks order ROUND
drip BORE; FALL; GIT; LEAK; WIMP; ■ TRICKLE
dripping FAT
drips, lots of SPLASH

drive DR; EGG; GO; IMPEL; FORCE; LUST; PUSH; RAM; RUN; SPUR; STEER; TRIP; SPIN; URGE; ■ AVENUE; MOTOR; THRUST; [◊ TEST]
drive a point home NAIL
drive aimlessly TOOTLE
drive away/out CHASE; OUST ROUT; SHOO
drive back REPEL
drive down hard RAM
drive off REPEL; ROUT; SHOO; ■ ESTRANGE; REPULSE
drive off, we hear SHOE
drive out OUST
drive, prepared to FEED
drive through TOUR
drivel PAP; ROT
driver CLUB; ENGINE; HERD (as in shepherd); MOTOR; WOOD; ■ TEAMSTER
driver, demon TOAD (character in "Wind in the Willows")
driver, inexperienced L
driver, place for DICKY
driver's can indicate something to do with golf as "driver's place" → TEE
drivers AA; RAC
drivers, new LL
driving competition RALLY
driving, help for person TEE
driving, no condition for FOG
drizzle RAIN
droit CLAIM; RIGHT
droll FUNNY; MERRY; WITTY; WRY
drone HUM; IDLER
drool GUSH; SLAVER
droop FALL; FLAG; FLOP; HANG; SAG; TIRE; WILT; ■ DECLINE
drooping LIMP
drop BEAD; BIT; DIP; DRAM; DUMP; FALL; HANG; JUNK; LOSE; LOWER; OMIT; POUR; RAIN; SAG; SCRAP; SHED; SLIP; SLUMP; SPOT; TASTE; TEAR; TOT; ■ DECLINE; REJECT (qv); omission indicator; can signify an animal giving birth as "Drop a little lower" →

CALVE; can indicate something to do with a parachute drop; [◊ GUM]

drop a line ANGLE; FISH; WRITE

drop behind LAG

drop, little CC

drop of first letter indicator, as "drop of water" → W

drop off KIP; NAP; NOD; SLEEP

dropout PROD (i.e. anag.)

dropped FELL; SHED; anagram indicator; omission indicator

dropping in CALLING; IN to be omitted; nesting indicator

drops SPRAY

drops suspended can refer to icicle or stalactite

dross SCUM; SLACK; ■ REFUSE

drove CROWD; FLOCK; HERD; HOST; SENT

drove noisily ROAD (i.e. sound-a-like for RODE)

drover HUGH (opera)

drown DIE; KILL; ■ DELUGE; DRENCH

drowned valley RIA

drowsy, be NOD

drub BEAT

drubbing DEFEAT

drudge DEVIL; HACK; SERF; SLAVE; TOIL; TOILER; can indicate something to do with Dr Johnson

drudgery SWEAT; *see* TEDIOUS TASK

drug ACID; COKE; CRACK; CURE; DOPE; DOWNER; E; GRASS; H; HEMP; HORSE; POT; SMACK; SPEED; UPPER; WEED; ■ BANG; OPIATE; OPIUM; POPPER; SPLIFF; STEROID

drug-abuse anagram of DRUG

drug addict FIEND; JUNKIE; USER; *see* DRUG TAKER; [◊ TRIP]

drug agent NARC

drug dealer PUSHER

drug dose SHOT; SPLIFF

drug, hard CRACK

drug, having taken UP

drug injection E to be nested

drug, instance of E; *see* DRUG

drug-pusher DEALER

drug repeatedly, inject EE to be nested within component(s)

drug session TRIP

drug, soft POT

drug taker TRIPPER; USER; ■ JUNKIE

drug supplier DEALER; PUSHER

drugged STONED

drugs DOPE; *see* DRUG

drugs agent NARC

drugs, amount of DOSE; SHOT

drugs, on HIGH

drugs, take USE

drugs, taking USING

drugs, use of TRIP

drum BEAT; MASS; TAP; TUB; ■ NAKER; TABLA; [◊ ROLL; STICK]

drummer's performance ROLL

drunk BLIND; CUT; GONE; HAPPY; HIGH; LIT; LUSH; MERRY; OILED; RIPE; SOAK; SOT; STONED; TIGHT; TOPER; ■ BLOTTO; BOTTLED; CANNED; FULL; LOADED; PICKLED; PLASTERED; ROLLING; SMASHED; SOAKED; SODDEN; SOUSED; SOZZLED; SQUIFFY; STEWED; STINKO; TIDDLY; WINO; anagram indicator; can indicate that a word is slurred

drunk up in a DC, a synonym for "drunk" (qv) to be reversed, e.g. TOS, TUC etc

drunkard BINGER; BOOZER; LUSH; SOAK; SOT; SOUSE; TOPER; ■ DIPSO

drunken *see* DRUNK

drunken state, in a *see* DRUNK

dry AIR; ARID; BARREN; BORING; BRUT; SEC; SERE; THIRSTY; TT; can indicate something to de with being "on the wagon"

dry, become PARCH

dry land BANK; SHORE

dry off DRAIN

dry surroundings, in a component to be nested within TT

dry up FAIL; WITHER

dryer *see* DRIER

dual DOUBLE; can indicate that a component is to be repeated, or two components of similar meaning are to be used, probably consecutively

dub NAME

dubious FISHY; IFFY; ■ UNCLEAR; anagram indicator

dubious shape, in BLUR

dubiously anagram indicator

duchess MALFI

duck AVOID; BOB; DEAR; DIP; DODGE; DRAKE; ELUDE; FABRIC; LOVE; O; NIL; TEAL; TERN; ZERO; ■ EIDER; EVADE; SCAUP (bird); SCOTER; SMEE; WIGEON; [◊ DOWN]

ducking-stool [◊ WITCH]

ducks OO; OS

duct CHANNEL; FLUE; PIPE; TUBE; ■ CHANNEL;

dud BOMB; *see* FAILURE

dude CAT; DANDY; FOP; TOFF

Dudley LEICESTER

duds can indicate something to do with clothes

due FIT; FOR; OWED; OWING; ■ COMING; DESERT; EXACT; FITTING; PROPER

due course TIME

due to be recited ODE

due, when one is ETA

duel FIGHT

duet SONG; [◊ TWO; PAIR]

duff FAKE; PUDDING; anagram indicator

dug DELVED; MINED; TEAT

dug up UNEARTHED; anagram indicator

duke D; FIST

Duke of Milan PROSPERO

dull BLAND; DEAD; DENSE; DREAR; DRAB; DRY; FLAT; GREY; LAME; MAT; MATT; SLOW; TAME; THICK; TRITE; ■ BANAL; BLEAR; BLUNT; BORING; DINGY; DREARY; STUFFY

dull American GRAY

dull appearance MAT; MATT

dull brown DUN

dull for American GRAY

dull, go TARNISH

dull, grow FADE

dull person PUDDING

dull report CRUMP

dull speaker BORE

dull speech PROSE

dull writing PROSE; [◊ HACK]

dullard DUNCE

dumb MUTE; THICK

dumb show MIME

dumbfound STUN

dumbstruck AWED

dummy CLOT; MODEL; SAMPLE; SHAM; ■ COMFORTER; SUCKER; can refer to an exposed hand at cards, and so something to do with laying one's cards on the table

dump CHUCK; DROP; REJECT; TIP

dump in, dumped in nesting indicator

dumped SHED; *see* DUMP; omission indicator

dumping omission indicator

dumpster SKIP

dumpy SQUAT

dun DEMAND; HORSE

dunce ASS

Dundee CAKE

dunderhead ASS; D; DOLT

dune SAND

dunk DIP

dunking nesting indicator

duo BRACE; PAIR; TWO

dupe CHEAT; GULL; PAWN; STING; ■ FOOL (qv); SUCKER

duplicate COPY

duplication can call for a letter or component to be repeated, as "a second duplication" → ASS

duplicity CHEATING; LYING; TREASON; *see* SCAM; also note the compiler may be invoking the word's archaic meaning of "state of being double" as in the example "Craft necessarily entailing duplicity" to clue CATAMARAN

duration of, for the OVER
duress FORCE
Durham COW
during IN; ON; OVER; WHILE; WHILST; nesting indicator
during French EN
during the course of nesting indicator; *see* DURING
dusk, after NIGHT
dusky UMBER
dust ASH; CLEAN; DIRT
dust-free STUD
dust-up STUD (i.e. anag.)
duster FLAG
dustman can indicate something to do with Doolittle, the character in "My Fair Lady"
Dutch D; DU; WIFE; ■ MISSUS
Dutch coast HOOK
duty CHARGE; FEE; OFFICE; TAX; TOLL; ROLE; SHIFT; ■ EXCISE; JOB; ONUS; can indicate something to do with Customs and Excise
duty list ROTA
duty to pay, have a OWE
duty, without FREE
duvet QUILT
dwarf DOC; HAPPY; LITTLE; SLEEPY; SMALL; STAR; STUNT; TROLL
dwell ABIDE; LIVE; LODGE; RESIDE; STAY
dwelling ABODE; FLAT; HOME; HOUSE; SEMI; TENT; ■ CABIN; SHANTY
dwelling, crude SHACK
dwelling, one-roomed CELL
dwelling, small COT; HO
dye COLOUR; STAIN; TINT; ■ HENNA; INDIGO; WOAD
dying, be END
dyke DITCH; WALL
dyke-builder OFFA
dynamic DRIVING
dynamism GO
dynamite HE; TNT

dynasty HAN; HOUSE; KING; *see* HOUSE
dynamite HE
dysprosium DY

Ee

e-mails, unsolicited/unwanted SPAM
each APIECE; EA; EVERY; ONE; PER
'eadgear AT (i.e. 'at)
eager AGOG; AVID; FAIN; HOT; KEEN; PANTING
eagle ERNE
eagre BORE
ear INTEREST; LUG
ear, by homophone indicator
ear hairs TRAGI
ear, in one's homophone indicator
ear, of the/to do with the OTIC
ear, on the homophone indicator
ear, part of DRUM; LOBE
ear-piece MUFF
earl E; PEER
earlier AGO; BACK; PRE; PRIOR; preceding indicator
earliest can refer to the early years of a user (*see* EARLY) for example where "earliest form of transport" calls for PRAM
early AM; RATHE (from A.S.); consider the word 'early' carefully even when it is used in what appears to be its ordinary sense, for instance "early transport" may call to mind penny-farthings etc but it may be referring to the early years of its users e.g. pram, push-chair, "early costume" can refer to playsuit and so on; similarly an "early bird" can refer to a flying creature from the dinosaur age
early bird LARK
early hours, into the LATE

early in the morning IAM (i.e. one a.m.)

early light DAWN

early part of day AM; MORN

early piece PRELUDE

early stage ACTI (i.e. Act 1); PARTI (i.e. Part 1)

early stage of competition HEAT

early, very IAM (i.e. one a.m.)

earn GET; MAKE; MERIT; NET; PULL; WIND; ■ DESERVE; GAIN; WORK

earned MADE

earner PRO

earnest GRAVE; INTEREST; PLEDGE

earnest, in DEVOUT

earnings INCOME; INTEREST; PAY; WAGE

ears, all can indicate something to do with attending, listening etc

ears, by the homophone indicator

ears, of the OTIC

ears, on the homophone indicator

earshot homophone indicator

earth CLAY; DEN; DIRT; DUST; EA; HOLE; LAIR; LAND; SOD; SOIL; TERRA; ■ GLOBE; GROUND; PLANET; SETT; WORLD

earth, foot of SPIT

earth, piece of CLOD; PLOT; SOD; ■ DIVOT]

earth's crust SIMA

earth, sticky CLAY; MUD

earth, wet MUD

earthenware POTTERY

earthwork DYKE

earthwork builder OFFA

earthy COARSE; CRUDE; LUSTY

earthy pigment UMBER

ease FREE; RELENT; REST; sounding like E's this word can, with a homophone indicator, call for EE

ease, it's said EE

easel FRAME; STAND

easily anagram indicator

easily carried PORTABLE

easily led/manipulated/persuaded PLIANT

easily remembered CATCHY

east E; can indicate a component is to be used reading from right to left (i.e. east to west)

East Anglia, town in DISS

East Anglian BROADS

East End D; T; can also indicate that the initial H should be omitted from a word, or the final G from an -ing word (i.e. supposed East Ender's pronunciation)

East European SLAV; CROAT

east, from the reversal indicator, as "American marksman watched a man from the east" → DEADEYE (i.e. EYED-A-ED reversed)

East German OST

East London DON

east of can indicate that the last letter of the ensuing word is to be used

east of France EST

East, out E to be omitted

East Standard Time EST

east to west reversal indicator

Eastcheap can refer to a Shakespearean character associated with the area e.g. PISTOL

Eastender T (i.e. end of 'east')

Eastenders in the supposed manner of the speech of East End Londoners can denote the dropping of H, or that TH is to become F;

Easter PASCH; [◊ EGG; PASSION]

Easter, first Sunday after LOW

Easter, seventh Sunday after WHIT

Easter, some time before LENT

eastern, Eastern E

eastern game GO

eastern half of can indicate that the last half of the ensuing word is to be used

eastern representative EMP

eastern state can refer to an eastern state of the U.S. (e.g. VA) as well as an eastern country

Eastwood CLINT
easy LIGHT; LOOSE; PAT; SIMPLE; ■ COMFY
Easy capitalized in this way, can refer to the eponymous hero of Marryat's novel, hence midshipman, reefer etc
easy catch SITTER
easy pace AMBLE
easy piece* CAKE
easy shot/target SITTER
easy, take it IDLE; LOAF; REST
easy task CINCH
easy thing PIE
easy victory ROMP
easy-going PLACID
easy task CINCH; DODDLE
easy to raise LIGHT
eat BITE; DINE; ETCH; FEAST; FEED; GOBBLE; GORGE; GRAZE; SUP; TASTE; ■ CHAMP; CONSUME; INGEST; SWALLOW; TAKE; nesting indicator; [◊ MESS]
eat, a little to BITE
eat a lot PIG; see EAT GREEDILY
eat away ERODE
eat daintily PECK
eat grain PECK
eat greedily/ravenously CRAM; GORGE; SCOFF; WOLF
eat hurriedly BOLT
eat lavishly FEAST
eat leaves GRAZE
eat noisily CHAMP
eat out ETCH
eat quickly BOLT
eat ravenously PIG
eat sparingly PECK
eat too much GORGE
eatables FOOD; see FOOD
'eated OT (i.e. 'ot)
eaten DINED; ROTTED; ROTTEN
eater APPLE; BITER; DINER
eating FEAST
eating-house CAFE; CAFF
eating out ETCHING
eating-place MESS
eats FOOD; GRUB; TUCK; see EAT, FOOD; nesting indicator

eats late SUPPER
ebb DECLINE; FALL; FLOW; RUN; see DECLINE
ebbing reversal indicator
ebullient HEARTY
eccentric CAM (eng.); CAMP; CARD; CASE; CRANK; NUT; ODD; RUM; anagram indicator; ■ DOTTY; CHARACTER; OUTRE; WEIRDO
eccentric Oxford don can signify a spoonerism (after The Rev. Spooner, see Introduction)
eccentricity anagram indicator
ecclesiastic DD
ecclesiastical garment HABIT; ■ CASSOCK
echelon LEVEL
echo APE
eco-friendly GREEN
ecological GREEN
ecologically correct GREEN
economic development, place of rapid TIGER
economical, be see ECONOMISE
economies CUTS
economies, make SAVE
economise SCRIMP; ■ RETRENCH; SKIMP
economise, feel keen to MISER
economist BRIGHT; MILL; SAVER; ■ KEYNES
economy CUT; THRIFT
economy-minded TIGHT
economy of truth LIE
ecstasy BLISS; E
ecstasy, form of TRANCE
ecstatic HIGH; SENT; anagram indicator
eddy RIP; ■ CURRENT
Eden GARDEN
edge BITE; BLADE; BRIM; BRINK; END; HEM; INCH; LIMIT; LINE; LIP; MARGIN; RIM; SIDE; VERGE; ■ FRINGE; KERB; RIDGE; first or last letter indicator
edge, give HONE
edge, put on HONE
edge, rounded NOSING
edge, sharp BLADE

edged nesting indicator

edges first and last letters indicator

edges of first and last letters indicator; note it may be necessary to insert the implied AND as "edges of high" → H AND H = HANDH (on the way to building up HANDHOLD for instance)

edging nesting indicator

edgy JUMPY; TENSE

edict BULL; ORDER

Edinburgh Festival/audiences FRINGE

edit CHECK; EMEND; REVISE; anagram indicator

edited/editing anagram indicator

edition BOOK; ED; ISSUE; PRINT; ■ COPY; NUMBER; VERSION; anagram indicator

edition, special EXTRA

editor ED; can indicate something to do with LEADER

editor, lowly SUB

editorial LINE

editorial assistant SUB

editorial work, do EMEND; ISED (i.e. is Ed); SUB

educate SCHOOL; TEACH; TRAIN

educated ED; TAUGHT; TRAINED; ■ LITERATE

educated man DON; *see* GRADUATE

educated people LITERATI

education CLASS; ED; LEARNING; TRAINING

education, person of BA

educational establishment LSE; POLY; *see* COLLEGE, SCHOOL, UNIVERSITY

educational publication TES

educationalist, trained BED

Edward ED; NED; TED

Edward, King SPUD

EE with a homophone indicator can call for EASE

eerie WEIRD

efface DELE

effect CAUSE; END; TONE; ■ ENGINEER; IMPACT; anagram indicator

effect, general TONE

effect, had an BIT

effect, lasting SCAR

effecting can indicate that the definition immediately follows

effective NEAT; NET; NETT; TELLING; ■ ACTIVE

effective, are/be BITE; COUNT

effective, not LAME; *see* INEPT

effective, more BETTER

effective, was/were BIT

effectively, acted BIT

effectual SOUND

effeminate man CISSY

effeminate type PONCE

effervescent anagram indicator

efficient GOOD; ■ CLEAN

effigy BUST

effort PUSH; STRAIN; TRY; ■ DINT; TROUBLE; [◊ HERCULEAN]

effort, make STRAIN

effort, one making TRIER

effort, requiring HARD

efforts TRIES

effrontery FACE; *see* NERVE

effuse GUSH

effusive type GUSHER

'efty UGE (i.e. 'uge)

Egad!* OATH

egg DUCK; NIT; O; POKE; PROD; SPUR; URGE; ■ BOMB; CHEER; GOAD; PRESS; [◊ CUP; LAYER; TIMER]

egg collection CLUTCH

egg-farm BATTERY

egg-flip NOG

egg-head BRAIN(S); E

egg on PRESS; URGE

egg-part SHELL; WHITE; YOLK

egg-producer HEN; LAYER

egg-shaped OVOID

egg, size of an GLAIR (i.e. viscous substance)

eggs OVA; ROE; SPAT; SPAWN; ■ CLUTCH

eggs, produce LAY

ego I

egotist can indicate a word beginning with SELF

egotistical can indicate some construction involving I or ME

Egypt ET
Egypt once UAR
Egyptian COPT
Egyptian god RA; ■ HORUS
Egyptian river NILE
Egyptologist CARTER
eider DUCK
eight CREW; CUBE
eight German ACHT
eight, group of CREW; OCTET
eight, one over the COX
eight pints GALLON
eight short OCT
eighteen holes ROUND
eighteen, under MINOR
Eisenhower IKE; ■ DWIGHT
either way can indicate the answer
  is a palindrome (see *Introduction*)
eject BOUNCE; OUST; OUT
ejected OUT
eke out RATION
elaborate RICH; anagram indicator
elaborate, not PLAIN
elaborating anagram indicator
élan DASH; GRACE
elapse PASS
elastic YIELDING
elasticity GIVE
elate CHEER; DELIGHT;
  PLEASE
elation LIFT; ■ JOY; DELIGHT
elbow NUDGE
elder SENIOR; TREE
elderly AGED; OLD
elderly relative GRAN
elder, group of* WOOD
Eleanor ELLIE
elect OPT; PICK; VOTE
elected IN
election POLL; VOTE; ■
  BALLOT; OPTING; OPTION; [◊
  PRIMARY]
electoral division WARD
electoral process VOTE
electoral system PR
electric SHOCKING; anagram indicator
electric current AC; DC; I
electric tool DRILL
electric wire ELEMENT

electrical device BULB; FADER;
  FUSE; LAMP; LIGHT; PLUG;
  SWITCH
electrical fault SHORT
electrically dangerous LIVE
electrician GAFFER; SPARKS
electricity AC; DC; HYDRO;
  JUICE; MAINS; POWER
electricity, break in OUTAGE
electricity, discharge ARC
electricity supply *see*
  ELECTRICITY
electrified LIVE
electrify CHARGE
electrode ANODE
electronic communication IT
electronic component CHIP
electronic device BUG; CHIP;
  MODEM; TIMER
electronic point of sale EPOS
electronic tracking device TAG
electroplated EP
elegance CHIC; FLAIR; GRACE;
  STYLE
elegant CHIC; SMART; SPRUCE
elegant, make REFINE
elegy DIRGE; LAMENT
element ARGON; AS; FIRE;
  IRON; LEAD; NEON; PART;
  RADON; RESPECT; TIN; U; ■
  FACTOR; SPHERE; WATER;
  when a chemical element is specified, it usually calls for the use
  of the technical symbol for the element, AS for arsenic etc [◊
  PERIODIC; TABLE]
element, noble ARGON
elemental SPIRIT
elementary BASIC; PRIME; can
  indicate a chemical element; or
  something to do with the weather
elementary work PRIMER
elephant DUMBO; JUMBO
elevate RAISE
elevated HIGH; UP; reversal indicator, as "elevated knight" →
  RIS
elevated, not very LOW
elevated, was ROSE
elevation HILL; LIFT; MOUNT;
  reversal indicator; ■ UPLIFT

elevation, in reversal indicator
eleven II; SIDE; TEAM; XI; ■ ONE BY ONE
eleven abroad XI
eleven, before TEN
eleven, first K (i.e. position in the alphabet)
eleventh hour LATE
elf FAIRY; TROLL; ■ PIXIE
elfin SMALL
elicit DRAW; EXTRACT
elide CUT; OMIT
eliminate END; ERASE; OMIT; SCRATCH
eliminating omission indicator
elite BEST; CREAM; PICK; SAS; SELECT; TOP
elite body of troops SAS
Elizabeth BET; BETTY; ER; LIZ
elk MOOSE
elliptical OVAL; OVOID; anagram indicator
elocution DICTION
elope BOLT
elsewhere GONE; OFF; OUT; anagram indicator
elude AVOID; ESCAPE
elusive anagram indicator
emanate ISSUE; SPREAD
embankment DAM; DYKE
embargo BAN; BLACK; BLOCK; STOP
embark BOARD; ENTER
embark on military action ENGAGE
embarked OFF
embarking on nesting indicator
embarrass ABASH
embarrassed RED; SHY; anagram indicator
embarrassing anagram indicator
embarrassingly anagram indicator
embarrassment FLUSH; SCRAPE (qv)
embarrassment, in anagram indicator
embarrassment, show BLUSH
embarrassment, sign of BLUSH; FLUSH
embassy MISSION
embassy office CHANCERY

embattled anagram indicator
embed SET
embellish LARD
embellished anagram indicator
embellishment FRILL
embellishment, without PLAIN
embellishments DECOR
ember GLOWER
embers ASHES; CINDERS
embezzlement PECULATION (convenient for reaching the answer "speculation"); anagram indicator
emblem BADGE; CREST; LEEK; LOGO; MARK; ROSE
emblem of authority STAFF
emblem, spiritual TOTEM
emboss CHASE
embrace CLASP; GRASP; GRIP; HOLD; HUG; ■ CLINCH; CUDDLE; ENFOLD; ESPOUSE; run indicator; nesting indicator
embraced, embraces run indicator; nesting indicator
embraced by run indicator; nesting indicator
embraces nesting indicator
embracing nesting indicator
embrocation OINTMENT
embroidery CREWEL
embroidery, bit of PICOT
emcee HOST
emending anagram indicator
emerge ARISE; PEEP; SHOW
emergency NEED; SPARE (i.e. as an adj.)
emergency appeal SOS
emergency take-off SCRAMBLE
emigre EXPAT
Emily, Little EM
eminence HILL; MOUNT; PEAK; RIDGE; TOR; ■ STATURE; can refer to the name of a particular mountain
emissary LEGATE
emit ISSUE; SEND; SHOW
emmer WHEAT
emoted RAGED
emotion HATE; IRE; LOVE; PANG; ■ FEELING; PASSION

emotion, show CRY; SOB; WEEP
emotion, showed WEPT
emotion, showing no STOLID
emotional HOT ▪ INTENSE; TORRID
emotional, less DRIER
emotions, state of MOOD
emperor EMP; NERO; OTTO; TITUS; ▪ CAESAR; CSAR; HADRIAN; TRAJAN; TSAR
emphasis ACCENT; STRESS; TONE
emphasise ACCENT; STRESS
emphatically can indicate a word is to be repeated (as "Emphatically know how to dance → CANCAN)
empire-building anagram of EMPIRE
employ HIRE; USE
employed PAID; USED
employed in nesting indicator
employed, one HAND
employee HAND; MAN ▪ EARNER
employees MEN; STAFF; *see* STAFF, TEAM
employer BOSS; USER
employing anagram indicator; nesting indicator
employment JOB; PLACE; POST; USAGE; USE ▪ EXERCISE; TRADE
employment, in USED
empower ENABLE
emptied omission indicator, all but first and last letters of associated word to be omitted, as "emptied bottle" → BE
empty BARE; DRAIN; IDLE; VAIN; ▪ FLAT; HOLLOW; VOID; omission indicator where all but first and last letters of associated word to be omitted as "empty container" → CR; can also indicate the nesting of O within a word or component, as "Chap's empty complaint" clues MOAN (i.e. M-O-AN)
empty bed BD; CT
empty space VOID
empty talk GAS (qv)

empty threats BLUSTER
empty tin TN
Empyrean can indicate something to do with sky, heaven
emulate APE; COPY; MATCH
emulate betters WAGER
emulsion PAINT
enable ALLOW; LET; ▪ EMPOWER
enamour CHARM
encase SHEATHE
encased in nesting indicator
enchant CHARM; DELIGHT
enchantress CIRCE; FAIRY; SIREN; WITCH
enclose CORRAL; PEN; nesting indicator
enclosed ENC; nesting indicator
enclosed space YARD
enclosure CAGE; CIRCLE; ENC; ENCL; FOLD; PALE; PEN; PIT; RING; WALL; YARD; ▪ COMPOUND; CORRAL; FRAME; WEIR; [◊ GROUNDS]
enclosure, animal CAGE; CORRAL; PEN; POUND; STY; ZOO
enclosure, course RING
enclosure, small ENC; PEN; STY
encoded anagram indicator
encomium PRAISE
encompass/ed, nesting or run indicator
encompassed in nesting or run indicator
encompassing nesting indicator
encore AGAIN; BIS (mus.); MORE
encore, give an REDO; REPEAL
encounter FACE; INCUR; MEET; [◊ BRIEF; COWARD]
encounter, brief can indicate something to do with Noel Coward
encountered MET
encountered in nesting indicator
encourage BACK; CHEER; EGG; PRESS; PROD; PUSH; URGE; ▪ HEARTEN; INCITE
encouragement FILIP; NUDGE; PUSH; can indicate a word beginning with DO (as "encourage-

ment to take a chance" signals DOWAGER)

encouragement, give/provide CHEER; INSPIRE; *see* ENCOURAGE

encouragement (word of) DO (as in "Old woman's encouragement to take a chance" gives DOWAGER)

encroachment INROAD

encrypted a component to be nested within CODE

end AIM; BACK; BOUND; CHECK; CLOSE; DEATH; DIE; EDGE; EXPIRE; FINIS; GOAL; LAST; RUIN; STOP; TAIL; TIP; Z; ■ CLOSURE; CURTAINS; DESIGN; EXTREME; FINALE; OBJECT; OMEGA; indicator of first or last letter(s); in conjunction with a homophone indicator the sound of the last letter or letters of a word may be required, for instance "told about family's end" clues WISE (i.e. y's).

end, came to an DIED; STOPPED

end, come to an DIE

end, from end to THROUGH

end of last letter indicator (as "back of queue" clues E)

end of book FINIS; K

end of game MATE; ■ WHISTLE

end of piece, wood TENON

end of sequence E; Z; ■ OMEGA

end of the E

end of the line, at the can indicate the name of a specific railway station

end, towards the LATE

end up LAND; MIA (i.e. reversal)

endearment, term of PET

endeavour ATTEMPT; TRY

Endeavour MORSE

ended DONE; OFF; OVER; UP

ending CODA; DEATH; last letter indicator; ■ OUTRO (mus.); TERMINATION

ending, game's MATE

endless EVER; S (i.e. end of the word itself); last letter(s) to be omitted from associated word;

can indicate that first and last letters of the succeeding word are omitted (example: "endless lines" → INE)

endless

endorsement OK; STAMP; ■ APPROVAL; VISA

endless fuss D; FUS

endlessly AY; EVER; last letter(s) to be omitted from associated word; can indicate that both first and letters are to be omitted

endorse BACK; OK; RATIFY; SECOND; SIGN

endorsement OK

endowed GIVEN

ends indicator of first and last letters

endue CLOTHE; INVEST

endurance, show LAST; *see* ENDURE

endure BEAR; LAST; STAND; STICK; WEAR; ■ SUFFER; TOLERATE

enduring LASTING; LONG; STABLE; STEADY

Endymion poet KEATS

enemy FOE; TIME

energetic person DOER; GOER

energise POWER

energy DRIVE; E; ELAN; GO; LIFE; PEP; POWER; STEAM; VIM; ■ OOMPH; ZING

energy, amount of KW

energy, conserving E to be nested within a component

energy, full of LUSTY

energy, lacking TIRED; WEAK; letter E to be omitted

energy-provider BATTERY; CHARGER; can indicate a water-wheel, mill-race etc; also *see* ENERGY, SOURCE OF

energy, source of COAL; E; GAS; OIL; ■ PETROLEUM

enfold HUG

engage BOOK; CHARM; DRAW; ENLIST; HIRE; LOCK; MESH; SIGN

engaged PLEDGED

engaged, become PLIGHT

engaged by nesting indicator

engaged, get MESH

engaged in AT; nesting indicator;

engagement ACTION; DATE; WAR; can indicate something to do with battle, fighting, sporting contest, etc

engagement, one fixing (making) FIANCE

engagements, series of WAR

engaging nesting indicator

engender BREED

engenders anagram indicator

engine LOCO; MOTOR; TRAIN

engine cover BONNET

engine failure STALL

engine, increase speed of REV

engine, part of SUMP

engine's sound WHIRR

engineer CE; EFFECT; ENG; SAPPER; WATT; ■ BRUNEL

engineering anagram indicator

engineering graduate BE

engineers CES; RE; REME

England E; ENG; REALM

English E; ENG

English Channel EDUCT

English Channel, part of SOLENT

English coins EP

English in Spain INGLES

English navy ERN

English, Old OE

Englishman abroad/in Australia POM

engrave CHASE; ETCH; STAMP

engrave into, to nesting indicator

engraver BLAKE; ETCHER

engraver, work of CHASING; ETCHING

engraving PRINT

engrossed RAPT

engulf SWAMP

enjoin ORDER

enjoy DIG; HAVE; LIKE; LOVE; SAVOUR

enjoy book READ

enjoy life BE

enjoyable FUN

enjoyable time BALL; FLING; PARTY

enjoyment FUN; GLEE; KICK

enjoying, show sign of GRIN; SMILE; ■ LAUGH

enjoys HAS

enlarge BLOAT; FATTEN; GROW; INCREASE; SWELL

enlarged, become GROW; INCREASE

enlightened WISE

enlightenment can indicate a light source e.g. lamp; lamppost etc

enlist JOIN

enlist support, try to CANVASS

enlisted in nesting indicator

ennoblement ERMINE

enormous HUGE; MEGA; OS; VAST

enough AMPLE; ENOW

enough, had/having had SATED

enough, not UNDER

enquire ASK

enquiry can indicate that the answer is in the form of a question and so is likely to begin with an interrogative pronoun (what, where, where, etc); if the answer is one word then it may mean the answer itself is simply an interrogative (what, etc)

enraged IRATE; MAD; ■ ANGRY; anagram indicator

enraptured SENT

enrobe CLAD; CLOTHE

enrol MUSTER

ensconced nesting indicator

ensemble anagram indicator; *see* GROUP

enshroud COVER; HIDE; VEIL

ensnare TRAP (qv)

ensnared, ensnares, ensnaring nesting indicator

ensue COME; FOLLOW

ensure SEE

ENT specialism EAR

entangled anagram indicator

entanglement KNOT

entangling anagram indicator

enter LIST; LOG; START; ■ LAY; PIERCE

entered WENT; nesting indicator; ■ INCAME (i.e. in came)

entered by nesting indicator

entering nesting or run indicator
enterprise DRIVE; GO; ■ SPIRIT; VENTURE
enters nesting indicator
entertain AMUSE; FETE; HOST; TREAT; ■ DIVERT; HARBOUR; REGALE; nesting indicator
entertain lavishly FETE
entertained nesting indicator
entertainer ARCHIE (Osborne character, first name); ARTISTE; COMIC; HOST; RICE (Osborne character, second name); STAR; SINGER
entertainer, radio DJ
entertaining FUN; FUNNY; anagram indicator; nesting indicator
entertaining person CARD; HOST
entertainment FAIR; FUN; PANTO; PLAY; PORT (Gael.); REVUE; SHOW; TREAT; ■ SPECTACLE
entertainment, free TREAT
entertainment, place of (venue etc) CLUB; FAIR
entertainment, provide REGALE
enthral HOOK
enthralled by nesting indicator
enthralling nesting indicator
enthuse FIRE; RAVE
enthusiasm FAD; FIRE; GO; GUSTO; MANIA; RAGE; ZEAL; ■ ENERGY; SPIRIT
enthusiasm, exude GUSH
enthusiasm, feel BURN
enthusiasm, filled with FIRED; can indicate that GO is to be nested within a component
enthusiasm, show LIKE; LOVE
enthusiasm, wild RAVING
enthusiast BUFF; FAN; NUT; ■ ADDICT
enthusiast, keen NUT
enthusiastic AVID; HEARTY; HOT; INTO; KEEN; MAD; MANIC; WARM; ■ CRAZY
enthusiastic about INTO
enthusiastic, not *see* UNENTHUSIASTIC

enthusiastic, someone *see* ENTHUSIAST
entice BAIT; DRAW; LURE; TEMPT
enticement BAIT; DRAW; LURE
enticed LED (ON)
entire ALL; FULL; WHOLE
entire range AZ
entirely ALL; CLEAN (as in "clean cut"); QUITE
entitled can indicate something to do with the peerage, or a book title; ■ ALLOWED; NAMED
entitled, be DESERVE
entitled, one LADY; *see* NOBLE
entitlement RATION; RIGHT; SHARE (qv)
entitlement, legal LIEN
entomb INTER
entourage TRAIN
entrance ADIT; DOOR; CHARM; GATE; PASS; ■ APPEARANCE; BEWITCH; DELIGHT; ENCHANT; MOUTH; PORCH; PORTAL; nesting indicator; initial letter indicator
entrance hall FOYER; LOBBY
entrance to initial letter indicator
entranced RAPT
entrap CATCH; NET; TRICK
entreat ASK; BEG; PLEAD; PRAY
entreaty PLEA; PRAYER
entrée COURSE; STARTER
entries GATE; GATES
entry DOOR; GATE; ITEM; PASS; ■ ADMISSION; COMPETITORS; INGRESS; LOBBY; nesting indicator
entry in ledger ITEM
entry permit PASS; TICKET; VISA
entwined anagram indicator
enumerate COUNT; DETAIL; LIST
envelope SAE
envelope, put in WRAP
envious GREEN; ■ JEALOUS
envious, be COVET

environment HOME; MILIEU; SETTING; nesting indicator, as "in modern environment" requires a component to be nested within NEW or RECENT

environment, concerned with GREEN

environmental GREEN

environmentally-friendly GREEN

environmentalist GREEN

environs of first and last letters indicator

envisage SEE

envy COVET; RESENT; SIN

ephemeral DAY

epic BIG; GRAND; SAGA; STORY; VERSE

epidemic RIFE; SARS; ■ PLAGUE

epidermic eruption BOIL; PIMPLE; SPOT

epiglottis FLAP

epilogue END

episode EVENT; PAGE; STORY

epistle ELI; EP; LETTER; TIM

epistler PAUL; PETER

epitaph RIP

Epsom* SALTS; can indicate something to do with the racecourse, racing etc

equal EVEN; LIKE; MATCH; PEER; ■ EGAL

equal outcome DRAW; TIE

equal to, be MATCH

equalised EVEN

equality PARITY

equally AS

Equator LINE

equestrian RIDER

equine establishment STUD

equip ARM; KIT; RIG; SUPPLY

equipment GEAR; KIT; PLANT; RIG; TACKLE; ■ CLOBBER; FITTING; can indicate some kind of instrument (qv)

equipment, provide KIT

equipment, riding TACK

equipment, winter sports SKI

equipped KITTED; RIGGED

equipped, dangerously ARMED

equitable FAIR; JUST; RIGHT

equity RIGHT; SHARES

Equity UNION

equity, in accordance with JUST; *see* EQUITABLE

er UM

era AGE; TIME

era, our AD

eradicate omission indicator

erase WIPE

'ere ENCE

erect BUILD; PITCH (i.e. tent); RAISE; ■ STANDING

erected UP; reverse indicator

ergo SO

eric FINE

Eric AMBLER

erica HEATHER

ermine STOAT

erne EAGLE

Ernest ERN

'ero ECTOR

erode EAT; ROT

eroded edges, with first and last letters to be omitted

eroding anagram indicator

Eros LOVE; [◊ CIRCUS]

Eros, beloved of PSYCHE

erotic SEXY; STEAMY

erotic desire EROS

err FALL; SIN; SLIP; STRAY; ■ WANDER

errand MISSION; TASK; ■ ORDER

errant anagram indicator

erring SINNING; SLIPPING; anagram indicator

error BLIP; BOOB; BUG; FLAW; GAFFE; LAPSE; OUT; SIN; SLIP; TYPO; ■ BISH; BLOOMER; BLUNDER; OMISSION; OVERSIGHT; WRONG

error, in AMISS; ASTRAY; OUT; ■ WRONG; anagram indicator

error, minor BLIP

erroneous, erroneously anagram indicator

ersatz FAKE

Erse IRISH

erstwhile EX; LATE; OLD; ■ FORMER

erupt FLARE; anagram indicator

erupting anagram indicator

eruption RASH; SPOT

escalation RISE; SURGE

escapade ANTIC; STUNT

escape AVOID; BOLT; BREAK; ELUDE; FLEE; FLIGHT; FLY; GO; LAM; LEAK; RUN; VENT; [◊ OUT]

escape (US) LAM

escape, arrange SPRING

escape, means of OUT

escape mechanism RELEASE

escape, narrow SQUEAK

escaped FLED; FLEW; GONE; WENT

escaping out of omission indicator

escarp SLOPE

eschew AVOID

escort BEAU; BRING; DATE; LEAD; SQUIRE; TAKE; USHER; [◊ SHIP]

escorted LED; TOOK

escorting nesting indicator

esker RIDGE

Eskimo INUIT

especially ESP

espionage activity BUGGING

espionage device BUG

espouse BACK; ■ CHAMPION; EMBRACE; MARRY

esprit WIT

espy SPOT; NOTE

essay GO; TRY WORDS; ■ ARTICLE; PAPER; THEME; anagram indicator

essayist ELIA (pen-name of Lamb); LAMB; STEELE; ■ BACON

essence CORE; GIST; GUTS; HEART; NUB; OIL; POINT; ROOT; SCENT

essential BASIC; KEY; MUST; ROOT; VITAL; can indicate that the middle letter of a word is to be used as "what's essential to house" signals U, and "minimum essential" → NIM

essential data see ESSENCE

essential element PITH; THREAD; see ESSENCE

essential for (in, to) run indicator

essential ingredients only the middle letters of a word to be used as "essential ingredients of meal" clues EA

essential oil OTTO; ■ ATTAR

essential quality see ESSENCE

essential, something MUST

essentially this can mean that the middle of a word is to be used; more rarely, and a little more complicated, it can mean that the middle run **between** two words constitutes the necessary set of letters as "Essentially Royal Society rescheduled party" cues an anagram of ALSOCI leading to SOCIAL

essentially wasted middle letter(s) to be omitted

essentials anagram indicator

establish FOUND; DEFINE; FIX; FORM; ROOT; SET; SETTLE; ■ DEPLOY; INSTIL

established E; EST; HARD; SET; STABLE; SURE; ■ FIXED; PROVEN

established actor, performer STAR

established, more OLDER

established, was DWELT

establishment BODY; CE; FIRM; PLACE; STAFF; ■ FOUNDATION; FOUNDING; LOCATION; see RESIDENCE;

Establishment SYSTEM

establishment, anti- RED

establishment, small COTTAGE

estate CAR; EST; LAND; MANOR; ■ GROUNDS

estate, cattle RANCH

estate manager STEWARD

esteem RATE; ■ HONOUR; REGARD; RESPECT; SALUTE; VALUE

estimate ASSESS; COST; RATE; THINK; ■ GUESS

estuary HUMBER

ET ALIEN

etch EAT

eternally EVER
eternity AGE; AGES; EON
ethical MORAL; RIGHT
ethical standards CODE
ethics, of MORAL
Ethiopian prince RAS
ethnic group RACE; TRIBE
ethos SPIRIT
etiquette CODE(S); FORM
eulogise PRAISE
euphoria BLISS
euphoric HIGH; anagram indicator
euphoric feeling/state HIGH; RUSH
Euphrates city UR
euphuist LYLY
Europe EC; EU; EUR
European E; EC; EUR; can indicate a European nationality e.g. BALT, DANE, FINN, GREEK, LAPP, POLE, SLAV, ROMAN
European city PARIS; ROMA; ROME; TURIN
European Commission EC
European, East SERB
European, from a can indicate a European word as "discouraging sign from a European partner" cues NON
European, North LAPP
European, northern LETT
European Parliament EP
European project EMU
European question EQU; *see entries under* FRANCE *and* FRENCH
European said CHECK (i.e. homophone of CZECH)
European river ODER; *see* RIVER
European's voiced CHECK
European Union EU
European, we hear CHECK
evade AVOID; DODGE; PARRY
evaluate ASSESS; APPRAISE; MARK; RATE; SCORE
evaluation MARK; RATING; SCORE
evangelist JOHN; LUKE; MARK
evasion PARRY

evasive COY; SHIFTY; ■ SLIPPERY
evasive, appear SHUFFLE
even EEN; ENE; FLAT; FLUSH; IRON; LEVEL; PAR; PLANE; SLACK; SQUARE; STILL; YET; ■ JUST; QUITS; REGULAR; UNIFORM
even if THOUGH
even in can indicate that the even letters be taken from the word that follows (as "even in Bedlam" clues ELM)
even now STILL; YET
even so BUT
even-tempered EQUABLE
even the score AVENGE
even though IF
even up ALIGN
evening EEN; EVE; LATE; NIGHT
evening in Paris SOIR
evening out can indicate something to do with ironing
evening wear GOWN; TAILS
evenly the even-numbered letters to be used or omitted
evensong SERVICE
event DO; FETE; HEAT; PARTY; RACE; RALLY; RESULT; ■ CONTEST; INCIDENT
event, distance MILE
eventually LATER
ever AY; AYE (Mid. Eng.); KEEPS
ever-changing anagram of EVER
Everest MOUNT; PEAK
every EA; EACH; PER
every one PER
every respect, in FULLY
every second can indicate that only the even-numbered letters of the indicated words are to be used (as "Vessel just being still every second" → UTENSIL)
every side, on ROUND
every thoroughfare EAST
every year PA
everybody ALL
everybody else REST
everybody in France TOUT

everybody is about the word (or component) which follows to be nested within ALL

everyone ALL; E; EACH; WORLD

everyone, concerning NATIONAL

everyone, for APIECE

everything ALL; LOT; POT; SUM; TOTAL; TOUT; ■ THE LOT

Evesham area VALE

evict OUST

evidence CLUE; PROOF; SIGN; TRACE; ■ GROUND; GROUNDS; HINT

evidence of debt IOU

evidence of disease RASH

evident CLEAR; PLAIN; OVERT; ■ OBVIOUS

evident in, among, etc run indicator; anagram indicator

evident therein run indicator; nesting indicator

evil BAD; BASE; CRIME; HARM; ILL; MALIGN; SIN; VICE; VILE; WRONG; anagram indicator

evil act CRIME; SIN

evil doer IMP

evil event CRIME

evil woman WITCH

evince SHOW

evolution anagram indicator

evolve CHANGE; anagram indicator

ewer JUG

ewes sounding like U's this word can, with a homophone indicator, call for UU

ex LATE; OLD; ■ FORMER; PREVIOUS

ex- *see* EX

ex officio EO

ex-PM DERBY; *see* PRIME MINISTER

ex-rail BR

ex-student GRAD; OB

exact DUE; EVEN; RIGHT; ■ DEMAND; PRECISE

exactly DUE

exaggerate STRETCH; can signpost a word beginning with OVER

exaggerated CAMP; OTT; ■ STRETCHED; can signpost a word beginning with OVER

exalt PRAISE

exalted HIGH; RAISED; UP; reverse indicator; can indicate something to do with a means of being elevated e.g. being on stilts

exalted, not LOW

exam *see* EXAMINATION

exam answer(s) SCRIPT

exam, get through PASS

exam, repeat RESIT

exam result GRADE; MARK; MERIT; SCORE

exam, second go at RESIT

exam success PASS

exam, take SIT

exam, took SAT

examination AUDIT; CHECK; MOCK; MOT; ORAL; PAPER; SCAN; STUDY; TEST; TRIAL; VIVA; ■ ASSAY; HIGHER; MEDICAL; PHYSICAL; PRELIM; SEARCH; VETTING; anagram indicator

examination body BOARD

examination, medical SCAN

examine CASE; CHECK; EYE; SCAN; STUDY; TEST; TRY; VET

examine cursorily SKIM

examine judicially HEAR; TRY

example CASE; IDEAL; MODEL; ONE; ■ INSTANCE; LESSON

example, by way of SAY

example, fine ONER

example, following AFTER

example, for AD; EG; SAY

exams FINALS

exams, those setting BOARD

exasperate ANGER; BAIT; GALL; TRY

exasperation IRE

excavate DIG; DISINTER

excavation DIG; MINE; PIT; QUARRY

excavations, do DIG

exceed TOP; ■ CAP; OUTDO; SURPASS; can indicate a verbal phrase ending in OVER (e.g. go over)

exceeding OVER

excel BEAT; CAP; SHINE; STAR; TOP; can indicate a word beginning with OUT-, as "excel in egg production" → OUTLAY

excelled LED

excellence CLASS

excellent ACE; AI; BEST; CLASS; COOL; DIVINE; FAB; FINE; GOOD; GRAND; GREAT; MEGA; PRIME; RIPPING; STRONG; SUPER; TOP; TOPPING; ■ BRAVO; GOLDEN; RARE; SUPERB

excellent one ACE

excellent position FIRST; LEAD; TOP

excellent, something really TOPPER

excellent specimen RATTLER

excellent thing PEACH

except BAR; BUT; SAVE

exception BAR

exception of BUT; SAVE

exceptional RARE; SUPER; ■ ESPECIAL; NOTABLE; anagram indicator

exceptionally anagram indicator

exceptionally good RARE

excerpt PART; SCRAP

excess GLUT; OTT; SPARE; [◊ OVER]

excess, in OVER

excess, to can indicate a verb beginning with OVER

excessive HIGH; OTT; THICK; UNDUE; WILD; can indicate the use of TOO; can indicate a word beginning with OVER

excessive amount LASHINGS

excessively OTT; OVER; TOO; ■ UNDULY; can indicate an element to be repeated

excessively high STEEP

excessively large OS

exchange BARTER; DEAL; SWAP; SWITCH; SWOP; TRADE; TRUCK; ■

CONVERSION; anagram indicator

exchange of words can indicate something to do with translation

exchange, Parisian stock BOURSE

exchange rate anagram of RATE

excising omission indicator; can indicate something to do with tax

excite INFLAME; ROUSE; ROUST; WOW

excited AGOG; ASTIR; HOT; RANDY; SENT; UP; anagram indicator

excited expression WHEE

excited, get PEP; WHET; WOW

excited state FEVER; FLAP; TIZZY; WHIRL

excited, unnaturally MANIC

excitedly anagram indicator

excitement ADO; BUZZ; FEVER; FLAP; HEAT; HUM; KICK; STIR; THRILL; ZING; ■ FERMENT; MUST (i.e. amongst animals)

excitement, cause AROUSE

excitement, in a state of AGOG

excitement in Ireland TRILL

excitement of anagram indicator

excitement, sense of BUZZ

exciting HOT; anagram indicator

exclaim CALL; CRY; ■ SHOUT; YELL; *see* CRY

exclamation AH; AW; CRY; GOSH; HA; MY

exclamation of annoyance BOTHER; DRAT

exclamation of disapprobation TUT

exclamation of disapproval BOO; TUT

exclamation of dismay LOR

exclamation of distaste UGH; YUCK

exclamation of joy WHEE

exclamation of pain OUCH; OW

exclamation of surprise, pleasure AH; BOY; COR; GEE; MY; WOW

exclamation, Spanish OLE

exclamation, vexed PHEW

exclude BAN; BAR; BLACK; DEBAR

excluded ALONE; OUT

excluding EX; NO; omission indicator

exclusion BAN; BAR

exclusion order BAN

exclusive INNER; SOLE; SCOOP

exclusive group ELITE; SET

exclusively WHOLLY; ■ SOLELY

excrement, piece of PAT

excursion DRIVE; OUTING; TOUR; TRIP

excuse ALIBI; PLEA; REASON; ■ OUT; PRETEXT

execute ACT; DO; HANG; KILL; TOP; ■ IMPLEMENT

executed initial letter to be omitted, as "executed villain" → ROOK

execution can indicate CAPITAL (as in capital punishment); can indicate the first letter is to be omitted as "The issue is execution for treason" → EDITION (i.e. initial S omitted)

execution, means of ROPE

executive EXEC; SUIT

executive, chief DG

exemplary EG; IDEAL; MODEL

exempt FREE; ■ CLEAR

exemption WAIVER

exercise APPLY; BIKING; DRILL; EXERT; JOG; PE; PT; RUN; SPORT; TRAIN; USE; WIELD; anagram indicator; ■ EMPLOYMENT; OPERATION; RUNNING

exercise choice PICK; SELECT

exercise regime, follow TRAIN

exercise soldiers DRILL

exercise, do SKIP

exercised anagram indicator

exercises USES; YOGA; anagram indicator

exercising anagram indicator

exercising, person USER

exercising power REGNANT

exert EXPEND

exert force PRESS

exertion, show PANT

exhaust DRAIN; TIRE; WEAR; ■ POOP

exhausted ALLIN (i.e. all-in); BEATEN; DEAD; OUT; HOT; SPENT; TIRED; USED; WAN; WHACKED; in the sense of being "well-worn" can indicate words such as TRITE

exhaustion WEARINESS

exhibit BOAST; HANG; SHOW

exhibit distress CRY; SOB; WEEP

exhibited in run indicator

exhibition EXPO; FAIR; SHOW; SPECTACLE; anagram indicator

exhibition centre NEC

exhibition equipment STAND

exhibitor SHOWER

exhort *see* URGE

exile DEPORT; EJECT

exist AM; ARE; BE; LIVE

existed BEEN; LIVED; WAS; WERE

existed previously WAS

existence LIFE

existence, have *see* EXIST

existing BEING

existing circumstances ASIS

exists IS; LIVES

exit DIE; DOOR; GATE; EGRESS; GO; LEAVE; LEAVING

exonerate CLEAR

exotic ALIEN; anagram indicator

exotic, we hear ALIAN

expand DILATE; GROW; PAD; SWELL

expanse SEA; SPREAD; STRETCH

expansion SPREAD; SWELL STRETCH; ■ SWELLING

expansive VAST; WIDE

expatiate ENLARGE

expatiate on RAMBLE

expect AWAIT; HOPE

expectant AGOG; in relation to a person (e.g. hero) can indicate something to do with Dickens' 'Great Expectations' e.g. PIP

expectantly AGOG

expectation HOPE; ■ PROSPECT

expectation in a component to be nested within HOPE

expected DUE; PAR; ■ LABOUR; NORMAL

expected time of arrival ETA

expected to win TIPPED

expecting HOPING; ■ IN THE CLUB; PREGNANT; UP THE SPOUT

expectorate SPIT

expedition HASTE; MISSION; TOUR; TRIP; ■ DESPATCH

expedition, with FAST; can indicate that something is done quickly e.g. 'move with expedition' can clue RUN, RUSH

expel EJECT; OUST; OUT; REMOVE

expelled RID

expels omission indicator

expend EXERT

expense COST; PRICE; RENT

expense, bear the AFFORD

expenses EXES

expensive DEAR; HIGH; STEEP

expensive coat FUR

expensive, not CHEAP; FRUGAL

expensive, now more UP

experience FEEL; HAVE; KNOW; LIVE; MEET; SEE; SENSE; SUFFER; TASTE; TOUCH; TRY; USE; ■ ENCOUNTER; WISE

experience, brief SAMPLE; TASTE

experience, dreary BIND; CHORE; DRAG; FAG

experience, harrowing ORDEAL

experience life BE

experience, short of GREEN; RAW

experience strong emotion BURN

experience, without GREEN

experienced ABLE; FELT; HAD; KNEW; PROVED; SAW; SEEN; ■ SEASONED

experiences HAS

experiment PILOT; TEST; TRIAL; TRY

experimental anagram indicator; *see* EXPERIMENT

experimenting TRYING; anagram indicator

expert ABLE; ACE; ARCH; BUFF; CRACK; DAB; DEFT; DEMON; MASTER; ONER; PRO; ■ HOTSHOT; WHIZ

expertise ART; SKILL

expertly ABLY; WELL

expiate ATONE

expire DIE; END; LAPSE; PASS

expired DEAD; ENDED; GONE; OVER; UP

explain SHOW; TELL

explain away GLOSS

explained SHOWED; SHOWN

explanation KEY; MOTIVE; REASON

expletive BLAST; CURSE; DAMN; HECK; OATH

explicit PLAIN; ■ OPEN

explode GOOFF (i.e. go off)

exploded, explodes, exploding anagram indicator

exploit ACT; DEED; FEAT; MILK; STUNT; TAP; USE; ■ ADVENTURE; anagram indicator

exploit, daring STUNT

exploitation USE

exploited USED; anagram indicator

exploited, someone TOOL

exploiting USING

explore PROBE

explorer BYRD; COOK; CABOT; OATES; PARK; ROSS; SCOTT; ■ TASMAN

exploring anagram indicator

explosion BANG; BOOM; REPORT; anagram indicator

explosive H; HE; MINE; SHELL; TNT; ■ JELLY; *see* EXPLOSIVE DEVICE

explosive device BOMB; CAP; MINE; SHELL

explosive, lay down MINE

explosive, use BLAST

exponent LOG; POWER

export omission indicator as "ice, one for export" clues CE (i.e. 'i' to be omitted)

exported anagram indicator

expose AIR; BARE; OUT; SHOW; STRIP; ■ OPEN; REVEAL

expose briefly FLASH

expose, do not COVER; HIDE; SHIELD

exposed AIRED; BALD; BARE; NUDE; OUT; anagram indicator; *see* EXPOSE

exposing can indicate that the definition follows

exposition SHOW

expounds, so to speak TENNER

express FAST; PUT; SAY; STATE; TALK; UTTER; VENT; ■ COMMUNICATE; homophone indicator

express a preference VOTE

express annoyance TUT

express contempt BOO; MOCK

express disappointment, pain GROAN

express disapproval BOO; HISS; OBJECT; TUT

express discontent CARP

express dissatisfaction BOO; CARP; JEER

express despair SIGH

express doubt QUESTION

express emotion EMOTE

express glee CROW

express gratitude to THANK

express hesitation ER

express pleasure PURR

express regret SIGH

express relief SIGH

express reluctance ER

express sadness SIGH

express scorn HISS

express self-satisfaction GLOAT

express sorrow REGRET

express triumph GLOAT

express view OPINE

express weariness SIGH

expressed homophone indicator

expressed glee CREW

expressed, not COVERT; INNER; SECRET

expression FACE; LOOK; TERM

expression, lacking BLANK; GLASSY

expression of aggression SNARL

expression of amazement WOW

expression of amusement HA; HAH; LAUGH

expression of annoyance HOOT(S)

expression of approval AY; AYE; BRAVO; YES

expression of astonishment GEE; WOW

expression of contempt BAH

expression of delight AH; WHEE; WOW

expression of derision BOO; HA; YAH

expression of disapproval AHEM; BOO; TUT

expression of discontent BAWL; BOO; FIE; GROAN; SIGH; YAH

expression of disdain POOH

expression of disgust BAH; FIE; UGH; YUCK

expression of dismay FIE; HECK

expression of dissatisfaction BOO

expression of exultation WHOOP

expression of gratitude TA

expression of grief CRY; WEEPING

expression of horror UGH

expression of impatience TUT; ■ PSHAW

expression of joy AH

expression of pain AGH; AW; OUCH; OW

expression of refusal NO

expression of regret SIGH

expression of relief ALACK; PHEW

expression of surprise AH; AW; COR; EH; GAD; GOLLY; GOSH; LOR; MY; OH; OHO; OOH; WELL; WOW

expression of sympathy THERE

expression of triumph AHA

expression of triumphant surprise OHO

expression of weariness SIGH

expression of wonder GEE (U.S.)

expression, relieved SIGH

expression, style of DICTION

expression, suggestive LEER

expression, sulky MOUE

expression, sullen SCOWL

expression, suspicious HA

expulsion OUT; OUTING

exquisitely anagram indicator

extempore, extemporised anagram indicator

extend GROW; REACH; SPREAD; STRETCH

extend all round RING

extend loan RENEW

extended LONG

extended (Scottish) LANG

extension STRETCH; STRETCHING; [◊ EXTRA]

extensive LARGE; LONG; HIGH

extent AMBIT; AMOUNT; AREA; LENGTH; RANGE; SIZE; SCOPE (qv)

extent, of great HUGE; LONG; VAST

extent (to some extent) run indicator

exterior nesting indicator

exterior, tough SHELL

exterminated omission indicator

external OUTER; nesting indicator

extinguish DOUSE; SNUFF

extort WRING

extorted WRUNG; anagram indicator

extortionate anagram indicator

extra ACTOR; BONUS; BYE; GASH; MORE; ODD; OVER; PLUS; RISE; RUN; SPARE; SUR (as in surcharge); WIDE; ■ GARNISH; RELIEF (i.e. as a relief bus); SPECIAL

extra fifty changes an L to a C

extra, five changes a V to an X

extra five hundred changes a D to an M

extra money TIP

extra note PS

extra payment BONUS

extra, provide ADD

extra, unexpected BONUS

extract DRAW; EXT; MILK; OUST; PART; PRESS; PUMP; ■ DERIVE; ELICIT; REMOVE; run indicator

extract, appetising TRAILER

extract from, in run indicator

extract metal SMELT

extract money TOUCH

extracted DREW; OUT; TOOK; omission indicator

extraction DESCENT

extractor MINER

extraordinary E; anagram indicator

extraordinarily anagram indicator

extravagance, burst of SPLURGE

extravagant FANCY; OTT; ■ LAVISH; OUTRE; anagram indicator

extravagantly anagram indicator

extravaganza anagram indicator

extreme EDGE; POLE; POLAR; UTTER; ■ HARSH; MEGA; UNDUE; first or last letter indicator; can indicate an adjective ending in MOST

extreme characters AZ; *see* EXTREMES OF

extreme measures, favouring ULTRA

extreme, not MIDDLE

extremely EDGY (i.e. having extremes); MOST; TOO; ULTRA; VERY; ■ FILTHY (as in "filthy rich"); MEGA; first and/or last letter indicator, as "extremely secure" leads to SE; can indicate that the first and last letters of a word are used while linked by AND as "extremely coy" clues CANDY (i.e. C-AND-Y)

extremely expensive EE; *see* EXPENSIVE

extremely large LE; OS

extremely rare RE

extremely rude RE

extremely trendy TY

extremely unpopular UR

extremely unusual UL

extremely useful UL

extremely tacky TY

extremes AZ; *see* EXTREMES OF

extremes of indicator of first and last letters of associated word(s); can also require AND to be inserted between the end letters of indicated word e.g. "extremes of rascality" gives RANDY, "extremes of paranoia" gives PANDA; can indicate something to do with fingertips, nails, toes, etc

extremis, in OTT; *see* EXTREMES OF

extremist ULTRA

extremists AZ; ZA; first and last letters only to be used (example "nasty extremists" → NY)

extremity END

exuberance BRIO; PEP

exudes anagram indicator

exult CROW; GLOAT

exultation, cry of WHOOP

eye LOOK; OGLE; ORB; REGARD; SCAN; SEE STUDY; [◊ SIGHT]

eye movement BLINK; WINK

eye-opener E; LID

eye protector VISOR

eyelid sore STYE

eyepiece LENS

eyepiece, with OCULAR

eyes sounding like I's this word can, with a homophone indicator, call for II

eyewash SALVE; ROT; *see* RUBBISH

Ezra POUND

Ff

F LOUD

fab SOUND

fable LIE; STORY (qv); TALE

fable, lesson of MORAL

fabric CHINO; CLOTH; DUCK; LACE; LAME; LINEN; LISLE; NET; RAYON; REP; SATIN; SERGE; TOILE; TWILL; ■ ANGORA; CREPE; DENIM; DIMITY; FELT; LAWN; NINON; SCRIM; TISSUE; TWEED; VOILE

fabric, delicate/flimsy LACE

fabric join SEAM

fabric, woven TWILL

fabricated LIED; anagram indicator

fabrication LIE; LYING; MYTH

fabulous GREAT

fabulous bird ROC

fabulous female PERI

facade FRONT; SHOW

face BRASS; BRAVE; CLOCK; DIAL; FRONT; LOOK; MEET; MUG; PAN; RISK; SIDE; ■ ASPECT; BEARD; RESIST; TYPE; can refer to coal-face

face disruption anagram indicator

face down PRONE

face-lift anagram indicator

face of initial letter indicator

face, part of BROW; CHEEK; EYE; LIP; MOUTH; NOSE

face-saving device VISOR

face up to DEFY

faced MET

faceless initial letter omission indicator

facet SIDE; ■ ASPECT

faces initial letters to be used

facial disorder TIC

facial feature BROW; CHIN; CHEEK; LIP; NOSE; *see* FEATURE

facial hair BEARD; GOATEE; TACHE

facile GLIB; LIGHT; WEAK

facility EASE; ROOM

facility, recreational CLUB

fact DEED; TRUTH; ■ DATUM; GOSPEL

faction GROUP (qv); PARTY; SECT; SET; SIDE; TEAM

factor AGENT; PH; REASON; ■ BROKER

factory MILL; PLANT; WORKS

facts DATA; GEN; INFO; TABLE; TRUTH

facts, brief INFO

faculty FLAIR; TASTE

fad CRAZE; RAGE

fade DIE; FLAG; GO; PALE; TIRE; ■ WITHER

fade away DIE; EBB

faded EX; PASSE; RUSTY

fading DYING; GOING; LOW; *see* FADE

fag CHORE; TIRE; WEED; can indicate some kind of servant; [◊ CIGARETTE]

fag-end ROACH (U.S.)

Fahrenheit F

fail DIE; FLOP; FLUNK; LAPSE; LOSE; MISS; OMIT; ■ BOMB; CUT; PLOUGH (univ. slang); anagram indicator; can indicate a verb beginning with UNDER

fail, likely to DICKY; IFFY; *see* DICKY

fail to can indicate a word beginning with NOT, as "Fail to come up" → NOTARISE

fail to answer PASS

fail to do SKIP

fail to see/observe MISS

fail to win DRAW; LOSE

failed DIED; LOST; MISSED; anagram indicator (e.g. "has failed" → SHA)

failed, we hear MIST (i.e. homophone of "missed")

failing CRASH; DYING; ERROR; FLAW; GREED; LAPSE; SIN; VICE; ■ DEFECT; INFIRM; LOSING; MISSING; anagram indicator; omission indicator; can indicate an adjective ending in -LESS; *see* ERROR

failing at the start first letter to be omitted

failing finally last letter to be omitted

failing half half a word to be omitted

failing to open first letters to be omitted

failing to see BLIND

faille SILK

failure BOMB; BREACH; DUD; FLOP; LAPSE; LOSER; ■ CROPPER; OMISSION; anagram indicator

failure, admission of ICANT (i.e. I can't)

failure to hit ball STRIKE

faint DIM; PALE; SWOON; VAGUE; WAN; ■ FEEBLE; GENTLE; HAZY; SLIGHT; WEAK

fair BRIGHT; CLEAN; CLEAR; DUE; EVEN; FINE; JUST; LIGHT; MARKET; PALE; PRETTY; RIGHT; SALE; SHOW; WELL; ■ DISHY; GOOD; HONEST; RIGHTFUL; SPORTING

fair-haired type BLONDE

fairground attraction RIDE

fairies ELVES

fairly PRETTY; QUITE

fairly big TIDY

fairy ELF; FAY; HOB; PERI; PUCK; SPRITE; ■ PIXIE

fairy, male PERI

fairy tale LIE

faith BELIEF; TRUST

faithful TRUE

faithful woman NUN

fake BUM; COD; COPY; DUFF; ERSATZ; FRAUD; MOCK; PASTE; SHAM; ■ CHARLATAN; DOCTOR; FUDGE; PHONY; PHONEY; SWINDLE

faked anagram indicator

falcon SAKER

Falkland Islands FI

fall DIE; DIP; DIVE; DRIP; DROOP; DROP; ERR; LAPSE; MISS; RAIN; SAG; SIN; SLIP; SNOW; SPILL; TRIP; ■ ABATE; CHANCE; FLOP; SETTLE; SHOWER; STUMBLE; TUMBLE; can require a verb followed by DOWN or OFF

fall and rise TIDE

fall apart CRUMBLE

fall behind LAG; TRAIL

fall heavily POUR; SHEET; TEEM

fall, likely to TOTTER

fall out FIGHT; SCRAP; ■ QUARREL; anagram of FALL

Fall story, feature of APPLE; SNAKE; TREE

fallacious UNSOUND

fallen anagram or reverse indicator

falling anagram indicator

falling apart anagram indicator

falling out anagram indicator

fallout anagram indicator; ■ SPIN-OFF

fallow IDLE

falls apart from being in the sense of the verb (*see* DROP) can also indicate a waterfall (e.g. cascade) or a particular waterfall e.g. Victoria, Niagara; anagram indicator

falls in nesting indicator

false SHAM; ■ PSEUDO; anagram indicator; *see* FAKE

false beard anagram of BEARD

false hair WIG; anagram of HAIR

false impression LIE

false information LIE

false teeth DENTURE

false, was LIED

false witness LIAR

falsehood FICTION; LIE; TALE

falsely anagram indicator

falsetto, intermittent YODEL

falsified anagram indicator

falsified the facts LIED

falsify LIE; ■ FIDDLE; can indicate a verb beginning with MIS

falter FLAG; HALT

faltering anagram indicator

falteringly, go DODDER

fame NAME; NOTE; ■ CELEBRITY; REPUTE

fame at last E

familiar OLD; PAL; *see* FRIEND

familiar, perhaps CAT

familiar with, was KNEW

family BROOD; CLAN; FAM; HOUSE; ILK; KIN; KIND; LINE; OWN; RACE; SEPT; STRAIN; TRIBE; ■ BLOOD; DESCENT

family chart TREE

family chronicle SAGA

family emblem CREST

family line DESCENT

family member AUNT; GRAN; RELATION (qv); SIS; SON; UNCLE; ■ RELATIVE; *see* FATHER, MOTHER

family, member of *see* RELATIVE

family member, young SCION

family record TREE

family, royal ORANGE; HOUSE

family tendency STRAIN

famine DEARTH

famous NOTED; STAR

famous person CELEB; NAME; VIP; ■ LION

famous performer/player STAR

famously WELL

famous group FIVE (i.e. from Enid Blyton)

famous horse ARKLE; BESS

fan BUFF; CAT; COOL; NUT; ■ ADMIRER; COOLER; DEVOTEE; FREAK; LOVER; anagram indicator; [◊ ROTARY]

fanatic NUT; ■ BIGOT; *see* FAN

fanatical MAD (qv); RABID

fancied to win HOT

fanciful AIRY

fancy DREAM; FAD; GUESS; IDEA; ITCH; LIKE; LOVE; NOTION; WHIM; anagram indicator

fanfare TUCKET

fang TOOTH

fans, number of GATE

fantastic FAB; MAGIC; SUPER; WOW; ■ GRAND; OUTRE; anagram indicator; can indicate something to do with a well-known legend or myth

fantastically anagram indicator

fantasy DREAM

far-fetched TALL

far from REMOTE

far off REMOTE; anagram of FAR

far side of last letter indicator (as "far side of room" clues M)

far, too OVER

farce COMEDY

fare BREAD; CHEER; CHOW; DIET; DO; EATS; FOOD; MEAL; MEAT; MENU; PRICE; TABLE; ■ PASSENGER; RATIONS; TRAVEL; can indicate a specific food; *see* MEAL, FOOD

fare, child's HALF

fare, quick SNACK

farewell ADIEU; ADIOS; AVE; BYE; VALE; ■ CONGE

farm CROFT; GROW; RANCH; SPREAD; STUD; ■ HOLDING

farm animal BULL; COW; CROFT; EWE; GOAT; PIG; RAM; SHEEP; SOW; STEER

farm animals FLOCK; HERD; KINE; STOCK; *see* FARM ANIMAL

farm building BARN; BYRE; STY

farm labourer *see* FARM WORKER

farm machine/machinery COMBINE; HOPPER; TRACTOR

farm overseer in Scotland GRIEVE

farm policy CAP

farm shop DAIRY

farm store BARN; SILO

farm vehicle CART

farm worker HIND (Sc.); REAPER; SHEARER

farmer SOWER

farmhouse BREAD; GRANGE; LOAF

farming concern *see* FARM

farming policy CAP

farming scheme, European CAP

farming, type of ARABLE

farmland ARABLE

farmstead GRANGE

farmyard produce EGG

fascinated SMITTEN

fascinated by INTO

fascist leader DUCE

fashion CULT; DRESS; FAD; FORGE; FORM; HEW; MODE; RAGE; SHAPE; TON; TONE; TREND; WAY; WISE (arch.); ■ ALA (i.e. a la); MODAL; STYLE; VOGUE; anagram indicator

fashion, after a anagram indicator

fashion designer DIOR

fashion, man of RAKE; SWELL

fashion, people of TON

fashionable CHIC; HIP; HOT; IN; POP; SMART; SWELL; TON; TRENDY; U; anagram indicator

fashionable crowd TON

fashionable, more HIPPER

fashionable society TON

fashioned anagram indicator

fast FIRM; FLEET; LENT; NIPPY; PACY; QUICK (qv); SPEEDY; STUCK; SWIFT; ■ ABSTAIN; EXPRESS; FIXED; NIPPY; RAMADAN; SECURE; SLIM; [◊ BUCK]; can indicate something to do with Lent, Ash Wednesday

fast behaviour, showing LOOSE

fast days EMBER

fast delivery EXPRESS

fast food apart from hamburgers, pizza etc., this can refer to traditional food that is quickly cooked e.g. minute steak

fast-food outlet CHIPPY

fast, held STUCK

fast, move DART; RACE; RUN; RUSH; SPEED; ■ HASTEN

fast, not LOOSE; *see* SLOW

fast pace LICK

fast talking LEANT (i.e. homophone)

fast time LENT

fast, moved RAN; SPED

fast, went RAN; SPED

fasten BIND; CLIP; CLOSE; FIX; LACE; LASH; LOCK; NAIL; PIN; REEVE; ROPE; SCREW; SEAL; TAG; TAPE; TIE; ZIP

fastened ROVE; ■ FIXED; TIED

fastener CATCH; CLIP; FROG; HASP; HOOK; LOCK; NAIL; NUT; PIN; SCREW; STAPLE; STUD; TIER; ZIP; ■ BUTTON; TOGGLE

fastening KNOT; LATCH; LOCK; SEAL; TAPING; TIE

fastening device *see* FASTENER

fastest TOP; WINNER

fastidious CHARY; NICE; PICKY; ■ DAINTY

fat ESTER; FLAB; GROSS; HUGE; LARD; PLUMP; RICH; STOUT; SUET; ■ BUTTER; DRIPPING; DUMPY; GREASE; TALLOW; TUBBY

fat, extremely GROSS

fat, not *see* SLIM

fat, very OS

fatal, without LEAN

fatal DIRE; [◊ BANE]

fate DOOM; LOT; ■ KARMA; NORN (Scand).

fated to die FAY; FEY; FIE

fateful day IDES

father DA; DAD; FR; PA; POP; SIRE; ■ BEGET; ELDER; PAPA; PATER

Father Christmas SANTA

Father, Old usually refers to the Thames

fathom PLUMB

fatigue TIRE; WEAR

fatigued DRAWN; TIRED; WEARY

fatuous DUMB

fault BLIP; ERR; ERROR; FLAW; HITCH; MISS; PRIDE; RIFT; SHORT (i.e. elec.); SIN; SLIP; VICE; ■ BLUNDER; DEFECT; can indicate something to do with earthquake

fault, at anagram indicator

fault, find CARP; ■ CENSOR

faultfinder CRITIC

faulty DUFF; OUT; anagram indicator

faulty item DUD; REJECT

faux pas ERROR; GAFFE; SLIP; ■ BLOOMER; CLANGER

favour BOON; GRACE; HELP; LIKE; ■ ADVOCATE; PARTIAL; ROSETTE

favour, in FOR; PRO

favour of, not in AGIN; ANTI; CON

favourable NICE; PRO; ■ BOON

favourable review PUFF

favourable slant SPIN

favourable vote AYE; FOR; YES; ■ PLACET; PRO

favoured IN; PET; POPULAR

favouring FOR; PRO

favourite CERT; PET

favourite, one who has LOVER

fawn CREEP; FLATTER; ■ ECRU

FBI GMEN

FBI agent FED

FBI agents GMEN

FBI man FED

fear ALARM; AWE; DREAD; SCARE; TERROR; ■ PANIC

fear, extreme PANIC

fear, show QUAKE; SHAKE; TREMBLE

fear, sudden PANIC

fearful TIMID; anagram indicator

fearless BRAVE

fearless hero HERO

feast DO; EAT; EATING; SPREAD; ■ GAUDY; GORGE; JUNKET; REGALE

feat ACT; DEED; EXPLOIT; STUNT

feather HACKLE; ■ PLUME

feathers DOWN

feathers, grow FLEDGE

feathery accessory BOA

feature MARK; PROPERTY; STAR; TRAIT; often indicates a facial feature commonly CHIN, EAR, LIP, NOSE; also can indicate a distinctive part of anything (e.g. with reference to a limb can indicate a particular bone) or something essential (e.g. as a ball is to snooker); can refer to a geographic feature e.g. plain; when related to a named place (e.g. as a geographic feature) can refer to a specific river, mountain, etc; anagram indicator

feature, distinguishing STAMP; TRAIT

feature, facial HAIR; *see* FEATURE

feature, geographic PLAIN; *see* FEATURE

feature of run indicator; can indicate some grammatical feature of whatever follows e.g. apostrophe, hyphen

featured BILLED (i.e. as on a poster)

features FACE; MOVIES; STARS; *see* FEATURE; run indicator

features, set of FACE

February FEB; within the context of a clue which has some reference to omission, can indicate FIVE or FIFTH (i.e. it is the month usually missing the fifth week!)

fed PAID

fed-up BLUE; BORED; DEF; FULL; LOW

federal agents CIA; GMEN (i.e. G-men)

federal district of America DC

federation FED; UNION; ■ ALLIANCE; AXIS

fee CHARGE (qv); COST; PAY; RATE; SUM; TOLL

feeble DAMP; FAINT; FRAIL; LAME; LIMP; PUNY; SAD; SLIGHT; WEAK; WET; ■ ABJECT; PATHETIC

feeble, grow LANGUISH

feeble individual WIMP

feeble performer RABBIT

feeble person NERD; WIMP

feed DINE; EAT (qv); PAY; STOKE

feed fire STOKE

feed greedily *see* EAT GREEDILY

feeding nesting indicator

feeding system HOPPER

feeding, was ATE

feel BE; FINGER; GROPE; PROBE; SENSE; TOUCH

feel afraid FEAR

feel bad AIL; RESENT;

feel bad about LIA (i.e. reversal); RESENT; RUE

feel bitter RESENT

feel ill AIL

feel insulted RESENT

feel longing YEARN (qv)

feel sick AIL

feel the loss of MISS

feeling HEART; HUNCH; MOOD; SENSE; ■ EMOTION; HUMOUR; SENTIENCE; SENTIMENT

feeling, bad ODIUM

feeling, not DEAD; NUMB

feeling pain ACHE

feeling, passionate HATE; *see* PASSION

feeling, without CRUEL; DEAD; HARD; NUMB

feeling, induce EMOTIVE

feelings, arousing EMOTIVE

feelings, show EMOTE

feet HOOVES; IAMBI

feet, several YARD

feign ACT; SHAM

feline CAT; LYNX; *see* CAT

fell CHOP; CUT; DIED; DOWN; HIDE; HILL; MOOR; SKIN; ■ ABATED; anagram indicator; can indicate something to do with the felling of trees

felled CHOPPED; DOWN; anagram indicator

felling anagram indicator

fellow BOD; CHAP; CO (i.e. co- as in co-worker)); COVE; DON; F; GENT; GUY; LAD; MALE; MAN; MATE; PEER; ■ GEEZER; can refer to a man's name; *see* MAN

fellow American FUS

fellow, Aussie SPORT

fellow-citizen BRIT

fellow in blue TAR; *see* POLICEMAN, SAILOR

fellow left F (or some other synonym for fellow) to be either omitted or followed by L (e.g. FL)

fellow-member HON (i.e. MP's title)

fellow's HIS

fellow, sound GEYSER

fellow, that/the HIM

fellows FF; MEN

felony CRIME

felt CLOTH

female DAM; DOE; F; GAL; HEN; HER; LASS; MISS; MS; SHE; SISTER; ■ BITCH; MAIDEN; MATRON; can refer to a woman's name, *see* WOMAN; can indicate that a word ends in -ESS, as "Value of the female donkey?" → ASSESS

female, a French UNE

female body WI

female, characterised as DISTAFF

female, common BIRD

female community HAREM

female dress, gear DRAG

female, enchanting CIRCE

female, fiendish/monstrous OGRESS

female of unknown marital status MS

female ox COW

female principle, universal YIN

female relative AUNT; DAUGHTER; GRAN; SIS; SISTER; *see* MOTHER

female teacher MISS

female's HER

female, vulgar HUSSY; TART; TIT

females WOMEN; *see* FEMALE

feminist LIB

fen BOG

fence HEDGE; LIMIT; PALE; PALING; PICKET; RAIL; ■ BARRIER; OXER; RAILING; RECEIVE

fence, bit of RAIL

fence material WATTLE

fencing KENDO; PALING; RAIL; RAILING; [◊ TOUCHE]

fend off WARD

feral BRUTAL; WILD

ferment BREW; anagram indicator

ferment, cause of YEAST

fermented, fermenting anagram indicator

fermenting agent YEAST

ferocious WILD

ferret RIFLE

ferret, male HOB

ferry BOAT; [◊ CROSS; OVER]

fertile RICH

fertiliser PEAT; ■ COMPOST; MULCH

fervour ARDOUR; FIRE; HEAT; ZEAL; ■ HWYL (Welsh)

fester RANKLE; *see* ANNOY, NEEDLE

festival EASTER; FETE; GALA; WHIT; can indicate something to do with Mardi Gras

festive GAY; JOLLY

festive meal SPREAD

festive occasion GALA; *see* FESTIVAL

festive season NOEL; YULE

festivity GALA

fetch BRING; DOUBLE; GET

fetch up LAND

fetched BROUGHT; GOT

fetish TOTEM

fetter HOBBLE

feud FIGHT

fever AGUE; HEAT

feverish HECTIC; anagram indicator

feverish cold CHILL

few SOME; small number, TWO, THREE, FOUR or a low Roman numeral viz. IV, V, VI

few feet, a YARD

few feet, up a DRAY

few lines, a MEMO; NOTE; VERSE

few, they say FU

few words NOTE

few words, with TERSE

fewer LESS

Fiat UNO

fib LIE

fibre ISTLE; JUTE; RAFFIA; RAYON; STRAND; *see* FILAMENT

fibrous STRINGY

fibrous stuff, some HANK

fiction FIB; LEGEND; LIE; NOVEL; STORY; TALE; ■ FALSEHOOD

fiddle BOW; CHEAT; CON; FIX; LIFT; POTTER; RIG; SCAM; SCRAPE; STRAD; TINKER; TOY; VIOL; ■ CHISEL; RACKET; SWINDLE; TAMPER; anagram indicator; [◊ BOW; NERO]

fiddle cash LAUNDER

fiddle, fellow on the NERO

fiddle, part of NECK; STRING

fiddle, play the BOW

fiddle with FIX; RIG; ■ FINGER

fiddled, fiddles, fiddling anagram indicator

fiddlesticks BOWS; ROT

Fido DOG

fiddly anagram indicator

fidgeting, finish SETTLE

field ACRE; AREA; ENTRY; DOMAIN; GROUND; LAND; LEA; PITCH; STOP (cric.); can indicate the name of a specific football or cricket field e.g. OVAL; ■ RANGE; REALM; SPHERE

Field can refer to the composer

field event DISCUS; HAMMER

field officer FO

field, one in *see* FIELDER

field, one on the REF; *see* CRICKETER, FOOTBALLER, PLAYER

field, part of OFF; ON

field, take from the SCRATCH

fielder GULLY; POINT; SLIP; ■ CATCHER

fielding OUT

fielding position COVER; GULLY; MIDON (i.e. mid-on); POINT; SLIP

Fielding's novel AMELIA

fieldwork TILLING

fiend DEMON; DEVIL

fiendish EVIL; GRIM; anagram indicator

fiery HOT; RED

fiesta BEANO; PARTY (qv)

1500m-equivalent (race) MILE

15th of month, Roman IDES

fifth change to V, or the fifth letter of a word, to be changed as instructed

fifth-rate E

fifties LL

fifties, boy of TED

fifty L

fifty cents being half a dollar can thus signify the three letters DOL (or LAR)

fifty extra changes an L to a C

fifty-nine LIX

fifty-one LACE (i.e. L+ACE); LI

50% DEMI; HALF; SEMI; or half a word is to be used

fifty pounds LL

fifty-two cards DECK; PACK

fig DECK; DRESS

Figaro BARBER

fight ACTION; BOUT; BOX; BRAWL; CLASH; DUEL; FENCE; FEUD; MATCH; MILL; ROW; SCRAP; SPAR; TIFF; TILT; ■ AFFRAY; BATTLE; COMBAT; MELEE; SETTO (i.e. set-to); anagram indicator

fight, prepare to ARM

fighter BOXER; FENCER; GI; MIG; ZERO; *see* SOLDIER

fighter, old VET

fighters ARMY; WING

fighting ACTION; FRAY; WAR; ■ BATTLE; JUDO; SUMO; anagram indicator

fighting area RING

fighting-cocks can indicate the use of MAIN

fighting-fit *see* HEALTHY

fighting force ARM; ARMY (qv); TA; UNIT

fighting man BOXER; FENCER; *see* SOLDIER

fighting, people *see* ARMY

figure BUILD; CIRCLE; CONE; COVER; DIGIT; FIG; FORM;

M; NUMBER; OBLONG;
PRICE; SHAPE; SQUARE;
SUM; TRIANGLE; ■ MODEL;
POLYGON; PUPPET; STATUE;
see NUMBER

figure-head (or figurehead)
BUST; F; FRONT; TOKEN

figure in the sky can refer to a
constellation e.g. Orion

figures in run indicator

★ **figures of speech** are instances of
where we distort or exaggerate
our statements to make an effect.
Top writers of the day will be
creating new figures of speech
but many old ones have become
so embedded in our everyday
speech and writing that we are
not aware of their figurative origin (such as "paying cash on the
nail"). Figures of speech are
common in crosswords as in "De-
teriorated down at the track?" →
GONE TO THE DOGS

figures, set of TABLE

Fijian capital SUVA

filament HAIR; STRAND;
THREAD

filch PINCH; STEAL

file LINE; LIST; MARCH; RASP;
ROW; ■ FOLDER; STREAM

fill CHARGE; MEAT (as in sausage); PACK(IN); STOCK

fill between tiles GROUT

fill up BRIM; TOP

filled, we hear PACT

filled with run indicator

fillet BONE

filling STOCKING; nesting indicator; run indicator

filling, sandwich HAM

fillip LIFT; RISE

filly HER; SHE

film CINE; COAT; COVER; EPIC;
ET; FLICK; LAYER; LOOP;
MIST; MOVIE; PANC; PIC;
PSYCHO; REEL; ROLL;
SCUM; SHINE; SHOOT;
SHORT; SKIN; SPOOL; ■
GREASE; IRIS; KODAK;
MEMBRANE; VIDEO

film actor EXTRA

film actress GARBO; LOREN

film director LANG; LEAN;
REED; TATI

film director's milieu SET

film excerpt, extract CLIP

film for everyone U

film, long EPIC

film, make SHOOT

film music SCORE

film part BIT; EXTRA; LEAD;
REEL; ROLE; STAR

film, part of REEL

film, part of proposed TAKE

film, piece of CLIP; FRAME;
REEL; TAKE F

film premiere F

film, section of *see* FILM, PIECE
OF

film, short PIC; VID; can indicate
an abbreviation of anything listed
under FILM

film shot TAKE

film, some REEL

film star ACTOR; CHAPLIN;
COOPER; GABLE

filming, location (place) of SET;
STUDIO

filming, stop CUT

filter STRAIN

filth DIRT; GRIME; MUCK;
SMUT

filthy BAD; BLUE; DIRTY; ■
SQUALID

filthy accommodation/place
STY

final CLOSE; END; EXAM; HEAT
(as in a sports event); LAST;
NET; NETT; ULT; ■ MATCH;
last letter(s) indicator

final check MATE

final letter Z

final piece CODA; END; TIP

final point END

final score TOTAL

final words PS

finale END; ENDING; last letter(s)
indicator

finalise charges BILL

finalise, to component or word to
go at end

finalist last letter indicator as "cup finalist" → P

finally last letter(s) indicator; ■ AT LAST

finally dropped last letter to be omitted (as "Penny finally dropped" → COI)

finally failing last letter to be omitted

finally get TUMBLE

finally going last letter to be omitted

finally gone ahead last letter of word to be relocated to the beginning

finally made E

finance BACK; FUND; RESOURCE

finance house BANK

financial adviser CA

financial analysis AUDIT

financial backer ANGEL

financial centre N; NY

financial district CITY

financial obligation DEBT; IOU

financial obligations IOUS

financial ratio GEARING

financial relief AID

financial resources CHEST; FUND

financially support FUND

finch SERIN

find TRACE; ■ DISCOVER; LOCATE; UNCOVER; UNEARTH

find answer CRACK; SOLVE

find fault CARP; ■ UPBRAID

find new job for REUSE

find new place RESITE

find not guilty CLEAR

find, one who manages to TRACER

find out HEAR; SUSS; anagram of FIND

fine ACE; AI; CATCH; DANDY; F; FAIR; GOOD; GRAND; NICE; OK; OKAY; RIGHT; SHEER; SUPER; THIN; WELL; ■ COOL; PENALTY; SCONCE

fine chase FETCH

fine fabric LACE

fine once in Ireland ERIC

fine one PEACH

fine rain, spray MIST

fine, really SUPER

fine Scottish BRAW

fine specimen PEACH

finesse ART; SKILL

finest BEST; TOP; ■ ELITE

finest product FLOWER

Fingal's Cave, island of STAFFA

finger INDEX; PINKIE; SHOP; TOT; ■ HANDLE

finger on, lay a TOUCH

finger tip TOUCH

fingered FELT

fingertip NAIL

fingertips can signify something to do with nail polish, nail varnish, manicure etc

finish AMEN; CEASE; CLOSE; DIE; DO; EDGE; END; ENDING; KILL; LEAVE; STOP; last letter indicator

finish off END; KILL (qv); SCOTCH; SEAL

finish off, something to ENDER

finish to game MATE

finished DEAD; DONE; GONE; OFF; OVER; PAST; READY; UP; USED; ■ ENDED; THROUGH

finished early last letter to be omitted

finishing END; last letter(s) indicator

Finland, Finnish SUOMI

fir PINE

fire ANGER; FLAME; INGLE; LIGHT; LOB; PYRE; SACK; SHOOT; ■ ENTHUSE; HEARTH; [◊ ARSON]

fire, bit of EMBER; FLAME; SPARK

fire, consequence of ASH; EMBER

fire goes out anagram of FIRE

fire, on ALIGHT; FLAMING; LIT

fire-raising ARSON

fire, start LIGHT

fire to, set LIGHT; TORCH

fire up STOKE

fire when told LITE

firearm GUN; GAT; RIFLE

fired LIT; SHOT; anagram indicator

fired again RELIT

fired up TIL

fireman [◊ HOSE; STATION]

fireplace GRATE; INGLE; HEARTH; HOB

fireside HEARTH

firewood FAGGOT

firewood, load of CORD

firework CRACKER; SQUIB

firing ARSON; SACKING; ■ REPORT; SHOOTING; omission indicator

firing, result of SHOT

firm CO; COY; FAST; HARD; SET; SOLID; STABLE; STEADY; STIFF; STRICT; STRONG; SURE; TIGHT; ■ BUSINESS; CONCERN; CONSTANT; HOUSE; STAUNCH; STURDY

firm, are not QUAVER; SHAKE; WAVER (qv)

firm hold CINCH; GRIP

firm, make CEMENT; ENSURE

firmness STEEL

firms COCO

first A; ALPHA; ARCH; BEST; FORE; GOLD; HEAD; I; IST; LEADING; ONE; ORIGIN; PRIME; PROTO; START; TOP; WINNER; ■ LEADER; MAIDEN (as in "maiden speech"); OPENER; ORDINAL; ORIGINAL; initial letter(s) indicator; ordering indicator

first and second ISTS

first, be B; BEAT; LEAD; WIN

first-born B

first class AI; C; GRAND; SUPER; TOP; ■ TOPPING

first-class return IA; SPOT

first couple of first two letters of subsequent word to be used

first eleven E; K (i.e. position in the alphabet)

first few, among the PLACED

first, go G; LEAD

first, gone G; LED

first lady EVE; L

first light DAWN; L

first love L

first man ADAM; M

first mate EVE; M

first mate on boat MARK

first of month can indicate I in combination with the abbreviation of a month e.g. IDEC, DECI, JANI

first off O; initial letter(s) to be omitted

First Officer O

first person ADAM; I; P; ■ CHAMP; WINNER

first person in France JE

first person killed ABEL

first person's MINE; MY

first place GOLD; LEAD; P; TOP; VAN; ■ FRONT

first place, man in CHAMP

first rate A; ACE; AI; AONE (i.e. AI); CLASS; CRACK; GOOD; PRIME; R; TOP

first sign ARIES; S

first signs of initial letters to be used

first sixteen letters ATOP (i.e. A to P)

first son CAIN; S

first thirteen letters ATOM (i.e. A to M)

first thoughts PLAN; T

first three, in the PLACE

first to T; can indicate the first letter of the word that follows

first to last the first letter of a word to be moved to the end of the word (as "Despatch first to last objects" → ENDS)

first two letters AB

first, was LED; W; WON

first week W; can refer to Genesis

first wife EX; W

first woman EVE; W; ■ PANDORA

fish ANGLE; BARB; BASS; BIB; BLEAK; BREAM; BRILL; BRIT; DAB; CARP; CATCH; CHAR; CHUB; COD; DORY; EEL; FLUKE; GAR; GOBY; HAG; HAKE; HUNT; ID; IDE;

KIPPER; LING; LOACH;
LUCE; PARR; PERCH; PIKE;
PLAICE; POPE; POUT; RAY;
ROACH; RUDD; RUFF; SCAD;
SCHOOL; SHAD; SHINER;
SKATE; SMELT; SOLE;
SPRAT; TAI; TENCH; TOPE;
TRAWL; TROLL; TROUT;
TUNA; ■ ANGLER;
BLOATER; CHARR; ELVER;
FLOUNDER; GROPER;
GROUPER; HERRING; ORFE;
RUFFE; SNAPPER;
SWIMMER; TETRA; TUNNY;
TURBOT; [◊ COURSE; ROD;
WANDA]

fish, amount of CATCH;
DRAUGHT

fish, attraction for *see* BAIT

fish basket CREEL

fish, bit of FIN; FINGER

fish-catcher NET

fish-eater GULL

fish eggs ROE

fish, little MINNOW

fish, part of, piece of GILL; FIN;
SCALE

fish-plate SCALE

fish product ROE

fish, some SCHOOL

fish, type of PERCA (genus for
perch)

fish, way to catch TICKLE

fish, young ELVER

fisherman ANGLER; WALTON

**fishing aid (equipment, tackle
etc)** HOOK; LINE; NET; REEL;
ROD

fishing boat SMACK

fishing, go ANGLE; TRAWL

fishing-spear GAFFE

fishnet TRAWL; ■ TRAMMEL;
see NET

fishy ODD; RUM; anagram indicator

fishy feature FIN; GILL

fishy, something CRAN (a measure of fish catch)

fissure CRACK; GAP; RENT;
SPLIT

fist DUKE; HAND; PUNCH

fist full, having a HANDED

fit ABLE; AGUE; AI; APT;
BOUT; GO; HALE; HEALTHY;
MEET; MOOD; PET; RIGHT;
SOUND; SPELL; SUIT; TRIM;
TURN; WELL; ■ ADAPT;
ANSWER; STROKE

fit for drinking POTABLE

fit for employment ABLE;
USABLE

fit of anagram indicator

fit of depression, pique HUMP

fit of temper SNIT; *see* TEMPER

fit out EQUIP

fitfully anagram indicator

fitly ABLY

fitness FORM; ■ APTITUDE;
HEALTH

fitted ABLE; anagram indicator

fitter BETTER

fitting APT; MEET; PROPER;
RIGHT; ■ EQUIPMENT; ana-
gram indicator

Fitzgerald ELLA

five V; ■ PRIME; QUIN

five centavos COLON

five digits HAND

five extra changes a V to an X

five hundred D; MONKEY;
THOU (i.e. half a thousand!)

501 DI

five hundred extra changes a D to
an K

five hundred pages REAM

five hundred pounds MONKEY

five-o, the big L

five years LUSTRE; ■ LUSTRUM

fiver FIN

fix AMEND; CLAMP; CLIP;
CURE; FASTEN; HOLE; JAM;
LOCK; NAIL; PICKLE; PIN;
PLACE; PLANT; REPAIR; RIG;
RIVET; SCRAPE; SCREW;
SET; SPOT; STAPLE; STEW;
TIE; ■ ARRANGE; CEMENT;
EMBED; WANGLE; anagram in-
dicator; *see* PICKLE

fix firmly CEMENT; PLANT; *see*
SECURE

fix up RIG; a synonym of fix (*see*
FIX) to be reversed e.g. LIAN

fixation THING

fixed FAST; SET; STABLE; ■ PRESET; SEWN; STEADY; STUCK; SURE; anagram indicator

fixer HYPO; RIGGER

fixing anagram indicator; ■ CEMENT

fixing device BOLT; CLIP; NAIL; PIN; RIVET; SCREW

fixing pin *see* FIXING DEVICE

fixture AWAY; DATE; HOME; MATCH; TIE; VENUE; ■ MEETING

fixture, part of LEG

fizzle out DIE

fizzy anagram indicator

flab FAT

flabbergasted anagram indicator

flabby LIMP

flag COLOUR; DROOP; FADE; FALTER; HAIL; IRIS; JACK; PAVE; PIN; SAG; TAG; TIRE; WAVE; WILT; ■ BANNER; DUSTER; ENSIGN; PENNON; STANDARD; STREAMER; can indicate something to do with pavement; [◊ POLE]

flagrant GROSS; RANK

flags BUNTING; *see* FLAG

flags, group of HOIST

flags, put out PAVE

flair STYLE

flak STICK

flaky anagram indicator

flame BEAU; FIRE; LOVER

flame, old EX

flames FIRE

flames, in AFIRE; *see* FIRE, ON

flaming ALIGHT; CROSS; HOT; RED ■ DARNED; STEAMING

flan DISH; FLY; TART

Flanders MOLL

flank SIDE; WING

flanks first and last letters indicator

flanks, both LR; RL

flap BUSTLE; COVER; TAB; TODO (i.e. to-do); ■ PANIC; SPOILER; [◊ WING]

flapping anagram indicator

flare BLAZE; LIGHT; WIDEN

flare-up, result of EMBER

flash GLEAM; LINE; SECOND; STREAK; STRIP; TICK; ■ GLINT

flash fellow SPIV

flash of run indicator

flash socket SHOE (i.e. on a camera)

flashing light STROBE

flashy BRIGHT; LOUD; SHOWY; ■ JAZZY

flashy clothes, man who wears DUDE

flat BANAL; DEAD; DOWN; DULL; EVEN; HOME; LOW; LEVEL; MAT; MATT; OUT; PAD; PLAIN; PRONE; STALE; ■ BORING; PLANAR; SMOOTH; TAME; UNIFORM; VAPID

flat land PLAIN

flat surface TABLE; ■ RINK

flatfish PLAICE; SKATE

flats can indicate something to do with theatrical scenery

flatter SUIT; TOADY; ■ BLANDISH

flatterer TOADY

flattery BUTTER; SOAP; UNCTION

flaunting anagram indicator

flavour SPICE; TANG; TASTE; ■ MINT

flavour enhancer ADDITIVE

flavouring ANISE; MINT; SPICE; THYME

flavoursome TASTY

flaw BLEMISH; *see* BLEMISH

flawless CLEAN; IDEAL; PURE

flaws, without *see* FLAWLESS

flay FLOG; SKIN

fleck SPOT

fled RAN

flee BOLT; FLY; RUN

fleece CHEAT; COAT; COVER; GULL; HAIR; ROB; SHEAR; SKIN; STRIP; WEB; WOOL can indicate something to do with the Golden Fleece, Jason, Argonauts etc

fleeced SHORN

fleet ARMADA; FAST; NAVY; PACY; RAPID; RN; SWIFT

fleet, one in AB; BOAT; SHIP *see* SAILOR

Fleming's hero BOND

flesh MEAT; SKIN

flesh, loose WATTLE

fleshly CARNAL

fleshy PLUMP

flew FLED

flex BEND; CABLE; CORD

flexible LIMP; LITHE; ■ ELASTIC; PLIANT; SUPPLE; anagram indicator

flexible, more SUPPLER

flick FILM

flickering anagram indicator

flier BADER; BAT; GNAT; PILOT; PO; TIT; WING; *see* BIRD

flier, low OWL

flier, old BEA

fliers RAF

flies JETS

flight FLOCK; LAM; TRIP; WING; ■ ESCAPE; can indicate something to do with stairs e.g. caracole, newel, stair, step; can indicate something to do with Exodus, Moses etc; can require that a word is to be followed by UP e.g. 'catch flight' can clue TRIP UP; [◊ STAMPEDE; TEST]

flight, component/part of RISER; STAIR; STEP; TREAD

flight, disorderly ROUT

flight leader MOSES

flight, put to ROUT

flight, short HOP

flight, start ROUT

flight, unaccompanied SOLO

flighty creature *see* BIRD

flighty type PILOT; *see* AIRCRAFT, BIRD

flimsy FRAIL; LIGHT; WEAK (qv)

fling CAST; HURL; PARTY (qv); PITCH; SHY; TOSS; ■ AFFAIR; DANCE (qv); THROW

flint ROCK; STONE; ■ LIGHTER

flip SPRING; anagram indicator

flippancy AIRINESS

flippant AIRY

flipped SPRUNG; anagram indicator; reversal indicator

flipper FIN

flipping SPRINGING; anagram indicator; reversal indicator

flipping rubbish! TOR

flirt SPOON; TOY; VAMP

flirtation DALLIANCE

flit FLEE

flitted FLED

flitting anagram indicator

float BOB; LAUNCH; ■ BUOY; CHANGE

float around anagram indicator

floater BOAT (qv); RAFT; SHIP (qv)

floating anagram indicator

flock DROVE; TROOP

flog BEAT; BELT; FLAY; HIDE; LASH; LICK; SELL; ■ HAWK; SCOURGE; THRASH

flood FLOW; SPATE; SWAMP; ■ POUR; WASH; WATER; can indicate something to do with Noah's Ark; can indicate something to do with lighting (i.e. floodlight)

Flood, survivor of the HAM

flood-survivor HAM

flooded AWASH

floodland FEN; MARSH

floor BASE; DECK; DOWN; FL; KO; STOREY; ■ GROUND; LEVEL

floor covering MAT; RUG; ■ LINO; CARPET

floor, covering for *see* FLOOR COVERING

floored, one can refer to a rug, mat, carpet etc

floozie TART; ■ STRUMPET

flop BOMB; FAIL; FALL; SAG; WILT; ■ DROOP; SLEEP; TURKEY; *see* DISASTER; anagram indicator

floppy LIMP

flora PLANTS; *see* FLOWER, PLANT

flora and fauna NATURE

floral BLOOMING

floral tribute WREATH

Florence FLO

florid RED; SHOWY; ■ ORNATE
Florida FL
Florida Keys FLAG
Florida town TAMPA
flounder DAB; FLUKE; WALLOW; anagram indicator
floundering anagram indicator
flour MEAL
flour, mixed BATTER
flour, source of WHEAT
flourish BLOOM; SHAKE; WAVE; ■ FLOWER; THRIVE; TUCKET
flourished FL; anagram indicator
flourishing PALMY; anagram indicator
flow CURRENT; EBB; FLOOD; RUN; STREAM; SURGE; ■ SCAPA
flow, gentle TRICKLE
flowed RAN
flowed around anagram and/or nesting indicator
flower ASTER; BELL; BLOOM; FLAG; GLAD; PICK; PLANT; POPPY; PRIME; ROSE; STOCK; TULIP; ■ ANNUAL; CAMPION; CARNATION; ORRIS; see PLANT; also an old standby to signal a river, see RIVER; in this way it can also signal any other kind of waterway, as "Artificial flower" → CANAL
flower, artificial CANAL
flower, blue NILE
flower-bud CLOW
flower garland LEI
flower-girl IRIS; LILY; ROSE; VIOLET; see GIRL, WOMAN
flower-part PETAL; STAMEN; STEM
flower's corolla BELL
flower, unopened BUD
flower, white NILE
flowers BUNCH; LEI; SPRAY; see FLOWER
flowers, bunch of SPRAY; see FLOWER
flowery can indicate something to do with flowers, see FLOWER-PART

flowing RUNNY; anagram indicator
fluctuate SWING
flue DUCT; VENT
fluent GLIB
fluent, insincerely GLIB
fluently anagram indicator
fluff BOTCH; BUNGLE; DOWN; NAP
fluffing anagram indicator
fluid FL; anagram indicator; see LIQUID
fluke CHANCE; ■ FLOUNDER
flummox STUMP
flung CAST; PITCHED; anagram indicator
flunk FAIL
flurry, in a anagram indicator
flush LEVEL; RED; SCOUR; START; SWILL; ■ ROLLING
flushed RED
flustered anagram indicator
flute PIPE; WIND
flutter BET; HOVER; WAGER; WAVE; see BET; can indicate something to do with a bird, moth or a flag
flutter, have a BACK; BET; GAMBLE
fluttering anagram indicator
fly BOT; CADDIS; FLAP; FLEE; FLIT; GLIDE; GNAT; HARE; HOVER; JET; RUSH; SHARP; SOAR; WING; ■ COACH; DRAKE; HACKLE; MIDGE; SHREWD; SMART; STREAK; ZOOM; anagram indicator; can indicate a colloq. imper. such as "get lost", "push off", "vamoose"
fly-by-night BAT; MOTH; OWL
fly, give help to IMP
fly off GLANCE; SOAR; anagram of FLY
fly-trap WEB
fly, unable to GROUNDED
flyer AD; BAT; PILOT; ■ AIRMAN; can indicate a bird, butterfly, moth etc; see BIRD, FLIER
flyers RAF; see AIRCRAFT, BIRD
flyers' decoration AFM

flying UP; ■ AVIATION; RUSHING; WINGING; anagram indicator

flying ace BADER

flying manoeuvre LOOP

flying, one can indicate a bird, *see* BIRD

flying saucer UFO

flying, send SCRAMBLE

Flynn ERROL

foam HEAD

focus AIM; HUB; ■ CENTRE

fodder CLOVER; GRUB; HAY; ■ STRAW; VETCH; anagram indicator

fodder crop HAY

fog BLEAR; FRET; MIST; ■ HAZE; MURK

fog, in a anagram indicator; also can indicate that something is not seen (e.g. indiscernible) or that someone cannot understand

fogy, old SQUARE

fogeyish PASSE

foil BAFFLE; BEAT; CHECK; METAL; SWORD; ■ SCOTCH; SCUPPER

foil, use FENCE

fold BEND; CLOSE; PEN; PLEAT; TUCK; ■ CHURCH; CREASE; FLOCK

folded anagram indicator; reversal indicator

folder BINDER; FILE; can indicate something to do with origami

foliage FROND

folio F; LEAF; PAGE

folk KIN; MEN; ■ SET

folks KIN

follow CHASE; DOG; SHADOW; STALK; TAG; TAIL; TRACE; TRACK; TRAIL; ■ ENSUE; OBEY

follow, closely ATTEND; HEED

follower BUFF; FAN; LACKEY; NUT; TAIL; can indicate the next in some familiar sequence (example: "March follower" signifies APRIL); can indicate the surname of some noted person when the first name is given in the clue

as "a follower of Calvin" clues COOLIDGE

follower, a B

follower, enthusiastic FAN; *see* FOLLOWER

followers SCHOOL; TAIL

following AFTER; F; NEXT; POST; ■ LATTER; SECOND; can indicate that one component is to be placed behind another

following almost every FEVER

following example AFTER

fomented, fomenting anagram indicator

fond of, be LIKE; LOVE

fond of, be foolishly DOTE

fondness BENT

fondle STROKE

food BOARD; BRAN; BREAD; BUN; CAKE; CHOP; CHOW; CROP; DIET; DISH; EATS; EGG; FARE; FISH; FODDER; GRUB; HAM; MEAL; MEAT; OATS; PASTA; PIE; RICE; STEAK; TABLE; TART; TOAST; TRIPE; TUCK; ■ BEEF; CHEER; COURSE; ENTREE; HONEY; NOSH; SCAMPI; TACK; WAFFLE; *see* COURSE, MEAL, MEAT

food and drink CHEER

food, Australian TUCKER

food container ASPIC

food, cooked DISH; *see* FOOD, MEAL

food enhancer SPICE

food enhancers, use SEASON

food, fatty CREAM

food from heaven MANNA

food, go without FAST; [◊ LENT]

food-hall MESS

food, health(y) BRAN

food, hot CHILLI; TOAST; ~TOASTY

food, invalid PAP

food, particular DISH

food, prepare DRESS; *see* COOK

food, processed PATE

food-processor can indicate a tooth (e.g. MOLAR), the stomach, intestines etc

food provided TABLE

food recycled HASH
food regime DIET
food, semi-liquid PAP
food, selection of DIET
food, served DISH
food shop DELI
food, soft PAP
food, sweet JAM
food store DELI; ■ LARDER; PANTRY
food, traditional English BEEF
fool ASS; CHEAT; CHUMP; CLOD; CLOT; COD; CON; DILL; DOLT; DOPE; DUPE; GIT; GOOSE; GULL; JESTER; KID; LOON; MUG; NIT; NOODLE; NUT; OAF; PRAT; SAP; SUCKER; TRICK; TWIT; WALLY; ■ BERK; CLOWN; CUCKOO; DELUDE; DESSERT; DOLT; DONKEY; DORK; DUMMY; DUNCE; GOON; IDIOT; JERK; MORON; NERD; NINNY; NUTTER; PUDDING; TWERP
fool, Australian DILL
fool of, made a HAD
fool, pale-faced AUGUST
fool, upper-class ASS
foolery ANTIC
foolhardy RASH
foolish CRASS; DUMB; MAD; POTTY; RASH; SILLY; SIMPLE; anagram indicator
foolish later life DOTAGE
foolish person ASS; *see* FOOL
foolish talk YAK; ■ TWADDLE
foolishly anagram indicator
fools ASSES; GEESE; *see* FOOL
foot BASE; FT; HOOF; PAD; PAW; PAY; ■ PAEON; SPONDEE; TOOTSY; TROTTER
foot, bottom of SOLE
foot of page, written at PTO
foot, one seen on can call for any type of footwear
foot, part of ARCH; INCH; SOLE; TOE
foot soldiers LI; INFANTRY
football RU; ■ SOCCER

football club FC; FOREST; MANU; ORIENT; SPURS; UNITED; XI
football facility GROUND
football kit STRIP
football match TIE
football pitch PARK
football, place for GROUND; PITCH
football team FC; XI; *see* FOOTBALL CLUB
football team, most of TEN
footballer BACK; HALF; WING; ■ FORWARD; HIB; KEEPER; KICKER; PELE; STRIKER; WINGER; *see* RUGBY PLAYER; [◊ NET]
footballers FA; *see* FOOTBALLER
footer can indicate a dancer
footfall TREAD
footing last letter indicator
footing, losing can indicate that the last letter is to be omitted, as "walker losing footing" → RAMBLE
footing, on equal PAR
footloose last letter to be omitted, as "footloose traveller" → TRAM
footman LACKEY
footnote PS
footpath TRAIL; WAY
footsore CORN
footwear BOOT; CLOG; HOSE; MULE; OXFORD; PUMP; SHOE; SLIPPER; SOCK; TRAINER
fop DUDE (qv)
for ON; PER; PRO; TO; can indicate that the definition follows; can indicate a substitution as "given shelter for one" requires I to be replaced by LEE
for a poet THO (i.e. though)
for all to see U
for church FORCE
for each PER
for every PER
for example EG; SAY
for French AU; POUR
for instance AS; EG; SAY

for me MY
for nothing FREE
for sale GOING
for this reason HENCE
for us OUR
for, Spanish POR
forage DELVE
foray RAID
forbid BAN; BAR; VETO
forbidden OUT; ■ BANNED
forbidden to speak BAND (i.e. homophone of "banned")
forbidding DOUR; GRIM; STERN
force ARMY; BRUNT; CRAM; DRIVE; F; FLEET; G; JAM; MAKE; MIGHT; POWER; PRESS; PRISE; RAF; RAM; RUC; SQUAD; STRAIN; STRESS; TA; UNIT; WEIGHT; WREST; ■ BRANCH; COERCE; DURESS; DYNE; EDGE; EXERT; MUSCLE POLICE; POSSE; SERVICE; TEETH; THRUST; TORQUE; can indicate something to do with the police; [◊ ACTION]
force, elite (British, special) SAS
force, fighting TA etc; *see* ARMY
force, in ING (i.e. in + g); RULING; VALID
force into shape BEND
force of law POSSE; *see* POLICEMEN
force one's way PUSH
force, oppressive WEIGHT
force out GOUGE
force, positive YANG
force, remove by OUST; REAVE
force, rotating TORQUE
force, sort of TASK
force 10 STORM
force to flee, fly ROUT
force, using PRISING; *see* FORCE
force, without GENTLE; ■ GENTLY
forced MADE; anagram indicator
forceful HARD; PUNCHY; STERN; STRONG; TELLING
Forces'sweetheart VERA

forcible restraint GAG
forcibly anagram indicator
forcing anagram indicator
ford CROSS; WADE
Ford's preferred colour BLACK
fore FRONT; VAN
forecast TIP; ■ PREDICT
forecaster SEER
forego PASS
forehand SHOT
forehead BROW
foreign ALIEN; ODD; STRANGE; anagram indicator
foreign, a EIN; UN, UNE
foreign agent SPY
foreign article DER; EIN; EL; IL; LA; LE; LES; UN; UNE
foreign articles UNDER (i.e. un + der)
foreign city AIX; ROME; PARIS
foreign coin *see* FOREIGN CURRENCY
foreign currency COLON; DM; FRANC; GUILDER; LEU; LIRA; LIRE; MARK; ROUBLE; RAND; SEN; YEN
foreign dignitary KHAN
foreign friend AMI
foreign hotel PENSION
foreign land *see* COUNTRY
foreign language LANGUE
Foreign Office FO
foreign parts, in ABROAD
foreign private GI
foreign royalty ROI
foreign soldier GI
foreign, the DER; EL; IL; LA; LE; LES
foreign title PASHA
foreigner ALIEN; STRANGER; beware that this can refer to any nationality other than British (some compilers seem to assume that 'foreigners' don't attempt their crosswords!)
foreman GAFFER; ■ GANGER; can indicate something to do with jury
foremost BEST; TOP; first letter(s) indicator
forepart FRONT; PROW

foreshore, part of HARD
forest ARDEN; BLACK; DEAN; JUNGLE; WOOD; ■ TAIGA; TREES
forest clearing GLADE
forest, small WOOD
Forester's book GUN (i.e. *The Gun*)
forfeit WAIVE
forge COIN; SMITHY
forged MADE; anagram indicator
forger SMITH
forget LEAVE; MISS; OMIT
forgetful ABSENT
forgetting omission indicator
forgiving disposition MERCY
forgot LEFT; MISSED
forgot to mention PS
forgotten LOST; omission indicator; *see* FORGOT
fork BRANCH; Y; ■ CRUTCH
forked, something *see* FORK
form BED; BENCH; CAST; CLASS; FOUND; MAKE; SEAT; SHAPE; VERSION; ■ CREATE; FIGURE; GROUP; OVAL; anagram indicator
form of anagram indicator for the word or words that follow
formal DRY; PRIM; STIFF; ■ STARCHY
formal attire TAILS
formal gathering BALL; DANCE; MEET
formal guidance CLASS; LESSON; ■ COURSE; TUITION
formal pronouncements DICTA
formal, stiffly PRIM
formal wear DRESS; SUIT
formality ICE; RESERVE; STARCH
format PATTERN
format, in new anagram indicator
formation anagram indicator; ■ CREATION
formation, in anagram indicator
formed MADE; anagram indicator
formed in run indicator
former EX; LATE; OLD; ONCE; OLDEN; PAST

former days BC; ONCE
former pupil OB
former pupils OBS
former student OB; *see* GRADUATE
formerly EX; LATE; NEE; ONCE; ■ ERST; can indicate that a component is to be placed at the front; can indicate some device or institution in the past which has now been superseded
formerly named NEE
formers CLASS
formidable GRIM
formidable type TERROR; ■ DRAGON
forming anagram indicator
formula SECRET; anagram indicator
formula, magic SPELL
formulated anagram indicator
forsaken LORN
forsaking omission indicator
fort KEEP
fortepiano FP
forth ON
forthcoming attraction TRAILER
forthcoming, not COY; SHY
forthright BLUNT
Forties SCORES; [◊ ROARING]
fortification CAMP; KEEP; REDAN; WALL
fortified place KEEP
fortitude COURAGE; GRIT
fortress CASTLE; TOWER
fortunate HANDY; HAPPY; LUCKY
fortunately WELL
fortune BOMB; DOOM; FATE; LOT; LUCK; MINT; PILE; ■ CHANCE; WEALTH
fortune, good LUCK
fortune, having good LUCKY
fortune, reverse of DOWN
fortune-teller PALMIST; SEER; ■ SYBIL
forty XL
forty-five inches ELL
forty-nine IL
forty ponies GRAND

forty winks NAP

forward AHEAD; EARLY; LOCK (rugby); ON; PERT; SEND; can indicate a component is to be placed at the front as "spectators surge forward to barrier" → FLOODGATE

forward play RUCK

forwarded SENT

fosse DITCH; TRENCH

fossick MINE

foster BACK; NURSE; ■ HARBOUR; SUPPORT

foul BREACH; DIRTY; EVIL; RANK; VILE; anagram indicator

foul-mouthed F

fouled, fouling anagram indicator

found BASE; CAST; FORM; MET; START; TRACED; ■ BEGIN; CREATE; LAUNCH; run indicator; anagram indicator

found, are LIE

found everywhere COMMON

found here run indicator

found in run indicator; nesting indicator; can mean that the answer is contained in what follows as a run or anagram; or that instructions and components follow to build up the answer as a compound

found out nesting indicator

foundation BASE; BED; CAUSE; FOOT; REASON; ROCK; START; can indicate the first or last letter of a word

foundation, given a new first or last letter to be changed

foundation, without the first or last letter to be omitted

founded anagram indicator

founder SINK; anagram indicator

foundered SANK

foundering anagram indicator

fountain JET; SODA

four IV

four, one of QUAD

four, reportedly FOR

four pints GAL

four points TRY

14 lb STONE

fourth D

fourth-rate D

fowl HEN; SULTAN

fowl, water GANDER; *see* BIRD

fox CON; TOD; ■ REYNARD; VIXEN; *see* CON; [◊ EARTH]

fox-hunt fixture MEET

foxhole EARTH

fracas SCRUM

fraction BIT; PART; PORTION; RATIO; TITHE; can also refer to ordinary fractions e.g. half, third, quarter etc; [◊ (IM)PROPER; VULGAR]

fractured anagram indicator

fracturing anagram indicator

fragile TENDER; ■ DELICATE

fragment BIT; CHIP; PIECE; SCRAP; SHRED; SNATCH; SPLINTER; ■ IAMB; anagram indicator

fragments ORT

fragrance AROMA; SCENT

fragrant air *see* FRAGRANCE

frail BASKET; WEAK(qv)

frame CASE; CHASE; EASEL; GRID; MODEL; PLAN; SASH; ■ MOULD; PLANT; STILL (i.e. cinema film); YOKE; nesting indicator; run indicator

frame (under skirt) BUSTLE

frame of mind MOOD; TEMPER

framed, frames nesting indicator; run indicator

framing nesting indicator

France, and in ET

France, close by in PRES

France, first person in JE

France (formerly) GAUL

France, from (in) DE

France in EN

France in, or OU

France, part of MIDI

France, said in DIT

France, summer in ETE

France, that in QUE

France, these in CES

France, town in LENS; *see* TOWN

France, well in BIEN

France, you in TU; VOUS

Francis DRAKE

frank BLUFF; BLUNT; OPEN; PLAIN; STAMP; ■ CANDID; DIRECT; HONEST; MARK; SINCERE; STRAIGHT

frantic MAD; WILD; anagram indicator

frantically anagram indicator

fraternity ORDER

fraud CON; FAKE; RACKET; SCAM; STING; ■ PSEUD; SWIZZLE; anagram indicator

fraudster CON

fraudsters CONMEN

fraudulent FAKE; PHONY

fraudulent type PSEUD

fray RUB; STRAIN

frayed RAGGED; TATTY; anagram indicator

freak FAN; WEIRDO; anagram indicator

freakish WEIRD; ■ ODD; RUM; anagram indicator

free CLEAR; EASE; LOOSE; OFF (as "mark free from parasite" cues TICK OFF); OPEN; OUT; RID; UNTIE; ■ ACQUIT; DELIVER; EXEMPT; GRATIS; RELEASE; SPRING; UNDO; anagram indicator; can indicate a verb beginning with UN (as "Become free of habit" signals UNDRESS); can indicate a phrase beginning with NO (e.g. no charge)

free entertainment TREAT

free entertainment, provide TREAT

free entry PASS

free-lance anagram of LANCE

free, not BOUND; CAGED; ENGAGED; TIED

free offer, we hear TREET

free passage VENT

free play VENT

free transport LIFT

free travel HITCH; LIFT

freedom EASE; PLAY; ■ LATITUDE; LIBERATION

freedom of movement PLAY; see FREEDOM

freeholder LETTER

freeloader SPONGE

freemartin CALF

freely LIEF; anagram indicator

freer SAVER; SAVIOUR

freewheel COAST

freeze ICE; STILL

freezer ICER

freezing BITTER; GELID

freezing point F; O; ■ ICICLE

freezing temperature IC (i.e. one Centigrade)

freight LOAD

French F; FR; the use of a French locality in a clue, commonly Paris, Nice, can indicate that a French word is required, see some of the combinations below

French accent ACUTE; GRAVE

French actor TATI

French alternative OU

French are ES

French art ES

French aunt TANTE

French author see FRENCH WRITER

French authoress SAND

French beach PLAGE

French bed LIT

French biography VIE

French book ROMAN

French bread PAIN

French, by DE

French Canadian native CREE

French capital F; PARIS; can also indicate the French spelling of London i.e. Londres

French cat CHAT

French, certain SUR

French city CAEN; NANCY; NANTES; NICE; NIMES; ROUEN

French coast COTE

French coin, old SOU

French collaborator PETAIN

French comic actor TATI

French company CIE

French complaint MAL

French Connection, The TUNNEL

French count ODO

French dear CHER

French deep MER

French department MARNE; OISE

French drink VIN

French, during EN

French eleven ONZE

French fashion TON

French fashion, in the ALA (i.e. a la)

French father PERE

French, first person in JE

French for POUR

French friend AMI

French good BON

French here is VOICI

French horn COR

French house MAISON

French husband MARI

French, in DE; EN

French inn AUBERGE

French is EST

French island ILE

French king ROI

French kiosk TABAC

French land TERRE

French maid BONNE

French name NOM

French naval base BREST

French nobleman CONTE; DUC

French novel ROMAN

French novelist HUGO; PROUST; SAND; ■ DUMAS; VERNE; *see* FRENCH WRITER

French, of DE; DES; DU

French or OU

French plainsong CHANT

French port BREST

French priest ABBE; CURE

French provincial, old NORMAN

French pussy CHAT

French queen REINE

French refusal NON

French resort NICE

French river OISE; SEINE

French school ECOLE; LYCEE

French sea MER

French, second person in TU

French she ELLE

French, some DES

French, speaks in DIT

French state ETAT

French station GARE

French street RUE

French, the LA; LE; LES

French, this CE

French to A; ALA (i.e. a la); AU; AUX

French town BREST; NANCY; NICE; PAU; TOURS; VILLE

French trip TOUR

French, very TRES

French veto NON

French wall MUR

French water MER

French way, the RUE

French, we translated into NOUS

French what QUOI

French where OU

French wine VIN

French woman ELLE

French writer CAMUS; GIDE; SAND; ZOLA; *see* FRENCH NOVELIST

Frenchman FROG; IL; M; RENE; ■ JULES; LOUIS; PIERRE

Frenchman, said by the DIT

frenzied MAD; anagram indicator

frenzied excitement MUST (with regard to animals)

frenziedly anagram indicator

frenzy, in a anagram indicator

frequency F; PITCH

frequency, high OFTEN

frequent COMMON; ■ REGULAR; VISIT

frequently FR; OFT; OFTEN

fresco PAINTING

fresh BRACING; CLEAN; CHEEKY; CHILLY; FORWARD; GREEN; LATE; NEW; NOVEL; PERT; RECENT; SAUCY; ■ IMPRUDENT; MINT; VERNAL; anagram indicator; can indicate a verb beginning with RE- (as "Put fresh string around document" → RECORD)

fresh display of anagram of letters that follow

fresh, get *see* FRESHEN

fresh, no longer *see* FRESHNESS, LACKING

fresh, not STALE

fresh-sounding NEU; NOO; PNEU

fresh, when anagram indicator

freshen AIR; RALLY; REVIVE

freshening up, in need of anagram indicator

freshly can indicate a word beginning with RE as "freshly directed" → RESENT

freshness, lacking OFF; OLD; USED

fret BAR; CHAFE; EAT; FOG; FUSS; MIST; MOPE; PINE; RUB; WORRY

Freudian concept ID

friar AUSTIN; TUCK

friary CONVENT

friction RUB; ■ STRIFE; [◊ OIL]

friction, cause RUB

friction, reduce OIL

Friday via the nursery rhyme can refer to LOVING, GIVING

fried food CHIP

friend ALLY; AMI; BUD; BUDDY; CHINA; CHUM; COCK; CRONY; MATE; PAL

Friend QUAKER

friend, American BUD; BUDDY

friend, best DOG; can also refer to a particular breed, *see* DOG

friend, familiar COCK

friend from France/Paris AMI

friend from US BUD

friend, French AMI

friend, like a *see* FRIENDLY

friendly KIND; PALLY; ■ AFFABLE; AMICABLE; PLEASANT

friendly gesture PAT

friendly spirit AMITY

friendly terms, on WELLIN (i.e. well in)

friends ALLIES; *see* FRIEND

friends upset SLAP (i.e. reversal)

friendship AMITY

fright PANIC; SHOCK; TERROR

frighten CHILL; COW; SCARE; ■ ALARM; INTIMIDATE

frightened SCARED; ■ PSYCHED

frightened, seem WHITEN

frightening SCARING; SCARY

frightening noise BOO

frightening story CHILLER

frightfully anagram indicator

frigid COLD; ICY

frigidity ICE

frill RUFF; TUCK

fringe BANG (i.e. hairstyle); BORDER; EDGE; VERGE; *see* HAIR; can indicate something to do with Edinburgh (i.e. via The Fringe)

fringe benefit PERK

fringes of first and last letters to be uses as "fringes of society" → SY

frisk FROLIC

frisky anagram indicator

fritter away time POTTER

frivolous LIGHT; SHALLOW; ■ GIDDY

frivolously, act TRIFLE

frock DRESS

frolic CAPER; FRISK; LARK; PRANK; ROMP

from EX; OFF; OUT; run indicator; can indicate that the definition precedes (i.e. before the word "from"); can indicate that an adjective is required as "Rich son may come from the county" signals the adjective CORNISH; can indicate that the word(s) that follows is an anagram; can indicate that the word that precedes "from" in the clue should be placed last as "In the break see girl from Bury" → INTERVAL

from French DE

from Latin AB

from start to finish AZ

from that day on SINCE

from the French DU

from within RO (i.e. a run within FROM)

front BOW; FACE; FACADE; FORE; HEAD; LEAD; NOSE; PRE; PROW; SHOW; VAN; WAR; ■ BRASS; IMPUDENCE;

TEMERITY; first letter/word indicator; preceding indicator; can indicate something to do with weather, meteorology

front, hinged DOOR

front, in AHEAD; HEADING; LEADING

front page RECTO

front seat STALL

front, to the last letter of a word to moved to the beginning (as "Run to the front – hear this bird" → RHEA)

front, was in LED; WON

frontage first letter indicator

frontal first letter/word indicator

fronted first letter/word indicator; preceding indicator

frontier BORDER; MARCH

frost HOAR; RIME

frosty coating ICING

froth FOAM; HEAD; SCUM; SUDS

froth, bear HEAD

frown LOUR

frozen COLD; FRIGID; ICE; ICY; NUMB; STATIC

frozen, girl partly MIMI

frozen, more NUMBER (one of the classic chestnuts)

frozen water ICE

frugal SPARE

fruit ACORN; APPLE; BERRY; CONE; CROP; DATE; FIG; GRAPE; HAW; HIP; ISSUE; LIME; MAST; NUT; OLIVE; PEACH; PEAR; PLUM; PRUNE; SLOE; ■ ANANAS; CRAB; GOURD; MELON; QUINCE; RAISIN; SWEETIE; TANGELO; TOMATO; anagram indicator

fruit cake NUT; NUTTER

fruit drink CRUSH; SQUASH

fruit, large MELON

fruit of oak trees ACORN; MAST

fruit-picker HOPPER

fruit product JAM

fruit stone PIP; PIT

fruits CROP; *see* FRUIT, PROFIT

fruity RICH; RIPE

frumpish DRAB; DOWDY

frustrate BAFFLE; DASH; FOIL; SCOTCH; ■ COUNTER

frying material BATTER

frying pan SKILLET

FT PAPER; can indicate something to do with PINK (as the newspaper)

fuddled anagram indicator

fudge COOK; FAKE; SWEET; anagram indicator

fuel COAL; COKE; DERV; FIRE; GAS; OIL; PEAT; PETROL; STOKE

fuel, add STOKE

fuel pipeline PLUTO

fuel, place for BUNKER; FIRE; GRATE; LIGHTER; SCUTTLE

fuelling, tanker for BROWSER

fugitive RUNNER; ■ RUNAWAY

full FAT; ■ COMPLETE; GENERAL; PACKED; THOROUGH

full amount SUM; TOTAL

full-bodied RICH

full choice RANGE

full complement SET

full of nesting indicator

full of energy E to be nested

full of wind a synonym of "wind" (e.g. GAS) to be nested

full range AZ (i.e. range of alphabet)

full set BEARD

full strength NEAT

full-toned RICH

fully ALL

fulminate RAGE; RAIL

fumble GROPE

fumbled anagram indicator

fume BOIL; RAGE; SMOKE

fun FLING; GLEE; JAPES; JEST; LARK; PLAY; SPORT

fun, bit of LARK

fun, have REVEL

function DO; EVENT; GO; JOB; PART; PARTY; ROLE; USE; WORK; anagram indicator; can refer to a mathematical function, commonly COS, COT, LOG, SINE

functioning ON

fund KITTY; MINE; POOL; STORE; SUB; ■ ACCOUNT; RESOURCE

fund-raising event RAG

fundamental BASIC; PRIME; ROOT; *see* IMPORTANT

fundamental part ROOT

funding *see* FUNDS

funds AID; BACKING; PURSE

funds, way of accessing PIN

funeral bell KNELL

funeral car HEARSE

funeral fire PYRE

funeral gathering WAKE

funeral stand BIER

funerary receptacle URN

fungi CEP

fungus CEP; ROT; ■ MILDEW; MUSHROOM; TOADSTOOL; TRUFFLE

fungus reproducer SPORE

funnel HOPPER

funnily anagram indicator

funny COMIC; DROLL; ILL; ODD; RUM; ■ AMUSING; QUEER; STRANGE; anagram indicator

funny character CARD; *see* JOKER

funny fellow FISH; WAG; WIT

funny, something HOOT; JOKE; LAUGH

funny story JOKE; anagram of STORY

funny, they're *see* COMEDIAN, COMIC, JOKE, JOKER

funny, very KILLING

fur COAT; NAP; SABLE

fur covering TIPPET; *see* FUR, HIDE

furious CROSS; MAD; RED; ■ IRATE; LIVID; RAGING; anagram indicator; *see* ANGRY

furious, be RAGE; RANT

furious, become SEERED (i.e. see red)

furious speech RANT

furiously anagram indicator

furnish GIVE; EQUIP; ■ PROVIDE; SUPPLY

furniture BED; BUNK; CHAIR; COT; COUCH; DRESSER; PRESS; SOFA; STAND; STICK; STOOL; SUITE; TABLE; ■ COMMODE

furniture, old LUMBER

furniture, old-style REPRO

furniture, set of SUITE

furrow RIDGE; RUT

further AGAIN; ALSO; ELSE; EXTRA; MORE; OVER; SERVE; ■ PROMOTE (qv); can indicate a verb beginning with OVER or OUT; in conjunction with verb can indicate the use of RE as a prefix

furtiveness STEALTH

fury ANGER; IRE; RAGE; ■ ALECTO; WRATH; anagram indicator

furze GORSE; WHIN

fuse JOIN; SHORT; SOLDER; WELD

fuse, cause to blow a SHORT

fusillade SALVO

fusing anagram indicator

fusion BLEND; ■ MERGER

fuss ADO; DO; DUST; LATHER; POTHER; RACKET; RANT; ROW; STINK

fuss, make a CREATE

fuss over MOTHER; can indicate the reversal of a synonym for "fuss", and so: OD, ODA, STUD, WOR etc

fussed anagram indicator

fussy PICKY; ■ PARTICULAR; anagram indicator

future COMING; can indicate something to do with tense i.e. future tense in grammar

fuzz BLUR

Gg

G-string GROPE
gab CHAT; ■ CHATTER
gab, with the gift of FLUENT
Gabriel ANGEL
gad WANDER
gadget DEVICE; HOOK; TOOL (qv)
Gael SCOT
Gaelic ERSE
gaffe BLUNDER; ERROR
gaffer BOSS (qv); SUPER
gag JOKE; QUIP; RETCH; VOMIT
gain GET; EARN; LAND; NET; WIN
gain access HACK
gainfully employed, be EARN
gait CANTER
gaiter SPAT
gala FETE
gale BLOW; WIND
gall ANGER; CHEEK; ■ WORMWOOD
gall bladder [◊ BILE]
gallery GODS; TATE; ■ LOUVRE; can indicate something to with rogue i.e. via rogue's gallery
gallery, contents of ART
gallery, modern ICA
galley SLIP (printing)
Gallic FRENCH
gallivant GAD
gallon G
gallop CANTER; DASH; RUN; anagram indicator
galloped RAN; SPED
gallows trapdoor DROP
gambit PLOY
gamble BACK; BET; CHANCE; DICE; LAY; PLAY; PLUNGE; PUNT; SPEC; STAKE; WAGER
gambled DICED; LAYED
gambler BETTER; PUNTER; STAKER; TAKER

gambler's need CHIP; STAKE
gambling LOTTO
gambling behaviour STAKING
gambling centre RENO
gambling device TOTE
gambling equipment CARDS; DICE
gambling game CRAPS; *see* CARD GAME, GAME
gambol FROLIC; PRANCE; ROMP
gambolling anagram indicator
game BINGO; BOWLS; BRIDGE; DARTS; DEER; FARO; FIVES; FOWL; FRAME; GO; HALT (i.e. lameness); LAME; LOO; LOTTO; MATCH; MEAT; MONTE; NAP; NIM; PLAY; PLUCKY; POLO; POOL; RAG; RU; RUSE; SNAP; SOLO; SPORT; TAG; TIE; TIG; TRICK; WHIST; ■ BEETLE; CHESS; CONTEST; CRAMBO; DRAUGHTS; FOOTER; GROUSE; HOCKEY; PIQUET; QUOITS; RUGGER; SCRABBLE; SQUASH; *see* CARD GAME, SPORT; can indicate something to do with hunted animal, bird etc [◊ PANEL]
game bird GROUSE; PHEASANT
game, board GO
game, card *see* CARD GAME
game, children's MARBLES
game, easy SUCKER
game, finish MATE
game of chance DICE; LOTTO
game of golf ROUND
game, old gambling EO
game over a synonym of "game" to be reversed so we get STRAD, UR etc
game over! MATE
game, possibly MEGA
game point RUN
game, pursuit of COURSE
game, shot BAG
game taken BAG
game's ending MATE
games PE; PT; RUBBER; SET; SPORT
games, at least six SET

games, number of RUBBER; SET

games period INNINGS

gamin STRAY

gammon ROT

gamut RANGE

gander GOOSE; LOOK; PEEK

gang BAND; CREW; CROWD; LOT; MOB; RING; SQUAD; SWARM; TEAM; ■ BUNCH; GROUP; HORDE

gang-leader G

gangster AL; CAPONE; HOOD

gangster's friend MOLL

ganja POT

gap BREACH; BREAK; CLEFT; GORGE; HOLE; RIFT; ROOM; SPACE; VENT

gap in printing EM; EN

gap, narrow SLIT

gap, wide GULF; ■ CHASM

gape YAWN

gape at EYE

gaper CLAM

gaping OPEN

garage, job in MOT

garb RIG; WEAR; see CLOTHING, GARMENT

garble JUMBLE

garbled anagram indicator

garden BED; EDEN; HOE; KEW; PARK; PATCH; PLOT; WEED; YARD; ■ GARTH; GROUNDS; ROCKERY; [◊ FLOWER; PLANT]

garden equipment FORK; HOE; MOWER; RAKE; SPADE

garden feature FLOWER; LAWN; ROCKERY

garden, part/section of BED; PLOT

garden pest SLUG

garden, prepare TILL

garden suburb KEW

garden tool see GARDEN EQUIPMENT

garden, work in DIG; HOE; WEED

gardener ADAM

gardener, contrary MARY

gardener's son ABEL; CAIN

gardening, do HOE; WEED

gardens HOES; KEW; ■ GROUNDS

garish LOUD

garland LEI

garlic ALLIUM

garlic, segment of CLOVE

garment BRA; CAPE; CLOAK; COAT; DRESS; GOWN; HABIT; LUNGI; MINI; MAXI; ROBE; SHIFT; SKIRT; SLIP; STOLE; TOGA; TOP; VEST; ■ JACKET; SWEATER; TUNIC; VESTMENT; see CLOTHING

garment, church COTTA

garment maker TAILOR

garment, old TOGA

garment, scant MINI; THONG

garment, singular DUD; TIGHT; TOG

garment, tiny THONG

garments SHORTS; see GARMENT

garner GATHER

garret ATTIC

garter ORDER; [◊ BELT; SNAKE; STITCH]

gas A; AIR; ARGON; CHAT; CL; CS; H; HE; N; NE; O; TALK; XE; ■ CHATTER; NEON; RADON; SPEECH; WAFFLE

gas, escape of VENT

gas unit THERM

gash CUT; REND; RENT; SPARE; TEAR; WOUND

gasket SEAL

gasp PANT; SOB

gat GUN; ROD; TOOL

gate CROWD; ENTRY; PORTAL; WAY; WICKET; ■ ATTENDANCE; POSTERN

gate-crashing nesting indicator

gatehouse LODGE

gatekeeper PORTER

gates ENTRIES

Gateshead G

gateway DOOR; PORTAL

gather AMASS; DRAW; GLEAN; HEAR; INFER; MEET; ■ COLLECT; CONTRACT; GARNER; HOARD; LEARN; MARSHAL; MUSTER

gathered MET; anagram indicator
gathered by nesting indicator
gathering BALL; CROWD; DO; GROUP MASS; MEET; PARTY; RALLY; SOCIAL; anagram indicator
gathering, formal BALL; ■ MEETING
gathering in nesting indicator as "before gathering in" → ERINE
gaudy FEAST (college); FLASHY; SHOWY; ■ GARISH
gauge METER; TIMER
gauge, sort of OO
gaunt SPARE; THIN
gauntlet GLOVE
gave PAID
gave birth BORE
gave off SHED
gave up QUIT
gavel HAMMER
gawp STARE
gay [◊ OUT]
gay, openly OUT
gaze EYE; GLARE; STARE
gaze at EYE
gazelle GOA
gear COG; DRESS; KIT; RIG; ■ HARNESS; NEUTRAL; STUFF can indicate something to do with clothes, or engine
gear, female DRAG
gear, not in *see* NAKED
gear, one in fancy MODEL
gearwheel COG
Gee! COO; COR
gee-gee, say GG
geese GAGGLE
geese, flock of SKEIN
gel BIND; SET
gelatine SETTER
gelatine-like substance AGAR
gelignite, bit of STICK
Geller URI
gem AGATE; OPAL; PEARL; ROCK; RUBY; STONE; ■ GARNET; QUARTZ; [◊ CARAT]
gemstone *see* GEM
gen DOPE
gender SEX

general AVERAGE; BROAD; COMMON; CUSTER; FULL; G; GEN; LEE; PUBLIC; RIFE; THUMB; WOLFE; ■ AVERAGE; COMPLETE; MASS; NORMAL; OVERALL; [◊ STAFF]
General Assembly GA
general effect TONE
general, small THUMB
general's assistant ADC
generally known OPEN; PUBLIC
generate BREED; CAUSE; START
generating anagram indicator
generation AGE
generous AMPLE; BIG; KIND; LARGE; NOBLE; OPEN; ■ LAVISH; PROFUSE
generous, be GIVE
generous character SANTA
generous, extremely GS
generous, hardly/not MEAN; TIGHT
Genesis BIRTH
genetic material DNA
genial KIND; SUNNY
genius BRAIN
Genoa SAIL
genre CLASS; KIND; SORT; STYLE
gent MAN (qv); NOB; SWELL; TOFF
Gentile GOY
gentle KIND; MILD; P; SOFT; TAME; TENDER; ■ FAINT; MAGGOT; MEEK; QUIET; SLIGHT
gentleman G; GN; MR; SIR(E); ■ SQUIRE
gentleman, gypsy RYE
gentlemen LOO; ■ CONVENIENCE; TOILET; *see* GENTLEMAN
gentlemen, one preferred by BLONDE
gently P
gently wash LAP
gents MEN; *see* TOILET
genuine ECHT; HONEST; REAL; RIGHT; STRAIGHT; TRUE; ■ PROPER

genuine, accepted as CANON
genuine, not SHAM
genus BREED; CLASS; SORT; TYPE
geological sample/specimen CORE; ROCK
George G; GEO; GR; can indicate something to do with the automatic pilot of an aircraft
George* SAINT
Georgia GA
Gerald JERRY
germ BUG; SEED; SHOOT
German D; G; GER; HANS; HERR; HUN; OTTO; VON; ■ PRUSSIAN
German, a EIN; EINE
German and UND
German article DAS; DER; DIE; EIN
German bread STOLLEN
German car AUDI
German chap heard HAIR
German child KIND
German city EMS; ESSEN; TRIER
German commander ROMMEL
German consent JA
German count GRAF
German cry of pain ACH
German currency DM; M; MARK
German dramatist SCHILLER
German east OST
German, famous GOETHE
German gentleman HERR
German how WIE
German is IST
German joiner UND
German leader G
German Mr HERR
German, old ALT; ANGLE; FRANK
German physicist PLANCK
German poet HEINE
German prince ELECTOR
German quarter OST
German songs LIEDER
German state LAND; REICH
German states LANDER
German, the DAS; DER; DIE

German town EMS; ESSEN; TRIER
German wine WIEN
German with MIT
German woman FRAU
German writer MANN
Germanic people, member of ANGLE
Germans, OK for the JA
Germany D; GER
Germany, east of OST
Germany, is in IST
Germany, new from NEU
Germany, part of LAND
Germany, parts of LANDER
Germany's leader G
Gershwin IRA; [◊ RHYTHM]
Gestapo SS
gesture MOTION; NOD; PASS; SHRUG; SIGN; WAVE; ■ BECKON
gesture, empty TOKEN
gesture of affection CARESS; KISS
gesture, suggestive WINK
get BUG (i.e. to irritate); CATCH; CLAIM; COP; EARN; FETCH; GRASP; MAKE; NARK; PEEVE; SEE; TAKE; TWIG; inclusion indicator; in the context of getting someone to do something, can indicate ORDER; can indicate that the clue's definition immediately follows (as "Get praise" can signify PLAUDIT)
get a goal SCORE
get a load of COP
get a move on *see* RUN
get airborne FLY
get angry RILE
get annoyed RILE
get away FLEE; FLY; ■ ESCAPE; anagram of GET
get back REGAIN
get beaten LOSE
get better RALLY; RISE; ■ IMPROVE; RECOVER
get better of BEAT; PIP
get by COPE; PASS; ■ MANAGE
get down EAT
get excited ELATE; WOW

get from run indicator
get going ROUSE; START
get heated RAGE
get hold of CLUTCH; GRAB; GRASP
get hot under the collar SEETHE
get imprisoned INTERN
get in ALIGHT; ELECT; ENTER
get into ENTER
get less TAPER
get lost SHOO
get money EARN
get moving STIR
get off ALIGHT; LIGHT
get on AGE; ALIGHT; BOARD; FARE; MOUNT
get on feet STAND; RISE
get on one's back NAG
get on well CLICK; PROSPER
get one going I to be omitted
get out ALIGHT; ESCAPE; EXTRACT; ■ EXIT; anagram of GET
get over CLEAR; VAULT
get ready DRESS; RIPEN; EARN
get rid of BIN; CLEAR; DITCH; DROP; DUMP; EJECT; FIRE; KICK; KILL; OUT; PURGE; SACK; SCRAP; SHED; SLING; TRIM; ■ DELETE; DROP; DUMP; ERASE; REMOVE; SCRATCH; SCRUB; ZAP; can indicate that the answer is a verb beginning with DE as 'get rid of shadow' clues DETAIL (i.e. de-tail)
get rid of mess CLEAN
get spotless CLEAN
get the better of can allude to a verb beginning with OUT-, e.g. outdo, outsmart
get things moving START
get through COPE; PASS; PIERCE
get to EAT; REACH
get to grips COPE; WRESTLE
get to know HEAR; LEARN
get to one's feet ARISE; RISE; STAND

get-together can suggest that a word is to be repeated as "seamen's get-together" → TARTAR
get together ALLY; BAND; CLUB; RAISE; UNITE
get up CLIMB; LIFT; REAR; RISE; STAND; STIR; reverse order indicator; anagram indicator
get-up *see* DRESS, GET UP
get very excited OVERHEAT
get weary FLAG; TIRE
get well CURE; HEAL
getaway ESCAPE
gets HAS; can indicate that the clue's definition immediately follows
gets better RALLIES
gets some run indicator
gets up reverse order indicator
getting hot HEATING; WARMING; H to be added
getting on AGED; AGEING; AGING; LATE; OLD; OLDER
getting on, person BOARDER
geyser SPOUTER
Ghana GH
ghastly WHITE
ghetto SLUM
ghost SHADE; SPIRIT; SPOOK; ■ SPECTRE; [◊ HAUNT]
ghost, give up DIE
GI's shop PX
giant GOG; HUGE; OGRE; TITAN
gibe BARB; CRACK; DIG; GUY; MOCK; SCOFF; TAUNT
Gibraltar GIB; ROCK; ■ STRAIT
Gibson MEL
giddy DIZZY; LIGHT; SPINNING; anagram indicator
giddy up GEE
gift DOWER; PRESENT; TIP; ■ ALM; TALENT
gift paper WRAPPING
gift, propitiatory BUNG; SOP
gift, speaker's GAB
gifted ABLE
gifts, with ABLE
gig CART; ■ CONCERT
giggle TITTER
gigot LEG

Gilbertian princess IDA
gilt-edged BEST
gimmick TRICK
gimp LIMP
gin SNARE; TRAP; [◊ SLOE]
gin cocktail anagram of GIN
gin sling anagram of GIN
gin-soaked a component to be nested within GIN, TRAP etc, as "Gin-soaked married woman who's promiscuous" → TRAMP
ginger SANDY; SPICE
ginger biscuit SNAP
gipsy queen MEG
giraffe BROWSER
girder(s) can indicate something to do with a form of clothing around the waist
girl DOLL; GAL; HER; LASS; MAID; MISS; WENCH; can signal a female proper name e.g. ANN, CLARE, *see* WOMAN'S NAME, but very often the use of "girl" calls for the diminutive of a proper name e.g. SUE, TESS, *see* LITTLE GIRL
girl, attractive DISH; DOLL
girl coming out DEB
girl, good GLASS
girl, good-time TART
girl, grown-up LADY
girl, high class DEB
girl, little DI; SAL; SIS; SUE; VAL; VI; *see* GIRL
girl, of the HER
girl, presentable DEB
girl, pretty BELLE; CUTIE
girl, promiscuous HUSSY
girl's DIS; HER
girl, slovenly SLUT
girl, small CHIT
girl, stunning PEACH
girl, US SIS
girl who marries BRIDE
girl, young DEB
girlfriend BIRD; DATE; FLAME; LOVER; STEADY
girlfriend, American BROAD
girlfriend, Peter's WENDY
girls, group of BEVY
giro DOLE

gist DRIFT; HEART; NUB; POINT
git DRIP
give ALLOT; DOLE; HAND; PLAY; PRESENT; ■ BESTOW; METE; RENDER
give a beating PASTE
give a hand AID; CLAP; HELP
give an order TELL
give and receive SWAP; ■ EXCHANGE
give away SHOP
give back RETURN
give details RETAIL; TELL
give in *see* YIELD
give in, don't RESIST
give instructions BRIEF; TEACH; TRAIN; TELL
give money to PAY
give name LABEL
give notice RESIGN
give off, out EMIT
give out YIELD
give over TURNIN (i.e. turn in)
give pleasure TICKLE
give title DUB
give, to RENDER; YIELD; can indicate the definition follows
give too little space to CRAMP
give up CEDE; DITCH; DROP; KICK; QUIT; WAIVE; YIELD; ■ FORSAKE; RENDER; RESIGN; TURNIN (i.e. turn in)
give voice SING
give way BREAK; CEDE; CRACK; DEFER; SAG; YIELD; ■ BUCKLE
give weapons ARM
given IF; ■ GRANTED
given away omission indicator
given, be GET
given orders BOSSED
gives anagram indicator
gives a different look anagram indicator
giving ELASTIC
giving up CESSION
glad HAPPY; PLEASED
glade ARBOUR
gladly FAIN; LIEF
glamorous GLAM

glamour CHARM; GLITTER; ■ ALLURE
glance LOOK; PEEK
glance at SCAN
gland LIVER; ORGAN
glare GAZE; GLOWER; LIGHT; LOUR
glaring PLAIN
glass FLUTE; JAR; LENS; PANE; PONY; ■ BALLOON; BUMPER; MIRROR; RUMMER; SCHOONER; TUMBLER
glass, fit with GLAZE
glass, large RUMMER
glass plate SLIDE
glasses SPECS
glaze SIZE
gleam FLASH; GLINT; SHINE; TRACE; ■ GLISTEN
glean GATHER; PICK
glee FUN; ■ DELIGHT; MIRTH
glee, expressed CREW
glen VALE
glib PAT
glide SKATE; SKIM; SOAR
glide along SWEEP
glider PLANE; SKATE; can indicate a snake
glimmer INKLING; LIGHT
glimpse SIGHT
glint FLASH
glisten GLEAM; SHIMMER
glittering GARISH
glitzy GLAM
globe BALL; EARTH; O; ORB; ■ SPHERE
gloom DAMP; DARK; DUSK; SCOWL
gloom, former DOLE
gloom, period of NIGHT
gloomy DARK; DISMAL; DOWN; DREAR; DULL; GREY; LOW; SABLE; SAD; ■ BLUE; DISMAL; EERIE; MOROSE; SULLEN
gloomy, become CLOUD
gloomy dean INGE (one-time Dean of St Pauls)
gloomy type MOPER
glory PRAISE; ■ LUSTRE

gloss SHEEN; SHINE; SPIN
gloss over PAINT
gloss over, doesn't STRESS
glossy SLEEK
glove MITT; MITTEN
glove, type of OVEN
glow BEAM; BLUSH; SHEEN; SHINE
glower EMBER; STARE; can indicate anything that emits a light, (lamp, firefly etc)
glowing coal EMBER
glowing with heat RED
glue PASTE; SIZE; STICK
glum MOROSE
glut GORGE
glutton HOG; PIG
gluttony GREED
gnarl KNOT
gnash GRATE; GRIND
gnat FLY
gnaw CHEW
gnawed away EATEN
gnome MORAL; SAW; SAYING
go CRACK; DIE; DRIVE; EXIT; LEAVE; PEP; QUIT; SCAT; SHOO; SHOT; STAB; SWING; TRAVEL; TRY; TURN; VEND; WORK; ■ BEAT IT; BOUNCE; DEPART; ENERGY; MOVE; SALLY; can indicate a colloq. imper. such as "push off"
go about business CO to nested within a component
go across BRIDGE; SPAN
go after CHASE; ENSUE
go ahead LEAD; LEAVE
go-ahead OK
go along with TAG; ■ ACCEPT; AGREE
go around GAD; TOUR; TRAVEL; a component to be nested within GO or one of its synonyms
go ashore LAND
go astray ERR; SIN; WANDER
go away LEAVE; PASS; SCRAM; SHOO; ■ DEPART
go back OG; RETIRE; REVERSE; ■ REGRESS; RETURN; REVERT

go-between MEDIATE; GO to be nested within component(s)

go broke SHATTER

go by PASS

go carefully EDGE; INCH; NOSE

go cold CHILL; ■ FREEZE; ICE

go down DIE; DIP; EBB; FALL; SET; SINK; SWOON; ■ LOWER

go down quickly DIVE; SKILL; SLIDE

go downhill COAST

go fast BELT; HURTLE; NIP; TROT; *see* HASTEN

go for FAVOUR; HIT; LIKE; PREFER; ■ ATTACK

go from (one place) to (another) CROSS (Example: "Go from Mile End to Stratford East for weapon" → CROSSBOW)

go-getter DOER

go hard CAKE; SET

go, have a PLAY; TRY; ■ SHOOT

go in ENTER

go into ENTER

go mad FLIP; RANT; RAVE

go North of the Border GANG

go off ADDLE; ELOPE; LEAVE; ROT; SOUR; START; TURN; ■ DEPART; anagram indicator

go off course STRAY

go on PRATE; RABBIT; RANT; ROLL; *see* TALK

go on and on RAMBLE

go one better TRUMP

go out DIE; EXIT; LEAVE; SALLY; STRIKE

go over CROSS; OG; RECAP; TOP; VAULT; ■ TRAVERSE

go over again RECAP; RELIVE

go quickly BELT; NIP; *see* HASTEN

go round EDDY; LAP; ROLL; SPIN; TURN; nesting indicator

go round corner BEND

go separate ways PART

go slowly AMBLE; DALLY; LINGER

go so far as EVEN

go straight ARROW

go through RIFLE; ■ PIERCE; PEPPER

go to BASH

go to court, law SUE

go to ground EARTH

go to Paris ALLER

go to pieces SHATTER (qv); SPLIT; anagram indicator

go together AGREE

go topless first letter to be omitted

go up CLIMB; reverse indicator

go with speed WING; *see* MOVE FAST

go without LACK

go without food FAST; STARVE

go wrong ERR; anagram indicator

goad DRIVE; EGG; POKE; PRESS; PROD; PUSH; SPUR; URGE; ■ NEEDLE; ROWEL

goal AIM; CROSS; END; ■ OBJECT

goal, attempt at HEADER; SHOT

goal, put ball into NET; SCORE

goalie SAVER; ■ KEEPER

goalkeeper SAVER; [◊ BALL; NET]

goat BILLY; KID; NANNY; ■ BUTTER; IBEX; IZARD

goat, young KID

gobbling anagram indicator

goblet CUP

goblin TROLL

god ARES; D; FAUN; IDOL; LAR; MARS; ODIN; PAN; RA; SOL; THOR; TITAN; ■ DEITY; HORUS; INDRA; KAMA; PLUTO; TRITON; WODEN

God-fearing PI

God, speak to PRAY

God, Thank DG

God Willing DV

goddess ATE; HEL; MUSE; VESTA; ■ DIANA; HEBE; HERA; ISIS; KALI; VENUS

Godiva, one like LADY

godly man ST

godly style, treat in DEIFY

godparent PATRON

gods can indicate something to do with theatre seats

goes across one element to span another

goes out DATES; LEAVES; anagram indicator, especially of GOES

goes to one's head a component to be placed before INESS

Goethe can indicate something to do with Faust

Gog* GIANT

goggle STARE

going EXIT; OFF; ON; ■ LEAVING; SPEED

going away omission indicator

going by VIA

going down DESCENT

going down, person DIVER

going for ON

going in ENTRY

going into nesting indicator

going off BAD; HIGH; RANK; ROTTING; TURNING

going out EGRESS

going round reversal indicator; nesting indicator; anagram indicator

going through nesting indicator

going to a A to be added to the end (or sometimes the beginning)

going to pieces anagram indicator

going up reverse indicator

goings-on ACTIONS

gold AU; BULL; OR; SPECIE; WEALTH; ■ BULL'S EYE

gold and diamonds ORD

gold-backed can indicate that AU or OR are to be reversed (RO, UA) or that AU or OR are to be included at the end of a word or component

gold coin SOV

gold, covering of GILT

gold cross AUX

gold, get WIN

gold measure CARAT

gold-plated an element to be nested within O and R

gold, source of MINE

golden AURIC; BRIGHT; can indicate that the answer is a word beginning with AU or OR

golden retriever can indicate something to do with Jason, Argo, fleece etc

Golden State CAL

golf GAME; SPORT; ■ BIRDIE; CLUB; EAGLE; GREEN; HOOK; IRON; PRO; TEE; [◊ ROUND]

Golf CAR

golf-ball GUTTA

golf course TROON

golf club BRASSY; DRIVER; IRON; SPOON; WOOD; WEDGE ■ BRASSIE; MASHIE; NIBLICK

golf, game of ROUND

golf, play PUTT

golf shot PUT; PUTT

golf, some ROUND

golf tournament OPEN; MASTERS

golfer PALMER; PUTTER

golfer, good PRO

golfer's achievement ACE

golfer's need CADDY; CLUB; TEE; *see* GOLF CLUB

golfer's position STANCE; TEE

golly GOSH; *see* EXPRESSION OF SURPRISE

gone BY; LATE; LEFT; PAST; SPLIT; WENT

gone ahead LED

gone back reversal indicator

gone down FELL; SUNK

gone first LED

gone in front LED

gone off HIGH; LEFT; TURNED; anagram indicator; anagram of GONE

gone round nesting indicator

gone through MET

Goneril's father LEAR

gong MC; MEDAL

goober NUT

good ABLE; BON; FAIR; FINE; G; GRAND; HIGH; HOLY; KIND; MORAL; OK; PI; PIOUS; PLUM; RIGHT; ■ CHASTE; PRODUCT; SKILLED; can indicate some religious association as "good

book" for Bible, "good man" for
saint etc; [◊ WELL]

good at heart G to be nested
within a word or component

good, be too can indicate a verb
beginning with OUT (e.g. outdo,
outmatch)

good bloke SPORT

good book AV; BIBLE (qv); JER;
JUDGES; MATT; *see* BOOK

good book, section of NT; OT;
see BIBLE

good condition FIT

good deal BAGS; LOT; MANY;
TON

good deal of, a most of a word to
be used

good definition, with CLEAR

good, exceptionally HOLY; *see*
GOOD

good for eating PI to be nested

good fortune LUCK

good French BON

good gracious EGAD; GEE; MY

good hand FLUSH

good health, in FINE; HALE;
WELL (qv); ■ BLOOMING

good heavens GOSH; MY

good in Scotland GUID

good, jolly SUPER; TOPPING

good-looking DISHY; PRETTY

good man S; ST

good movement G to be relocated
within a word

good, not BAD; ILL; OFF

good opening G

good order, in TRIM

good, particularly TOPS

good party GRAVE (i.e. G +
RAVE)

good queen BESS

good, really SUPER

good reason, with RIGHTLY

good result GAIN; WIN; ■
CREDIT; SUCCESS

good result in race PLACE

good sense NOUS

good shot BULL; INNER

good sort BRICK

good start G

good terms, on IN

good thing ASSET; BOON

good time BALL; FUN; UP

good time girl TART

good time, in EARLY

good, very ACE; AI

good writing *see* BIBLE

goodbye TATA; VALE

goodness LORD; LUMME (con-
traction of 'Lord love me!'); MY
(i.e. exclamation)

goods GG; LINE; STUFF;
WARES; ■ FREIGHT;
PRODUCE; PRODUCTS;
PROPERTY

goods, cheap, shoddy TAT

goods for sale *see* GOODS

goods, one who delivers
SHIPPER

goodwill AMITY

Goodwood COURSE

goody-goody PI; PRIG

goof BOTCH; BUNGLE; *see*
MISTAKE

goose BRENT; EIDER; EMBER;
GANDER; IRON; MUTT;
NENE; SAP

gorge EAT; FEAST; GAP;
GULCH; NECK; ■ ABYSS;
BOLT; DEFILE; OVEREAT;
RAVINE

gorse WHIN

gory BLOODY; RED

gosh COR; GAD; GEE; LORD;
MY; OH; OOPS

gosh! (Scots) OCH

gospel FACT; can indicate a Biblical book e.g. LUKE, MARK

Gospeller MARK

gospels NT

gossip ANA; CHAT; CHATTER;
GAB; GAS JAW; NOISE; RAP;
RATTLE; YAP; ■ NATTER;
SLANDER; TATTLE; TATTLER

got back TOG

got over TOG

Gotham NY; can refer to some aspect of New York

got TOOK

got on AGED

got rid of FIRED; SACKED;
SHED; ■ KILLED

got together MET

got up ROSE; STOOD; TOG; reverse indicator

got up, having RISEN

gourmand PIG

govern DIRECT; LEAD; RUN; ■ COMMAND

governed, being UNDER

governed by UNDER

governess ANNA; EYRE

governing IN

governing body BOARD

government REIN; REIGN; RULE; STATE

government department FO; MOD

government leader G; PM

government official WHIP; ■ CONSUL

government, place in FO

government report PAPER

government study CIVICS

governess MISS

governor BEY; BOSS; DAD; HE; HEAD; PA; POP; ■ FATHER; GAFFER; RULER; *see* FATHER

gown DRESS; ROBE; SHIFT

GP DOC

grab CATCH; GRASP; SNATCH; ■ ANNEXE; CLUTCH

grab greedily HOG

grabbing nesting indicator; run indicator

grace POISE; ■ CHARIS; ELAN; UNCTION

graceful AIRY

gracious COR; KIND; MY(i.e. My!); PLEASING; *see* GOOD GRACIOUS

grade A; B; C; CLASS; D; E; MARK; LEVEL; RANK; STAGE

grades, decreasing DEF

gradual GENTLE

gradual progress, make INCH

gradually reduce TAPER

graduate BA; BE; BED; BSC; MA; MBA; PASS; ■ MARK

graft SPLICE

grail CUP

grain CORN; CROP; GR; MEAL; RICE; SEED; SPELT; WHEAT; ■ BARLEY

grain, remainder of BRAN

grain store SILO

grains SAND

grains, number of DRACHM

gram G

grand BIG; EPIC; FINE; G; GOOD; K; NOBLE; SUPER

Grand Master GM

grandma MOSES; *see* GRANDMOTHER

grandmother GRAN; NAN

granny KNOT; *see* GRANDMOTHER

grant ALLOW; AWARD; CEDE; CONFER; DOLE; LEND; LET; OWN; PRIZE; YIELD; ■ AGREE; ASSIGN; PRESENT

grant, don't REFUSE; *see* VETO

grant to tenant LEASE; LET

granted LET; ■ ALLOWED

grape juice MUST

graph CHART; PLOT

grapple with TACKLE

grasp CLING; GET; GRAB; HOLD; SEE; SEIZE; TAKE; ■ SNATCH

grasp firmly CLAMP

grasped GOT; SAW

grasping MEAN

grasping thing CLAW

grass BENT; CANE; CEREAL; HAY; JOINT; LAWN; NARK; NOSE; OAT; OATS; PANIC; PEACH; POT; REED; REEFER; RYE; SEDGE; SEED; SHOP; SING; SNEAK; SNOUT; SOD; SPILL; SWARD; TALK; VERGE; WEED; ■ BLADES; MARRAM; RICE; WHEAT

grass bordering fairway ROUGH

grass by seaside MARRAM

grass, chewed CUD

grass, cover with TURF

grass leaf BLADE

grass, long REED

grass, lots of LEAS

grass, mown LAWN

grass, some of the BLADE

grassland LAWN; LEA; LEY; MEAD; PARK; SWARD

grassy area FIELD

grate FILE; FRAME; GRIND; JAR; RIDE; RUB; WEAR

gratify PLEASE; SATE

grating COVER; GRID; GRILL(E); HARSH; JAR

gratis FREE

gratitude THANKS

gratitude, expression of TA

gratitude, show THANK

gratuitous FREE

gratuity TIP

grave ACCENT; CHASE; PLOT; STERN; SAD; TOMB; ■ MAJOR; SERIOUS; SOMBRE; [◊ EPITAPH; RIP]

grave letters RIP

grave, put into BURY; INTER

grave situation, put someone in a BURY; INTER

gravel GRIT; SHINGLE

graves STYLE

Graves* POET; WINE

Gravesend E

gravitational centre SUN

gravy SAUCE

gravy, container for BOAT

Gray POET

graze BARK; EAT; FEED; SCRAPE

grazed FED

grazing area FIELD; LEA

grease FAT; LARD; OIL; SMARM

grease, covered in OILY

greasy OILY; WAXY

greasy spoon CAF; CAFF

great BIG; FAB; GOOD; GRAND; GT; HIGH; HUGE; LARGE; MAIN; MAJOR; MEGA; MOST; OLD; OS; SUPER; TOPS; VAST; ■ FULL; GREAT; INTENSE; TOPPING

Great Bear PLOUGH

great deal LOT; LOTS; OODLES; SIGHT; TON; TONS

great force GALE; MAIN

great in extent HUGE; LONG; VAST

great man can indicate a giant, Cyclops etc

great many HOST; SLEW; *see* GREAT DEAL; M or some combination with other Roman numerals e.g. IM, MI, ML, MD

great-sounding JAR

great time BALL

greater EXTRA; MORE

greatest BEST; TOP

greatest possible ALL

grebe DIVER

Greece, once area of DEME

Greece, we hear FAT

greedy AVID

greedy chap/person HOG; PIG

greedy episode BINGE

Greek ATTIC; GR; SOLON; TIMON

Greek character, letter 2 letters: EI, MU, NU, XI, OU, PI; **3 letters:** ETA, RHO, TAU, PHI, CHI, PSI; **4 letters:** BETA, IOTA, ZETA; **5 letters:** ALPHA, GAMMA, DELTA, THETA, KAPPA, LAMBDA; SIGMA, OMEGA; **7 letters:** EPSILON, OMICRON, UPSILON

Greek cheese FETA

Greek city SPARTA

Greek contest AGON

Greek god ARES

Greek heroine ELECTRA

Greek island COS

Greek maiden IO

Greek poetess SAPPHO

Greek, thinking can refer to an ancient philosopher e.g. Aristotle

Greek, wise old NESTOR

green CALLOW; COMMON; COURSE; ECO; LAWN; LEAFY; LIME; NEW; OLIVE; RAW; SAGE; SICK; TURF; VEG; VERT; YOUNG; ■ BICE; EMERALD; GARDEN; GROWING; can indicate a fruit or vegetable; can indicate something to do with golf; can indicate something to do with GO (i.e. traffic light);

green feature BUNKER; HOLE

green, kind of PEA

green light OK

green, not ADULT; ■ MATURE

green stone PRASE

green, type of CROWN

Greene character LIME

greenkeeper can indicate something to do with COURSE

greens VEG

greenstuff VEG

Greenwich, say TIME

greeny blue CYAN

greet FLAG; HAIL; KEEN; SALUTE; WAVE; ■ KISS

greeting AVE; CARD; HAIL; HAILING; HALLO; HELLO; HI; HOW; WAVE; YO

greeting card HIJACK

greeting, Cockney ALLO; ELLO

greeting, Indian HOW

greeting sent CARD

greetings HIS

grew ROSE

grey AGE; ASHEN; ASHY; DULL; DIN; GY; OLD; PALE; SAD; ■ BICE; GRIS

grey-haired OLD

grey in Paris GRIS

greyish ASH; STONE; ■ ASHY

greyish-brown DUN

grid FRAME; GRATING; LATTICE

grief SORROW; WOE; anagram indicator

grief, come to anagram indicator

grief, evidence/sign of TEAR

grief, express CRY; WEEP

grievance BEEF; GRUDGE; *see* GROUSE

grieve MOAN; MOURN; ■ SIGH; SORROW

grieves audibly SIZE

Griffin as the main character in H G Wells' *The Invisible Man* can indicate something to do with visible/invisible

grill BROWN; COOK; TOAST; ■ GRATING; QUESTION; TOASTER

grilled HOT; anagram indicator

grim DOUR; HARD; STARK; STERN

grim end M

grime DIRT

Grimes SWEEP

grin SMILE

grind CHEW; CRUSH; GNASH; GRATE; MILL; POUND

grinder MOLAR; POUNDER

grip BITE; CASE; HOLD; TREAD; VICE; ■ CINCH; CLINCH; nesting indicator

Grip's owner RUDGE (pet raven owned by Dickens' character)

gripe BEEF; BITCH; GROAN; GROUSE; MOAN; PAIN

gripped BIT; BITTEN; HELD; nesting indicator

gripped by nesting indicator; run indicator

gripper CLAM

gripping nesting indicator

grips run indicator

grips with, get to TACKLE; WRESTLE

grist [◊ MILL]

grit GUTS; NERVE; PIP; PLUCK; SAND; ■ GRAVEL; RESOLUTION; *see* COURAGE

gritty BRAVE; SANDY

grizzled GREY; ■ HOARY

groan GRIPE; SIGH; ■ BEEF

grog DRINK; RUM

groggy anagram indicator

groggy, make DAZE

grommet RING

groom COMB; CURRY; DRESS; PREEN; TRAIN [◊ BRIDE]

groomed TRAINED; anagram indicator

groove CHANNEL; CUT; RUT; SLOT

groovy COOL; HIP; IN

grope FEEL; FUMBLE

gross FAT; GR; RANK; SUM

gross, not NET

grotesque ANTIC; anagram indicator

grotto CAVE

ground CLAY; EARTH; FIELD; FLOOR; LAND; LOT; MOOR;

PARK; PLOT; SITE; SOD; TERRA; ■ CAUSE; CRUSHED; REASON; STRAND; TERRAIN; VENUE; anagram indicator (as "ground rice" calls for an anagram of RICE)

ground-breaking work, do DIG

ground, get your feet back on the ALIGHT

ground, on the ATERRE (i.e. terre)

ground, our HOME

ground, piece of LOT; SOD

ground, to the DOWN

ground, unstable BOG

grounds DREGS; DROSS; ESTATE; LEES; ■ CAUSE; GARDEN; PARK; can indicate something to do with coffee

groundwork BASIS

group BAND; BATCH; BEE; BLOC; BLOCK; BOARD; BODY; CASTE; CELL; CIRCLE; CLAN; CLASS; CLUB; FACTION; FORM; GANG; GP; LOT; MASS; ORDER; PACK; PARTY; RING; SECT; SET; SIDE; SORT; TEAM; TRIBE; TRIO; TROOP; WING; ■ BEVY; BRACKET; BUNCH; CLUSTER; COVEN; ENSEMBLE; FORCE; GENUS; LEAGUE; ROUT (arch.); SCHOOL; UNIT; *see* BUNCH; anagram indicator; as a run indicator can refer to a group of consecutive letters within the clue

group, breakaway/dissenting FACTION; SECT

group in run indicator

group, management BOARD; TRUST

group of companies CARTEL

group of conspirators CELL

group of flags HOIST

group of girls BEVY

group of horses STRING

group of lions PRIDE

group of organisms GENERA

group of people NATION; *see* GROUP

group of players BAND; CAST; LSO; ORC

group of pupils CLASS; FORM; ■ SCHOOL; STREAM; YEAR

group of quail BEVY

group of workers CREW; GANG; GUILD; SHIFT; STAFF; TU; UNION

group, organised FORCE

group, our US

group, political PARTY; CELL

group, small CELL; DUO; TRIO

groups GENERA; *see* GROUP

grouse BEEF; BITCH; CRAB; GRIPE; GRUDGE; MOAN; ■ GAME; GRUMBLE; MUTTER; WHINGE

grove BRAKE; HURST; THICKET

grovel CRAWL

grow BLOOM; FARM; RAISE; SWELL; THRIVE; WAX; [◊ PLANT; SOW]

grow old AGE

grow older AGE; RIPEN

grow large SWELL; WAX

growing LIVE; ■ BECOMING; GREEN

growing things FLORA

growl GNAR (arch.); GRUNT; SNARL

growler *see* DOG

grown-up, almost ADUL

grows in/into anagram indicator

growth BEARD; CROP; FLOWER (qv); MOSS; MOULD; PLANT (qv); POLYP; SPRIG; TREE (qv); WART; WEN; *see* VEGETABLE

growth area(s) FARM

growth, large TREE

growth, new BUD; SHOOT

growth point NODE

growth potential EGG; SEED

grub CHOW; EATS; FODDER; FOOD; LARVA; NOSH; ROOT; ROOTLE (i.e. to rummage in the manner of a pig); ROUT; TUCK; WORM; ■ DIG; MAGGOT

grudge RESENT

grudging regard ENVY

gruelling HARD; anagram indicator

gruff HOARSE ■ HUSKY

grumble BEEF; CARP; CRAB; CRIB; CHUNTER; GROUSE; MOAN; MUTTER; NAG; YAMMER; *see* GROUSE

grumpy CROSS; SURLY

grumpy expression RATS

Grundy *see* GRUNDY, MRS. and GRUNDY, SOLOMON

Grundy, Mrs PRUDE (character in play); *see* GRUNDY, SOLOMON

Grundy, Solomon indicates an activity or its associated day stemming from the nursery rhyme: Born on Monday, Christened on Tuesday, Married on Wednesday, Took ill on Thursday, Worse on Friday, Died on Saturday

grunt OINK

guarantee ENSURE; INSURE; SEAL; ■ ASSURE; PROMISE; WARRANTY

guaranteed CERTAIN; SURE

guard FENCE; KEEP; SCREW; SENTRY; WARDER; WATCH; anagram indicator; nesting indicator; ■ CAVE (Lat.); ESCORT; FENDER; SHIELD

guard, on one's WARY

guard's intended ALICE

guarded CAGY

guardian ARGUS; ■ CARETAKER

guarding nesting indicator

guck SLIME

Guernsey can refer to the island or breed of cattle

guerrilla CONTRA

guerrilla leader CHE; G

Guevara CHE

guess DIVINE; FANCY; OPINE; RATE; SHOT; STAB; THINK; ■ RECKON; ESTIMATE; THEORY

guest INVITEE

guests COMPANY

guests, receive ENTERTAIN; HOST

guide DIRECT; LEAD; LEADER; MAP; PILOT; PLAN; POINT; RUDDER; RULE; SCOUT; SHOW; STEER; TRAIN; USHER; ■ GILLIE; POINTER; RANGER; STANDARD; TEMPLATE

Guide Leader G

guide-line STANDARD

guided LED; SHOWN

guild uniform LIVERY

Guinness ALE; STOUT

guitar AXE

guitar, play STRUM

gulf SPLIT

Gulf state OMAN

gull CHEAT; CON; DELUDE; DUPE; MEW; SUCKER

gullible GREEN

gully PASS

gulp (down) SWALLOW

gum GLUE; STICK; PASTE

gummy, something MASTIC

gumption NOUS

gumshoe EYE; TEC

gun ARM; COLT; GAT; PIECE; PISTOL; REV; RIFLE; ROD; SHOT; STEN; ■ HEATER; LUGER; MORTAR; REVOLVER; SHOOTER; UZI

gun component COCK; HAMMER; STOCK; TRIGGER

gun-play anagram of GUN

gun, pull a DRAW

gun, with ARMED

gunman EARP; SNIPER

gunmen RA

gunners RA

Gunpowder Plot TREASON

guns (big) ORDNANCE

guru SWAMI

gush SPOUT; ■ DROOL; POUR

gust BLOW; RUSH; SQUALL; WIND

Gustave DORE (artist)

gusted BLEW

gusto BRIO; SPIRIT; VIM; ZEST

gusty anagram indicator

gut *see* GUTTED

gut feeling HUNCH; INSTINCT

gutless the middle of a word to be omitted, usually to leave just the first and last letters

guts GRIT; PLUCK; ■ BOTTLE; NERVE

guts, some COLON

gutted can indicate that the middle letter(s) to be omitted, possibly all but the first and last letters as, for example, "gutted salmon" → SN

gutter CHANNEL

guttering CHANNEL; anagram indicator

guy APE; BLOKE; CHAFF; DOPE; MALE; MAN; RAG; RIB; ROPE; STAY; TEASE; TRICK; can also signify a man's name e.g. SAM, STAN; *see* MAN; can indicate something to do with tent, camping, guyrope etc [◊ MICKEY; PEG]

Guy can indicate something to do with Fawkes, Bonfire Night, November 5th, Gunpowder Plot etc

guys MEN; [◊ CAMP; TENT]; *see* GUY

guys heard GUISE

guzzle SWILL

guzzler GANNET

gym PE; PT

gymnast's posture PIKE

gyp PAIN (qv)

gypsy ROM; TINKER

gypsy gentleman RYE

gyrate SPIN; TURN

Hh

haberdashery, item of NEEDLE; PIN

habit BENT; DRESS; SUIT; USE; WIMPLE; ■ VESTMENT; can indicate some specific item of clothing (*see* GARMENT); can indicate something to do with holy orders, or riding

habit, bad VICE

habit-forming ADDICTIVE

habitat HOME; RANGE

hack AXE; CHOP; HEW; HORSE; KICK; LOP; MANGLE; NAG; RIDE; SEVER; ■ DRUDGE

hackle FEATHER

hackneyed BANAL; STALE; TRITE

hackneyed idiom CANT

hackneyed stuff/work CORN

had D (i.e. 'd usually clued with an abbreviation indicator e.g. 'briefly'); OWNED; TRICKED

had been WERE

had, I ID (i.e. I'd)

had in mind THOUGHT

had on CARRIED; SPORTED; WORE

had somehow anagram of HAD

Hades HELL (qv)

hag FISH; WITCH

haggard DRAWN; GAUNT

Haggard woman SHE

haggle BARTER

hail AVE; CALL; CHEER; FLAG; WAVE; ■ ACCLAIM; GREET

hail-storm anagram of HAIL

hair BEARD; BRAID; BRISTLE; BUN; CREW; DOWN; LASH; LOCK; MANE; MOP; ROLL; SHOCK; STRAND; TACHE; TRESS; WIG; ■ KEMP (usually wool); THATCH; WHISKER; [◊ SHAMPOO]

hair, back-comb TEASE

hair dye HENNA

hair, fine FUZZ

hair, knot of BUN

hair, lacking BALD

hair, long MANE

hair, losing one's BALD; BALDER

hair-restorer COMB

hair, short BOB

hair of the dog usually indicates something to do with alcohol or where it is drunk

haircloth CILICE

haircut HAI (i.e. last letter of "hair" omitted); TRIM; *see* HAIRSTYLE

haircut, short BOB; CREW

hairdo PERM; RINSE; *see* HAIRSTYLE

hairdressing establishment SALON

hairless BALD

hairpiece WIG; ■ TRESS

hairpin BEND(S)

hairs, a few LOCK

hairstyle AFRO; BANG; BOB; BUN; CROP; CUT; TRIM; ■ FRINGE

hairstyle treatment PERM

hairy ROUGH; anagram indicator

hairy, less BALDER

hairy man ESAU

hairy, not BALD; ■ SHAVEN

Hal, like BLUFF

hale SOUND

half DEMI; SEMI; half of the indicated word to be used, as "left half" cues LE or FT

half a chance EVENS

half-a-dozen VI

half-a-dozen, less than V

half century L

half-cooked RARE

half-day SUN, MON etc

half-day closing FRIEND

half-door HATCH

half-forgotten half of word to be omitted

half-hidden half of word to be omitted

half-hearted AL; one of the two middle letters of an evenly-numbered word to be omitted as "half-hearted lawman" → COPER

half-heartedly one of the two middle letters of an evenly-numbered word to be omitted as "half-heartedly shout" → BELOW

half hour two letters to be used from HOUR

half-hundred L

half-inch CH; IN; STEAL

half-measure EN

half-mile LE; MI

half, more than MOST

half of F; O; half of the word that follows 'of' to be used

half of, failing half of succeeding word to be omitted

half of the weekend SAT; SUN

half-portions half the letters of the associated words to be used

half-score TEN

half-sister SIS or TER

half-term two consecutive letters of TERM to be used

half ticket TIC or KET

half-time two consecutive letters from TIME to be used (usually TI or ME, but IM is possible)

half-truth VERA

half-witted DAFT

half-wrecked anagram of HALF

hall LOBBY; ROOM; SEAT; ■ CHAMBER; HOUSE

hallow BLESS

halo RING

haloed nesting indicator

halt CEASE; END; LAME; STOP; ■ FALTER; LIMP

halt to, call a STOP

halt, come to a END; STOP; STALL

halting LAME

halve SHARE

ham THIGH

Ham can indicate something to do with Noah, Ark etc

Hamlet DANE; LEAD; PLAY; PRINCE; can indicate something Danish e.g. pastry; [◊ IDIOT; MADNESS; TRAGEDY]

hammer BEAT; DRIVE; GAVEL; HIT; RAM; SLEDGE; TILT; TOOL; ■ MALLET; STRIKE; TROUNCE; can indicate something about the inner ear

hammer-blow, deal KNAP

hammer, type of MAUL; SLEDGE; TRIP

hammered, hammering anagram indicator

hamper BAR; BLOCK; CLOG; CUMBER; DETER; TIE; ▪ BASKET; IMPEDE
hampered nesting indicator
Hampton Court, feature of MAZE
hand AID; DEAL; E; EAST; FIST; GIVE; MAN; MITT; N; NORTH; PALM; PASS; PAW; S; SOUTH; W; WEST; ▪ DELIVER; DUMMY; HELP; MEMBER; PRESENT; SCRIPT; WORKER; [◊ FINGER; PAW]; can indicate something to do with manicurist
hand around PASS
hand, clenched FIST
hand, could be on GLOVE
hand, give a AID; DEAL; HELP
hand, good FLUSH; STRAIGHT
hand, on CLOSE; NEAR
hand out DEAL; DOLE; ISSUE; METE; anagram of HAND; can indicate that a component is to be nested within HAND or a synonym such as PAW; *see* HANDOUT
hand, out of anagram indicator
hand out pieces SHARE
hand over GIVE; PASS; PAY; REFER; SIGN; WAP (i.e. paw reversed); ▪ CEDE; CONSIGN; PRESENT
hand, show one's VOTE
hand signals, give WAVE
hand, take in GRASP
handbook MANUAL
handcart BARROW
handcuffs SNIPPERS
handed down GENIC
handful FEW
handicap SADDLE
handiwork DIY
handkerchief TISSUE
handle COPE; CRANK; CROP (i.e. the handle of a whip); DO; HAFT; HILT; LEVER; NAME; RUN; STOCK; TACKLE; TAG; TITLE; TREAT; ▪ FINGER
handle roughly MAUL; PAW; SCRAG
handle well COPE

handled DID; FELT; RAN
handler COACH; TRAINER
handling TOUCH; anagram indicator
handout ALMS; DOLE; GIFT; GRANT
hands CREW
hands, in both a component is to be nested between L and R
handshake can indicate an anagram of HAND
handsome man HUNK
handsome youth ADONIS; APOLLO
handwriting FIST; SCRIPT
handy ABLE; CLEVER; CLOSE; DEFT; NEARBY
handy way of can indicate a blow delivered by hand e.g. punch, chop
hang DROOP; KILL; PEND; SAG; SLING; SWING; ▪ DANGLE; KNACK; LYNCH; SCRAG; SUSPEND
hang about/around HOVER; IDLE; LINGER; LOAF; STAY; TARRY; WAIT; ▪ LOITER
hang on TARRY; WAIT
hang onto KEEP; RETAIN
hang over BEETLE
hang up DRAPE; GAS; [◊ BAT]
hang-ups can indicate something to do with washing line e.g. peg
hanged, be SWING
hanger-on BAT; BURR; PARA
hanging ARRIS; can indicate something to do with paintings
hangman's rope NOOSE
hank COIL
hanker LONG; YEARN; ▪ DESIRE; WANT
Hannibal LECTER; can indicate something to do with elephants
haphazardly anagram indicator
hapless WRETCHED
happen BE; BEFALL; CHANCE; COME; OCCUR
happened CAME; ▪ BEFALLEN; BEFELL
happening AFFAIR; EVENT
happens, as it LIVE

happens, where something VENUE

happily in the past LIEF

happiness BLISS; GLEE; JOY

happiness, place of HEAVEN

happy GAY; GLAD; ELATED; OK; PLEASED; ■ BLESSED; BLITHE; CHUFFED; CONTENT; FINE; TIPSY

happy event DELIVERY; ■ BIRTH

happy, not SAD

happy sound PURR

harangue DECLAIM; ORATE; TIRADE

harass NAG; ■ HECKLE; HOUND; PESTER

harassed anagram indicator

harbinger HERALD

harbour BERTH; DOCK; FACE; FOSTER; HIDE; HAVEN; HOME; POOLE; PORT; ■ ENTERTAIN; MARINA; QUAY; SHELTER; *see* PORT

harbour we hear HYDE

harbouring nesting indicator; run indicator

harbour PIER(S)

harbours reportedly DOX

hard FIRM; GRIM; H; RAW; ROUGH; SET; STERN; STIFF; ■ GREAT; HEAVY; ILL (as "ill use" = "hard treatment"); IRON; ROCKY; SEVERE; STONY; STRONG; TOUGH; [◊ROCK]

hard area CALLUS

hard at work BUSY

hard-faced H

hard-fought CLOSE

hard-hearted AR; H to be the centre of an element

hard look GLARE

hard matter can indicate diamond, jasper etc

hard, not SOFT; H to be omitted

hard on, be SCOLD (qv)

hard place TOR

hard skin CORN

hard tissue BONE

hard to catch H to be nested within a component

hard to follow H to be inserted after a component

hard to open TIGHT

hard to put in H to be inserted

hard-up BROKE; SKINT; ■ INSOLVENT

hard wood EBONY; HELM (i.e. H + elm); TEAK

hard work FAG; GRAFT; HOP (i.e. H op.)

hard worker BEE

hardly worth mentioning MINOR; SLIGHT

harden SET; ■ ENURE; INURE

hardliner DRY (i.e. in politics as opposed to "wet")

hardship NEED; PINCH

hardware, article of SCREW

hardwood *see* HARD WOOD

hardy SPARTAN

Hardy OLLIE

Hardy hero JUDE

Hardy sergeant TROY

Hardy's girl TESS

hare CHASE; DASH; FLY; RACE; RUN (qv); RUSH

hare-brained SCATTY

hare, sort of MARCH

hared SHOT

harm EVIL; HURT; ILL; MAR; SPOIL; anagram indicator

harmed, not OK; *see* ALL RIGHT

harmful BAD; EVIL

harmful, very FATAL

harmonic ACCORD

harmonise/ harmonize CHIME; FIT; TONE; ■ KEY

harmonised WENT

harmonium ORGAN

harmony BLISS; ORDER; ■ ACCORD; CONCERT; KEEPING; UNITY

harness HITCH; REIN; TACK

Harrier FIGHTER

Harris ISLE; ROLF

Harris's brother BRER (i.e. Brer Rabbit)

harry HECKLE; NAG; ■ MOLEST; anagram indicator; *see* WORRY

Harry HAL; anagram indicator; *see* HARRY *above*

harsh CRUEL; GRIM; HARD ; ROUGH; RUDE; STERN; STRICT; ■ ACID; AUSTERE; EXTREME; SEVERE

harsh conditions RIGOUR

hart STAG

harvest CROP; GLEAN; REAP

harvester CROPPER; GLEANER; REAPER

has OWNS; S (i.e. 's abbr.)

has-been GONER

has cracked anagram of HAS e.g. ASH

has different anagram of HAS

has previously HATH

has to MUST

hash CHOP; MESS; MINCE; NUMBER (U.S.); POT; SPACE (pr.); anagram indicator

hasn't omission indicator, usually the following word to be omitted

hassle BOTHER; BUG; TROUBLE *see* ANNOY

haste HURRY; RUSH; SPEED; ■ CELERITY

haste, made RAN; SPED; SURGED; TORE

haste, make RUN; SURGE; TEAR

hasten BELT; HIE; NIP; RUN; RUSH; SPEED; TEAR; TROT ■ HURRY

hastened RAN; TORE

hastily assembled SCRATCH

Hastings area SE

hasty RASH

hat CAP; LID; TAM; TILE; ■ BERET; BOATER; BONNET; BOWLER; DERBY; LEGHORN; MITRE; TAM; TOPI; TOPPER; TOQUE; TRILBY; *see* HEADGEAR

hat, raised DIL; PAC

hatch PLOT; TRAP

hatchet CUTTER

hate DETEST

hate, do not LOVE

hating ANTI

hatred SPITE

haughty LOFTY; PROUD; ■ GRAND

haul DRAG; HEAVE; LUG; PULL

haul up HOIST

hauled HOVE

hauled up reverse indicator

haulier CARTER

haunch HIP

haunt FOLLOW; PLACE; SHADOW [◊ GHOST; RESORT]

hauteur PRIDE

Havana SMOKE; ■ CIGAR

have CON; HOLD; KEEP; OWN; TRICK

have a word with SEE

have existence ARE

have fun PLAY; SPORT

have, I IVE

have importance COUNT

have life BE

have power CAN; P to be nested

have, to WITH

haven PORT

having OWNING; WITH

having a ball BALL (or O etc) to be nested

having no can indicate an adjective beginning with UN or ending in LESS; can indicate that the definition follows immediately

having, no longer LOSING

having no power UNABLE; P to be omitted

having no record CLEAN

having potential ABLE

having problems anagram indicator

having spoken SAID

Hawaiian greeting ALOHA

hawk CRY; COUGH; SELL; TOUT; ■ BIRD; PEDDLE

hawser, use KEDGE

Hawthorn MAY

hay COCK; CROP; DANCE; FODDER; RICK; ■ GRASS

hay, bundle of BALE; *see* HAY

hay, make TED

haymaker BALER; PUNCH

haystack COCK; RICK

hazard BAR (i.e. sandbar); BERG; FOG; REEF; RISK; ■ CHANCE;

DANGER; GUESS; PERIL; WEIR

hazard for plane ICING

hazard, maritime BAR; BERG; REEF

hazardous *see* DANGEROUS; anagram indicator

haze FOG; MIST

Hazel* NUT

haziness *see* HAZE

hazy FAINT; UNCLEAR; anagram indicator

he can indicate a man's name, worker or occupation; in the same way, can indicate a word ending in ER describing the participator in some activity or who displays some characteristic, as "he seems happy" can cue SMILER; ■ PRONOUN

He as the symbol for helium can indicate something to do with chemical symbol

he had HED

he in France IL

he scored can indicate the name of a composer

he will HELL

he would HED

head BEAN; BLOCK; BONCE; BOW; BRAIN; CAPE; DOME; FIRST; FRONT; LEAD; LOAF; MIND; NESS; NOB; NUT; PATE; PEAK; POLL; PRES (for President); PROW; TIP; TOP; ■ CRANIUM; CROWN; DIRECTOR; FROTH; LEADER; NAPPER; NODDLE; NOODLE; ONION; POINT; PRECEDE; PRESIDENT; SKULL; initial letter indicator; can indicate something to do with head (e.g. hair, hat); can refer to a particular geographic head e.g. LIZARD; [◊ CAP; HAIR; HAIRBRUSH; LEAD; LED]

head, a EACH; PER

head branch ANTLER

head-butt GORE

head, cereal EAR

head covering HOOD; *see* HAT

head-dress D; *see* HEADGEAR

head first H

head lowered initial letter to be re-located further back into the word as with "Imposing gaze with head lowered" changes GLARE (i.e. gaze) into the solution LARGE (i.e. imposing)

head of can indicate that the initial letter of the ensuing word is to be used, as "head of lab" → L

Head of Division D

head of faculty DEAN; F

head of family DON

head of government G; PM; PRES

head of house PRIOR

head of state ER; KING; S; ■ PRESIDENT; QUEEN

head off first letter to be omitted

head over heels anagram indicator; reversal indicator

head-over-heels, go TUMBLE; reversal indicator

head, part of CHIN; FACE; ■ SKULL

head's supporter NECK

head scholar S

head, Scottish RECTOR

head to foot initial letter to be transposed to the end as "Shook head to foot" clues HOOKS

headache BOTHER; *see* PROBLEM

headed LED; first letter indicator

headed off first letter to be omitted

headgear BERET; BONNET; CAP; CROWN; G; HAT (qv); TOP; TOPI; VEIL; ■ BOWLER; TOPPER; TURBAN

heading BOUND (as "heading East" cues EBOUND); ■ DIRECTION; initial letter indicator (as "today's heading" → T); can indicate that a component is to go at the beginning

heading for initial letter of the word that follows

heading for the T

heading north reversal indicator in a DC

heading off first letter to be omitted

heading west reversal indicator in an AC

headland CAPE; L; POINT

headless first letter(s) to be omitted

headlight HALO

headline SPLASH

headlong RASH

headmaster HM; M

headquarters *see* HQ

heads TOPS; *see* HEAD; [◊ TAILS]

heads (all the) only the initials of indicated words to be used

heads off initial letters to be removed from adjacent words; anagram of HEADS

headwear HAT (qv); *see* HEADGEAR

headwind W

heady STRONG; RASH

heal CURE

health TOAST

health food BRAN

health, offer TOAST

health, propose TOAST

health centre AL; HYDRO; SPA

health risk CARRIER

health wing SAN

health-worker *see* DOCTOR, NURSE

healthy FIT; GOOD; HALE; SOUND; TRIM; WELL; ■ WHOLE

healthy, appearing less PALER

healthy food FRUIT

healthy, looking TRIM; *see* HEALTHY

healthy, not AILING; ILL PEAKY; SICK

healthy, opposite of ILL; TIF; *see* NOT HEALTHY

healthy town SPA

heap CAR; CLAMP (i.e. of vegetables); CRATE; HILL; LOAD; MOUND; PILE; RICK; STACK; anagram indicator

heap of vegetables CLAMP

heaped LADEN; STACKED; anagram indicator

heaps, in PILED; STACKED

hear CATCH; GATHER; TRY; homophone indicator; can indicate a word of phrase sometimes uttered by the subject; similarly; can indicate a sound associated with the subject (BARK for dog, MEW for cat and so on)

hear about anagram of HEAR

hear, we homophone indicator

heard TRIED; homophone indicator

hearing SESSION; TRIAL; homophone indicator

hearing aid EAR

hearing, in homophone indicator

hears TRIES

hears about anagram of HEARS

heart CENTRE; CORE; GIST; H; NUB; PITH; TICKER; ■ BOSOM; CRUX; ESSENCE; GUTS; MIDDLE; MORALE; the middle letter(s) of a word is to be used, as "heart of gold" → OL

heart* ORGAN

heart, at *see* AT HEART

heart, having a A to be nested within a component

heart, lose DESPAIR; middle letter(s) of a word to be omitted

heart of America CENTER

heart-throb PULSE

heartbreak anagram of HEART

heartbroken anagram of HEART e.g. EARTH

hearted indicates an element to be inserted in middle of a word

heartens previous word to be nested in word that follows

hearth HOME; INGLE; [◊ FIRE]

hearth-frame FENDER

heartily the middle letter(s) of a word to be used

heartily sick IC

heartless STERN; ■ CRUEL; can indicate that one should omit the middle of a word, usually one letter (as "heartless man" → MN) but can mean several letters (as "heartless lady" → LY, "heartless rogue" → RE and so on)

heartless bloke GY; MN

heartless, not KIND (qv); NT

heartless woman SE

heartlessly omit the middle of a word, for example, "heartlessly cool" → CL, *see* HEARTLESS

hearts H; *see* HEART

hearty WELL

heat ANGER; BAKE; BOIL; EVENT; FEVER; H; MULL; RACE; WARM; ■ FINAL (as in a sports event)

heat, get BURN

heat injury BURN

heat, source of SUN

heated HOT; WARM; ■ ANGRY

heater BOILER; FIRE; KETTLE; OVEN; STOVE

heater, small RAD

heath BRIER; MOOR; (COMMON

heathen PAGAN; [◊ IDOL]

heather ERICA; LING; [◊ PURPLE]

heats H; RACES

heave CAST; DRAG; LIFT; PULL; PUSH; RAISE; RETCH; SWELL

heaven BLISS; SKY

heaven, in ABOVE

heavenly being ANGEL

heavenly body COMET; EARTH; MOON; PLANET; STAR; SUN; ■ ASTEROID

heavenly body's LUNAR; SOLAR; ■ VEGA

heavenly creature ANGEL

heavenly food MANNA

heavenly life HEREAFTER

heavenly surroundings, in a component to be nested within SKY

heavens GOSH; SKY; ■ SKIES

Heavens! COR; GEE

heavenwards reversal indicator

heaviness WEIGHT

heaving motion SWELL

heavy BOLD; HARD; THUG; ■ LEADEN; ROUGH; WEIGHTY; can indicate some kind of tough guy, bodyguard, villain in play or film etc

heavy demands, make TAX

heavy metal LEAD; PB

heavyweight TON

Hebridean island HARRIS

Hebrew measure COR

heckle HARRY

hectic, hectically anagram indicator

hector BADGER; BULLY

hedge FENCE

heed NOTE; RECK; ■ ATTEND; WATCH

heel CAD; CANT; LEAN; LIST; RAT; SWAY; SWINE; ■ BOUNDER; LOUSE; ROTTER; ROGUE

heel, with square S to be added at the end

heedless of omission indicator

heft RAISE

height H; HILL; HT; MOUNT; RIDGE; TOR; ■ ALTITUDE; STATURE; can require a specifically named mountain

height, more than average TALL

heighten RAISE; UPRAISE

Heights GOLAN

heights, reach new VAULT

heinous EVIL; WICKED

heir SUCCESSOR; [◊ WILL]

heiress, Venetian PORTIA

heist ROB; STEAL; ■ ROBBERY

held HAD; PENT; nesting indicator

held by nesting indicator

held by the a component to be nested within THE

held captive nesting indicator

held fast STUCK

held in run indicator; nesting indicator

held on CLUNG

held, to be TENABLE

held up HUNG; LATE; PENT; ■ ONICE (i.e. on ice); reversal indicator; UP to be nested within a component

Helen's mother LEDA

helium HE; GAS

hell DIS; HADES; ■ ABYSS; INFERNO

hell, feature of PIT

hell-hole ABYSS

hellfire PI (as "hellfire sermon" gives PIRANT – i.e. pi-rant – to construct ASPIRANT)

hellish anagram indicator

hellish place DIS

hello *see* GREETING

helm, man at the LEADER

helmet CREST; LID

helot SLAVE

help ABET; AID; BACK; HAND; HINT; SERVE; SOS; ▪ ASSET; ASSIST; AVAIL; FAVOUR; MAYDAY; RELIEF; RELIEVE; SERVICE; can indicate some kind of device (as "current help" might refer to a water-wheel, mill-race etc)

help, inside AID to be nested within a component

help out can indicate an anagram of HELP (qv)

help, outside a component to be nested within AID

help, request for SOS

helper AID; AIDE; ALLY; HAND; MATE; can indicate a device or instrument, *see* HELP

helper at wedding USHER

helpers can indicate a device or instrument as "seeing helpers" can lead to spectacles, pince-nez

helpful AIDING; KIND; WILLING; ▪ INSTRUMENTAL

helpful, be ABET; *see* HELP

helping RATION; SHARE; SLICE; ▪ PORTION; SERVICE

helpless omission of the letters AID

helter-skelter anagram indicator

hem COUGH; EDGE (qv); PEN; SEAM; VERGE

hen LAYER; POULE; PULLET

hence SO

henna DYE

hennery COOP; RUN

henpeck NAG

Henry FORD; H; HAL; HANK; HY; can indicate something to do with the Martini-Henry rifle

Henry VIII, wife of ANNE

Her Majesty ER; HM

Herald SIGNAL

heraldic band FESS

heraldic device CREST

heraldic designs ARMS

heraldry [◊ ORDINARY, SINISTER, CHEVRON]

heraldry flower LIS

herb CHIVE; DILL; RUE; SAGE; SIMPLE; THRIFT; THYME; ▪ CICELY; FENNEL; PARSLEY

herb, aromatic MINT

Herbert LOM

Hercules can indicate something to do with labour, labourer, labours etc

herd CROWD; DROVE; FLOCK

herd, one of the COW; HORSE; PIG

here GRID (i.e. the puzzle itself); LOCAL; NOW; PRESENT

here and there ABOUT

here in France ICI

here in Germany HIER

here in Paris ICI

here in Rome HIC

here, not THERE

hereditary element GENE

heretic ARIAN; ARIUS (ancient priest)

Hereward [◊ FEN]

hermit CRAB

hero BADER; FAUST; IDOL; LEAD; LION; STAR

heroic BRAVE; EPIC

heroic exploit FEAT; DEED

heroin H; HORSE; SMACK

heroine BECKY; BESS; DIDO; EMMA; MOLL; NELL; NORMA; SHE (from Rider Haggard's novel); TESS

heroine, tragic MIMI

heron EGRET

herring KIPPER

Hertfordshire town WARE

hesitancy *see* HESITATION

hesitant UNSURE; WAITING

hesitant expression/utterance ER; UM; UR

hesitate ER; HOVER; HEM; UM; WAVER; ▪ DITHER; FALTER; TEETER

hesitate to take off ER or UM to be omitted from as word (as "Hesitate to take off sweater") → JUMP)

hesitation DOUBT; ER; UM; UR; ■ STAMMER

hesitation about MU; RE

hesitation, express ER

het-up anagram of HET; *see* ANGRY

★ **heteronyms** words with the same spelling but different meanings and pronunciations e.g. pol-ish/Polish. In clues they will be used without an indicator and in such a way as to put you onto the wrong meaning

hew CHOP; CUT (qv); HACK

hewn AXED; CYT

hex AXE; SPELL; WITCH

hi-fi, piece of AMP

hiatus BREAK; GAP

hibernation SLEEP

Hibernian IRISH

hiccup BUG; GLITCH; SNAG

hick YOKEL

hidden INNER; SECRET; UNDER; ■ COVERT; DOGGO; nesting indicator; run indicator

★ **"The Hidden 'And'"** with this device the word AND has to be assumed, for example the solution to "The girl who has my letters" is MANDY (i.e. M and Y)

hidden by run indicator

★ **hidden clue** another name for the type of clue in which the answer is a run of letters within the clue; *see* RUN

hidden danger TRAP

★ **hidden word clue** *see* RUN *and* RUN INDICATOR

hide BURROW; CACHE; COAT; COVER; DEN; FELL; FLOG; KID; KIP; LAIR; LEATHER; PELT; SCREEN; SKIN; SUEDE; ■ HARBOUR; SECRETE; anagram indicator; nesting indicator; run indicator

hide in order to be found PLANT

hide, some THONG

hideout DEN; HOLE; LAIR; anagram of HIDE

hider of pain ETHER

hides run indicator

hidey-hole DEN

hiding BEATING; ROUT; nesting indicator

hiding, give BEAT; SPANK; ■ THRASH

hiding-place CACHE; DEN; HOLE

hiding-place for can indicate that the component that follows is to be nested

hie URGE

higgledy-piggledy anagram indicator

high GREAT; H; MANIC; OFF; STEEP; STONED; TALL; TOP; UP; ■ ECSTATIC; LOFTY; SMELLING; SPACED OUT; anagram indicator; can indicate something to do with being drunk or on a drug-trip; can refer to an elevated location as "high water" can clue TARN; similarly with regard to the body e.g. "high level habit" can indicate some kind of headwear

high class U

high cost BOMB

high explosive HE

high-flier EAGLE; PILOT; ■ ICARUS; *see* BIRD; [◊ AIR]

high-fliers RAF; *see* BIRD

high-flying can refer to a bird, cloud, aircraft, pilot etc

high-flying singer LARK; MARTIN; *see* BIRD

high frequency OFTEN

high, get RISE

high, got ROSE

high ground HILL; MOUNT; TOR; ■ EMINENCE

high-level RIDGE; ROOF

high-level cover-up HAT

high living can indicate a people or breed of animal living in mountainous region

high, on ALOFT

high on drugs STONED

high place HILL; MOUNT; STATUS; RIDGE; TOR
high-point APEX
high position, in ALOFT; UP
high-quality AI; FINE; TOPS
high-ranking TOP
high regard, held in RATE
high-rise RIDGE
high shot LOB
high sound HI
high speed, at *see* FAST
high-speed train APT; HST
high-spirited FRISKY
high spirits ELATION
high spot TOR
high temperature, having a HOT
high tension HT
high-up can indicate something to do with flying, aircraft or a bird esp. eagle
high voice TREBLE
high water TIDE
high winds GALE
highball LOB
higher BETTER; UP; ■ SUPERIOR
higher degrees HEAT
higher, get CLIMB
higher in price UP
highest BEST; TOP; ■ SUPREME
highest level, at the ATOP
highest medal GOLD
highest place TOP
highest point APEX; PEAK
highflyer *see* HIGH-FLIER
highflyer, legendary ROC
Highland area ROSS
Highland dress KILT; ■ JABOT
highland feature RIDGE
Highland gathering MOD
Highland town WICK
Highlander SCOT; *see* HIGH LIVING
highlight STRESS; STAR
highly can indicate something or someone in a physically high position as "Highly-reclusive sort" → STYLITE; [◊ TOP]
highly desirable PLUM
highly priced DEAR
highway ROAD

hike RAISE; RAMBLE; RISE
hiker RAMBLER
hiking club YHA
hilarious person RIOT
highlight VERY (i.e. from Very pistol)
hill BERG; BRAE; BROW; DOWN; FELL; HEAP; MOUND; PEAK; RISE; TOR
hill, northern BEN
hill-range RIDGE
hill top BROW; H; ■ RIDGE
hill, top of H; PEAK; PIKE
Hillary [◊ ASCENT; EVEREST]
hills MOORS; RANGE
hillside FELL; BANK; BRAE
hilltop H; RIDGE
hilly area DOWNS
Hilton can indicate something to do with Shangri-La
hind BACK; DEER; REAR; STERN
hinder BLOCK; CUMBER; ■ IMPEDE
hindered LET
hindquarters HAUNCH; RUMP
hindrance LET; *see* IMPEDIMENT
Hindu goddess KALI
Hindu status CASTE
hinge MOUNT; ■ DEPEND
hint CUE; CLUE; DASH; IMPLY; TIP; TRACE; ■ BREATH; INKLING; can signal that only a small part (usually one letter) of the indicated word is to be used
hint, give a CUE; INTIMATE
hint of first letter of the word that follows to be used
hint of colour C; TINGE
hip COOL; HAUNCH; [◊ CHEER]
hippy BROAD (i.e. in the beam!)
hippy gathering LOVE-IN
hips BOTTOM (as in "To wiggle one's hips is the nadir" (4,6) → ROCK BOTTOM)
hire LEASE; LET; RENT; ■ CHARTER
hired LEASED; LET; RENTED
hired man HAND

hired out a component to be nested within LET

hires LET

hirsute HAIRY

hirsute growth BEARD; TACHE

hirsute, not BALD

his new form ISH

his or her ONES

his undoing ISH

hiss SCOFF

historian BEDE; LIVY; ■ HERODOTUS; TACITUS

historic OLD

historic city TROY; UR

history PAST; ■ ACCOUNT; RECORD

history oral PASSED

history, sort of POTTED

hit BANG; BASH; BAT; BELT; BLOW; BUTT; CLIP; CLOCK; CLOUT; CLUB; CUFF; LAM; LASH; PAT; POUND; RAM; RAP; SLAP; SLOG; SLUG; SMASH; SMITE; SOCK; STRUCK; SWIPE; ■ BRAIN; BUTTED; RAPPED; SLAPPED; SLOGGED; SMASHED; SMITTEN; SUCCESS; WALLOP; WELT

hit ball high in the air SKY

hit, big ACE; SIX

hit forcefully SOCK

hit gently PAT; TAP

hit hard RAPH (i.e. rap H); *see* HIT

hit high in the air SKY

hit it off CLICK

hit-man PAT

hit on head CLOCK

hit out HIT to be omitted; anagram of HIT; a component to be nested within HIT, LASH etc

hitch TIE; TETHER; can indicate a knot; *see* SNAG

hitching can indicate something to do with getting married

hitherto unknown NEW; NOVEL

Hitler's deputy HESS

Hitler's bully boys/men, some of SS

hitting, keep FLOG

HM ER

hoard SAVE; STASH; STOCK; STORE; ■ COLLECT; GATHER; SAVINGS; SUPPLY

hoarse GRUFF; HUSKY; ROUGH

hoax BLUFF; CON; DUPE; GULL; KID; SPOOF

hob RANGE; SHELF

hobble FETTER

hobby INTEREST; note, this is a bird as well as meaning 'pastime'

hobby-horse can indicate something to do with morris dancing

hock PAWN; POP; WINE

hoe WEED; ■ GARDEN

hog SWINE; ■ CORNER

hogshead BUTT; CASK

hogsheads, two PIPE

hoist LIFT

hold BIND; GRASP; GRIP; HAVE; HUG; KEEP; LOCK; OWN; PIN; STAY; STORE; ■ CARRY; CLAIM; CLINCH; CLING; CONTEND; CLASP; NELSON; RESERVE; RETAIN; can indicate a wrestling hold e.g. armlock; nesting indicator; run indicator

hold-all BAG

hold back DAM; DEFER; DELAY; REIN; STEM; WAIT; WAVER; ■ RESTRAIN; RETAIN; can indicate a synonym of "hold" is reversed, e.g. PIN

hold back, to the component which follows is to be reversed and nested

hold, do not DROP

hold down PIN

hold firmly GRIP; GRASP; [◊ VICE]

hold forth ORATE

hold in run indicator

hold in regard RESPECT; *see* ESTEEM

hold in respect REGARD; *see* ESTEEM

hold line L to be nested

hold on CLING; GRASP; LAST

hold on to CLASP; GRIP; KEEP

hold out OFFER; RESIST

hold sway REIGN

hold tight CLASP; CLING; GRIP

hold, to nesting indicator

hold up BLOCK; DEFER; DELAY; PROP; ■ DELAY; IMPEDE; reversal indicator

hold-up DAM; DELAY; GLITCH; HEIST; HITCH; SNAG; reversal indicator

hold-up, device for HANGER; HOOK

holdall BAG

holder CUP; HOD; PEN; ■ KEEPER; see CONTAINER

holding nesting indicator; run indicator

holding on ON to be nested

holding one back ENO to be nested

hole CELL; CORNER; CRATER; CUP; DEN; DENT; EARTH; GAP; GORE; JAM; LAIR; MINE; O; PIT; POCK; PORE; PORT; SLOT; SPACE; SPOT; VENT; VOID; ■ ABYSS; CAVE; SITUATION

hole in one ACE

hole in one, got a ACED

hole, make a BORE; DRILL; GORE

hole, small PORE

holiday BREAK; EASTER; FEAST; HOL; JAUNT; LEAVE; REST; TRIP; VAC; WHIT; ■ CRUISE; OFF; PACKAGE; RECESS; VACATION

holiday centre RESORT; SPA

holiday destination RESORT

holiday, Northern WAKE

holiday, on AWAY; OFF

holiday period EASTER; SUMMER; see HOLIDAY

holiday, prepare for PACK

holiday region MED; SW

holiday souvenir TAN

holidaymaker CAMPER; TRIPPER; [◊ RESORT]

Holland, place in EDAM

holler CALL

hollow CAVE; COMBE; COOMB; CRATER; DELL; DENT; DIP; HOLE; PAN; PIT; ■ DIMPLE; GUTTER; SOCKET; TOKEN; can indicate the use of first and last letters only as "hollow sound" → SD

hollow in ground PAN

hollow sound BONG

hollow victory VY; WN

hollowed BORED

hollows ANTRA; see HOLLOW

holly ILEX

Hollywood LA; [◊ STAR, MOVIE]

Hollywood spectacular EPIC

Hollywood star COOPER; GABLE

holm OAK

Holst usually refers to "The Planet Suite" and so calls for one of the planets in the solar system mentioned in the work

holster CASE

holy GOOD; PI; ■ BLESSED; can indicate a word beginning with ST; [◊ ORDERS]

holy book BIBLE (qv); KORAN; can call for a specific book from the Bible, esp. its abbreviation e.g. GEN, EX – see BIBLE, BOOK

holy books NT; OT

holy city ROME; SION

holy, make HALLOW

holy man MONK; SAINT; ST; ■ FAKIR

holy orders can refer to the ten commandments, the Decalogue etc

holy person SAINT; ST

holy place SHRINE; see CHURCH

Holy See ROME

holy writ NT; OT

homage, do KNEEL

home BACK; BASE; COT; DEN; EARTH; FLAT; HOUSE; IN; LAIR; NEST; PAD; VILLA; ■ HEARTH; INTERIOR

home again BACK; ININ

home before midnight ING

home, bring STRESS

Home Counties SE

home, get a SETTLE

home help CHAR

home improvement DIY
home-made anagram of HOME
home of monster LOCH
Home Office HO
home, stately HALL; PILE
home team INSIDE (i.e. IN-SIDE)
homeless, make EVICT
homer COR (a Hebrew measure); can refer to the pigeon
Homer can indicate a Greek letter as "last character in Homer" → RHO; note, despite the capital letter, Homer can refer to the pigeon as well as the poet
homestead FARM
homework DIY; PREP
homicide KILLING
homo sapiens MAN
★ **homophone** a word that is pronounced like (or very much like) another such as 'might' and 'mite', 'gate' and "gait'. Its use in a clue will be signalled by the use of a homophone indicator which has the connotation of being restricted solely to sound (examples: "on the radio", "heard"). In this way, for example, "Sound money order test" calls up CHECK (i.e. sounding like 'cheque')
homosexual GAY
homosexuality, reveal OUT
honed SHARP
honest FAIR; FRANK; JUST; OPEN; RIGHT; STRAIGHT; TRUE; UPRIGHT; WORTHY; ■ CANDID; CLEAN
honestly REALLY; TRUE; TRULY
honesty TRUTH
honey COMB; DEAR; LOVE; MEL
honey-badger RETAL
honey, source of COMB
honour CBE; CH; DBE; DUB; LAUD; MBE; OBE; OM; ORDER; ■ AK; CREDIT; CROWN; MERIT; can refer to an honour card i.e. ACE, JACK, QUEEN, KING
honourable HON

honoured FETED
honoured companion CH
hood BONNET; COWL; COVER; ROUGH; with a capital initial can refer to Robin Hood
hood, wearing a COWLED
hooded can refer to something to do with (i) a monk (ii) a cobra (iii) Robin Hood
hoodlum GANGSTER; ■ THUG
hook GAFF; ■ CATCH; SHOT; STROKE
Hook PIRATE
hooker TART
hooligan LOUT; ROUGH; TED; THUG; YOB; ■ ROWDY
hoop BAND (qv); RING
hooter HORN; NOSE; OWL; SIREN; ■ CONK; SIGNAL
hop BOUND; DANCE; LEAP; NIP; REEL; SKIP; SPRING
hop off PHO
hop the twig DIE
hope TRUST; YEARN; ■ ASPIRE; YEARNING
Hope can refer to the author and his work; [◊ ZENDA]
hope for a response FISH
hope, lose DESPAIR
hopeful ROSY; ■ PROMISING
hopeless DEAD
hopelessly anagram indicator
hopelessness DESPAIR
hopper FROG; ROO
Horace, characteristic of his poetry ODIC
Horatio can indicate something to do with philosophy (i.e. from *Hamlet*)
horde ARMY; DROVE; GANG; MASS; MOB; SWARM
horizon KEN
horizontal FLAT; LEVEL; LYING; can indicate something to do with sleeping; ■ PRONE
horizontal, was LAY
horn CORNET; HOOTER; LUR; ■ BASSET
horn, sound TOOT
horns BRASS
horns, trim POLL

horrible FRIGHTFUL; VILE; anagram indicator; *see* NASTY

Horrible! UGH

horribly anagram indicator

horrid anagram indicator

horrid thing NIGHT

horrific GORY; anagram indicator

horrify APPAL

horrid NASTY; *see* HORRIBLE

horror FRIGHT

horror, sound of UGH

horse ARAB; BARB; BAY; BESS; CHASER; COB; COLT; DAM; DRIER; DRUG; DUN; FILLY; FOAL; GG; GREY; H; HACK; KNIGHT; MARE; NAG; PACER; PINTO; PONY; PUNCH; ROAN; SHIRE; STUD; ■ AMBLER; AIRER; ARKLE; CHARGER; COURSER; DRIER; HUNTER; JADE; MOKE; WHEELER; *see* RACEHORSE; [◊ RIDE; SADDLE; TRIP (i.e. as in a "bad trip")]

horse, back of CROUP

horse, black/dark BESS

horse, child's GG

horse chestnut COB

horse, concerning EQUINE

horse, cowboy's TRIGGER

horse-dealer COPER

horse entered in minor race PLATER

horse-feed BRAN; CORN; HAY; OATS

horse, food for, stuff for *see* HORSE-FEED

horse, frame for difficult TRAVE

horse, like a EQUINE

horse, on a RIDING; UP

horse, resembling a EQUINE

horse sure to win CERT

horse-trader *see* HORSE-DEALER

horseback GAN (i.e. nag reversed)

horseback, on UP

horseback, travel on RIDE

horseback, went on/was on/were on RODE

horseman RIDER

horses HERD; STABLE; STRING; STUD

horses, some *see* HORSES

horseshoe PLATE

hose LINE; SOCK(S); STOCKING(S)

hose, single TIGHT

hospital BARTS; ENT; GUYS; H; MASH; SAN; ■ CLINIC

hospital admission H to be nested within a component

hospital department ENT

hospital drama ER

hospital facility WARD

hospital, military MASH

hospital, part of ENT; WARD; WING

hospital patient CASE

hospital room WARD

hospital unit BED; ENT; WARD

hospitality CHEER

hospitality, one receiving GUEST

host ARMY; CROWD; LOT; MASS; MC; SWARM; nesting indicator; ■ ENTERTAIN

hostelry INN

hostile ANTI; AVERSE; COLD; COOL; ICY; ILL; ■ ADVERSE; ALIEN; HARSH

hostile promise THREAT

hostile reaction BOO

hostilities STRIFE; WAR

hostility ANGER; FEUD; MALICE; SPITE

hosting nesting indicator

hot BAKED; CROSS; H; IN; NEW; ■ BAKING; BIG; LIVE; RED; STEAMY; STOLEN; SULTRY; TROPICAL

hot and humid STEAMY; *see* HOT

hot, get unpleasantly SWELTER

hot-headed RASH

hot issue LAVA

hot meal CHILLI

hot potato ISSUE

hot spot OVEN

hot stuff LAVA

hot, very RED; SEARING

hot weather HEAT; SUN

hotel H; HYDRO; INN; PORTER; ■ RITZ

hotel employee PAGE

hotel guest RESIDENT

hotelier HOST

hothead H ■ MADCAP; *see* HOTLY TIPPED

hotheaded H; *see* HOTLY TIPPED

hotly tipped can indicate a volcano e.g. ETNA

hotpot STEW

hound HUNT; ■ BADGER; *see* DOG

hour H; HR; TIME; ZERO; can indicate any figure up to twelve

hour in which something starts (take-off, ascent etc) ZERO

hour of prayer SEXT

hourly HORAL

hours of darkness NIGHT

house BINGO; BULL (i.e. Taurus); CASTLE; CO; CROWD; DIET; DRUM; FIRM; GRANGE; H; HO; HUT; INN; LEO; LODGE; LOTTO; MANOR; MANSE; ORANGE; RES; SEMI; SIGN; STABLE (as a verb); VILLA; YORK; ■ FRIARY; GAFF; HALL; HANOVER; LANCASTER; TUDOR; WINDSOR; run indicator (as a verb); can indicate something to do with theatre; can indicate something to do with astrological houses e.g. Cancer, or their signs e.g. crab

house, big GRANGE; MANOR; MANSE

house, European/French MAISON

house, large country HALL

house limit WALL

house, little COT; H

house, minister's MANSE

house, part of big WING

house, secluded part of DEN

house, section STOREY

house, small HO; HUT

house, Spanish CASA

house, splendid CASTLE

house vacated HE

household FAMILY; MENAGE

householder, small SNAIL

houseman MEMBER

houseman, US INTERN

houses ESTATE; nesting indicator; run indicator; *see* HOUSE

housewife HOW; ■ ETUI

housing nesting indicator

housing complex ESTATE

housing development CITY; ESTATE; TOWN

hovel HUT; SHACK; SHED; STY

hover FLY; WAIT; WAVER

how annoying! PISH

how Frenchman COMMENT

how German WIE

how old AGE

how old one is AGE

how Parisian COMMENT

how to can indicate the answer is an adverb, usually ending in LY; can indicate a word in which the first component is a self-standing verb (as "Informant – how to put the kids to sleep" signals TELLTALE)

Howard's End D

Howdy HI

however BUT; THO; YET; ■ THOUGH; anagram indicator

howl CRY; ROAR; WAIL

howler BLUNDER; MONKEY

HQ BASE; DEPOT; ■ STATION

hub FOCUS

hubbub DIN; *see* NOISE

Huck FINN

huddle CROWD

Hudson RIVER; ROCK; can indicate something to do with film star

hue SHADE; TINCT; TONE

huff PET; PIQUE

hug ENFOLD; LOCK; nesting indicator; run indicator

huge BIG; FAT; GREAT; TALL; TITAN; ■ JUMBO

huge amount PILE; TON

hugged by nesting indicator

Hugh DROVER (opera)

Hugh, we hear HEW; HUE

hugs nesting indicator; run indicator

hull BOAT ■ BILGE; KEEL

Hull note, as well as the town can refer to a boat

hullabaloo DIN

Hulot, Monsieur TATI

hum BO; BUZZ; DRONE; ODOUR; PONG; REEK; SMELL; STINK (qv)

hum, humming can indicate something to do with smell

human being MAN

human beings MAN; MEN

humane studies ARTS

humanity MEN

humanity, show ERR

humble ABASE; DEMEAN; LOW; LOWER; MEEK; MODEST

humble person HEEP (i.e. from Dickens)

humble place HOVEL; HUT; SHED

humbug CANT; FUDGE; PHONY; ROT; SHAM

humdrum BANAL; TRITE

humid CLOSE; MOIST

humiliate DEMEAN; GALL; TEASE

humiliation GALL

humming NIFFY

humorist CARD; LEAR; WAG; WIT

humorous COMIC; DROLL; FUNNY; WITTY

humorous material, feeble CORN

humorous, quietly DRY

humour MOOD; WIT; ■ FEELING

humour, object of BUTT

Humpty Dumpty, like OVOID

humus MOR

hunch CLUE; HINT; HUMP

hundred C; TON

114 cm ELL

100 mph TON

hundred-odd acres HIDE

hundred, one short of IC; OO

hundred pence POUND

hundred sheets REAM

hundreds CC; D

hung DRAPED; *see* HANG

hung about, around WAITED

hunger GREED; ITCH; NEED; YEARN(ING)

hunger, suffer STARVE

hungry EMPTY; NEEDY; this is one of the old chestnuts where, if a person or animal is involved in the clue, 'hungry' can signify the insertion of O into the person or animal (i.e. "has nothing inside"!); note, the last comment can apply to any living creature

hungry, extremely HY

hunt CHASE; FISH; HOUND MEET; QUEST; SCOUR; SEARCH; SEEK; SHOOT; ■ COURSE; POACH

hunt illegally/illicitly POACH

hunt protester SAB

hunt's objective FOX

hunted animals GAME

hunter HORSE; MOUNT; WATCH; ■ ORION; TRAPPER

hunting expedition/party SHOOT

hunting trophy BRUSH

huntsman PEEL

hurdle JUMP

hurl FLING; LOB; PITCH; THROW; TOSS

hurled anagram indicator

hurly-burly BUSTLE

hurrah CHEERS

hurried RAN; RACED; SPED; TORE

hurry BELT; DASH; HASTE; HIE; NIP; RACE; RUN; RUSH; SPEED TEAR; URGE; ■ BEETLE; HASTEN; LEGIT (i.e. leg it); SCRAMBLE

hurry along *see* HURRY

hurry, in a RUSHED; RUSHING

hurry up TRAD (i.e. reversal of "dart" in a DC)

hurst GROVE

hurt ACHE; HARM; ILL PAIN; SMART; STAB; STING; ■ ACHED; HARMED; STUNG; WOUND

hurt, appeared BLED
hurtful remark BARB
hurting SORE
hurtle PLUNGE; *see* RUSH
hurtled SPED; TORE
hurts, that OUCH
husband GROOM; H; MAN; MATE; SAVE; STORE; ■ CONSERVE; RESERVE; SPOUSE; USELESS (i.e. use less)
husband, French MARI
husband no longer EX
hush SH
hush money BRIBE; BUNG
hush up CONCEAL
husk AWN
husks BRAN; CHAFF
husky GRUFF; HOARSE; THROATY
husky, sounds HORSE
hussy WANTON
hut CABIN; HOGAN; HOVEL; SHACK; SHED; ■ SHANTY
hybrid ASS; MULE; anagram indicator
hydrocarbon TERPENE
hydrophobic RABID
hygienic CLEAN
hymn PAEAN; ■ ANTHEM; SEQUENCE
hymn-writer DAVID
hymnbook MISSAL
hype PUFF; SPIN
hyperactive MANIC; anagram indicator
hyphen DASH; LINK
hypnotised UNDER
hypocrisy CANT
hypocrisy, showing SLY
hypocrite PRIG
hypocritical SLY
hypocritical words CANT
hypotenuse* SIDE
hypothetical NOTIONAL
hysteria PANIC

I i

I EGO; ONE; ■ PRONOUN; beware that the first person 'I' can itself be an element in the answer; as the symbol for iodine can indicate something to do with chemical symbol
I admitted I to be nested within a component
I agree YES; ■ TRUE
I am IM
I am proposing to ILL
I am unable ICANT
I don't half IDO; INT
I'd put up DI (in a DC)
I, for example PRONOUN
I had ID
I had kept ID to be nested
I have IVE
I have to secure the following word to be nested within IVE
I hear homophone indicator
I heard EYE
I in France JE
I, in Paris JE
I intend ILL
I introduced I to be nested within a word or component
I leave I to be omitted
I'll leave I or ILL to be omitted
I'll say ISLE
I'll set up LLI (in a DC)
I'm IAM; IM; can indicate a word made up of I plus a verb as "I'm a trader" clues IDEAL
I'm going to ILL
I'm half D (i.e. in Roman numerals D is half of one M!)
I'm out I to be omitted
I object ME
I reported(ly) EYE
I royally WE
I run about IRRE
I say EYE; IGH
I see, reportedly IC
I shall ILL

I will ILL
I would ID
Ibsen can indicate something to do with his plays e.g. BRAND, GHOSTS
Ibsen heroine GABLER; HEDDA
Icarus can call for something to do with sun, wax
ICBM MISSILE
ice BERG; CHILL; RINK; ■ RESERVE; can indicate something to do with diamonds
ice, break the CALVE
ice, kind of BLACK; CREAM; PACK
ice-cream CHOC; CONE; SCOOP; TUB; ■ CORNET; GLACE
ice-cream container CONE
ice, mass of BERG
ice, quantity of BERG; CONE; RINK; SCOOP;
ice venue RINK
icebox FRIDGE
Iceland IS
icon IDOL
ictus FIT; STRESS; STROKE
icy COLD; COOL
ID NAME
Idaho ID
idea DREAM; NOTION; PLAN; ■ FANCY; THEME; VISION; THEORY; THOUGHT
ideal BEST; DREAM; MODEL; VISION; ■ EXAMPLE; PERFECT
ideal situation THEORY
ideally BEST
idem SAME
identical EQUAL; SAME
identical statement EQUATION
identification ID; LABEL; MARK; NAME; STICKER; ■ BRAND; TITLE
identification, means of DNA
identify FINGER; NAME; PLACE; SPOT; ■ LABEL
identifying feature NAME; NUMBER; TITLE
identifying, way of TEST
identity ID

identity card ID
idiot ASS; CLOT; GOON; NIT; SAP; TWIT; ■ DIMWIT; DOLT; TWERP; anagram indicator; *see* FOOL
idiotic INANE; anagram indicator
idle FALLOW; LAZE; LAZY; LINGER; LOAF; LOLL; REST; SLACK; VAIN; anagram indicator
idle, be LOAF
idle chatter GAS
idle fellow *see* IDLER
idle-sounding LAYS
idle talk GAS; YAK; ■ PRATTLE
idler DRONE; SLOB; WASTER; ■ CABBAGE; SKIVER
idling LAZING; SLACKING; anagram indicator
idol BAAL; ICON; JOSS; ■ IMAGE
idols appear SOLID (anag.)
idolise LOVE; REVERE
if CONDITION
if, say WEATHER
if turned up FI (in a DC)
iffy RISKY
igloo HOME; HOUSE; [◊ ICE; ROUND]
ignite BURN; LIGHT
ignited LIT; anagram indicator
ignoble BASE; CHEAP; LOW; MEAN
ignorance, state of LIMBO
ignore CUT; DEFY OMIT; PASS; SLIGHT; omission indicator
ignored CUT; omission indicator
II with a homophone indicator can call for EYES
ilex HOLLY
ill AILING; BAD; FUNNY; POOR; POORLY; SEEDY; SICK; ■ AGUE; EVIL; anagram indicator, as "ill-starred" → TRADERS
ill-advised RASH; ■ MAD
ill-advisedly anagram indicator
ill-assorted anagram indicator
ill, become AIL
ill-behaved anagram indicator
ill-bred type BOOR; CAD; OAF; LOUT; YOB

ill-defined HAZY; VAGUE; anagram indicator; ■ BLURRED

ill-feeling can refer to illness as "widespread ill-feeling" → PANDEMIC

ill-fitting anagram indicator

ill-gotten anagram indicator

ill-gotten gains LOOT

ill-humour ANGER; BILE; PET; SPLEEN; TEMPER

ill in Australia CROOK

ill-mannered CRUDE; ROUGH; RUDE

ill-manners in speech RUED

ill-mannered, someone BEAR; OAF; ■ LOUT

ill-matched, be CLASH

ill-natured CROSS

ill-starred TRADERS

ill, taken anagram indicator

ill-temper SPLEEN; *see* TEMPER

ill-tempered CRABBY; SURLY

ill-treat can indicate something to do with treating the ill, hence nurse, tend, dose etc

ill-used anagram indicator

ill-written anagram indicator

illegal HOT

illegal act CRIME

illegal business RACKET

illegal enterprise RACKET

illegal occupation SQUAT

illegal substance *see* DRUG

illegally anagram indicator

illegally, raise money ROB (qv)

illegally record BUG

illegitimate NATURAL

illicit BLACK; anagram indicator

illicit gains LOOT

illicitly anagram indicator

illiterate anagram indicator; homophone indicator; *see* ILLITERATES, FOR

illiterate signature X

illiterates, for can indicate a deliberate misspelling as "school for illiterates brought back" → LOOKS

illness AGUE; BUG; FLU; MAL; TB; ■ AILMENT; INFECTION; QUINSY

illness, minor COLD

illness, mystery/unidentified LURGY

illuminated LIT

illumination BEAM; LAMP; LIGHT; RAY; ■ CANDLE

illumination, form of LED; SPOT

illumination, provided LIT

illusion DREAM; MIRAGE; can refer to an enduring myth e.g. yeti, Loch Ness Monster

illustration PIC

illustrative GRAPHIC

illustrator, French DORE

illustrious FAMED; LOFTY; NOBLE

image ICON; IDOL; RINGER; ■ DOUBLE

imaginary number I

imaginative American POE (recalling his *Tales of the Imagination*)

imagine DREAM; FANCY; *see* THINK

imbecile ANILE

imbibe DRINK; SIP; SUP

imbibed DRANK; DRUNK; nesting indicator

imbibed by nesting indicator

imbibing nesting indicator

imbued with nesting indicator

imitate APE; COPY; FORGE; ■ ECHO; MIMIC

imitation COPY; PASTE; SHAM; SPOOF

imitative of recent past RETRO

imitator APER; COPIER

immaculate PURE

immature CALLOW; EARLY; GREEN

immediate PROMPT; ■ INSTANT; NEAREST

immediate action, need for URGENCY

immediately ANON; NOW; STAT (Lat.)

immediately after NEXT; ON

immense HUGE; STEEP

immerse BATHE; DIP; PLUNGE

immersed in nesting indicator

immigrant ALIEN; INCOMER

immigrate INCOME (i.e. in come)
immobile STATIC; STILL;
  STUCK
immobilise car CLAMP
immoral LOOSE
immoral act SIN
immoral woman TART
immorality EVIL; VICE
immune PROOF
imp SPRITE; *see* CHILD,
  NAUGHTY
impact BUMP; DENT; HIT; RAM;
  ■ EFFECT
impact, have an TELL
impact, make an TAP
impaired anagram indicator
impale SPEAR; SPIKE
impart REVEAL
impartial FAIR; JUST; ■
  NEUTRAL
impassioned MAD; STORMY; ■
  FERVENT; *see* PASSIONATE
impassive BLAND; STOLID
impatience ITCH
impatience in driving, show
  HOOT; TOOT
impatient AGOG
impatient, be ITCH
impatient expression PISH
impecunious BROKE; POOR;
  SKINT; can indicate that an associated word is to lose a
  money-related letter/component
  such as P, L
impede BLOCK; CRAMP;
  HAMPER
impediment BAR; BLOCK; LET;
  RUB; ■ SHACKLE
impel DRIVE; FORCE; GOAD;
  MAKE; URGE
impend LOOM
imperceptible, almost SLIGHT
imperfect SKETCHY
imperial IMP
imperial unit FT; INCH; OUNCE
  see MEASURE
imperialist RHODES
impersonate APE
impersonating, one APER;
  MIMIC; RINGER

impertinence CHEEK; LIP;
  SAUCE
impertinent COOL; FORWARD;
  LIPPY; SASSY; SAUCY *see*
  CHEEKY
impetuous HASTY; RASH; can
  indicate a word beginning with
  HOT e.g. hot-headed,
  hot-tempered
impetuosity ELAN
implausible TALL
implement AWL; AXE; HOE;
  POKER SPADE; SPIKE; TOOL;
  USE; ■ AGENT; EXECUTE; *see*
  INSTRUMENT, TOOL
implement, kitchen PESTLE
implication TONE
implicit anagram indicator
implied in anagram or run indicator
implore BEG; PLEAD; ■
  ENTREAT
imply HINT; MEAN
impolite RUDE; ■ IMPUDENT;
  PERT
impolitic RUDE; ■ IMPRUDENT
import DRIFT; FIT (i.e. verb);
  GIST; MEAN; NUB; POINT;
  WEIGHT; ■ MATTER;
  MEANING
import into nesting indicator
importance WEIGHT; ■
  GRAVITY; MOMENT; STRESS;
  VALUE; can indicate something
  to do with Wilde's play e.g. Ernest; *see* IMPORT
importance, have COUNT
importance, of minor LIGHT
important BIG; GREAT; HIGH;
  KEY; MAJOR; PRIME; VITAL;
  WEIGHTY; ■ CAPITAL
important, are MATTER
important, more HIGHER; *see*
  IMPORTANT
important, not quite the most
  can indicate a secondary position
  beginning with SUB
important person LION; VIP
imported MEANT; nesting indicator; can indicate a foreign word
  as "imported article" clues LE,
  UN, etc

importune BEG; PLEAD; PRESS

impose FOIST; LEVY; SET

imposing GRAND; STATELY; TAXING; ■ AUGUST

imposition LINES; TAX

impostor SHAM

impound nesting indicator

imprecise VAGUE

impress CHARM; STAMP; TYPE; ■ AFFECT; AWE; STRIKE

impress deeply INGRAIN

impress, try to BRAG

impressed AWED; STAMPED; *see* IMPRESS

impression AIR; DENT; FEEL; IDEA; MARK; PRINT; SEAL; SENSE; STAMP; ■ DENTING; IMAGE

impression, create a BRAG

impression, indistinct BLUR

impression, made an ETCHED; STAMPED

impression, make an DENT; ETCH; PRINT; SEAL; STAMP

impression of speed BLUR

impressive EPIC; LARGE

imprint SEAL; STAMP

imprison CAGE; GATE; INTERN

imprisoned INSIDE; PENT; nesting indicator; can indicate that a component is to be nested within a synonym for prison e.g. PEN or GAOL as in "Doctor could be imprisoned for caper" → GAMBOL (i.e. GA-MB-OL)

imprisoned, get INTERN

imprisoned, not FREE; OUT

imprisons CAGES; nesting indicates

improbable, improbably anagram indicator

improper CRUDE; RUDE; anagram indicator; *see* CHEEKY

improper, not PURE

improperly anagram indicator; can indicate an adjective beginning with NON

improve BETTER; EMEND; MEND; RALLY; REFORM; TWEAK

improve on CAP; TOP

improved BETTER; anagram indicator

improvement REFORM; UP; anagram indicator; [◊ GOOD]

improvement, make an AMEND; MEND

improvements DIY

improvise JAM; RIG

improvised, improvising anagram indicator

imprudent RASH

impudence CHEEK; CRUST; FRONT; GALL; LIP

impudent BOLD; BRASH; CHEEKY; FRESH

impudent language LIP

impudent youngster BRAT; CHIT; IMP

impulse INSTINCT; ITCH; THRUST; URGE; WHIM

impulses ID

impulses in check, keeping can indicate that ID is to be nested within a component

impulses, set of ID

impulsive RASH

impurities, remove LEACH; REFINE

in AT; BATTING; HOME; LIT; TRENDY; nesting indicator; run indicator; can indicate that whatever follows is synonymous with the answer; note that, like all small innocent looking words, IN itself can be part of the answer as "Element unknown in club" gives ZINC (i.e. Z-IN-C); used as a prefix can indicate NOT

in a way anagram indicator

in accordance with ASPER (i.e. as per)

in addition AND; PLUS; TOO; ■ ALSO

in advantageous position UP

in, be BAT

in between INTER; nesting indicator

in care of nesting indicator

in case LEST

in certain ways a component to be nested within some combination of N, E, W and/or S

191

in charge IC

in charge of OVER

in company a component to be nested within CO

in court UP

in demand HOT

in difficulties anagram indicator

in extremis first and last letter indicator

in error OUT

in fact REALLY

in favour FOR; PRO

in foreign DE; EN

in former days THEN

in French DE; EN

in French a UN; UNE

in front AHEAD

in good time EARLY

in grip of nesting indicator

in hearing homophone indicator

in, is BATS

in-joke GAG to be nested within a component

in many cases OFTEN

in motion GOING

in my case a component to be nested within MY

in no hurry PATIENT; SLOW

in order to get FOR

in other words IE

in our opinion TOUS (i.e. to us)

in panic anagram indicator

in Paris a UN; UNE

in pieces anagram indicator

in place ON

in question anagram indicator

in real trouble a component to be nested within an anagram of REAL

in respect of ABOUT; ON; RE

in role of AS

in rows TIERED

in some way anagram indicator

in South INS

in such a way anagram indicator

in that case THEN

in the air ABOVE; ALOFT; anagram indicator

in the case of FOR

in the form of AS

in the grip of nesting indicator

in the manner of ALA (i.e. a la); AS

in the matter of RE

in the open OUT

in this case HERE

in this manner SO; THUS

in this place HERE

in this way SO; THUS

in three parts a component to be nested within an anagram of THREE

in tune ONKEY (i.e. on key)

inaccurate OUT; anagram indicator

inaccurate statement LIE

inactive ASLEEP; FALLOW; IDLE; RUSTY

inactive, be IDLE; LAZE; SLEEP

inactivity, affected by *see* INACTIVE

inadequacy LACK

inadequate POOR; SCANT; SLENDER; THIN; WEAK; ■ MEASLY; ROPY; SCANTY; anagram indicator

inadvertently anagram indicator

inapplicable NA (i.e. not applicable)

inattentive, be SKIP

inaugurate FOUND; LAUNCH; START

inbuilt nesting indicator

incandescent AGLOW

incantation SPELL

incapacitated LAMED

incarcerate GATE; *see* IMPRISON

incautious RASH

incense ANGER; JOSS

incensed, be FUME; RANT; RAVE

incentive BAIT; BUNG; GOAD; MOTIVE; SPUR; ■ CARROT

inch EDGE; I; IN

incident EVENT

incidental SIDE

incise SCORE

incision CUT

incision, make an LANCE

incisive SHARP; can refer to the incisor tooth

incisor TOOTH

incite BAIT; DRIVE; GOAD; TEMPT; SPUR; URGE; ■ STIMULATE

incited DROVE; SPURRED

inclination BENT; CANT; GRAIN (as in "against the – "); HUMOUR; LEAN; LIST; SLOPE; TILT; TREND; RAMP; ■ CAMBER; LIKING; PENCHANT; RAKE; TENDENCY

inclination, have LEAN (qv); *see* INCLINE

incline ANGLE; BEND; LEAN; LIST; RAKE; SLANT; SLOPE; TEND; TILT; RAMP; ■ ASCENT

inclined ANGLED; BENT; LEANED; TENDED; ■ ASLANT; GIVEN; PARTIAL; STEEP; TILTED

inclined, be TEND; ■ LEAN (qv)

inclined to, be PREFER

include ADD; COVER; ■ EMBRACE

included IN; HAD; ON; nesting indicator; run indicator

includes nesting indicator

incognito ANON

incoherent anagram indicator

income FEE; PAY; SCREW; TITHE; WAGE; ■ CUT; EARNINGS; LIVING; MEANS; SALARY

incomer SETTLER

incoming nesting indicator

incomplete PARTIAL; omission indicator; run indicator

incompletely omission indicator (especially of last letter); run indicator

inconclusive last letter to be omitted

incongruous, be JAR

inconsistent FADDY

incontrovertible SOUND

inconvenient way, in an anagram indicator

inconveniently anagram indicator

incorporate nesting or run indicator

incorporated INC; anagram indicator; nesting indicator; run indicator

incorporates, incorporating anagram indicator; nesting indicator; run indicator

incorrect AMISS; OUT; WRONG; anagram indicator

incorrectly anagram indicator

increase BREED; GROW; RAISE; RISE; SURGE; UP; ■ ACCRUE; APPRECIATE; BOOST; DOUBLE; ENLARGE; RALLY

increase, pay RAISE; RISE

increase rapidly TREBLE

increase speed GUN

increased ROSE; UP

increases UPS; *see* INCREASE

incredible FAB; TALL

incredibly anagram indicator

incriminate SET UP

incriminating factor PLANT

incubate HATCH

incur MEET; ■ ENCOUNTER; SUFFER

incursion RAID

indecent BLUE; RACY

indecent talk SMUT

indecision ER; UM

indecision, position of FENCE

indecisive, be HEDGE; WAVER

indecisive game DRAW

indeed AY; TRULY; VERILY; YEA; YES; a component to be nested within DEED; *see* YES

indefinite number N; X

indent HASH (pr.)

indentation BAY; BIGHT

independent I; IN; IND

indeterminate VAGUE

index AZ; LIST; POWER; TABLE; ■ DIRECTORY; FINGER

India I; IND

India, authority in RAJ

India, fare from RAITA

India, rule in RAJ

Indian I; IN; INCA; IND; can indicate something to do with tea; *see* AMERICAN INDIAN; [◊ CURRY]

Indian, American *see*
  AMERICAN INDIAN
Indian bread NAN
Indian city AGRA
Indian cooking BALTI
Indian drums TABLA; ■
  TOM-TOMS
Indian food BALTI
Indian greeting HOW
Indian leader GANDHI; NEHRU
Indian princess RANI
Indian state, territory GOA
Indian title SRI
Indian tourist centre AGRA
indicate MEAN; NOD; POINT;
  SHOW; SIGN; ■ DENOTE;
  SIGNAL
indicated MEANT
indication OMEN; SIGN; ■
  POINTER
indicating anagram indicator
indicator ARROW; POINTER;
  SIGN; TIMER
indicator of weather COCK;
  GLASS; VANE
indict CHARGE; ■ ACCUSE
indifference, show SLIGHT;
  SNUB
indifferent COLD; COOL
indifferently anagram indicator
indigent POOR
indignant CROSS; IRATE
indigo ANIL
indirectly anagram indicator
indiscreet remark GAFFE
indiscriminately anagram indicator
indispose AIL
indisposed ILL; anagram indicator
indisposition, slight CHILL;
  COLD
indistinct BLEAR; BLEARY;
  BLUR; FAINT; VAGUE
individual EACH; I; MAN;
  NAME; ONE; OWN; PERSON;
  SINGLE; SOLE; SOUL; UNIT
individual, for ONES
individuality SELF
indolent IDLE; LAZY

induce GOAD; LEAD; LULL;
  LURE; SPUR; TEMPT; URGE
induced LED; anagram indicator
inducement BRIBE; SOP
indulge PANDER; PET; TREAT
indulgence BINGE; TREAT
indulger *see* DRUNKARD
industrial action STRIKE
industrial area ESTATE
industrial magnate BARON
industry LINE; TRADE; WORK
industry, growth FARMING
ineffective DUD; LAME; *see*
  INEPT
ineffectual DUD
ineffectual person DUD; PRAT;
  TWIT
inefficient anagram indicator
inept WET; WIMPISH; anagram
  indicator; *see* THICK
ineptly anagram indicator
inert STILL; ■ LAZY
inexpensive CHEAP; ■
  ECONOMIC; PENNY (as in
  penny whistle)
inexperienced GREEN; NEW;
  RAW; ■ CALLOW; FRESH
inexperienced person L
infant BABE; CHILD; CUB; TOT;
  ■ MINOR; TODDLER
infantry FOOT; LI
infatuation PASH
infect TAINT
infected BITTEN; SEPTIC
infected by CATCH
infection BUG; CHILL; COLD;
  FLU; STYE; TAINT
infer DEDUCE; GATHER;
  REASON
inferior BAD; BASE; BELOW;
  LESS; LOW; LOWER; POOR;
  ROPY; SUB; UNDER; ■
  BENEATH; CHEESY;
  CRUMMY; DOG; MINOR;
  NAFF; can indicate NO followed
  by a word as "inferior violin" →
  NOSTRAD (for example to build
  up NOSTRADAMUS)
inferior status, give DEMOTE
inferior to can indicate that one
  component is to to follow another

infernal NETHER

inferno FIRE; HELL; *see* HELL

infest FILL; SWARM

infestation, suffering NITTY

infiltrate nesting indicator

infinite ALL

infinity C

infirm FAILING; FEEBLE; anagram indicator

inflame ANGER; HEAT; RILE; SWELL

inflamed AFIRE; LIT; RED

inflammation BOIL; ■ CROUP

inflate SWELL

inflation SWELLING

inflation, affected by AIR to nested within a component

inflexible HARD; RIGID; STERN

inflict DEAL

inflict defeat BEAT; WORST

influence AFFECT; CHARM; CLOUT; DRAG; FACTOR; FORCE; HOLD; LEAD; PULL; REACH; SAY; SWAY; SWING; WEIGHT; ■ CHARISMA; HOLD; IMPACT

influence, area of REALM; ■ FIELD; PATCH

influence, has COUNTS

influenced LED; ■ AFFECTED; SWAYED; SWUNG

influential TELLING

info DOPE; GEN

inform GRASS; NARK; TELL; PEACH; RAT; RUMBLE; SHOP; SING; SPLIT; TELL; ■ SNITCH

inform on FINGER; SHOP; SPLIT

informal CASUAL; FREE; can indicate (i) the shortened form of a proper noun e.g. BILL; (ii) the nickname of an historical figure e.g. IKE for Eisenhower (iii) casual speech, slang etc

informally anagram indicator

information DATA; DATUM; DOPE; FACT; FILE; GEN; GRIEF; INF; NEWS; SECRET; TIP; WORD; ■ LOWDOWN

information, attempt to get GRILL; PUMP

information, give TELL

information, inside TIP

information, provide GRASS; SHOP; TELL

information, scandalous DIRT

information, special LORE

Information Technology IT

information, try to get SNOOP; PRY

information unit BIT

informed AWARE; HIP; RATTED; SANG; SHOPPED; TOLD; UP

informed, be HEAR

informed, was HEARD

informer GRASS; NARK; NOSE; RAT; SPY

infra BELOW

infraction BREACH; BREAKING; anagram indicator

infrared IR

infrequent RARE

infringement *see* INFRACTION

infuriate ANGER

infuriated ANGERED; RILED

infuse BREW; STEEP

infusion BREW

ingenious DEFT

ingenious devices GADGETRY

ingenuity ART; CRAFT; SKILL

ingenuous GREEN; NAVE; PLAIN; SIMPLE; ■ ARTLESS

ingest EAT; SWALLOW

ingle FIRE; HEARTH

ingratiate oneself CRAWL

ingratiating SMARMY

ingredients anagram indicator

ingress ENTRY

inhabit DWELL; LIVE; ■ RESIDE

inhabitant NATIVE

inhaled, inhaling nesting indicator

inheritance GENE; LEGACY

inherits, he HEIR

inhibit DETER; STUNT

inhibit growth STUNT

inhibited SHY

inhibiting nesting indicator

iniquity, place of DEN

initial FIRST; SIGN; initial letter indicator; can indicate the initial state of something e.g. "initial child" can clue BIRTH

initial discount first letter to be omitted

initially FIRST; initial letter(s) indicator; adjacent word or element to go to the front of the other element; can indicate the first in some historical line as "woman, initially" can refer to Eve

initially dismissed first letter to be omitted

initiate SPARK; START

initiated, initiation first letter indicator

initiative DRIVE; LEAD; first letter indicator; ■ RESOURCE

initiative, showed LED

inject JAB; PUMP

injected nesting indicator

injection IV; JAB; SHOT

injection in nesting indicator

injure HARM; HURT; LAME; MAR; ■ GRAZE; WOUND

injured GAME; HARMED; HURT; LAME; anagram indicator

injury BURN; CUT; HARM; HURT; SORE; SPRAIN; STRAIN; WOUND; ■ LASH; LESION

injury, leg LIMP

injury, minor/slight GRAZE; NICK; SCRATCH; SPRAIN

injury, sign of SCAR

injury to anagram indicator

inkling HINT; IDEA; NOTION

inky DARK

inland HINTER

Inland Revenue IR

inlet BAY; COVE; CREEK; RIA; WASH

inmate CON; INTERN; ■ RESIDENT

inn HOTEL; LOCAL; MOTEL; *see* PUB, HOTEL; ■ SERAI

innards WORKS

inner ENDO; RED (i.e. target)

inner cover LINING

inner part can indicate an internal organ

inner ring RED

innings KNOCK; STAND

innkeeper HOST

innocent CHASTE; CLEAN; GREEN; PURE; WHITE; ■ CANNY

Innocent POPE

innocent, declare CLEAR

innocent person LAMB

innovation anagram indicator

inoffensive a component to be nested within RUDE

inordinate anagram indicator

inordinately anagram indicator

input DATA

input to nesting indicator

inquire ASK

inquisitive NOSY; ■ NOSING

inquisitive, be NOSE; PRY

inquisitive, is NOSES; PRIES

inquisitive, was PRIED

inroad RAID

insane MANIC; *see* NUTS

inscribe WRITE

inscribed nesting indicator

inscribing tool GRAVER

insecure anagram indicator

insect ANT; BEE; BUG; FLEA; FLY; GNAT; LOUSE; MIDGE; MITE; MOTH; WASP; ■ CRICKET; HORNET; IMAGO; INSTAR; LARVA; LOCUST; MANTIS

insects ANTS; LICE; with a homophone indicator can call for BB (i.e. bees)

insects, lots of SWARM

★ **insertion** *see* NESTING

inserts nesting indicator

inset a component is to be nested within SET

inside GUT; INNER; run indicator; nesting indicator; can indicate something to do with prison; can indicate the middle letters of a word are to be used (as "walk inside" cues AL) can indicate that a component is to be nested within SIDE

★ **inside and outside** *see* NESTING

inside, go LINE

inside help, with AID to be nested within a component

inside layer LINING

inside, person CON
insidious DEEP
insignia BADGE; CHAIN
insignificant PETTY; SMALL; TINY; WEE
insignificant person SQUIT
insincere FAKE; GLIB; PHONY; SHAM; ■ LYING
insincerely fluent GLIB
insincerity CANT
insinuating SLY
insinuation HINT; ■ INNUENDO
insipid BLAND; DULL; ■ TASTELESS; VAPID
insist DEMAND; STRESS
insist on EXACT
insolence CHEEK; LIP
insolent CHEEKY; LIPPY; PERT; RUDE; SHORT
insolvent SKINT; ■ BROKE; BUST
inspan YOKE
inspect CHECK; EXAMINE; EYE; SCAN; TEST; VET; VIEW; ■ AUDIT
inspect carefully CASE
inspection CHECK; LOOK; MOT; TEST; ■ SCREEN; VET; *see* EXAMINATION
inspection, make inspection *see* INSPECTION
inspiration MUSE; ■ BREATH; ERATO
inspiration, take BREATHE
inspire FIRE; PUSH; URGE; ■ BREATHE; KINDLE; PROMPT
inspired FIRED; LIT
install SITE
installation of nesting indicator
installed SET
installed in nesting indicator
instance CASE; EXAMPLE
instance, for AS; EG; SAY
instant FLASH; MO; NOW SEC; TICK; TRICE; ■ SHAKE; TWINKLE
instead a component to be nested within STEAD
instinct DRIVE; EAR; ID; IMPULSE; URGE

institute FOUND; INST; LAUNCH; START
institution HOME; HOUSE; INST
instruct BRIEF; ORDER; PRIME; TEACH; TELL; TRAIN; ■ ENJOIN
instructed TAUGHT; TOLD
instruction BRIEF; LESSON; ORDER; RULE; STET (from printing); STOP; ■ CHARGE; COMMISSION; TRAINING; [◊ SCHOOL]
instruction, faithful RI
instruction, give TEACH; TRAIN
instruction to turn PTO
instructions BRIEF; ■ RUBRIC
instructions, issue ORDER; RULE; TELL; *see* INSTRUCT
instructor TEACHER; ■ TRAINER
instrument AWL; CLOCK; LEVER; METER; PROBE; TOOL; ■ BALANCE; DUPE; MEANS; PUPPET; *see* MUSICAL INSTRUMENT
instrument, ancient LUR
instrument of torture GADGE
instrument, percussion DRUM; GONG
instrument, pointed AWL
instrument, stringed REBEC
instrument, surgical PROBE
instrument, textile CARD
instrumentalist PIPER; PLAYER
instruments BAND; BRASS; REEDS; STRINGS; ORC
instruments of restraint CHAINS; CUFFS; IRONS
insubstantial AIRY; LIGHT
insufficiency of can indicate the last letter is to be omitted as "insufficiency of backbone" → SPIN
insufficient SCANT; SHORT
insufficiently UNDER; can indicate a verb beginning with UNDER
insulate LAG
insulated cable FLEX
insult ABUSE; AFFRONT; CUT; DISS; SLAG; SLIGHT; SLUR; SNUB

insulting RUDE; *see* CHEEKY; IMPERTINENT
insurance COVER; INS
insurance guarantee COVER
insurance premium LOADING
insure COVER
insurgent REBEL
insurrection RISING
integrate FUSE
intellect BRAIN; MIND; NOUS
intellectual TITAN
intelligence BRAIN; CIA; GEN; INFO; MI; NEWS; NOUS; SENSE; WIT; ■ ADVICE; IQ
intelligence agency CIA
intelligence, those with CIA
intelligence, U.S. CIA
intelligent BRIGHT; CLEVER; QUICK; SHARP; SMART
intelligent, not very SLOW
intemperate speech RANT
intend AIM; MEAN; PLAN; ■ DESIGN; DESTINE; TRY
intend to WILL
intended MEANT; ■ AIMED; FIANCE; anagram indicator
intended for the auditor MENT
intended to do FOR
intense ACUTE; GREAT; STRONG
intensify HEIGHTEN
intent BOUND; KEEN; ■ DESIGN; *see* INTENTION
intent, with MEANT
intention AIM; END; OBJECT; PLAN
intention, with TRYING
inter COVER; ■ BURY
inter alia a component to be nested within ALIA
interbreed CROSS
intercede MEDIATE
interchange anagram indicator
interchanging INERT (i.e. anagram of "inter"); indicated letters to be swapped
interdiction BAN
interest CUT; INT; SHARE; SIDE; SLICE; SPICE; STAKE; USURY; ■ ARP; BEHALF; CONCERN; GAIN; HOBBY; MONEY; RETURN
interest, be of APPEAL
interest, lack of APATHY; FREE
interest rate, low can indicate something to do with being boring
interest, sphere of FIELD
interest, with little IDLY
interested in INTO
interested, very RAPT
interesting, not very DRY; DULL; *see* BORING, DULL
interesting object CURIO
interfere AFFECT; TAMPER; ■ MEDDLE; TINKER
interference SNOW; STATIC; anagram indicator
interferes PRIES
interfering with anagram/nesting indicator
interior INNER; INT
interior design DECOR
interjection EEK
intermediary BROKER
interment, place for GRAVE; TOMB; VAULT
interminable last letter to be omitted (i.e. unending); ■ UNENDING
intermission BREAK
intermittent PATCHY
internal ENDO; INNER; run indicator
internal organs VITALS
internally nesting indicator
international CAP; INT; TEST; UN
international conference DIET
international group BLOC; EC; NATO; UN; WHO
international language NEO
international league IL
international medical group WHO
international organisation *see* INTERNATIONAL GROUP
international peacekeepers UN
international show EXPO
internet WEB
internet address URL

internet, use the SURF
interpret READ
interpretation ANGLE; SLANT; SPIN; VERSION; VIEW; ■ OPINION
interpreted READ
interrogate GRILL; PUMP; QUIZ
interrupt BREAK; HECKLE; anagram indicator; nesting indicator
interrupt movement PAUSE
interrupted nesting indicator
interrupting nesting indicator; run indicator
interruption BREAK
interruption in service LET
interruptions can indicate that several components are to be nested
interrupts nesting indicator
intersect CUT
intertwine WREATHE
interval BREAK; GAP; LULL; PAUSE; RECESS; REST; SPACE; ■ FIFTH
intervene MEDDLE
intervene, to nesting indicator
intervening nesting indicator
interview ASK; SEE
interwoven anagram indicator
intestinal infection CHOLERA
intestine GUT
intimacy SEX
intimate BOON; CLOSE; HINT; IMPLY; MEAN; STATE; ■ BOSOM; INFORM
intimation CLUE; HINT; WIND
intimidate AWE; BULLY; COW
into nesting indicator
into action anagram of INTO (especially TION); can indicate a component is nested within ACTION or one of its synonyms e.g. DEED
into wildly anagram of INTO (especially TION)
intoxicated DRUNK (qv); anagram indicator
intoxication HEADY
intractable individual MULE; TARTAR
intrepid BOLD
intricacy WEB

intricate anagram indicator
intrigue CABAL; PLOT; ■ AFFAIR
intrigues anagram indicator
intriguing anagram indicator
intriguing character PLOTTER
intro START
introduce LAUNCH; PRESENT; START; nesting indicator
introduce oneself, attempt to can indicate a word beginning with ME (in the style of "Me, Tarzan") as "Physician's attempt to introduce himself to non-English tipple" clues the wine MEDOC (i.e. Me, Doc)
introduced first letter indicator; nesting indicator
introduced by the component that follows to be placed first
introducing nesting indicator
introduction IM (i.e. I'm); START; ■ PREAMBLE; can indicate that the word alongside should be placed at the beginning; initial letter indicator
introduction for/of/to initial letter indicator
introduction, with no first letter to be omitted
intrusive NOSY; nesting indicator
intuition INSTINCT
inundated nesting indicator
inure TRAIN; ■ ACCUSTOM; HARDEN
invade LAND
invader ANGLE; GOTH; HUNT; JUTE
invades nesting indicator
invading nesting indicator
invalid ILL; NULL
invaluable RARE
invariably ALWAYS; EER; EVER
invasion RAID
inveigh RAIL
inveigle CON
invent LIE; ■ DEVISE
invention LIE; FICTION; [◊ PATENT]; anagram indicator
inventive ORIGINAL
inventiveness ART

inventor BELL; MORSE; NOBEL; [◊ PATENT]
inventory LIST; [◊ ITEM]
invertebrate WORM
inverted anagram indicator; reversal indicator
invest SINK; ■ ENDUE; INDUE nesting indicator
invest in BACK; FUND; SUPPORT; nesting indicator
invested in nesting indicator
investigate CHECK; NOSE; PROBE; PRY; STUDY; SUS; TEST
investigation CASE; PROBE; STUDY; ■ CHECK; HEARING; SEARCH
investigator DC; DI; DS; EYE; PI; TEC
investigators CID
investing apart from the financial meaning, can indicate something to do with donning clothes
investment SPEC; STAKE; ■ CAPITAL; HOLDING; SEED; SPECULATION (convenient for reaching the answer "peculation"); TRUST; nesting indicator
investment, make ENDUE
investment, small some synonym for "small" (e.g. WEE) to be nested within a component
investor ANGEL; SAVER; ■ FINANCIER
invigorating BRACING
invigoration TONIC
invisible, being omission indicator
invitation COME
invite ASK; BID
invited BADE
invited in nesting indicator
invited person GUEST
inviting nesting indicator
invocation KYRIE
invoice BILL
involved (in) INTO; anagram indicator; nesting indicator; run indicator
involved with INTO
inwardly, poets' INLY
involves, involving anagram indicator; nesting indicator

iodine I
Iolanthe [◊ PEER]
ion CHARGE
iota FIG; JOT
Iowa IA
Iranian, old MEDE
Iraqi typically ARAB
irascibility CHOLER
irascible *see* IRRITABLE
irate CROSS; MAD
Ireland EIRE; I; ■ ERIN
Ireland, house in DAIL
Ireland, place in TARA; *see* IRISH TOWN
Ireland, part of DOWN; *see* IRISH COUNTY
iridescent substance NACRE
iridium IR
iris FLAG; ORRIS
Irish ERSE; I; IR; TEMPER; can refer to some aspect of Irish culture, history or language, such as CEILIDH, CONACRE, etc; can indicate the dropping of H as "Irish thinking discussed" clues TAUT (i.e. thought)
Irish accent BROGUE
Irish author BEHAN; ■ JOYCE
Irish boy *see* IRISH FELLOW
Irish broadcasting RTE
Irish city DERRY
Irish county CLARE; CORK; DOWN; MAYO; ■ KERRY; LOUTH
Irish fellow LIAM; PADDY; PAT; SEAN
Irish lady BRIDGET
Irish location TARA
Irish lough ERNE
Irish politicians DAIL
Irish pound PUNT
Irish town BALLA; BRAY; CORK
Irish water LOUGH
Irishman PAT; PADDY; ■ DECLAN; RORY; RYAN; with some reference to speech can indicate 'H' to be eliminated in 'TH', for example THREE to become TREE
irk ANGER
irksomely anagram indicator

iron CLUB; FE; MASHIE; PRESS; SMOOTH; SPOON; ■ DECREASE (i.e. de-crease); GOOSE; [◊ ORE]

ironclad F and E to be placed either side of element or word

ironed anagram indicator

ironic DRY

irrational, irrationally anagram indicator

irrational (number) E; PI

irregular PATCHY; SPOTTY; anagram indicator; can indicate that the odd-numbered letters in a word are to be used (as "very irregular" → VR)

irregularly anagram indicator

irrelevant TRIFLING

irreverent RUDE; *see* CHEEKY

irrigate WATER

irritability BILE; CHOLER

irritable EDGY; LIVERY; RATTY; SORE; TESTY; ■ CRABBY; *see* IRRITATED

irritant BUG; THORN

irritate ANGER; BUG; EAT; FRET; GET; GRATE; IRK; ITCH; RILE; ■ ANNOY; CHAFE; MADDEN; NEEDLE; PEEVE; PIQUE; RANKLE

irritated CROSS; CRUSTY; EDGY; GOT; IRKED; ITCHY; RATTY; SORE; TESTY; anagram indicator; *see* IRASCIBLE

irritated, be ITCH

irritated, easily TESTY

irritating GRATING; IRKING; ITCHY; SORE; anagram indicator

irritating, be *see* IRRITATE

irritating youngster BRAT

irritation BIND; BUG; ITCH; PEST; PRICK; SORE; ■ NUISANCE; PIQUE

irritation, cause *see* IRRITATE

irritation, causing ITCHY

irritation, express SNAP

irritation, source of NEEDLE; *see* IRRITATE

is S (i.e. 's); note that IS can be innocently placed in clue while actually constituting an element in building up the solution; can act as the link between the two definitions in a double definition clue

is able CAN

is back SI

is French EST

is German IST

is hard ISH

is, it TIS

is no longer WAS

is not half I or S to be used

is turning over SI

Isaac IKE

Ishmael can indicate something to do with being an outcast

isinglass MICA

island AIT; ATOLL; BARRA; CAY; COS; CUBA; ELBA; I; INCH; IOM; IS; KEY; MALTA; MAN; MULL; SARK; SKYE; STAFF; ■ ARRAN; BALI; CRETE; EYOT; HERM; IONA; IOW; JAVA; LEWIS; SICILY; SKERRY; TIMOR; TIREE; TONGA; *see* ISLE; can refer to Great Britain or Ireland etc; note ELBA is very common with a reverse indicator because it usefully provides ABLE for the end of an adjective

island, American ELLIS

island, Celtic INCH; *see* ISLAND

island group CI; GB

island, holy IONA

island, little AIT

island race TT

island retreat ABLE (i.e. Elba reversed)

island, rocky SKERRY (Scot.)

islander ARIEL

islands CI; II

isle MAN; WIGHT; *see* ISLAND

islet KEY; *see* ISLAND

Islington area NI

isn't AINT; NOT

isn't, commonly AINT

isn't in OUT

isn't normal anagram indicator

isn't out IN; anagram of ISNT

isn't that so? RIGHT

Israel HANDS; ZION

Israel's leader DAVID; I
Israeli city ACRE
Israeli, old *see* BIBLICAL CHARACTER
Israeli parliament KNESSET
Israelite JEW
issue BROOD; CAUSE; EDITION; EMERGE; EMIT; FLOW; MATTER; NUMBER; POINT; PRINT; SEED; SON; SPAWN; TOPIC; UTTER; YOUNG; ■ EMANATE; EMISSION; LITTER; QUESTION; RESULT; can indicate something to do with children, offspring; anagram indicator
it ARTICLE; SA (i.e. sex appeal); THING; ■ APPEAL; VERMOUTH; note that, although innocently placed, IT itself can be an element in constructing the solution; can refer to a drink as in 'gin and it'
IT design CAD
it is ITS; TIS
it is past ITS or IT IS to placed at the end of a word
it isn't commonly TAINT
it raised TI
it's TIS
it's easy anagram of ITS
it's necessary to can indicate that a run is hidden in what follows
it's not commonly AINT
It's Not Unusual anagram using the letters ITS NOT
it's possibly anagram of ITS
it's said homophone indicator
it, with COOL; HIP; SEXY
Italian I; IT; ITAL; ■ ROMAN
Italian agreement SI
Italian article IL
Italian capitalist ROMAN
Italian city COMO; ROMA; ROME; ■ GENOA; MILAN; TURIN
Italian dictator DUCE
Italian fare PESTO
Italian food PASTA
Italian footballers INTER

Italian gentleman SIGNOR
Italian leader (former) DUCE
Italian master TITIAN
Italian one UNA
Italian poet DANTE
Italian restaurant TRAT
Italian river ARNO
Italian, the IL
Italian wine VINO
Italian writer ECO
itch URGE (qv); YEN; ■ HUNGER; YEARN; *see* DESIRE
itchiness *see* ITCH
item ARTICLE; BIT; COUPLE; ENTRY; IT; PIECE; POINT; THING; UNIT
item, auction LOT
item, faulty DUD; REJECT
item for sale LOT
item in sports programme EVENT
item, newspaper CUTTING
item of property ASSET; EFFECT
item, per EACH
itemise LIST; TABLE
items available MENU
items, number of LIST
itinerary ROUTE; WAY
itinerary, planning ROUTING
itself, by ALONE
Ivan the Terrible VANI (i.e. anagram)
ivories usually indicates something to do with a piano or piano-playing
ivory WHITE; can indicate something to do with elephant's tusk; can indicate something to do with a piano or piano-playing
IVR denotes international vehicle registration letters (as, for example, "Dutch IVR" clues NL)
ivy CREEPER

Jj

jab BLOW; DIG; POKE; PROD; SHOT; STAB; ▪ INJECT

jabber GAS; POKER; *see* CHATTER

jack AB; BALL; BOWL; CARD; FLAG; HAND; J; KNAVE; LIFT; NOB (cribbage); RAISE; SPRAT; TAR; ▪ ASS (i.e. jackass); KITTY; PIKE; STANDARD; *see* SAILOR; can indicate something to do with the nursery rhyme about Jack Sprat; or the proverb "All work and no play makes Jack a dull boy"; or money (U.S.); or the game of bowls; or lumberjack

Jack FLAG; KETCH; MAN; RIPPER; [◊ JILL]; *see* JACK *above*

Jack Sprat can indicate something to do with fat, lean

jacket COAT; COVER; PARKA; TUX; ▪ BLAZER; BLOUSE; REEFER; TABARD

jacket, sort of TWEED

Jacob can indicate something to do with Jacob having no hair e.g. bare-faced

Jacob's son ASHER

jade HACK; NAG; STONE

jag BINGE; BOUT; BENDER; PRICK

Jag CAR

jagged ROUGH; anagram indicator

jaggedly anagram indicator

jaguar CAT

jail CAN; CLINK; NICK; PEN; QUAD; ▪ GAOL; PRISON; QUOD; SLAMMER

jail sentence BIRD; LIFE; TERM; TIME; ▪ STRETCH

jail term BIRD; LIFE; TIME; ▪ SENTENCE; STRETCH

jailbird CON; LAG

jailed INSIDE

jalopy BANGER; CAR; CROCK; HEAP

jam BIND; BLOCK; CLOG; CORNER; CRAM; LOCK; PICKLE; PRESS; SCRAPE; SPOT; STICK; STUFF; WEDGE; ▪ CONSERVE; PRESERVE

Jamaican cult member RASTA

jamb POST

James BOND; JAS; JIM; SID

jammy CUSHY

Jane EYRE; GREY

jangle anagram indicator

Japan J; can indicate something to do with wood-finishing; [◊ GLOSS]

Japanese commander SHOGUN

Japanese currency SEN; Y; YEN

Japanese drama NO

Japanese drink SAKE

Japanese fencing KENDO

Japanese fighting SUMO

Japanese game GO

jape CAPER; FUN; PRANK; TRICK; ▪ JOKE; SCREAM

jar CLASH; GLASS; GRATE; POT; ROCK; SHOCK; [◊ POTTER]

jargon BULL; CANT; PATTER; LINGO; SLANG

Jason's ship ARGO

jaundiced SALLOW; YELLOW

jaunt TRIP

jaunty PERKY; PERT; ▪ RAKISH

jazz RAG; RIFF; STRIDE; SWING; TRAD; [◊ TATUM]

jazz dance BOP; JIVE; STOMP

jazz drums TRAPS

jazz enthusiast/fan/type CAT

jazz group COMBO

jazz music, piece *see* JAZZ

jazz pianist WALLER

jazz piece INTRO

jazz songstress ELLA

jazz style *see* JAZZ

jazzman BASIE;

jazzy anagram indicator

jealous GREEN

jealousy ENVY

Jedi, renegade VADER

jeer BOO; FLOUT; HOOT; MOCK; TAUNT; ■ BELITTLE; HISS; SCOFF

jelly BRAWN; GEL; ■ AGAR

jennet ASS

Jenny ASS; DONKEY; [◊ SPINNING]

jeopardy, in anagram indicator

jerk CLOD; CURE; HITCH; TIC; TUG; YANK; ■ NERD; TWITCH; *see* FOOL

jerker anagram indicator as in "no tear-jerker" → ORNATE

jerks PE

jerry POT

Jersey COW; SPUD; ■ POTATO; can refer to either the island or breed of cattle (and so, by implication, some general feature of cattle as "New Jersey?" → CALF)

Jerusalem SION

jess STRAP

jest COD; CRACK; JOKE (qv); SALLY

jester FOOL; WAG; WIT; ■ FESTE

Jesuits (etc) ORDER

jet BLACK; FLY; PLANE; SHOOT; STREAM; SPOUT; SPRAY; ■ FIGHTER; STONE

jete SPRING

Jethro TULL

jettison DROP; DUMP

jetty MOLE; PIER

jewel AMBER; GEM; OPAL; PEARL; ROCK; RUBY; STONE; ■ SARD

jewellery *see* JEWEL, JEWELLERY, ITEM OF

jewellery, cheap PASTE

jewellery, item of BANGLE; CLIP; CORAL; RING; ROPE; STUD; *see* JEWEL

Jewish SEMETIC

Jewish roll BEGEL

jibe CRACK; DIG; JEER; SCOFF

jiffy MO; SEC

jig BOB

Jill FERRET; [◊ JACK]

jingle RHYME; VERSE

job BILLET; CHORE; LINE; POST; ROLE; TASK; WORK; ■ CAPACITY; CAREER; DUTY; ERRAND; LIVING; POSITION; STATION; TRADE; VOCATION; can indicate a specific job, e.g. fitter; anagram indicator

Job can indicate something to do with patience

job, boring/uninteresting CHORE; GRIND

job, assess CASE

job centre O

job, give a APPOINT; PLACE; USE

job, given a PLACED; USED

job not started OB

job, type of TRADE; *see* JOB

Jock SCOT; can refer to something Scottish as "Jock's interjection" clues OCH; *see* SCOT

jockey RIDER

Joe GI

joey ROO

jog NUDGE; RUN; TROT

jogger can refer to some kind of reminder, so "A jogger in France" → AIDE-MEMOIRE

jogging anagram indicator

John CAN; HEAD; HEADS; JACK; LAV; LOO; PRIVY; ■ TOILET; can refer to the painter Augustus John

John* BULL; can refer to the disciple or biblical book of the same name

join ABUT; ADD; BRAID; BRIDGE; ENTER; FUSE; KNIT; LINK; MEET; SCARF; SEAM; SEW; SPAN; SPLICE; TIE; UNITE; ■ COUPLE; MARRY; MERGE; RIVET; SOLDER; STAPLE; WELD; YOKE; can indicate something to do with marriage; can indicate that two components in a clue are to be set side by side

join in nesting indicator

join securely RIVET; *see* JOIN

join together ALLY

join up KNOT; LINK; TIE; ■ BIND; CONNECT; ENLIST; MARRY; WED

joined up LINKED; can refer to being a member

joined up with MET

joined violently AMAIN (archaic)

joiner AND; ■ UNITER

joining UNION; can indicate the use of AND

joins LINKS etc – *see* JOIN; can indicate that one component in a clue is to be placed alongside another

joint ANKLE; BEAM; BEEF; BRAWN; CUT; DIVE; HINGE; HIP; HOCK; KNEE; LEVEL; LINK; LOIN; NECK; PLACE; RACK; RIB; SCARF; SHIN; SPLICE; ■ BRISKET; COLLAR; ELBOW; HAUNCH; KNUCKLE; MITRE; REEFER; ROAST; SEAM; SHOULDER; STIFLE; TALUS; TENON; WRIST; can indicate that AND is to be used as a component; [◊ CARVE]

joint exercise HIPPE (i.e. HIP + PE)

joint, metal WELD

joint near the end ROACH

joint of meat LOIN etc – *see* JOINT

joint, part of TENON

joint stake SKEWER

jointly can signal a word beginning with CO (co-worker etc)

joints CHINE; SPINE

joints, relating to ARTICULAR

joist BEAM

joke CRACK; GAG; JAPE; JEST; PUN; QUIP; RIB; TEASE; TRICK; ■ CHESTNUT; HOAX; JOSH; PLEASANTRY; SCREAM

joke, practical TRICK

joker CARD; FOOL; WAG; WIT; ■ CHARACTER; FUNSTER; PUNSTER

jokes HUMOUR; WIT; *see* JOKE

jokes, fellow making *see* JOKER

jokes, old/trite CORN

joky COD

jollification BEANO; PARTY (qv)

jollity GLEE

jolly FESTIVE; GAY; HAPPY; MERRY; RM (i.e. Royal Marine); TAR; VERY; can indicate something to do with sailors; *see* DRUNK

Jolson AL

jolt JAR; SHAKE; SHOCK

Jonathan APPLE

Jones INIGO

Joplin piece RAG

Joseph JO; JOE

Josephine JO

josh *see* JOKE

jostle BUFFET

jostled anagram indicator

jostling anagram indicator

jot BIT; NOTE; WHIT

jotting NOTE; ■ NOTING

jottings, make NOTE

journal LOG; MAG; ■ DIARY; PAPER; PERIODICAL; RECORD

journalism PRESS; WRITING

journalism, example of REPORT

journalist CUB; ED; HACK; SUB; ■ EDITOR

journalist, part-time STRINGER

journalist, routine HACK

journalists PRESS

journey DRIVE; GO; RIDE; SPIN; TOUR; TRIP; WAY; ■ JAUNT; ROUTE; TRAVEL; TREK

journey, make a TRAVEL (qv)

journey, part of LAP; STAGE

journey, short HOP

journo *see* JOURNALIST

jousting weapon LANCE

Jove in the exclamation "By Jove!" can refer to one of the satellites of Jupiter namely Io, Ganymede, Europa, Callisto

jovial MERRY

jowl CHEEK

joy BLISS; GLEE; ■ DELIGHT; ELATION; EUPHORIA; TRANSPORT

Judah, king of ASA

Jude note Jude is the patron saint of lost causes

judge DEEM; HEAR; J; LUD; RATE; REF; SAY; SEE; TRY; UMP; ■ ASSESS; MEASURE; TESTER; TRIER

judge, act as HEAR; SIT; TRY

judge, acted as SAT

judge, old GIDEON

judge, part-time RECORDER

judged SAT

judges BENCH

judgment DOOM; SENSE; ■ SENTENCE

judicial enquiry CASE

judicial investigation HEARING

judiciary BENCH

judicious WISE

judo expert DAN

jug EWER; POT; URN; ■ PITCHER; note this can also mean prison, e.g. CAN, STIR see PRISON

juice SAP

juicy MOIST

Jules VERNE

Juliet J; LOVER

Juliet, perhaps WENCH

jumble HEAP; MIX; ■ GARBLE; WELTER; anagram indicator

jumble sale anagram of SALE

Jumbo BIG; HUGE; LARGE; OS; PLANE; can indicate something to do with an elephant

jump BUCK; CLEAR; HOP; LEAP; SKIP; START; ■ AXEL; BOUND; POUNCE; SPRING; VAULT

jump, kind of HIGH; LONG

jump over CLEAR

jumper FLEA; FROG; ROO; TOAD; TOP (i.e. garment); ■ CRICKET; HOPPER; JOEY

jumping HOPPING etc – see JUMP; anagram indicator

jumping across can indicate that the component that follows is to be nested within what precedes – example: "Mister jumping across river to pet cat" → MOUSER

jumps, without FLAT

jumpy anagram indicator

junction ANKLE; T; see JOINT

jungle BUSH

junior COLT; JUN; LESS; LOW; SON; SUB; ■ LITTLE; LOWER; MASTER; MINOR; UNDER; YOUNG

junior counsel DEVIL

junior editor SUB

junior employee COG

junior officer ALT

junk BIN; BOAT; DROP; DRUG; DUMP; LUMBER; MEAT; SMACK; SPURN; TRASH; TRIPE; see RUBBISH

junk mail SPAM

junk meal BURGER

junked anagram indicator

junket FEAST; TRIP

junkie USER

jurisdiction REACH

jurors PANEL

jury PANEL

jury's recommendation RIDER

just BUT; DUE; EVEN; FAIR; MERE; METE; MORAL; ONLY; RIGHT; ■ LICIT; ONLY; RIGHTFUL; SIMPLY

just not on OFF

just, only HARDLY

just open AJAR

just over fifty LI

just over a hundred CI

just over a thousand MI

just right APT; PAT

just so PAT

just the same DO; ■ DITTO

just the thing TICKET

justice RIGHT; RECORDER; SHALLOW (i.e. Shakespearean character); SILENCE (from same play); can indicate something to do with NEMESIS; [◊ BENCH]

justification GROUND(S); REASON; RIGHT

justified FAIR

justify WARRANT

juvenile CHILD; MINOR

Kk

kaleidoscope TOY; ■ PATTERN
kangaroo HOPPER; ■ JUMPER
kangaroo, male BUCK
Kansas KS
karma FATE
Kate SHREW
Katherine SHREW
Kay K
kebab, type of SHISH
keck RETCH
keel LIST; SHIP
keel over DIE; LEEK; LIST
keen ACUTE; ARDENT; AVID;
    COLD; CRY; GREET; HOT;
    INTO; LAMENT; LOW (e.g.
    price); MAD; SAVE; SHARP; ■
    CHEAP; BITTER; can indicate
    something to do with mourning;
    [◊ WHET]
keen, be LONG
keen, be very RAVE
keen, not COOL; LOTH
keen on INTO
keen on, be DIG
keen type FAN
keen, very AVID; MAD
keenness EDGE
keep FORT; GUARD; HOLD;
    LAST; MIND; STOCK; STORE;
    TOWER; ■ CASTLE;
    DEFENCE; OBSERVE;
    PRESERVE; REMAIN;
    RESERVE; RETAIN; nesting in-
    dicator; run indicator
keep an eye on GAZE;
    OBSERVE; WATCH
keep away from AVOID; SHUN
keep back RESERVE; ■
    RESTRAIN
keep close CLUTCH; HUG
keep, do not ROT
keep down COW; REPRESS
keep fit PE; PT; ■ EXERCISE
keep going LAST
keep in GATE; LIMIT; PEN

keep in touch WRITE
keep left L to be inserted
keep lid on CAP
keep on at HARRY
keep on complaining GRIPE
keep out BAN; BAR
keep out of clutches ELUDE
keep pushing PLY
keep quiet HIST; SH; WHIST
keep score TALLY
keep talking DRONE
keep things to sell STOCK
keep under lock and key
    INTURN
keeper RING; nesting indicator as
    "steal book in titled person's
    keeping" → NOBBLE
keeping nesting indicator
keeping up HIP
keeps EVER; nesting indicator;
    run indicator
keepsake TOKEN
Kelly GENE
Kelvin K
ken KNOW; RANGE
Kenneth KEN; KENNY
Kent can refer to Clark Kent and
    hence something to do with Su-
    perman
Kent area SE
Kent, in SE
Kent town DEAL
Kentish SE
Kentucky KY
kept HELD; HAD; PENT;
    STORED; nesting or run indica-
    tor
kerb EDGE
kernel NUT
kernel of the middle letter(s) of the
    word that follows
Ketch JACK
kettle DRUM; ■ DIXIE; HEATER
key A; B; BEST (as best man at a
    wedding is a key man); C; CAY;
    D; B; E; G; LEVER; MAJOR;
    MINOR; NOTE; PIN; PITCH;
    REEF; TONE; TYPE (i.e. verb,
    as on a keyboard); ■ CLUE;
    LOCKER; SEMINAL; can indi-
    cate a computer key e.g. DEL,

ESC; can indicate something to do with an island, islet etc; [◊ LOCK]

key mechanism PIANO

key, off FLAT

key ring BO, CO etc (i.e. a musical key to be followed by O, *see* KEY)

keyboard, at the TYPING

Khan AGA

kick BLOW; BOOST; BOOT; BUCK; BUZZ; CROSS; HACK; PASS; SHIN; THRILL; ■ RECOIL; anagram indicator

kick bucket DIE

kick oneself RUE

kick out EJECT; EXPEL; OUST

kick up TOOB

kickback reversal indicator

kicked/kicking anagram indicator

kid BILLY; CHILD; COD; CON; DUPE; FOOL; GOAT; JOSH; MITE; RIB; TEASE; TOT; TWIT; ■ LEATHER; NIPPER; SUEDE; YOUTH

kid* SON

kid, American BUB

kidnap, kidnapping SNATCH

kidneys, of the RENAL

kids ISSUE

kill BAG; DOIN (i.e. do in); END; HANG; ICE; PREY; RUIN; SLAY; STOP; SWAT; ■ DROWN; ZAP

kill in America ICE

kill without legal sanction LYNCH

killed SLAIN; SLEW; STONED

killed, be DIE

killed, was FELL

killer ASP; CAIN

killer-whale ORCA

killing MINT; PILE; POT; STACK can indicate something to do with laughing, something very funny

kiln OAST; OVEN; STOVE

kin OWN; STOCK; ■ RELATION

kin, next of RELATED

kind BRAND; BREED; CLASS; CLEMENT; GOOD; NICE; RACE; SORT; STAMP; TYPE; ■ GENTLE; TENDER

kind deed FAVOUR

kind-hearted TENDER; a synonym for kind (e.g. GOOD) to be inserted into a component

kind person ANGEL; BRICK; LAMB

kindle INSPIRE

kindling FAGGOT

kindly GOOD; ■ BENIGN; GENTLE

kindly fashion, in a GENTLY

kindness FAVOUR

kindred OWN

king CARD; COLE; ER; GR; K; LEAR; MAN; R; REX; VIP; ■ ARTHUR; GEORGE; OFFA; PIECE; PRIAM; RULER; SAUL; [◊ REIGN]

king and his advisors COURT

king and queen KER; RER

King Arthur's seneschal KAY

King Edward ER; SPUD; TATER

King Edward I ERI

King Lear PLAY; can signify a character from the play e.g. Fool, Regan

King of the Forest OAK

king, old OFFA; ■ DAVID; *see* KING

King, Old COLE

king once CR; *see* KING

king's ERS; KS; MANS; REGAL; ROYAL; RS

King's Cross STATION

king's son HECTOR; PRINCE

king said, the WRECKS (i.e. homophone of REX)

kings, one of six GR

kingdom NEPAL; REALM; STATE; UK; with a capital letter can signify something to do with Brunel

kinked anagram indicator

kinsman RELATION (qv)

kink CURL

kinky anagram indicator, as "kinky fun" → UNF

kinky, not STRAIGHT

Kipling novel KIM

Kipling verse IF

kipper CURE

kiss BUSS; CROSS; NECK; PECK; SMACK; TOUCH; X; ■ GREET; SMACKER

kiss passionately SNOG

kiss, quick PECK

kisser MOUTH

kisses, give NECK

kit CLOTHE; GEAR; RIG; SET; STRIP; can indicate something to do with clothing; being the name of a small violin, can indicate something to do with violin-playing

kitchen GALLEY

kitchen cabinet UNIT

kitchen equipment GRILL; OVEN; STOVE

kitchen, part of SCULLERY

kitchen stove RANGE

kitchen utensil GRATER

kitchen wrap FOIL

kittens LITTER

kitty BANK; FUND; JACK; POOL; POT

Klemperer OTTO

knack ART; CARD; HANG; HONOUR (i.e. card); SKILL; TRICK; WAY

knave CAD; JACK; ■ BOUNDER

knead MASSAGE; PUMMEL; WORK

knee BENDER

kneel BEND

kneeler HASSOCK

knees-up DO

knew long ago WIST

knife BLADE; CUT; STAB; ■ CUTTER; LANCET

knife wound STAB

knight DUB; KT; MAN; N; PIECE; SIR; ■ CHAMPION; HORSE

knighthood K

knit BOND; JOIN; LINK; anagram indicator

knitted anagram indicator

knitting BONDING; [◊ NEEDLE]

knitwear JUMPER

knob BOSS; NODE; PAT (i.e. of butter); STUD

knock BANG; BASH; BAT; HIT; PAT; PINK; RAP; TAP; ■ INNINGS; STRIKE

knock back DOWN; DRINK; EAT

knock down DECK; FLOOR

knock drink back a synonym for drink to be reversed, hence MUR, PAL, PUS etc

knock, gently TAP

knock hard can indicate a synonym for "knock" followed by H e.g. BATH, PATH, RAPH

knock off DISCOUNT; KILL

knock on the head BRAIN

knock out *see* KNOCK-OUT

knock-out HIT; KO; STUN; ■ SUCCESS; can indicate something to with anaesthetic; an anagram indicator (for example "his knock-out" requires an anagram of HIS)

knock unconscious KO; STUN

knock up LOB; ROUSE; ■ SCORE

knocked back ATE; DRUNK; reversal indicator

knocked HIT

knocked about a component to be nested within HIT

knocked out GONE; anagram indicator

knocked out of shape anagram indicator

knocked over reversal indicator

knockout *see* KNOCK-OUT

knoll HILL

knot BEND (naut.); BIRD; BOND; BOW; KT; MAT; REEF; SLIP; TIE; ■ GNARL; GRANNY; HITCH

knot in handkerchief REMINDER

knots anagram indicator; *see* KNOT

knots, in anagram indicator

knotted MATTED; TIED; anagram indicator

know CAN; CON; KEN; ■ REALISE

know from the past WOT

know, get to LEARN

know-how ART

know, let TELL
know once WIST
know, want to/ would like to ASK
knowing ARCH; AWARE; FLY; SLY; WISE ■ AWARE; SHREWD
knowing about ONTO
knowledge KEN; LORE; ■ SCIENCE; can indicate something to do with a cab-driver (a requirement of the job being to have "the knowledge")
knowledge, fount of all ORACLE
knowledge, having *see* KNOWLEDGEABLE
knowledge, impart INFORM; TEACH
knowledge, range of KEN
knowledge, slight SMATTERING
knowledge, sphere of AREA; FIELD; SCENE
knowledgeable ABLE; HIP; INTO; SAGE; WISE
known once WIST
known, one of those ONION
known OPEN
knows how to CAN
KO'd OUT
Koran, part of SURA
Koranic passage SURA
Kosovan SERB
kris DAGGER

Ll

la! AH; LO; SEE
label TAG; TALLY; ■ TICKET
label attached TAGON (i.e. tag on)
labour GRAFT; SLOG; TOIL; WORK; can indicate something to do with birth, baby etc.
Labour LAB; LEFT; PARTY; RED

Labour, not fond of IDLE; ■ LAZY
labour organization GUILD; TU
labour schedule STINT
laboured ORNATE; anagram indicator
labourer HAND; PEON
labourer, unskilled COOLIE
labours can indicate something to do with Hercules
lace SPIKE; TIE; ■ TATTING
lace, make TAT
lace-maker TATTER
lack NEED; WANT; ■ DEARTH; OMISSION; can indicate a word ending in OFF (as "lack of performance" → TURNOFF)
lack of NO
lack of clarity in speech SLUR
lack of money, hampered by TIGHT
lack of rain/ water DROUGHT
lackey MINION; PAGE; VALET; ■ SERVANT
lacking BARE; FREE; LESS; NO; SINE (legal); omission indicator as "lacking skill" requires ART to be omitted; can indicate a phrase involving NOTHING; can indicate an adjective ending in LESS
lacking capacity UNABLE
lacking cover NUDE; first letter to be omitted; synonym for "cover" (e.g. LID, CAP) to be omitted – *see* COVER
lacking energy E to be omitted
lacking experience GREEN; RAW
lacking finish last letter to be omitted; END to be omitted
lacking in self-confidence SHY
lacking morals EVIL; *see* BASE
lacking refinement CRUDE; RUDE; *see* CRUDE
lacking spirit AILING
laconic CURT (qv); FRANK (qv); TERSE
lad BOY; SON; YOUTH; ■ FELLOW; *see* BOY
lad in hearing BUOY
ladder RUN; STEPS
laden HEAPED

ladies LOO; WC; ■ CONVENIENCE; *see* LADY, TOILET

ladies' group WI

ladies' man ROUE

ladies' organisation WI

lady DAME; HER; LASS; LUCK; SHE; WIFE; *see* WOMAN

lady doctor DRESS (i.e. dr-ess!)

lady, for HER

lady, foreign FRAU

Lady Jane GREY

lady, lovely BELLE

Lady MacBeth can indicate something to do with SPOT

lady, nasty CAT

lady, old GRAN; GRANNY; MUM

lady, pert young CHIT

lady's HER; HERS

lady's man BEAU

lady, titled DAME

lady, young GAL; *see* GIRL

lag CON; COVER; LATH; STAKE; STAVE; WRAP

lag behind TRAIL

lager PILS; ■ BEER; STELLA

Lagos, money in NAIRA

laid SET

laid-back COOL; DIAL (i.e. rev.); reverse indicator

laid down SET; PLACED

laid out FLAT; SET; anagram indicator

laid up ILL; reversal indicator; component to be nested within BED (i.e. in bed)

lair DEN; HOLE; HOLT; HOME; NEST

laity LAY

lake COMO; ERIE; L; LAC; LOCH; MERE; TARN; WATER; ■ BALA; LOUGH

Lake District NW

lakes LL

lam BEAT; FLIGHT; PUNCH

lamb DEAR; EWE; RAM

Lamb ELIA

Lamb-like ELIAN

lamb partly RACK (i.e. cut of veal)

Lambeth can indicate something to do with archbishop or palace

lame GAME; POOR; THIN; WEAK

lament ELEGY; KEEN; MOURN; WAIL; WEEP; ■ BEWAIL; DIRGE; MONODY; YAMMER

lamina PLATE

lamp LIGHT

lampoon SATIRE; SQUIB; *see* PARODY

lance CUT; OPEN; PIERCE; SPEAR

land ALIGHT; BAG; DOCK; ESTATE; FIELD; GAIN; LIGHT; NATION; PARK; PLOT; PROPERTY; REACH; SOIL; STATE; TERRA; TRACT; ■ AREA; ASHORE; COUNTRY; EARTH; GROUND(S); SETTLE; SHORE; TERRAIN

land in America REALTY

land, low-lying VLEI

land mass ASIA; ISLE

land, native HOME

land, on ASHORE

land, open COMMON; LEA

land, piece of ACRE; LOT; PLOT; SOD; TRACT; ■ ISLE

land, poor HEATH

landed LIT; can indicate some form of landowner, *see* LANDOWNER

landed property ESTATE; REALTY

landholder THANE

landing DOCK; JETTY; QUAY; can indicate something to do with stairs; can indicate an historical military operation such as Gallipoli

landing place/stage DOCK; JETTY; PIER; ■ QUAY (plus note its old spelling: KEY)

landlord HOST; LETTER

landowner LAIRD; SQUIRE

lands ESTATE

lane ALLEY; ROAD; TRACK; WAY

Langley CIA

language LANG; LINGO; SLANG; TALK; WORDS; ■

ARGOT; can indicate a specific language e.g. BASQUE, ERSE, FRENCH, HINDI, NORSE, PUNIC, TAMIL, THAI

language, African IBO

language class, group NORSE

language, computer JAVA

language, empty LE; RANT

language, Indian HINDI; PALI

language, informal SLANG

language, old ERSE; LATIN

language, ordinary PROSE

language, special CANT; JARGON

language, vulgar ARGOT

language, with command of FLUENT

languages ROMANCE

languish FADE; PINE; ■ WITHER

languishing PINING; anagram indicator

lanky RANGY; TALL; THIN

lap CIRCLE; DRINK; LEG; ROUND; STAGE; SUP; can indicate something to do with racing as "Lap-dog" cues GREYHOUND; ■ CIRCUIT

lapse ERROR; FAIL; FALL; PASS; SIN; SLIP; TRIP; ■ EXPIRE; omission indicator

lapse morally SIN

lard FAT; GREASE

large AMPLE; BIG; BROAD; FAT; GRAND GREAT; HUGE; L; LG; MEGA; OS; WIDE; ■ JUMBO; ROOMY; TIDY

large amount TON

large amounts LOTS; POTS

large, at FREE

large company ICI

large enough AMPLE

large family, member of QUIN

large group MASS

large, grow WAX

large helping of several letters from the following word to be used

large number C; K; M; MANY

large portion of can indicate all but the last letter of what follows (or a synonym) is to be used as

"Large portion of spaghetti" → PAST

large quantity LOT; ■ OODLES; PILE; REAM(S)

large scale EPIC; MASS

large size OS

large sum MINT; POT

large town CITY

large, very OS

large wave ROLLER

larger MORE

lark ANTIC; CAPER; FUN; JAPE; PLAY

larva BOT; BOTT; GRUB

lasagne* PASTA

laser BEAM

lash CAT; FLOG; WHIP

lashed by nesting indicator

lashings LOTS

lass GAL

lassie GAL; *see* GAL

lasso CATCH; ROPE; KNOT; LOOP

last END; ENDURE; FINAL; REAR; STAND; STICK; TAIL; WEAR; ■ BOTTOM; can indicate something to do with cobbler, shoes, etc; by implication can indicate the last of something e.g. Z, OMEGA, AMEN; last letter indicator

last (as in 'last of a kind') SOLE

last bit ENDER

last bit of last letter indicator

last character Z; ZED; ■ OMEGA; last letter indicator

last course AFTERS

last letter *see* LAST CHARACTER

last minute LATE

last minute, at the LATE

last month ULT

last, not quite the last-but-one component to be used

last of last letter indicator

last one ENDER

last ones going last letters to be omitted

last pair YZ

last pair, almost the XY

last say, has/have the Y

last unknown Z
last wishes RIP
last word AMEN
last, work at/on HEEL; SOLE; ■ COBBLE
latch LOCK
late EX; DEAD; GONE; OLD; SLOW; ■ BEHIND; FORMER; NEW; NIGHT; PAST; RECENT; TARDY; WITCHING (as in witching hour); can indicate something to do with death, e.g. autopsy, funerals, heaven, meeting one's maker, as "late transport" → HEARSE
late activity NIGHT
late, became DIED
late, become DIE; *see* DIE
late eats SUPPER
late edition EXTRA
late, extremely E; LAST
late in the day EVEN; NIGHT; ■ EVENING
late in the evening ATTEN (i.e. at ten); TEN
late news OBIT
late party WAKE
later AFTER; NEXT; NEW; THEN
latest HOT; NEW; NEWEST; NEWS; last letter indicator
latest odds SP
lathe TOOL; ■ TURNER
lathe worker TURNER
lather STATE; STEW; SWEAT
lather, in a anagram indicator
Latin L; LAT; can refer to some Latin word or phrase e.g. "in Latin thus" clues HOC
Latin bird AVIS
Latin, but in SED
Latin country RUS
Latin epigrams, source of MARTIAL
Latin, from AB
Latin name NOMEN
Latin, this HIC
Latin type ROMAN
Latin, works in OPERA
latitude PLAY; ROOM; SCOPE; SPACE
latitude, warm TROPIC

latter RECENT
latter part of day EVE; NIGHT
lattice GRID
Latvian LETT
laud PRAISE (qv)
laugh HA; HOOT; MOCK; SCREAM; TITTER
laugh loudly ROAR
laugh quietly NICKER
laugh, real/great GAS
laughable RICH
laughter MIRTH
laughter-maker COMIC; HYENA; JESTER
laughter, some PEAL
launch FLOAT; HURL; OPEN; PITCH; START
launch, fast JATO (i.e. jet-assisted take-off)
launched PITCHED; SENT
launching first letter indicator
launder CLEAN; WASH
laundered CLEANED; anagram indicator
laundry CLEANERS; WASH; WASHING; [◊ MANGLE]
laurel *see* PRIZE
Laurel STAN
lavished anagram indicator
lava, particles of ASH
lavatory CAN; HEAD; HEADS; JOHN; LAV; LOO; WC
lavish RICH; ■ LIBERAL
lavish affection DOTE
lavish money SPEND
lavish style, in PLUSH
law DECREE; EDICT; LEX; ORDER; RULE; ■ STATUTE; [◊ BILL; OHM; POOR]
law, agreeing with LICIT
law expert LLD
law, go to *see* LAWMEN
law group *see* LAWMEN
law, lay down the DICTATE
lawbreaker anagram of LAW; *see* CRIMINAL
lawful LEGAL; LICIT; ■ FAIR
lawgiver MOSES
lawlessness CRIME
lawless type *see* CRIMINAL

lawmaker MP; OHM; ■ SENATOR

lawman DA; MOSES; MP

lawman, Wild West EARP

lawmen MPS; POSSE; *see* POLICE

lawn CLOTH; GRASS; GREEN

Lawrence DH; ROSS; TE

Lawrence initially DH; L; TE

lawsuit ACTION; CASE

lawyer BL; DA; LLB; SILK; ■ COUNSEL; MASON; NOTARY; [◊ BRIEF]

lawyers BAR; INN; INNS

lawyer, US DA

lax LOOSE; SLACK; ■ CASUAL; anagram indicator

laxity LATITUDE

lay AIR; BET; CIVIL; PLACE; POEM; POSE; PUT; SET; SONG; SPREAD; [◊ EGG]

lay claim to BAG

lay hand on FINGER; GRAB

lay on THRASH

lay out ARRAY; DECK; FLOOR; KO

layer BED; COAT; CRUST; FILM; HEN; LEVEL; PLY; ROW; TIER; ■ CARPET; COATING; SHEET; STOREY; [◊ EGG]

layer of dirt SCUM

layer of ore VEIN

layout PLAN

laze IDLE; LOAF; LOLL; REST

lazily IDLY

laziness SLOTH

lazy IDLE; SLACK; ■ INERT; anagram indicator

lazy lot SHOWER

lea FIELD

lead FRONT; GUIDE; HEAD; HERO; OPEN; PILOT; PB; STAR; STEER; USHER; VAN; ■ LEASH; METAL; can indicate that an adjacent word goes to the front; can indicate the use of UP as "to lead at Wimbledon" can clue SET-UP

lead astray *see* TEMPT

lead, in the AHEAD; FIRST; VAN; UP; a component to be nested within PB

lead off START; anagram of LEAD; *see* START

lead, sort of DOG

lead, take the lead STAR; START

lead, taking the HEADING; STARRING; WINNING; can indicate that one component goes in front of another

leaden HEAVY; WEIGHTY

leader AGA; BOSS; CHIEF; ELDER; HEAD; KING; POPE; PRIME; STAR; TOP; ■ DUCE; FIRST; WINNER; initial letter indicator; can indicate something to do with a newspaper's leading article

leader being deposed first letter to be omitted

leader demoted the first letter of a word to be transposed to the end

leader, political PM

leader's disqualified initial letter to be omitted

leaders initial letters indicator, either the initial letters of several words or the first two letters of one word; can require AND to be inserted between the initial letters as "Leaders of Royal Society" clues RANDS; can indicate something to do with a newspaper's leading article(s)

leadership, change of first letter to be changed

leading AHEAD; ARCH; BIG; CHIEF; HEAD; PRIME; STAR; TOP; UP; initial letter(s) indicator; in conjunction with lady, man, etc. can indicate a ruler or the office of ruler

leading actor, player, role STAR

leading character A; ALPHA; first letter indicator; *see* LEADING ACTOR

leading characters can indicate an anagram of the first letters of the alphabet ABC etc

leading duo first two letters to be used

leading group G; VAN

leading fighters VAN

leading journalist ED; J

leading lady L; STAR
leading light BEACON; L
leading man HERO; KING; M; STAR; ■ BOSS
leading monk M; PRIOR
leader of the mob DON
leading, one HEAD; O; *see* LEADER
leading part P; SOLO; STAR
leading partner COSTAR (i.e. co-star); P
leading performer P; STAR
leading player P; can indicate something to do with the leading player in an orchestra e.g. violin, violinist, fiddle
leading position FRONT; HEAD; P; STAR; TOP; VAN
leading seaman S
leads initial letter indicator
leaf BRACT; F; FOLIO; PAGE; SHEET
leaf, part of VEIN
leaflet TRACT
leafy borders LY
leafy one PALM; *see* TREE
leafy street AVENUE
league ALLY; CLASS; GROUP; UNION; ■ ALLIANCE; AXIS; MEASURE
league, first in L; TOP
leak BLEED; ESCAPE; SEEP; DRIP; ■ WATER
leakage EMISSION
leaked BLED; anagram indicator
Leamington SPA
lean BEND; HEEL; LIE; LIST; POOR; RELY; REST; SPARE; TEND; THIN; TILT; TIP; ■ DEPEND; STOOP
lean-framed a component to be nested within LIST (or LEAN)
lean on ABUT
lean period can indicate something to do with dieting
lean-to SHED
lean towards FAVOUR; LIKE
Leander can indicate something to do with HERO
leaning BENT

leaning, exhibit some HEEL; LIST; TILT
leant BENT; BOWED; LEANED
leap HOP; JETE; JUMP; ■ BASKET; SPRING; VAULT
leap forward BOUND
leapt SPRANG
lear OVEN
Lear can refer to Shakespeare's play (and so Regan, Goneril, Cordelia) or Edward Lear, the latter suggesting something to do with nonsense
Lear's daughter REGAN
learn CON; HEAR; ■ GATHER
learn a trade TRAIN
learn of HEAR
learn, ready to APT
learn, try to STUDY
learned WISE
learned people BAS; MAS
learner L; ■ PUPIL; TIRO; TRAINEE; TYRO
learner in driver's place TELE
learners CLASS; STREAM
learning LORE
learning method/process/way of ROTE
lease HIRE; LET; RENT
leased LET
leaseholder TENANT
leash LEAD
least amount WHIT
least familiar RAREST
least suitable LAST
leather BEAT; HIDE; KID; STROP; ■ CALF; OXHIDE; PATENT; THRASH; WELT
leather, type of CALF; *see* LEATHER
leathery HARD; ROUGH; TOUGH
leave BREAK; DEPART; DROP; DESERT; EXIT; GO; LET; OFF; PART; QUIT; REST; SHOO; SPLIT; STRAND; RETIRE; WILL; ■ BEAT IT; DECAMP; EXEAT; FINISH; FURLOUGH; PERMISSION; *see* ABANDON
leave behind WILL; ■ STRAND
leave car PARK

leave decision to chance TOSS
leave it be STET
leave of absence EXEAT; *see* LEAVE
leave off STOP; PROP
leave out OMIT; SKIP
leave suddenly VANISH
leaves COPY; FF; GOES; SALAD; omission indicator; can indicate something to do with autumn, fall etc; can indicate something to do with a plant known for its leaves e.g. cabbage, lettuce, tea, mint, tobacco; *see* LEAF, PAGE
leaves producer TREE (qv)
leaving OFF; omission indicator
leavings ASH
lecher GOAT; RAKE; ■ ROUE; SATYR
lechery LUST
lector READER
lecture CHIDE; LECT; TALK; ■ ADDRESS; CARPET; SERMON; SPEECH
lecture series COURSE
lecturer DON; L
lecturers STAFF
lectures COURSE
led astray anagram of LED
ledge SHELF; SILL
ledger BOOK; ■ ACCOUNT
lee SHELTER
leer OGLE; STARE
leery SHY
lees DREGS
left GONE; L; LABOUR; OFF; NEAR (i.e. side of car in UK); ODD; PORT; QUIT; RED; SIDE; SPLIT; WENT; ■ LORN; PARTED; SINISTER; omission indicator; run indicator; can indicate the initial letter of a word (i.e. the leftmost letter) as "left alone" → A; [◊ HEIR]
left abandoned L to be omitted
left behind PASSE; L or PORT to be at end of word
left in charge LIC
left-hand L; VERSO
left on board PORT; SPORTS (i.e. PORT nested within SS)

left on road NEAR
left out L to be omitted
left-over COLD (as in cold meat); ■ RELIC; a component to be nested within LEFT
left-overs REST
left side VO (i.e. paper)
left to be last L to be moved to the end of the target word
left unfinished last letter to be omitted
left-wing PINK; RED
left-winger RED; TROT; ■ COMMIE
leftie *see* LEFT-WINGER
leftist RED
leftover END; DREG; SCRAP; ■ RESIDUE; L to be at the front
leg ON (i.e. cricket); LIMB; PIN; SHANK; SIDE; STAGE
leg, bit/part of CALF; SHIN; ■ ANKLE
leg injury LIMP
leg on each side ASTRIDE
leg, opposite OFF
leg-protection SOCK; STOCKING; ■ GAITER
leg, say SIDE
leg, upper THIGH
legacy BEQUEST
legal LICIT; ■ LAWFUL; [◊ ACTION; CASE; SUE; SUIT]
legal action CASE; SUIT; TRIAL; ■ LITIGATION (useful to get mitigation)
legal action, take CHARGE; SUE
legal authority COURT; JUDGE; POWER; *see* AUTHORITY
legal case/proceeding/process ACTION; APPEAL; SUIT
legal claim DROIT; TITLE
legal claim, basis for TITLE
legal concern INTEREST
legal document/paper ACT; DEED; WRIT; WILL
legal document, part of CLAUSE
legal entitlement LIEN
legal profession BAR; LAW
legal removal OUSTER
legal right LIEN

legal type WIG
legal validity FORCE
legend FABLE; FOOT (i.e. leg end); G (i.e. last letter of leg); MYTH; YETI
legendary bird ROC
legendary figure TITAN
leghorn FOWL; HEN
legible PLAIN
legion MYRIAD
legislation ACT; BILL; LAW
legislative assembly DIET
legislative body COUNCIL
legislator MP; ■ DRACO
legislature DAIL; HOUSE
legitimate FAIR; LEGAL; LICIT; ■ PROPER
legs PINS; STAGES
legume POD
legwear TIGHTS
Leicester CHEESE; SHEEP; [◊ SQUARE]
lend ADVANCE; LOAN
lend uncle PAWN
lender BANK(ER)
length FOOT; INCH; L; MILE; SIZE; YARD
length of, the ALONG
lengthen EKE; STRETCH
lengthy LONG
lengthy period AGE; ERA
lens GLASS
Lent FAST
lentil PULSE
Leo HOUSE; SIGN
Leonard LEN
Leonardo VINCI
Leopold BLOOM
Les Anglais THE
Leslie LES
less FEWER; LACKING; MINUS; UNDER; omission indicator
-less as a suffix "less" can be an omission indicator for the element to which it is attached as; for instance, "artless" signifies that ART be dropped; can indicate a word ending in FREE
less loud F to be omitted
less on top BALDER
less so SO to be omitted

less than BELOW; UNDER; omission indicator; can indicate that the last letter is to be omitted as "less than one" → ON
lessee RENTER; TENANT
lessened LOWER
lesson CLASS; MORAL; ■ EXAMPLE; FORM; PERIOD; READING; TEACHING
lessons/series of COURSE
lest INCASE (i.e. in case)
let ALLOW; ALLOWED; BLOCK; GRANT; LEASE; LEASED; HIRE; HIRED; RENT
let down DEFLATE; LOWER
let go DROP; FREE; ■ RELEASE
let in ADMIT
let it be AMEN; STET
let it remain/stand STET
let loose FREE; anagram indicator
let me think UM
let off FREE; FREED; LOOSE; anagram of LET
let-off anagram of LET
let out EMIT; FREE; FREED; HIRE; LEASED; VENT; anagram of LET
lethargic INERT; LAZY
lethargic type CABBAGE
letter EP (abbr. for Epistle); NOTE; RUNE; ■ MISSIVE; SCREED; can indicate the use of a character (A, B, C etc., or in full e.g. EM, ESS, KAY, AITCH); note that "letter" is also an old standby for referring to something to do with a landlord
letter, official MISSIVE
letter, old RUNE; THORN
letter opener L
letter, short LINE; NOTE
letter-writer PAUL
letters MAIL; POST; anagram indicator; can indicate a run of letters within the alphabet as "nine letters" clues ATOI (i.e. A to I, the first nine letters of the alphabet) which is the device used in "Nine letters recalled in one" to yield IOTA; PRINT; *see* HIDDEN 'AND

letters from anagram indicator; run indicator; can indicate two letters linked by AND, thus "letters from father" clues PANDA (i.e. P and A)

letters, give out SPELL

letters said BEES; CEASE; EASE; ELLS; PEAS; TEASE; USE

letters, send POST

letting LEASING; ALLOWING

lettuce COS

level AIM; EVEN; FLAT; FLOOR; FLUSH; GRADE; PAR; PLANE; POINT; RANK; RASE; RAZE; STOREY; TIE; TIED; TIER; TRAIN; ■ ABREAST; BALANCE; MARSH

level ground FLAT; PLAIN

level-headed SENSIBLE

level, make EVEN; ROLL

level, not on the BENT; CROOKED; TILTED

level of water TABLE

lever BAR; PRISE; STICK; ■ HANDLE; RELEASE; TREADLE

lever, sort of COCK

Leviticus etc OT

levy RAISE; RATE; TAX

liability anagram indicator

liability, not a ASSET

liable APT; BOUND; PRONE

liable to UNDER

liaison AMOUR; BOND

liar can indicate something to do with Ananias (the liar from the Biblical story)

libel DEFAME

libel action anagram of LIBEL

liberal AMPLE; BROAD; FREE; LAVISH; OPEN

Liberal L; LIB

Liberal, old WHIG

liberate FREE

liberated FREE; anagram indicator

liberation anagram indicator

Liberia LIB

Libra SIGN; ■ SCALES

libertine RAKE; ROUE

liberty CHANCE; SCOPE; ■ LICENCE; FREEDOM; anagram indicator

liberty, at FREE; LOOSE; anagram indicator

libido LUST

library equipment SHELF

licence ALLOW; GRANT; PERMIT; RIGHT; anagram indicator

licentious FREE; RIBALD

licit LEGAL

lick BEAT (qv); THRASH; can indicate something to do with tongue

licking can indicate something to do with tongue

lid CAP; COVER; HAT (qv); ROOF; STOPPER; TOP

lid on, putting the ROOFING

lie FABLE; FIB; FICTION; LINE; REST; TALE; ■ LOUNGE; REPOSE; RESIDE; STORY; WHOPPER

lie back RECLINE

lie, big WHOPPER

lie in bed KIP

lie in the sun BROWN; TAN

lie in wait LURK

lie low HIDE

lie still REST

Liechtenstein FL

lied can indicate something to do with a song

lied about anagram of LIED

lien RIGHT

lies FICTION; STORIES; *see* LIE

lies about/around anagram of LIES; a component to be nested within LIES; the preceding word to be nested within LIES

lies in LIES to be nested within a component; nesting indicator; run indicator

lies, lot of TISSUE

lieu PLACE

lieutenant L; LT

life BIO; GO; PEP; SPAN; VALE; ZIP; ■ BIOGRAPHY; SENTENCE; SPIRIT; [◊ BIOGRAPHER; BOSWELL; BREATH]

life, account of BIO
life after death OBIT
life, enjoy BE
life force CHI (Chin.); QI (Chin.)
life, full of LUSTY
life, have BE
life in France VIE
life in Rome VITA
life of Caesar VITA
life-preserver ARK
life, Roman VITA
life support AIR
lifeless DEAD; NUMB; TAME; ■ INERT
lifeless state DEATH
lifetime DAY; SPAN
lift HEAVE; HITCH; HOICK; HOIST; JACK; NICK; RAISE; RIDE; RISE; STEAL; SWIPE; reversal indicator
lift-shaft WELL
lift, sort of SNATCH
lift, to nesting indicator
lift to, giving reversal indicator
lift up see LIFT
lift weight in a Down clue can indicate the reversal of a "weight" e.g. BL, NOT, ZO
liftable run indicator
lifted PINCHED; RAISED; STOLE; reversal indicator
lifted up PU; reversal indicator
lifting reversal indicator (as "lifting lid" → TAH)
lifting device CRANE; HOIST; ROTOR; WINCH
ligament SINEW; TENDON
light AIRY; AMBER; BEAM; BRIGHT; CLUE (technical term from crosswords); DAY; FAIR; FIRE; FLARE; GLEAM; GREEN; LAMP; LAND; LOW; LT; MATCH; MOON; PALE; PLANE; RAY; RED; SHINE; SMALL; SOFT; SPILL; SPOT; STAR; SUN; TAPER; THIN; TORCH; UV; VESTA; ■ BEACON; CANDLE; FEEBLE; GIDDY; GLARE; KINDLE; NEON; SETTLE; SHAFT; SIMPLE; STROBE; VERY (i.e. Very Light); WICK; WINDOW;

as "light" has the technical meaning within crosswords of "answer to clue" it thereby can indicate something to do with crosswords
light, artificial CANDLE; LAMP; TORCH
light, bring to EXPOSE
light, cautionary AMBER
light, colour ECRU
light, failing DUSK
light-headed FAIR; L; see GIDDY
light meal BITE; TEA
light, natural SUN
light of danger RED
light, particle of PHOTON
light period DAY
light, poor GLOOM
light, sort of HEAD; SIDE; SPOT; VERY
light, source of BULB; CANDLE; FLAME; LAMP; SUN ■ FIRE; TORCH
light speed C
lighter BARGE; BOAT; CRAFT; FLINT; MATCH; PALER; SCOW; SPILL
lighter, make EASE
lighting LAMP; see LIGHT
lightly cooked RARE
lightning BOLT; FLASH
lights LUNGS
lights, put out the FUSE
lightweight GR; GRAM; OUNCE; OZ
like AS; DIG; LOVE; ■ EVEN (arch.); TOAST; can indicate some adjective (e.g. ending in -ISH)
like, do not DETEST; HATE; LOATHE; MIND
like, really DIG; LOVE
like that/this SO; THUS; anagram indicator
likeable NICE; PLEASANT
liked DUG
likely APT; PRONE; SET
likely, are/be TEND
likewise AS; SO; TOO
liking CRUSH; FANCY; TASTE; ■ PALATE; PENCHANT; [◊ KEEN]

liking for, show KISS
lilt SWING; TUNE
lily, type of ARUM
limb ARM; BRANCH; LEG; WING; ■ MEMBER
limber LITHE
limbo PARADISE
lime TREE; ■ GREEN
limelight, in the LIT
limerick JINGLE
limerick writer LEAR
Limey BRIT
limit BORDER; BOUND; BOURN; BRINK; CAP; CHECK; EDGE; END; FENCE; LINE; RATION; RIM; TIE; TOP; ■ CONSTRAIN; RESTRAIN; RESTRICT; TERMINATE
limit availability CUT; RATION
limit, beyond OTT
limit, within a component to be nested inside a synonym for "limit" e.g. PALE
limit, without ALL
limitation nesting indicator; ■ DIET
limited LOCAL; NARROW; abbreviation indicator; ■ SPECIFIC
limited amount RATION
limited by nesting indicator
limiting nesting indicator
limits AMBIT; RANGE; ■ TERMS; first and last letters indicator; nesting indicator; can indicate something which surrounds; see LIMIT
limits of first and last letters of succeeding word to be used (as "limits of Europe" cues EE)
limo CAR
limp GIMP
limping HALT (arch.); LAME
Lincoln ABE; GREEN; ■ PRESIDENT
linden tree LIME
line ANGLE; ARY (i.e. a RY); BAND; BAR; BARB; CLASS; CORD; DASH; DRESS; EDGE; EM; EN; FILE; JOB; L; LEY; LIST; MARK; NOTE; PAD; RANGE; RANK; RAY; ROPE; ROW; RY; SCORE; SHEET; TACK; TIER; TRACK; VIEW; ■ CABLE; CAREER; COURSE; CREASE; HOSE; NOOSE; OCHE (darts); PAINTER; POLICY; QUEUE; REINFORCE; ROUTE; RULE; STREAK; STRING; STRIPE; THREAD; TRADE; TROPIC; WAY can indicate something to do with fishing; can indicate the policy of a particular group or organ e.g. editorial; [◊ HOOK]
line, brush STROKE
line-dance CONGA
line, get into DRESS
line of workers ASSEMBLY
line, part of EM
line, put into ALIGN
line, short BRANCH; L; NOTE; RY; SIDING
line, small DASH; EM; EN; L; RY
line stated/told/voiced CUE (homophone of "queue")
line, straight RAY
line, thick CABLE
line up DRESS; ■ FALLIN (i.e. fall in)
line-up FIELD
lined EDGED; see LINE
lined up FELLIN (i.e. fell in)
lineage BREED; STOCK
linen CLOTH; SHEETS
linen, colour of ECRU
liner SS; ■ TITANIC; note: this can refer to anything that lines something as "Ocean liner?" → COAST
lines BAR; LL; ODE; ODES; POEM; R; RY; SONNET; TRACK; VERSE; ■ ECLOGUE; RADII; RHYME; STANZA
lines, part of FEET
lines, some PARA
lines told CCUSE (i.e. homophone of "queues" as "a lines told" leads to ACCUSE i.e. A+CCUSE); see LINE TOLD
linesman BARD; POET
ling HEATHER
linger LAG; STAY; TARRY; ■ DELAY; DRAGON (i.e. drag on)

lingerie KNICKERS
lingerie, item of BRA
lining nesting indicator; run indicator
link BOND; BRIDGE; KNOT; NEXUS; SPAN; THREAD; TIE; YOKE
★ **linked clues** different clues in a grid may be linked in various ways. For instance you may be told that part of the answer to one clue is to be used to build up the answer to another. A common ploy is for two consecutive clues to be written as one, with the first ending in a row of dots and the second beginning with a row of dots. There may be a connection between the two. For example, the answer to one (say, HORSE) is an example of the other (say, ANIMAL). But be wary: the compiler may be nudging you to think there is a connection when there isn't one
links CHAIN; MAIL; *see* LINK
links carrier CADDY
lion CAT; LEO; SIGN
lion, little CUB
lion-tamer DANIEL
lioness ELSA
lions PRIDE
lip BRASS; CHEEK; EDGE; RIM; SAUCE; VERGE
lipid FAT
liqueur CASSIS
liquid INK; LOTION; RAIN; WATER; ■ HUMOUR; RUNNY
liquid, amount of *see* LIQUID MEASURE
liquid food SOUP
liquid from well INK
liquid measure DRAM; FINGER; GILL; LITRE; NIP; PINT; QUART; SHOT; TOT
liquid mess SLOSH
liquid, tiny amount of DROP; SPOT
liquid, without ARID; DRY
liquidation anagram indicator
liquefy MELT

liquor ALE; GIN; MEAD RUM; RYE; SAKE; *see* DRINK
liquor measure FINGER
lissom AGILE; LITHE
list BANK; CANT; FILE; HEEL; LEAN; ROLL; ROSTER; ROTA; TABLE; TILT; TIP; ■ CHOOSE; DETAIL; ENTER; INDEX; KEEL; MANIFEST; MENU; RECORD; REGISTER
list of candidates ENTRY
list, itemised TABLE
list, official ROLL
listed LEANING
listen HARK; HEAR; HEED; HIST; ■ ATTEND; homophone indicator
listen to HEAR; HEED
listen to you U
listened (to) HEARD; homophone indicator
listener EAR; HEARER
listeners, for homophone indicator
listening EAR
listening device BUG; EAR; TAP
listening equipment EAR
listening to reason CENSE (i.e. homophone of sense)
listing ROTA; ■ LEANING; *see* LIST
listless, appear MOON; MOPE
Liszt ABBE
lit FIRED; IN; ON
lit-up HIGH; *see* DRUNK
literal extremes AZ
literary [◊ BOOK]
literary collection ANA (i.e. suffix as in Americana, for example)
literary drudge HACK
literary gathering SALON
literary man *see* WRITER
literary work BOOK (qv); PLAY; POEM; TOME; VERSE
literature LIT
lithe SPRY; ■ LIMBER; SUPPLE; anagram indicator
lithium LI
litmus TEST
litre L
litter BED; BROOD; STRETCHER; ■ BEDDING;

REFUSE; *see* RUBBISH; [◊ PUP]

litter-holder STY

litter, part of PUP

little BIT; DASH; DROP; FINE; MINI; O; PETITE; PUNY; SHORT; SHRED; SLIGHT; SMALL; SPOT; TAD; TRACE; WEE; WHIT; ■ DWARF; MITE; PETIT; abbr. indicator (as "little old" → O); run indicator (as "little gallery's OK" → LEGAL)

little, a BIT; MITE; OUNCE; first letter to be used, as " a little cry" → CRY

little American TAD

little animal RUNT

little bit OUNCE; WHIT

little brother BRO; SIB

little boy diminutive of male name (e.g. AL, ED, TED) *see* MAN

little chap IMP; TITCH; TOM; ■ TIDDLER; *see* LITTLE BOY; can indicate something to do with midget etc

little child BABY; TOT; *see* CHILD

little, comparatively LESS

little creature can indicate either the young of some creature or a physically small creature (e.g. insect)

little drink DRAM; HALF; SHORT; TOT

little girl SIS; diminutive of woman's name (e.g. DI, MO) *see* WOMAN

little house COT; H

little ladies can refer to toilet, particularly short words for same, so LAV, LOO etc, *see* TOILET

little left L

little man PAWN

Little Mary a term coined by Barrie for the stomach

little money CENT; IP (i.e. one penny) L; P

little one CUB; MITE; TITCH; TOT; *see* CHILD

little path BYROAD

little room CELL; DEN

little, saying QUIET

little Scottish SMA

little swimming, a STROKE

little sister SIB; SIS

little time HR; MO; SEC; T; YR

little, very MINUTE; TRACE; ■ NOMINAL

little water DRIP; DROP; SPOT

little woman JO (from novel); W; can require the diminutive of a woman's name (e.g. MO, SUE), *see* WOMAN

Little Women W; can refer to toilet, particularly short words for same, so LAV, LOO etc, *see* TOILET

little woman's JOS

little work ERG; OP

liturgy RITE

live ABIDE; ARE; BE; DWELL; LODGE; QUICK; RESIDE; ■ GROWING; HOT; THRIVE

live appearance in, make BE or ARE to be nested within a component

live, go to SETTLE

live show CONCERT

lived DWELT; WAS; WERE

liveliness BRIO; ESPRIT; GO

lively AGILE; BRIGHT; BRISK; GAMY; PACY; RACY; SPRY; ■ ALLEGRO; anagram indicator

lively type SWINGER

livened up anagram indicator

liver MEAT; can indicate a word beginning with HEP

Liverpool* PORT

Liverpudlian SCOUSE

lives IS

living IS; QUICK; ■ BEING; CURACY; INCOME

living, some BE

Lizzie BET; BETH

lo-calorie LITE

load CARGO; FILL; HEAP; LADE; LOT; ONUS; PILE; STACK; ■ CHARGE; FREIGHT; LOAD; WEIGHT

load, say WAIT

loaded FULL; HIGH; LADEN; RICH; anagram indicator; nesting indicator; *see* DRUNK

loaded with nesting indicator

loaf BEAN; BREAD (qv); COB; HEAD; IDLE; LAZE; LOUNGE; NOB; NOODLE; NUT; PATE; [◊ BAKE]

loafer BUM; DRONE; SHOE

loam SOIL

loan LEND; SUB; ■ LENDING

loan, beg a TOUCH

loan, extend RENEW

loan shark USURER

loan, type of BRIDGING

loaned LENT

loathe, loathing HATE

lob LOFT; SHY; *see* THROW

lobby HALL; FACTION; GROUP; ■ ENTRANCE; ENTRY; PASSAGE

local CLOSE; INN; NEAR; NUMBER (i.e. anaesthetic); PUB (qv); ■ HERE; NATIVE; TOPICAL; can be disguised as an adjective while still referring to a pub as where "local vessel" calls for TANKARD

local area PATCH

local area, one from NATIVE

local authority COUNCIL

local-born NATIVE

local office BRANCH

locality AREA

locality, in this HERE

locatable in nesting indicator

locate FIND; PLACE; SEE; SIGHT; SITE; TRACE

located SET; *see* LOCATE

located in nesting indicator

location PLACE; SITE; SPOT; ■ ADDRESS; CORNER; SITUATION; VENUE

location of can indicate a set of letters beginning with compass points as "location of Florida" → SEUS (i.e. South-east U.S.)

loch L; LEVEN; NESS

lock BOLT; CLOSE; FIX; FORWARD (rugby); HUG; LATCH; SEAL; SECURE; STRAND; UNION; *see* HAIR; [◊ KEY]

lock, end of GATE; K

lock-keeper HAIRNET

lock up CAGE; JAIL; ■ INTERN; nesting indicator; can call for a synonym of hair to be reversed e.g. SSERT

locked TRESSED

locker KEY

locked in nesting indicator; run indicator

locked up INSIDE; ■ BARS

locking device HITCH; KEY

locks HAIR (qv); QUIFF, TRESS

locks, remove CUT

loco MAD

locomotive TRAIN; ■ ENGINE

locum TEMP

locus PLACE

lode ORE; REEF

lodge DWELL; HOUSE; LIVE; PLACE (qv); STAY; STOW; ■ SETTLE

lodged in nesting indicator

lodger RENTER; RESIDENT

lodging CAMP; HOSTEL; HOTEL; HYDRO; INN; REST

lodging-place REST; *see* LODGING

lodgings DIGS; PLACE; ■ QUARTERS

loft ATTIC; CHIP; LOB; [◊ TOP]

lofted shot CHIP; LOB

loftiness PRIDE

lofty HIGH; TALL; UP; [◊ CAP; TOP]

log ENTER; LOG; NOTE; ■ BILLET; RECORD

log, bit of POWER; ■ EXPONENT; MANTISSA

log-book DIARY

logarithm LOG

logarithmic ratio SINE

logic REASON

logic, piece of PREMISE; PREMISS

logical process DEDUCTION; INDUCTION; REASON

logo BRAND; MARK

logs, collection of RAFT

loiter DELAY; LOAF; MOOCH; TARRY

loitering with intent SUSS

loll LAZE; LOUNGE

lollipop, lolly ICE; SUCKER
London CAPITAL; CITY;
SMOKE; TOWN; WEN; note, a
fair knowledge of London land-
marks, stations and suburbs is as-
sumed, e.g. ACTON, POPLAR,
SOHO
London* CITY
**London area (borough, district,
part of, etc)** ACTON; BOW;
BRENT; C; E; EALING; EC;
KEW; N; NE; NW; POPLAR; S;
SE; SOHO; SW; ■ BALHAM;
BARNET
London attraction EYE
London club REFORM
London college LSE; UCL
London coppers/police MET;
YARD
London dock WAPPING
London, from DOWN
London, heading for UP
London hospital BARTS; UCH
London road STRAND
London theatre GLOBE
London, to UP
London tourist attraction EYE
lone SINGLE; SOLO
long ACHE; DIE; HANKER;
ITCH; L; LANK; PANT; PINE;
REMOTE; SIGH; TALL; WANT;
YEARN
long ago ERST; OLD; YORE
long-ago PAST
long ago, knew WIST
long and thin LANK
long, before ANON
long-delayed SLOW
long-distance LEAGUE
long-distance runner STAYER
long-established OLD; ■
CHRONIC
long for COVET; MISS
long-legged LANKY; RANGY;
TALL
long live VIVA
long live the Spanish VIVA
long, not BRIEF; SHORT
long period see LONG TIME
long-suffering PATIENT
long term LIFE; see LONG TIME

long time AEON; AGE; AGES
CENTURY; EON; EPOCH; ERA
long way AFAR; FAR
long way off, a OUT
long while see LONG TIME
longer MORE
longer-established OLDER
longer, no ONCE; EX
longing ACHE; DYING; ITCH;
PAIN; URGE; WISH; YEN
Longleat BATH
longs DIES; see LONG; can refer
to trousers e.g. TREWS
loo GENTS; see TOILET
look AIR; APPEAR; EYE; FACE;
FROWN; GANDER; GAPE;
GAZE; GLANCE; GLARE; LA;
LEER; LO; MIEN; OGLE;
PEEK; PEEP; PEER; SCAN;
SEE; STARE; WATCH
look after CARE; MIND; TEND
look after baby SIT
look after the kids SIT
look angry LOWER
look around KEEP
look at READ
look briefly GLANCE
look closely EYE; PORE; see
STUDY
look curiously PEER; PRY
look daggers GLOWER
look, dirty LOUR
look for (future event) AWAIT
look forward to AWAIT; LIKE
look hard STARE
look, have a PRY; see LOOK
look glum POUT
look happy GRIN
look hard PEER
look-in, get a LO to be nested
look inquisitively PEEK; PEER;
PRY
look into AUDIT; see CHECK
look menacing SCOWL
look, oppressive LOUR
look out CAVE; WARE; LO to be
omitted
look-out SENTRY; LO to be omitted
look over PERUSE; READ;
SCAN

look pleased BEAM; SMILE
look, quick SCAN
look quickly GLANCE
look threatening LOWER
look, unpleasant LEER
look up CALL; VISIT; in a down clue can indicate the reverse of a synonym for look, so EES, KEEP, RIA etc
look, sly PEEK
look suggestively LEER; OGLE
look sulky POUT
look worried FROWN
lookalike DOUBLE; RINGER
looked EYED; GAZED
looked for SOUGHT
looked older AGED
looked on EYED
looker EYE
looking after nesting indicator
looking healthy RUDDY
looking in run indicator
looking round can indicate someone who is fat (as "Person looking round" → ROLY-POLY)
looking sickly PALE
lookout, be on the STALK
looks curiously PRIES
looks for gold PANS
looks silly anagram indicator
looks, sly PEEKS
looks up and down SEES
loom APPEAR
looming NIGH
loon FOOL
loony ASS; anagram indicator; *see* LUNATIC
loop BIGHT; NOOSE; RING; ■ PICOT
loose ADRIFT; FREE; LAX; SLACK; UNTIE; VAGUE; anagram indicator
loose stones SCREE
loose woman TART
loosely anagram indicator
loosen EASE; FREE; UNTIE
loot ROB; SACK; STEAL; SWAG; ■ BOOTY
looted anagram indicator
lop CUT (qv); DOCK; HACK
lop off SEVER; anagram of LOP

lope RUN; ■ BOUND; STRIDE
lopped omission indicator
lord BARON; BOSS; COUNT; EARL; LD; LUD; MASTER; PEER; TITLE
Lord Lieutenant LL
Lord Mayor LM
Lord's GROUND; can indicate something to do with cricket as "side at Lord's" → OFF
lord's partner LADY
lords and ladies ARUM
Lorna DOONE
Lorraine CROSS
lorry ARTIC; TANKER; TIPPER; TRUCK; WAGON
lose DROP; MISS; WASTE; *see* DROP
lose colour FADE; RED to be omitted
lose direction N, E, W or S to be omitted
lose figure SAG
lose footing SLIP
lose force DIE; can indicate omission of F (force), G (gravity)
lose no time HASTEN; *see* RUN
lose out MISS
lose pounds can indicate something to do with metrication
lose vital forces DIE
lose way ERR; STRAY; can indicate that a component listed under WAY (e.g. ST) is to be omitted
loses anagram indicator
loses heart middle letter(s) to be omitted
losing DOWN; FAILING; omission indicator; anagram indicator
losing 1-0 an indicator that I and O are to be omitted
losing backing last letter to be omitted
losing good looks AZES
loss COST; DEATH; MISS; TOLL; ■ WASTAGE; anagram indicator; omission indicator; can indicate that the word OUT is incorporated in the solution
loss, big ROUT
loss of power FALL

loss, without FREE

lost ASTRAY; SHED; omission indicator; anagram indicator, as "lost at sea" → an anagram of AT SEA; [◊ CAST]

lost blood BLED

lot ALL; CO (for company); CROWD; DEAL; DOOM; FATE; GANG; GROUP; LUCK; MANY; MASS; MUCH; PILE; PLIGHT; SET; SIGHT; SITE; STACK; ■ AMOUNT; BUNCH; KISMET; PORTION; in its meaning of "fate" can lead to associated words such as FATALIST; can indicate something to do with AUCTION, SALE

lot, a BAGS; MUCH

lot different, a anagram of LOT

lot of can indicate that one is to use most of the letters in what follows to provide either a component (as "a lot of bother" → FUS), or the complete answer (as "A lot of beverage for the sports venue?" → RINK

lot of, a MANY

lot of birds FLOCK

lot of money BOMB; GRAND; WAD

lot of paper/writing REAM

lot of sheep FLOCK

lotion, cosmetic TONER

lots MANY; MASSES; MUCH; REAMS; SIGHT; STACKS; TON; ■ HATFUL; OODLES; SCORES; can indicate something to do with auction, sale etc

lots of can indicate that most of a word is to be used

lots of dollars G

lots of people CROWD (qv); GANG; RACE

lottery CHANCE; DRAW; GAMBLE; SWEEP

lotto BINGO

loud BRASH; BRASSY; BRIGHT; F; FLASHY; NOISY; VOCAL; homophone indicator

loud abuse FLIP

loud broadcast anagram of LOUD

loud, not *see* QUIET

loud, very FF

loudly F

loudly, not softly F to replace P

loudspeaker TWEETER

loudspeaker, through the homophone indicator

lough ERNE; LAKE

Louis JOE

lounge IDLE; LAZE; LIE; LOLL; SIT

lounge* ROOM; SUIT(E)

louse BUG; HEEL (qv)

lousy CRUMMY; anagram indicator

lout OAF; BOOR; SLOB; THUG; YOB; ■ YAHOO

lovable SWEET

lovable rogue SCAMP

love ADORE; DEAR; EROS; FANCY; LIKE; NIL; NOUGHT; O; PET; SEX; ZERO; ■ DEARIE; NOTHING; POINTLESS; *see* DARLING, DEAR

love* PASSION

love affair AMOUR

love-bite NIP

love, classic AMOR

love-god EROS

love, possible evidence of BITE

love upset LIN (i.e. rev.)

loveless indicates the omission of O from an associated word, as "loveless marriage" → UNIN

lovely DEAR; FAIR; NICE; SUPER; SWEET; ■ ANGELIC; CUTIE

lovely French BEL

lovely girl DISH; PEACH

lover AMOUR; BEAU; BUFF; FAN; FLAME; SWAIN; ■ DARLING; ROMEO; LEMAN (arch.)

lover boy EROS

lover, classical HERO

lover former/old EX

lover, taken out by DATED

lover, tragic LEANDER

loves OO
lovesick anagram of LOVE
loving FOND; ■ AMATORY; AMOROUS
low BASE; BLUE; CHEAP; DOWN; FLAT; LIGHT; MEAN; MOO; POOR; SAD; SHORT; UNDER; ■ HUMBLE
low alcohol LITE
low-calorie LITE
low down *see* BASE, DIRTY
low-down GEN; INFO
low place, in DOWN
low point between peaks COL
low position, in BELOW; DOWN; UNDER
low quality CHEAP
low river MOOR (i.e. MOO + R)
low tone MOO
low voice BASS
low water NEAP
low water, time of DROUGHT
lowdown *see* INFORMATION
lower ABASE; BELOW; COW; CUT; DIM; DOWN; DROP; LUFF; NETHER; OX; SCOWL; SINK; UNDER; ■ ABATE; DEMOTE; DEPRESS; can indicate something to do with cattle
lower, a little CALF
lower bottom SIT
lower class NON-U
lower classes DE
lower grades ED
lower head BOW; NOD
lower standard INFERIOR
lowers CATTLE
lowest part BASE; BED (i.e. of river); FOOT
lowland VALE
loyal TRUE
loyal person BRICK
loyalty TRUST; ■ ALLEGIANCE; FAITH
LSD ACID; CASH; DOPE; DRUG; MONEY; specifically it can refer to some aspect of pre-decimal currency
lubricant OIL
lubricate OIL

lubrication GREASE; OIL; *see* DRINK
lucid CLEAR; PLAIN; SANE
lucifer MATCH
luck BREAK; CESS (Irish); CHANCE; HAP; LADY; LOT
luck, bit of STROKE
lucky CHARMED
lucky, it's FLUKE
lucre *see* MONEY
ludicrously anagram indicator
lug DRAG; EAR; HAUL; PULL; SAIL
luggage BAG; CASE; TRAPS; ■ EFFECTS
luggage carrier PORTER; RACK
luggage compartment BOOT
luggage, piece of BAG; CASE
luggage, put in PACK
lull CALM; SOOTHE
lumbar BACK
lumber SADDLE; WOOD
lumberjack LOGGER
luminary LIGHT; STAR
lump CHUNK; CLOD; LOBE; MASS; ■ DOLLOP; NUGGET
lump (of butter) PAT
lump, small PAT
lunar excursion module LEM
lunatic KOOK; LOCO; MAD; NUT
lunch EAT; MEAL
lunch, out to MAD; NUTS
lunch time IPM
lunch-time, at ATI; ATONE
luncheon* MEAL
luncheon meat SPAM
lunchtime, around I; ONE
lunge CHARGE; PASS; RUSH
lung ORGAN; note "lung" can refer to open space near a city
lungs LIGHTS (as food)
lurch PITCH; ROLL; ■ SHAMBLE; STAGGER; TOTTER; note this can refer to a difficult situation as "to leave in the lurch"
lure DRAW; TEMPT; ■ SEDUCE
lurk behind DOG
lush DRUNK; GREEN; RICH; SOT; TOPER

lust DRIVE; SIN; ■ CRAVING
lustful LEWD; RANDY
lustful, be LECH
lustre GLOSS; SHEEN; SHINE; also can refer to five years (from Roman days)
lustreless MAT; MATT
lusty EARTHY
lusty young man STUD
lutetium LU
Luton person HATTER
luxuriant LUSH; PLUSH; RICH
luxurious *see* LUXURIANT
luxury CLOVER; EXTRA; ■ EXCESS
luxury car GT; LIMO; ROLLS; RR
luxury, in some WELL
lying ABED; FLAT; ■ FIBBING; PRONE; RESTING; can indicate something to do with sleep
lying, was LAY
lyric AIR; ODE; VERSE; WORDS; ■ EPODE; LIN

Mm

macabre SICK
macaroni FOP; PASTA
Macbeth OPERA; PLAY; THANE; [◊ COVEN; LADY; WITCH]
Macbeth **character** WITCH
Macbeth, Lady [◊ SPOT]
Macbeth **nobleman** ROSS
Macbeth, **part of** ROSS
MacDonald FLORA
mace CLUB; SPICE; STAFF
machination PLOT
machine GIN; LATHE; LOOM
machine gun emplacement NEST
machine part BEARING; COG
machine, sound of HUM
machine tool LATHE
machinery PLANT
machinery, piece of CAR; COG

macho MALE; MANLY
macho types HEMEN
mackerel TINKER; [◊ SPRAT]
mackintosh MAC; with a capital letter can indicate something to do with a Scotsman
mackle SPOT
mad BARMY; BATS; CROSS; FRANTIC; GAGA; LOCO; LOONY; NUTS; RABID; RAGING; WILD; ■ BATTY; INSANE; LUNATIC; MENTAL; TOUCHED; ZANY; [◊ HATTER]; anagram indicator
mad behaviour *see* RAGE
mad character HATTER
mad cow anagram of COW
mad, go RAVE
mad, not SANE
mad party member HATTER
Madagascar MR
Madam Butterfly OPERA
madcap anagram indicator; can indicate an anagram of CAP
maddened, maddening anagram indicator
made DID; DONE; GOT; SENT (as in made/sent one mad); anagram indicator
made badly TRASHY
made by anagram indicator
made fun of RAGGED
made out anagram indicator
made redundant SHED
made up LIED; anagram indicator
made use of HAD
made way WENT
madly anagram indicator
madman NUT; ■ HEADCASE; MANIAC; can indicate an anagram of MAN (similarly madmen, madcap, etc)
madmen NUTS; anagram of MEN; *see* MADMAN
madness RAGE
Madonna MARY
Madrid, team from REAL
Mafia chief CAPO
magazine COMIC; GLOSSY; ISSUE; MAG; ORGAN; specific titles e.g. ELLE, HELLO, LIFE,

PUNCH, NATURE, TIME, WHICH; ■ PRINT

magazine, Paris MATCH

magazine, U.S. LIFE; TIME

maggot GENTLE; GRUB

magic ART

magic concoction POTION

magic formula SPELL

magical feat TRICK

magical power MANA

magician WIZARD; [◊ TRICK]

magistrate BEAK; CONSUL; DOGE; JP; REEVE; ■ ARCHON; EPHOR; JUSTICE

magistrate, before/facing UP

magistrate, chief DOGE

magistrate's assistant LICTOR

magistrates BENCH

magnanimous NOBLE

magnate BARON; TYCOON

magnet DRAW

magnificence GLORY

magnificent NOBLE; REGAL

magnum BOTTLE

maid GIRL; MISS

maid, old PRUDE

maiden FIRST; M; MISS; can indicate something to do with OVER (i.e. cricket)

maiden, divinely transformed IO

maiden name NEE

mail ARMOUR; POST; [◊ DELIVERY; POSTER]

mail, convey/distribute DELIVER

mail distribution anagram of MAIL

mail, regarding POSTAL

mailer POSTER

maim WOUND

main CHIEF; HEAD; SEA; STAPLE; STAR; WATER; ■ BRINY; TIDE; usually has some sea connotation

main addition SEA to be added

main container can indicate the name of a particular sea

main line SEAL

main point CRUX; GIST; HUB

main part BODY; LEAD

main road A; AI; ARD (i.e. A-road); ■ ARTERY

Maine ME

maintain AVER; KEEP; PLEAD; FIX; ■ AFFIRM; ALLEGE; HARBOUR; SUPPORT

maintain firmly FIX

maintaining nesting indicator

maintenance CARE

majestic LORDLY; REGAL; ROYAL

major BIG; GRAVE; GREAT; KEY; MAIN; STAR

majority MASS; MOST; ■ EIGHTEEN; can indicate that all but one letter of a word is to be used, thus "religious majority can clue HOL (i.e. first three letters of "holy"); can refer to coming of age (in U.K. now 18) and so can indicate some aspect of adulthood

make BRAND; CAUSE; DO; EARN; FORCE; FORM; GET; SORT; TYPE; ■ CREATE; DELIVER (i.e. as with speech); MARQUE; anagram indicator; run indicator

make a face POUT

make a move ACT

make a point SCORE

make a record NOTE; *see* RECORD

make a scene EMOTE

make amends ATONE

make an alteration EDIT; MEND; REPAIR

make an effort TRY

make an effort to see CRANE

make an impression ETCH

make arrangements ORDER

make assessment RATE

make beastly noise GROWL; LOW; MOO

make better CURE; ENHANCE; HEAL; IMPROVE

make changes AMEND; *see* CHANGE

make coins MINT

make contact *see* CONTACT

make corrections AMEND; EDIT; EMEND

make, could anagram indicator

make cuts LANCE; *see* CUT

make dynamic progress BOUND

make for HEAD

make formal SETTLE

make fun of RAG; RIB; TEASE; ■ JOSH

make good MEND; ■ RESTORE

make haste RUSH; TEAR

make hay TED

make heavy demands TAX

make improvements BETTER

make large numbers SPAWN

make last EKE

make merry PARTY; ■ REVEL

make money EARN

make more UP

make much of FETE

make notes SING

make off ELOPE; *see* LEAVE

make off with ROB; ■ ABDUCT; *see* STEAL

make official SIGN

make one's way WEND

make out SEE; ■ SCAN

make preparation PLAN

make progress MOVE; ROLL; ■ ADVANCE

make progress socially CLIMB

make provision CATER

make ready EARN; ■ PREPARE; REALISE

make recording TAPE

make signal NOD; WAVE

make short journey HOP

make slow progress PLOD

make solid FREEZE

make smaller REDUCE

make sure CLINCH; SEE

make tea MASH

make the most of resources EKE; ■ ECONOMISE

make-up LINER; ROUGE; anagram indicator; [◊ AD-LIB]

make use of TAP

make way STEP; *see* TRAVEL

make well BORE; CURE; DRILL; HEAL

make worse MAR; SPOIL; ■ COMPOUND

makeover anagram indicator

makers anagram indicator

makes anagram or run indicator

makes mistakes anagram indicator

makeshift anagram indicator

making anagram indicator; run indicator

making cuts AXING

Malawian statesman BANDA

Malay [◊ PENINSULA; SARONG]

Malay dagger KRIS

Malaysian capital KL; M

male BOY; BUCK; BULL; COCK; HE; LAD; M; MACHO; MAN; RAM; STAG; TOM; TUP; *see* MAN

male, a French UN

malediction CURSE

malefactor FELON; *see* CRIMINAL

malicious talk SCANDAL

malformation anagram indicator

malfunction BUG; FAULT; FLAW; GLITCH

malfunctioned/ing anagram indicator

malice SPITE

malicious BAD; EVIL; SNIDE

malign DEFAME; EVIL; ■ SLANDER

malignant person DEVIL

malleable PLIABLE; SOFT

mallet CLUB; PRIEST; ■ HAMMER

Malta M

maltreated anagram indicator

maltreatment anagram indicator

mammal ANIMAL; can call for the name of a specific mammal, frequent examples used in word construction include COATI, MOLE, SEAL, SLOTH

mammal, aquatic OTTER

mammal, flying BAT

mammal, marine SEAL

mammoth BIG; HUGE

man AGENT; BLOKE; BOD; CHAP; GENT; GUY; HAND; HE; HIM; HOMO; LAD; MALE; ONE; STAFF; VALET;

■ DRAUGHT; FELLOW; HANDLE; HOMBRE; *see* FELLOW; can refer to a man's name, often shortened – *see* MAN'S NAME; can refer to a chess piece in full or abbreviated form i.e. B, BISHOP, CASTLE, K, KING, KNIGHT, KT, N, P, PAWN, PIECE, Q, QUEEN, R, ROOK

Man I; IOM; IS; ISLE; ■ FRIDAY; note that this is a favourite with compilers, referring to the island, usually with 'Man' at the beginning of the clue so the solver may not realise the added significance of the capital letter

man about town TOFF

man, admired HERO

man, associated with HIS

man at crease BAT

man at the controls DRIVER; PILOT

man, big/handsome HUNK

man, classical VIR

man-eater OGRE; TIGER

man, first ADAM

man, good ST

man in BATTER (cric.)

man in America CHECKER (as in checkers, the term used in the U.S. for the game of draughts)

man in charge HEAD; KING; MASTER; *see* CHIEF

man in love MINO (i.e. m-in-0)

man, little PAWN; can call for the short form of man's name e.g. LES, TIM, *see* MAN'S NAME

man, most powerful QUEEN

man of action DOER; HERO

man of cloth CURATE; DRAPER; REV; ■ TAILOR; *see* PRIEST, VICAR etc

man of fashion RAKE

man of muscle HUNK

man of note often calls for a composer's name

man of straw RICK

man of the match GROOM

man on board DRAUGHT (i.e. the board game); HAND; *see* CHESSMAN, SAILOR

man on field PLAYER; REF; *see* PLAYER

man's HES (i.e. he's); HIS

Man's device LEGS (i.e. Manx emblem)

man's name AL, ALF, ART, BEN, DAN, DEN, DES, DON, ED, EMIL, GREG, GUS, HERB; IAN, JACK; KAY, KIT, LEN, LES, MILES, NAT, NED, NICK, PAT, PHIL, RAY; REG, RICK, RON, ROY, SID, TED, THEO, TIM; RAY; VIV; ■ ALAN; ALEX; ANGUS; BERT; CARL; COL; COLIN; DAVE; ERIC; ERNEST; FELIX; FRED; GARY; HECTOR; LESTER; MICK; MIKE; NEIL; PETER; ROGER; ROLF; SERGE; TERRY

man's, the HIS

man, strong TITAN

man, the HIM

man, typical JACK

man uncouth LOUT; OAF

man, violent BRUTE

man, young LAD; MASTER

manage BOSS; COPE; DO; FEND; HANDLE; RUN; SHIFT; SWING; TEND; TREAT; ■ ADMINISTER; WANGLE

manage, do not FAIL

manage for oneself FEND

manage to retain SALVE; SAVE

managed DID; DONE; RAN; SWUNG; anagram indicator; *see* MANAGE

management ADMIN; BOARD; ■ EXECUTIVE; RUNNING; anagram indicator

management graduate MBA

management group BOARD; TRUST

manager BOSS; CHIEF; COPER; EXEC; HEAD; RUNNER; anagram indicator

managers BOARD

manages, person who COPER

managing COPING; anagram indicator

managing director MD

managing, one BOSS; HEAD

Manchester orchestra HALLE
Manchester, part of SALE
mandarin DRAKE
mandate CHARGE
mane HAIR; SHOCK
maneater OGRE; TIGER
manger TROUGH
mangle HACK; PRESS; WRINGER
mangled RENT; TORN; anagram indicator
Manhattan as well as the district in New York can indicate something to do with the cocktail or drinking
mania CRAZE; RAGE
manifest LIST; PLAIN; ■ OBVIOUS; [◊ CARGO]
manifesto LINE
manipulate FIX; HAND; RIG; USE; ■ MANAGE; MASSAGE; anagram indicator
manipulated USED; anagram indicator
manipulating anagram indicator
manipulation anagram indicator
manipulates USES; anagram indicator
mannequin MODEL
manner AIR; FRONT; MODE; STYLE; TONE; WAY; WISE; ■ BEARING; MIEN
manner, condescending AIRS
manner, hypocritical UNCTION
manner, in this SO; THUS
manner in which can indicate the answer is an adverb (usually ending in LY)
manner of ALA (i.e. A LA)
manner of saying/speaking BROGUE; DRAWL; DICTION; ■ ACCENT
manner, old-fashioned WISE
mannered TWEE
mannerisms STYLE
manoeuvrable NIPPY
manoeuvre FEINT; GAMBIT; PLOY; TACTIC; anagram indicator
manoeuvre little by little EASE; INCH

manoeuvres anagram indicator
manoeuvring anagram indicator
manor HALL
manor, grounds of ESTATE
manpower STAFF
manservant VALET
manservant, Dickensian WELLER
mansion PALACE
mansion, country SEAT
mantle PALL
mantra CHANT; OM
manual CONSOLE
manual workers can indicate something to do with audience, clappers etc
manufacture BRAND; MAKE; anagram indicator
manufactured MADE; anagram indicator
manufacturer MAKER; anagram indicator
manure MUCK; ■ GUANO; HUMUS
manuscript MS
Manx cat can indicate that "cat" or one of its synonyms has its last letter omitted (and so is tailless like a Manx cat) e.g. CA, PUS, TO
many BAGS; LOT; LOTS; M; MASS; MUCH; MULTI; POTS; ■ MASSES; OODLES; can be used to signal a Roman numeral for a large number, such as L, C, D, K etc; *see* GREAT MANY
many, great SLEW; *see* MANY
many occasions, on OFTEN
many people HOST
many years AGE; *see* LONG PERIOD
map CHART; GUIDE; PLAN; PLOT
map-making department OS
map, type of OS (i.e. Ordnance Survey); RELIEF
maple ACER
mar BLIGHT; SPOIL; STAIN; TAINT
marauder RAIDER

marble AGATE; ALLEY; ALLY; ROCK; STONE; TAW; with a capital letter can indicate ARCH

marbles can indicate something to do with brains, intelligence

march BORDER; DEMO; FILE; STEP; STRIDE; STRUT; WALK; ■ PARADE; PROTEST

March [◊ IDES]

March Hare, like the MAD

march, on the anagram indicator

march past PARADE

March past PARADE; can indicate something to do with April (e.g. April Fools' Day) or the season of spring

Marco Polo note that this is also the name of an airport as well as a famous explorer

mare DAM

Margaret MEG; PEG

Marge's rival BUTTER

Margery PEG

margin CUT; EDGE; RIM; ■ BORDER

marginal explanation GLOSS

Marie CURIE

marijuana GRASS

marina DOCK; HARBOUR

marinate SOAK

marine RM

marine creature SEAL; WHALE; see FISH

marine growth CORAL

mariner MASTER; see SAILOR

mariner, senior CAPT; SKIPPER

mariners ABS; NAVY; RN; see SAILOR

Marines RM

maritime environment SHORE

mark BADGE; BLAZE; BLOT; BRAND; CHECK; DENT; DOT; EMBLEM; GRADE; LINE; LISTEN; M; MK; MODEL; NOTCH; NOTE; POINT; RATE; SCAR; SCUFF; SEE; SIGN; SMEAR; SPOT; STAIN; STAR; TALLY; TEE; TICK; WEAL; WELT; ■ ACCENT; CARET; FRANK; GRADUATE; PRINT; RECORD; STIGMA; STRIPE; can indicate something to do with

money (i.e. the former German currency) e.g. change; with a capital letter can refer to the gospel; can indicate a punctuation mark (exclamation, question etc)

Mark TWAIN; ■ ANTONY; GOSPEL

mark, black BLOT; STAIN

mark, make DENT; see MARK, SCORE

mark, make one's SIGN

mark of distinction STAR

mark of rank BADGE; PIP; STRIPE

mark on body/skin SCAR

mark, second best B; SA

mark, slight TOUCH

mark, top A; STAR

mark of rank PIP

mark on horse's face BLAZE

marked SEEN

marked "special" STARRED

marker SIGN; ■ ARROW; BUOY; CAIRN; POST

market AGORA; FAIR; MART; SALE; SELL; TRADE; ■ EXCHANGE

market leader M

marketed SOLD

marketing PR; TRADE

marketplace MALL; MART

marks M; see MARK

marksman SNIPER

Marlborough can indicate something to do with Churchill

Marlene LILY

marmalade CAT; ■ LEMON; ORANGE; SQUISH

maroon DESERT; LEAVE; STRAND

marque BRAND; MAKE

marquetry BUHL

Marquis SADE

marred anagram indicator

marriage ALLIANCE; BOND; MATCH; PAIRING; UNION; WEDDING; ■ NUPTIALS; [◊ MARITAL]

marriage certificate LINES

marriage settlement DOWER; ■ DOWRY

married M; MATED; SPLICED; WED; [◊ SHELF]

married, get MATE; WED

married, not M to be omitted

married ladies WIVES

marrow GIST

marry HITCH; PAIR; UNITE; WED; ■ ESPOUSE

Mars ARES

marsh BOG; FEN; MIRE; SWAMP

marsh plant RUSH

marshal NEY; ■ ARRANGE

marshland FEN; *see* MARSH

marshy PLASHY

marshy land FEN; *see* MARSH

marsupial ROO; ■ TUAN

martial artist DAN

Martin Luther King [◊ DREAM]

martyr ST

martyr, English ALBAN

martyrdom END

marvel WONDER

marvellous BRILL; FAB; SUPERB; SWELL

Marx CHICO; GROUCHO; HARPO; ■ KARL

Marxist RED

Maryland MD

mask COVER; HIDE; VISOR

Masons LODGE

masquerading anagram indicator

mass BODY; BULK; CRAM; CROWD; GLOB; GRAM; HEAP; LUMP; M; PILE; RUCK; STACK; TON; ■ DRUM; SERVICE; TONNE; WHOLE; can signify a specific mountain or mountain range; can signify the general population as "Mass in Greek" clues HOI POLLOI

mass mailing SPAM

mass meeting RALLY

mass, part of CREDO

mass stuck together CLOT

Massachusetts MA; MASS

massacre KILL; SLAUGHTER; SLAY; anagram indicator

massacred KILLED; SLAIN; SLEW; anagram indicator

massage KNEAD; anagram indicator

massaged anagram indicator

masse STROKE

masses, the PROLES; ■ HOI POLLOI

masseur RUBBER

mast POLE; STAFF

mast, up the ALOFT

master ACE; BEAT; BETTER; BOSS; HEAD; LEARN; LORD; M; MA; MAN; SIR; ■ TAME; SKIPPER; TEACHER; can indicate something to do with a dog

master of ceremonies EMCEE

masterful ACE

masters MAS; *see* MASTER

masterstroke COUP

mastery ART; CRAFT; SKILL

masticate CHEW

masts, arrangement of RIG

mat RUG

match AGREE; BOUT; FIT; FUSE; GAME; GO; LIGHT; PAIR; PEER; SET; SO; SUIT; TALLY; TEAM; TEST; TIE; VESTA; ■ BEST; COMPARE; CONTEST; EQUAL; FINAL; LIGHTER; SAME; anagram indicator; can indicate something to do with wedding, marriage; [◊ DRAW]

match, big TEST

match, boxing BOUT

match, football TIE

match in series LEG

match-making, consequence of ARSON

matched MET

matches CUP; RUBBER

matching TWIN

mate ALLY; BRIDE; BUD; CHINA; COCK; CHUM; COBBER; GROOM; HEN; OPPO; PAL; TOSH; WIN; ■ MUCKER; SPORT; SPOUSE; can indicate something to do with chess

mate, American BUD

mate, Australian SPORT

mate down under COBBER

material CHINO; CLOTH; CREPE; DENIM; FELT; ISTLE; LACE; MATTER; PRINT; REP; SERGE; STUFF; TERRY; TICKING; TOILE; TWEED; TWILL; WOOL; ▪ APPROPRIATE; CONTENT; EARTHLY; GERMANE; *see* FABRIC; anagram indicator

material, delicate LACE

material, roofing SLATE; THATCH

material, striped TICKING

material, strong TICKING

material, surfacing MACADAM

material, vitreous GLASS

material, woollen FELT

mates PAIR; SIDE

mathematical quantity LOG

mathematical section CONIC

mathematical shape CONE

mathematician ADDER; ▪ EULER; FERMAT; GAUSS

mathematician's line ORDINATE; ▪ TANGENT; [◊ FUNCTION]

mathematician's power LOG

mathematician's table LOG

mathematics, bit of GRAPH

maths, simple SUM

Matilda can signal something to do with lies, lying

matinee actor/star IDOL

matrix WOMB

matt DULL; FLAT

matter COUNT; ISSUE; PUS; TOPIC; WEIGHT; ▪ AFFAIR; BUSINESS; STUFF; THEME

Matthew and the rest NT

mattress BED

mattress cover TICK

mature ADULT; AGE; AGED; FLOWER; RIPE; RIPEN

mature, become AGE; RIPEN

maturity AGE

maudlin SLOPPY

maudlin behaviour, display SLOBBER

maul SCRUM

mauled anagram indicator

maunder RAMBLE

Maureen MO

maverick anagram indicator

maxim MORAL; SAW; SAYING; ▪ MOTTO; TRUISM

maximum BEST; HEIGHT; LIMIT; TOP

maximum number LIMIT

maximum speed C

may CAN; MIGHT; along with another verb (be, have etc) can be an anagram indicator

May BLOSSOM; MONTH

may be anagram indicator

may be used to make anagram indicator

may come from anagram indicator

May French MAI

may have anagram indicator, as in the neatly constructed clue "She may have dresses cut beguilingly" (10) where the answer is SEDUCTRESS. (Note the all-round cleverness in choice of words here: the clue reads well, the scenario (qv) is relevant, and then there is the way in which the two words "dresses cut" do double-duty (qv), serving both as the basis for the anagram and as part of the definition.)

may not CANT

maybe anagram indicator; can indicate that the clue contains an example of the answer (as "China disrupted American radar, maybe?" leads to ACRONYM); can indicate that the clue contains an example of a component (as "London maybe" clues CITY)

Mayday SOS

Mayfair WI

mayonnaise DRESSING

mayor's insignia CHAIN

maze WARREN; anagram indicator

MC HOST

me SETTER

Me MAINE

me, belonging to MINE

me, for MINE; MY

me, you and US

meadow LEA; LEY

meagre LEAN; SLENDER; SLIM; SPARSE; THIN; WEAK

meal COURSE; CURRY; DINNER; DISH; FARE; FEAST; FEED; FLOUR; GRAIN; LUNCH; OAT; OATS; PULSE; SNACK; SUPPER; TEA; ▪ BRUNCH; PIZZA; REPAST; SPREAD

meal, gave FED

meal, had ATE; FED

meal, have a EAT (qv)

meal, having a EATING; ▪ DINING

meal, hot CHILLI; CURRY

meal, reheated HASH

meal-starter M

meal, take EAT; FEED

meal ticket LV

meal, took ATE; FED

meals EATS; BOARD

meals, have BOARD; EAT

mealy PALE

mean AIM; BASE; CLOSE; DIRTY; IMPLY; INTEND; LOW; NEAR; NORM; PAR; PLAN; STINGY; TIGHT; ▪ DENOTE; DESIGN; GRASPING; INTIMATE; LOWDOWN; MEASLY; PROPOSE; SHABBY; SKINNY; SPARING

mean, comparatively LOWER

meandering anagram indicator

meaning DRIFT; GIST; IMPORT; INTENT; SENSE

means MEDIA; WAY; ▪ AGENCY; INCOME; RESOURCES; see MONEY

means of access WICKET; see ACCESS

means of bearing LITTER; see TRANSPORT

means of, by VIA

means of controlling REIN

means of raising money TAX; VAT

means to buy see MONEY

means to secure NAIL; SCREW; TACK

meant AIMED; FATED; IMPLIED

measly SPOTTED; SPOTTY; see TIGHT

measure ACT; AMP; BAR; BOLT; CARAT; CC; CL; DANCE; DOSE; DRAM; DROP; ELL; EM; EN; ERG; FOOT; FT; GILL; HAND; INCH; JUDGE; METE; METER; MIL; MILE; MM; OPTIC; PACE; PECK; PH; PINT; POLE; QUART; ROOD; RULE; RULER; STEP; TUN; UNIT; YARD; ▪ CUBIT; DOSAGE; EPHA; GIRTH; LEAGUE; PINCH; WATT; can refer to a particular dance; can indicate a cardinal number e.g. ONE, TEN; see QUANTITY

measure, imperial OUNCE; see MEASURE

measure of brightness IQ

measure, medicinal DOSE

measure of cloth BOLT; ELL

measure of grain PECK

measure of horse HAND

measure of insulation TOG

measure of noise BEL

measure of power WATT

measure of rhythm FOOT

measure of speed KNOT; MACH; MACHI; MPH

measure of viscosity STOKE

measure, old ELL; LEAGUE

measure, short EM; EN; FT; INCH; MM; see MEASURE, SMALL

measure, small DASH; IMM (i.e. one MM); SNORT; SPLASH; can indicate abbreviation of standard measures see MEASURE

measure up some unit of measurement to be reversed e.g. DRAY

measured amount DOSE

measured lines usually indicates something to do with poetry e.g. verse

measurement SIZE; see MEASURE

measurement, angular LATITUDE; [◊ DEGREE]

measurement of about 45' ELL

measurements, system of SI

measures FEET; see MEASURE

measuring device/instrument
METER

meat BARON; BEEF; CHOP;
FARE; FISH; FLESH; GAME;
HAM; LAMB; LEAN; LIVER;
LOIN; MINCE; NUB; OX;
PORK; RIB; RUMP; SPAM;
STEAK; VEAL; ■ CAPON;
CLAM; HAUNCH; MUTTON;
OFFAL; SATAY; see JOINT

meat, cooked anagram of MEAT;
see MEAT, MEAT DISH

meat dish PATE; ROAST; see
MEAT

meat, joint of BRAWN,
COLLAR; see MEAT

meat paste PATE

meat, piece of CHOP; HAUNCH;
STEAK; see MEAT

meat, type of HAM; see MEAT

meat with no fat LEAN

meaty product SPAM

meaty snack BURGER

mechanic FITTER

mechanical procedure ROTE

mechanical, something DEVICE

mechanical repetition ROTE

mechanism GEAR; SERVO

Med SEA

medal AWARD; BEM; BRONZE;
DSO; GC; GM; GOLD; MBE;
MM; OBE; SILVER; VC; ■
PRIZE

medallion DISC

meddle NOSE

media PRESS

medic DOC; DR; see DOCTOR

medic, famous GALEN

medical degree MB

medical journal LANCET

medical officer MO; see
DOCTOR

medical specialist/speciality
ENT

medical treatment PILL

medicament DRUG; see
MEDICINAL PREPARATION

medication PILL

medicinal extract ARNICA

medicinal preparation DOSE;
LOTION; PILL; SHOT

medicine CURE; DOSE; MED;
PILL; TONIC; ■ CURATIVE;
DRAUGHT; POTION; TABLET

medicine bottle PHIAL; VIAL

medicine-box CHEST

medicine, branch of ENT

medicine man see DOCTOR

medicinal measure DOSE

medico DOC; DR; see DOCTOR

medics MA (i.e. Medical Association)

medieval copyist SCRIBE

medieval historian PARIS

medieval writer ROMANCER

mediocre POOR; ■ AVERAGE;
SOSO

meditate BROOD; MUSE;
PONDER

meditation, place for RETREAT

meditative technique YOGA

meditator YOGI

Mediterranean MED

Mediterranean area LEVANT

medium AGENT; ETHER;
NORM; OIL; ORGAN; ■
MIDDLE; TEMPERA; [◊
SPIRIT]

medley anagram indicator

medley-race anagram of RACE

Medusa GORGON

meek HUMBLE

meet ABUT; APT; FACE; FIT;
FITTING; GATHER; HUNT;
PAY; RALLY; SEE; ■
COUNTER; ENCOUNTER;
JOIN; SATISFY; TOUCH

meet my needs, to TOME

meeting AGM; BEE; CONTACT;
DATE; MATCH; RALLY;
SEANCE; SESSION; ■
ASSEMBLY; CONVENTION;
ENCOUNTER; JUNCTION;
TRYST

meeting announced TRIST

meeting for work BEE

meeting place CLUB; DEN;
VENUE

meeting, run/take CHAIR;
PRESIDE

mega ACE; GREAT; SUPER

melancholy, tending to MINOR
(mus.)

mêlée SCRUM; anagram indicator
mellow RIPE; THAW; ■ RIPEN
melodic sequence LINE
melodious SWEET
melody AIR; STRAIN; TUNE
melon OGEN
melt SOFTEN; THAW; anagram indicator
melt down RENDER
melted anagram indicator
melting snow SLUSH
Melville HERMAN
member ARM; BONE; BRANCH; JOIST; LEG; LIMB; M; MP; PART; PEG; TOE; [◊ CLUB]
member, crew HAND; *see* SAILOR
member of IN
member of family RELATION; *see* RELATIVE
member's end FOOT
member, younger SCION
members ARMS; LIMBS; anagram indicator; *see* MEMBER
members of run indicator
members of band BRASS
members of church FOLD
membership, evidence of BADGE
membership fee SUB
membrane CAUL (physio.); FELL; FILM; SKIN
member, supporting BONE; RIB
memento RELIC; TOKEN
memo NOTE
memo, write JOT; NOTE
memoirs STORY
memoranda NOTES
memorandum NOTE
memorial RELIC
memorial tablet PLAQUE
memory RAM; ROM; ROTE
memory, aid to CRIB
memory, sort of ROM
Memphis area TENN
men ARMY; STAFF; this can require the names of two men to be used together to form a new component or word e.g. PATRON; *see* MAN, REGIMENT
men at work CREW

men, for STAG
men only STAG
men's a synonym for man with the addition of S, e.g. ALS, LENS, CHAPS (*see* MAN)
men with guns RA
menace THREAT
menacing look LOUR; SCOWL
menagerie ZOO
mend DARN; FIX; KNIT; PATCH; REPAIR; ■ COBBLE; IMPROVE; anagram indicator
mendacious LYING
mendacious, be LIE
mendacity LYING
mended anagram indicator, as "thing mended" → NIGHT
Mendelssohn can indicate something to do with ITALIAN (one of his symphonies)
mendicant BEGGAR
menial BASE; SERF
menial work, one in CHAR
menswear TIE
mental BATS; MAD; ■ CRACKED; *see* MAD
mental suffering ANGUISH
mentally acute BRAINY; SHARP
mention CITE; OBSERVE; REFER; ■ REFERENCE
mentioned SAID; homophone indicator
mentor SAGE
menu BILL; CARTE; FARE; LIST; TABLE; [◊ DISH]
menu, item on COURSE; DISH
merchandise GOODS; LINE; WARE; WARES
merchant MONGER; ■ DEALER; TRADER; [◊ TRADE]
Merchant Navy MN
merciless IRON
mercurial MOODY
mercury HG
mercy QUARTER; RUTH
mercy of, at the nesting indicator
mere BARE; JUST; LAKE; LITTLE; POND; POOL; SMALL; WATER; can indicate a specific stretch of inland water
merge FUSE; JOIN; UNITE

merger FUSION

meringue SWEET; ■ DESSERT; PAVLOVA

merit EARN; OM; RATE; WORTH; ■ CREDIT

Merlin WIZARD

merriment GLEE; ■ HILARITY

merry GAY; HAPPY; anagram indicator; *see* DRUNK; [◊ COLE]

merry-go-round RIDE

merry, make PARTY; ROISTER

mesh GRID; NET; SIEVE

mess BOTCH; HASH; PAP; SLOSH; ■ CLUTTER; SHAMBLES; TANGLE; anagram indicator; can refer to a place reserved for eating (as in the services); *see* CONFUSION

mess, in a anagram indicator

mess up FLUFF; MUFF

message CABLE; LETTER; LINE; MEMO; MORAL; NOTE; SIGN; SIGNAL; SOS; WIRE; WORD; ■ CALL; COMMUNICATION; FAX; RING; can indicate a word ending in GRAM e.g. telegram, kissagram

message received ROGER

message, urgent SOS

messed up, messing about, messy anagram indicator

messenger ANGEL; PAGE; ■ COURIER; ENVOY; HERALD; RUNNER

messily anagram indicator

messing about anagram indicator

messing up anagram indicator

messy anagram indicator

messy room STY

messy situation STY

met FOUND

Met YARD; can indicate something to do with opera (i.e. via New York Metropolitan)

metal AG; AU; BA; CU; DY; FE; FOIL; GOLD; HG; IRON; K; LEAD; NI; ORE; PLATE; SN; TIN; ■ COPPER; STEEL

metal, bit of BLADE

metal box TIN; *see* BOX

metal container ORE; TIN

metal, lump of PIG

metal man ROBOT

metal, thin FOIL

metallic TINNY

metallic sound TING

metals, mix of ALLOY

metalworker BEATER; SMITH

metamorphose into anagram indicator

metamorphosis anagram indicator

metaphor IMAGE

mete DOLE; SHARE

methane GAS

method HOW; LINE; MEANS; MODE; ORDER; STYLE; WAY; ■ COURSE; MANNER; PLAN; SYSTEM; anagram indicator (as "knew a method" → WAKEN)

meticulousness CARE

★ **metonym** this is where a single aspect of something is used to stand for the thing as a whole as "glass" can stand for "drink", or "the ring" can stand for "the sport of boxing"

metre M

metre, nearly a YARD

metre, one millionth of a MICRON

metres can indicate something to do with verse

metric can indicate something to do with verse

metrical form/text VERSE

metropolis CAPITAL; CITY

mettlesome GAMY

mew GULL

Mexican HOMBRE

Mexican food TACO

Michael MIKE

Michigan MI

Mickey GUY; MOUSE

Mickey Finn to, give a DOPE; DRUG

mickey out of, take the *see* TEASE

micro SMALL; TINY

microphone MIC; MIKE

mid- as a prefix (e.g. mid-July) usually signifies that the middle letter(s) should be taken from the associated word e.g. "mid-July" indicates UL, "mid-afternoon" indicates R, "mid-off" indicates F; can indicate a run of letters within a word or phrase, as "Point, mid-south or north" → THORN

mid-afternoon R
mid-day A; NOON
mid-day, after PM
mid-day, before AM
mid-evening N
mid-life IF
mid-month IDES; N
mid-morning N; TEN; ■ ATTEN (i.e. at ten)
mid-stream RE
mid-week EE
Mid-West ES
midday, after PM
midday, before AM
midday, one hour after ATI (i.e. at one)
middle CORE; HEART (qv); TUM; WAIST; *see* MIDDLE OF
middle-age G
middle-aged GE
Middle East AS; ME
Middle Eastern ME; T; ■ ISRAELI
Middle Easterner ARAB
middle, in the AMID; can indicate that only the middle letter or letters be used (as "wrong in the middle" clues RON)
middle of can signify that the middle letter(s) should be taken from the associated word as "middle of dinner" is a cue for NN
middle of day A; NOON
middle point MEDIAN
middle, the H
Middle-West ES
middleman A
middlemen E
middling SOSO
midfielder SCARECROW
midge* FLY
Midlands city STOKE
midnight G; LATE

midnight, after AM
midnight, hour after IAM
midshipman EASY; REEFER
Midsummer Night's Dream can indicate a character from the play e.g. Bottom, Oberon, Puck, Titania
mien AIR; MANNER
MIG JET
might BEEF; CLOUT; MAY; POWER
migrant ALIEN
Mike can indicate something to do with a microphone; depending on context (e.g. "as heard by Mike") can be a homophone indicator
mild GENTLE; LIGHT; LOW; SLIGHT; WEAK
milder LESS
mile M
mile or so KNOT
miler RUNNER; [◊ LAP]
miles MM
miles away M to be omitted
militant MARTIAL
militant action WAR
military ARMY; MIL
military accommodation QUARTERS
military action OP; WAR; ■ BATTLE
military actions OPS
military advance PUSH
military alliance NATO
military arm NAVY
military base STATION
military branch ARM
military cadets RMA
military commander AGA
military display/entertainment TOURNEY; ■ TATTOO
military group NATO; TA
military honour MEDAL; VC; *see* MEDAL
military HQ BASE; SHAPE; STATION
Military Intelligence MI
military leader M; *see* OFFICER
military man *see* OFFICER, SOLDIER
military music MARCH

military offender DESERTER
military operation MISSION
military personnel ARMY; *see* SOLDIERS, REGIMENT etc
military prisoner POW
military punishment FATIGUE
military quarters BASE; CAMP ■ BARRACKS
military slog YOMP
military station CAMP
military status RANK; SITREP (i.e. situation report)
military, the ARMY; *see* ARMY, REGIMENT
military training group OTC
military unit COY; TA; *see* REGIMENT
military vehicle JEEP; TANK
military zone SECTOR
milk PINT; SQUEEZE; WHITE; ■ EXPLOIT; EXTRACT; [◊ DAIRY]
milk cart FLOAT
milk producer/provider COW; EWE; SOW; UDDER
milk pudding SAGO
milk, thickened CURD
milk, top of the CREAM; M
milksop WIMP
milky WHITE
mill GRIND; [◊ GRIST; HOPPER; RACE]
millennium building DOME
millennium year MM
Miller GLENN; MICK (racing dog)
Milligan SPIKE
millilitre ML
milliner HATTER
milling about, around anagram indicator; can simultaneously indicate an anagram and nesting
million M
millions M; MM
Milne can refer to any of the author's characters e.g. Winnie, Pooh, Tigger, Roo etc
Milne's bouncer TIGGER, as "run into Milne's bouncer" → TRIGGER
mimer ACTOR
mimic APE; COPY; MINA

mince CHOP; CUT; GRIND; HASH; anagram indicator
mince-tart anagram of TART
minced CUT; GROUND; anagram indicator
mind BRAIN; CARE; HEAD; HEED; NOUS; RESENT; TEND; ■ BOTHER; [◊ FANTASY]
mind, in MENTAL
minder NANNY; NURSE; ■ ESCORT
mindless activity ROTE
mine BOMB; BORE; DIG; FUND; PIT; ■ LIMPET; TUNNEL; WHEAL (Cornish)
mine, entrance to ADIT
mine, product of ORE
Minehead M
miner DIGGER
mineral MICA; OPAL; SPAR
mineral aggregate ORE
mineral resource MINE; PIT
miners NUM
Ming POT
mingle BLEND; MIX; ■ MELL
mingled MIXED; anagram indicator
mini CAR; SKIRT; SMALL
miniature MINI; SMALL; TOY; ■ LITTLE
minimal LIGHT; SMALL; can indicate the use of only one letter from an indicated word, usually the first letter
minimal piece of can indicate the first letter of the word that follows, as "minimal piece of apparel" → A
minimal amount/sum IP; P
minimally, minimum can indicate use of only one letter from an indicated word
minimum LEAST; MIN
mining land CLAIM
minion TOOL; ■ LACKEY; SERF; UNDERLING
minister CARE; DD; ENVOY; MIN; PARSON; PASTOR; PRIEST; REV; SERVE; TEND; TREAT; ■ CURATE; LECTOR; PRELATE; RABBI; RECTOR

minister, former foreign GREY
minister's house MANSE
minister, junior CURATE
minister's office CURACY
ministers CLOTH
ministry MIN; MOD
mink FUR
mink-like FURRY
minor CHILD; KEY; LESS; LIGHT; PETTY; SIDE (as in "a side issue"); SLIGHT; SMALL; TINY; WARD; ■ CHARGE; INFANT; LITTLE; can call for an abbreviation as "minor street" clues ST; first letter indicator; can indicate something to do with a child or children
minor character PAWN
minor hit PAT
minor illness COLD
minor personality CELEB
minor player EXTRA
minor route BROAD (i.e. B road)
minority can refer to the condition or fact of being under age (in U.K. below 18) and so can signal teenage, youth etc
mint COIN; NEW; POT; TOP; ■ FLAVOUR; FRESH; *see* CASH RESOURCES
minus LESS; SIGN; omission indicator
minute M; MIN; NOTE (i.e. as in take minutes); TINY; WEE; ■ BABY; MO; SEC; TICK
minutes ACTA
miracle was performed, where CANA
Miranda usually refers to Shakespeare's character (hence, "Brave new world") or some aspect of "The Tempest"
mire BOG; MARSH; MUD
mirk DARK
mirror GLASS; can indicate something to do with reflection, face or Snow White
mirth GLEE; ■ HAHA; HILARITY
mirthless DOUR
mis- words beginning with mis- can indicate that the remaining letters

of the word are an anagram, as "miscue" calls for an anagram of CUE
mis-sorted anagram indicator
misanthrope TIMON
misappropriate STEAL
misappropriation can refer to a particular form of stealing e.g. embezzlement, mugging, piracy, robbery
misbehave, misbehaved, misbehaving, misbehaviour anagram indicator
miscalculation ERROR
miscast anagram indicator
miscellany ORIO
mischief HARM
mischief, do SIN
mischief-maker ATE (Greek goddess); ELF; IMP; SCAMP
mischievous ARCH; ELFIN; ELFISH; IMPISH
mischievous child ELF; IMP; SCAMP
mischievous type IMP; MONKEY
misconduct anagram indicator
misconstrued anagram indicator
miscreant WRETCH; anagram indicator; *see* CRIMINAL
miscue anagram of CUE
misdemeanour SIN
misdirected anagram indicator
miser SNUDGE
miserable BLUE; DOWN; GLUM; SAD; SORRY; ■ ROTTEN; anagram indicator
miserable place HELL
miserably anagram indicator
miserly STINGY; TIGHT
misery GLOOM; WOE
misfire PINK; REBOUND; RIFE (anag.)
misfortune BLOW; ILL; ■ REVERSE
misgiving PANG
misguided/misguiding anagram indicator
mishandle BLOW; MUFF
mishandled anagram indicator
mishap, likely to cause RISKY

misheard anagram of HEARD

misinterpretation anagram indicator

misinterpreted anagram indicator

mislaid LOST; omission indicator; anagram indicator; anagram of LAID

mislaid, is IS to be omitted

mislay LOSE; anagram of LAY

mislaying, one LOSER

mislead CON; DEAL (anag.); DELUDE; DUPE; LIE

misleading anagram indicator

misleading statement LIE

misled LIED; anagram indicator (especially of LED)

mislocated anagram indicator

misplaced anagram indicator

misread anagram indicator; anagram of READ

misrepresent BELIE; TWIST; anagram indicator

misrepresented anagram indicator

misrepresentation LIBEL; LIE; SLANDER; SPIN; STORY; TALE; anagram indicator

misrepresents anagram indicator

miss AVOID; FAIL; LACK; LASS; LOSE; LOSS; MAID; MUFF; NEED; OMIT; SKIP; ■ SINGLE

miss, modern MS

Miss Peacham POLLY

missed omission indicator

missed, not can signify something to do with a married woman

misshapen anagram indicator

missile ARROW; DART; SAM; SCUD; ■ IBM

missile-launcher BOW; EROS; SLING

missing ASTRAY; GONE; LACKING; LOST; omission indicator

missing end last letter to be omitted

missing nothing omission of O

missing the can indicate that the word THE is to be omitted

mission AIM; QUEST; RAID; TASK; ■ ALAMO; DELEGATION

missionary PAUL

missionary, Irish AIDAN

Mississippi MISS

Mississippi traveller HUCK

missive LETTER

misspelled anagram indicator

missus *see* WIFE

Mrs Mopp CHAR

Mrs Trollope FRANCES

mist DAMP; DIM; FOG; FRET; HAZE

mistake BISH; BOOB; ERR; ERROR; FLUFF; GAFF; GOOF; LAPSE; MUFF; NOD; SIN; SLIP; ■ BLUNDER; BONER; BOTCH; BUNGLE; CLANGER; HOWLER; anagram indicator

mistake, by anagram indicator

mistake, make ERR; MUFF; NOD; *see* MISTAKE

mistaken, mistakenly anagram indicator

mistakes ERRORS; anagram indicator

mistakes, without CLEAN; CLEAR

mister MR

Mr Chips can indicate something to do with school e.g. MASTER

mistiness FILM

mistook anagram indicator

mistreated anagram indicator

mistreatment, after anagram indicator

mistress LOVER; TEACHER

mistress, royal NELL

mistrust DOUBT

misused, misuses, misusing anagram indicator

mitigate EASE

mitt GLOVE

mix BLEND; GARBLE; MINGLE; anagram indicator

mix up JUMBLE; TANGLE; anagram indicator

mixed anagram indicator

mixed school COED

mixed-up type PI; PIE

mixer BLENDER; TONIC

mixing anagram indicator

mixture BREW; MASH; anagram indicator

mo SEC; SHAKE; ■ MINUTE; *see* TIME, LITTLE

Moabite woman RUTH

moan BEEF; GROUSE; SIGH; ■ GRUMBLE; PLAINT

moat DITCH

mob GANG; HERD; HORDE; LOT; ■ CROWD; RABBLE

mobile ACTIVE; PHONE; anagram indicator; can indicate something to do with transport, cars, or people on the move e.g. nomad, ambler

mobile, message on TEXT

mobilise MARSHAL

mock FAKE; RAG; SCOFF; SCORN; SHAM; TAUNT; ■ DERIDE; JEER; anagram indicator

mockery CHAFF

model COPY; CRIB; DOLL; FORM; FRAME; IDEAL; LAST (i.e. cobbler's); MARK; POSE; POSER; SIT; T (i.e. from Ford Model T); TOY; TYPE; anagram indicator; ■ DUMMY; PATTERN; SITTER; TEMPLATE

modelling FORMING; POSING; SITTING; anagram indicator

moderate BLAND; CHAIR (i.e. meeting); CURB; EASE; LOWER; MILD; TEMPER; ■ SOFTEN; SO-SO; anagram indicator

moderate Conservative WET

modern AD; LATE; LATTER; MOD; NEW; RECENT; ■ NOVEL

modern day AD

modern girl MILLIE

modern style HIP

modern times AD

modest CHASTE; COY; DECENT; HUMBLE; LITTLE; PURE; SHY; SLIGHT; SMALL ■ DEMURE

modification CHANGE; ■ UPGRADE; anagram indicator; can indicate that one letter has to be changed

modified anagram indicator; can indicate that one letter has to be changed

modify ALTER; CHANGE; TEMPER; ■ ADAPT; PREPARE

modish IN

Mogul capital AGRA

moist DAMP

moisten BASTE; WET

moisten joint BASTE

moisture DAMP; DEW

moisture from, take DRY

moisture, remove AIR; DRY

moke ASS

mole JETTY; PIER; SPY

mole's work SPYING

molest ACCOST; *see* ANNOY, HARRY

mollusc CLAM; GAPER; ORMER; SNAIL; SQUID; UNIO; WINKLE

Molly BLOOM

molten anagram indicator

molten rock LAVA

moment MO; SEC; TICK; TRICE; WINK; ■ INSTANT; JIFFY; SECOND

moment, this, of the NOW

momentary BRIEF; SHORT

momentous SIGNAL

momma MUM

monarch ANNE; COLE; ER; GR; HM; KING; QUEEN; R; RH

monarchy CROWN

monastic clique, group etc ORDER

monastic singing CHANT

Monday MO; MON; via the nursery rhyme can indicate FAIR

Mondeo FORD

Mondrian PIET

monetary union EMU

money ANNA; BILL; BRASS; BREAD; BUCK; BUCKS; CASH; CENT; COIN; DOUGH; DOSH; ECU; FEE; FLOAT; FUND; GRANT; GREEN; KITTY; L; LOLLY; LOOT; LY; MEANS; NOTE; NOTES; P;

PAY; READY; RIAL; ROLL; SEN; SOU; TAKE; TENDER; TIN; WAD; ■ CAPITAL; BOODLE; CHANGE; COPPER; INTEREST; LUCRE; OOF (Yid.); RHINO; SCRATCH; TALENT; [◊ MINT]; *see* CURRENCY and various MONEY *entries below*

money, a little TIP

money, a lot of GRAND; *see* MONEY, LOAD OF

money advanced LOAN ■ IMPREST

money, American BUCK; CENT; DIME; JACK; ROLL ■ DOLLAR

money, amount of FUND

money, appearance BAIL

money, attempt to make SPEC

money, bundle of WAD

money demand BILL; FEE; PRICE; ■ CHARGE; RANSOM

money earned SCREW; *see* INCOME

money, European DM; FRANC; GUILDER; LIRE; LIRA; MARK

money, extra BONUS; TIP; ■ INTEREST

money for immediate use CASH; READY

money foreign/from overseas LEU; *see* FOREIGN CURRENCY

money, gambler's CHIP

money, get EARN

money, give PAY

money given PAID; TIP

money, having enough SOLVENT

money, having no BROKE; POOR; a synonym for money (e.g. P for pence) to be omitted

money in America JACK; *see* MONEY, AMERICAN

money in hand FLOAT

money, in the PLUSH

money instantly needed FLOAT

money, lacking BROKE; *see* MONEY, WITHOUT

money, large amount of *see* MONEY, LOADS OF

money, little CENT; MITE; PENNY; ■ FLOAT; can indicate the abbreviation of a monetary unit, hence D, L, P, S

money, load(s), lot(s) of BOMB; MINT; PILE; STACK; WAD; ■ BUNDLE; PACKET

money, made EARNED

money, make EARN; GROSS; MINT

money-makers MINT

money, more RISE

money, old BOB; CROWN; D; DUCAT; GROAT; JOEY; LSD; S; TANNER; ■ NOBLE; SHILLING; apart from an historically ancient currency, can refer to the former monetary unit of a European country now converted to the euro, MARK, FRANC etc

money, one taking CASHIER

money order CHEQUE; GIRO; PO

money order, sound CHECK

money out of, get TAP

money provided LIF; MIF; PIF

money, put down EARNEST

money raised a synonym for money, particularly in a DC (i) to be reversed; or (ii) to be brought forward within a word as "money raised in Northern Ireland" → LUSTER

money, short of STUCK; *see* MONEY, HAVING NO

money, some COIN; NOTE; *see* MONEY

money supply FUND

money, take CHARGE; ROB

money, tiny sum of ICENT; IP

money, try to get DUN

money, very little SOU

money, with RICH

money, without BROKE; BUST; SKINT; ■ INSOLVENT; a synonym for money to be nested within a component (as "Transported traitor without money" clues RAPT); *see* MONEY, HAVING NO

moneybag PURSE

moneymaker MINTER

moneyman CA
Mongol ruler KHAN
mongrel CUR; CROSS; TIKE
monitor SCREEN
monk DOM; LAMA; TUCK (i.e. Friar Tuck); ■ BROTHER; FATHER
monk, leading PRIOR
monk, title of DOM
monkey APE; MONA; ■ HOWLER; RHESUS; SAI
monks ORDER; *see* MONK
monogram CIPHER
monograph PAPER
monologue RAP
monopolise HOG; nesting indicator
monotonous SAMEY
monotonous speech DRONE
monotony TEDIUM
monsoon RAIN
monster DRAGON; FIEND; HYDRA; ORC; OGRE; TROLL; ■ BRUTE; NESSIE
monster's home NESS
monstrosity anagram indicator
month MO; MOON; abbreviations for months are common: JAN, FEB, MAR, APR, MAY, JUN, JUL, AUG, SEPT, OCT, NOV, DEC; ("two short months" can signal a word made up wholly in this way e.g. DECOCT)
month in arrears ULT
month in France/Paris MAI
month, last DEC; ULT
month, this INST; INSTANT
month we are in INST; INSTANT
months SEASON; YEAR
months, several *see* MONTHS
monthly MAG
monument CAIRN; GRAVE
moo LOW
mooch MOSEY
mooch about *see* WANDER
mood AIR; FIT; KEY; STATE; TONE; TEMPER; VEIN; ■ FEELING
mood, bad PET; *see* TEMPER
mood, change of anagram of MOOD

moody PENSIVE
moon LIGHT; LUNA; MOPE; PINE; ■ SATELLITE
moon about MOPE
moon cavity CRATER
moonshine HOOCH
moor BERTH; DOCK; FELL; HEATH; ■ ANCHOR
moored TIED
mooring BERTH
mooring site BERTH; DOCK
moorland FELL; HEATH
moose ELK; ■ DEER
mop CLEAN; CLEANER; SWAB
mope FRET; MOON; PINE
moral GOOD; JUST; MAXIM; POINT; RIGHT
moral guidelines CODE
moral principles ETHICS
Moral Re-armament MRA
moral slip SIN
moral tale FABLE; PARABLE
morale HEART; SPIRIT
moralise PREACH
morally wrong IMPURE
moran BOG
morass MARSH
moratorium FREEZE
more AGAIN; EXTRA; LONGER; OVER; PLUS; ■ ANOTHER; ENCORE; can suggest the answer is a word ending in ER; with a capital letter can refer to something to do with Sir Thomas More e.g. Utopia; can signal a verb beginning with OUT (e.g. "gape more" → OUTSTARE); [◊ PLUS]
more absurd DAFTER
more dubious anagram, of MORE
more, fifty changes an L to a C
more, five changes a V to an X
more, five hundred changes a D to an M
more or less ABOUT; C; ■ PRETTY; ROUGHLY
more, say ADD
more than OVER; run indicator (the suggestion being that the word or phrase containing the run has more letters than necessary)

more than enough AMPLE

more than enough, to have SATED

more than half MOST

more than one can indicate the answer is a plural noun and so ends in S etc

Morecambe ERIC

moribund DYING

morning AM; MORN

morning, in the component(s) to be nested within AM

moron FOOL (qv)

morose GLUM; SOUR

Morocco LEATHER; [◊ BIND, BINDER, BOUND]

Morse CODE

Morse feature *see* MORSE SIGNAL

Morse signal, unit DASH; DIT; DOT

morsel BIT

mortar GROUT; GUN

mortgage LOAN

mortified SICK

Moslem ALI

moss* PLANT

most can indicate that most letters of a word are to be used, either in a run or as an anagram as, for example, "most profound" clues DEE (i.e. DEEP minus its last letter); can indicate an adjective ending in ER; in conjunction with an opposite can indicate LEAST as "most injudicious" → LEASTWISE; can signify an adjective ending in EST

most confused anagram of MOST

most desirable BEST

most important CHIEF; MAIN; TOP

most of run indicator

most part MAIN

most part, for the a word to be used less one letter (usually first or last)

most successful BEST; TOP

mostly all but one letter (sometimes two letters) of a word to be

used, as "mostly to arrive" → COM

mostly silent DUM

motel INN

mothball STORE

mother DAM; MA; MATER; MAMA; MUM

Mother NATURE; ■ SUPERIOR

mother* HEN; MARE; PARENT

mother, ancient THETIS

mother and child MACH; MAD; MASON

mother, be BEAR; POUR

mother, beastly DAM

mother country HOME

mother-in-law NAOMI

mother, reverend MARIA

mother's MAS

mother's mother GRAN

mother's ruin GIN

mother superior a synonym for "mother" (*see* MOTHER or MOTHER*) to be placed in front of a component

Mothers' Union MU

motherland HOME

motif DESIGN; THEME

motion SIGNAL

motivate DRIVE; FIRE; ROUSE; SPUR; URGE; ■ EGG ON

motivation BUG; DRIVE; FIRE; GO; URGE; ■ ROUSING; URGING

motivation, give *see* MOTIVATE

motive REASON; SPUR; *see* MOTIVATION

motor CAR; DRIVE; DRIVER; ENGINE; TURBO; can refer to a particular marque commonly: JAG, FORD, MINI, RR, ROLLER

motor-sport event RALLY

motor vessel, yacht MY

motorbike rally SCRAMBLE

motorcyclist BIKER

motoring DRIVING

motorist DRIVER

motorist, awful TOAD

motorists AA; RAC

motorway AI; M; MI; ROAD

motorway organisation AA; RAC

mottled DAPPLE

motto MAXIM; SAW

mould CAST; FORM; FRAME; FUR; MUST; SHAPE

moulded CAST; anagram indicator

mouldering anagram indicator

moulding, hollow SCOTIA

mouldy OFF; STALE

mouldy-smelling MUSTY

moult SHED

mound BANK; HEAP; HILL; PILE; ■ CAIRN; BARROW

mount ASS; CLIMB; HILL; HORSE (qv); MULE; RAISE; RIDE; RISE; SCALE; STAGE; TOR; ■ BUILD; HINGE; can indicate that the name of specific mountain is required e.g. ATHOS, OSSA, RIGI

mountain ALP; BEN; BERG; FELL; IDA; PEAK; SION; ■ ATHOS, IDA, RIGI

mountain climb PLA (i.e. reversal of Alp) in a DC

mountain, part of PEAK; RIDGE

mountain pass COL; GATE; ■ GHAT

mountain road PASS

mountain side FACE

mountain-top ALP; M; PEAK

mountain water TARN

mountaineer CLIMBER; [◊ UP]

mountaineer's intent ASCENT; CLIMB

mountaineer's requirement CRAMPON; PITON

mountainous area MASSIF

mountains ANDES; CHAIN; RANGE

mounted UP; reversal indicator

mounting reversal indicator

mourn RUE; ■ GRIEVE; LAMENT

mournful PLANGENT

mournful cry WAIL; WOE

mourning GRIEF

mouse MICKEY

mouse, use CLICK

mouser CAT

mousetrap CHEESE

mousse GEL

mouth MAW; GOB; SAY; SPEAK; STOMA; TRAP; ■ KISSER; can indicate the use of an initial letter as "mouth of the Nile" clues N

mouth, by ORAL; ORALLY

mouth, of the ORAL

mouth off RANT

mouth, part of GUM; LIP; ROOF

mouthed first letter indicator, as "foul-mouthed" → F

mouthpiece CHEEK; GUM; LIP; ORGAN

move ACT; AFFECT; BETAKE; BUDGE; CASTLE (as in chess); EDGE; FLIT; GO; HURRY; LUNGE; LURCH; ROLL; ROUSE; SELL; SHIFT; SHOVE; SIDLE; SLIP; STIR; SWAY; TOUCH; ■ REHOUSE; anagram indicator

move about an anagram of either ABOUT or MOVE

move aimlessly MILL

move along the ground TAXI; *see* MOVE

move awkwardly LUMBER

move boat ROW

move carefully EDGE; INCH

move cautiously EASE; EDGE; INCH; NOSE

move, decisive MATE

move elsewhere RESITE

move fast/quickly/swiftly DART; FLY; HURRY; RIP; RUN; RUSH; SCUD; SPEED; SPRINT; STREAK; WHIP; ZOOM; ■ BOMB; CANTER; DIVE; CAREER; HIE; *see* RUN FAST

move, final MATE

move forward SURGE; ■ ADVANCE

move from side to side SWING

move furtively CREEP; SIDLE

move gently ROCK

move in game CASTLE

move, make a ACT

move, on the ABOUT; ASTIR; GOING; anagram indicator

move, opening GAMBIT

move out VACATE
move painfully LIMP
move quickly *see* MOVE FAST
move quietly FLIT
move rapidly *see* MOVE FAST
move round TURN; anagram indicator
move slowly AMBLE; CRAWL; EDGE; INCH
move smoothly FLOAT; GLIDE; SKATE
move suddenly DART; LUNGE; NIP
move to side SHUNT
move to next page PTO
move towards APPROACH; NEAR
move two pieces CASTLE
move unsteadily LURCH; REEL; ■ STAGGER
move up and down BOB
move vessel KEDGE
moveable steps RAMP
moved RAN; SENT; anagram indicator
moved quickly FLEW; HIED; RAN; RUSHED; SPED; TORN
moved silently STOLE
movement ACTION; LUNGE; MOTION; STEP; TIC; TWITCH; ■ BOBBLE; GROUP; LARGO; anagram indicator as "counter-movement" → TROUNCE
movement, in anagram indicator
movement, quick DART
movement, slow LARGO
movement, sudden LUNGE; LURCH
movement, uncontrollable/uncontrolled TIC
movements TROTS; *see* MOVEMENT
movie CINE; EPIC; ET; FILM; PIC
movie actor *see* FILM STAR
moving ASTIR; MOTIVE; anagram indicator; can indicate that the position of a letter in a word is to be changed as "moving east" means E has to be relocated

moving, not STABLE; STILL; ■ IMMOBILE; STATIC
mow CUT
Mozart, catalogue of K
MP MEMBER; ■ REDCAP
MP, is SITS
MP, was SAT
MPs, group of PARTY
much FAR; LOT; LOTS; WELL; ■ OFTEN
much of run indicator as in "Too much of coal's on" → ALSO
much, too OVER
much-travelled BEATEN
muck GUNGE; MUD
Muck ISLE
mucked up anagram indicator
mud LUTE; MIRE; OOZE; SLIGHT; SLIME; SLUR; SLUSH; ■ MUCK; SLANDER; [◊ CLART; SLICK]
mud, application of CAKE
mud, covered in SOILED
mud, roll in WALLOW
muddle ADDLE; HASH; MESS; STEW; TANGLE; anagram indicator
muddled ADDLED; STEWED; TANGLED; anagram indicator
muddled, become ADDLE
muddy MIRY
muddy ground BOG; MIRE
muff MAR; MISS; ■ BUNGLE; *see* SPOIL
muffin ROLL
muffled anagram indicator
mug ASS; DUPE; FACE; NOODLE; PAN; POT; PUSS; ROB; SAP; STEIN; ■ CLOCK; *see* FOOL
Muggins *see* FOOL
mugshot PIC
mule ASS; SLIPPER
mull HEAT; MUSE; THINK
mullet, type of RED
multinational ICI; UN
multipart programme SERIAL
multiply BREED; DOUBLE; TRIPLE; ■ TREBLE
multitude HOST; MASS
multitudinous MANY

mum MA; MOTHER; SH; ■ SILENCE; SILENT

mum, isn't TALKS; TELLS

mum, keep HUSH; SH; SHUSH

mumble SLUR

munch CHAMP; CHEW

municipality TOWN

Munro SAKI

mural PAINTING

murder CHOKE; DOIN (i.e. do in); DROWN; KILL; SLAY; ■ STRANGLE; anagram indicator

murder, arrangement to CONTRACT

murder penalty ERIC (Irish law)

murder victim ABEL

murdered man ABEL

murderer CAIN; ■ ASSASSIN; KILLER; STRANGLER; see MURDER

murderer, become see MURDER

Murdoch publication (THE) BELL

murmur COO; HUM; WORD ■ BUZZ; RUMOUR

murmuring HUM

Murphy can have something to do with potatoes

muscle BEEF; BRAWN; CLOUT; MIGHT; PEC; POWER

muscle-man HUNK

muscle pain CRAMP

muscle, pulled SPRAIN

muscular BEEFY

muscular chap HEMAN

muscular flap LIP

muscular spasm TIC

muscular trouble CRAMP

muse MULL; PONDER; THINK; ■ ERATO

muse about can indicate an anagram of MUSE; see MUSE

muse of history CLEO

muses NINE

museum VA; VANDA (i.e. V and A); ■ LOUVRE

mush SLO ■ SCHMALTZ

mushroom CEP (an edible variety;) ■ BUTTON; MOREL

mushy anagram indicator

music AIR; CHANT; M; MUS; PIECE; POP; RAP; REEL; ROCK; SCORE; SONG; STRAIN; SWING; TANGO; TUNE; ■ CONCERTO; FUGUE; LARGO; PIECE; REGGAE; SUITE

music, ability to appreciate EAR

music, arrange SCORE

music, black RAP

music, church MASS

music going the rounds DISC

music group BAND; COMBO

music, item of see MUSICAL ITEM

music, kind of DANCE; DISCO; see MUSIC

music, line of STAVE

music maker/producer can indicate an instrument or a particular kind of musical performer; see INSTRUMENT, INSTRUMENTALIST, PLAYER, SINGER

music, perform PLAY; SING

music, piece of BAR; SNATCH

music, pop MOTOWN; RAP; ROCK

music producer BAND; DJ; see COMPOSER

music, slow LARGO

music, some PIECE

music, sort of ROCK; ■ COUNTRY; see MUSIC

music with strong beat ROCK

music, write COMPOSE

musical CATS; CHESS; EVITA; GIGI; HAIR; OLIVER; SHOW; ■ CAROUSEL; GREASE; OPERA

musical composition PIECE; WORK

musical drama see MUSICAL, OPERA

musical entertainment DISCO; see MUSICAL

musical family TRAPP

musical gang, member of JET; SHARK

musical group BAND; DUO; TRIO; ■ NONET; OCTET;

ORCHESTRA; QUARTET; QUINTET; SEPTET; SESTET

musical instrument BASS; BELL; CELLO; DRUM; FIFE; FLUTE; GONG; GRAND; HARP; HORN; LUTE; LYRE; ORGAN; PIPE; REED; SAX; SPINET; TUBA; UKE; VIOL; ■ BUGLE; CORNET; FIDDLE; REBEC; RECORDER; SITAR; TRUMPET; VIOLA; VIOLIN

musical instrument, old STRAD

musical item NUMBER; PIECE; SONG

musical piece LIED; SONG; TUNE; VERSE

music, piece of RIFF

musical pieces LENTI

musical performance CONCERT; ■ RECITAL

musical performer PLAYER; RAPPER

musical prince IGOR

musical show OPERA; *see* MUSICAL

musical tail CODA

musical talent EAR

musical technique BOWING

musical, very ASSAI (Ital.); MOLTO (Ital.)

musical work CHORALE; OPERA *see* MUSIC

musically Italian musical terms (and their abbreviations) are used commonly as components, and are frequently signalled by the word *musically; see* the phrases starting with MUSICALLY *below*

musically broad and slow LARGO

musically loud F

musically, quiet P

musically rapid/rapidly MOSSO

musically slowly LENTO

musically very loud FF

musically very quiet PP

musician DRUMMER; FIDDLER; PIPER; PLAYER; SINGER; *see* COMPOSER

musician, leading CONDUCTOR

musicians BAND; COMBO; GROUP; ORC; ■ ORCHESTRA

musicians' go-slow LARGO

musicians, group of LSO; *see* MUSICIANS

musicians' union MU

musketeer ATHOS; SAM (from an old song)

Muslim SHIA; SUNNI

Muslim council ULEMA

Muslim judge CADI (Arabic)

Muslim leader IMAM; M; ■ SULTAN

Muslim state EMIRATE

Muslim student SOFTA

Muslim women HAREM

Mussolini DUCE; FASCIST

must MOULD

mustard, like KEEN

mutate ALTER; CHANGE anagram indicator

mutated anagram indicator

mutation can indicate that one letter is to be changed; anagram indicator

mute DUMB

muted P

mutineer REBEL; SILVER; ■ CHRISTIAN

mutiny, scene of NORE

mutt CUR; DOG; GOOSE

mutter DRONE; GROUSE; GRUMBLE

mutton, joint of SADDLE

muzzled MUTE; SILENT

my (my!) can indicate some exclamation e.g. CRUMBS, GOSH; HA; *see* EXPRESSION OF SURPRISE etc

my partner and I WE

my way TOME (i.e. to me)

My Word! WELL

myself I; ME

myself included I or ME to be nested within component(s)

mysterious DARK; anagram indicator

mysteriously anagram indicator

mystery POSER; PUZZLE; RIDDLE; anagram indicator

mystic symbol RUNE

myth FABLE; SAGA; STORY; TALE

mythical figure TITAN

Nn

Naaman LEPER

nab *see* CATCH

nabbed CAUGHT; PINCHED

nabbing nesting indicator

nag CARP; HACK; HORSE; MOAN; PESTER; SCOLD; ■ GETAT (i.e. get at); GRIPE; GRUMBLE; HARRY; TROUBLE; *see* HORSE

nagging anagram indicator

nail BRAD; CATCH; CLAW; CLOUT; HIT; PIN; SPIKE; TACK; ■ SPRIG

nail-biting TENSE

nail polish remover ACETONE (convenient for constructing ACT ONE)

naive GREEN; RAW; ■ ARTLESS

naked BARE; BUFF; NUDE; OPEN; RAW; ■ PATENT; STARKERS; STRIPPED

name CALL; CITE; DUB; N; NOUN; STAR; STYLE; TAG; TERM; TITLE; ■ HANDLE; QUOTE; *see* MAN, WOMAN, BOY, GIRL

name, add SIGN

name, another ALIAS

name, bad MUD

name-calling DUBBING; ■ BAPTISM

name, common SMITH

name-dropping N to be omitted

name, false ALIAS

name from Ireland RYAN

name, Latin NOMEN

name on, put SIGN

name, unpopular MUD

name, without ANON

named CITED; *see* NAME

named, also AKA

named alternatively AKA

nameless omission of N as "nameless individual" gives OE (i.e. "n" from "one")

namely SC

nan GRAN

nanny GOAT; NURSE; *see* GOAT

nap DOZE; DOWN; FLUFF; KIP; PILE; SLEEP; TIP; ■ SIESTA

nape SCRUFF

Napoleon PIG; ■ BONY; BONEY; CONSUL

narcissistic VAIN

Narcissus, like VAIN

narcotic DRUG; ■ DOWNER; UPPER

nark ANGER; GRASS; ■ ANNOY; NEEDLE; TELLER

narrative ACCOUNT; STORY; TALE; TELLING

narrow TAPER; THIN; TIGHT; ■ SLENDER

narrow escape SQUEAK

narrow part NECK

narrow passage ALLEY; GUT; *see* PASSAGE

narrowly-defined STRICT

nasal bone BRIDGE

nasal intonation TWANG

nasty BAD; EVIL; ICKY; ROTTEN; SEPTIC; ■ AWFUL; anagram indicator

nasty lady CAT

nasty smell BO

nasty waste CRUD

nation LAND; RACE; STATE; or, of course, can mean any country

national DAILY; NAT; PAPER; or can refer to any specific national, usually French, Irish, Scot

national emblem EAGLE; LEEK

national organisation NT

national representative BULL (i.e. John Bull)

nations UN

native LOCAL; SON; ■ NATURAL; can indicate a person or animal associated with a particular country, area or region; can indicate something to do with oysters

native American *see* AMERICAN INDIAN

native servant BEARER

natter CHATTER

natty *see* SMART

natural PURE; RAW; ■ NATIVE

natural light SUN

natural, not FLAT; SHARP (music)

nature KIND; SORT; TYPE; ■ CHARACTER; BENT; ESSENCE; DISPOSITION; can indicate a word ending in -NESS i.e. describing a quality; [◊ MOTHER]

naturist NUDE

naughtily anagram indicator

naughty BLUE; OFF; RACY; RUDE; anagram indicator

naughty child IMP

nauseous QUEASY

naval officer HOOD; MATE; PO; *see* ADMIRAL, CAPTAIN, OFFICER

naval officers POS

navigable OPEN

navigate SAIL; STEER

navigating around anagram indicator; nesting indicator

navigation system DECCA

navigational aid/equipment COMPASS; HELM; LORAN; RADAR; RUDDER; SEXTANT; SONOR; STAR

navigator DRAKE; PILOT

navy FLEET; N; RN

navy, part of FLEET

Nazi HESS

NCO CORP; CORPORAL; SM

ne'er-do-well IDLER; WASTER

near BY; CLOSE; LOCAL; MEAN; NIGH; ON; STINGY; TIGHT; ■ LOOMING; MISERLY

near, come LOOM

Near East BYE (i.e. BY + E); ■ LEVANT

near fellow MISER

near French PRES

near future OFFING

near, one that's MISER

nearby CLOSE; HANDY; LOCAL; NIGH

nearly ABOUT; ■ ALMOST; omission indicator, specifically for an associated word to be reduced, usually by one letter at the end, as "nearly correct" clues AMEN (i.e. last letter omitted from AMEND); or for a number to be reduced as "nearly all soccer team" clues TEN

nearly all AL (i.e. "all" minus last letter); MOST

nearly everyone AL; MOST

nearly new NE

neat BULL; COW; DEFT; OX; SMART (qv); TIDY; TRIM; ■ CATTLE (qv) STEER; STRAIGHT

neat, get it *see* NEATEN

neat, make *see* NEATEN

neaten ORDER; TIDY; TRIM

Nebraska NE

necessary MONEY; READY; run indicator

necessitate ENTAIL

necessity NEED

neck BRASS; DRINK; CHEEK; COL; GORGE; SCRAG; *see* AUDACITY; can refer to some aspect of romancing e.g. bill, coo, canoodle

neck, adornment RUFF

neck and neck EVEN

neck, back of NAPE

neck, pain in CRICK; *see* IRRITATION

neck-cloth *see* NECKWEAR

necklace RUFF; [◊ BEAD]

neckwear SCARF; TIE; ■ CRAVAT; MUFFLER; *see* NECKLACE

need CALL; LACK; MISS; WANT; ■ HAVE (as in "have to"); HUNGER; REQUIRE; with a homophone indicator (as in "need reportedly" i.e. knead) can indicate something to do with a masseur, masseuse

need for can indicate a word beginning with NOT, as "Exceptional

need for furniture" →
NOTABLE

need no can indicate a phrase incorporating WITHOUT

need to MUST

needed DUE; anagram indicator

needed, just what is IT

needing to be paid DUE

needle IRK; LEAF; NETTLE;
PIQUE; POINT; SEW; ■ NARK;
PEEVE; POINTER; RUFFLE;
see ANNOY; [◊ STITCH]

needle, use SEW

needles, use KNIT

needlework STITCH

needlework, do SEW; STITCH

needs making up anagram indicator

needs repair anagram indicator

needs to travel anagram of
NEEDS

needy POOR

ne'ertheless THO; *see*
NEVERTHELESS

negate DENY

negative NAY; NEG; NO; NOPE;
NOT; ■ ADVERSE

negative comment NAY; *see*
NEGATIVE

negative indicator NO

neglect FORGET; OMIT

neglect, state of LIMBO

neglected LEFT; omission indicator

negligent REMISS

negligible TINY

negotiate DEAL; TREAT

negotiated anagram indicator

negotiating anagram indicator

negotiation PARLEY; TALKS

neigh CRY; NICKER; WHINNY

neighbour ABUT

neighbourhood AREA; ZONE

neighbouring NEAR

Nell GWYN; can indicate something to do with oranges

Nelly DEAN

Nelson HOLD; HORATIO; [◊ COLUMN; HARDY]

neo-Nazis NF

nerd SAP; TWIT; WIMP

Nero can indicate something to do with fiddle, emperor, Rome, lyre

Nero's capital N; ROME

nerve BOTTLE; CHEEK; FACE;
LIP; NECK; STEEL; ■
DARING; GRIT; GUTS; SAUCE

nerve cell NEURON

nerve gas SARIN

nerveless BRAVE; DEAD;
INERT

nerves STRESS

nervous EDGY; JUMPY; SHY;
TENSE; WARY; WINDY; ■
AFLUTTER; TIMID;
TWITCHY; anagram indicator

nervous about, most IMIT (i.e.
rev. with last letter omitted)

nervous, be TWITCH

nervous disorder STRESS

nervous flutter TWITTER

nervous, make RATTLE

nervous reaction TIC

nervous state JITTERS

nervous symptom TIC; TWITCH

nervously anagram indicator

nervousness, show TWITCH

ness CAPE; HEAD

nest DEN; DRAY; HOME; LAIR

nested nesting indicator

★ **nesting** a device in which one
component is to be nested within
another for the solution. It can be
in the form of one component being
inserted into another e.g.
"Sweet little Daniel is in place of
baptism" → FONDANT (i.e.
FON-DAN-T); or one component
is required to go round another
e.g. "Support that is gathered by
prince" → PIER (i.e. P-IE-R)

net BAG; CATCH; EARN; LACE;
MESH; TRAP; TRAWL; WEB;
WIN; ■ CLEAR; ENTRAP;
SNARE; TOIL; TRAMMEL; [◊
FISH]

Net WEB

net advantage GOAL

nether LOWER

Netherlands NL

nett FINAL

nettle ANGER; IRK; NEEDLE; RILE; STING; TEASE; WEED; ■ STINGER; *see* ANNOY

network GRID; MAZE; TISSUE; WEB; ■ MESH; RETE (anat.)

network, complex GRID

neuralgia, cause of NERVE

neutral WIRE; ■ IMPARTIAL

Nevada NEV

Nevadan city RENO

never NARY; NEER

never-ending R; ■ FORAY (i.e. for ay); last letter to be omitted

never mind THERE

nevertheless BUT; EVEN; STILL; THO; YET; ■ EVENSO (i.e. even so)

new FRESH; MINT; N; NOVA; NOVEL; RAW; RECENT; ■ CHANGED; GREEN; HOT; MODERN; UPDATED; anagram indicator; can indicate that RE is to be placed before a word as a prefix

New Age anagram of AGE

new arrival BIRTH

new couple ITEM

new deal anagram of DEAL

new deal, in anagram indicator

new delivery anagram indicator

new design for an anagram to be made from the word(s) that follow(s)

new driver L

New England state CT; MASS; ME; NH; RI; VT

new form of anagram indicator

new from Germany NEU

new ground, break HARROW

new growth SHOOT

New Hampshire NH

new heading, under/with first letter to be changed

new idea INVENTION

new layout anagram indicator

new, no longer USED

new style NS; anagram indicator

New Testament (NT) book ACTS; EPH; COR; GAL; HEB; JAS; JOHN; JUDE; LUKE; MARK; PETER; PHIL; REV; ROM; TIM

New Year, before the DEC; INDEC (i.e. in Dec)

New Year's Day JANI

New York NY

New York area BRONX; QUEENS

Newcastle area NE

newly anagram indicator (thus "newly-rich" requires an anagram of RICH)

newly-arrived JUSTIN

newly-issued anagram indicator

newly-wed BRIDE; GROOM

news DOPE; GEN; GRIFF; WORD; ■ REPORT; STORY

news agency TASS

news broadcast anagram of NEWS

news channels MEDIA

news media PRESS

news time GENT

newsman ED

newsmen PRESS

newspaper DAILY; FT; ORGAN; RAG; SUN; TIMES; ■ NATIONAL; SHEET; SUNDAY; WEEKLY

newspaper article LEADER; ■ COPY; ITEM; PIECE

newspaper boss/chief ED

newspaper coverage PRESS

newspaper feature COLUMN

newspaper item CUTTING; REPORT

newspaper leader ED; N

newspaper, send to FILE

newspapermen PRESS

newspapers PRESS

newsworthy, something COPY

next THEN

next day MORROW

next in line SUCCESSOR

nexus LINK

nib POINT; TIP

nibble BROWSE; EAT; PICK

nibbled BIT; FED

nice FAIR; FINE; PLEASING; ■ PLEASANT

Nice can indicate something to do with the French resort or its locality e.g. Cote D' Azur; or can

255

indicate a French word is required as "Nice young lady?" → MADEMOISELLE

Nice way RUE
nicely WELL
niche BAY; RECESS
Nicholas NICK
nick CELL; COP; CUT; NAB; PINCH; ROB; STEAL; SWIPE; ■ ABSTRACT; COLLAR; NOTCH; PRISON; SCRUMP; SNAFFLE; STATION; *see* PRISON
nick, in good WELL
nicked nesting indicator
nickel NI
nicker NEIGH
nickname TAG
Nietzsche can indicate something to do with Superman
niff STINK; *see* SMELL, STENCH
Nigerian state OGUN
niggardly MEAN; NEAR
niggardly person MISER
nigh CLOSE; NEAR
night BLACK; DARK; EVE; LATE
night, at LATE
night before EVE
night-bird OWL
night flier/flyer BAT; MOTH; OWL
night in Calais, France etc NUIT
night jar PO
night spot CLUB; STAR
nightclub DISCO; DIVE
nightlight MOON; STAR
nightwatchman can indicate something to do with batting in cricket
nil *see* NOTHING
nimble AGILE; DEFT; SPRY; ■ LITHE
nimble-fingered DEFT
nimbus HALO
nincompoop ASS; DOLT; NINNY; TWIT; *see* FOOL
nine IX
nine players NONET
Nineteen-eighty-four (1984), character from SMITH

1960's teenager MOD
ninety XC
ninety-nine IC
90 Romans XC
nip BITE; DASH; DRAM; HOP (as in hop over); PINCH; POP; RUN; SHOT SNAP; SPLASH; TOT; ■ CATCH; TASTE
nipped BIT; BITTEN; RAN; ■ CAUGHT
nipper BITER; CLAW; CRAB; FANG; TOOTH; *see* CHILD, TOOTH
nippers PLIERS; TEETH; *see* CHILD, CHILDREN, TOOTH
nippy COLD; FAST; SHARP
nippy type BITER; RACER
no NAY; O (i.e. zero); with an initial capital can indicate PLAY, DRAMA, etc (i.e. Japanese theatre); can indicate a word ending in -LESS; can indicate a phrase ending in OFF, as "No end to warning" → TIP OFF
no admission NO to be nested
no approval NOOK
no back chat OKAY (i.e. rev. of yak-O)
no backing ON; a word to end in NO
no backtracking ON; YAN (i.e. reversal of "nay")
no bid PASS (cards)
no charge FREE; ■ GRATIS
no doubt SURE
no end of last letter of following word to be omitted
no future, one with no GONER
no good NG; G to be eliminated from indicated word; anagram indicator
no-good CAD; HEEL; ROGUE; ROTTER; *see* NO GOOD
no handicap SCRATCH
no-hoper JERK; LOSER
no leader first letter to be dropped from indicated word
no leaders either first two or three letters to be dropped from the indicated word or the first letter to be dropped from each of several words

no longer DEAD; EX; FORMER; OLD; ONCE; PAST

no longer available OVER

no longer fresh AGED; OFF; OLD; STALE

no longer in fashion OUT; PASSE

no longer keen OFF

no longer performing well STALE

no longer kept OFF

no longer young AGED; OLD

no lover of can indicate a noun ending in -PHOBE

no matter which ANY

no mistake ON

no more ENOUGH; LESS

no more than ONLY

no-one NOI (i.e. No.1)

no-one backed/backing ION

no opening NO to be at the beginning; first letter to be omitted

no Parisian NON

no parking P to be omitted

no place NP

no points NOSE (i.e. no SE)

no problem SURE

no return, point of ACE

no right NOR; usually indicates R is to be omitted

no, say DENY

no score LOVE; NIL; O; OO

no special ANY

No. 10 see NUMBER 10

no topping on first letter of target word to be omitted

no trump/s NT

no two ways about it SNOW (i.e. S-no-W)

no variety can indicate a phrase starting with ALL

no way NOST (i.e. "no St"); OST (i.e. zero ST); can indicate that a component meaning "way" (e.g. AVE, RD, ST) is to be omitted

Noah* BOATMAN; [◊ ARK]

Noah's son HAM

Noah's vessel ARK

nob HEAD; SWELL; TOFF; VIP

nobble BRIBE

nobbled, nobbling anagram indicator

nobility LORDS; PEERS

nobility, foreign COUNT

noble BARON; COUNT; DUC; DUKE; EARL; GRAND; HIGH; LOFTY; LORD; PEER; THANE; TITLED

noble, not BASE

noble said LAUD

nobleman see NOBLE

nobleman from France DUC

noblewoman DAME; LADY; ■ CONTESSA; COUNTESS

nobody NONE; NOONE (i.e. no-one)

nobody heard NUN

nocturnal NIGHT

nocturnal mammal BAT

nodding SLEEPY

noddle HEAD

nodule LUMP; SWELLING

nog PEG

noise BANG; BOOM; CLINK; COO; DIN; HUM; RACKET; ROAR; ROW; SOUND; ■ BRUIT; CACKLE; CLANG; DING; RATTLE; REPORT; TING

noise, animal BARK; BLEAT; MEW; PURR; ROAR; WHINNY

noise from motorist HOOT; TOOT

noise, harsh BRAY

noise, lots of DIN

noise, loud BOOM; THUNDER

noise, low RUMBLE

noise, metallic CLANG

noise, noisy homophone indicator

noise of gunfire BANG; REPORT

noise, weary SIGH

noiseless DUMB; MUTE

noises, horrible DIN; RACKET

noises off anagram of NOISES

noisily homophone indicator

noisily finished OVA

noisy F; FF; LOUD; VOCAL; homophone indicator as "noisy boys" → GUISE

noisy bird STARLING

noisy scene CIRCUS

nomad KURD; ROVER
nominal TOKEN
nominate NAME
nominated MADE
non- NOT; can indicate that the word (or its abbreviation) to which it is hyphenated is to be omitted as "non-Eastern" signals the omission of E
non-amateur PRO
non-British omission of B or BR
non-cleric LAIC
non-clerical LAY
non-Communist countries WEST
non-coms OR; *see* NCO
non-conformist REBEL
non-consonant VOWEL
non-ecclesiastical LAY
non-edited anagram of NON
non-ersatz REAL
non-European omission of E
non-factual account FICTION
non-Jew GOY; ■ GENTILE
non-member GUEST
non-professional LAY
non-ruling OUT
non-speaking DUMB; MUTE
non-specialised GENERAL
non-specialist GENERAL
non-starter first letter(s) to be omitted
non-striker SCAB; ■ BLACKLEG
non-U OFF; OUT; U to be omitted
nonconformist REBEL
nondescript GREY
nondescript colour NEUTRAL
none LOVE; NIL; NOUGHT; O; ZERO
none the less *see* NONETHELESS
none too bright DIM (qv)
nonentity CIPHER
nonplus BEWILDER
nonsense BOSH; BULL; BUNK; COD; PAP; RATS; ROT; STUFF; TRIPE; ■ BILGE; FLANNEL; FUDGE; GUFF; TOSH; TUSH; anagram indicator; *see* RUBBISH, JUNK

nonetheless omit O from indicated word
noodle HEAD; IDLE; LOAF; MUG; PASTA
nook CORNER
noon N; ■ AMEND (i.e. "a.m. end"); TWELVE
noon, about two hours before TEN to be nested within a component
noon, at AMEND (i.e. am end)
noon, before AM; a component to be placed ahead of N
noose LINE; LOOP; ROPE; TRAP
Nordic verses EDDA
Norfolk can signify something to do with The Broads
Norfolk town DISS
norm MEAN; NORM; PAR; STANDARD
normal PAR; RIGHT; ■ GENERAL; STANDARD; USUAL
Norman can refer to something to do with the Conquest e.g. WILLIAM
Normandy town CAEN
Norse poems/story EDDA
North N; initial letter indicator (as "the northern" clues T); reversal indicator; ■ ARCTIC
North African MOOR; RIFF
North American NA; *see* AMERICAN, AMERICAN INDIAN
north and south, going when in a Down clue can indicate the answer is a palindrome
North, Northern N; initial letter indicator; reversal indicator
North of Paris NORD
North of the Border, one ANE; SCOT
North Sea, part of WASH
Northern LAPP; *see* NORTH
northern bank BRAE
Northern European LETT
northern hillside BRAE
Northern holiday WAKE
Northern Ireland NI; ULSTER; ■ PROVINCE
northern region ARCTIC

northerner LAPP; SCOT; ■ INUIT; SCOUSE

Northumberland area NE

northwards UP

Norwich can signify something to do with The Broads

Norwich town DISS

nose FRONT; BEAK; PRY; SNOUT; ■ DETECT; FEATURE; HOOTER; MEDDLE; SNOOP

nose, part of BRIDGE

nosegay POSY; SPRAY

nosey NASAL

nosing EDGE; [◊ SILL; STAIR; STEP]

nostalgic for, be MISS

nosy, be PRY

nosy parker PRIER

nosy parker, heard PRIOR

nosy, was/were PRIED

not NARY; NON; NOR; NT; ■ NE (arch.); omission indicator (usually the following word or its synonym); when followed by a gerund (e.g. skating) can signal OFF (for example to yield OFFICE i.e. "off ice"); can indicate solution ends in -LESS; can indicate a word beginning with UN as "not encountered" clues UNMET

not a O

not a lot BIT

not above BELOW; UNDER

not active RESTING; ■ DORMANT; INERT

not all PART; SOME; run indicator

not allow BAN; BAR

not allowed BANNED; OUT

not altogether PARTIAL; one or two letters to be omitted (usually the last), as in "Murderer falls? Not altogether" → CASCA (i.e. "cascade" minus its last two letters)

not, and NOR

not applicable NA

not as can indicate an adjective ending in LESS or ER

not at all NEVER

not at home AWAY; OUT

not at work AWAY; OFF

not available OFF

not back TON

not bad DECENT; FINE; GOOD; OK; anagram of NOT

not badly placed FINE; OK

not begun first letter to be omitted

not being served OFF

not bound FREE; LOOSE

not certain MAY

not charged FREE

not circulated TON

not closing last letter to be omitted

not concerned omission of RE

not connected APART; OFF

not crazy SANE

not deep PALE; SHALLOW

not done RAW

not drinking DRY; TT

not eat/eating FAST

not elected OUT; IN to be omitted from a word

not empty NT

not enough SHORT; UNDER; can require TOO followed by an adjective as "Not enough left" can call for TOO RIGHT

not entirely SEMI; ■ PARTIAL; omission indicator, particularly indicating that an incomplete word is to be used as "not entirely honest" → PUR (i.e. last letter of "pure" omitted); run indicator

not even ODD; ROUGH

not everybody SOME

not evident at first initial letter to be omitted

not exactly anagram indicator

not exalted BASE; LOW

not expressed COVERT; INNER; SECRET

not far CLOSE; NEAR; NIGH

not fashionable OUT; PASSE

not fat LEAN; THIN

not favouring ANTI; CON

not feeling NUMB

not finished last letter to be omitted

not fit UNABLE; *see* ILL

not following omission indicator, usually in conjunction with some other indicator pinpointing what element is to be omitted (as "Roman man not following" → RO)

not for ANTI; CON

not functioning *see* NOT WORKING

not get MISS

not going STILL

not good BAD; ILL; G to be omitted

not gross NET

not half only half of word to be used

not hard EASY; SIMPLE; SOFT; can signal the omission of H from the indicated word

not hard-hearted can signal the omission of H from the centre of a word

not healthy AILING; ILL; PEAKY

not heartless NT

not hitched can indicate a bachelor or spinster; can indicate the same in a foreign country as "This girl's not hitched in Italy" → SIGNORINA

not hot COLD (qv); H to be omitted

not in AWAY; OUT; IN to be omitted

not in fashion OUT; PASSE

not in favour ANTI; OUT; can indicate that FOR or PRO should be omitted from a word

not in favour of AGIN; AVERSE

not initially identified first letter to be omitted

not interested BORED

not interested, we're told BOARD

not keen LOTH

not known NK

not listened to KNOT

not making moves INERT; STILL

not many FEW

not missed can refer to a woman and her marital status

not mistaken RIGHT

not much LITTLE; SLIGHT; SMALL; SOME; TRIFLE; ■ MEAGRE

not much to spend P; SOU

not named ANON

not new OLD; USED; N to be omitted

not nice FOUL

not noble BASE

not notice MISS

not now LATER; THEN

not occupied FREE

not occurring OFF

not old NE (arch.); ■ YOUNG; *see* MODERN, NEW

not on OFF; ON to be omitted

not one PAIR; TWO

not opening can indicate the omission of first letter

not ordinary SPECIAL (qv)

not out ALIGHT; IN; LIT

not outstanding LOW

not over/overly TON

not paid HON (i.e. honorary)

not paid for OWED; OWING

not plentiful LEAN; SCARCE

not popular IN to be omitted

not prepared GREEN; RAW; anag. of NOT

not prepared to listen DEAF

not present NOW or HERE to be omitted from a word; ■ ABSENT

not preserving anagram indicator; omission indicator

not pretty PLAIN

not previously used GREEN; NEW; STRANGE; VIRGIN

not pro ANTI

not properly ILL

not qualified UTTER; *see* UNQUALIFIED

not quite ALMOST; NEARLY; anagram indicator; letter sequence to be cut short, usually by one letter

not quite finished the last letter to be omitted from a synonym of "finished" e.g. GONE, OVER, hence GON, OVE etc

not real SHAM; *see* FAKE

not reasonable STEEP

not recorded LIVE
not reported KNOT
not required OVER; SPARE
not returned TON
not right AMISS; BAD; EVIL; ■ OUT; WRONG; anagram indicator; can indicate that R is to be omitted from associated word; can indicate that the right half of a word is to be omitted
not serious FLIP
not settled DUE; OWED; OWING
not so NAY; NO; ■ FALSE; WRONG; SO to be omitted
not so bad BETTER
not so many LESS
not so much LESS
not standing LYING
not started first letter to be omitted
not stiff LIMP
not stopping last letter to be omitted
not straying RIGHT
not that much LESS
not the can refer to the opposite of the word that follows, as "not the worst" can cue BEST; or can refer to something which is close but not the same, as "Not the final temperature" cues HEAT i.e. a heat of a sports event is not the final
not to begin indicates omission of first letter
not to worry anagram of NOT
not-too-near future OFFING
not unknown COMMON; X or Y to be omitted
not up TON; UP to be omitted; *see* DOWN
not up to BELOW; UNDER
not used anymore EX
not very V to be omitted
not very good can indicate that a synonym for "very good" (e.g. PI) is to be omitted; *see* POOR
not vulgar PURE
not wanting AGAINST; OFF
not well AILING; ILL
not well done RARE
not wild TAME

not willing AVERSE; LOTH; can indicate something to do with being intestate
not winning DRAW; LOSING
not without heart NT
not working DOWN; FREE; IDLE; OFF; OUT; ■ AVAILABLE
not worth considering OUT
not worthy of consideration TRIFLING
not written on BLANK
not yet LATER
notable BIG; STAR
notable, nothing SILENT
notation SIGN
notch CUT; MARK; NICK; SCORE
note A; B; BILL; C; CHIT; D; DO; DOH; E; F; FAH; FAME; FIVER; FLAT; G; HEED; IOU; LAH; LINE; LOG; ME; MEMO; MI; MINIM; N; PS; RAY; RE; SEE; SHARP; SO; SOH; SOL; TE; TI; TONE; ■ BREVE; EMINENCE; LETTER; NATURAL; QUAVER; RECORD; SOUND; TENNER; TONIC; WRITE; can indicate something to do with music; can indicate something to do with money
note added PS; can indicate a synonym for "note" (*see* NOTE) is to be included
note, brief MEMO
note, make a (quick) JOT
notebook PAD
note free omission of a synonym for note (usually A-G or N); *see* NOTE
noted SAW; can indicate something to do with music, song etc.; can indicate that a note be placed before a component as "noted member" → ELEG
noted, he usually calls for the name of a composer
notedly can indicate something to do with music, song etc
notepad JOTTER

notepaper can indicate something to do with musical score or scoring

notes ROLL; WAD; ■ can indicate some combination of components listed under NOTE (for instance ME + RE to give MERE); this is also common shorthand for a piece of music so it can indicate some general word (such as air, tune, march, sonata, symphony) or it can require the title of a specific piece of music; *see* SONG, TUNE

notes from bird TRILL

notes, group of CHORD; *see* NOTE

notes, make PLAY; SING; ■ LOG; RECORD; WRITE

notes, producer of *see* MUSICAL INSTRUMENT

notes, successive AB; DE; DEF

notes, supply SING

noteworthy SIGNAL

nothing BLANK; LOVE; NIL; O; ■ NIX; NONE; NOUGHT; NOUT; NULL; ZERO; ZILCH; ; can indicate a phrase starting with ALL followed by the opposite, as "OK, nothing left" → ALL RIGHT; [◊ FREE]

nothing but JUST; PURE

nothing ensues/follows O to be added to end

nothing figuratively ROUND

nothing, for FREE

nothing for the French RIEN

nothing good OG

nothing, having EMPTY; O to be inserted into, or attached to, a component; can indicate that the answer is an adjective ending in -LESS (e.g. penniless)

nothing in America ZIP

nothing in French RIEN

nothing in return, getting LIN (i.e. rev.)

nothing left OL; RIGHT; can indicate that O (or synonym e.g. NIL) is to be omitted

nothing less O (or other synonym e.g. NIL) to be omitted

nothing more O (or other synonym e.g. NIL) to be added, usually at the end

nothing more than MERE

nothing on OON (i.e. O on); *see* NUDE

nothing on, having/with NUDE; O to be added to the beginning or end; *see* NUDE

nothing other than SHEER

nothing, person saying CLAM

nothing put away O to be omitted

nothing, say SH

nothing, showing DEAD

nothing's gained O to be included

nothing's left/missed/omitted can indicate that O (or synonym e.g. NIL) is to be omitted

nothing visible O to be nested

notice AD; MARK; SEE; SIGN; SPOT; SPY; ■ BOARD; CIRCULAR; HEED; MIND; NOTE; OBSERVE; POSTER; REMARK; REVIEW

notice, take HEED; OBSERVE; *see* NOTICE

noticed SAW

noticed in nesting indicator; run indicator

notify TELL

notion FANCY; IDEA; INKLING; THOUGHT

notion, vague CLUE; INKLING

notorious ARRANT

notwithstanding STILL; THOUGH

nourish FEED; FOSTER

nourishment FOOD (qv)

nourishment, take EAT

nourishment, took ATE

nous BRAINS; WIT (qv)

nova anagram indicator

Nova Scotia NS

novel NEW; ■ FRESH; RECENT; ROMAN; anagram indicator; can indicate some short titled novel commonly EMMA, KIM, SHE, SCOOP, TRILBY

novel, French ROMAN

novelist BATES; HOPE; MANNE; READE; SNOW; STERNE; WELLS; WOOLF; ■ COOPER;

DRABBLE; FORSTER; GREENE; JAMES; KAFKA; WAUGH

novelty CHANGE; FAD; anagram indicator

November, fifth of M

novice L; LAY; TIRO; TYRO; ■ AMATEUR; [◊ GREEN; RAW]

now AD; HERE; PRESENT

now, before ALREADY

now expected DUE

now expected to go first solution to begin with DUE

now (then) NONCE

nowadays AD

NT *see* NEW TESTAMENT

nuance SHADE

nub GIST; MEAT; POINT

nude BARE; BUFF; NAKED

nude, appear in the/appearance in the STREAK

nudge POKE; PROD; PUSH; ■ PROMPT; REMIND

nuisance BIND; BORE; BOTHER; BRAT; IMP; ORDEAL; PAIN; PEST; PILL; ■ MENACE; SCOURGE; TRIAL

numb DEAD

number AIR; C; COUNT; D; EDITION; I; ISSUE; K; L; M; N; NO; PI; PIECE; PRIME; RANGE; SONG; SUM; TUNE; V; X; ■ DIGIT; FIGURE; INSTRUMENTAL; followed by an actual number can indicate a chemical element as "number 77" clues IRIDIUM; *see* SONG; can of course indicate the use of any arithmetic number but the following are commonly used as components: ONE, SEVEN, EIGHT, TEN; plus this is an old crossword warhorse, based on the fact that the unwary solver will overlook the secondary meaning of the word with a silent 'b', indicating a specific painkiller or anaesthetic e.g. ETHER

number, any N

number, large C; D; K; M; MANY; RAFT; SLEW; ■

CROWD; MASS; SCORES; STREW; *see* CROWD, MASS

number losing height TREE

number of Germans LIED (i.e. German for "song")

number of people killed TOLL

number of performances RUN

number of suits FOUR

number of varieties RANGE

number one SELF

number shot BAG

Number 10 can denote something to do with prime minister; can denote something to do with a bus

number, unknown X; Y; Z

number, unspecified SOME

numbers NOS (i.e. no's)

numerous MANY

numskull DORK; FOOL (qv)

nun SISTER

nunnery CONVENT

nuns ORDER

nun, short SIS

nurse EN; REAR; SEN; SISTER; SRN; TEND; ■ ANGEL; AYAH; CARER; DRESS; HARBOUR; NANNY; RGN; SUCKLE; TENDER; [◊ WARD]

nurse, trained anagram of NURSE

nursemaid ALICE

nursery CRECHE; can indicate something to do with plant-growing, skiing (e.g. ski-slopes) as well as children; [◊ CHILD]

nursing CARE; nesting indicator

nursing home SAN

nurture REAR

nut ASS; BEAN; BUFF; CASE; COB; CRANK; FAN; HAZEL; HEAD; LOAF; SNAP

nutcracker anagram of NUT

nuts BARMY; MAD; POTTY; ■ CRACKERS; CUCKOO; ZANY; anagram indicator

nymph ECHO; OREAD

Oo

O'Hara's boy KIM
oaf FOOL (qv); LOUT
oak HOLM
Oaks CLASSIC; RACE
oar BLADE; ROW; STROKE; SWEEP
oar, long SWEEP
oar, manoeuvre FEATHER; ROW
oarsman BOW; ROWER; STROKE
oarsmen EIGHT
oast OVEN
oath CURSE; EGAD; GAD; PLEDGE; VOW; WORD
oath, ancient EGAD; ODS
oatmeal BROSE
oats FOOD
obedient GOOD
obeisance, make/show BOW; KNEEL
obese FAT
obesity FAT
object AIM; DEMUR; END; IT; MIND; RESENT; THING; ■ ARTICLE; CAVIL; GOAL; INTENT; PROTEST
object of devotion GOD; IDOL
object to MIND; RESENT
objecting to ANTI
objection BUT; DEMUR; OB; ■ CAVIL; PROTEST
objection raised TUB
objectionable, find RESENT
objections raised STUB
objective AIM; CASE; END; GOAL
objector ANTI; CON
obligation DEBT; DUTY; TIE
obligation, had an MUST; OWED
obligation to pay IOU; OWING; ■ DEBT
obligation to pay, have OWE
obligatory BINDING
oblige FORCE

obliged BOUND; MADE
obliged, be OWE
obliged, is MUST
obliged, was HAD
obliging EASY
obliging person, type ANGEL
oblique ASKEW; INDIRECT; anagram indicator; [◊ SKEW]
obliquely ASKEW; anagram indicator
obliquely, move SKEW
obliterate ERASE
obscene BLUE; RUDE; ■ INSULTING; LEWD
obscene matter/pictures/publication PORN; SMUT
obscenity OATH; SMUT
obscenities SMUT
obscure BEFOG; BLEAR; BLUR; CLOUD; DIM; FOG; HIDE; MIST; ODD; SMOKE; ■ SHADOW; anagram indicator; also can indicate that one element in the clue is to replace another
obscuring omission indicator as "obscuring what's above" calls for the omission of a first letter
obscurity anagram indicator
obsequious OILY; SMARMY
obsequious, be FAWN
observable OPEN; OVERT; PLAIN
observant SHARP
observation SIGHT; ■ COMMENT; SIGHTING
observe BEHOLD; EYE; HEED; KEEP; LOOK; MARK; NOTE; SEE; SPOT; WATCH; ■ CELEBRATE; NOTICE; STARE
observed SAW; SEEN
observer EYE; SEER; ■ STARER
obsession BUG; MANIA; THING
obstacle BAR; BARRIER; BLOCK; HITCH; LET; SNAG; WALL
obstinate DOUR
obstinate fellow MULE
obstreperous anagram indicator
obstruct BAR; BLOCK; STALL; STOP; ■ HINDER
obstruction BAR; LET; STOP

obtain EXIST; GAIN; GET; HAVE; LAND; STAND ■ ACQUIRE; PREVAIL; SECURE

obtain by threat EXTORT

obtainable from anagram indicator; run indicator

obtained GOT

obtuse can indicate something to do with an angle

obviate AVOID

obvious CLEAR; OPEN; OVERT; PLAIN; ■ MANIFEST; PATENT

occasion DATE; DAY; DO; EVENT; NOW; PARTY; REASON; ROOM; THEN; TIME; ■ CHANCE; ENTAIL; INDUCE; NEED

occasion, have NEED

occasion, on one ONCE

occasional ODD

occidental W

occupant INMATE

occupant of seat MP

occupation LINE; TRADE; ■ CAREER; run indicator

occupational therapist, therapy OT

occupied FULL; nesting indicator

occupied, be WORK

occupied by nesting indicator

occupied with AT

occupies FILLS; ISIN (i.e. is in); see OCCUPY

occupies, one who TENANT

occupy DWELL; FILL; SQUAT; nesting indicator

occupy, illegally SQUAT

occupying nesting indicator

occur ARE; FALL; ■ HAPPEN

occurred CAME

occurrence EVENT

occurring in nesting indicator; run indicator

occurs IS

ocean DEEP; MAIN; SEA (qv); ■ ARCTIC

ocean-going vessel accommodates a component to be nested within SS

octet from Germany ACHT

oculus EYE

odd DROLL; LEFT; RUM; STRANGE; ■ ATYPICAL; CURIOUS; QUEER; UNTYPICAL; anagram indicator

odd assortment DOD

odd bits see ODD CHARACTERS

odd characters can signal that only the odd-numbered letters in an indicated sequence are be used e.g. "odd bits of iron traps" clues IOTAS

odd couple anagram of COUPLE

odd parts of see ODD CHARACTERS

odd person see ODDBALL

odd-shaped anagram of ODD

odd type of see ODD CHARACTERS

oddball CARD; CRANK; WEIRDO; anagram indicator

oddity anagram indicator

oddly anagram indicator; indicator for odd numbered letters to be used as "croft oddly" clues COT

oddly disqualified/neglected odd-numbered letters in indicated word/s to be omitted

oddly reduced see ODD CHARACTERS

oddment SCRAP

odds EVENS; PRICE; SP; can indicate the odd numbered letters (as "Wild play, ignoring the odds? In vain" → IDLY)

odds and ends ORT; TRUCK (Sc. and U.S.)

odds to fall SPRAIN (i.e. SP + rain)

Odin, son of BALDER

odium HATE

odour BO; HUM; SMELL

of RE; can indicate a run in what follow (as "perpetual sound of a screech owl" → ECHO)

of course SURE; NATCH; can indicate something to do with food e.g. menu

of French DE; DU

of note OFF (i.e. of F)

of rising FO

of us OUR

off AWAY; BAD; DOWN; GONE; HIGH; OUT; START; SOUR; ■ LEAVING; NOTON (i.e. not on); RANCID; anagram indicator; omission indicator; can indicate a word beginning with LACK (as "24 hours off" → LACKADAY)

off colour ILL; PALE; SEEDY; SICK; ■ PASTY

off course ADRIFT; ASTRAY; ERRING; anagram indicator

off course, to be DRIFT; ERR; STRAY

off-day anagram of DAY

off duty FREE; ■ TAX-FREE

off-form anagram indicator

off, is GOES; LEAVES; ■ DEPARTS; PONGS; REEKS; WHIFFS see SMELL

off-key FLAT

off-limits OUT

off, opposite LEG

off-peak can indicate something to do with activity on mountain e.g. yodelling

off-piste anagram of PISTE

off-putting anagram indicator; can refer to delay, defer, later, etc

off target MISS; OUT; see WRONG; anagram indicator

off the ground UP

off the rails anagram indicator

off-track anagram indicator

off-white CREAM

offal LIVER; TRIPE

offence ARSON; CRIME; HUFF; SIN; SLIGHT; ■ ABUSE; FAULT

offence, give MIFF; SLIGHT

offence, take RESENT

offend HURT; INSULT; SIN; STING

offender SINNER

offensive BLUE; PUSH; RUDE; ■ ATTACK; can indicate something to do with military attack

offensive, one favouring HAWK

offer BID; EXTEND; PRESENT; SALE; SELL; TENDER; TRY; ■ PROPOSE; anagram indicator

offer bait LURE; ■ TEMPT

offer free TREAT

offer, make an TENDER

offer period SALE

offered BID; GAVE

offering GIFT; PRESENT; ■ COLLECTION

offertory ALMS

office BRANCH; DUTY; POST; ROOM; SERVICE; SEXT; ■ AGENCY; CENTRE; POSITION

office, at the IN

office, bishop's SEE

office block, feature of LIFT

office building BLOCK

office, give up RESIGN

office, in SITTING

office worker FILER; SEC; TEMP; ■ CLERK

officer AIDE; ALT; BRIG; CAP; CAPT; CO; COL; COP; DI; GEN; LT; MAJOR; MATE; NCO; OC; PO; SUPER; SM; ■ BOSN; BOSUN; CORNET; ENSIGN; GENERAL; JAILER; MARSHAL; PURSER

officer* PETTY

officer commanding OC

officer, platoon LT

officers COS; DIS; POS

Officers' Training Corps OTC

official AGA; ELDER; OFF; REF; USHER; ■ CLERK; CONSUL; DIPLOMAT; FORMAL; REEVE

officials BRASS

offpeak can indicate something to do with activity on mountain e.g. yodelling

offset anagram of SET

offshoot BRANCH; SUCKER

offspring BROOD; ISSUE; LITTER; SEED; SON(S); SPAWN

offtrack anagram indicator

often MUCH

Ogden NASH

ogle LEER; STARE

ogre GIANT

oh MY; ■ EXCLAMATION

oh dear see OH DEAR!

Oh dear! ALAS; MY; OOPS; WELL

Oh, you've heard! homophone indicator for "Oh" i.e. its sound, so a component such as EAU, O, OUGH (as in "dough") or OW is required

Ohio O

oik *see* LOUT, YOB

oil CASTOR; CRUDE; DERV; EASE; ESTER; ■ ATTAR; OTTAR; VIRGIN; can signal something to do with painting as "Oil off the coast" → SEASCAPE

oil container SUMP

oil, essential ATTAR; OTTO

oil mess SLICK; ■ GREASY

oil product TAR

oil reservoir SUMP

oil, source of GUSHER; WELL; can indicate some kind of nut or seed

oil spill anagram of OIL

oilman RIGGER

oily SLICK

oily manner UNCTION

oink GRUNT

ointment BALM; SALVE; UNCTION

OK, okay ALLOW; FAIR; FINE; GOOD; KOSHER; RIGHT; SWELL; TICK; WELL

OK, show TICK

Oklahoma OK

old AGED; ARCH; AGED; DATED; EX; FORMER; GREY; LATE; O; OVER; PAST; RUSTY; STALE; USED; ■ AULD; PASSE; YORE; can indicate something historical (example: "old chucker" clueing BALLISTA); [◊ AGE]

'old AVE

old, a bit DATED

old agreement YEA

old American OUS

old, anything but MINT

old article YE

old Austrian ALT

old bird DODO

old boat ARK

Old Bob S

old boy OB; OLAD

old boys MEN

old chap COVE

old city TROY; UR

old copper D

old counsel REDE

old craft ARGO

old days PAST

old dodderers anagram of OLD

Old English OE

Old English, in a component to be nested within OE

old-fashioned CORNY; DATED; OUT; PASSE; TRAD; SQUARE; STEAM; ■ QUAINT; anagram using the letters OLD

old-fashioned denial NAY

old-fashioned entertainment CORN

old-fashioned individual/type FOG(E)Y; SQUARE

old-fashioned way WISE

Old Father usually refers to the Thames

old fighter VET

old flame EX

old German ALT

old, grow AGE

Old Harry DEVIL; NICK

old hat SQUARE; *see* OLD-FASHIONED

old Iranian MEDE

old item RELIC

old jokes CORN

Old King COLE

old lady GRAN; MUM

old letter RUNE

old lover EX

old maid PRUDE

old man PA; POP; ■ BUFFER; CODGER; HUBBY; *see* FATHER

old man's PAS

old money D; LSD; S

old partner EX

old people AGED; ELDERS; OAPS; can refer to a race or tribe from historical times (e.g. Iceni, Angles)

old person ANGLE; OAP

old ring OO

old ring binding component to be nested within OO

old Scottish AULD

old soldier VET

old sovereign GR

old-style REPRO

Old Testament OT

Old Testament book DAN; DEUT; EXOD; EZ; GEN; HAB; HAG; HOS; IS; JER; JO; JOB; JOSH; KINGS; LAM; LEV; MAL; MIC; NUMB; OBAD; PROV; PS; RUTH; SAM; ZEPH

Old Testament character LOT

old, the YE

old, that YON

old-time ONCE

old timer apart from an old person can refer to a grandfather clock, hourglass etc

old times BC; PAST; ■ HISTORY

old vehicle CRATE

old wife EX

old woman CRONE; GRAN; HAG; MA; *see* MOTHER

old, you THEE; THOU; YE

older SENIOR

oldest, the YE

olive [◊ STONE]

Oliver HARDY; REED; TWIST; can signify something to do with the musical Oliver or the novel *Oliver Twist*; or can indicate something to do with Cromwell, Goldsmith

Oliver's friend STAN

Olivier ACTOR; LARRY

olla podrida STEW (Sp.)

Olympian can indicate a Greek god e.g. HERA

'ome OUSE

omen SIGN

omen, be an BODE

ominous BAD; DIRE; EVIL

omission ERROR; LACK

★ **omission** most cryptic puzzles will contain more than one example where you are required to omit a component from a word. You may be required to omit (i) the first letter, say to turn CRAVE into RAVE; (ii) the last letter, say to turn BRAND into BRAN; (iii) the first and last letters, say to turn SPINS into PIN; (iv) the middle letter, say to turn PAINT into PANT, and so on. Each manipulation will be signaled by an indicator. Common examples of the above in turn: (i) 'headless, 'topless; (ii) 'detailed', 'endless'; (iii) 'trimmed', 'topped-and-tailed'; (iv) 'heartless'

omit CUT; DROP; ELIDE; FAIL; MISS; SCRATCH; SKIP; omission indicator

omitted CUT; OUT; SKIPPED; omission indicator; can indicator a word or phrase beginning with NO

omitted, with filling the middle letter(s) from a word to be omitted

omnibus COACH

omnivore COATI

on AT; LEG (i.e. cricket); OVER; RE; ■ ABOARD; ABOUT; AHEAD (as in "get on"); ASTRIDE; ordering indicator (the component preceding ON to be directly followed by the next component, as "sent on course" clues HIGHWAY); nesting indicator (for example: "Excessive footprint on earth" calls for E to be nested to provide STEEP); note that, although innocently placed in the clue, ON itself can be part of the answer

on all sides ROUND

on behalf of FOR

on behalf of king FORK

on being engaged ON to be nested

on board nesting indicator; commonly an element to be nested between S and S (i.e. Steamship); can refer to chess, pieces etc

on boat ABOARD

on edge TENSE

on hand CLOSE; NEAR

on high ALOFT; OVER; UP

on holiday AWAY; OFF

on no account NEVER

on one's own LONE; SOLE; SOLO

on reflection reversal indicator

on-screen display can indicate something to do with car parking (and ticket on windscreen)

on show OUT

on that account THEREAT

on the go DOING

on the loose FREE; anagram indicator

on the move AFOOT; anagram indicator

on the rocks AGROUND

on the side WITH

on the spot HERE; THERE

on the way back can indicate a component is to precede TS, DR, etc, *see* WAY BACK

on top of ABOVE; OVER; preceding indicator

on top of everything TOO

on tour ROVING; anagram indicator; can indicate something to do with nomads

once EX; FORMER; ■ AFORE (arch.); can signal the use of an archaism, *see* ONCE KNOWN for an example

once again RE; can indicate a verb beginning with RE

once knew/known WIST

once more AGAIN; can call for a verb beginning with RE

once very SORE

one A; ACE; AN; ANE (Scots); EACH; I; SINGLE; SOLE; SOLO; UNIT; UNITY; when accompanied by a colloquialism indicator (commonly, in speech, when talking etc) can signify UN

one adding COUNTER

one and all EACH

one after another two synonyms for "one" juxtaposed, so AI, ANI, IA, IAN, II

one arrested I to nested within a component; *see* PRISONER

one aspiring HOPER

one bit of first letter of word that follows

one born in NATIVE; or can require a specific nationality

one bound SERF

one by one II; ■ ELEVEN

one casual UN (i.e. 'un, slang)

one crafting SMITH

one crossing ELECTOR

one despising inferiors SNOB

one, every PER

one existing BEING; LIVER

one flying can indicate a bird

one for Beethoven EIN

one Frenchman IM

one hears homophone indicator

one in I to nested within a component as "one in the way" clues SIT

one in court CIT

one in eight OAR

one in five QUIN

one in France UN; UNE

one in Germany EIN

one in pack CARD; DOG; HOOKER; WOLF; *see* RUGBY PLAYER

one in Scotland ANE; YIN

one in suit SPADE etc

one looking PEEKER; SEEKER

one missing from school TRAN

one more ANOTHER

one much disliking HATER

one-night stand GIG

one-nil IO

one occupying seat IMP; MP

one of the Scots ANE

one of two DOUBLE; EITHER; TWIN

one-off NONCE

one on the way out GONER

one ordered anagram of ONE

one paid to work PRO

one quarter empty FUL

one rising REBEL

one's IS; MY; YOUR

one's depressed KEY

one's heart N; NE

one's time ONEST

one seen hanging can indicate a pub-sign or a painting

one short ON

one short of century, hundred
OO

one taking instruction L; PUPIL;
TRAINEE

one that belongs MEMBER

one that lifts JACK

one time ONCE

one-time EX

one-time partner EX

one upset ANTI

one way to describe anagram indicator

one we hear WON

one who can indicate a word ending in ER (or IST)

one who's been had SUCKER

one who holds up ROBBER

one who is owed a favour
OBLIGEE

one who likes to be seen
POSER

one who's in BATTER

one who succeeds HEIR;
WINNER; ■ HEIRESS

one with no centre OE

one who wanders NOMAD;
ROVER

one who's fallen TART

one with special interest
FANCIER

one worth supporting CASE

oneness UNITY

ones II; IS

ones here, the THESE

ones there, the THOSE

oneself AUTO; EGO; I; ID

onion BULB; ■ SCALLION; *see*
HEAD

onlooker SEER

only ALONE; BUT; JUST; LONE;
MERE; SINGLE; SOLE; can indicate O, as "Sign cryptically indicating females only?" →
OMEN

only for men STAG

only just BARELY

only off NOON (i.e. no "on")

only remaining LAST

onrush SURGE

onset (of) initial indicator

Ontario ONT

oodles LOTS

oodles of money *see* MONEY,
LOTS OF

oomph ZING

ooze MUD; SEEP

opaque SMOKE; SMOKEY

opal RING

open AIRY; AJAR; BARE;
BROACH; FRANK; FREE;
LANCE; LEAD; OUT; OVERT;
PRISE; RAISE; START; UNDO;
UNLOCK; ■ CANDID;
LAUNCH; NAKED; PATENT;
PUBLIC; first letter indicator

open air, in the OUT

open country PLAIN

open, doesn't first letter to be
omitted

open for poets OPE

open, in the OUT

open, just AJAR

open land DOWN

open mouth GAPE

open-mouthed AGOG

open, not completely AJAR

open shop S

open space FIELD; GLADE;
PARK; ■ GARTH; YARD

open tennis match SERVE

open to change anagram of
OPEN

Open University OU

open up LANCE

open wide YAWN

opened UNDID; anagram indicator; initial letter indicator

opened, to be anagram indicator

opener BAT; KEY; initial letter indicator; can indicate the first letter of a word

openers can indicate the first two
(or three) letters of a word, or the
first one (or two) letters of several words

opening ADIT; CHINK; CLEFT;
DOOR; ENTRY; GAP; GATE;
HOLE; INTRO; MOUTH;
PORE; PORT; RENT; START;
VENT; ■ BREACH; CHANCE;
CRANNY; GAMBIT; HATCH;
LANCING; NOOK; ONSET;
OPPORTUNITY; ORIFICE;

PORTAL; STOMA; anagram indicator; initial letter indicator; precedence indicator

opening, American PROLOG

opening lost L; first letter to be omitted

opening move GAMBIT; M

opening section INTRO; S

openly gay OUT

opera AIDA; NORMA; MET (i.e. the opera company in New York); OP; WORKS; ■ CARMEN; SALOME; THAIS; THE RING; [◊ SOAP]

opera character *see* OPERATIC PART

opera company ENO

opera house (US) MET

opera, part of ARIA

opera singer DIVA

opera, sort of SERIA

operas RING

operate USE; WORK

operated anagram indicator

operatic extravaganza RING

operatic heroine MANON; MIMI; NORMA

operatic part AIDA; ARIA; LULU; MIMI; NORMA

operating ON; anagram indicator

operating room OR

operating system DOS

operation OP; PLAY; USE; ■ AGENCY; anagram indicator

operation, in ON

operations research OR

operator DRIVER; USER; ■ SURGEON; WORKER

opinion ANGLE; NOTION; POINT; SAY; SLANT; TAKE; VIEW; VOICE; ■ SENTIMENT; THOUGHT

opinion, in our TOUS (i.e. TO US)

oppo COLLEAGUE; MATE; *see* FRIEND

opponent ANTI; FOE

opponent mentioned FAUX; PHO

opponents ANTIS; EN (from bridge); NE; SW; WS

opponents, our THEM; THEY

opponents' ground AWAY

opportunist CHANCER

opportunity BREAK; CHANCE; ROOM; SCOPE; SHOT; can indicate BUS, COACH in phrases such as "miss the bus" etc

oppose BUCK; FACE; PLAY; RESIST; ■ COUNTER

opposed AVERSE

opposed (to) AGIN, ANTI; V; ■ AGAINST

opposer NOE

opposing ANTI; CON; V; ■ COUNTER

opposing pair SE

opposing sides variations of LR, NS, EW etc

opposite ABEAM; COUNTER; REVERSE; can indicate that words or components are to be in reverse order; reversal indicator

opposite sex, liking STRAIGHT

opposite side OFF

opposition ANTIS; CON; FOE; NOES; opposing sides in bridge e.g. EN; [◊ OPPOSITION]

opposition, being in V

opposition, in COUNTER

opposition leader O

opposition, member of ANTI

oppress BULLY; IMPOSE

oppression, sense of WEIGHT

oppressor DESPOT; ■ IMPOSER

opt CHOOSE; ELECT

opted for CHOSE; ELECTED; PICKED

optic in conjunction with another word e.g. "optics expert" can signal something to do with bars or drinking

optical character recognition OCR

optimum BEST

opting ELECTION

option CHOICE; HEADS; TAILS; anagram indicator

options MENU

optimism HOPE

optimistic ROSY; UPBEAT

opulence WEALTH

opulent RICH

or note that, although innocently placed in the clue, OR itself can be part of the answer

or, France OU

or rather NAY

oral SAID; SPOKEN; homophone indicator

oral contraceptive PILL

oral examination VIVA

oral statement SPEECH; WORD(S); ■ PAROLE

orally homophone indicator

orange AMBER; FLAME; LEVAN; NAVEL

Orange HOUSE

orange-peel ZEST

orate TALK

orator's homophone indicator

orb GLOBE (qv); O; ■ EYE

orbit BEAT; FIELD; PATH; ROUND; can indicate something to do with EYE

orchestra BAND; LSO; [◊ PIT]

orchestra, part of BRASS; FIDDLES; STRINGS; WIND

orchestra, place of PIT

orchestra section PIT; *see* ORCHESTRA, PART OF

orchestrated anagram indicator

ordain RULE; STATE; ■ APPOINT

ordeal TEST; TRIAL; STRAIN

order BATH; (i.e. order of knighthood); BID; BIDDING; CH; DECREE; DEMAND; DIRECT; DO; EDICT; ENJOIN; FIAT; FILE; LAW; O; OBE; OM; ORD; PO (i.e. postal order); RANGE; RULE; SET; SORT; TELL; TRIM; ■ BOSS; CHARGE; COMMAND; COMMISSION; DICTATE; ERRAND; GARTER; INDENT; MARSHAL; NEATEN; STATUTE; STRAIGHTEN; WARRANT; anagram indicator; an architectural order e.g. IONIC, DORIC; can indicate a religious order e.g. Benedictine; can indicate a word or phrase beginning

with DO as "order for matricide" yields DOMAIN (i.e. "do ma in")

order, in OK

★ **order indicator** is a word that tells us the order in which letters or components are to be used. They are of two kinds. One type tells us in what order components should be placed. For example "Give instruction in the square before bad weather" tells us to place T before RAIN to get TRAIN. These are quite straightforward (such as "preceding, "after" and "following") but there can be difficulty in spotting that the words are functioning as ordering indicators. The other kind consists of reversal indicators which are discussed under that heading.

order, member of MONK; NUN; ■ BROTHER; FRIAR; SISTER

Order of the British Empire OBE

order to pay CHEQUE

order to start shooting ACTION

order to stop DONT

order, out of LAY; anagram indicator

ordered BADE; BID; anagram indicator

orderly NEAT; SISTER; TIDY

orders anagram indicator

ordinance BULL

ordinary PLAIN; ■ COMMON; NORMAL; as a class of armorial charges can indicate something to do with heraldry e.g. chevron

ordinary charge can indicate something to do with heraldry

ordinary language PROSE

ordnance ORD

ore ROCK

Oregon OR

organ BRAIN; EAR; EYE; GLAND; HEART; LIVER; LUNG; NOSE; SKIN; ■ CORTEX; SPLEEN

organ, breathing GILL; LUNG

organ knob STOP

organ, of an RENAL

organ, portable REGAL

organic food HAY

organisation ADMIN; BODY; CIA; CO; FIRM; UN; ■ COMPANY; OUTFIT

organisation, national NT

organise BUILD; DIRECT; HAVE; RUN

organised HAD; RAN; anagram indicator

organised properly TRIM

organised workers TU

organiser, party WHIP

orgy REVEL

Oriel can indicate something to do with Oxford

orient E; EAST; PEARL

oriental E; EASTER; ■ ASIAN; EASTERN; EMAN (i.e. E-man, eastern man); THAI

oriental coppers can indicate eastern currency e.g. sen, yen

oriental criminals TONG

oriental dress SARI

oriental drink SAKE

oriental-sounding TIE

oriental vessel JUNK; WOK

origami, do some FOLD; ■ CREASE

origin BUD; ROOT; SOURCE; START; ■ GENESIS

origin of initial letter indicator

original CARD; EARLY; EX; FIRST; MASTER; NEW; OLD; ■ PRIMAL; initial letter indicator; anagram indicator

original American see AMERICAN INDIAN

originality, lacking first letter to be omitted

originally initial letter indicator; in conjunction with a homophone indicator can indicate a word with the sound of a word's initial letter as "originally thinking aloud" can clue TEA; anagram indicator

originally called NEE

originally cancelled first letter to be omitted

originate CREATE; SPRING; START; STEM

originating BORN

originator of first letter indicator

origins anagram indicator; first letters indicator

Orion STARS

ornament ADORN; DECOR; TRIM; ■ BANGLE; BROOCH; VASE

ornament, supply ADORN; DECK

ornamental FRILLY; anagram indicator

ornamental, doesn't sound PLANE

ornamental, not PLAIN

ornamentation TRIM

ornate DRESSY; ■ BAROQUE; FANCY; FLOWERY; PURPLE; anagram indicator

orphan ANNIE; OLIVER; TWIST; WARD

'orrible can indicate that the associated word has initial H omitted

orris IRIS

orthodox NORM; ■ NORMAL; STANDARD; USUAL

Oscar O; PRIZE

oscillate SWING

osier WICKER; WILLOW; WITHY

Osiris, sister of ISIS

ostentation POMP; SHOW; SWANK

ostentatious CAMP; SHOWY

ostentatious, not HUMBLE

'ostile, to feel ATE (i.e. (h)ate)

ostler GROOM

ostracise BAN

OT see OLD TESTAMENT

OT book DAN; NUMB; see OLD TESTAMENT BOOK

Othello MOOR; PLAY; can indicate something to do with the play e.g. Iago, Desdemona, jealousy

other anagram indicator

other people REST

other ranks OR

other than NOT

other things ETAL (i.e. et al)

other things, and ETAL; ETC

other words, in can indicate something to do with translator, translation etc

other-worldly FEY

others ETAL; REST; ■ MORE; THEM

others, and ETAL; ETC

otherwise AKA; ELSE; OR; anagram indicator

Otis can indicate something to do with regret (from Cole Porter song)

otologist [◊ EAR]

Ottoman TURK

OU course PPE

Ouch! OW

ought SHOULD

ounce CAT; OZ

our ONUS (i.e. on us); on the assumption that readers are British (mainly) "our" can refer to some aspect of Britain, thus "our country" → UK; or the "us" can be inhabitants of earth, so "our way" → MILKY

our country UK

our ground HOME

our group US; WE

our home EARTH

our part of the world WEST

our side US

our side will WELL (i.e. we'll)

our time AD

our years AD; AGE

ourselves US

'ouse OME

oust EJECT; ■ SUPPLANT

ousting omission indicator

out ABSENT; BAN; GONE; OFF; OVER (i.e. no longer available); UNDER; ■ ALOUD; ASLEEP; DEAD; EXCUSE; SLEEPING; anagram indicator (as "let out" cues an anagram of LET); nesting indicator; omission indicator; can refer to being absent, insensible, being asleep e.g. DREAM

out- beware of words beginning with out-, as they may signify an anagram of the rest of the word where, for example, "outlet" can call for an anagram of LET

out-and-out RANK

out at first initial letter to be omitted

out, be ABROAD; AWAY; STRIKE

out East E to be omitted

out for can indicate some kind of hunting activity as "out for a duck" clues FOWLING

out in Amsterdam UIT

out in the middle U

out, is BLOOM; BLOOMING

out more INLESS

out, not IN; anagram of OUT

out of EX; anagram indicator; nesting indicator; run indicator; can indicate that the components necessary to construct the answer follow, a clever example being: "Run out of gas, visiting U.S. physicist" → HENNERY (a hennery being a chicken run, achieved by nesting gas NE in the name of American physics scientist HENRY)

out of bed UP

out of breath, be GASP

out of control ADRIFT; anagram indicator

out of date OLD; PASSE

out of date, almost OL; PASS

out of fashion PASSE

out-of-form anagram indicator

out of joint anagram indicator

out of one's mind MAD; STONED; *see* DRUNK, MAD, NUTS, CRAZY etc

out of order US (i.e. useless); anagram indicator

out of place anagram indicator

out of this world ALIEN; ET

out of tune anagram indicator

out of turn AMISS; anagram indicator

out of water DRY

out of work IDLE

out to lunch MAD (qv)

out to lunch? EATING

out West W to be omitted

outbreak anagram indicator; anagram of OUT (e.g. TOU)

outbreak of initial letter indicator

outbuilding BARN; SHED
outburst FIT; GUST; RANT; anagram indicator; run indicator
outcast LEPER
outcome END; *see* RESULT
outcome, level DRAW; TIE
outcry NOISE
outdated EX; OLD; PASSE
outdo BEAT; CAP; TOP; ■ BETTER
outdoes anagram of DOES
outdoor facility CAMP; TENT
outer clothing, removing first and last letters to be omitted
outer cover/ing SKIN (qv); *see* OUTER SURFACES
outer surfaces SKINS; can indicate the first and last letters of a sequence of words as "Outer surfaces of sauna need another acrylic resin for varnishing" → SANDARAC
outerwear COAT; MAC
outfit DRESS; FIRM; GANG; GARB; GEAR; LOT; RIG; TEAM; ■ BUNCH; SQUAD; SUIT; anagram indicator (especially of FIT)
outgoing ISSUE
outhouse BARN; SHED
outing AMBLE; RAMBLE; TOUR; TREAT; TRIP; anagram indicator
outlandish ALIEN; anagram indicator; *see* STRANGE
outlaw BAN; BAR; BLACK; HOOD; ROBIN; anagram of LAW
outlawing BAN; omission indicator
outlay COST; PRICE; SPEND
outlet FLUE; HOLE; SHOP; STORE; VENT; ■ DRAIN; DUCT; HYDRANT; PIPE; anagram of LET
outlet, sales DELI; MART; SHOP; STORE
outline BORDER; DRAFT; ETCH; SKETCH; TRACE; ■ PROSPECTUS; SCHEME
outline, make TRACE

outlook ASPECT; SCENE; VISTA; ■ PROSPECT
outlying part RIM; *see* BORDER
outmanoeuvred BEAT; ROUTED
outmoded DATED; *see* OUTDATED; anagram of MODED
outperform CAP; TOP
outpost PICKET
output CROP; WORK; YIELD
outrage AFFRONT; APPAL; FURY; anagram of RAGE
outrageous GROSS; OTT; ■ ARRANT; OUTRE; anagram indicator
outrageously anagram indicator
outré SHOCKING
outright SHEER; UTTER; RT to be omitted or nested within a component
outset EST (abbr. of establishment); OFF; START; anagram of SET; *see* START
outset, at initial letter indicator (as "grabbing ball at outset" signals that B is to be nested within a component)
outset, of/from the initial letter indicator
outshine CAP
outside EXTERNAL; nesting indicator (as "outside America" requires US to be nested within a component); can indicate the outer letters of an adjacent word (as "slept outside" → ST)
outside broadcast OB
outside, on the the first and last letters of word(s) to be used; ■ EXTERNAL; *see* OUTSIDE
outsider nesting indicator; can indicate first or last letter
outsiders first and last letters are to be used or deleted
outskirts of *see* OUTSIDERS
outskirts, on the nesting indicator
outspoken BOLD; FRANK; PLAIN; ■ BLUNT; CANDID
outstanding ACE; DUE; HIGH; OWED: OWING; SUPER; TALL; ■ ESPECIAL; LEADING; PROUD; SPECIAL;

TODO (i.e. to do);
UNSETTLED; can refer to some kind of relief work e.g. rilievo; nesting indicator, as in "I dispose of outstanding firm" where I has to be nested within SOLD to give SOLID; [◊ RELIEF]

outstanding example LULU; ■ CRACKER

outstanding, not LOW

outstanding person ONER

outstandingly OVER; VERY

outstrip TOP

outward appearances, to first and last letters indicator

outward movement EBB

outwardly indicates first and last letters as "outwardly sensible" → SE

outwit BEAT; BEST; TRUMP

Oval can indicate something to do with cricket (as "Oval headgear" → BOWLER)

ovation HAND

oven KILN; LEAR (i.e. glass-annealing); OAST; STOVE

oven, just out of HOT

oven-ready bird ROASTER

over ACROSS; ALONG; ATOP; BY; DEAD; DONE; DOWN; ENDED; FOR; GONE; OLD; ON; OUT; PAST; RE; TOO; UP; ■ FINISHED; THROUGH; anagram indicator; reversal indicator; preceding indicator; can indicate something to do with cricket e.g. balls, bowling, maiden

over-amorous RANDY

over-barbecue/cook BURN; CHAR

over-cooked anag. of OVER e.g. ROVE

over-dressed anagram of OVER; OVER to be nested within a component

over-effusive, be GUSH

over-familiar STALE

over-formality STARCH

over, go CROSS; FORD

over-hasty RASH

over-indulge BINGE

over-infuse STEW

over-luxuriant RANK

over-ripe STRONG

over the limit OTT

over the moon ELATED

over the top OTT; a component to precede T, as "Stop over the top party" clues DOT (i.e. a "full stop")

over there YON; YONDER; ■ THAT

over there, the things THOSE

overabundant RIFE

overact HAM

overacted HAMMED; HAMMY

overactive HYPER

overall SMOCK; TOP; ■ GENERAL; SUPREME; reverse or anagram of ALL; *see* CHIEF, HEAD, MAIN

overalls CHAPS; SMOCK(S); TOP(S)

overbalance TOPPLE

overcame BEAT; nesting indicator

overcast CLOUDY; DULL

overcharge OC; ROOK; RUSH

overcome BEAT; STUN; WORST; anagram indicator; nesting indicator; reversal indicator

overcook BURN; CHAR

overdose OD

overdrawn OD

overdue LATE; reverse or anagram of DUE

overeat GORGE; WOLF; ■ ENGORGE; reverse of, or anagram of, EAT

overenthusiastic, be RAVE

overexcited GIDDY

overfill CRAM

overflow BRIM; SLOP; WOLF

overgrown REEDY; WEEDY

overhanging, something FLAP

overhasty RASH

overhaul SERVICE

overhaul, in need of anagram indicator

overhead ABOVE; ALOFT; HIGH; UP; can indicate an item of headgear; can indicate that a synonym of "head" is to be reversed, for example NUT becomes TUN

overhead railway EL (i.e. in U.S.)

overheads can indicate something associated with space, the night sky, ceiling etc as in "Model with astronomical overheads, perhaps?" → PLANETARIUM

overheard homophone indicator – in a special case it can indicate TWO i.e. homophone of TOO, synonym of "over"

overindulge PIG

overindulgence BINGE

overland a component to be placed before a synonym of "land" (qv), as "Take away warship overland" → SUBTRACT

overlay nesting indicator

overlook NOD

overlooked FORGOT

overmuch TOO

overplay HAM

overprecise FUSSY

oversaw RAN; anagram or reversal of SAW

overseas ABROAD; anagram of SEAS; can indicate something to do with a pier (it is "overseas"!) or entertainment found on a pier e.g. pierrot, Punch and Judy

overseas, go SAIL

overseas visitor ALIEN

overseas, went SAILED

oversee RUN; anagram or reversal of SEE

overseer BOSS

oversight CARE; LAPSE; OMISSION; *see* ERROR

overt CLEAR; OPEN; OUT; PLAIN

overtake CATCH; PASS

overthrow EVERT; USURP; anagram indicator; reversal indicator

overthrown anagram indicator; run indicator; *see* OVERTHROW

overtime OT; reverse indicator for time (EMIT) or for synonyms for time, hence ARE, EGA, etc

overtips OR (i.e. the end letters of "over"); OS (i.e. the end letters of "overtips")

overture START; initial letter(s) to be used

overtures to initial letters to be used

overturn TIP

overturned anagram indicator; reversal indicator

overweight AMPLE; FAT; STOUT; TON; reversal indicator for measures of weight, hence MARG, NOT, ZO, etc; can indicate some component has to be placed before synonym of "weight" as, for example, "Save overweight page" → BUTTONS

overwhelm AWE; SMOTHER; SWAMP

overwhelmed AWED; nesting indicator

overwhelmed by nesting indicator

overwrought anagram indicator

ovum EGG

Ow! OUCH

owed DUE

owing DUE

owl HOOTER

owl, sound of HOOT

own HAVE; GRANT; ■ PERSONAL; POSSESS

own goal OG

owned HAD; LETON (i.e. let on)

owner of estate LAIRD

ownership TITLE

owning HAVING

owns old HATH

ox NEAT; STEER; YAK; ■ URUS

Oxbridge distinction BLUE

oxen, two YOKE

Oxford OU; SHOE (hence can indicate something to do with shoe); [◊ CIRCUS]

Oxford, at UP

Oxford course GREATS; PPE

Oxford Street HIGH

oxidation, oxidise RUST

oxygen O; OZONE

oxymoron can indicate that the answer consists of a combination of two contradictory terms, ante-post (a racing term), subject-object (a term from philosophy) for example

oyster spawn SPAT
oysters, source of STEW

Pp

pa *see* FATHER; with a capital letter can refer to Pennsylvania
pace AMBLE; CLIP; RATE; SPEED; STEP; TEMPO; TROT; ■ CANTER; CELERITY; STRIDE; TREAD
pace, fast CANTER; RUN
pace, go at a steady TROT
Pacific area RIM
Pacific state TONGA
pack BAG; BALE; BOX; CRAM; DECK; FILL; KIT; LOAD; ROUT; STOW; TAMP; TIN; ■ GROUP; SET; TAROT; STUFF; anagram indicator (as "pack of lies" cues an anagram of LIES); can indicate something to do with a pack of cards, a suit (e.g. SPADE), or a specific card (e.g. ACE); *see* ONE IN PACK; [◊ WOLF]
pack animal BURRO; MULE
pack in LEAVE; RESIGN; nesting indicator
pack, member of HUNTER; *see* CARD
pack, one PROP
pack up can indicate that PACK (or a synonym) is to be reversed, and so: ELAB, GAB, MARC etc
package BALE; PACKET; PARCEL
packaging WRAPPING
packed FULL
packed in LEFT; RESIGNED; nesting indicator
packed up DOWN; GONE; LEFT; OFF; RESIGNED; WENT
packed with nesting indicator
packet BOMB; COST; SHIP; ■ CARTON; PARCEL; SACHET; STEAMER

packing nesting indicator
packing case CRATE
pact DEAL; TREATY
pacy SMART
pad BLOCK; FLAT; FOOT; SWELL; TRAMP; TREAD; WAD; ■ CUSHION
Paddington BEAR; STATION
paddle DIP; OAR; ROW; WADE
paddy IRE; PET; RAGE; TEMPER; [◊ FIELD]
paediatrician SPOCK
page BOY; CALL; LEAF; P; SHEET; ■ BUTTONS; SUMMON
page boy/page-boy BUTTONS; PSON (i.e. p-son)
page, edge of MARGIN
page, look at the next PTO
page size QUARTO
pageant TABLEAU
pages, lots of REAM; QUIRE
pages, two LEAF
paid GAVE; MET; PD; STOOD
paid, be EARN
paid, being EARNED
paid for MET
paid, get EARN
paid player PRO
paid, still to be DUE; OWING
paid worker PRO
paid, yet to be OWING
pain ACHE; CRAMP; GRIPE; SORE; STING; ■ BALE (arch.); COLIC; GYP; PANG; PERISHER; STITCH
pain, cause ACHE; HURT; SMART; STING
pain, cry of OUCH
pain, emotional WRENCH
pain, exclamation of, indication of OW
pain, experience AIL; HURT; SUFFER; *see* HURT
pain, experienced HURT; TWINGED; *see* PAIN, EXPERIENCE
pain, feel HURT; SMART
pain in the neck CRICK; DRIP
pain, inflict HARM; HURT; TORMENT

pained ACHING; ENSORED
painful ACHY; SORE
painful affliction GOUT; SPRAIN
painful parting WRENCH
painful, something GOUT
painful toe GOUT
painful, very SPLITTING
painful, was BIT
painfully anagram indicator
painstaking THOROUGH
paint BICE; OIL; TEMPERA; ■ COLOUR; DAUB; DECORATE
paint ingredient RESIN
paint, one using RA; *see* ARTIST
painter ARA; BACON; HALS; INGRES; MASTER; RA; ROPE; SARGENT; TITIAN; TURNER; ■ ARTIST; DEGAS; DURER; LELY; ROUSSEAU; SPENCER
painter, amateurish DAUBER
painter's first application PRIMER
painting, abstract OPART (i.e. op art)
painting ART; MURAL; OIL; ■ DAUB; FRESCO; ICON; TURNER
painting medium OIL; TEMPERA; ■ ACRYLIC
painting, method of *see* PAINTING MEDIUM
paintings ART
pair BRACE; COUPLE; DUO; PR; TWIN; TWO; repetition indicator; can indicate two components to be used with AND as "Pair of initials between Lowry's" clues LANDS (i.e. L-AND-S)
pair of can indicate the first two letters of the succeeding word as "pair of tights" clues TI
pair of fives TEN; TENNER
pair off MATCH
pal ALLY; BUD; CHUM; COCK; FRIEND; MATE; OPPO; PARD; *see* FRIEND
palace [◊ ROYAL]
palace servants COURTS
palate ROOF
pale ASHY; DRAWN; DOUGHY; FADED; FAINT; FAIR; FENCE; LIGHT; MEALY; PASTY; POST; SALLOW; STAKE; WAN; WHITE; ■ ASHEN
pale ale LIGHT
Palestine group PLO
Palestrina can refer to one of his works e.g. MASS
palindrome can indicate that a word or the answer reads the same both ways, popular ones in crosswords being OTTO, LEVEL, MADAM, NOT ON
paling FENCE
pall BORE
pallet BED
pallid WAN
palm HAND; HIDE; ■ PRIZE; [◊ OIL]
paltry CHEAP; TIN
pampas PLAIN
pamphlet TRACT
pan BOWL; DISH; FACE; KNOCK; MUG; ROAST; *see* CRITICISE
Pan PETER
Panama CANAL; HAT; PA
pancake CREPE
pane GLASS; LIGHT
panel BOARD; JURY; TEAM
pang PAIN; TWINGE
Pangloss a character from Voltaire's *Candide* so can refer to the book itself or optimism (the feature of the character)
panic ALARM; FLAP; FRIGHT; SCARE; TERROR; ■ FUNK; GRASS; note "panic" is also a plant
panic, in anagram indicator
panorama VIEW
pansy VIOLA
pant GASP; LONG
pantheistic PAGAN
pantry LARDER; STORE
pap MESS; MUSH; *see* RUBBISH
paparazzi can indicate something to do with the press
paparazzo SNAPPER
paper FT; LEAF; MS; ORGAN; PAD; PAGE; QUIRE; RAG; REAM; ROLL SHEET; SUN; TIMES; TISSUE; ■ DAILY;

ESSAY; EXAM; MIRROR; STANDARD; THESIS

paper for publication ARTICLE; COPY; MS

paper, in the WRAPPED

paper, individual COPY

paper, official FORM

paper, piece of SLIP

paper size QUARTO

paper, twenty-five pieces of QUIRE

paper worth money BILL; CHEQUE; NOTE

papers FILE; PRESS; QUIRE; REAM

papers, many REAM

par EQUAL; EVEN; LEVEL; NORM; NORMAL

par, be on a MATCH

par, below EAGLE

para LANDER; can indicate words associated with jump, fall, drop

parable can indicate something to do with a story from the New Testament; or a more modern work seen to have the nature of a parable such as *Animal Farm*

parachutist [◊ DROP; JUMP]

parade AIR; MARCH; SHOW; ■ DISPLAY; TATTOO

paraded AIRED

paradise EDEN; HEAVEN; LIMBO

paradoxically anagram indicator

parallel classes STREAM

paralyse NUMB; STUN

paramour LOVER

paraphrased anagram indicator

parasite DRONE; LOUSE; MITE; TICK; ■ FLEA; VERMIN; WORM; [◊ HOST]

parasite, one with HOST

parasites LICE

parcel PLOT

parcel (out) ALLOT

pardon SPARE

pare CUT; PRUNE; SHAVE; TRIM

parent DAD; DAM; FATHER; MA; MAMA; MOTHER; MUM; PA; PAR; POP; RAISE; SIRE

parentage DESCENT

parental guidance PG

Paris apart from the French capital can also refer to Paris, the Classical figure, and in this context can indicate something to do with the Trojan War, death of Achilles, heel, Helen, Hector, etc

Paris, all in TOUT

Paris and ET

Paris correspondent can indicate the French equivalent of an English word; *see* FRENCH

Paris, description of GAY

Paris, first person in JE

Paris, in can indicate the use of a French word, *see* FRENCH for the common ones

Paris, old man of PRIAM (myth.)

Paris paper PAPIER; ■ FIGARO; LE MONDE

Paris, say CITY

Paris so much, in TANT

Paris suburb ORLY

Paris who QUI

Paris, who in QUI

parish CURE

parish of time-serving vicar BRAY

parish priest PP; *see* VICAR

Parisian, a UN; UNE

Parisian copper SOU

Parisian life VIE

Parisian, of the DE; DES; DU

Parisian station GARE

Parisian, that QUE

Parisian, the LE

Parisian to go ALLER

Parisian who QUI

Parisienne ELLE

park HYDE; PUT; STOP

park-keeper/warden RANGER

parked, parking P

Parker, Charlie BIRD

parking area LOT

parking area for Americans LOT

parking facility PEASE

parlance DICTION

parley TALK; TREAT

Parliament DIET; P; PARL; RUMP; [◊ ACT; LAW]

parliament, edict of ACT
parliament, house of CHAMBER
Parliamentarian MP; ■ MEMBER
parliamentary group
  OPPOSITION
parliamentary seat BOROUGH
parliamentary session, held
  SAT
parlour [◊ FLY]
parody COD; SKIT; ■
  TRAVESTY; *see* LAMPOON
parole WORD
parrot LORY; KEA; ■ KAKA;
  MIMIC; RECITE
parsimonious MEAN (qv)
parsnip ROOT
parson CLERIC; REV; *see*
  CLERGYMAN
part AREA; BIT; HALF; LEAVE;
  PIECE; PT; MEMBER; ROLE;
  SEMI; SEVER; SHARE; SIDE;
  SNAP; SOME; SPLIT; UNIT;
  run indicator; ■ FRACTION;
  PORTION; QUARTER;
  RATION; SECTION; SUNDER;
  TRANCHE
part company with, to can indicate that the word that follows is
  to be nested within CO
part for actor ROLE; SCRIPT;
  WORDS
part in play INNINGS
part of IN; run indicator
part of Bible NT; OT; VERSE; or
  a book from the Bible e.g. JOB,
  MARK
part of body ORGAN etc
part of circle ARC
part of foot ANKLE; HEEL;
  SOLE
part of member THIGH
part of orchestra BRASS; WIND;
  see ORCHESTRA, PART OF
part of revellers ROUT
part of speech LINE; NOUN;
  TENSE; VERB; can indicate adjective, adverb, preposition etc
part of theatre APRON; STAGE
part of town QUARTER;
  SECTION
part of work EXCERPT
part, play a ACT

part, render ACT
part, small remaining STUMP
part-time TEMP; ■ TEMPORARY
part-time soldiers TA
parterre BEDS
partial SOME
partial to, be EYE; LIKE; LOVE;
  PREFER
partiality for, have a LIKE;
  LOVE
partially HALF; one or two letters
  to be omitted; run indicator
participant, willing SPORT
participate SHARE
participated in anagram indicator
participating in nesting indicator,
  as "participating in song" requires a component to be nested
  within ARIA
particle ATOM; BOSON (physics);
  ION; MOTE; PIECE; ■
  NEUTRON; PHOTON
particle, charged ION
particles, stone GRIT
particular ASPECT; CERTAIN;
  DETAIL; FOG; PET; POINT;
  RESPECT; STRICT; ■ ELITE;
  EXPRESS; FUSSY; SPECIAL;
  SPECIFIC; can indicate a noun
  preceded by THE
particular way, in a anagram indicator
particularly ULTRA (as "particularly reliable" →
  ULTRASOUND)
parties united BLOC
parting, painful WRENCH
partition CLEAVE
partly SOME; run indicator
partner ALLY (qv); BUD; DATE;
  E (from bridge); FELLOW (in
  the sense of fellow-worker)
  LOVER; MAN; MATE; N;
  OPPO; PAL (qv); PARD; S; W; ■
  CONSORT; SPOUSE; STEADY;
  see FRIEND; can indicate one's
  opposite number in the card game
  of bridge as "West's partner"
  calls for E; can refer to one of the
  partners in a specific partnership
  e.g. DUCK/DRAKE,
  STALLION/MARE,

EMPEROR/EMPRESS;
HUSBAND/WIFE
partner, find SCORE
partner no longer EX
partner, take a MARRY; WED
partner, with a PAIRED
partners ALLIES; ITEM;
COUPLE; PAIRING; PALS; very
often indicates a bridge partnership namely EW, NS, SN or WE;
see ALLY, FRIEND, PAL,
PARTNERSHIP
partnership CO; FIRM; STAND;
■ CAHOOTS; LEAGUE; *see*
PARTNERS
parts of/in anagram indicator
party ANC; BALL; BASH;
BEANO; BINGE; CAMP; CON;
CROWD; DANCE; DISCO; DO;
FETE; FLING; GANG; GREEN;
LAB; LIB; RAVE; REVEL;
SECT; SET; SIDE; SNP;
SOCIAL; SPREE; STAG;
THRASH; TORIES; WAKE; ■
BUST; FACTION; FUNCTION;
GROUP; RECEPTION; ROUT
(arch.); [◊ FIESTA]; can have
something to do with one of the
characters from the party scene in
Alice in Wonderland e.g. Alice,
Mad Hatter, Dormouse
party, African ANC
party, Aussie DING
party-giver HOST
party, illegal RAVE
party, kind of STAG
party, late WAKE
party man HATTER; MEMBER
party member GREEN
party official/organiser WHIP
party, old ROUT; WHIG
party organiser WHIP
party policy in America TICKET
party, riotous/wild RAVE
party's policy LINE; TICKET
party, section of/some of WING
party, sort of BOTTLE; HEN;
SEARCH; STAG
party supporters CAMP
party time DOT (i.e. DO-T)
party type MEMBER
partygoer RAVER

parvenu UPSTART
Pasch EASTER
pass ALLOW; COL; CROSS; DIE;
ELAPSE; GAP; GATE; GO;
HAND; LAPSE; LUNGE;
ROAD; ROUTE; SPEND; WAY;
■ GHAT; GOBY (i.e. go by);
PERMIT; RELAY; TICKET;
VISA
pass, mountain COL; GATE
pass off FOIST
pass on HAND; REFER; RELAY;
see DIE
pass out FAINT; METE; ■
GRADUATE; QUALIFY
pass over CROSS; DIE; FORD;
JUMP; LEAP; SKIP
pass quickly FLIT
pass through a hole REEVE
pass up LOC (i.e. rev.); SHUN
passable DECENT; FAIR
passage AISLE (or, with a homophone indicator, ISLE); ALLEY;
CODA; DUCT; EXCERPT;
EXIT; HALL; LANE; ROAD;
STRAIT; TUNNEL; VENT;
WAY; ■ ADIT; DEFILE;
EXTRACT; GUT; LOBBY;
TRANSIT; run indicator
passage for cables DUCT
passage in, a run indicator
passage in, has nesting indicator
passage, slow LARGO
passageway HALL
pass OLD; OVER; *see*
HACKNEYED, STALE; can signify an archaic word as "have become pass" cues HAST
passed on DEAD; DIED; LATE
passed quickly RAN; TORE
passenger FARE; RIDER; ■
SLACKER; note, this is also a
breed of pigeon; nesting indicator
(i.e. where the "passenger" is
some component to be carried or
nested)
passing DEATH; GOING;
SHORT; ■ BRIEF; DYING;
TEMPORARY; anagram indicator

passing of time indicates the omission of T in an associated word

passion ANGER; DESIRE; EMOTION; FIRE; HEAT; IRE; LOVE; LUST; RAGE; WRATH

passion, with HOT; WARM; ▪ AVIDLY

passion, with less PALER; ▪ COOLER

passionate AVID; HOT; ▪ BURNING; KEEN; SULTRY

passionate about, be LOVE

passionate, be BURN

passionately anagram indicator

passover dinner SEDER

passport endorsement VISA

password SIGN

past AFTER; AGO; EX; FORMER; GONE; LATE; OLD; OVER; PT; TENSE (i.e. grammatical form); ▪ ANCIENT; HISTORIC; can indicate that a component is to be placed at the end as in "A quarter past twelve" which clues NO-ONE i.e. NOON (twelve) + E (E being the "quarter"); *see* PAST, IN THE

past, at some time in the ONCE

past, from time long OLDEN

past, in the AGO; GONE; OVER; can indicate that an element is to be nested within AD (i.e. Anno Domini); can indicate that the immediately preceding word (or component) is to be added at the end to get the solution, as "Man in the past to trip qualified worker" → JOURNEYMAN

pasta DOUGH; NOODLE(S); ▪ FUSILLI; ORZO; SPAGHETTI

pasta, some NOODLE

paste BEAT; GLUE; GUM; PATE; STICK; ▪ STRASS (in gem trade)

Pasternak heroine LARA

pastime HOBBY

pastor P; ▪ MINISTER

pastry CAKE; CRUST; FILO (Gk.); FLAN; PIE; PUFF; TART

pastry dish PIE

pasture-land LEA; LEY

pasty PALE; PIE

pat CLAP; KNOB (i.e. of butter); STROKE; TAP

pat firmly TAMP

patch BED; DARN; MEND; ORBIT; PLACE; PLOT; REPAIR; SPOT; TRACT; ▪ AREA; PERIOD

patch up DEB (i.e. reversal of bed); MEND; TOPS (i.e. reversal of spot); ▪ COBBLE; REPAIR

patchy UNEVEN

pate HEAD

pat PASTE

paten PLATE

patent CLEAR; OPEN; OVERT; ▪ NAKED; OBVIOUS

path ALLEY; COURSE; ROUTE; TRACK; TRAIL; WAY

path, garden ALLEE

path, short PAT; ROUT

pathetic LAME; SAD; WEAK; anagram indicator

pathological anagram indicator

patience WAIT(!); ▪ GAME; can indicate something to do with JOB

patient CASE; can indicate something to do with JOB; [◊ WARD]

patient man JOB

patients ILL (i.e. the ill)

patina FILM

patio YARD; ▪ PAVING

patna RICE

patriarch JOB; JACOB; LEVI; ▪ NOAH

Patrick PAT

patrimony HERITAGE

patriotic LOYAL

patriotic John BULL

patrol PROWL

patrol leader P; PL

patrol, those on POLICE

patron ANGEL; CLIENT; ▪ CUSTOMER; USER

patronising, be DEIGN

patter PITCH; SPIEL; ▪ SPEECH

pattern CHECK; GRID; MODEL; NORM; ▪ DESIGN; FORMAT; TRACERY

paucity DEARTH

Paul Newman film HUD
Pauline disciple TITUS
paunch BELLY; POT; TUM
pause BREAK; DELAY; STOP; WAIT
pavement PATH
pavilion MARQUEE; TENT
paving SETT; ■ PATIO; SLABS; [◊ CRAZY]
paving slab/stone FLAG; SETT
paw FOOT; HAND
pawn GAGE; HOCK; P; PIECE; PLEDGE; POP; ■ DUPE; SURETY
pawnbroker UNCLE
pay BONUS; DO; FEE; FOOT; MEET; RATE; REMIT; SETTLE; STAND; WAGE; ■ DISCHARGE; EARNINGS; MONEY; SCREW; TAR (as with a boat); *see* PAYMENT
pay attention HEED; LIST; MARK; RECK; ■ LISTEN; RESPECT
pay for (another) TREAT
pay heed MARK; RECK; ■ LISTEN
pay out SPEND; anagram of PAY
pay rise YAP (in Down clue)
pay up SETTLE; YAP (in a Down clue)
pay increase RAISE; RISE
pay, way to HP
payable DUE
payment ANTE; BONUS; CHARGE; COST; FEE; GIRO; PRICE; RATE; RENT; SALARY; TITHE; ■ ACCOUNT; CHEQUE; DOLE; EARNEST; *see* PAY
payment, advance ANTE
payment, American means of CHECK; *see* AMERICAN MONEY
payment, demand DUN
payment, extra BONUS
payment, method of CASH; CHEQUE
payment token RECEIPT
payment, token EARNEST
payout DIVI
PC facility MOUSE

pea PULSE; SEED
pea container POD
peace ORDER; PAX; ■ QUIET; SILENCE; SERENITY; TRUCE
peace agreement TRUCE
peaceful CALM; STILL; ■ QUIET; SERENE; SILENT
peacemaker DOVE
peacemakers UN
peach CLING; DISH; GRASS; SING; SNITCH; *see* INFORM, SHOP
peak ACME; ALP; BEN; CAP; TIP; TOP; TOR; ■ HEAD; VISOR
peaky DOWN
peal RING; TOLL; ■ CHIME
pear TUNA (i.e. prickly pear)
pear drink PERRY
pearl GEM
pearler DIVER
pearls ROPE
peas sounding like P's this word can, with a homophone indicator, call for PP
peasant COTTAR; HIND; RUSTIC
peasant, Arab FELLAH
peaty area BOG
pebble STONE
pecan NUT
peccadillo SIN; *see* MISTAKE, SIN
peccavi SINS
peck KISS; PICK
pecked BIT; BITTEN
peculiar ODD; OWN; RUM; ■ SPECIAL; STRANGE; anagram indicator
pedal CYCLE; ■ CLUTCH
peddle TOUT
pedestal BASE
pedestrian BANAL; DULL; LAME; P; TRITE; ■ PROSAIC
pedestrianised the letters CAR to be omitted from word
pedigree BREED; LINE; TREE (as in family tree); ■ FAMILY; STEMMA
pediment GABLE
pedlar HAWKER

peel RIND; SKIN; STRIP; with a capital letter can indicate something to do with (1) the Isle of Man (Manx cats, three-legged emblem etc) or (2) the former prime minister

peel off SHED; STRIP

peeling STRIPPING; ■ SUNBURNT; TANNED

peels from first and last letters from the word that follows to be used

peeping, man caught TOM

peer EARL; EQUAL; LOOK; LORD; NOBLE; PRY; ■ BARON

peeress LADY

peerless BEST

peeve ANGER

peeved CROSS; SHIRTY; *see* CROSS

peevish CROSS (qv); TESTY; TOUCHY

peevishness *see* IRRITABILITY

peg CLIP; NOG; PIN; TEE; THOLE; ■ DOWEL

peg-leg STUMP

peg out DIE; *see* DIE

Pegasus HORSE

pell-mell anagram indicator

pellet BALL; O; PEA; SHOT; SLUG

pelt FUR; RAIN; RUN; SHOWER; SKIN (qv); STONE

pelt, remove FLAY; SKIN

pen BIRD; COOP; DOCK; FOLD; NIB; POUND; STY; WRITE; ■ CRIB; QUILL; can call for the name of an author; can indicate something to do with SWAN

penal system NICK; *see* PRISON

penal reform anag. of PENAL

penalise FINE

penalty COST; FINE; PRICE

penance, do ATONE

pence D; P

pence, new NP; P

penchant LIKE

pencil, some letters on HAND (i.e. H and B); HB

pencil, sort of B; H; HB

pencil, very soft BB

pendent HANGING

penetrate ENTER; PIERCE

penetrating ACUTE

peninsula IBERIA

penitent shirt material HAIR

pennant FLAG; STREAMER

penned in nesting indicator

penniless BROKE; P to be omitted; *see* BROKE

penning nesting indicator

Pennsylvania PA

penny D; P

penny-pinching MEAN; STINGY; TIGHT

pens nesting indicator

pension scheme SERPS

pensioner OAP

pensive MOODY

penultimate N; indicator for last but one letter

penury NEED

people BODS; CHAPS; CLAN; DEMOS; FOLK; GATE; KIN; MEN; NATION; ONES; PUBLIC; RACE; SOME; THEY; TRIBE; the proper names of some peoples (1) provide useful material for word-building e.g. IRISH, DANES, FRENCH, LAPPS, POLES; (2) while others are useful in providing complete answers in themselves as heteronyms (alternative meaning) e.g. POLISH; or (3) provide useful homophones e.g. CZECH (for CHECK); ■ SETTLE (i.e. as a verb)

people, different OTHERS

people in general THEY

people, leading LIGHTS

people, lots of MANY

people, many HOST

people, of the LAIC; NATIONAL

people on board MEN to be nested within component(s)

people, other REST

people, those THEM; THEY

people watching game GATE

pep GO; LIFE

pepper CHILLI; SEASON; ■ RIDDLE (i.e. make holes in); SEASONING

per A; BY; THROUGH

per item EACH

perceive SEE

perception ANGLE; SENSE; VIEW

perception, uncanny ESP

perch ALIGHT; BASS; POLE; ROD; ROOST; SEAT; SETTLE; SIT

perchance *see* PERHAPS

perched up TAS (i.e. "sat" reversed)

percussion DRUM

perennial HARDY; can indicate some flower such as lupin

perfect HONE; IDEAL; MINT; UTTER; ■ FLAWLESS; can indicate something to do with the verb tense

perfect, most BEST

perfect shot BULL; WINNER

perfection IDEAL

perfectly PAT

perform ACT; DO; PLAY; RUN; SING; ■ RENDER

perform again REDO

perform better than CAP

perform duty SERVE; ■ MINISTER

perform, those who ACTORS; CAST; PLAYERS

performance ACT; DEED; DUET; FEAT; GIG; SHOW; TURN; ■ ACTING; CONCERT; DRAMA; MIME; RECITAL; anagram indicator

performance, great BLINDER

performance, in ON

performance, live CONCERT

performance, musical GIG

performance on stage ACT; PLAY; OPERA

performed ACTED; DID; DONE; SANG; anagram indicator

performed, being ON

performer ACTOR; ARTISTE; TURN; ■ DIVA; PLAYER; SINGER

performer, brilliant, leading STAR

performer, skilful ACE; MASTER

performing ON; anagram indicator

performs ACTS; anagram indicator; *see* PERFORM

perfume SCENT

perfume ingredient ORRIS

perfunctory TOKEN

perhaps SAY; can indicate that we have been given an example and we should look for a general category e.g. "mother perhaps" calls for PARENT, "perhaps Siamese" can call for CAT; can act as an accessory to a homophone indicator; can act as an acknowledgement that the compiler is stretching a point; anagram indicator; can indicate you are expected to suggest the clue, *see* WRITE YOUR OWN CLUE in the *Introduction*

peril DANGER; RISK

perilous RISKY

perilously anagram indicator

perimeter BORDER

period AGE; BOUT; CLASS; DATE; DAY; ERA; POINT; SHIFT; SPACE; SPAN; SPELL; STAGE; STOP; TERM; TIME; WHILE; ■ DECADE; INNINGS; PHASE; *see* TIME

period, dark NIGHT

period, historical AGE; DATE; ERA

period of abstinence LENT

period of calm REST

period of control REIGN

period of delay HALT

period of duty STINT; TOUR; WATCH

period of expansion, growth BOOM; UP

period of play OVER; RUN

period of progress LEG; STAGE; ■ PHASE

period of prosperity BOOM

period of study CLASS; TERM

period of work STINT

period, prosperous BOOM

period taken to finish TIME

periodic REGULAR; ■ ANNUAL; [◊ TABLE]

periodic review, subject to ROLLING

periodical MAG; RAG; REVIEW; *see* MAGAZINE

peripatetic ROVING

peripheral OUTER

perish DIE

perisher PAIN; *see* NUISANCE

perishing COLD; DAMN

perjury, commit LIE

perk BONUS

perky JAUNTY

permanent memory ROM

permanent way RAIL; RY

permeate nesting indicator

permed SET

permission LEAVE; OK; OKAY

permission, get/obtain CLEAR

permission to enter PASS

permission to go LEAVE; ■ EXEAT

permit ALLOW; CLEAR; LET; PASS

permit to go ahead CLEAR

permitted LET; OK; ■ ALLOWED; LEGAL; LICIT

permitted to CAN

perpendicular ERECT; PLUMB

perpetual EVER

perplex BAFFLE; BOTHER; ■ CONFUSE; NONPLUS; PUZZLE; STUMP; TROUBLE

perplexed anagram indicator

Perry MASON

persecutor BULLY

Persian CAT; RUG

Persian fairy PERI

persist HOLD

persistence PLUCK

persistent CHRONIC; HARD

persistently can indicate a verb followed by ON, as "persistently preserve the rule" → CANON

persisting CHRONIC

person BODY; BEING; BOD; MAN; ONE; PARTY; PER; SORT; ■ HUMAN; SOUL; TYPE

person, admired IDOL; TRUMP; ■ ANGEL; BRICK

person advancing LENDER

person, amusing CARD; CHARACTER; *see* COMIC

person, chubby PUDDING

person, dreadful PILL

person eating DINER

person, extraordinary ONER

person, ferocious TARTAR

person, first I

person harassing PEST; ■ BADGERER; HARRIER

person, helpful ANGEL; BRICK

person holding sway RULER; *see* RULER

person, hopeless GONER

person, ignorant MUTT; *see* FOOL

person, ill-bred CHURL

person in debt OWER

person, ineffectual DRIP; DUD; WIMP; *see* WIMP

person, kind/generous/loyal ANGEL; BRICK; GEM

person, inexperienced TIRO; TYRO

person living in RESIDENT

person, nasty GIT; *see* PERSON, TREACHEROUS

person no longer working OAP

person of breeding GENT

person of distinction DAME; SWELL; VIP; *see* LORD

person one may no longer care for EX

person opposing ANTI; CON

person, presiding CHAIR

person putting on airs DJ

person, qualified BA

person, remarkable DILLY; ONER; SAINT

person, responsible CARER; *see* HEAD

person, sad NERD

person, second YOU

person, silly ASS; CLOD; DUNCE; PRAT; PUDDING; TWERP; TWIT; *see* FOOL

person, skilful ACE; MASTER

person, small TITCH

person standing in for VICE

person, stupid *see* PERSON, SILLY

person, supportive ANGEL; BRICK

person that amuses *see* COMIC

person transfixed STARER

person, treacherous CRUD; CUR; RAT; WEASEL

person, uninteresting BORE

person unpleasant CREEP; GIT; PIG

person, untidy SCRUFF

person, violent ROUGH

person who is foolish *see* FOOL

person who matters VIP

person, wonderful *see* PERSON, KIND

personal ONES; OWN; ■ PRIVATE; can indicate a word beginning with SELF; *see* PRIVATE

personal advice AGONY

personal aptitude BENT; FLAIR; ■ TALENT

personal assistant PA

personal column can indicate something to do with spine, vertebrae, leg

personal domestic activity DIY

personal problem BO

personality EGO; ID; SELF; ■ NATURE

personnel CREW; STAFF (qv); TEAM (qv)

perspiration BO; SWEAT

perspiration, covered in DAMP; MOIST; WET; ■ SWEATY

persuade GET; URGE

persuaded, easily PLIABLE

pert CHEEKY; FRESH; SAUCY; ■ IMPUDENT

perturb SHOCK

perturbed anagram indicator

perusal READING

peruse READ

Peruvian/old INCA; INCAN

perverse ODD; RUM; ■ WARPED; anagram indicator

perversely anagram indicator

perversion WARP; anagram indicator

perverted WARPED; anagram indicator

pest BORE; BOTHER; BUG; LOUSE; MOUSE; RAT; ■ VERMIN; *see* NUISANCE

pest, American ROACH

pester BADGER; BOTHER; PLAGUE

pestilence PLAGUE

pests LICE; MICE; *see* PEST

pet BATE; CARESS; CAT; DOG; HUFF; PEKE; RAGE; TIFF

pet, Darling NANA

pet lamb CADE

pet shelter HUTCH

peter SAFE; can indicate something to do with diminishing (i.e. to peter out)

Peter PAN; SELLERS; *see* PETER (above); [◊ GREAT]

peter out DIE (usually Peter has a capital initial to confuse you)

petite LITTLE; SMALL

petition BEG; CASE; SUE; SUIT

petitioner SUPPLICANT

petrified SCARED; STONED

petrol GAS; FUEL; JUICE; ■ LEADED

petrol provider ESSO; MOBIL; SHELL

petrol pump BOWSER

petty MINOR (qv)

petty complaints, make CARP

petty cash CHANGE; FLOAT; P; PENCE

petty criminal anagram of PETTY

Petty Officer PO

petulant SURLY

petulant gesture, make STAMP

phase LEG; PERIOD; STAGE; ■ CYCLE

phantom GHOST

pharmacist MPS

pheasants NIDE (from Fr. *nid*)

Phil as an abbrev. for Philharmonic can indicate something to do with orchestra or musical instrument, as "Behave like Phil?" → FIDGET (i.e. a synonym for 'fiddle')

Phileas FOGG

Philip PHIL; PIP; [◊ ARMADA]

Philip, young PIP

philosopher AYER; LOCKE; MILL; PLATO; SAGE; ■ BACON; HEGEL; KANT; OCCAM; ROUSSEAU; RUSSELL; SARTRE; STEINER; STOIC; THALES

philosophy VIEW

Phineas, Trollope's FINN

phlegmatic PLACID

phobia FEAR; THING

Phoebe MOON

phone BLOWER; CALL; DIAL; LINE; MOBILE; RING; TEL

phone book DIRECTORY

phone, by homophone indicator

phone call BUZZ; RING

phone connection LINE

phone, use DIAL; RING

phoned RANG

phony, phoney MOCK; *see* FAKE

phosphorus P

photo PIC; SHOT; SNAP; STILL

photograph SHOOT; *see* PHOTO

photographic developer SOUP

photography can indicate something to do with lighting

photogenic PRETTY

phrase MOTTO

phrase, familiar/oft-repeated CLICHE; MANTRA; MOTTO; SAYING; *see* PROVERB

phwoar! COR

physical education, instruction, training PE; PT

physical qualification BSC

physician DOC; GALEN; LUKE; *see* DOCTOR

physicist CURIE; LODGE; MACH; PAUL; ■ HENRY

physics establishment CERN

physique BODY

pi SMUG

pianist once, female HESS

piano GRAND; P; QUIET; SOFT; UPRIGHT; [◊ KEY; NOTE]

piano part KEY

piano piece ETUDE

pick BEST; CREAM; ELECT; ELITE; FLOWER; GLEAN; OPT; PECK; PLUCK; POKE; PRIME; SELECT; TOOL; TOP; ■ CHOOSE

pick for one's country/team CAP

pick-me-up TONIC

pick up LEARN; RESUME; SPOT

pick-up UTILITY (i.e. truck)

picket FENCE

picking up reversal indicator

pickings, make GLEAN; SELECT

pickle BIND; CORNER; CURE; HOLE; IMP; JAM; MESS; PLIGHT; SCRAPE; SPOT; STEW; anagram indicator; *see* CHILD, NAUGHTY

pickle, in a CURRIED

pickled HIGH; ■ PRESERVED; STEWED; *see* DRUNK

pickpocket DIP

picnic SPREAD; can indicate something being easy, piece of cake, etc; [◊ AL FRESCO]

picot LOOP

picture FILM; IMAGE; MOVIE; MURAL; OIL; PHOTO; PIC; PRINT; SKETCH; SNAP; VIEW; ■ DRAWING; IDEA; IMAGINE

picture, big EPIC; POSTER

picture blacker, make SHADE

picture, small INSET

picture-postcard VIEW

pictures ART; PIX

pictures, some TATE; ■ GALLERY

picturesque anagram indicator

pie DISH; PASTRY; PASTY; TART; anagram indicator

pie-cooking EPI (i.e. anagram of pie)

pie-eyed *see* DRUNK

pie top CRUST

piece BIT; CHIP; CHUNK; CUT; FLAKE; GUN; ITEM; LUMP; MAN; MORSEL; PART; PATCH; PORTION; SHARD; SHEET; SLAB; SLICE; STRIP; TAG; TUNE; WEDGE; ■ ARTICLE; EXCERPT; PARTICLE; can indicate that a sequence of letters within a word is to be used, as "concert piece" → ERT; *see* CHESSMAN

piece, narrow BAND; SLIVER; STRIP

piece of initial letter indicator; run indicator

piece of advice TIP

piece of cake EASY

piece of film CLIP

piece of ground/land LOT; PARCEL; PATCH; PLOT; ■ FEUD (archaic)

piece of material RAG; ■ CLOTH

piece of news ITEM

piece of paper SHEET; TICKET

piece of wood BOARD; PALE; PLANK

piece, short EXTRACT; ■ PASSAGE

piece, small SLIVER

piece, thick SLAB

piece, tiny PARTICLE

piecemeal anagram indicator

pieces MEN

pieces, go to FLAKE

pieces, in/to anagram indicator

piecework COLLAGE

pieceworker, a ABITANT (i.e. a-bit-ant, useful for making 'habitant' or 'inhabitant')

pier JETTY; [◊ DOCK; MOLE]

pierce BORE; CLEAVE; CUT; ENTER; GORE; LANCE; SPEAR; SPIT; STAB; ■ BROACH; IMPALE

pierced CUT

piercing tool AWL

pierhead P

piers HARBOUR

Piersporter VIEN; WINE

piety DEVOTION

piffle *see* RUBBISH

pig BAR; BOAR; HOG; RUNT; SOW; SWINE; ■ BEAST; POKE; PORKER; can indicate something to do with iron, iron-works etc; [◊ FARROW; STY; SWILL]

pig, bit of a *see* PIG-MEAT

pig, cured BACON

pig food MAST; SWILL

pig-meat HAM; ■ BACON; PORK; RASHER

pig-pen STY

pig's origin P; STY

pig, smallest RUNT

pig sound GRUNT

pigeon CARRIER; HOMER; ■ CONCERN; PASSENGER; [◊ LOFT]

piggish noise OINK

piglet* RUNT

pigment UMBER; ■ BISTRE

pigment, brownish BISTRE

pigs SWINE

pike LUCE; SPEAR; STAFF

pile HEAP; HILL; MASS; MINT; NAP; POT; RICK; STACK; STAKE; TOWER; ■ MOUND; REACTOR

pile, combustible PYRE

pile of combustible PYRE

pile of hay RICK

pile of papers REAM

pile of rocks CAIRN; TOR

pile of sheaves STOOK

pile up AMASS; GATHER; HEAP; STACK; *see* PILE-UP

pile-up SMASH; CRASH; ■ ACCIDENT; *see* PILE UP

pilfer RIFLE; ROB; STEAL

pilgrim PALMER

pilgrimage HAJ

pill TAB; TABLET

pill-box INRO

pillage ROB; SACK; ■ REAVE (arch.)

pillar PIER; POST; STELE; ■ COLUMN

pilot ACE; FLY; FLYER; GUIDE; LEAD; STEER; TEST; TRIAL; USHER

piloted FLEW; LED

pimple SPOT

pin CASK; CLIP; FLAG; NAIL; PEG; RIVET; SPIKE; STICK; TACK; ■ AXIS; SKITTLE; THOLE; [◊ PANEL]

pin down NAIL

pin one's faith on TRUST

pin-up LIAN (i.e. nail reversed); NIP (i.e. pin reversed); SNAP; ■ POSTER

pinafore PINNY

Pinafore can indicate something to do with Gilbert and Sullivan, D'Oyly Carte

pinch BIT; CRAMP; FILCH; NIP; ROB; STEAL; SWIPE

pinched DRAWN; STOLE

pinching nesting indicator

pine DEAL; FRET; LONG; MOON; TREE

pine leaf NEEDLE

pinion COG; WING; ■ FEATHER

pink CORAL; KNOCK; ROSE; ROSY; RUDDY; THRIFT

pink, look BLUSH

pink paper FT

pinned NAILED; TACKED

pins LEGS

pint ALE; BEER; JAR; PT

pints, sixteen PECK

pints, two QUART

pioneer BLAZE

pious DEVOUT; GOOD; HOLY; PI

pious hope RIP

pious man ST; ■ SAINT

pip BEAT; FIT; GREED; SEED; SPOT (i.e. on a playing card)

Pip can clue the word EXPECTATIONS (from Dickens)

Pip's beloved ESTELLA (i.e. from *Great Expectations*)

pip, we hear CEDE

pipe BUTT; CASK; DUCT; FLUE; FLUTE; HOSE; OAT; REED; SEWER; TUBE; ■ BONG; BRIER; CHANTER

pipeline HOSE

piper's son TOM

pipes, like some REEDY

piping HOT; REEDY; ■ TUBES; TUBING

pippin* APPLE

piquancy TANG

piquant TANGY

pique HUFF; PET

piracy CRIME; THEFT

pirate FLINT; HOLE; HOOK; KIDD; MORGAN; PEW; ROVER; SILO; SILVER

pirouette TURN

Pisa, tower of usually indicates LEAN, LEANS or LEANING

piste SLOPE

piston ROD

pit BED; MINE; STONE; TRAP; ■ ABYSS; HOLLOW

pit-worker DIGGER; MINER; ■ COLLIER

pitch CAST; DIP; FIELD; HURL; KEY; LOB; SHY; SLING; SPIEL; TAR; THROW; TONE; TOSS; ■ FLING; PATTER; can indicate something to do with music or sound; [◊ NOTE]

pitch, on another AWAY

pitch, on the IN; ■ BATTING; PLAYING

pitch, over the normal SHARP

pitch, side of END

pitched CAST; FLUNG; SLUNG; TARRED

pitcher DIPPER; EWER; URN

pitchfork [◊ TUNE]

pith CORE; HEART

pithy TERSE

pitiable POOR

pity SHAME; RUE; RUTH; ■ QUARTER

pivot AXLE; TURN

placard POSTER (qv); SIGN

placate CALM; ■ APPEASE

place AREA; BED; CELL; CITY; FLAT; HOME; LAY; LIEU; LODGE; PAD; PL; POINT; POSE; POST; PUT; ROOM; SET; SHOP; SITE; SPOT; SPACE; ■ LOCATE; LOCUS; NICHE; POSITION; STEAD; ZONE

place, all over the anagram indicator

place, awful DUMP; STY

place below BURY; INTER

place, cleric's BRAY

place, cosy NEST; ■ NICHE

place for discussion FORUM

place for entertainment CLUB; FAIR

place for fighting RING
place for reading AMBO
place for street vendor PITCH
place, high EYRIE; PEAK
place, in ON; anagram indicator
place in France/Paris LIEU
place in office INVEST
place in opposition PIT
place in society CASTE; CLASS
place in the field *see* FIELDING POSITION
place, in the same IB
place, in this HERE
place, iniquitous DEN
place of birth NATAL
place of convalescence SPA
place of debauchery STY
place of duty POST
place of entertainment CLUB; FAIR
place of great beauty EDEN
place of match VENUE; ■ PITCH
place of seclusion LAIR
place of unspoiled beauty EDEN
place of vice DEN
place of worship CH; TEMPLE
place often visited HAUNT
place on board CABIN; CHAIR; DECK; SQUARE
place, out of anagram indicator
place overseas LIEU
place, perfect NICHE
place, relaxing HAVEN
place, safe ARK
place setting COVER
place, small BOOTH
place, that THERE
place, that's the THERE
place, this HERE
place to confine PEN
place to eat CAFE; CAFF; MESS; TABLE; ■ RESTAURANT
place to exercise GYM
place to hide LAIR
place to live, stay *see* ACCOMMODATION
place to play PITCH
place to stop BERTH; PORT
place, uncomfortable HOLE
place to watch STAND

place where workers are seen *see* WORKPLACE
placed LAID; PUT; SAT; SET
placid COOL
placing SITING; ■ SETTING
placket SLIT (in a skirt)
plagiarise COPY; STEAL
plagiarised STOLEN
plagiarism CRIB; THEFT
plagiarist COPIER; PIRATE
plague DOG; PRESS; ■ SCOURGE; *see* ANNOY
plague-carrier RAT
plaid CHECK; ■ CHECKED; TARTAN
plain BALD; BARE; BLUNT; FLAT; OVERT; SIMPLE; SOBER; STARK; STEPPE; ■ CANDID; CLEAR; EXPLICIT; FRANK; UGLY; UNPAINTED
plain language PROSE
plain-spoken BLUNT; FRANK
plaintiff DOE
plait BRAID
plaits, with BRAIDED
plan AIM; CHART; DEAL; DESIGN; DRAFT; FRAME; IDEA; INTEND; MAP; MEAN; PLOT; PLOY; THOUGHT; ■ BREW; METHOD; PROPOSITION; SCHEME; anagram indicator
plan, prepare DRAFT
plan to steal CASE
plane BUS; DRESS; EVEN; FLAT; JET; KITE; LEVEL; MIG; SHAVER; SOAR; TREE; TOOL; ■ FIGHTER; GLIDER
plane control RUDDER
plane, get on BOARD
plane in, bring LAND
plane journey FLIGHT
plane, take a (travel by) FLY
plane, took a (travelled by) FLEW
planet EARTH; MARS; WORLD
plank BOARD
planking BOARDS
planned MEANT; anagram indicator
planners OS

planning DESIGN
plant ARUM; ASTER; BROOM; BURY; BUSH; CHARD; CHIVE; CRESS; DILL; DOCK; FERN; FIX; FLAG; GORSE; GRASS; HEATH; HEMP; HERB; HOLLY; HOP; HOSTA; INTER; IVY; JUTE; LAY; MALLOW; MILL; MINT; MOSS; PEA; PLUNGE; PUT; REED; RAPE; ROOT; RUE; RUSH; SAGE; SEDGE; SOW; STOCK; TARO; THRIFT; VINE; WEED; WORKS; YARROW; ■ ALOE; ANNUAL; BUGLE; FACTORY; FRAME; HEATHER; LOVAGE; MEU; NETTLE; OCA; ORRIS; PARSLEY; PINK; SENNA; SET; SETTLE; SPURGE; STATICE; STOCK; *see* FLOWER, SHRUB, VEGETABLE
plant, aromatic ANISE
plant, bog SEDGE
plant disease BLIGHT
plant, fodder EMMER
plant, garden ANNUAL; *see* PLANT
plant, intrusive WEED
plant juice SAP
plant, large TREE
plant, leguminous GUAR
plant life FLORA
plant, marsh REED; RUSH
plant, North American SEGO
plant, oil RAPE
plant, part of ANTHER; ROOT; STALK; STEM
plant, poisonous SPURGE
plant, tropical LIANA
plant, wild ANISE
plant, woody VINE
plant, yellow RAPE
planted SOWN; anagram indicator
planter SEEDER; SOWER
plaque PLATE; TABLET
plaster RENDER; STRIP; ■ DAUB; TEER (building)
plastered DRUNK (qv); STONED
plastic SOFT; anagram indicator
plate COAT; COVER; DISC; DISH; LAMINA; METAL; SCALE; ■ CHARGER; COURSE; PATEN; SCUTE (zool.); can indicate baseball plate and so calling up PITCHER etc.
plate, metal FISH
plate, small SCALE
plateau FLAT; TABLE
plates SCUTA (zool.); *see* PLATE
plates of meat FEET (rhyming slang)
plates, small SCALES
platform CAGE; DECK; RAFT; RIG; STAGE; ■ DAIS; GANTRY; PODIUM; STADDLE
platform, mobile DOLLY; LIFT
platform, part of PLANK
plating silver AG to be nested
platoon PL
platter DISH; RECORD; *see* PLATE
play ACT; BAT; BET; BRAND; CAST; FRISK; FUN; GAME; GIVE; LARK; ROOM; SCOPE; SKETCH; SHOW; SPORT; STRUM; TOY; TRIFLE; VENT; WORK; ■ DISPORT; DRAMA; GAMBLE; PIPE; PLUCK; ROMP; anagram indicator; can signal a famous play, often by Shakespeare, and often abbreviated in the clue e.g. MND; [◊ ACTOR; CAST]
play area BOARD; COURT; PITCH; REC
play around MONKEY; a component to be nested within PLAY (or a synonym e.g. TOY)
play at first *see* PLAY FIRST
play, be in ACT; APPEAR
play casually STRUM
play, end of ACTIV (i.e. Act IV); Y
play first LEAD; START; TOP
play football DRIBBLE
play for time STALL
play game anag. of GAME
play ground COURT; ■ PITCH; REC
play, in anagram indicator
play, late part of ACTIV
play leading role STAR

play on words PUN; anagram indicator

play opening ACTI; P

play, part of ACT; SCENE

play, preferring to SPORTY

play, present STAGE

play quaveringly TRILL

play regularly LY

play school RADA

play, section of ACT

play, start of ACTI (i.e. Act I); P

play the fool DAFF

play violin BOW

play with words PUN

playboy RAKE

played anagram indicator

played first LED

player ACTOR; BLACK; BLUE; PIPER; STRIKER; WHITE; WING; WINGER; *see* FOOTBALLER; can signify an orchestra member, usually a musical instrument, e.g. oboe, tuba, *see* MUSICAL INSTRUMENT; anagram indicator; [◊ PART; ROLE]

player, best CHAMP

player, bit EXTRA

player, defensive BACK

player, extra RESERVE

player of pipes PAN

player, poor RABBIT

player, sidelined WING; WINGER

player, top ACE; SEED; STAR

player, unskilful HAM

player's warning FORE

players BAND; CAST; GROUP; LSO; SIDE; SQUAD; TEAM; can indicate something to do with orchestra, music; [◊ PITCH; STAGE]

players, group of *see* PLAYERS

players, groups of SIDES; *see* PLAYERS

players' union EQUITY

playful FRISKY

playground REC; ■ COURT; PITCH

playing ON; SPORT; anagram indicator

playing area PITCH

playing cards DECK; PACK

playing-field PITCH

plaything DOLL; TOY

playtime BREAK

playwright BOLT; FRY; PINTER; RICE; SHAW; TRAVERS; WILDE; ■ BEHAN; BRECHT; WILDER; *see* DRAMATIST

plea APPEAL; CALL; SUIT

plea for mercy MITIGATION (useful to get litigation)

plead ASK; BEG; CLAIM; SUE; ■ ENTREAT

pleasant GOOD; KIND; NICE; SWEET; ■ AMICABLE; AMIABLE; FRIENDLY

pleasant surroundings, in a component to be nested within a synonym for pleasant e.g. NICE

pleasantness AMENITY

please CONTENT; DELIGHT; ■ GRATIFY; TICKLE

pleased CONTENT; GLAD; HAPPY; ■ PROUD

pleased, look SMILE (qv)

pleasure BLISS; DELIGHT; FUN; JOY; WILL

pleasure, gain ENJOY

pleasure, give DELIGHT; TICKLE; TREAT

pleasure-seeker RAVER; ■ HEDONIST

pleat FOLD; TUCK

plebeian RED

plectrum [◊ PLUCK]

pledge GAGE; OATH; PAWN; TOAST; TROTH; WORD; ■ EARNEST; can signal something to do with pawnshops

plentiful AMPLE; ■ COPIOUS

plentiful, be ABOUND

plenty ALOT (i.e. A LOT); AMPLE; LOT

plenty, with RICH; *see* RICH

pliant SUPPLE; ■ ELASTIC; GIVING; LITHE

plied STROVE; TOILED

plight LOT; PICKLE

plimsoll PUMP

plinth SOCLE

plod TRAIL; TRUDGE; WADDLE

plonk BOOZE; DUMP; SIT; WINE

plonked SAT

plot BED; GRAPH; GRAVE; GROUND; HATCH; LAND; PLAN; RUSE; TRACT; ■ GARDEN; INTRIGUE; MAP

plot, clerical GREBE

plots anagram indicator

plotter CASCA

plough SHARE; TILL

ploughed anagram indicator

ploughed, may be ARABLE

ploughing anagram indicator

ploy CABAL; DODGE; GAMBIT; PLAN; RUSE; TRICK; WILE

ploy, deceptive SELL

ploy, winning MATE

pluck GRIT; PICK; ■ GUTS; PLAY; TWANG; TWITCH; [◊ PLECTRUM; STRING]

plucky BRAVE; GAME; can indicate something to do with the player of a string instrument

plug AD; BUNG; PUSH; SHOOT; STOP; STOPPER; TAMP; as a form of tobacco can indicate something to do with smoking a pipe

plum CREAM; GAGE; TOP

plumb LEAD; SOUND; WEIGHT; ■ FATHOM

plumber PIPER

plume WISP; ■ FEATHER

plummet DROP; FALL; PLUNGE; SOUND

plump FAT; ROUND; STOUT; ■ ROTUND; ROUNDED

plunder LOOT; PREY; RIFLE; ROB; SACK; SWAG

plunge DIP; DIVE; RUSH; ■ GAMBLE

plunged DOVE

★ **plural** a plural word can indicate that a word or component is to be repeated. In this way the plural "firms" can signify COCO for example as in "Firms connected with a beverage" is solved by COCOA

plus AND; ASSET; CROSS; MORE; SIGN

plus, give a ADD; ■ CREDIT

plush RICH

Pluto DIS

plutonium PU

pluvial RAINY

ply BEND; LAYER; STRAND; THREAD

Plymouth, feature of HOE

PM can call for the name of a specific prime minister, see PRIME MINISTER; can indicate something to do with the afternoon

PM, former LAW

poach STEAL; ■ COOK; HUNT

pocket KEEP; POUCH; RETAIN; ■ PURSE; can indicate something to do with snooker

pocket, in UP

pocketing, pockets nesting indicator

pod CASE

podium STAGE; ■ ROSTRUM

Poe's visitor RAVEN

poem CANTO; EPIC; IF; LAY; LINES; LL; ODE; SONNET; VERSE; ■ BALLAD; IDYLL; [◊ ODIC]

poem, part of VERSE

poet BARD; BRIDGES; BROOKE; BURNS; CLARE; DONNE; GRAY; HOMER; HOOD; HUNT; KEATS; LEAR; MARVEL; OWEN; POPE; POUND; PRIOR; TATE; VIRGIL; YEATS; ■ AUDEN; BROWNING; CHAUCER; COWPER; DANTE; ELIOT; HEINE; MARTIAL; OVID; RILKE; SHELLEY; SKELTON; SPENDER

poet, Italian DANTE

poet's work ODE; POEM; VERSE; see POEM

poetic element IAMB; VERSE; ■ RHYME

poetic rhythm METRE

poetic usage VERSE; can indicate poetic versions of words e.g. tho

poetry LL; VERSE; see POEM

poetry, of ODIC

poetry, short FOOT

point AIM; BARB; CAPE; DOT;
E; END; GIST; HEAD; ISSUE;
LEAD; MARK; N; NESS; NIB;
NODE; NUB; PEAK; PIN;
PRONG; PT; REASON; S;
SHOW; SPIKE; SPOT; STOP;
THORN; THRUST; TICK;
TINE; TIP; TRAIN; W; ■
DETAIL; GUIDE; MORAL;
PRICKLE; STAGE; TUSK; first
letter indicator as "freezing
point" clues F; first or last letter
indicator (example: "has no good
points" requires G to be omitted
from the beginning and end of a
word such as GANG to give AN)

point, at every ALL

point, at that THERE

point, at this HERE

point, central HUB; NUB

point in journey GEO (i.e. E in
"go")

point, main CRUX; GIST; HUB;
NUB

point of view ANGLE; SLANT;
TAKE

point of writing, the NIB

point out N, E, W or S to be omitted

point to FINGER

point-to-point can indicate two
points of the compass connected
by TO (e.g. ETON, STON,
STOW); or simply two points of
the compass juxtaposed e.g. EN

pointed ACUTE; SHARP; ■
TAPERED; TAPERING

pointed remark BARB; DIG

pointed structure SPIRE

pointer ARROW; CLUE; DOG;
HAND (as on a clock);
NEEDLE; SETTER

pointless BLUNT; INANE;
LOVE; O; VAIN; ■ INEPT; see
POINTLESSLY

pointlessly can indicate that N, E,
W, and/or S should be omitted

points some combination of N, E,
W and S; [◊ TRACK]

points, with no NOSE (i.e. no
SE); see POINTLESSLY

poise BALANCE

poison BANE; ■ MALICE;
TOXIN; anagram indicator

poisoned TOXIC

poisoner ASP

poisonous TOXIC

poisonous plant SPURGE

poke BAG; EGG; GOAD; JAB;
PICK; PROD; ROOT; STAB;
URGE; ■ SPORRAN

poke fun at MOCK

poker STUD

poker hand FLUSH; STRAIGHT

Poland PL

polar might indicate something to
do with ice, cold, bear, penguin
etc

polar explorer ROSS; SCOTT

Polaris STAR; SUB

pole BEAM; BOOM; MAST; N;
NORTH; POST; ROD; S;
SOUTH; SPAR; SPRIT; STAFF;
STAKE; STICK; ■ ANODE;
PERCH; ROOST; can indicate
something to do with stylite

polenta MEAL

police BILL; CID; COPS; DIS;
FORCE; LAW; MET; MPS;
RUC; YARD; ■ CONTROL;
GARDA; GUARD

Police Department PD

police force MET; MP; YARD

police force, former RUC

police informer GRASS; NOSE

police officer DI; DS; PC;
SUPER; see POLICEMAN

police operation ARREST

police post BOMA (E.Afr.)

police, secret KGB

police spy NARK

police station NICK

police suspicion SUS

police trap STING

policeman COP; COPPER;
GARDA; MOUNTIE; MP; PC;
PLOD; SPECIAL; SUPER; ■
BUSY; DIXON; [◊ LOT, PATCH]

policeman, old PEELER;
RUNNER; ■ CATCHPOLE

policeman, plain-clothes DI; DS

policeman, senior SUPER

policemen CID; MPS; *see* POLICE

policy LINE; PLAN; PLANK; TACK; can indicate the answer is a familiar advisory proverb

polish BUFF; CLASS; FINISH; GLOSS; RUB; SAND; SHINE; WAX; ■ REFINE; SMOOTH

polished SLICK; WAXED; ■ SHONE; SMOOTH

polished off ATE

polite CIVIL; SUAVE

politer NICER

politic DISCREET; ■ DIPLOMATIC; TACTFUL; [◊ TACT]

political PARTY; STATE

political activists CELL; PARTY

political allies BLOC

political control POWER

political division CENTRE; LEFT; RIGHT

political enforcer WHIP

political gathering RALLY

political group BLOC; CELL; PARTY; WING; ■ FRONT; SENATE

political leader P; PM; *see* PRIME MINISTER

political leaders POL

political opponents SIDES

political organisation PARTY

political power STATE

political spokesman's words SPIN

politically correct PC

politician CON; LAB; LIB; MP; TORY; WHIG; ■ GREEN; MAYOR; MEMBER

politician, American DEM

politician, senior MINISTER; PM

politicians PARTY

politicians, removal of PURGE

politics [◊ PARTY]

poll COUNT; CUT; HEAD; VOTE

pollute DEFILE; DIRTY; MAR; ■ INFECT

polluted anagram indicator

pollution anagram indicator

pollution, create *see* POLLUTE

Polo CAR

polo mallet STICK

Polonius can indicate something to do with lending (character in *Hamlet*)

pommel HORN

pompom BALL; CANNON

pompous STUFFY

pond MERE; POOL

ponder MULL; MUSE; THINK; WEIGH; ■ DEBATE

pontiff POPE

pony HORSE

pooch DOG

Pooh BEAR

Pooh's friend ROO

Pooh said BARE (i.e. homophone)

pool BATH; CESS; FUND; KITTY; LIDO; MERE; POND; *see* CASH RESOURCES; anagram indicator

pool, heated SPA

pool, open-air LIDO

pool, work in the TYPE

pools entries DIVES

poop DECK; TIRE; ■ EXHAUST

poor BAD; BLEAK; ILL; LAME; LEAN; LOW; NEEDY; OFF; ROPEY; THIN; WEAK; ■ BUM; DISMAL; RAGGED; SHODDY; anagram indicator

poor actor HAM

poor area SLUM

poor fellow WRETCH

poor grade D; E

poor grades DD; DE; ED; EE

poor growth SCRUB

poor health, in ILL; SICK

poor performer RABBIT

poor quality, stuff TAT

poor reception STATIC

poor relief ALMS

poor soul WRETCH

poor trading figure LOSS

poor, very LOUSY; *see* POOR

poorer quality, of LEANER; ROPIER

poorest LEAST

poorly AILING; ILL; anagram indicator

poorly drafted anagram indicator

poorly dressed RAGGED

poorly-made BAD

Pooter signals something to do with the book *The Diary of a Nobody*

pop BURST; DAD; FATHER; HOCK; NIP; PA; PAWN; *see* FATHER

pop artist RAPPER

pop back AP

pop concert GIG

pop figure IDOL

pop-group BAND

pop music RAP

pop off DIE; PA or POP to be omitted

pop star STING

Pope LEO; URBAN; ■ ADRIAN; CLEMENT; MARTIN

Pope at turn of century POLE

Pope's document BULL

popinjay FOP

poplar ASP; with its initial letter capitalised (Poplar) can indicate something to do with London

popped anagram indicator

poppycock ROT; *see* RUBBISH

popular IN; HOT; LAY; LIKED; MASS; ■ FAMED; can indicate the colloquial version of a word, for instance "popular game" → FOOTER

popular demonstration DEMO

popular, most TOP

popular music MOTOWN; POP; RAP; ROCK

popular, not IN to be omitted

popular person/record/thing HIT

popular, something very CULT

popular success HIT

popular team INSIDE

popular, very HOT

porcelain, Chinese MING

porcelain container MING

porch ENTRANCE

pore over CON; STUDY

pork PIG

pork, bit of RUMP

pork-pie HAT; LIE; UNTRUTH

porker PIG (qv)

porkies LIES

pornographic BLUE

porridge BIRD; GRUEL; OATS; STIR

porridge, ingredient of SAMP

port HAVEN; HOLE; L; LEFT; PT; STOP (i.e. port of call); sea port, commonly RIO; also ACRE, ADEN, AYR, BARI, BREST, CORK, DEAL, DOVER, HULL, OBAN, ORAN, POOLE, RYE, SPLIT, TYRE

port* WINE

port authority PLA

port, Cornish LOOE

port, prepare MULL

port, Scottish OBAN

port authority PLA

port, prepare MULL

portable LIGHT

portal GATE

portend BODE

portent OMEN; SIGN

porter ALE; BEER; CARRIER; STOUT

Porter COLE

Porter's can refer to a song or musical by Cole Porter

porter's house LODGE

portico STOA

portion BIT; DOLE; LOT; PART; PIECE; RATION; SHARE; SLICE; SOME; ■ CHUNK; FRACTION

portly FAT; STOUT

portraitist LELY

portray SHOW; SKETCH; ■ DEPICT

Portsmouth POMPEY

pose ACT; LIE; MODEL; PUT; SIT; ■ STANCE

posed SAT; anagram indicator

poses anagram indicator; *see* POSE

poseur PSEUD

posh SMART; TOP; U; UPPER

posh car LIMO; ROLLER; ROLLS; RR

posh chap/ person NOB; SNOB; TOFF

posh fellows UFF

posh frock ROBE

position GRADE; LAY; LIE; OFF; ON; PLACE; POSE; POST; PUT; SEAT; SET; SITE; SLOT; SPOT; STANCE; STAND; ■ BERTH; OFFICE; POINT; SITUATE; STANDING; STATION; STEAD

position, assign to PUT; SITE; ■ LOCATE

position, awkward CORNER; SPOT

position, commanding TOP

position, fill APPOINT

position, in advantageous UP

position of authority CHAIR

position of cross STATION

position, paid POST; *see* JOB

position relative to ship ABEAM; AFT; PORT; ■ FORWARD; STARBOARD

position, taking new anagram indicator

positioned ON; PUT; SAT; SET

positioned around nesting indicator

positions LOCI; *see* POSITION

positive PLUS; POS; SURE; YES

positive photo PRINT

positive reaction AY; AYE; JA; OK; OUI; YES

positive result GAIN; WIN

positive sign PLUS

possess HAVE; HOLD; KEEP; OWN

possessed HAD; OWNED

possessed of nesting indicator

possesses HAS; OWNS

possession, be in *see* POSSESS

possession, in nesting indicator

possession, in our a component to be nested within OUR

possession, was in HAD

possessions ESTATE

possessions, enjoy HAVE; OWN

possessive female HER

possessive male HIS

possessive sort OWNER

possessor OWNER; ■ HOLDER

possibilities anagram indicator (as "ten possibilities" calls for an anagram of TEN)

possibility CHANCE; MIGHT

possible ON; anagram indicator

possibly MAYBE; anagram indicator; can indicate that the general category of the example given is called for (Example: "Whip Tom, possibly?" → CAT); can indicate that the definition given in the clue is indirect (Example: "The first to filch – one put inside, possibly" leads to THIEF)

possibly true anagram of TRUE

post AFTER; CHAIR; JAMB; JOB; MAIL; OFFICE; PLACE; POLE; RAIL; SEND; STAKE; STUD; ■ NEWEL; PILLAR; SITUATION; STATION

post, in the SENT

postage CHARGE; STAMP

postal order PO

postal service RM

posted MAILED; SENT

poster AD; BILL; STICKER

postern DOOR; GATE

postman PAT

postpone DEFER; DELAY; SHELVE

postponed OFF; ■ DEFERRED

postulate POSIT

posture POSE; SET; STANCE; STAND

posturing CAMP

posy SPRAY

pot BELLY; CROCK; DOPE; GRASS; HASH; JAR; MING; MUG; SHOOT; TUB; TUM; URN; WEED; WOK; ■ CATCH; COOKER; DIXIE; KITTY; PAUNCH; PRIZE; [◊ STAKE]

pot-bellied ROUND

pot, broken CROCK

pot shot, take SNIPE

potassium K

potato SPUD; TUBER; YAM; ■ EDWARD; MURPHY; [◊ CHIP; CRISP; ROOT]

potato, battered CHIP; FRITTER

potato dish MASH

potato, portion of CHIP
potatoes MASH
potatoes, pile of CLAMP
potboiler HOB; STOVE
potent STRONG
potentate PRINCE
potential MAKINGS; VOLT; anagram indicator
potential growth BUD; SEED
potential, having ABLE
potentially anagram indicator
pother FUSS
pothole CAVE
pots CROCKERY
Potter can indicate something to do with Harry Potter e.g. magic, broomstick
potter MESS; TINKER; can indicate something to do with Wedgwood
potter about FOOTLE; a component to be nested with POTTER
pottery CHINA; CRAFT; DELFT; MING
pottery centre STOKE
pottery material CLAY
pottery, piece of SHARD
potting can indicate something to do with snooker, etc.
pouch POCKET; SAC; ■ PURSE
poultry GOOSE; HEN; HENS
poultry disease ROUP
poultry product EGG
pounce JUMP; SPRING
pounced STRUCK
pound BEAT; BELT; GRIND; HIT; L; LB; LAM; ONER; PEN; QUID; RAM; THUMP; WEIGHT; ■ BATTER; CAGE; NICKER; ONCER; STRIKE
pound coin/note ONCER; ONER; QUID
£1 debt, to have OWEL (i.e. owe L)
pounds L; LL; *see* POUND
pounds, a few LL; STONE
pounds, having lost L or LL to be omitted
pounds, shillings and pence ACID; LSD

pour DROP; GUSH; LASH; RAIN; SERVE; SPOUT; STREAM; TEEM; TIP
pour away DRAIN
pour noisily TEAM (i.e. homophone)
pour out DECANT; anagram of POUR
pout BIB; MOUE; SULK
POW camp STALAG
powder FLOUR; MEAL; TALC; ■ SNUFF
powder, reduced to GROUND
powdered GROUND
power AC; AMP; DC; ARM; CLOUT; FORCE; LIVE (i.e. as in live cable); MIGHT; P; STEAM; SWAY; TEETH ■ EXPONENT; NUCLEAR
power, classically VIS
power cord FLEX
power cut OUTAGE
power, extraordinary ESP; MAGIC
power, governing STATE
power, great US
power, having the ABLE
power, in REIGNING
power, increase REV
power, lacking *see* POWERLESS
power, lose DIE; FADE
power, source of COAL; GRID; STEAM
power supply AC; COAL; DC; GAS; STEAM
power symbol MACE
power unit KW; WATT
power, with ABLE
power, without WEAK; ■ FEEBLE; P to be omitted
powerful MIGHTY; STRONG; ■ POTENT
powerful man TITAN; ■ SAMSON
powerful, was most LED
powerless WEAK (qv); P to be omitted; ■ UNABLE
PP with a homophone indicator can call for PEAS
PR *see* PUBLIC RELATIONS
practicable, practical ON

practical joke TRICK
practice DRILL; HABIT; PE; PT; USE; ▪ CUSTOM; USAGE; can indicate something to do with law or medicine
practice, out of/without RUSTY
practise DO; DRILL; SPAR; USE;
practised ABLE
prairie PLAIN
praise EXTOL; GLORY; LAUD; ▪ COMMEND; CREDIT; FLATTER; TOAST
praise insincerely FLATTER
praise, song of [PAEAN]
prance SWAGGER
prank CAPER; DIDO (i.e. U.S.); JAPE; TRICK; ▪ FROLIC
prate GAB; *see* CHATTER
prattle BABBLE
prawns SCAMPI
pray ASK; BEG; ENTREAT
prayer AVE; GRACE; PLEA; WISH; ▪ COLLECT; ENTREATY; LITANY; ORISON
prayer, aid to MAT; ▪ ROSARY
prayer book MISSAL
prayer, end/finish to AMEN; R
prayer, hour of PRIME; SEXT
pre-Christian BC
pre-constructed anagram of PRE
pre-Easter period LENT
pre-eminent ARCH; TOP
pre-match can indicate something to do with the period before marriage e.g. stag night
pre-prepared envelope SAE
precariously anagram indicator
precaution CARE; DRILL (as in fire, kerb etc)
precede HEAD; LEAD
preceded LED
precedence, took LED
precinct MALL
precious TWEE
precious little can indicate something to do with a precious stone
precious metal AG; AU; GOLD; OR; SILVER
precious, something GEM; *see* GEM, PRECIOUS METAL
precious stone *see* GEM

precious stones ICE
precious thing *see* GEM, PRECIOUS METAL
precipice EDGE
precipitate RAIN
precipitation RAIN
precipitous SHEER; STEEP
précis SUM
precise EXACT; NICE; PRIM; ▪ EXPRESS; STRICT
precisely DEAD
precocious child BRAT; IMP
predator OWL; LION
predetermined SET
predict AUGUR
predilection TASTE
preen GROOM; PRIMP
preface INTRO
prefer FAVOUR; LIKE; ▪ ADVANCE
preferable BETTER
preferably RATHER
preference LIKING; TASTE
preference, by SOONER
preference, express OPT
★ **prefixes** although these are small groups of letters which usually only make sense as affixes added at the beginning of a word, compilers will treat them as words in the construction of an answer. So, "old" or "without" can signal the use of EX, "before" can signal ANTE or PRE
pregnant GREAT; can indicate PRE as in – "Award – one accepted by pregnant woman?" → PREMIUM where "one" is nested in "pre-mum"
prejudice BIAS
prejudice, without OPEN
prejudiced SEXIST
prejudiced, someone, person BIGOT
preliminary PILOT
preliminary passage/section INTRO
prelude initial letter indicator

premature, prematurely EARLY
premier CHIEF; FIRST
premonition OMEN
prepare DO; DRESS; EQUIP; FIX; PLAN; PRIME; READY; TRAIN; anagram indicator
prepare bread KNEAD
prepare for exam CRAM; REVISE; SWOT
prepare for getaway PACK
prepare for re-surfacing SCRAPE
prepare for war ARM
prepare the way PAVE
prepare to drive TEE
prepare to fight again REARM
prepare to fire COCK
prepare to fight ARM
prepare to shoot COCK
prepared ARMED; BOUND; CUT; GAME; LAID; ON; PAT; READY; SET; anagram indicator
prepared food DISH; MEAL
prepared, not GREEN; RAW; ■ AD LIB (i.e. "ad lib"); UNREADY; UNFIT
prepared to fight ARMED
prepared to fire COCKED
prepared to fly FEATHERED
prepared to row OARED
prepares anagram indicator
preparing anagram indicator
preposterous anagram indicator
prequel, as a the indicated word or component to go at the front
presbyter ELDER
prescribe ORDAIN; SET
prescribed SET
prescribed amount DOSE
prescribed, what's DOSE
prescription DOSE; anagram indicator
presence AIR; BEARING; GHOST
present AD; AT; GIFT; GIVE; GRANT; HAND; HERE; NOW; OFFER; SHOW; STAGE; TIP; ■ SOP
present* TENSE
present, at NOW
present chap SANTA

present circumstances ASIS
present day can refer to Christmas
present favourably SPIN
present left LEGACY
present play STAGE
present source GIVER; SANTA
presentation anagram indicator
presented GAVE
presented in anagram indicator; run indicator
presently NOW; SOON
preservative TAR
preserve CAN; CURE; JAM; KEEP; PICKLE; POT; SAVE; SMOKE; SPARE; TIN; ■ EMBALM; MUMMIFY
preserved CANNED; nesting indicator, specifically that an element is to be nested within CAN or TIN, as "Preserved in Irish grave?" → CAIRN
preserving, means of CAN; TIN
preside RULE
preside (over) CHAIR
president CHAIR; P; *see* PRESIDENT, U.S.
president, former PERON; TITO; *see* PRESIDENT, U.S.
President Roosevelt TEDDY
president's wife EVITA
president's wife rebuffed AVITE
President, U.S. ABE; BUSH; FORD; GRANT; IKE; POLK; TAFT
presidential office OVAL
press CLAMP; CRAM; CROWD; DAB; FORCE; HUG; IRON; JAM; MANGLE; MEDIA; OUP (i.e. Oxford UP); PAPERS; PRINT; PUSH; SPUR; SURGE; URGE; ■ SQUASH; SQUEEZE; can indicate something to do with key (i.e. which is pressed)
Press Association PA
press briefly DAB
press down TAMP
press employee SUB
press gently TAP
press hard COMPACT
press measure EM; EN
press operator PRINTER

press, prepare for EDIT

press release PR; anagram of PRESS

pressed nesting indicator

pressing SORE; ■ INSTANT; URGENT

pressing need can indicate something to do with device which needs pressing e.g. keyboard, TV remote control

pressman *see* JOURNALIST

pressure P; STRAIN; STRESS; ■ COERCE; FORCE; can signify something to do with weather maps e.g. BAR

pressure, apply EXERT; FORCE; LEAN; PRESS; URGE; ■ PUSH; SOFT SOAP (phrase); P to be added

pressure, exert LOBBY

pressure group FACTION

pressure, means of exerting LEVER

pressure on king PIN (chess)

pressure on, put STRESS

pressure to get, use EXTORT

prestige STANDING; ■ CACHET; KUDOS

presumption THEORY

presumptuous FORWARD

pretence BLUFF; POSE; SHAM; ■ ACTING

pretend ACT; FAKE; FEIGN; PLAY; POSE; SHAM; ■ AFFECT; IMAGINE

pretended SHAM

pretension SIDE

pretentious ARTY; PHONY

pretentious chap/person/type PSEUD; SNOB; ■ POSEUR

pretext FRONT; PLEA; ■ EXCUSE

prettified TWEE

pretty FAIR; QUITE; SWEET; TWEE; ■ BONNIE; COMELY; DEAR; LOVE; RATHER

pretty boy PUTTO

pretty creature PERI

pretty girl/ woman BELLE; CUTIE; DISH; DOLL; LOOKER

pretty, not PLAIN

prevail REIGN; WIN; ■ OBTAIN

prevail upon GET

prevailed WON

prevalent RIFE

prevaricate LIE

prevent AVERT; BAN; BAR; BLOCK; CHECK; DETER; FOIL; STEM; STOP

prevent a ship's loss SALVE

prevent entry LOCK

prevented LET; STOPPED; *see* STOP

preview TASTE; TASTER

previous BACK; EX; OLD; FORMER; LATE; PAST; ■ FIRST

previous night EVE

previously ALREADY; ANTE; EX; ONCE; can indicate that one component should precede another; *see* PREVIOUS

previously cooked COLD

prey KILL; ■ VICTIM

price COST; FARE; FEE; PR; RATE; SP; TOLL; ■ CESS; CHARGE; EVENS; FIGURE; ODDS

price-fixers RING

price-fixing group RING

price, increase in APPRECIATE

price, low IP (i.e. one p)

price, pay the ATONE

priced at 50% can indicate half of the word 'priced', hence PRI or CED

priceless FREE; *see* EXPENSIVE

pricey DEAR; STEEP

prick STING; TINGLE

prickle SPINE; THORN

prickling sensation TINGLE

prickly SPINY

prickly pear TUNA

pricy *see* PRICEY

pride can indicate something to do with lions; [◊ SIN]

pride, one with LION

pride, source of P; ■ CREDIT

priest ABBE; CURE; ELI; FATHER; FR; LAMA; LEVI; P; PASTOR; PR; PRIOR;

RECTOR; REV; ■ CANON; CLUB; MALLET; MINISTER

priests MAGI

prig PRUDE

prim COY; PROPER; ■ DEMURE; FORMAL

prima donna DIVA

primarily initial letter(s) indicator

primary BASIC; CHIEF; MAIN; first letter indicator

primate APE; CHIMP; ■ MONKEY; POTTO

prime ACE; LOAD; PLY; STAPLE; ■ BRIEF; CHARGE; FIRST; LEADER; *see* FIRST RATE

prime minister BLAIR; DERBY; EDEN; HEATH; LAW; MAJOR; NORTH; PEEL; PITT; PM; ■ CANNING; DISRAELI; PREMIER

primed SET

primitive CRUDE; UR (Germ.); ■ STONE-AGE

primp PREEN

prince HAL; IGOR; P; PR; ■ ELECTOR; RAJA; ROYAL

prince, German/Hanoverian ELECTOR

prince's friend HORATIO (from *Hamlet*)

princess AIDA; ANNA; ANNE; DI; IDA; RANA; ■ AMIR; BEGUM

principal ARCH; CHIEF; FIRST; HEAD; LEAD; MAIN; STAR; TOP; ■ CENTRE; LEADING; MASTER; [◊ INTEREST]; first letter indicator

principal role LEAD; STAR

principal way AROAD (i.e. A-road)

principally first letter(s) indicator

principle CAUSE; IDEA; IDEAL; PLANK; RULE; WAY; ■ AXIOM; BASIS; ELEMENT; TAO; TENET

principles WAY; *see* PRINCIPLE

print COPY; DAB; DRAFT; ETCHING; PRESS; PROOF; TYPE

print-out COPY; PROOF

print size PICA

print, something to COPY

printed RAN

printer's sign DELE

printing, gap in EM; EN

printing term STET

printing unit EM; EN

prints RUSHES

prior EARLY; PAST; preceding indicator; can signpost a word beginning with ANTE

priority, given the indicated component to be placed at the front

priority, had LED

priority, have LEAD

prise FORCE; *see* PRIZE (an alternative spelling)

prison BIRD; BRIG; CAN; CAGE; CELL; CLINK; GAOL; JAIL; JUG; NICK; PEN; STIR; ■ COOLER; FLEET; LIMBO; NEWGATE; SLAMMER; STALAG; [◊ BARS; LOCKS; SCREW]

prison, half of SING

prison, in CANNED; JUGGED; a component to be nested within a synonym for prison (CAN etc) as "left in prison" leads to CLAN

prison officer SCREW

prison, old FLEET; QUAD; QUOD

prison, old London FLEET

prison, part of CELL

prison, put in PENT; can indicate a component to be nested within a synonym of prison – *see* PRISON

prison sentence/term BIRD; LIFE; STRETCH; TIME

prison, time in *see* PRISON SENTENCE

prisoner CON; LAG; LIFER; POW; TRUSTY; ■ INMATE; INTERN

prisoner, long-term LIFER

prisoner, privileged TRUSTY

prisoner's room CELL

prisoners do, what TIME

private GI; INNER; OWN; PTE; ■ HIDDEN; INTERNAL;

PERSONAL; RANKER; SECRET; TOMMY

private American GI

private American, a AGI (i.e. a GI)

private investigator PI

private one OWN

private secretary PS

private transport CAR

privateer CRUISER

privilege PERK; RIGHT

privileged group ELITE

privileged prisoner TRUSTY

privy SECRET; *see* TOILET

prize AWARD; CUP; MEDAL; NOBEL; PALM; PEARL; PLATE; PLUM; POT; PURSE; ■ REWARD; VALUE; *see* PRISE, (an alternative spelling)

prizegiver NOBEL

prizes, gain WIN

pro FOR

probe SOUND

probing nesting indicator

problem BIND; CATCH; FAULT; HOLE; ILL; KNOT; NIGGLE; P; POSER; PROB; RUB; SNAG; SPOT; STEW; STRAIN; SUM; TANGLE; TEASER; ■ MAZE; HITCH; QUESTION; STICKER; TICKLER; anagram indicator (as "small problem" calls for an anagram of SMALL)

problem afoot CORN

problem for pilots ICING

problem, no SURE

problem, personal BO

problem, small HITCH, WRINKLE; *see* PROBLEM

problematic anagram indicator

problems HASSLE; anagram indicator

problems, with anagram indicator

proboscis NOSE

procedure COURSE; FORM; ORDER; SYSTEM; WAY; ■ ROUTINE; STEP(S)

procedure, tedious CHORE; RUT

proceed ACT; GO; HEAD; LEAD; LEAVE; ON

proceed laboriously PLOD

proceed quickly *see* RUN

proceeds GAIN; RETURN; TAKE; YIELD

process SWIPE (i.e. "to process credit card"); TREAT; anagram indicator

process of, in the WHILE

process, part of STAGE

processed, processing anagram indicator

procession FILE; LINE; MARCH; STRING

proclaim CRY; STATE; ■ ANNOUNCE; TRUMPET

proclaimed homophone indicator

proclamation EDICT

proclivity BENT

procrastinate TARRY; ■ TEMPORISE; *see* DELAY; [◊ LATE; LATER]

procrastinator DELAYER; [◊ LATER]

Procrustes as the character from mythology, can refer to stretching one's legs, pulling one's leg etc

procurator PIRATE

procure BUY; EARN; GET; NET

prod DIG; EGG; GOAD; JAB; NUDGE; POKE; PUSH; URGE

prodigal LAVISH; WASTER; ■ SPENDER

produce BEAR; CAUSE; CROP; DO; FORM; GOODS; GROW; ISSUE; MAKE; RAISE; SPAWN; STAGE; YIELD; ■ CREATE; GENERATE; anagram indicator; manipulation indicator

produce an effect ACT

produce better BEAT

produce, can anagram indicator

produce form SHAPE

produce newspaper PRINT

produce notes SING

produce young BEAR; CALVE

produced BORE; DID; MADE; anagram indicator

produces anagram indicator; *see* PRODUCE

producing MAKING; anagram indicator

product BRAND; GOOD; SON; YIELD

product of mine ORE
production WORK; anagram indicator
productive RICH
products, group of LINE
products, various LINES
profane DEFILE
profanity OATH
profess CLAIM
profession CALLING; can refer to "profession" as a statement starting with I followed by a verb (thus "Perfect profession for an entrepreneur" leads to IDEAL)
professional PRO; ■ EXPERT; TRAINED
professional, not LAY; ■ AMATEUR
professional post CHAIR
professionally, not LAY
professor PROF; ■ HEAD; [◊ CHAIR]
professorship CHAIR
proficient ABLE; ADEPT; see ABLE
profile SHAPE
profit BOOT; GAIN; NET; SERVE; YIELD; ■ ADVANTAGE; CASH; INTEREST; PROCEEDS; RETURN; WINDFALL
profit, clear NET
profit, in UP
profit, make a NET
profitable ROARING (as in success)
profligate ROUE
profound DEEP
profuse AMPLE; LAVISH; ■ GENEROUS
progeny ISSUE
programme BILL; CARD; COURSE; PLAN; ■ PILOT (i.e. on TV; anagram indicator)
programme, item in EVENT
programmer CODER
progress FARE; GO; WAY; ■ ADVANCE
progress, in ON; ONGOING
progress, make SCORE; ■ ADVANCE

progress, make slow CRAWL; INCH; PLOD
progress, slow CRAWL
progress, rate of MPH; PACE; SPEED
progressive LEFT; NEW; ■ FORWARD; RADICAL
progressive letters can indicate you are required to use the 1st letter of one word, then the 2nd of the next, 3rd from the next (and so on) from a sequence of words, as "God, taken by surprise by progressive letters" → TYR
prohibit BAN; BAR; ■ DEBAR
prohibited TABU; ■ INTERDICT
prohibited, not CLEAN
prohibition BAN; BAR; TABU
project CAST; HURL; IDEA; JOB; JUT; PITCH; PLAN; PUT; TASK; THROW; ■ BEETLE
projected THREW; see PROJECT
projectile BALL
projectiles AMMO
projection LEDGE; LUG; STUD; ■ LOBE; TENON
prolific LAVISH; RICH
prolific, be TEEM
prom FRONT; PIER; WALK
promenade AMBLE; WALK; ■ DANCE; PARADE; see PROM
prominence HILL (qv)
prominence, achieve RISE
prominence, achieved ROSE
prominent BIG
prominent, be most LEAD
promiscuous LOOSE
promise IOU; OATH; PLEDGE; PLIGHT; SAY; SWEAR; VOW; WORD; ■ COMPACT
promises to pay/settle IOUS
promising BRIGHT; RIPE; ROSY
promising, more ROSIER
promising person COMER
promissory note IOU
promontory CAPE; HEAD; NESS; ■ BILL
promontory in Scotland MULL
promote BACK; BOOST; FOSTER; HYPE; PEDDLE; RAISE; STAGE; UP; ■

FURTHER; MARKET;
UPGRADE

promoted UP; reversal indicator

promoted, was ROSE

promotion AD; BOOST; HYPE;
PLUG; SALE; ■ ASCENT; re-
versal indicator

promotion, extravagant HYPE

promotional material AD; PUFF;
■ BLURB; *see*
ADVERTISEMENT

prompt CUE; EARLY; EGG;
GOAD; PUSH; REMIND; ■
INSPIRE; JOG; NUDGE;
QUICK

promptly PAT

prone APT; LYING; ■ SUBJECT;
SUPINE

prone, be LIE

prone, is LIES

prong POINT

pronoun ONE, can also refer to
HE, I or another personal pronoun

pronounce SOUND; ■ AVER

pronounced ORAL; SAID; homophone indicator

pronouncedly homophone indicator (as "pronouncedly icy" → IC)

pronouncement homophone indicator

pronouncements DICTA

pronunciation homophone indicator

proof PRINT; TIGHT (as in water-
proof/tight;); ■ COPY (pr.);
READ (pr.); REPRO

proof, declaration of QED

proof of identity ID

prong TINE

prop LEG; REST; SCREW;
SHORE; STAY; ■ END (as in
book-end)

propaganda HYPE; SELL; ■
ANGLE; PITCH

propagandist EXPONENT

propagate BREED; RAISE

propagated BRED; RAISED; anagram indicator

propel DRIVE; PUSH; SEND;
ROW

propeller SCREW; note the propeller of a craft can be human, hence
oar, stroke etc

proper APT; DUE; FIT; PRIM;
PUCKA; REAL; RIGHT; U; ■
GOOD; STAID; STRAIGHT;
UPRIGHT

proper English U

proper form (time), in DULY

proper in China TAO

properly RIGHT; WELL

properly controlled anagram indicator

properly, not do BOTCH;
BUNGLE

property ASSET; ESTATE; FLAT;
GOODS; HOUSE; LAND;
REALTY; ■ QUALITY; SHARE;
can indicate a particular kind of
house e.g. vicarage

property charges RENT

property, income from RENT

property, U.S. REALTY

property right LIEN

prophet AMOS; ELI; MOSES;
SEER ■ AUGUR; ELISHA

prophetic VATIC

propitiatory gift BUNG; SOP

proponent of war HAWK

proportion PART; RATIO;
SCALE; SHARE

proportion, out of RATIO to be
nested within a component

proportionate DUE

proposal MOTION; MOVE;
OFFER; PLAN; ■ SCHEME

propose MEAN; MOVE; OFFER;
PLAN; TENDER; ■ INTEND;
anagram indicator

proposed MEANT; *see* PROPOSE

proposition IDEA; OFFER;
PLAN; POINT

propping up can indicate a
word/component is to follow the
succeeding word/component

proprietary TRADE

proprietor OWNER; ■ LAIRD

prosaic DULL (qv); FLAT; TAME

prosecute SUE; WAGE

prosecutor DA

prosecutor, American, U.S. DA

prospect HOPE; ■ CHANCE; OUTLOOK; VIEW; VISTA

prospecting for water, one DOWSER

prospector DIGGER; MINER

prospectus SPEC

prosper GROW

prosperity LUCK; SUCCESS; WELFARE

prosperity, formerly WEAL

prosperous RICH

prosperous-looking SLEEK

prosperous period BOOM

prospector can indicate something to do with gold prospecting e.g. PAN

prostrate PRONE

protect COVER; HIDE; MASK; SAVE; nesting indicator; ■ DEFEND; MOTHER; PRESERVE; SHIELD

protect pipes LAG

protected by nesting indicator (as "protected by iron" requires a component to be nested within FE)

protected minority WARD

protected species BAT

protecting nesting indicator

protection BIB; CAP; FENCE; GLOVE; HAVEN; JACKET; MAC; MASK; NET; SHELL; VISOR

protection against the sun TOPI

protection for nesting indicator for the word or component that follows

protection for face MASK; VISOR

protection, offering LEE

protective cloth APRON; BIB

protective clothing APRON; BIB; MAC; MAIL

protective cover LID; MAC; MAIL; SHEATH; *see* PROTECTIVE CLOTHING

protective covering MASK

protective gear *see* PROTECTIVE CLOTHING

protector APRON; BIB; CASE; GLOVE; MAC; VISOR; ■ PATRON

protégée WARD

protein, source of usually refers to SOYA BEAN

protest AVER; DEMO; MARCH; OBJECT; RAIL; ■ ASSERT; REVOLT; SITIN (i.e. sit-in)

protest abusively RAIL

protest, noisy SHOUT

Protestant LUTHER; ORANGE

protester, hunt SAB

protesting ANTI

proton constituent QUARK

prototype MODEL

protracted LONG

protuberance BUMP; HUMP; KNOB; LUMP; ■ HUNCH

protrude JUT

proud HAUGHTY

prove wrong REBUT

proverb ADAGE; MOTTO; SAW; SAYING

provide BRING; CATER; DO; FEND; GIVE; OFFER; SUIT; ■ AFFORD; ENDUE; EQUIP; FURNISH; LAYON (i.e. lay on); SUPPLY; anagram indicator

provide, can anagram indicator

provide cover for nesting indicator

provide extra ADD

provide information SHOP; SING

provide lessons TEACH

provide money FUND

provide teachers STAFF

provide with food CATER; SERVE

provide with hands DEAL

provide workers MAN; STAFF

provided GAVE; GIVEN; IF; anagram indicator

provided by anagram indicator; compound indicator; run indicator

provided nourishment FED

provider AGENT; ■ DONOR; SUPPLIER

provider of meat COW etc

providing IF; anagram indicator

providing backing FI (i.e. rev.)

providing cover for nesting indicator

providing support BRACING

province AREA; BAG; BC; FIELD; LAND; NATAL; NI; ULSTER

province, European TYROL

provision RIDER; SUPPLY

provision of meals BOARD

provisional arrangements, make CATER

provisionally anagram or initial letter indicator

provisions BOARD; EATS; FOOD; GRUB; *see* FOOD

provocation GALL; REASON; ■ EXCUSE

provocative girl TART

provoke ANGER; MOVE; NEEDLE; TAUNT; TEASE; ■ AROUSE; INFLAME

provoked anagram indicator

provoking anagram indicator

prow BOW; STEM

prowl ROVE

prowl, on the anagram indicator

proximate NEAR

proxy PP (i.e. at the end of letter)

prude PRIG

prudent SAGE; WISE

prudish PRIM

prune CLIP; CUT; DOCK; PARE; TRIM

pruned first or last letter to be omitted, as "Gardener's son pruned tree" → ABEL (where the last letter of ABELE is dropped)

pry NOSE; PEER; SNOOP

prying NOSY

Prussian BLUE

psephology [◊ POLL]

pseud FAKE; FRAUD; SHAM

pseudonym ALIAS

Pshaw, mon! OCH

PSV BUS

psyche MIND

psychiatrist SHRINK; *see* PSYCHOLOGIST

psychic sense, skill etc ESP

psychologist ADLER; FREUD; JUNG; SHRINK

pub BAR; INN; LOCAL; PH; ■ TAVERN

pub, City Road EAGLE

public OPEN; OUT; OVERT; ■ GENERAL; can refer to a public house, or something to do with a public house, *see* PUB

public address system PA

public admission OUT

public display *see* EXHIBITION

public domain, in the OUT

public gaze, put into OUT

public house *see* PUB

public land COMMON

Public Record Office PRO

public relations PR; can indicate something to do with SPIN

public relations officer PRO

public school ETON; HARROW; STOWE

public school boy FAG

public transport BUS; TRAIN; TRAM; ■ SHUTTLE

publication BOOK; ISSUE; MAG; ORGAN; PAPER; PRINT; RAG; TRACT; ■ EDITION; VOLUME

publication, improve for EDIT

publications PRESS

publicise AIR

publicist HYPER; PRO

publicity AD; ADVERT; HYPE; PLUG; POSTER; PR; PUFF

publicity agent/person PA; PRO

publicity brief AD

publicity event STUNT

publicity seeking escapade STUNT

publicity, wild HYPE

publish AIR; ISSUE; RUN; UTTER

published RAN; OUT

publisher OUP

publishing firm HOUSE

publishing house OUP

publisher, work for EDIT

Puccini opera TOSCA

pucker WRINKLE

pudding DUFF; RICE; SAGO; SWEET; TART; ▪ CRUMBLE; DUMPLING; anagram indicator

pudding* COURSE

pudding, half of POLY; ROLY

puff AD; BLOW; BLURB; DRAG; HYPE; SMOKE; WIND; can indicate something to do with advertising e.g. poster, billboard, skywriting

puff up BILLOW; SWELL

puffed BLEW; WINDED

puffed up VAIN

pug BOXER; DOG

pugilism BOXING

pugilist BOXER

pull CLOUT; DRAG; DRAW; HAUL; LUG; ROW; TOW; TUG; YANK; ▪ HEAVE; WREST

pull in PARK

pull leg of *see* TEASE

pull on weed SMOKE

pull out EXTRACT; LEAVE; QUIT

pulled DREW; *see* PULL

pulled off anagram indicator

pulled out of omission indicator (as "Fellow, one pulled out of sea" → MAN where I is dropped from MAIN)

pulling TOWING

pulled to bits anagram indicator

pullover JERSEY

pullulate TEEM

pulp MUSH; PAP; PUREE; anagram indicator

pulpit AMBO

pulse BEAN; BEAT; DAL (alt. spelling of dhal); LENTIL; PEA; SEED(S); THROB; ▪ BEATING

pulverise GRIND

pummel KNEAD

pump HEART; SHOE; TICKER

pumpkin GOURD

pun RAM; can indicate something to do with wordplay

punch BASH; BIFF; BLOW; CHIN; CHOP; CROSS; DIE; DRINK; FIST; HOOK; HORSE; JAB; LAM; LEFT; RIGHT; SLUG; SOCK; STINGO; STRIKE; [◊ BOX]

Punch PUPPET; [◊ TOBY]

punching (...) in nesting indicator

punctuation mark COLON; COMMA; DASH; STOP

puncture FLAT

puncturing nesting indicator

pundit SAGE

pungency BITE; TANG

pungent ACRID; BITTER

punish BEAT; CANE; FINE; FLOG; GATE; TAN; TAX; ▪ AMERCE

punish soundly CAIN

punished BEAT; FINED; GATED; ▪ FLOGGED; anagram indicator

punishment CANE; FINE; LINES; ROD; ▪ BEATING; FLOGGING; HIDING; LASHING; anagram indicator

punishment, corporal CANE; LASH

punishment, old form of STOCKS

punitive measure SANCTION

punt BET; GAMBLE; WAGER

punter BETTER; GAMBLER

punter's activity GAMING; *see* PUNT

pupil L; ▪ BOARDER; BOY; GIRL; SCHOLAR; can indicate something to do with the eye

pupil, former/once OB

pupil, very keen SWOT

pupils CLASS; FORM; STREAM

pupils, a lot of SCHOOL; *see* PUPILS

puppet JUDY; PAWN; PUNCH

puppies LITTER

puppy RUNT; WHELP

purchase BUY; GRIP; HOLD; ▪ LEVERAGE; PRISE; PRIZE

purchase, say BI

purchaser can indicate a form of money as "Japanese purchaser" clues Y or YEN

purchases SHOPPING; WARE(S)

purchasing power LEVER

pure CHASTE; CLEAN; WHITE; ▪ CLEAR; MERE; SIMPLE

pure PULP; anagram indicator
pured anagram indicator
purge CLEAR; FREE; RID
puritan PI; PRIG; PRUDE
puritan, smug PRIG
puritanical PRIM
puritanical person PRUDE
purple PLUM; PUCE; ■ MAUVE
purplish-brown PUCE
purpose AIM; END; GOAL; USE; ■ DESIGN;INTENT; INTENTION; MISSION; OBJECT; POINT
purpose, lack DRIFT
purpose, not having ADRIFT
purse BAG; POCKET; REWARD
purse, relentlessly HOUND
pursue BAG; CHASE; DOG; HUNT; WOO; *see* PURSUING
pursuing indicator that one component should follow another
pursuit CHASE; HUNT; ■ CAREER; HOBBY; INTEREST; QUEST
purveyor can indicate a tradesman such as a grocer etc.
purview KEN
push BUMP; BUTT; HEAVE; JAM; NUDGE; PLUG; PLY; POKE; PRESS; PROD; SHOVE; THRUST; TOUT; URGE; [◊ BUTTON]
push-button, use PRESS
push forward THRUST
push off LEAVE; SHOO
push with horns BUTT
pusher SCREW (i.e. propeller)
pushy individual SHOVER
pusillanimous YELLOW
puss CAT; MUG; TOM; *see* CAT
pussy *see* PUSS
pussy, French CHAT
put ADD; FIX; LAID; LAY; PARK; PLACE; PLANT; SET; SLIP (i.e. as in slip clothing on); ■ PARKED
put about anagram of PUT
put an end to KILL; SCOTCH; SLAY; TIP
put another way anagram indicator

put aside STORE(D)
put at danger IMPERIL; RISK; ■ ENDANGER
put away EAT; DINE; DRINK; HIDE; omission indicator
put back RETURN; reversal indicator; can indicate that "put" (or a synonym e.g. "set") be reversed, hence TUP, TES
put by SAVE; STORE
put cards on the table DEAL
put coat on DON; PAINT; VARNISH
put down INTER; LAID; LAY; LOWER; NOTE; PAN; PARK; REST; SET; SNUB; STATE; ■ CRUSH; DEGRADE; REPRESS; SUBJECT
put-down RELEGATION
put down firmly PLANT
put down on paper PEN; WRITE
put down roots SETTLE
put extra ADD
put foot down STAMP; TREAD
put forward POSE; TABLE
put in ENTER; nesting indicator
put in order SETTLE
put in the picture INFORM; PRIME; TELL; TOLD
put inside INTERN; JAIL
put into service USE; USED
put money on BET; STAKE; WAGER
put name down ENTER
put off DELAY; DETER; DETER; SHIFT; STALL; anagram of PUT
put on ADD; BEAR; DON; PLAY (as a record); SHAM; STAGE; WEAR; WORE; ■ ADOPT; APPLY; DRESS;
put on years AGE
put on hold REST
put on paper PEN; WRITE
put on play STAGE
put one's foot down STAMP; TREAD
put out AIR; CROSS; DOUSE; EJECT; EMIT; ISSUE; TED; ■ AIRED; HYPNOTISE; PIQUE; SNUFF; a general anagram indicator but can specifically call for an anagram of PUT

put out of joint anagram indicator
put questions to POSE
put right CURE; MEND; REDO; ■ REPAIR; anagram indicator
put secretly in PLANT
put the boat out PARTY; REVEL; ROISTER
put to flight ROUT
put to sea LAUNCH; SAIL
put together ADD; PIECE
put underground BURY; INTER
put up BOARD; ERECT; HANG; RAISE; STAND; TUP (i.e. "put" reversed); reversal indicator
put up with ABIDE; BEAR; LUMP; STAND; ■ SWALLOW; *see* TOLERATE
put years on AGE
putrefied OFF
putrefy ROT
putrid OFF
puts off anagram of PUTS; *see* PUT OFF
puts out anagram of PUTS; *see* PUT OUT
putsch COUP
putt HOLE
putter CLUB
putting forward article A or AN in word to be relocated to the beginning of the word
putting it right HOLING
puzzle FLOOR; MAZE; POSER; PROB; REBUS; RIDDLE; STUMP; anagram indicator
puzzle, little PROB
puzzle writer SETTER
puzzle's first part ACROSS
puzzle's second part DOWN
puzzled anagram indicator
Pylos, king of NESTOR
Pyrenean city PAU
pyromaniac [◊ ARSON; FIRE; BLAZE]

Qq

qua AS
quack SHAM; ■ EMPIRIC
quack, no PRO
quadrangle COURT; QUAD
quaff DRINK (qv); SUP
quag BOG
quagmire BOG
quail BEVY; BIRD; FLINCH
quaint CUTE; TWEE; ■ STRANGE; anagram indicator
quaintly pleasing CUTE
quake ROCK; ■ SHUDDER; TREMBLE
Quaker PENN; FRIEND
qualification *see* DEGREE
qualification, without LAY; UTTER; VERY
qualified ABLE; FIT
qualified, not LAY; UTTER
qualified teacher BED
qualify PASS
quality AIR; TONE; TRAIT; ■ NATURE; POINT; PROPERTY; can indicate a word ending in -NESS
quality, delightful CHARM
quantity AMOUNT; BATCH; GRAM; LOT; MASS SIZE; TON; ■ OMER (Heb.); can indicate a number; *see* MEASURE, WEIGHT
quantity, great/large BULK; GROSS; OODLES
quantity of drink CASK; CUP; DRAM; GLASS; PINT; SHOT; TUN; ■ BARREL
quantity of fish CRAN
quantity, smaller LESS
quantity, unspecified SOME; *see* UNKNOWN AMOUNT
quarrel ARROW; BOLT; BRAWL; CLASH; DUEL; ROW; SPAT; TIFF; ■ BICKER; DISPUTE; FEUD; RUNIN (i.e. run-in);

SCRAP; can refer to something
to do with archer

quarry BAG; CHASE; DIG;
GAME; GLASS; MINE; PREY;
STONE

quarter AREA; BILLET; E; EAST;
FOURTH; MERCY; N; NORTH;
S; SOUTH; W; WEST

quarter to ten EX (i.e. E-X)

quarterdeck SUIT (i.e. one of
four, a quarter of the pack!)

quartermaster's domain STORE

quartern* BREAD; LOAF (made
from a quarter of a stone of flour)

quarters BERTH; PAD; ■
BILLET; HOME; LODGING;
ROOMS; some combination of
N, E, W or S

quartet FOUR; IV

quartet heard FOR; FORE

quartz STONE

quash ANNUL; CRUSH;
REJECT; SCOTCH

Quasimodo note that, apart from
the character in Victor Hugo's
The Hunchback of Notre Dame,
this also refers to Low Sunday

quaver NOTE; SHAKE; TRILL;
WARBLE

quay CAY; DOCK

queasy IFFY; ILL; ■ AVERSE;
TENDER; anagram indicator

Quebec QUE

queen ANNE; BEE; BESS;
CARD; CAT; DIDO; E; ER;
MAN (as in chess); MARY;
PIECE; PUSS; Q; QU; R; VIP; ■
KITTY; RANI; REGINA;
TITANIA

Queen ELLERY; HM; *see* QUEEN

queen, beauty MISS

Queen Elizabeth BESS; ER; note,
can also refer to the liner as well
as the monarch

Queen Catherine PARR

queen, maybe BEE

Queen's English RP

queer ODD; RUM; ■ FUNNY;
SHADY; STRANGE; anagram
indicator

quell CRUSH

quench SLAKE

query ASK; WHAT; WHY

quest HUNT; SEARCH; ■
MISSION

question ASK; GRILL; HOW;
ISSUE; POINT; POSE; POSER;
PRY; PUMP; Q; QU; ■
MATTER; QUERY; RIDDLE;
TOPIC; WHICH; WHY; can indicate that the solution has the
appearance of a question and so
begins with something like IS, as
in "Question whether a flower
corolla's a drab colour" →
ISABELLA

question, it is said WEAR;
WEN; Y

question mark can imply that an
example is being given; or can
imply some humour in the clue
construction; or that the compiler
is stretching a point

question, pose ASK

question, put the ASK; ■
PROPOSE

question, put the same REPOSE

questionable FISHY; IFFY;
SHADY; can call for EH which is
the sound we might make to
emphasise a question

questioning ASKING; POSING

questions ASKS; PAPER; *see*
ASK, INVESTIGATE,
QUESTION

questions, set of PAPER; *see*
EXAMINATION

questions, ask a lot of GRILL;
PUMP

queue CHAIN; FILE; LINE;
TAIL; WAIT

queue, we hear WEIGHT (i.e. homophone of wait)

quick ALIVE; BRISK; DEFT;
FAST (qv); FLEET; LIVE;
LIVING; NIPPY; SHARP;
SHORT; SMART; ■ ACUTE;
CLEVER; PACY; PRESTO;
RACING; RAPID; READY

quick drawing/painting SKETCH

quick, not DEAD; LATE; SLOW;
see SLOW

quick, was RACED; RAN; SHOT;
SPED

quicken PEP

quickly APACE; FAST; SOON; ■ EXPRESS; PRESTO; PRONTO

quid L; PLUG; POUND; can signal something to do with tobacco, pipe etc

quiet DEAD; FAINT; LOW; MUM; P; PEACE; SH; SOFT; STAID; STILL; WHIST; WHISK; ■ CALM; GENTLE; HUSH; SILENCE; TACITURN

quiet about PRE

quiet, keep SEDATE

quiet, not kept P to be omitted

quiet, order to be SH; *see* QUIET

quiet pair PP

quiet pair, a APP

quiet person MOUSE

quiet, request for SH

quieten EASE

quietly P; SH

quiff HAIR; LOCK

quill PEN

quilt COVER

quintet FIVE; TROUT (i.e. by Schubert); V

quip JOKE (qv); PUN; SALLY

quires, twenty REAM

quirk TRAIT

quirky anagram indicator

quit CEASE; LEAVE; LEFT; RESIGN; SCRAM; STOP; ■ CEDE; DEPART; omission indicator

quitch GRASS; WEED

quite ALL; CLEAN; FULLY; ■ PRETTY; RATHER; WHOLLY

quite a few MANY

quite a/an SOME (as "Quite an effort to follow one having the same elevation" → ISOMETRY)

quits EVEN; LEVEL; SQUARE; ■ LEAVES

quite SOME; VERY

quiver TREMBLE; [◊ ARROW]

Quixote DON; *see* DON QUIXOTE

quiz ASK; GRILL; PUMP; TEST

quod *see* PRISON

quoin CORNER; EDGE

quoit RING

quota SHARE; ■ NUMBER

quotation TAG

quotation marks bear in mind that quotation marks are commonly used to confuse, so they can be placed around a single word to disguise its function in the clue, such as an indicator; or they can be used to break the connection between adjacent words, thereby putting you off the track; or to make you think about a book or play when the solution is nothing of the sort!

quotation, trite TAG

quote CITE; COPY; NAME; PRICE; ■ REPEAT

quote back ETIC (i.e. rev.)

quotient RATIO

Rr

R RIGHT

Rabelaisian COARSE

rabbit BUCK; CHAT; CONY; DOE; TALK; ■ BLATHER; JAW; RATTLE; WAFFLE; YAK; YAMMER; YATTER

rabble CROWD; MOB; ROUT

rabid MAD; WILD

race BELT; BLOOD; BREED; DART; DASH; EVENT; FLAT; HARE; HEAT; MILE; OAKS; RALLY; RELAY; RUN; RUSH; SCUD; SPEED; STOCK; TT; ■ DERBY; HUMAN; NATION; NATIONAL; SPRINT; STRAIN; WATERWHEEL; [◊ MILL]

race* EVENT

race against time RUNT

race competitor ENTRY

race, had a RAN

race meeting TT

race, part of LAP

race, start of OFF; R

racecourse ASCOT; EPSOM; REDCAR (useful in building RED CARPET!); TRACK

raced SPED

racehorse ARKLE; CHASER; STAYER

racehorses STABLE; STRING

races HEATS; TT; ■ REGATTA; anagram indicator; *see* RACE

racetrack COURSE; *see* RACECOURSE

racing TURF; *see* RACE, RUN etc

racing event HEAT; MILE; RALLY; ■ DERBY

racist NAZI

racket BAT; CON; DIN; DODGE; NOISE; RAMP; ROW; SCAM; ■ BOOMING; FIDDLE; FUSS

racy PAST

radiating member SPOKE

radiation REM

radiation mark, leave a TAN

radiation marks TAN

radiation, type of UV

radical RAD; RED; ROOT; can refer to a radical chemical e.g. methyl; ■ AMYL; ARYL; BASIC; COMMIE; INHERENT; LEFT; METHYL; ULTRA

radical, young TURK

radio SET; ■ MEDIUM; SOUND; TRANNY; homophone indicator in phrases like "on the radio"

radio company STATION

radio entertainer DJ

radio expert/operator/receiver HAM

radioactive HOT

radioactive element U

radius BONE; R

RAF man ERK

RAF officer FO; PO

RAF unit FLIGHT

raffle DRAW

raft CRAFT; STACK; *see* PILE

rafter BEAM

rag BIT; CLOTH; DAILY; PAPER; PRANK; RIB; SCRAP; TEASE; ■ TATTER

rag-roll anagram of RAG

ragamuffin URCHIN

rage ANGER; BATE; PAD; FURY; IRE; PET; RANT; STORM; TEMPER; ■ CRAZE; FASHION; FUME; PADDY; WRATH

rage, in ANGERED

ragged FRAYED; POOR; ROUGH; TATTY; TEASED; TORN; anagram indicator; note that "ragged" has two separate pronunciations and meanings, so it is likely to be used one way, say as a verb, when you should really see it as an adjective

ragged, get FRAY

raid BUST; FORAY; MISSION; SACK; SORTIE; STORM; SWOOP

raid, carefully planned STING

rail BAR; BIRD; BLAST; FENCE; LINE; RACK; RAGE; RY; TRACK; TRAIN; may refer to a specific breed of rail (bird) e.g. notornis

rail against REVILE

rail fare can indicate something to do with dining car

rail formerly BR

rail junction CREWE

rail, progress by TRAIN

rail system METRO; TRACK

railing FENCE

railings FENCE

raillery BANTER; ■ SATIRE

railroad COERCE

rails, go off the ERR; SIN

railway EL (i.e. US); LINE; RLY; RY; TRACK; TRAIN

railway carriage CAR

railway company, old LMS

railway, raised EL; YR

railwaymen NUR

rain POUR; R; SPIT; TEEM; WET; ■ PELT; SHOWER; [◊ MAC;]

rain, fine MIST

rain, sounds like REIGN; REIN

rainbow TROUT

raincoat MAC

rainstorm can indicate an anagram of RAIN

rainwear MAC

rainy WET

raise BOOST; BREED; GROW; HEFT; JACK; LIFT; LUFF; REAR; UP; ■ PARENT; ROUSE

raise glass TOAST

raise help DIA (i.e. rev. in a DC)

raise objection MIND

raise spirits ELATE; LACE

raise voice *see* SHOUT

raised BRED; HOVE; UP; reversal indicator (in a DC), as "raised stake" → ETNA; ■ GROWN

raised money abroad in a DC, can indicate a reversed foreign currency e.g. NEY

raised objection TUB (i.e. "but" rev. in a DC)

raised soundly GROAN

raiser JACK

raising reversal indicator

raising agent YEAST

rake COMB; GATHER; ROUE; SCRAPE; SLOPE; TOOL; [◊ GARDEN; SOIL; TILL]

rake-off CUT; SHARE; TAKE

raked anagram indicator

rakish JAUNTY

rally EVENT; MEET; MEND; RACE; RISE; anagram indicator

ram ARIES; BEAK; CRASH; DRIVE; TUP; ■ FORCE; PUN (i.e. consolidate); WETHER

Ramadan* FAST

ramble HIKE; ROVE; ■ WALK; WANDER

rambler ROSE; [◊ TRELLIS]

rambling anagram indicator; ■ LENGTHY

ramp SCAM (qv); SLOPE

rampage RIOT

rampage, on anagram indicator

rampaging anagram indicator

rampant RIFE; anagram indicator

rampant, frequently LION

rampart WALL

ramshackle anagram indicator

ran BLED; FLED; FLOWED; LOPED; SPED; *see* RUN

ran amok anagram indicator

ran away FLED

ran round a component to be nested within RAN or one of its synonyms e.g. SPED; *see* RAN

ranch FARM; SPREAD

rancid RANK

random SPOT (as in spot check); STRAW (as in straw poll); anagram indicator

randomly anagram indicator

randy young male STUD

range AMBIT; AREA; BAND; CHAIN; HOB; KEN; LINE; ORDER; ROW; SET; SCOPE; SPAN; STOVE; SWEEP; ■ COMPASS; EXTENT; GAMUT; SPREAD; TRAVEL; WANDER; can call for a specific mountain range e.g. ANDES, URAL

range, entire AZ (i.e. A to Z)

range of knowledge KEN

ranger GUIDE; SCOUT; WARDEN

ranges SPECTRA

rangy LANKY

rank GRADE; LEVEL; ORDER; PIP; RATE; ROW; TIER ■ RANCID; STATION; STATUS; STINKING; anagram indicator

rank-and-file man ROOK

rank, high NOBILITY

rank, mark of STRIPE

rank, one of the top DUKE

rankle CHAFE; FESTER; GALL

ranks SOLDIERS; anagram indicator

ransack RIFLE; ■ PLUNDER

ransacked anagram indicator

rant RAGE; RAVE; STORM

rant and rave THUNDER

rap BAT; BLAME; CHAT; CRACK; HIT; KNOCK

rapacity GREED

rapid PACY; QUICK; SWIFT; *see* FAST, QUICK

rapid eye movement REM

rapidity SPEED

raptor EAGLE; ■ TALON

rapture BLISS

rapturous SENT

rare R; RED; SCARCE; ■ BLOODY; anagram indicator

rascal IMP; LIMB (old word); ROGUE; SCAMP; *see* ROGUE

rascally anagram indicator

rash HASTY; HEADY; HIVES; SPOTS; ■ IMPRUDENT

rasp FILE

rat BETRAY; DESERT; GRASS; ROGUE; STINKER; WEASEL; ■ RENEGADE; ROTTER; TRAITOR; *see* ROGUE

rate BAT; CHECK; CLASS; COUNT; DEEM; FEE; LICK; MARK; PACE; PRICE; RANK; SCOLD; SPEED; TEMPO; ■ ABUSE; TERMS; WORTH

rate, first A

rate of progress MPH; PACE; SPEED

rate, set PACE

rather QUITE; ■ PRETTY; SOONER

rather, or NAY

ratify APPROVE; BACK

rating CLASS; ERK; HAND; LEVEL; MARK; SCORE; WORTH

ration PORTION; SHARE; ■ RESTRICT

rational SANE; ■ LOGICAL

rationale LOGIC; REASON; ■ BASE; BASIS; GROUND

rationed anagram indicator

rationing, time/years of WAR

rations FARE; SHARE; ■ FOOD; anagram indicator

Rats! DRAT

rattle SHAKE; ■ CLATTER; JANGLE; YAK; anagram indicator

rattled SHOOK; anagram indicator

ratty SHIRTY

Ratty can indicate something to do with the book *The Wind in the Willows* or Graham, its author

raucous cry CAW

rave RANT

ravel TANGLE; TWIST; anagram indicator (note it may be presented with a capital letter as "Ravel" to divert attention to the composer but it can still be indicating an anagram)

Ravel can indicate something to do with *Bolero*, his popular work

raven BLACK

ravine CHINE; GORGE; GULLY

raving MAD; RANT; ■ RANTING

ravioli, portion of SQUARE

ravished anagram indicator

raw GREEN; HARD

raw material ORE; STOCK

raw meat, like RED

ray BEAM; LIGHT; RE (alternative spelling of the 2nd note of the scale); SHAFT; SKATE (i.e. fish)

Raymond RAY

re ABOUT; ON; can signify an anagram indicator (e.g. re-used)

re-built anagram indicator

re-employed anagram indicator

re-enacted anagram indicator

re-established anagram indicator

re-jigged anagram indicator

re-penning anagram indicator

re-united anagram indicator

re-used anagram indicator

reach GET; HIT; LAND; MAKE; SPAN; ■ ATTAIN

reach land LIGHT

reach 99 GETIC (i.e. get-IC)

reach the end DIE

reached MADE

react angrily BRISTLE

react badly TRACE (i.e. an anagram)

reacted anagram indicator

reacting anagram indicator

reaction, automatic/nervous TIC

reactivated anagram indicator

reactor, part of PILE

read CON; SCAN; STUDY; ■ BROWSE; PERUSE

read, aloud homophone indicator

read carefully CON

read, out homophone indicator

read quickly SCAN; SKIM

read rapidly SCAN; SKIM

read up NOC (i.e. rev. of CON in a DC)

reader PRIMER; LECTOR

reader* DON

readily PAT; SOON

readiness, in ONICE (i.e. on ice); *see* PREPARED

reading VERSION; ■ LESSON; PERUSAL; VIEW

reading and writing RR

reading, bit of PAGE

reading-desk AMBO

reading of letter can indicate the sound of a letter e.g. ESS for S, TEE for T and so on

readjusted anagram indicator

ready BOUND; BRASS; CASH; COCKED; DONE; DUE; FIT; EURO; GAME; MONEY; ON; PAT; RIPE; SET; TENDER; TIN (i.e. money) *see* FOREIGN CURRENCY, MONEY; anagram indicator; can indicate any collective term for money or money for a specific purpose (as "Ready to go in" → ENTRANCE FEE)

ready for business OPEN

ready for immediate use INSTANT

ready for picking RIPE

ready for the French PRET

ready for war ARM; ARMED

ready, get EARN; PAWN; RIPEN

ready, getting PREPARATION

ready, got EARNED; RICH

ready, make DRESS; TRIM

ready to broadcast INCAN (i.e. in can)

ready to eat RIPE

ready to fight ARMED

ready to fire, shoot ARMED; COCKED

real ACTUAL; TRUE; ■ ECHT; PROPER

real estate GROUND

real, not FALSE; PASTE; PSEUDO; SHAM

realise CASH; KNOW; NET; SEE; TWIG

reality FACT; TRUTH

reallocated anagram indicator

really VERY; ■ INDEED; SURELY; TRULY

really big OS

really fine SUPER

realm AREA; FIELD; REGION; ■ DOMAIN

ream BORE

reappeared anagram indicator

rear BACK; BUM; END; HIND; LAST; RISE; STERN; TAIL; TRAIN; ■ TOWER

rear, at the AFT; last letter indicator; can indicate that a component should be placed at the end

rear of last letter indicator

rear, part of last letter indicator

reared BRED; ROSE

rearrange(d) anagram indicator

reason CAUSE; END; MIND; POINT; SENSE; SPUR; WHY; ■ FACTOR; GROUND; INFER; LOGIC; MOTIVE; SANITY

reason against CON

reason to take a bath BO

reasonable CHEAP; FAIR; JUST; OK; ■ DECENT; LOGICAL

reasonable, far from MAD

reasoned THOUGHT; ■ LOGICAL

reassembled anagram indicator

reassessed, reassessment anagram indicator

rebate CUT; ■ DISCOUNT; REDUCTION

Rebecca, Dame WEST

rebel CADE (an insurgent during time of Henry VII); RISE; ■ REVOLT

rebel leader CADE; R

rebel, young TURK

rebelled ROSE; anagram indicator

rebellion COUP; FIGHT; REVOLT; RISING

rebellious(ly) anagram indicator

rebels anagram indicator

rebound, on the reversal indicator

rebuff, severe NOSE

rebuffed, rebuffing reversal indicator

rebuild, rebuilding, rebuilt anagram indicator

rebuke BERATE; CHIDE; RAP; RATE; SCOLD; ■ EARFUL; RATING; TRIM; UPBRAID

rebuked CHID; CHIDDEN

rebut CHECK; REFUTE; REJECT

recalcitrant anagram indicator

recall EVOKE; ■ REMEMBER

recalled, recalling reversal indicator

recast anagram indicator

recasting anagram indicator

recede EBB; FALL; WANE; ■ RETREAT; reversal indicator

receipts TAKE

receive GET; SEE; TAKE; ■ ACCEPT; COLLECT; REAP

receive information HEAR; LEARN

receive, to anagram indicator

received HAD; GOT;

receiver CATCHER; EAR; FENCE; SET (i.e. TV or radio; ■ AERIAL; RADIO; TV

receiving nesting indicator

recent LATE; MOD; NEW; ■ LATTER; NOVEL

recent arrival BABY

recent, comparatively, more LATER

recent, more LATER; NEWER

recent setting a component to be nested within LATE

recently JUST; LATE

recently-made NEW

receptacle BAG; BIN; BOWL; DRAWER; HOPPER; PAIL; TRAY; *see* CONTAINER

reception LEVEE; SIGNAL; ■ WELCOME; can indicate something to do with TV reception e.g. aerial, antenna, dish

reception area HALL

reception, great OVATION

reception, poor STATIC

recess APSE; BAY; BREAK; CLOSET; NICHE; NOOK

recession DIP; SLUMP; TROUGH; reversal indicator

Rechabite TT (Rechabite was a non-drinking character in the Bible)

recipe DISH; PLAN; R; anagram indicator

recipient USER

reciprocal/ly reversal indicator

recite PARROT; SAY (qv); UTTER

recited anagram indicator; homophone indicator

reciting homophone indicator

reck CARE

reckless MAD; RASH; anagram indicator

recklessly anagram indicator

reckon ADD; COUNT; FANCY; REEL; RATE; TALLY; THINK; TOT; ■ GUESS; TELLER

reckoning BILL; COUNT; SUM; TALLY; ■ COSTING

reclaim SAVE; ■ SALVAGE

reclassification, requiring anagram indicator

reclassified anagram indicator

reclining LYING; reversal indicator

recluse LONER; ■ HERMIT; STYLITE

reclusive sort/type *see* RECLUSE

reclusive type LONER

recognise KNOW; OWN; SEE; SPOT

recognised KNEW; ■ STANDARD

recognition lacking BLIND

recoil FLINCH; KICK; SHY

recollect RECALL; ■ REMEMBER

recollected anagram indicator; reversal indicator

recommend TIP; URGE; ■ SUGGEST

recommendation PLUG

recommended TIPPED

recompense PAY (qv); ■ REWARD (qv)

recompensed PAID

reconciliation DETENTE

reconciliation, for anagram indicator

reconnoitre CASE

reconsider(ed) anagram indicator

reconstituted anagram indicator

reconstructed, reconstruction anagram indicator

reconstructed form, in anagram indicator

reconvened anagram indicator

record ANNAL; BOOK; CAN; CARD; CD; DEMO; DIARY;

DISC; ENTER; ENTRY; EP; FILE; FORM; LIST; LOG; LP; MARK; MONO; NOTE; REC; ROLL; STAMP; TABLE; TALLY; TAPE; TRACE; TRACK; ■ ACCOUNT; ALBUM; CASSETTE; FASTI (Latin); PLATTER; REPORT; SHEET; SINGLE; [◊ GROOVE; LABEL]

record, betting BOOK
record company INDIE; LABEL
record, half of SIDE
record holder FILE
record illegally BUG
record, made a LOGGED; TAPED
record minutes TIME
record, old OLP; PLATTER
record, part of TRACK
record presenter DJ
record, produce PRESS
recorded, not LIVE
recorded song TRACK
recording TAPE; ■ LOGGING; TAPING; *see* RECORD
recording attempt TAKE
recording, old way of EP; LP
recount RETAIL; TELL
recourse, have TURN
recover MEND; RALLY
recover from what follows to be used as an anagram
recovering BETTER; OVER
recovering from illness BETTER
recovery RALLY
recreant CRAVEN
recreated anagram indicator
recreation area COMMON; PARK; REC
recruit, raw ROOKIE
recruit, to nesting indicator
recruitment DRAFT
rectangle OBLONG
rector R; ■ MINISTER
recurrent, recurring reversal indicator
recurrent idea THEME
recycled anagram indicator
recycling anagram indicator

red FLAME; LAKE; LEFT; RARE; SORE; ■ BLOODY; CHERRY; FLAMING; ROUGE; TITIAN; can indicate something to do with embarrassment
red, become BLUSH; BURN; TAN
red-blooded MACHO
red-faced FLUSHED; RUDDY
red-headed R
red, in the DEBT; OD; OWING
red-light NOGO (i.e. no-go)
Red Rum anagram of RED
red, see RAGE
Red, The ERIC
redact EDIT
redcap MP
redcoat can indicate something to do with Santa Claus
redden BLUSH; FLUSH
reddish RUSTY
reddish-brown RUSSET
redecorated/redecorating anagram indicator
redefined anagram indicator
redeem ATONE
redefined anagram indicator
redemption, in need of HOCKED
redesign CHANGE; anagram indicator
redesigned anagram indicator
redesigning anagram indicator
redhead R
redirected anagram indicator
rediscovered anagram indicator
redrafting, in need of anagram indicator
redrafts anagram indicator
redress REPARATION; anagram indicator; apart from the sense of "to set right" can also refer to putting on clothes again as in "What drivers often do to make redress" → CHANGE GEAR
reduce CUT; DAMP; DOCK; EASE; LESS; LOP; LOWER; PARE; REMIT; ■ DECREASE; LESSEN; abbreviation indicator; can indicate a verb finishing with DOWN; can indicate an adjective ending in -LESS
reduce, drastically AXE

reduce in rank DEMOTE; ▪ RELEGATE

reduce intake DIET

reduce risk HEDGE

reduced CUT; DOWN; LOW; LOWER; LESS; THIN; abbreviation indicator; can indicate that the last letter is to be omitted (as "reduced charge" → TOL)

reduced in temperature T to be omitted

reduced risk CHANC

reduction CUT; DROP; PALL; abbreviation indicator; can call for a word ending in -LESS

redundancy, redundant omission indicator

redundant, make FIRE; SACK; ▪ DISMISS

reed GRASS; RUSH

reedy LEAN; THIN

reef ATOLL; BANK; CAY; ROCKS; SAIL; ▪ SHOAL; can indicate something to do with adjusting sails

reefer GRASS; JOINT

reek HUM; PONG; SMELL; SMOKE; STENCH

reel DODDER; HOP (i.e. dance); ROCK; ROLL; SPIN; SPOOL; TURN; WIND; ▪ STAGGER; TOTTER; anagram indicator

reeling anagram indicator

refashion, refashioned anagram indicator

refer SEE; ▪ ALLUDE; APPEAL; RELATE

refer to QUOTE; ▪ CONSULT

referee REF; ▪ MEDIATE; WHISTLER

reference NAME; ▪ CIT

reference book/work DICT; OED

reference line AXIS

referred to CIT

referring to ON; OVER; RE

refine POLISH

refined GENTLE; anagram indicator

refined man GENT

refinement POLISH

refinement, lacking CRUDE; RUDE; *see* CRUDE

refinery anagram indicator

reflect CHEW; GLANCE; MUSE; PONDER; THINK

reflection can indicate something to do with Narcissus, narcissist etc

reflection from/in combined reversal and run indicator

reflection, on reversal indicator

reflective reversal indicator; can indicate a palindrome (as "Girl's reflective article" → ANNA)

reform ALTER; AMEND; CHANGE; anagram indicator

Reformation anagram indicator

reformed EX (as "reformed pusher" → EXPRESSER); anagram indicator

reforming anagram indicator

refrain ABSTAIN; AVOID; CEASE; SONG (qv); STOP; VERSE; ▪ DESIST; MELODY

refrain from STOP; WAIVE; can refer to a combination of NOT followed by a verb (Example: "Refrain from taking action" gives NOT SUE which can be reversed to give EUSTON, the railway station)

refreshed anagram indicator

refresher DRINK; FEE

refreshing BRACING; ▪ WELCOME; anagram indicator

refreshment BUN; TEA; *see* DRINK, FOOD

refreshment room CAFF

refuelling, tanker for BOWSER

refuge DEN; HAVEN; HIDE; LAIR

refuge, place of ARK

refuge, seek HIDE

refuge, sought HID

refuge within, takes nesting indicator

refurbished anagram indicator

refusal NAY; NO; SHANT

refusal, French NON

refurbish anagram indicator

refurbishment, after anagram indicator

refuse ASH; BRAN; CHAFF; DENY; DROSS; SLAG; SWILL;

TRASH; VETO; WASTE; ■
DECLINE; DEMUR;
GARBAGE; JIB; LEAVINGS;
LITTER; MARC (wine); ORT;
SPURN; *see* RUBBISH
refuse admission BAN; BAR;
DEBAR
refuse-collector BIN
refuse container SKIP
refuse orders REBEL
refuse to SHANT; WONT
refuse to believe DISCOUNT
refuse to deal with BLACK
refuse to go (run etc) STALL
refuse to recognize CUT; SNUB
refuse to work STRIKE
refused to work STRUCK
refusing to work OUT
regain RECOVER
regain consciousness COME
TO
regale FEAST
regard EYE; SEE; WATCH; ■
ESTEEM; REGARD; RESPECT
regard to, with ON; RE
regarding ASTO (i.e. as to);
OVER; RE
regardless THOUGH
regardless of omission indicator
regatta town COWES
regime REIGN
regiment OR; R; RA; RE; REME;
RO
regimental HQ *see* HQ
region AREA; CLIME; LAND;
PLACE; REALM; SPOT;
TRACT; ZONE; ■ COUNTRY;
PART(S)
regime DIET
register LIST; LOG; NOTE;
POLL; R; ROLL; SIGN; ■
ENROL; RECORD; ROTA; *see*
RECORD
register points SCORE
regressed reversal indicator
regret MOURN; RUE; WEEP; ■
GRIEVE; LAMENT; SORROW
regret, express SIGH
regretful SORRY
regrettably ALAS; anagram indicator

regretting RUING
regroup anagram indicator
regular EVEN; FLAT; NORM;
OFTEN; SET; ■ CUSTOMER;
ORDERLY; STANDING;
STEADY; UNIFORM; USUAL;
anagram indicator
regular amount PAR
regular appearances, making
see REGULAR INTERVALS
regular date STEADY
regular intervals can indicate the
use of selected letters in a sequence – these are nearly always
the *evenly* numbered letters but
not necessarily (as in the following where the selection is in
threes: "Priest making regular appearances in the colonies" →
ELI)
regular performance ROUTINE
regular process CUSTOM
regularly OFT; can indicate the use
of the even letters in sequence as
"Fight ostentation regularly" →
SET-TO; apart from signifying
even letters can alternatively require the selection of other regu-
larly-numbered letters in a
sequence (as "Drink regularly offered by Telegraph" → TEA)
regularly discarded
evenly-numbered letters to be
omitted as in "Rubbish discovered in books he regularly
discarded" → BOSH
regulate CONTROL; RUN
regulated anagram indicator
regulation LAW; RULE; ■
ORDINANCE; anagram indicator
regulations CODE; *see* RULES
regulatory system CODE
regurgitated reversal indicator
rehabilitation anagram indicator
rehash, rehashed anagram indicator
rehearsal DRILL; RUN (as in "dry
run")
rehouse MOVE
reign RULE; SWAY

rein BRAKE; CURB; STRAP; ■ CONTROL

rein in CHECK

reincarnation anagram indicator

reindeer DASHER

reindeer-herder LAPP

reinforce BRACE; LINE; PROP; ■ CEMENT

reinforced nesting indicator

reinforcement BRACE; PROP; STRUT

reinterpreted, reinterpreting anagram indicator

reiterating reversal indicator; repeat indicator

reject DROP; DITCH; SCORN; SPURN; VETO; ■ DISCARD; REPEL

rejected LORN; OUT; reversal indicator

rejecting AGAINST; omission indicator

rejection NO; SNUB

rejection, blunt SHANT

rejig anagram indicator

rejoicing CHEER

rejoin anagram indicator

rejoinder RETORT

rejuvenate RENEW

rejuvenated anagram indicator

relate REFER; RETAIL; TELL; ■ CONNECT; JOIN; REPORT

related AKIN; TOLD; ■ AGNATE; FAMILY

related children QUINS; SIBS; ■ BROS

related to ABOUT; OF; ON; RE

relation AUNT; BOND; BRO; FATHER; GRAN; KIN; MA; MUM; NAN; NIECE; PI; PA; POP; RATIO; SIB; SIS; SISTER; SON; STORY; TALE; ■ ACCOUNT; BROTHER; DAUGHTER; RESPECT; see FATHER, MOTHER, KIN

relations KIN; TIES; ■ CLAN; FAMILY; NOOKY; TRIBE

relationship RATIO; TIE ■ AFFAIR

relative KIN; REL; ■ CONNECTION; [◊ ORDER]; see RELATION

relative, aged/elderly GRAN

relative, close BRO; see RELATION

relatively can indicate a word ending in -ER

relatives BROS; FOLK; KIN

relaunched anagram indicator

relax EASE; LOLL; REST; SIT; ■ LOUNGE; PATIENCE (i.e. exhortation); SOFTEN

relaxation EASE; REST; ■ EASING

relaxed COOL; EASED; EASY; LOOSE; SAT; SLACK; anagram indicator

relaxed, more LOOSER

relaxing EASING; anagram indicator

relay PASS; SWITCH; anagram indicator

relay of workers SHIFT

release DROP; FREE; ISSUE; SPARE; ■ ACQUIT; CATCH; DELIVER; EXEMPT; LEVER; UNLOCK; anagram indicator

release, on see RELEASED

released FREE; OUT; anagram indicator as, for example, "energy released" is an instruction to omit E

releasing omission indicator as "releasing new" requires the omission of N

relegate DROP; LOWER

relegation DROP

relentless STERN

relevant GERMANE

reliable HARD; SOLID; SOUND; SURE; TRUSTY; ■ STAUNCH; STEADY; STRAIGHT

reliable, more SURER

reliable, not SHAKY

reliable type BRICK; GEM; TRUMP

relief AID; BAS; EASE; HELP; ■ SUCCOUR

relief, kind of HIGH; LIGHT

relief, provide EMBOSS; see RELIEF

relief, that's a PHEW

relief work CAMEO

relieve AID; EASE; HELP

relieve soreness EASE
relieved EASED
relieved, sounded SIDE (i.e. hom.)
religion ZEN
religion class RE
religious HOLY; PI; PIOUS
religious adherent talking SEEK (i.e. homophone of Sikh)
religious authority POPE; ROME
religious belief ZEN
religious believers CULT
religious body *see* RELIGIOUS GROUP
religious celebration FEAST
religious centre ROME
religious ceremony MASS; RITE
religious community CHURCH; CONVENT; ■ ABBEY; CHAPEL; PRIORY; MONASTERY
religious experience VISION
religious figures PIETA
religious fraternity ESSENE; SECT
religious group CHURCH; CULT ORDER; SECT
religious house PRIORY
religious instruction, knowledge RE; RI
religious job CURACY
religious lady NUN
religious leader LAMA; POPE; PRIOR; R; RABBI; SWAMI; ■ ABBESS; MAHDI
religious man PRIOR
religious meeting MASS; SERVICE; ■ CHAPTER
religious order, member of MONK; NUN; TEMPLAR
religious outfit HABIT; MISSION; SECT; ■ VESTMENT
religious pamphlet TRACT
religious person MONK; NUN
religious school SECT
religious statement CREED
religious symbol CROSS
religious task MISSION
religious texts AV; NT; OT
religious work AV; TRACT

relinquish FORGO; YIELD
relish GUSTO; PICKLE; SAUCE; SPICE; ■ DRESSING; GOUT (Fr.); TASTE
relocate MOVE; anagram indicator
relocated anagram indicator
reluctance, express ER; UM
reluctant AVERSE; COY; LOATH; LOTH; SHY
rely BANK; COUNT; LEAN; STAND; TRUST; ■ DEPEND
rely on TRUST
remain ABIDE; BIDE; LAST; LIE; OVER; REST; STAY; STICK; TARRY
remain in the same place STAY
remain still FREEZE
remainder REST; OTHERS; ■ BALANCE
remainder, tree STUMP
remained LAY; ■ DWELT; LAIN; STAYED
remaining LEFT; ODD; OTHER; OVER
remains ASH; DUST; EMBERS; LEES; REST; RUMP; STUB; STUMP; ■ AFTERS; EMBERS
remark CRACK; NOTE; QUIP; SALLY; SAY; WORD; ■ COMMENT
remark, cutting BARB
remark, indiscreet GAFFE
remarkable RARE; SIGNAL; SOME; TALL; ■ (E)SPECIAL; anagram indicator
remarkable person ONER
remarkably anagram indicator
remedy BALM; CURE; SALVE; anagram indicator
remember RETAIN; ■ RECALL; RECOLLECT
remembered anagram indicator (i.e. re-membered!)
remind CUE; NUDGE; PROMPT
reminder CUE; MEMO; NOTE; NUDGE; PROD; PROMPT
remit BRIEF
remitted SENT
remix anagram indicator
remixing anagram indicator
remnant EMBER; RUMP; TRACE

remote BACK; FAR; LONG; OUT; *see* DISTANT

remodelled, remodelling anagram indicator

remorse, feel REPENT

remorse, felt RUED

remorseless HARD

remote AWAY (i.e. a way); FAR; ■ DISTANT; anagram indicator

remoteness can indicate a word beginning with TELE (Greek for "far"); *see* DISTANT

removal CUT; OUSTING

removal, legal OUSTER

remove CUT; DELETE; DOFF; ERASE; EVICT; FIRE; LOP; PEEL; SACK; STRIP; TAKE; ■ DELETE; EXCISE; EXTRACT; can indicate a verb to be preceded by DE, as "remove name from plan" clues DESIGN (i.e. de-sign); anagram indicator

remove appendage DETAIL

remove branches LOP

remove clothes STRIP

remove cover SHELL

remove impurities LEACH; REFINE

remove leader DEPOSE

remove moisture DRY

remove wallpaper STRIP

removed FAR; omission indicator; anagram indicator

removing anagram indicator; omission indicator

rend GASH; RIP; RIVE; SPLIT; TEAR; ■ PLASTER

render GIVE; YIELD; anagram indicator

render senseless STUN; ■ KAYO; KO

rendered anagram indicator

rendering VERSION; anagram indicator

rendez-vous, rendezvous MEET; VENUE

rendition VERSION; anagram indicator

renegade RAT (qv)

renegotiated, renegotiation anagram indicator

renounce QUIT; ■ DECLAIM; RECANT

renovate PAINT; anagram indicator

renovated anagram indicator

renovation REFIT; anagram indicator

renown FAME (qv); NAME

rent BREACH; BREAK; GASH; HIRE; LEASE; LET; SLIT; SPLIT; RIFT; RIP; TEAR; TORE; TORN; ■ CHASM; RAGGED

rental HIRE; LET

rented LEASED; LET

renting LET; *see* RENT

reorganisation anagram indicator

rep AGENT; MP

repast MEAL

repair FIX; MEND; PATCH; SEW; anagram indicator

repair, in need of anagram indicator

repair, temporary PATCH

repaired, repairing anagram indicator

repairman MENDER

reparation anagram indicator

reparations AMENDS

repartee QUIP; WIT

repartee, engage in FENCE

repast, take DINE; EAT

repatriate DEPORT

repeal REVOKE

repeat AGAIN; APE; COPY; ITERATE; PARROT; REDO; ■ ECHO; ITERATE

repeated AGAIN; DOUBLE; ■ DITTO; a component to be repeated

repeatedly AGAIN; OFT; OFTEN repeat indicator (for example, in "Repeatedly I act flexibly to meet new end?" one is required to repeat 'I act' in order to provide the main letters for the anagram to get TACTICIAN)

repeater GUN; ■ ECHO; PARROT

repel REJECT

repentant SORRY

repetition ROTE; repeat indicator

repetitive can indicate something to do with stammering, stuttering; repetition indicator

repetitive strain injury RSI

rephrased anagram indicator

replace anagram indicator

replaced CHANGED; TUP (i.e. rev. of PUT); anagram indicator

replacement SPARE; SUB; anagram indicator

replacing anagram or nesting indicator

replanted anagram indicator

replayed point/serve LET

replete FULL; SATED

replica DOUBLE; COPY

replicate APE; COPY

reply REJOIN ■ ANS; ANSWER

reply, affirmative *see* AFFIRMATIVE

reply, brief/short ANS

reply, negative *see* NEGATIVE

report BANG; BLAST; BOOM; CLAP; COVER; CRACK; PAPER; NOISE; POP; SAY; RELATE; STATE; STORY; TELL; ■ COMMUNICATE; NEWS; NOTE; RECORD; SOUND; homophone indicator

report, according to homophone indicator

report, source of GUN (qv)

reported as, what's homophone indicator

reported, it's homophone indicator

reportedly homophone indicator

reporter's homophone indicator (operating on the word that follows)

reporter's submission FILING

reporter, young CUB

reporting NEWS

repose REST

reposition RESET; anagram indicator; ■ ADJUST

repositioned RESET; anagram indicator

repository BANK; TILL

represent MEAN; SHOW; ■ LIMN; PORTRAY; RENDER; anagram indicator

representation IMAGE; STATUE; ■ ICON; PICTURE; anagram indicator (i.e. a re-presentation)

representative AGENT; ENVOY; MP; REP; ■ TYPICAL

represented anagram indicator

representing FOR

repress CHECK

reprimand CARPET; CHIDE; RAP; RATE; SCOLD; WIG; ■ HELL; RATING; REPROOF; ROCKET; WIGGING

reprimanded CHID

reprinted anagram indicator

repro PROOF

reproach TWIT

reprobate CUR; RAT; RIP; ■ SINNER

reproduce APE; COPY; anagram indicator

reproduced, anagram indicator

reproducing anagram indicator

reproducing letters from anagram of following word

reproduction COPY; FAKE; PRINT; anagram indicator

reproof, gave CHID

reprove RATE; *see* REPRIMAND

reptile CROC; EFT; SKINK; SNAKE (qv)

republic CHAD; EIRE; NIGER

Republican troops IRA

repugnance AVERSION

repugnance, show REBEL

repugnant ALIEN

repulse SPURN

repulsed reversal indicator

reputation FAME; NAME; REP; ■ ODOUR; RENOWN; STANDING

repute *see* REPUTATION

request ASK; BEG; ORDER; PLEA; PRAY; PRAYER; ■ ENTREAT; PETITION

request, forceful DEMAND

request, make ASK; *see* ASK

request meal ORDER

request to stop talking SH

require MAKE; NEED; ■ DEMAND

required MADE

required, not OVER; SPARE
required, what is SPEC; ■ EQUIPMENT
requirement MUST; NEED; WANT; ■ DEMAND; CONDITION; anagram indicator
requirements anagram indicator
requisition ORDER
rerun reversal indicator
rescue FREE; SAVE; ■ DELIVER
rescue vessel ARK
rescuer SAVER; SAVIOUR
research DIG
research centre/facility/place LAB
research institute CERN
research scientist BOFFIN
researcher BOFFIN
resembling LIKE
resent GRUDGE; MIND
resentful, feeling SORE; STUNG
resentment HUMP; IRE; ■ ENVY; PIQUE; GRUDGE
resentment, cause see ANNOY
resentment, show BRIDLE
reservation BOOKING; BUT; RES; can indicate something to do with American Indians
reservation, make BOOK
reserve BAG; BANK; BOOK; FUND; HOLD; ICE; PICK; RES; SAVE; SECOND; STORE; STOCK; SUB; TA; ■ EARMARK; RETAIN; TRACT
reserve eleven TAXI
reserve, in ASIDE; BY; SPARE
reserve player SUB
reserved COY; SHY; ■ BOOKED; anagram indicator (i.e. re-served)
reserved person OYSTER
reserves BOOKS; STOCK; STORE; TA
reservoir LAKE; SUMP; TANK; WELL
reset anagram indicator
resettled/resettling anagram indicator
reshuffle(d) anagram indicator
reside DWELL; LIE; LIVE; LODGE

residence ABODE; CASTLE; FLAT; GAFF; HOME; HOUSE; PAD; RES; SEMI; ■ ADDRESS; DWELLING
residence, change MOVE
residence, take up SETTLE
resident LODGER; ■ INMATE; NATIVE
residential area CITY; ESTATE; TOWN; VILLAGE
residential street CLOSE
residual fire EMBER
residual piece STUB
residue ASH; REST; RUMP; ■ REMAINS
resign QUIT; ■ DEMIT
resigned PATIENT
resilient BOUNCY; YIELDING; ■ ELASTIC; SPRINGY
resin LAC
resist BUCK; FACE; ■ COMBAT; OPPOSE
resistance R; STAND; ■ OPPOSITION
resistance unit OHM
resistant PROOF
resolute HARDY; STIFF; see FIRM
resolution RES; END; anagram indicator
resolve AIM; PLAN; WILL; ■ DETERMINE; SETTLE; anagram indicator
resolved SET; anagram indicator
resolving anagram indicator
resonant performance can indicate something to do with bell-ringing e.g. CHANGE
resort GO; HAUNT; SPA; anagram indicator; can refer to a specific popular resort e.g. in Britain: HOVE, POOLE, abroad: FARO, NICE, RIO; SPLIT
resorted anagram indicator
resound RING; ■ BOOM; ECHO
resounded RANG
resource ASSET; FINANCE
resources CAPITAL; STOCK; ■ FINANCE(S); MEANS; SUPPLY; anagram indicator
resources, make the most of EKE; ■ ECONOMISE

respect AWE; DEFER; HALLOW; HEED; REGARD; REVERE; WAY; ■ DETAIL; ESTEEM; PRESTIGE; RELATION; SALUTE

respect, fearful AWE

respect, high HONOUR

respect, show BOW

respect to IN; ON; RE

respect, with IN; ON; RE; PACE

respectable DECENT; FAIR; NICE; ■ STRAIGHT

respectable, not quite DECEN (i.e. 'decent' with last letter omitted)

respecting ON; RE

respire BREATHE

respite BREAK (qv)

respond PLEAD; REACT; YIELD; ■ REJOIN

response TIC; ■ ANSWER; REACTION

response at wedding IDO (i.e. I do)

response, basic GRUNT

response, disgusted UGH

response, involuntary (natural etc) TIC

responsible for OVER

responsible for, be CAUSE

responsibility CHARGE; DUTY; RAP; ■ GUILT; ONUS

rest BREAK; EASE; FF (i.e. following pages); IDLE; LEAN; LIE; NAP; PROP; REPOSE; SIT; SPIDER; STAY; ■ BREATHER; LEAVE; LOUNGE; RESPITE; STOOL

rest, and the ETC

rest-break PAUSE; an anagram of REST

rest, place of see RESTING-PLACE

rest, take a KIP; NAP; SIT

rest up synonym of "rest" to be reversed e.g. TIS

restaurant DINER; CAFE; CAFF; GRILL; ■ CARVERY; [◊ WAITER]

restaurant car DINER

restaurant, commonly/popularly CAFF

restaurant, part of BAR

restaurant worker CHEF; WAITER

rested LAY; LEANT; SAT

restful SERENE

resting place BED; COT; DEN; GRAVE; LAIR; ROOST

resting place anagram indicator

restoration anagram indicator

restore CURE; MEND; STET

restore balance COUNTER

restored MENDED; anagram indicator

restrain CURB; DAM; FETTER; HOLD; REIN; REPRESS; SMOTHER; STAY; STEM; ■ ARREST; CHAIN; LIMIT

restrained BOUND; TIED; anagram indicator; nesting indicator

restrained by nesting indicator

restrained in speech TIDE

restrained, not FREE; LOOSE; WILD

restrains nesting indicator

restraint BRIDLE; DAM; CURB; REIN; TIE; ■ CHAIN; FETTER; SHACKLE

restraint, lacking/without FREE; LOOSE; OTT

restraint, subjected to can indicate that a component is nested within a synonym of restraint such as CHAIN in "Mortification of king subjected to restraint" → CHAGRIN

restrict BAR; BIND; CHAIN; CLAMP; CRAMP; CURB; PEN; STUNT; TIE; ■ RATION

restrict, continue to KEEP

restrict movements GATE; HOBBLE; PEN

restricted PENT; TIED; ■ CUT; anagram, nesting or run indicator; can indicate that the last letter (and maybe the first) is to be omitted

restricted by nesting indicator

restricting nesting indicator

restriction BAN; BAR; CURB; LET; TIE; ■ BELT; LIMIT

restructured anagram indicator

restyle anagram indicator

result DRAW; END; ENSUE; EVENT; GAIN; ISSUE; SCORE; TIE; WIN ■ EFFECT; FOLLOW; IMPACT; UPSHOT

result, desired AIM; END; GOAL; ■ TARGET

result of day's shooting BAG

resurgence RALLY

retail SELL; TELL; ■ RECOUNT

retail outlet DELI; SHOP; STORE

retailer MONGER; SELLER; SHOP; STORE

retain HOLD; KEEP; RESERVE; SAVE; STET; ■ HOARD; nesting indicator

retain, manage to SAVE; SALVE

retain much water SEA to be nested within a component

retained KEPT

retainer KEEPER; *see* SERVANT

retaining nesting indicator

retaliation can indicate a word ending in BACK

retard SLOW

retch GAG; HEAVE; KECK

reticent CLOSE; COY; SHY

retinue SUITE; TRAIN

retire QUIT; ■ LEAVE; TURNIN (i.e. turn in)

retired ABED; EX; OLD; RET; reverse indicator; can indicate that a component is to be nested within the letters BED (i.e. in bed) as "A retired prayer-counter" → BEAD

retired person can indicate something with going to bed

retired soldier VET

retired vicar VER (i.e. reversal)

retirement BED; reversal indicator

retirement, in ABED; SLEEPING

retiring SHY; reversal indicator

retort SALLY; STILL (i.e. piece of equipment)

retouch EDIT

retracted/retraction reverse indicator

retreat BACK; DEN; EBB; FLEE; FLIGHT; LAIR; NEST; NOOK; RECEDE; RUN; SCRAM; STUDY; ■ ASHRAM; HERMITAGE; SHELTER; anagram indicator; reversal indicator

retreat, secure LIAN (i.e. reversal of NAIL)

retreated RAN

retribution REVENGE

retrieve BRING; FETCH; GET

retrieved reversal indicator

retro reversal indicator

retrograde reversal indicator, as "retrograde art" → TRA

retrogressive reversal indicator

retrospect, in BACK

retrospective, retrospectively reversal indicator

retsina WINE

retsina, like GREEK

retuned anagram indicator

return BACK; GAIN; PROFIT; NET; RET; YIELD; ■ ANSWER; EARNINGS; INTEREST; TICKET; reversal indicator

return game can indicate that a game is reversed, and so GAT, OG, PANS etc

return, say PROPHET

return, small RET

return, swift RETORT

returned BACK; GAVE; reversal indicator

returning BACK; BOUND (as in homebound, earthbound); reversal indicator

reuse, reusing anagram indicator

revamped anagram indicator

reveal BARE; OUT; SHOW; TELL; UNFOLD; VENT; ■ CONFIDE; DISCLOSE; EXPOSE; IMPART; PRESENT

reveal a gap YAWN

reveal one'end MOON

revealed OUT

revealing OUTING; SHOWING

reveals run indicator

revel PARTY; ORGY; ROIST; ■ ROLLICK

revelation, divine ORACLE

revelry RIOT

revels anagram indicator

revenue *see* EARNING

reverberating reversal indicator

revere HALLOW

revered figure IDOL

reverence AWE

reverence, inspire with AWE

reverence, producing AWING

reverend REV; REVD

reverent PI

reverie DREAM; TRANCE

★ **reversal** a ploy where (i) you have to reverse a whole word, so that PART becomes TRAP, for example; or (ii) you have to identify a reverse run in the clue, such as SING being a reverse run within "the sign isn't obvious". For examples of indicators, see below.

★ **reversal indicator** There are two kinds. One type (such as "back") tells us if a run of letters (see run indicator) within the clue is running backwards as "Time to go back to show" → EMIT. Terms like "receding", "retreating and "from right to left" can have this function while in the special case of a down clue, reversal can be indicated by "rising" or "ascending". The other type ("after" is a common one) instructs us to place letters or components in reverse order to construct the answer, as "Exclamation of pain after descent shows one to be uncultivated?" leads to FALLOW (i.e. FALL-OW)

reverse BACK; TURN; reversal indicator

reversed reversal indicator, so "is reversed" → SI, "was reversed" → SAW etc.

revert, reverted anagram indicator

reverts reversal indicator

review CHECK; CRIT; ■ JUDGE; PARADE; SUMMARY; TEST; VET; [◊ PUFF]; anagram indicator

review, enthusiastic RAVE

reviewed anagram indicator

reviewer CRITIC

revise AMEND; EDIT; EMEND; ■ CHANGE

revised anagram indicator

revision CHANGE; EDIT; anagram indicator

revision to book EDIT

revival RALLY; anagram indicator

revive RALLY; ■ FRESHEN

revived anagram indicator

revoke DELETE; REPEAL

revoked anagram indicator; reversal indicator

revolt REBEL; RISING; UPRISING

revolt, act of DEFECTION

revolt, in UP; anagram indicator

revolting RISING; UP; anagram indicator

revolution ROLL; ROUND; SPIN; TURN; anagram indicator; reversal indicator; [◊ WHEEL]

revolution, say TERN

revolutionary CHE; MAO; MARAT; RED; TROT; VILLA; ■ TURNER; reversal indicator (example: "revolutionary Italians" → TI); anagram indicator; can indicate something to do with left-wing politics; [◊ ROUND]

revolutionary leader R; *see* REVOLUTIONARY

revolutionary party LEVER (rev.)

revolutionary thinker MARX

revolutionary device WHEEL; ■ SPIN-DRIER

revolve ROLL; SPIN; TURN; TWIST; WHIRL

revolver ARM; COLT; GAT; GUN; ROTOR; SPINNER; TOP; WHEEL; ■ PISTOL; anagram indicator; can indicate anything which revolves e.g. gramophone turntable, platter, CD disc

revolving SPINNING; TURNING; anagram indicator

revue SHOW

reward FEE; PAY; PURSE; TIP; ■ BOUNTY; DESERT; DESERTS; PRIZE

reward, small TIP

rewoven anagram indicator

rewrite ADAPT; anagram indicator

rewriting, rewritten anagram indicator

Rex CAT; DOG; KING; R
Reynard FOX; [◊ EARTH]
rhetoric CANT; IRONY
rheumatic ACHY
rheumatoid arthritis RA
rhino BRASS; READY, can refer to a specific currency (qv)
rhyme JINGLE; VERSE; can indicate that the answer rhymes with a word in the clue as "Brief nursery rhyme" → CURSORY
rhymes VERSE (qv); ■ LIEDER; POEM (qv); can indicate the answer is a term consisting of two parts which rhyme with each other and, possibly, also a word in the clue. Examples: "silly rhymes" → WILLY-NILLY and "ruddy rhymes" → FUDDY-DUDDY
rhythm BEAT; LILT; ■ CADENCE
rib BAIT; BONE; CHAFF; GUY; KID; SCOFF; STITCH; TAUNT; TEASE; TWIT; can indicate something to do with wife; [◊ ADAM]
rib area CHEST
rib enclosure CASE
ribald BLUE
ribbing TEASE
ribbon BAND; BOW; STRIP; TAPE; ■ STREAMER
ribs can indicate an umbrella
rice GRAIN; ■ CEREAL; PATNA
rich CREAMY; FAT; FLUSH; FRUITY; HIGH; PLUSH; LUSH; ■ AFFLUENT; COMICAL; CREAMY; LOADED; ROLLING; THICK; WEALTHY
rich, extremely RH (i.e. first and last letters)
rich man DIVES
rich, to be ABOUND
riches WEALTH
Richard DICK; RICK
rick HAY; SPRAIN; STACK
rickety anagram indicator
ricochet reversal indicator
rid CLEAR; PURGE
riddle POSER; SIFT; STRAIN; ■ PIERCE; SIEVE

ride DRIVE; GRATE; HACK; LIE (as in "let it lie"); MOUNT; TRIP; ■ CYCLE; TRAVEL
ride in pursuit CHASE; HUNT
ride on horseback CANTER
ride, prepare for a SADDLE
ride, take for a CHEAT (qv)
rider CONDITION; JOCKEY; PS
rider, fast REVERE
rider's accessory BIT; HALTER; REIN; SADDLE; STIRRUP
ridge CREST; CHINE; EDGE; FRET; FURROW; REEF; ■ ARETE; ESKER
ridge near water's surface REEF
ridicule DERIDE; GUY; MOCK; SCOFF
ridicule, object of BUTT
ridiculous anagram indicator
riding UP
riding equipment TACK
riding in pursuit HUNTING
rife COMMON; CURRENT; GENERAL
riff-raff SCUM
rifle ARM; GUN; ROB; SACK; ■ FERRET
rifle butt E
rift BREAK; GAP; RENT; SPLIT; ■ CHASM; FAULT
rig COOK; EQUIP; GEAR; KIT; STRIP; ■ DRESS
rig-out anagram of RIG
rigged anagram indicator
rigger FIXER
rigging, old can indicate clothing from the past, or what is now considered an old-fashioned word e.g. apparel
rigging, part of STAY
right CLAIM; DUE; EXACT; JUST; LIEN; MEND; MORAL; OK; R; REAL; RT; SO; TORY; TRUE; YES; ■ ETHICAL; PROPER; anagram indicator (in the sense of make right); can indicate that what precedes it provides either the clue's definition or an example of the definition
right* SIDE

right answer, find CRACK; SOLVE

right away NOW; can indicate that R is to be omitted

right-back TR

right colour MATCH

right, exactly PAT

right hand RH

right-hand page RECTO

right, has R to be nested within a component

right, has no R to be omitted

right in HOME

right in China TAO

right, just FINE; PAT

right, legal LIEN

right, property LIEN

right of way LANE

right one MATCH

right over TR

right page RECTO

right people, the TORIES

right, say RITE

right to property LIEN

right, unconcerned about AMORAL

right up TR (i.e. rev. of RT in a DC)

right-wing BLUE; DRY; TORY

right-winger TORY

rightful JUST; PROPER; TRUE

rightist TORY

rigid FIRM; LOCKED; STERN; STIFF; STRICT; *see* STUCK

rigidly enforced STRICT

rigorous HARD; STERN; STRICT

rigorously anagram indicator

rile GALL; NAG; IRK; ■ ANGER; BOTHER

rill RUN; STREAM

rim BRINK; EDGE; LIP; ■ MARGIN

rim, wheel FELLOE

rind PEEL; SKIN

ring BAND; BELL; BUZZ; CALL; COIL; CYCLE; DIAL; DING; GANG; GONG; HALO; HOOP; LUTE (i.e. seal); O; OPAL; PEAL; PHONE; PING; ROUND; SEAL; SET; TING (i.e. bell noise); TOLL; ■ ARENA; CARTEL; CHIME; CIRCLE; CORONA; DOUBLE (darts); GROMMET; INNER; KEEPER; KNELL; OUTER; QUOIT; SET; SOUND; TREBLE (darts); WASHER; nesting indicator

Ring can indicate something to do with Wagner's *Ring Cycle*

ring back O to be placed at the end; synonym of "ring" to be reversed, hence LAID

ring, fixing SEAL

ring for saint HALO

ring-leader word to begin with O

ring of light HALO

ring off ONOTON (i.e. O not on); can indicate O to be omitted

ring once DIAL

ring-tailed O to be added to end

ringer BELL; ■ DOUBLE; IMAGE

ringing PEAL; nesting indicator

ringing sound PING; *see* SOUND

ringleader ARCH; R; *see* CHIEF

ringlet LOCK; TRESS

rings OO; OS; *see* RING

rink ICE

rinse SWILL; WASH

riot ROUT; SCREAM; ■ RUCTION; TUMULT; anagram indicator

riot control instrument MACE

rioting, riotous anagram indicator

riotous assembly ROUT

riotous spree REVEL

riot anagram indicator

rip CHEAT; EDDY; RAKE; REND; RENT; SCAMP; TEAR; TIDE; ■ CURRENT

rip off *see* RIP-OFF

rip-off ROB; SCAM; STEAL; TEAR; anagram of RIP

Rip Van Winkle as the character in the Washington Irving story, can indicate something to do with sleep, over-sleep etc

ripe READY

ripe, not GREEN

ripen MELLOW

riposte SALLY; ■ RETORT; can indicate something to do with fencing

ripped TORE; TORN

ripple WAVE

rippling anagram indicator

rise ASCENT; CLIMB; HIKE; HILL; KNOLL; LIFT; MOUNT; RALLY; REAR; REBEL; SLOPE; SOAR; STAND; START; STIR; SURGE; SWELL; TOR; UP; WAX; WELL; reversal indicator

rise and fall TIDE

rise effortlessly SOAR

rise rapidly ROCKET

rise up WELL

risen UP

rising HILL; UP; ■ STANDING; reversal indicator; *see* RISE

risk BET; CHANCE; DANGER; DARE; DICE; FACE; PERIL; ■ ENDANGER; HAZARD; THREAT

risk money BET (qv)

risk, reduce HEDGE

risk, take BET; CHANCE; DARE; DICE; GAME; WAGER

risking anagram indicator

risky IFFY; ■ DARING

risky opportunity SPEC; ■ VENTURE; *see* BET

risky venture *see* BET

risqu BLUE; DARING; RACY; SAUCY

rival FOE; VIE

rivalry BATTLE; CONTEST; OPPOSITION

riven SPLIT

river FLOW; FLOWER; R; can call for a specific river name – common British examples: AIRE, AXE, CAM, DEE, EXE, FAL, FORTH, OUSE, SEVERN, SPEY, STOUR, TAFF, TAMAR, TAY, TEE, TEES, TEST, TRENT, WEAR, YARE; common foreign examples: DON, INDUS, NILE, ODER, PLATE, PO, RHINE, RHONE, URAL, VOLTA; ■ CALE; DOURO; HUMBER; INN; ISIS; OB;

SALE; TIBER; TWEED; USK; RIBBLE; WESER

river barrier DAM

river bottom BED

river crossing can indicate a component is to be nested within the name of a river – *see* RIVER

river, crossing can indicate that R (or the name of a river) is to be nested within a component – *see* RIVER

river, European ODER; *see* RIVER

river excursion ROW

river, German MAIN; *see* RIVER

river in France OISE; ■ SEINE

river, infernal STYX

river mammal OTTER

river, Russian DON; NEVA

river, sacred ALPH

river, stretch of REACH

river transport BARGE; FERRY

river, varsity CAM

river wave BORE

river, Welsh NEATH; TAFF

riverside BANK

rivet BOLT; PIN; STUD; ■ FIXING

rivulet STREAM

road AI; AVE; CLOSE; DRIVE; LANE; M; MI; PASS; ROUTE; RD; ST; WAY; ■ ARTERY; BYPASS; [◊ RING]

road back DR

road, busy AI

road junction T

road, main ARTERY

road, minor B; RD

road, old VIA

road, private DRIVE

road repairs anagram of ROAD

road, Roman VIA

road sign SLOW; STOP; ■ HALT

road, small CLOSE; DRIVE; LANE; RD; *see* ROAD

road stone COBBLE

road, suburban CLOSE; DRIVE

road, type of RING; ■ A; B; BY

road up can indicate that a synonym for road is to be reversed e.g. DR, IM, TS

roadblock BARRIER
roadside VERGE; ■ KERB
roadside building MOTEL
roadside-emergency service AA; RAC
roadside facility KERB; can indicate street furniture, street lamp etc
roadside row, join PARK
roam RAMBLE; ROVE; WANDER; anagram indicator
roaming anagram indicator
roan BAY
roar BELLOW; BOOM; SHOUT
roast BAKE; BASTE; BEEF; BLAST; JOINT; PAN; SLATE (i.e. criticise)
roast meat JOINT
roasting anagram indicator
rob MUG; NICK; PINCH; SACK; STEAL; ■ BURGLE; RIFLE; ROLL
Rob ROY
robbed of omission indicator (as "robbed of grand" → G to be omitted)
robber MUGGER
robbery BLAG; HEIST; THEFT; ■ PILLAGE
robe GOWN
Robert BOB
Robin HOB (i.e. Robin Goodfellow); HOOD
Robin Goodfellow PUCK
robust HARDY; STOUT; ■ RUGGED; STRONG
rock CRAG; FLINT; GEM; GIB; ICE; JAR; LAVA; ORE; REEL; ROLL; SHAKE; SHOCK; STAGGER; STONE; SWAY; TOR; TUFF; WAVER; anagram indicator
rock formation CORK (i.e. anagram); SCAR
rock in the North Sea BASS
rock layers STRATA
rock, molten LAVA
rock music anagram of MUSIC
rock, siliceous SINTER
rocked, rocking anagram indicator

rocker CHAIR; STONE (i.e. Rolling)
rocker, old TED
rocker's opponent MOD
rocket RETRO; VI; with a capital letter, can indicate something to do with Stephenson or his locomotive
rocket, give a WIG
rocket launch SHOT
rocket launchers NASA
rocket organisation NASA
rocks ICE; REEF
rocks, on the can indicate a word ending in ICE
rocks, pile of TOR
rocky anagram indicator
Rocky BOXER; anagram indicator
rod BAR; CANE; CUE; GAT; PERCH; POLE; SPAR; SPIT; STAFF; STICK; SWITCH
rod, using ANGLING; FISHING
rodent CAVY; CONY; MOUSE; RAT; VOLE; ■ HAMSTER
rodent catcher RATTER
rodents MICE
Roderick ROD
Rodin mention of the name is likely to refer to one of the sculptor's famous statues such as *The Kiss* or *The Thinker*
Rodney ROD
roe DEER
Roger ROG
rogue CAD; CHEAT; CON; CROOK; CUR; DOG; IMP; SCAMP; ■ FIDDLER; ROUE
roguish ARCH
roist REVEL
role PART; TASK; ■ FUNCTION; STEAD
role, have a ACT
role of, assume PLAY
role, principal LEAD; STAR
role, small CAMEO
role, to be in ACT
roll BAP; BUN; CAKE; CARPET; COAST; LIST; ROB; ROCK; SPOOL; SURGE; SWELL; TURN; TWIST; WAD; WHEEL; WIND; ■ DRIFT; MUFFIN;

RECORD; ROSTER; STAGGER; SWISS

roll about WELTER

roll-about PODGY

roll, to anagram indicator; *see* ROLL

roll, type of SWISS

roll up FURL

rolled RAN; WOUND; anagram indicator; reversal indicator

roller BREAKER; SWELL; WAVE

rollick REVEL

rollicking anagram indicator

rolling FLUSH; RICH; anagram indicator; reversal indicator; can indicate other terms for "rich" e.g. well-to-do

rolling out anagram indicator

Rolling Stones BAND

rolls anagram indicator; reversal indicator; can indicate something to do with wallpaper

Rolls RR

roly-poly DUMPY; ■ CHUBBY

Roman R; RC; TYPE; ■ BRUTUS; CINNA; can indicate a Latin term, or Roman numeral (s); beware of the tricky use of Roman numerals as in "Eleven of the Romans turned back" which calls for the answer NINE i.e. XI reversed!

Roman art ARS

Roman chap VIR

Roman coin AS

Roman coins ASSES

Roman couple II

Roman date IDES

Roman emperor NERO; OTHO

Roman god DEUS; SOL; *see* GOD

Roman goddess VESTA

Roman historian LIVY

Roman, I am for ancient SUM

Roman law LEX

Roman, old ANTONY

Roman poet MARTIAL

Roman procurator PILATE

Roman road VIA

Roman, severe CATO

Roman's here HIC

Roman, this HIC

Roman, way for VIA

Roman, you TU

romance COURT; FICTION; NOVEL; WOO; with a capital letter can indicate something to do with Latin

romancer LIAR

Romans *see* ROMAN

Romans, number of CIVIC

romantic DREAMY

Rome, from/in can indicate that some Latin word or phrase is to be used, for an example *see* ROME, NOW IN

Rome, now in NUNC (Latin for now)

Rome, time in IDES

Rome's construction anagram of ROME; [◊ DAY]

Romeo LOVER; R; WOLF

romp ORGY; PLAY; SPREE

Romulus and Remus can indicate something to do with Rome, twins, common age

Ronald RON

rood CROSS

roof COVER; THATCH; TOP; ■ PALATE

roof-beam RAFTER

roof, part of EAVES

roof, sort/type of GABLE; THATCH

roof-top RIDGE

roofer TILER

roofing THATCH

rook CHEAT (qv); CON; MAN; PIECE; R; SKIN

rooked CHEATED

room ATTIC; CELL; CLOSET; DEN; GAP; HALL; LAB; LOFT; LOUNGE; RM; SALON; SCOPE; SPACE; STUDIO; STUDY; WARD; ■ CHAMBER; GAOL; PARLOUR; SHOP; VESTRY

Room At The Top ATTIC

room for concerts HALL

room for improvement WARD

room, little CELL; CLOSET; RM; ■ PANTRY

room, outer BUT

335

room, say SELL

room, small CLOSET

room under roof LOFT

rooms CELLS; FLAT; SUITE

rooms, set of *see* ROOMS

roost PERCH

roost, ruler of COCK

root BELIEF; CAUSE; POKE; ■ ORIGIN; SOURCE; TUBER; *see* ORIGIN

root crop BEET

rope CABLE; CAT; CORD; GUY; HEMP; LINE; NOOSE; PAINTER; SASH; SHEET; STAY; ■ PEARLS; SISAL; TETHER

rope, attachment for CLEAT

rope fibre ISTLE

rope maker ISTLE

rope trick anagram of ROPE e.g. PORE

rope up DROC (rev. in a DC)

ropes, use MOOR

ropey POOR

ropey piece of work can indicate the term for a particular knot

Rosalind ROS

rose BRIAR; PINK; TUDOR; ■ RAMBLER; reversal indicator; [◊ SPINE; THORN]

Rose* can indicate something to do with flowers as "arrangement involving Rose from Tokyo" → IKEBANA

rose-garden BED

rosette FAVOUR

Rossini opera TELL

roster LIST; ROLL; ROTA; TABLE

rostrum PODIUM

rosy PINK; RED

rot BULL; BUNK; ERODE; *see* RUBBISH

rota LIST; ROSTER; TABLE

rotate SPIN; TURN; WIND

rotisserie SPIT

rotor ARM

rotten BAD; NG; OFF; POOR; ■ ADDLED; EATEN; anagram indicator

rotten, become/get ADDLE; ROT; SOUR

rotten, made ADDLED

rotter CAD; HEEL (qv); RAT; ■ BOUNDER

rotting ADDLING

rotund PLUMP

rou RAKE; RIP; ROGUE

rouge RED; ■ BLUSHER

rough CRUDE; RAW; RUDE; THUG; VAGUE; ■ COARSE; HARSH; HEAVY; HOARSE; LEATHERY; RAGGED; RUGGED; UNCUT; anagram indicator; *see* HOOLIGAN

rough-haired SHAGGY

rough sea(s) anagram of SEA(S)

rough water anagram of WATER

rough water, patch of WAKE

rough water stretch RIP

roughed up anagram indicator

roughly ABOUT; ORSO (i.e. or so); anagram indicator

roughly made CRUDE; RUDE

roulette WHEEL; ■ GAMING

roulette wheel GAMING; [◊ BET; CHIP; GAMBLE]

round ABOUT; BALL; BEAT; BOUT; BULLET; C; CANON; DEAL; HEAT; LAP; O; PLUMP; RING; SHOT; SONG; STOUT; TURN; ■ CIRCLE; CIRCULAR; CYCLE; EDDY; NOUGHT; ORBIT; ZERO; anagram indicator; nesting indicator; reversal indicator; can indicate something to do with drink or drinking places

round-about anagram indicator; nesting indicator; a synonym for "about" e.g. C or RE to be nested within a component (Example: "Fears for the parents round-about" gives DREADS)

round, go ROLL; TURN

round of drinks SHOUT

roundabout *see* ROUND-ABOUT

rounded PLUMP; reversal indicator

rounded division LOBE

rounded object GLOBE (qv)

rounded up anagram indicator

Roundhead R

rounds BEAT; LAPS; OO; OS

rounds, do the EDDY; SPIN; TWIST; *see* TURN

rounds, making the can indicate something to do with whirlpool, eddy

rouse RAISE; START; STIR; WAKE

roused UP; ■ ABOUT

roused, be WAKE

roust STIR

rout BEAT; CRUSH; GRUB; PACK; RABBLE; RIOT; THRASH; ■ DEFEAT; HIDING

rout, in anagram indicator

route PASS; PATH; ROAD; WAY; ■ CANAL; COURSE; JOURNEY; LANE (as in bus-lane); LINE; TRACK

route, less frequented BROAD (i.e. B-road!)

route, part of STAGE

route, trade CANAL

routed anagram indicator

routine ACT; DRILL; HABIT; ROUND; RUT

routine, dull RUT

routine, established WAY

routine journalist HACK

routine task CHORE

routine work CHORE

rove RAMBLE; ROAM; ■ PROWL; TRAVEL; WANDER

rover RANGER

Rover* DOG; as Rovers is a popular name for a football club, can indicate something to do with an individual footballer (e.g. shinguard, football position)

row BANK; BRUSH; DIN; FILE; LINE; OAR; RACKET; RANGE; RANK; SCRAP; SCULL; SHINDY; SPAT; TIER; TIFF; ■ BOTHER; NOISE; POTHER; SETTO (i.e. set-to)

row, formed a LINED

row, get into a ALIGN

row, one involved in a OAR; STROKE

row, one leading a STROKE

rowan ASH

rowdy BULLY; TED; anagram indicator

rowel WHEEL

rowers CREW; EIGHT

rowing club LEANDER

rowing, one OAR; SCULLER

rowing people EIGHT

rowing position BOW

Roy ROB

royal R; ■ REAL; REGAL; REGIUS; can refer to a specific monarch, in full or abbreviated; *see* KING, QUEEN, MONARCH, RULER, or other member of royal family (prince etc)

royal address SIRE

royal, ancient REAL

royal characters ER; *see* KING, QUEEN, MONARCH, RULER

royal family HOUSE; *see* ROYAL HOUSE

royal house ORANGE; ■ HANOVER; TUDOR; WINDSOR; YORK

royal household COURT

royal status CROWN

Royalist [◊ COURT]

royalty ER; can indicate a court card

royalty, line of HOUSE

RPO PHIL

rub CHAFF; PRESS

rub away ERODE

rub out KILL (qv); SLAY; ■ ERASE

rubber can indicate something to do with masseur, masseuse

rubber product TYRE

rubber product, American TIRE

rubber, sort of INDIA

rubbish BIN; BOSH; BULL; BUNK; CHAFF; DRECK; DROSS; GASH; JUNK; MESS; PULP; ROT; TAT; TOSH; TRASH; TRIPE; ■ BILGE; COBBLERS; GARBAGE; JABBER; LITTER; PIFFLE; PRATTLE; TWADDLE; WASTE; *see* NONSENSE

rubbish container BIN; SKIP

rubbish, place for DUMP; HEAP; TIP; *see* RUBBISH CONTAINER

rubbish in US, place for DUMPSTER

rubbish, talk *see* TALK RUBBISH

rubbished BINNED; SCRAPPED; anagram indicator

rubbishing anagram indicator

ruby GEM; RED; STONE; ■ REDDY

ruck CROWD; SCRUM

ruction ROW; ■ AFFRAY; RIOT

rudder HELM

ruddy PINK; RED; ROSY; ■ BLOOMING; FLAMING; HEALTHY

ruddy, not PALE

rude BRASH; ROUGH; *see* CHEEKY

rude, do something POINT

rude, extremely RE

rude rejection SNUB

rudely anagram indicator

rudeness SLIGHT

rudeness, act of SLIGHT; SNUB

rudimentary BASIC; ROUGH

rue PITY; REGRET

ruff FRILL; TRUMP (at cards)

ruffian BULLY; LOUT; THUG; TOUGH

ruffle STIR; ■ NEEDLE; RUMPLE; anagram indicator

ruffled anagram indicator

rug MAT; WIG

rugby RU; with capital initial letter can refer to the SCHOOL

rugby competition SEVENS

rugby crowd RUCK

rugby final Y

rugby player CENTRE; HOOK; LOCK PROP; WASP; ■ FLANKER; HOOKER

rugby players PACK

rugby scores TRIES

rugby team BATH; WASPS

rugged exterior RD

ruin BREAK; DISH; DOOM; END; MAR; ROT; SMASH; SPOIL; WRECK; ■ RELIC; SCUPPER; SHATTER; TORPEDO; UNDO; anagram indicator

ruination anagram indicator

ruined BROKE; anagram indicator; *see* BROKE, RUIN

ruining anagram indicator

ruinous anagram indicator

ruins SPOILS; anagram indicator, as "ruins of Rome" → ROME; *see* RUIN

rule CANON; GOVERN; LAW; LINE; ORDER; REIGN; STRIP; ■ CHARGE; ORDINANCE; PRESIDE; REIGN

Rule Britannia can indicate use of ARNE, its composer

rule out BAN; BAR; BLACK; REJECT; anagram of RULE

rule soundly RAIN

ruled by UNDER

ruler ER; GR; KING; LORD; ■ AMIR; CSAR; EMIR; EMEER; KHAN; MEASURE; QUEEN; RAJA; REGENT; SULTAN; TSAR

ruler, current ER

ruler, Middle Eastern SULTAN

rules CODE; LAW; ■ CONSTITUTION; SYSTEM; *see* LAW, RULE

rules, set of CODE

ruling ACT; EDICT; IN; LAW; ■ REGNANT

rum GROG; ODD; OFF; STRANGE; anagram indicator

rumble TWIG

ruminant COW; DEER; ELAND

rummaged, rummaging anagram indicator

rummer GLASS

rumour CRY; NOISE; TALK; ■ BUZZ; *see* GOSSIP

rumour, according to/of homophone indicator

rumoured, it's homophone indicator

rump END; SEAT

rumple RUFFLE

rumpus FUSS; RIOT; ■ NOISE

run BELT; BOLT; BYE; CHAIR (i.e. a meeting); CHASE; COURSE; DART; DASH;

DRIVE; ESCAPE; EXTRA; FLEE; FLOW; FLY; GO; HARE; HIE; LOPE; NIP; PELT; R; RACE; RILL; RUSH; SCOOT; SHOOT; SINGLE; SNAG; SPEED; SPRINT; STREAK; TEAR; TROT; ZIP; ■ CANTER; CAREER; CONTROL; GALLOP; HENNERY; LADDER; MANAGE; SCAMPER; SUPERINTEND; anagram indicator; can indicate something to do with smuggling

★ **run** a device whereby the answer is a run or sequence of letters within the clue. Example: "Burden borne by son, usually" → ONUS (Also known as the hidden word clue.) However we may be required to select particular letters from a sequence (examples of such indicators being "oddly, "regularly") as "Hat, oddly in brown, with veil" tells us to take the odd letters from "brown" (BON) which we have to add to NET to get BONNET

run aground STRAND

run ahead R to be placed at the beginning

run-around anagram of RUN; a component to be nested within RUN or a synonym such as CANTER

run away *see* RUN OFF

run down REVILE

run-down PALE

run eye over READ; SCAN

run, famous CRESTA

run fast DART; DASH; PELT; ZIP; *see* RUN

run in COLLAR; NICK; ■ ARREST

★ **run indicator** a code word or phrase telling you the answer is a run or sequence of letters within the clue. Examples: borne by, carried in, part of, some

run into MEET; RAM; ■ ENCOUNTER; INCUR; R to be

inserted into word or component that follows

run naked STREAK

run off BOLT; ELOPE; FLEE; ■ FLY; LEVANT; SCATTER; anagram of RUN; R to be omitted

run, one taking part in RACER

run out LAPSE; RO; anagram of RUN; R to be omitted

run out of steam FLAG; TIRE

run over NUR; RECAP; REVIEW; SPILL; TRAD

run quickly RIP

run through EMPALE; IMPALE; PIERCE

run together ELOPE

run-up NUR; TRAD; can indicate an anagram in which R is included

runabout anagram of RUN; a component to be nested within RUN (or a synonym such as FLY, *see* RUN)

rung SPOKE; STEP

runner BEAN; COE; FOOT; MILER; R; SKI; VINE; ■ CARPET; HARRIER; LOPER; an old standby to indicate a river, *see* RIVER

runner* RUG

runner-up SECOND; SILVER

runners FIELD

running HARING; ON; can indicate something to do with smuggling; anagram indicator

running amok anagram indicator

running around nesting indicator; anagram indicator

running away FLIGHT

running, kind of TROT

running mate ELOPER

running water *see* RIVER

runny FLOWING; WET; anagram indicator

runs R; RR; anagram indicator; run indicator

runs away can indicate that R or RR to be omitted

runway STRIP

rupees R

Rupert BEAR; BROOKE

rupture BREACH; BREAK; ■ HERNIA
rural business FARM
Rural Dean RD
rural scene FARM
ruse DODGE; PLOY; SCAM; TRICK
rush CHARGE; CHEAT (colloq.); DART; DASH; FLY; HARE; HASTE; LUNGE; RACE; REED; RUN; SPATE; SPEED; SURGE; TEAR; ZOOM; ■ GUST; HUSTLE; PLUNGE; SCAMPER; SCUDDLE; SCUTTLE; *see* RUN
rush around anagram indicator; can indicate that a component is to be nested within RUSH
rush, don't DALLY
rush reportedly HAIR
rush through SKIM
rushed FLEW; HASTY; RAN; SPED; TORE
rushes PRINTS
rushing around anagram indicator
Russell RUSS
russet* APPLE
Russia once USSR
Russian IVAN; SERGE; ■ LENIN; SLAV
Russian before 1991, of RED
Russian commune MIR
Russian country house DACHA
Russian lady/woman RIASA; TAMARA
Russian plane MIG
Russian river OB
Russian, yes DA
rust can indicate something to do with fungus
rustic HICK; PEASANT; YOKEL
rustle STEAL; can indicate something to do with stock, stocktaking
rusty OLD
rut TRACK; ■ FURROW; GROOVE
ruth PITY
ruthless HARD
Ruth BABE
rye GRASS

Ss

's IS; when preceded by the name of the newspaper which is publishing the crossword it can indicate OUR (e.g. if in The Guardian then "Guardian's" → OUR); when functioning as an abbreviation for "is" it can act as the link between the two definitions in a double definition clue
's reportedly Z
S, we hear ES; ESS
SA can indicate something to do with South America *or* South Africa
Sabbath via the nursery rhyme can indicate being bonny, blithe, good or gay
sabot SHOE
sabotage anagram indicator
sabotaged anagram indicator
sac BAG; CYST
sachet BAG; PACKET
sack AXE; BAG; BOOT; CHOP; DRESS; DRINK; FIRE; LOOT; RAID; RIFLE; ROB; SPOIL; WINE
sacked anagram indicator; omission indicator; *see* SACK
sacked man SANTA
sacking JUTE
sacred HOLY
sacred pages/text AV; NT; OT
sacred writings AVESTA
sacrifice OFFER
sacrificed anagram indicator
sacrificial move GAMBIT
sacrificial slab ALTAR
sacrificing omission indicator
sacrosanct HOLY
sad BLUE; DOWN; GRAVE; LOW; ■ DISMAL
sad expression SIGH
saddle COL; LAND; LUMBER; PAD; SEAT
saddle, in the RIDING; UP

saddlery TACK
sadly ALACK; ALAS; anagram indicator
safe PETER; SURE; TILL; ■ SECURE; SOUND
safe-breaker anagram of SAFE
safe conduct PASS
safe place ARK
safe, not playing RISKY
safe to eat EDIBLE
safeguard PRESERVE; SURETY
safekeeping CHARGE
safety device FUSE; NET; ■ CATCH; VENT
sag DIP; DROOP; FALL; FLAG; SINK
saga EDDA; EPIC; FLOP; MYTH; STORY; TALE
sagacious WISE
sage WISE; ■ RISHI; SOLON; can indicate a particular title for a wise person e.g. maharishi
Sahara* DESERT
said ORAL; SPOKE; STATED; homophone indicator; *see* SAY
said "Hello" HIGH
said in France DIT
said to attract attention HOY
said yes? AYED
sail LUG; ROYAL; ■ CANVAS; [◊ LUFF; TACK]
sail, set RIG
sailing man *see* SAILOR
sailing, piece of TACK
sailor AB; HAND; JACK; MATE; OS; PO; SALT; TAR; ■ BOATER; HEARTY; LASCAR; MARINER; POPEYE; RATING; REEFER; SEAMAN; can indicate a famous sailor e.g. DRAKE, NELSON, ROSS
sailor, doomed BUDD
sailor, transatlantic CABOT
sailor's left PORT
sailors ABS; CREW; NAVY; RN
sailors, gang of PRESS
sails CANVAS
saint S; ST; ■ ALBAN; LUKE; MARTIN; PAUL; PETER; remember that many towns are prefaced by ST, e.g. St Albans, so

the reference might be pointing towards a geographical area e.g. county; when names such as St Joseph or St Paul, a US state might be called for
St Paul's, part of DOME
St Peters, part of DOME
saint, picture of ICON
salad dressing in America MAYO
salad food COS; CRESS; ■ CELERY
salad in U.S. SLAW
salad dressing OIL
salamander NEWT
salary CUT; PAY; SCREW
sale AUCTION; DEAL
sale, carry for HAWK
sale, for GOING
sale, have for STOCK
sale item LOT
sales-pitch AD; *see* SALES TALK
sales rep AGENT
sales talk PATTER; PITCH; SPIEL
salesman LOMAN (i.e. in Miller's play); REP; TOUT; ■ VENDER
salesman's line *see* SALES TALK
salesman, work as TRAVEL
salesperson REP
sally JEST; QUIP; RETORT; SORTIE
Sally SAL
salmon CHAR; COHO; PARR; PINK; [◊ LEISTER (i.e. salmon-spear)]
salmon, young PARR
saloon BAR; INN; PUB; also can indicate something to do with a car
salt AB; CURE; NACL; SEASON; TAR; WIT; *see* SAILOR
salt in France SEL
salt water *see* SALT-WATER *below*
salt-water BRINE; SEA; SWEAT; TEAR; TEARS
salute GREET; HAIL; TOAST; ■ ACCLAIM; SALVO

341

salvage collector TOTTER
salver TRAY
Salvation Army SA
Sam UNCLE
same DO; EQUI; ID; IDEM; LIKE; ■ DITTO; MATCH; repetition indicator; when associated with a reversal indicator can signal a palindrome
same again DO; ■ DITTO; repetition indicator
same, do the APE
same, doing the APING
same place, in the IB
same source, from the IB
sample SIP; TASTE; TASTER; TEST; TRY; ■ SWATCH; run indicator
sampled run indicator
samples SWATCH
Samuel SAM
Samuel's teacher ELI
sanctimonious PI
sanction ALLOW; FINE; OK; LET; PASS; ■ APPROVE; WARRANT
sanctioned OKED
sanctuary DEN; HAVEN; LAIR; ■ ASYLUM; HARBOUR; OASIS
sanctuary, animal ARK
sand BEACH; BUNKER; GRIT; SHORE
sand, bit of GRAIN
sand, lots of DUNE
sandal* SHOE
sandbank BAR
sandhill DUNE
Sandhurst RMA
sandpiper KNOT
sandwich PIECE; ROUND; TOASTY; WAD
sandwich filling HAM
sandwiches nesting indicator (as "pub sandwiches" signals that a component is to be nested within INN, BAR, PUB etc)
sandy GINGER; GRITTY
sandy area BEACH
sandy ground LINKS
sandy tract DENE

sane SOUND
sank putt, we hear HOLD
Santa CLAUS
sap DOPE; MINE; MUG; NERD; ■ COSH; JUICE; SUCKER; TRENCH
sapper(s) RE
Saracen's Head S
Sarah SAL
sarcasm IRONY
sarcastic ACID; BITING; DRY
sarcastic remark DIG
sarcastic, somewhat DRY
sardonic WRY
sash BAND; CORD; FRAME (i.e. as in window); OBI; ROPE
sash, Japanese OBI
sat POSED; SEATED
sat in nesting indicator
satchel BAG
satiate FILL; STUFF
satire IRONY
satirise MOCK; SQUIB
satirist MOCKER; SWIFT
satisfaction CONTENT; COMFORT; JOY
satisfaction, give PLEASE; SATE
satisfactory FINE; OK
satisfactory manner, in a WELL
satisfied FULL; MET; SMUG; ■ CONTENT; PLEASED
satisfy DO; MEET; PLEASE; SERVE
satisfy thirst QUENCH
satisfying MEETING; PLEASING; SATING
satisfying, was MET
saturate DRENCH; SOAK; STEEP
Saturday via the nursery rhyme can indicate "working hard for one's living"
satyr GOAT
sauce BRASS; CHEEK; DIP; GALL; GRAVY; LIP; PESTO; TOPPING; ■ DRESSING; NERVE
saucer CHINA

saucy FRESH; LIPPY; PERT; ■ INSOLENT

sauna BATH

saunter AMBLE; STROLL; ■ MOOCH

sausage BANGER; WURST; in junction with "land" can indicate CUMBER (i.e. Cumberland sausage); [◊ DOG]

sausage, German WURST

savage CRUEL; WILD; anagram indicator

savaged anagram indicator

savagely anagram indicator

save AMASS; BAR; BUT; KEEP; SKIMP; SPARE; STORE; ■ EXCEPT; RECLAIM; RECYCLE; SCRAPE; SCRIMP

save from wreck SALVE

save, try to SCRIMP

saving BAR; BUT; EXCEPT; nesting indicator

saving money THRIFT

savings HOARD; RESERVE

savings account ISA

savings plan PEP; TESSA

savour TANG

savoury PASTY; TASTY

savoury spread PATE

Savoy princess IDA

saw ADAGE; CUT; CUTTER; EYED; MAXIM; NOTED; RIP; SAYING; SPIED; SPOTTED; TOOL; ■ CAUGHT; EPIGRAM; GNOME; MOTTO; PHRASE; can indicate something to do with a proverb, saying, motto, etc. which often, in their full form, can be the required answer, especially in the larger crosswords

saw, sort of BAND; FRET; HACK; PANEL; RIP

say AS; AVER; EG (for example); MOUTH; OPINE; SPEAK; STATE; TELL; UTTER; VOICE; ■ EXPRESS; OBSERVE; REMARK; homophone indicator (as "I say" → AYE); can indicate that the reference word is an example of the required word, for instance "left, say" → SIDE, "wing, say" → LIMB

say excitedly PANT

say menacingly HISS

say more ADD

say no DENY

say nothing EGO (i.e. "e.g. zero"); HUSH; QUIET; SH; ■ SILENCE

say, they homophone indicator

say wearily SIGH

say, you might homophone indicator

saying PHRASE; ■ EGNOME; *see* SAW

saying, clever QUIP

saying little QUIET

saying nothing MUTE

sayings SUTRA

scab CRUST

scald BURN

scale CLIMB; KEY; PLATE; RATE; ■ MOHO; RATING; can indicate something to do with temperature scale e.g. C, F; can indicate something to do with mountaineering

scales LIBRA

scaling equipment LADDER

scalp TROPHY

scam CON; JAPE; PRANK; RACKET; RAMP; STING; TRICK; ■ FIDDLE; FRAUD; SWINDLE

scamp IMP; KNAVE; RIP; ROGUE;

scamper RUN; RUSH

scan EYE; LOOK; READ; TEST; ■ SEE

scandal DIRT

scandalise APPAL

scandalous anagram indicator

scandalous information DIRT

Scandinavian DANE; FINN; LAPP; NORSE; SWEDE

Scandinavian coin ORE

Scandinavian girl MIA

Scandinavian goddess HEL

Scandinavian monster TROLL

Scandinavian saga EDDA

scant SHORT; SLIGHT; STINT

scanty SPARSE

scape ERROR; SLIP

scar SEAM (geol.)

scarce LEAN; RARE

scarecrow BOGLE

scared WINDY; YELLOW

scarcely sufficient SCANT

scare FEAR; FRIGHT; UNMAN

scare away SHOO

scarf BOA; STOLE

scarlet RED

scarlet, turned DER

scathing BITCHY; SHARP; TART

scatter SOW; SPREAD; STREW; anagram indicator

scattered SOWN; SPARSE; SPREAD; STRAY; ■ RANDOM; anagram indicator

scatterbrained GIDDY

scattering anagram indicator

scatty DAFT; anagram indicator

scavenger RAT; TOTTER

★ scenario is a useful word to describe the picture being painted by the compiler. The scenario may be relevant as in "She's a minder working with us" (9) where "working" is indicating that an anagram is to be constructed from A MINDER and US to reach the answer NURSEMAID. (Note the clever way "working" here does double duty as an anagram indicator and as a main constituent of the definition.) But the scenario is just as likely to be misleading as in "Mount hotly tipped to run" (4) which strongly suggests something to do with horse-racing – yet the answer is ETNA(!)

scene PLACE; SET; SETTING; SPOT; VIEW

scene, disorderly RAG

scene of combat ARENA; LIST; RING

scenery FLAT(S); SET

scenes ACT

scent SMELL; SPOOR; TRAIL; ■ AROMA; MUSK

sceptic can indicate something to do with Thomas (i.e. Doubting Thomas) hence "a sceptic shortly" cues THOS

sceptical, be DOUBT

schedule FORM; LIST; ROTA

schedule, behind LATE

scheduled time SLOT

scheme CABAL; DODGE; IDEA; PLAN; PLOT; SCAM; THEORY

scheme, unrealistic BUBBLE

schism BREACH; BREAK; RIFT; SPLIT

schnozzle NOSE

scholar BA; MA; PUPIL; ■ LEARNER; MBA

scholarship LEARNING

school COACH; CLASS; COED (i.e. co-ed); ETON; FISH; FORM; GAM (i.e. of whales); HARROW; LYCEE; REPTON; STOWE; SCH; SECT; SET; TEACH; TRAIN; TUTOR; can indicate something to do with fish; anagram indicator

school building HOUSE

school curriculum, part of PE

school, go away to BOARD

school group/organisation PTA

school hall GYM

school leader HEAD; S

school lesson PE; RE

school-mate TEAM (i.e. anagram of MATE)

school member as well as pupil, teacher etc. can refer to whale, fish or a particular species of fish

school period CLASS; TERM

school, play RADA

school report EATEN (i.e. homophone of Eton)

school, secondary HIGH

school subject RE

school time TERM

school, type of PREP

schoolchild BOARDER; PUPIL

schoolboys HOUSE

schoolchildren CLASS; FORM; ■ BOARDERS

schoolgirl crush PASH

schoolmaster HEAD; SIR

schooner GLASS; SCH; SHIP

Schubert catalogue D

Schubert's work LIED

sc-fi movie ET

science SC; SCI
science exam PRACTICAL
science fiction SF
science man BSC
scientific establishment LAB
scientist BSC; PAULI; BOFFIN; [◊ LAB]
scintilla TRACE
scoff EAT; HISS; GIBE; JIBE; MOCK; SCORN; WOLF
scoffed ATE
scoffing EATING; SCORN
scold CHIDE; NAG; RATE; SLATE; ■ BERATE
scold, old SHEND
scolded CHID
sconce FINE
scone CAKE
scoop BAIL; STORY; TROWEL; ■ DIPPER
scooter rider MOD
scope AMBIT; PLAY; RANGE; REACH; ROOM; ■ BREADTH; EXTENT; LATITUDE
scorch SEAR; SINGE
score CUT; GOAL; LINE; MARK; NET (i.e. to put in net); NICK; NOTCH; POINT; RUN; TALLY; TRY; ■ ACCOUNT; ARRANGE; COMPOSE; COUNT; SCRATCH; WIN; can indicate something to do with music, composer
score, golf BIRDIE; BOGIE; EAGLE
score, half (of) TEN
score in darts BULL
score, part of NOTE
score, poor NIL; O
score, several EIGHTY
scored GOT; NOTED; RAN
scorer an old standby for a composer, so know your tunesmiths!
score, two-under EAGLE
scoreless O
scoreless draw OO
scores GOALS; a multiple of twenty particularly FORTY, EIGHTY
scorn SCOFF
scorn, express JEER

scorn, object of BUTT
scornful DERISIVE
scornful remark SNEER
Scot ANGUS; CELT; GAEL; IAN; KEN; MAC
Scot, old PICT
Scot's attire KILT; TARTAN
Scot's exclamation/expression OCH
Scot's historic AULD
Scot's own AIN
scotch BLOCK; DISH; END; STOP; WEDGE; ■ QUASH; SCUPPER
Scotch DRINK; RYE; SPIRIT *see* SCOTCH
scotched DEAD
Scotches DRINKS; SHORTS; anagram indicator
Scotland, child in WEAN
Scotland, resort in AYR
Scotland's extended LANG
Scotland's unmatched ORRA
Scotland, superfluous in ORRA
Scots church KIRK
Scots girl LASSIE
Scots group CLAN
Scots, known to KENT
Scots lawyer WS (Writer to the Signet)
Scots loch NESS
Scots, true RICHT
Scotsman MON; RAB; *see* SCOT
Scott WALTER
Scottish bank BRAE
Scottish beautiful BRAW
Scottish bog MOSS
Scottish chap, fellow MON; *see* SCOT
Scottish church KIRK
Scottish court official in MACER
Scottish dance FLING; REEL
Scottish dress KILT; PLAID
Scottish explorer ROSS
Scottish expression OCH
Scottish, fine for BRAW
Scottish footballers HIBS
Scottish gang GO
Scottish hall HA
Scottish head RECTOR

Scottish headland MULL
Scottish hillside BRAE
Scottish island BUTE; INCH; IONA; MULL; SKYE; ∎ ARRAN; ISLAY; SKERRY; TIREE; UIST
Scottish king DUNCAN
Scottish law LAUCH
Scottish little SMA
Scottish magistrate BAILIE
Scottish meeting MOD
Scottish mountain BEN
Scottish nobleman THANE
Scottish, odd ORRA
Scottish one ANE
Scottish order THISTLE
Scottish peak BEN
Scottish port AYR; OBAN
Scottish religious reformer KNOX
Scottish remark OCH
Scottish resort AYR
Scottish river DEE; SPEY; TAY
Scottish site, historic SCONE
Scottish tower BROCH
Scottish town AYE; WICK
Scottish water LOCH
Scottish youngster BAIRN; WEAN
scoundrel CAD; CUR; DOG; HEEL; RAT; ROGUE; ROTTER; SCALLY; *see* ROGUE
scour FLUSH
scourge BEAT; CAT; FLOG; WHIP; ∎ KNOUT; PLAGUE
scout CUB; GUIDE; ROVER; SPY; ∎ RANGER
scout leader S; SIXER
scout, potential/young CUB
scow LIGHTER
scowl LOUR; LOWER
scrabble piece TILE
scrag HANG; NECK
scraggy LEAN; THIN
scram GO; LEAVE; QUIT; ∎ BEATIT (i.e. beat it)
scramble anagram indicator; *see* HURRY
scramble awkwardly CLAMBER
scrambled, scrambles anagram indicator

scrambled egg GGE
scrambling anagram indicator
scrap BIN; BIT; BOUT; BRAWL; DITCH; DROP; FIGHT; ODD; ORT; PIECE; RAG; SHRED; SPAR; WASTE; ∎ EXCERPT; ODDMENT; *see* SCOTCH
scrap of cloth RAG; SHRED
scrape FIX; GRAZE; RAKE; SCORE; SPOT; ∎ CORNER; SAVE; TROUBLE
scrape legs BARK
scrapped FOUGHT; anagram indicator
scrappy WISPY; anagram indicator
scratch DITCH; DROP; ERASE; MARK; MONEY; OMIT; RUB; SCORE; SCRAP; SCRAPE; ∎ SCRABBLE; omission indicator; [◊ CARD]
scratch, having SCORED
scratch, needing a ITCHY
scratching anagram indicator
scrawled anagram indicator
scream CRY; LAUGH; ROAR; SHOUT; YELL; YELP; ∎ JOKE; RIOT
scream of pain OW
scree SLOPE
screech YELL
screen BLIND; CHECK; COVER; GRILL; GRILLE; HIDE; SHOW; SIFT; VEIL; VET; ∎ FILTER; SHIELD; VISOR; WINNOW; can indicate something to do with television, e.g. TV, show, soap opera
screen, move text across SCROLL
screenplay SCRIPT
screw CHEAT; CUT (i.e. share); FIX; GUARD; INCOME; PAY; PROP; TURN; WAGE; ∎ TWIST; TWISTER; WARDER; anagram indicator
screw, kind of GRUB
screw up TIGHTEN
screwed (up) anagram indicator
screwball NUT; ODD
Screwtape Letters can signal something to do with the Devil

scribble DOODLE; SCRAWL
scribe WRITER
scribe, was a WROTE
scrimmage MAUL
scrimp STINT
script HAND; MS; TEXT
scripture RE; R; ■ BIBLE
scripture, Ancient Hindu VEDA
scripture lessons RI
scriptures AV; BIBLE (qv); NT; OT; *see* BOOK
Scrooge MISER
Scrooge's partner MARLEY
scrounge BEG; CADGE
scrub BRUSH; CLEAN; SCOUR; WASH; *see* SCRATCH
scrub land HEATH
scruff NAPE
scruffy RAGGED; TATTY; anagram indicator
scrum MAUL; RUCK
scrump STEAL
scrupulous NICE
scrutineer CHECKER
scrutinise CHECK; CON; EYE; READ; SCAN
scrutiny MARK; *see* CHECK
scuba DIVER
scud RACE; RUSH
scuddle *see* SCUD
scuff BRUSH
scuffling anagram indicator
scull OAR; ROW
sculpted anagram indicator
sculptor MOORE; RODIN
sculpture BUST; IMAGE; STATUE; ■ CARVING
scum DROSS; FILM
scupper HOLE; SCOTCH; SINK
scurrilous COARSE; RIBALD
scurry BUSTLE
scurry off BEETLE
scuttle SINK
scuttled SANK; anagram indicator
scuttling anagram indicator
sea DEAD; DEEP; IRISH; MAIN; MED; OCEAN; RED; ROSS; S; WAVES; ■ ARAL; BALTIC; MARINE
sea, Antarctic ROSS
sea, arm of GULF

sea, at anagram indicator, as "lost at sea" → an anagram of LOST
sea-bird AUK; DIVER; ERNE; GULL; TERN; TEAL
sea-change anagram of SEA
sea channel STRAIT
sea cook SILVER
sea-dog SALT; TAR; *see* SAILOR
sea eagle ERNE
sea, European MER
sea-foam SURF
sea god TRITON; ■ NEPTUNE; POSEIDON
sea, home from the ASHORE
sea in France MER
sea legs PIER
sea-life CORAL; *see* FISH, MARINE CREATURE etc
sea, man going to SALT; *see* SAILOR
sea mollusc ORMER
sea passage STRAIT
sea-pink THRIFT
sea, put to sea LAUNCH
sea-sick anagram of SEA
sea trip anagram of SEA
seabird *see* SEA-BIRD, BIRD
seabound a component to be nested within SEA (or synonym e.g. MED)
seafood CLAM; CRAB; FISH; ORMER; PRAWN; SCAMPI; ■ MUSSEL; WINKLE
seal CLOSE; LOCK; RING; SHUT; STAMP; TOP; ■ GASKET; IMPRINT; SIGIL (i.e. a signet); SIGNET
sealant LUTE; SIZE
sealed TIGHT
sealing nesting indicator
seals POD
seam JOIN; JOINT
seaman AB; HAND; PO; RATING; *see* SAILOR
seaman, sort of ABLE
seamen ABS; CREW; NUS; RN; *see* SAILOR
seamstress TACKER
séance [◊ SPIRIT]
sear SCORCH

search COMB; FISH; FRISK; HUNT; LOOK; RIFLE; QUEST; RAKE; SCOUR; ■ DELVE; INSPECT; PROWL; ROOT

search around FORAGE

search for SEEK

search for gold PROSPECT

search in water FISH

searching THOROUGH

seas sounding like C's this word can, with a homophone indicator, call for CC

seaside BEACH; COAST; SHORE

seaside air OZONE

seaside place BEACH; PIER; PROM; SHORE

seaside, regular visitor to TIDE

seaside town HOVE; PORT; *see* RESORT

season FALL; LENT; SALT; TERM; TIDE; TIME; ■ ADVENT; SPICE; SPRING; SUMMER; TEMPER; WINTER

season for Americans FALL

seasonal *see* SEASON

seasonal ball, material for a SNOW

seasonal growth HOLLY

seasonal log YULE

seasonal presentation PANTO; can indicate the name of a specific pantomime

seasoning CHIVE; SAGE; SALT; SPICE; THYME

seat BASE; BENCH; CHAIR; FORM; HOME; PEW; REAR; RUMP; SADDLE; STALL; STOOL; ■ BOTTOM; POSITION; SETTLE; SOFA; THRONE; can indicate something to do with MP, election, estate or country house

seat in church PEW; STALL

seat in theatre STALL

seat of Irish kings TARA

seat, monk's STALL

seated SAT

seats BENCH; PEW; STALLS; *see* SEAT

seats in theatre CIRCLE

seaward OUT

seaweed KELP; LAVER; TANG; WRACK; ■ ALGA

sec INSTANT; MO; ■ TRICE

second AID; B; BACK; FLASH; HELP; LATTER; MO; OTHER; REJECT; S; SEC; TICK; TRICE; WINK; ■ AIDE; ASSISTANT; INSTANT; MOMENT; RESERVE; SILVER; can signal that the second letter of an indicated word is to be used as "second in command" clues O, "second-rate" clues A, etc.; can indicate something to do with a boxer or boxing; can indicate a verb beginning with RE (i.e. to do something again); can call for some component to be followed by II, as "Book's second chapter briefly" → GENII

second best E; STOP (i.e. S-TOP)

second-born O

second class B; L

second drink R; REFILL

second French person TU

second gospeller MARK

second-hand USED

second-hand market FLEA

second helpings MORE

second grade B; R

second mate A

second person E; YOU

second person in Paris/France TU

second person to talk EWE; YEW

second, placed in S to be nested

second prize R; SILVER

second rate A (i.e. second latter of "rate"); B; MINOR; ■ BELOW

second test RESIT

second time AGAIN; I

second time, a AGAIN

secondary LESS

seconds *see* DESSERT

secrecy STEALTH

secret COVERT; INNER; ■ CLOSED; HIDDEN; PRIVATE; PRIVY

secret agent BOND; MOLE; SPY

secret intrigue CABAL

secret, keep it SH

secret language CODE
secret police STASI
secret procedure STEALTH
secret service CIA; SS; ■ STASI
secret society TONG; TRIAD
secret, work out RUMBLE
secretarial work FILING
secretarial worker TEMP
secretary PA; TEMP
secrete HIDE
secreted HID
secretive CLOSE; TIGHT
secretive, very CLOSE
secretly follow TAIL
secretly in, put PLANT
secrets, divulge RAT
sect CLASS; CULT; FACTION; PARTY; SCHOOL
section BIT; CUT; DEPT; E (as in E-section); PART; PIECE; TEAM; UNIT; ■ CHAPTER; CONIC; ROOM; run indicator
section of firm DEPT; PR
section of poem (song, carol etc) VERSE
section of roof EAVES
section of track SIDING
section of tree LOG
section, short DEPT
sections of can indicate that a word is split into two parts which are then linked by "and" to yield the answer – as "case" requires "valise" to be split and re-presented in "Sections of a case for trash" to give V-AND-ALISE i.e. VANDALISE
sector BELT; PART; ZONE; ■ AREA
secular LAIC; LAY
secure BAG; BAR; BIND; CLAMP; CLOSE; FAST; FIX; GET; GRIP; HOOK; LAND; LOCK; MOOR; NAIL; NET; PIN; POT; REEVE; SAFE; SEAL; STITCH; STRAP; SURE; TIE; WIN; ■ AFFIX; ANCHOR; BATTEN; CEMENT; HEFT (Scot); KNOT; OBTAIN; RIVET; TETHER; TIGHT; [◊ BOLT]; nesting indicator
secure by rope REEVE; TIE

secure, make CLINCH
secure place CASTLE
secure, to nesting indicator
secured BOUND; GOT; SHUT; TIED; WON; ■ GRIPPED; LOCKED; NAILED; nesting indicator
secured by nesting indicator
secures TIES; nesting indicator
securing nesting indicator
securing, person TIER
security BAIL; BOND; GAGE; GILT; ■ LOCK; SAFETY
security device COTTER; KEY LOCK; NAIL; NUT; PIN; SEAL; ■ FUSE; *see* FASTENER
security, give up for LODGE
security organization CIA
sedate STAID
sediment LEES; SILT; ·WARP
sedition TREASON
seduce LURE; PULL; ■ ATTRACT; DRAW
seducer WOLF
seductress VAMP
see AS; BEHOLD; CLOCK; EYE; GET; GRASP; LO; LOOK; NOTE; READ; SIGHT; SPOT; SPY; TWIG; V; VID; VIDE; ■ MARK; OBSERVE; WATCH; WITNESS; can indicate something to do with religious diocese, commonly ELY, others: CHESTER, TRURO; "see" can merely act as a filler or separator indicating that the definition is to follow (and therefore the word may be ignored in actually constructing the solution)
see, able to SIGHTED
see fit DEIGN
see if CHECK; TEST; ■ DECIDE
see if it's all right CHECK; TEST; VET
see, make an effort to CRANE
see red RAGE
see the light LEARN
see-through GLASS; SHEER
see trouble anagram of SEE
seed BEAN; GERM; GRASS; ISSUE; OATS; PEA; PIP; SOW; STONE; ■ PULSE; SESAME;

seed covering ARIL; POD
seed-husks CHAFF
seed-vessel POD
seedcase POD
seeds PULSE
seedy ILL; anagram indicator
seedy bar DIVE
seeing SIGHT; VISION
seeing, not BLIND
seeing that AS; SINCE
seek ASK; COURT; FISH; HUNT
seek answer ASK
seek to win COURT
seek water DOWSE
seeking QUEST
seem APPEAR; LOOK; homophone indicator
seem different anagram of SEEM
seem done DUN
seemed FELT
seemly APT; FIT; RIGHT
seen EYED; SAW; SIGHTED; ■ OBSERVED; WATCHED
seen a disaster anagram of SEEN
seen in run indicator
seep LEAK; OOZE
seethe BOIL; ■ BUBBLE; FUME
seething BOILING; anagram indicator
segment CLOVE; PART; PIECE
seismology [◊ FAULT; QUAKE]
seize BAG; CLUTCH; GRAB; GRASP; NAB; PIN; POT; TAKE; ■ ASSUME
seized by two a component to be nested within II
seized, to be nesting indicator
seizes nesting indicator; run indicator
seizing nesting indicator
seizure CRAMP; FIT
seizure of power COUP
select CULL; ELITE; MARK; OPT; PICK; SORT; TAKE; VOTE; ■ CHOOSE
select a number DIAL
selected CHOSE; IN; PICKED; NAPPED; anagram indicator
selection NAP; PICK; ■ CHOICE; OPTION; TRANCHE; [◊ NATURAL]

selection from run indicator
selection of can indicate items linked by OR, as points of the compass in "A selection of points" → SWORN
selectivity TASTE
self AUTO; EGO; ID
self-assured PROUD
self-catering SC
self-esteem EGO
self image EGO
self-possessed COOL
self-regarding boast IMIT (i.e. I'm it)
self-righteous person PRIG
self-same VERY
self-respect PRIDE
self-satisfied SMUG
selfish GRASPING
selfish person HOG
selfishness GREED
sell FLOG; PUSH; RETAIL; VEND
sell for FETCH
sell publicly AUCTION
sell, something to LOT
sell, try to HAWK; TOUT
seller BEAR; *see* TRADESMAN
selling SALE
semblance IMAGE; ■ GUISE
semi HOUSE; PART; as a prefix can indicate half a word or element is to be used, as "semi-nude" gives NU or DE;
semi-detached half a word to be omitted
semi-nude use two letters from NUDE
semi-retirement IMES
seminal KEY
seminar CLASS
senator SEN
send EMIT; POST; REMIT; WIRE; ■ FORWARD
send account BILL
send back a synonym of "send" to be reversed e.g. TIME
send down RELEGATE
send off MAIL; POST; anagram of SEND
send on REFER

send payment REMIT
send up SQUIB
send-up reversal indicator
sender MAILER; POSTER
sending forth EMISSION
sends anagram indicator
senescence AGE
senile GAGA
senility AGE
senior ARCH; ELDER; HIGH; OLDER; can indicate one element is to precede another
senior citizen OAP
senior manager EXEC
senior officer/soldier GEN; SM *see* OFFICER
senior player CAP
senior teacher HEAD
seniority AGE
senor DON
sensation HIT; ■ FEELING; SPLASH
sensation, irritating ITCH
sensational LURID; YELLOW
sensational book BLOOD
sense HEAR; NOSE; NOUS; SIGHT; TASTE; WIT; WITS; ■ MEANING; RATION; REASON; TOUCH
sense, common NOUS
sense, lack of DRIVEL
sense, make CLICK
sense of exhilaration KICK
sense, one without ASS; *see* FOOL
sense organ EAR; EYE; NOSE
sense, sound CITE
senseless *see* STUPID
senseless, make KO
sensible AWARE; SAGE; SANE; SOUND; WISE; ■ RATIONAL
sensitive RAW; ■ DAINTY; TENDER
sensitive, less NUMBER
sensitive, not NUMB
sensitive reaction ALLERGY
sensitive, was FELT
sensory hair WHISKER
sensual CARNAL

sent DROVE; HIGH; ISLED (i.e. "is led" as in "up the garden path"); anagram indicator
sent back reversal indicator
sent off anagram of SENT; but can also be a general anagram indicator
sent up reversal indicator
sentence LIFE; TERM; TIME; ■ STRETCH; can indicate something to do with prison, penal code etc.
sentence, end of E; STOP
sentence, long LIFE
sentientious remark PLATITUDE
sentient AWARE
sentiment CORN
sentiment, sickly GOO
sentimental CORNY; MUSHY; SOFT; SOPPY; TWEE
sentimental, excessively/over SOPPY; SUGARY; *see* SENTIMENTAL; ■ MAUDLIN
sentimentality CORN; GOO; SLUSH; *see* SENTIMENTAL
sentimentally pretty TWEE
separate APART; ASUNDER; PART; SORT; SPLIT; SUNDER
separate from the chaff WINNOW
separated APART; can indicate something to do with an island
separated from omission indicator, as "once having been separated from female" → ORMER
separation RIFT
sepulchre TOMB
sequence CYCLE; RUN; SUITE; TRAIN; TURN
sequence of run indicator
sequence of events CHAPTER
sequence of shots RALLY
sequin SPANGLE
serenade SING
serene CALM
serenity CALM; PEACE
serf SLAVE
sergeant GO; NCO
sergeant-major SM
sergeant-major, regimental RSM

series CHAIN; LIST; ROW; RUN; SER; SET; STRING; run indicator

series from/of run indicator

series of games RUBBER; SET

series of jobs CAREER

series of lessons COURSE

serin FINCH

serious BAD; GRAVE; GRIM; HEAVY; STERN; ■ CHRONIC; EARNEST

serious, not LIGHT; ■ CASUAL; TRIVIAL

seriousness EARNEST; WEIGHT

sermon RANT; SER

sermonise SPOUT

servant AIDE; BUTLER; FAG; MAID; MAN; PAGE; VALE; ■ BEARER; FLUNKEY; LACKEY; RETAINER

servant boy FAG

serve ACE; DO; POUR; TEND; WAIT; ■ ANSWER; DISH; MINISTER; PROFIT; anagram indicator

serve, replayed LET

served DID; anagram indicator

served as WAS

served before can simply mean that one component is to precede another

served in nesting indicator; run indicator

served, not being OFF

served up anagram indicator; a reversal indicator in a DC

served up in run indicator; in a DC clue can indicate a reverse run within a sequence

service ACE; AID; FORCE; HELP; LET; MASS; REFIT; RITE; USE; ■ DUTY; MISSA; OFFICE; can indicate on of the military services e.g. NAVY, RAF, RM, RN, TA; can indicate something to do with a church service, or a tea service

service area COUNTER

service area, trackside PIT

service at sea NAVY; RN

service, bad FAULT

service, be of AVAIL

service, cancellation of LET

service, in USED

service, little RAF; RM; RN; TA

service, monastic TERCE

service, put into USE; USED

service, put out of DEMOB

service, we hear RIGHT

serviceman REV; VICAR; ■ MARINE; PILOT; *see* CLERGYMAN, SAILOR, SOLDIER

servicemen NAVY; OR; RA; RAF; RE; REME; RI; RM; RN; *see* REGIMENT

servicing, for anagram indicator

servile SLAVISH

serving Americans GIS

serving man RANKER; WAITER

serving men ARMY; NAVY; RAF; RM; RN; *see* REGIMENT

serving no useful function, purpose US

servitude YOKE

sesame TIL

session BOUT; SITTING; TERM; TIME; ■ MEETING

session, in SITTING

session, was in SAT

set BAND; CLOT; EMBED; FACTION; GEL; GROUP; KIT; LAID; LAY; LOT; PLACE; PUT; TACKY; ■ BATCH; FIRM; HARD; IMPOSE; PACK; PLANT; RING; SERIES; SYSTEM; anagram indicator

set about ASSAIL; TACKLE; anagram of SET; a component to be nested within SET

set across ABEAM

set again RELAY; REFIX; REPLANT

set against V

set aside SAVE; SAVED; ■ BOOK; RESERVE

set-back BLOW; COST; SNAG; reversal indicator; *see* SETBACK

set charges MINE(D); PRICE

set down LAND; LAY; LOG; TES; WRITE

set eyes on *see* SEE

set forth EXPOUND; STATE

set free CLEAR; LOOSE; ▪ UNDO; UNTIE

set, full BEARD

set in nesting indicator

set in motion TRIGGER

set limits STINT

set of books NT; OT

set of clubs* FLUSH

set of figures LIST; TABLE

set of parts for assembly KIT

set of rooms SUITE

set of rules CODE

set of values RANGE

set off FIRE; FIRED; GO; GRACE; TRIGGER; TRIP; ▪ EMBARK; IGNITE; can indicate an anagram of SET (e.g. EST, ETS, TES)

set out anagram indicator; can indicate an anagram of SET (e.g. EST, ETS, TES)

set sail EMBARK

set straight DRESS; REDRESS; RIGHT; ▪ ALIGN

set-to ROW; *see* FIGHT

set to explode ARM; PRIME

set to fight PIT

set up START; anagram indicator; reversal indicator in a DC

set-up RIG; anagram indicator; reversal indicator in a DC, hence DIAL, TES etc

set up once again RIGHT

set upon RAID

set with nesting indicator

set with diamonds D to be nested

setback REVERSE; TES (i.e. reversal of SET); reversal indicator; *see* SET-BACK

sett BLOCK; BURROW

settee SOFA

setter DOG; I; ME; SUN (i.e. in the west!)

setter's IS; MINE; MY

setting DECOR; MATCH; SCENE; TACKY; anagram indicator; runs indicator

setting off GRACING; *see* SET OFF

setting, tree FOREST; GLADE; WOOD

setting up reversal indicator, as "was setting up" → SAW

settle ALIGHT; BENCH; CLOSE; FALL; FIX; FOOT; LAND; LIE; LIGHT; LODGE; MEET; PAY; PERCH; ROOST; SEAT; SINK; SIT; ▪ DECIDE; PLANT; RESOLVE; SEATING; SQUARE

settle bill PAY

settled DONE; FIXED; LIT; MET; OVER; PAID; ▪ RESIDENT; anagram indicator

settlement CAMP; CITY; TOWN; anagram indicator

settlement, temporary CAMP

settler ANGLE; INCOMER; PAYER; can indicate the name of a specific currency

settlers COLONY

settles SEATING; *see* SETTLE

settling anagram indicator

settling in nesting indicator

Seurat can indicate something to do with dots, dotty, spots etc (i.e. characteristics of pointillism, his painting style)

seven PRIME; VII

seven-point ball BLACK

75p QUI (i.e. 75% of QUID)

sever CUT; HACK; PART

several SOME; ▪ DIVERS; can indicate a specific number (usually no more than ten)

severe BAD; DOUR; GRIM; HARD; STERN; ▪ ACUTE; AUSTERE; CRUEL; HARSH; SORE; STRICT

severely damaged, so to speak RECT

sew TACK; ▪ BASTE; STITCH

sewer DRAIN; NEEDLE; PIN; PIPE; ▪ CHANNEL

sex OATS

sex-appeal IT; SA

sex change/changing F to be substituted for M or vice versa; anagram of SEX

sex, of CARNAL

sex scandal anagram of SEX

sex symbol STUD

sexual gratification OATS

sexual orientation GENDER

353

sexual romp ORGY

sexual status GENDER

sexy RANDY

Seychelles SY

SF author VERNE; WELLS

SF film ET

shabby DINGY; DIRTY; DRAB; FRAYED; LOW; MEAN; anagram indicator

shabby articles TAT

shabby type BOUNDER (qv)

shack HUT; SHED; ■ CABIN; HOVEL

shackle CHAIN; FETTER; ■ ENCHAIN; TRAMMEL

shade BLIND; BUFF; CAST; COVER; GHOST; HUE; TINT; TONE; ■ AWNING; NUANCE; UMBRA; WRAITH; *see* COLOUR; [◊ COOL]

shade, put in the a component to be nested within a colour, usually RED

shadow DOG; FOLLOW; TAIL; TRACE; TRACK

shadowed by a component to be nested within the word that follows

shadowy DARK

shady dealer SPIV

shady nook ARBOUR

shaft ADIT; ARROW; BEAM; BOLT; MINE; PIT; TRAVE; WELL

shake MO; RATTLE; ROCK; SHOCK; WAG; WORRY; ■ INSTANT; QUAVER; QUIVER; SECOND; TREMBLE; TRICE; anagram indicator

shake-up anagram indicator

shaken anagram indicator

shaken, not easily STEADY; *see* RIGID

Shakespeare BARD; BILL; SWAN; WILL

Shakespeare's Queen BESS

Shakespearian actor KEAN

Shakespearean character DULL; NYM; PUCK; LEAR; ROMEO; SNUG; TIMON

Shakespearean fairy MOTH

Shakespearian production VERSE; can refer to the title of a particular Shakespeare play

Shakespearean villain IAGO

shakily anagram indicator

shaky WEAK; FEEBLE; anagram indicator

shallow FLAT

sham COD; FAKE; FRONT; ■ BLUFF; BOGUS; PRETENCE; SIMULATE; *see* DECEIT

shamble LURCH

shambles MESS; ROUT; anagram indicator

shame ABASH; ALAS; FIE; PITY; STAIN

Shame! AW

shameful VILE

shameful act CRIME; SIN

shamefully anagram indicator

shamelessly anagram indicator

Shanghai PRESS

shanty SONG ■ SEASONG; *see* HUT

shape CAST; CONE; CUT; FORM; HAMMER; ■ FIGURE; MOULD; anagram indicator

shaped WROUGHT; anagram indicator

shaping anagram indicator

shard CROCK

share CUT; DEAL; LOT; PART; SPLIT; WHACK; ■ HALF; HALVE; INTEREST; PLOUGH; QUOTA; RATION; THIRD; as a ploughshare can indicate something to do with farming

share out ALLOT

share, take unfair HOG

shared JOINT

shares STOCK

shark FISH; ■ NURSE; can indicate something to do with loan, lending, usury, etc

sharp ACUTE; BITTER; CHEAT; FLY; HARD; NIPPY; NOTE; SMART; SOUR; TART; ■ ACRID; CLEVER (qv); CUTE; KEEN; TANGY; can indicate something to do with cheating at cards

sharp, not BLUNT; DULL

sharp point TINE
sharp-tasting ACID; *see* SHARP
sharpen HONE; STROP
sharper *see* SWINDLER
shatter BREAK; BUST; SMASH; SPLIT
shattered BROKE; anagram indicator; nesting indicator
shattering anagram indicator
shave CUT (qv); PARE
shaver PLANE; TODD
shaw GROVE; THICKET; WOOD
Shaw ARTY
shawl STOLE; WRAP
she can indicate that the answer is a woman's name; can indicate an occupation ending in -ESS; where there is some reference to France (as "in Paris she"), can call for ELLE
She NOVEL; [◊ RIDER; HAGGARD]
she from Paris ELLE
she's French ELLE
she's heartless SE
shear CLIP; CUT
shears, type of PINKING
sheath, sheathe CASE
shed BYRE; CAST; DOFF; HOVEL; HUT; LOSE; LOST; SHUCK; SPILT; STORE; ■ LEAN-TO; MOULT; anagram indicator; omission indicator
shed light LIT
shed skin CAST; PEEL
shed tears CRY; WEEP
shedding omission indicator
sheen GLOSS; GLOW
sheep DOLLY; EWE; FLOCK; LAMB; RAM; TUP; ■ COTSWOLD; TEG; TEGG; [◊ FOLD; SHEPHERD]
sheep, castrated WETHER
sheep-like OVINE
sheep may be found, where *see* SHEEP REFUGE
sheep, number of FLOCK
sheep refuge FOLD; PEN
sheep's lungs LIGHTS
sheepdog COLLIE
sheepish OVINE

sheepish, sound BLEAT
sheer FINE; STEEP; TACK
sheet COVER; LAYER; LEAF; PAGE; PAPER
sheet of wood BOARD
sheets QUIRE; REAM
sheet of paper LEAF; PAGE
shelf BAR; HOB; LEDGE; RACK; SILL; TOP
shell CASE; CONCH; PEEL; SHUCK (i.e. to peel); ■ COVER; SHOT
shell, come out one's HATCH
shell, hard TESTA
shellfish CLAM; ■ LIMPET; PRAWN; TELLIN
shells AMMO
shelter BOWER; COT; COTE; COVER; HAVEN; HIDE; HOME; HOUSE; HUT; LEE; REST; RETREAT; SCREEN; SHED; TENT; ■ AWNING; HARBOUR; SHIELD; MARQUEE
shelter, animal BURROW; BYRE; DEN; LAIR; ZOO
shelter, crude HUT
shelter for animal EARTH; *see* HOME
shelter, temporary TENT
shelter, without BLEAK; OPEN
sheltered HID
sheltered by nesting or run indicator
sheltered side LEE
sheltering nesting or run indicator
shepherd TEND; [◊ CROOK]
shepherd, first ABEL
Shere Khan *see* TIGER
sheriff EARP
sheriff's men POSSE
sherry CREAM
Shetland tidal wave ROOST
shied CAST; *see* SHY, THROW
shield COVER; SCREEN; ■ BUCKLER; UMBRELLA; *see* SHELTER
shield, band on FESS
shielding nesting indicator
shift CHANGE; DODGE; DRESS; GOWN; LUG; MOVE; PERIOD;

ROBE; SPELL; TURN; WHILE;
■ CHEMISE; DUTY; anagram
indicator;

shifted, shifting, shifts anagram
indicator

shifty WILY; anagram indicator

shilling BOB; S

shilly-shally HEDGE

shimmer GLISTEN

shimmering anagram indicator

shine BRUSH; GLOSS; GLOW;
TWINKLE

shiner STAR

shindig PARTY

shingle TILE

shining, shiny AGLOW;
BRIGHT; GLOWING

ship ARGO; BARK; BARQUE;
BRIG; COASTER; CRAFT;
CUTTER; FERRY;
FREIGHTER; KEEL; LINER;
SLOOP; SS; STEAMER;
TRAMP; TUB; ■ RIGGER;
SCHOONER; TRADER;
VESSEL; VICTORY; *see* BOAT;
when "ship" is at the end of a
word in the clue it can call for a
word ending in -CRAFT, as "Mu-
sicianship of high fliers?" cues
AIRCRAFT

ship, American USS

ship, clumsy TUB

ship, old ARGO; ARK

ship, on ABOARD; component to
be nested within SS

ship, one jumping RAT

ship, part of BOW; DECK; KEEL;
MAST; PROW; STERN

ship's bottom KEEL

ship's company CREW

ship's loss, prevent a SALVE

ship's men CREW

ship's men, reportedly CRU

ship's officer MATE; PO; *see*
OFFICER

ship, side of PORT;
STARBOARD

ship, supply TENDER

shipbuilder NOAH

shipman MATE; *see* SAILOR

shipment CARGO; LOAD

shipping company LINE

shipping facility PORT; ■
HARBOUR

shipping order SO

ships FLEET; NAVY; SAIL; ■
ARMADA; *see* SHIP

shipwreck anagram of SHIP

shipwrecked anagram indicator

shire COUNTY; HORSE

shirk SLACK

shirt T; TOP; ■ DICKY; TEE

shiver SHUDDER (qv)

shivering anagram indicator

shivering fit AGUE

shivers, the AGUE

shoal BAR; SCHOOL

shock AMAZE; APPAL; BLOW;
DAZE; FRIGHT; HAIR; JAR;
JOLT; MANE; ROCK; SHAKE;
SHEAF; STAGGER; STUN;
TURN; anagram indicator; *see*
SHOCK TREATMENT

shock-absorber BUFFER

shock, bit of a HAIR; TRESS

shock, having HAIRY

shock therapy *see* SHOCK
TREATMENT

shock treatment ECT; can indicate some aspect of hairdressing
e.g. conditioner, haircutting,
shampoo, trichology

shocked anagram indicator

shocked cry OW

shocking OUTRE; anagram indicator; can signal something to do
with electricity

shocking, potential LIVE

shocking work ECT

shockingly anagram indicator

shoddy anagram indicator

shoddy articles/clothes/stuff
TAT

shoe BOOT; BROGUE; CLOG;
OXFORD; PUMP; ■
PLIMSOLL; SABOT;
TRAINER; can indicate some-
thing to do with foot; [◊ LACE;
SOLE; UPPER]

shoe, part of HEEL; SOLE;
UPPER

shoemaker SMITH

shoes, with SHOD

shoestring LACE

shoot BAG; BUD; DART; DASH; FILM; FIRE; GERM; GUN; HUNT; PLUG; POT; RACE; RUSH; SNAP; SPEAR; SPRIG; SPROUT; STEM; SWITCH; TEAR; ■ BOLT; SCION; SNIPE; SUCKER; TILLER (bot.); anagram indicator

shoot and wound WING

shoot down DROP

shoot, order to ACTION (i.e. film)

shoot, prepare to COCK

shooter SNIPER; *see* GUN

shooting anagram indicator; can indicate something to do with photography, example: "Anxious to keep out of shooting range" → CAMERA-SHY

shooting area RANGE

shooting party member GUN

shooting up reversal indicator

shop DELI; GRASS; PEACH; RAT; ROOM; SALON; SQUEAL; STORE; ■ BETRAY; BUY; INFORM; RATON (i.e. rat on)

shop assistant can indicate something to do with counter

shop, things in STOCK

shopkeeper BAKER

shopping [◊ BAG; LIST; MALL]

shopping area/facility/precinct MALL

shopping centre MALL; MART; ■ MARKET

shops EMPORIA; *see* SHOP

shore BANK; BEACH; BEAM; EDGE; LAND; PROP; STRAND

shorn CLIPPED; CUT

short BRIEF; BROKE; CURT; CUT; DRAM; DROP; FUSE; LOW; MINI; S; SHY; SCANT; SKINT; TERSE; TOT; UNDER; WEE; ■ INSOLVENT; LACKING; QUICK; SCOTCH; SMALL; SNAPPY; STUMPY; omission of first or last letter(s); abbreviation indicator, as "short period" clues BOU (i.e. last letter omitted from "bout")

short break RES

short cut BOB; CREW; this is an interesting phrase in crosswords as both "short" and "cut" are omission indicators so, beware, *either* can operate on the *other* word! Thus the phrase can indicate (i) that a word meaning "cut" is to be shortened, in which case we could have AX, NIC, SHAV and so on (*see* CUT); or (ii) that a word meaning "short" is to be cut, so TERSE becoming TERS, CURT becomes CUR etc. (*see* SHORT)

short distance EM; EN; FT; IN; INCH; YD

short distance, a AFT; AIN

short, falling UNDER

short film PIC

short man MA; MAL; can refer to the diminutive of a man's proper name e.g. REG; *see* MAN

short measure MIL; can indicate the last letter to be omitted as "short measure of beer" clues AL; *see* MEASURE, SMALL

short of cash STRAPPED; *see* BROKE

short of LACKING; LESS; can indicate an adjective ending in -LESS

short of experience GREEN; RAW

short of time T to be omitted

short of water DRY

short order DRAM; TOT; a specific short drink e.g. GIN, RUM

short piece STUB

short skirt MINI

short spells FITS

short story TAL

short stretch YARD; YD

short supply, in SCARCE; last letter to be omitted, as "wine in short supply" → HOC

short time HR; MIN; MO; SEC; SPELL; T; TICK; TRICE

short, very MINI

short while *see* SHORT TIME

short word TER (i.e. last M omitted)

shortage DEARTH; NEED; WANT

shorten CUT; REEF (i.e. topmast)

shortcoming FAULT; LACK

shortfall last letter to be omitted (as "shortfall in cash" → SPEC)

shortly ANON; SOON; omission of first or last letter(s); can indicate an abbreviation either an official one as "European organisation shortly" → EC, or a common shortening in speech as "shortly has" → S

shortly for FO

shorts PANTS

shot BULLET; CRACK; DRAM; DRIVE; GO; GUN; HARED; HIT; INNER; LEAD; LOB; NIP; OUTER; OVER; PUTT; ROUND; SLUG; SNAP; SPED; STAB; STILL; STROKE; SWIG; TOT; TURN; TRY; ■ BALL; BULLET; CLOSE-UP; MASSE; SHELL; SNAPPED; TONIC; WINGED; anagram indicator

shot, golf PUTT; STROKE

shot, high LOB

shot, highly effective LOB

shot in the arm TONIC

shot, lofted CHIP; LOB

shot, one may be BOLT

shot, snooker POT

shots, many RALLY

should AUGHT; MUST; OUGHT

should be can indicate that the clue's definition follows immediately (where the verb's object is the means for getting the answer – possibly an anagram as in "One hug should be sufficient" which leads to ENOUGH)

shoulder BEAR; CARRY; EDGE; [◊ ARM]

shout BARK; BAWL; BELLOW; CALL; CHEER; CRY; ROAR; SCREAM; YELL

shout of contempt BOO

shout of pain OUCH

shout to HAIL

shove PUSH

shovel SPADE

show ACT; AIR; FAIR; GALA; FAIR; HANG (i.e. paintings); PLAY; POINT; SPORT; USHER; ■ DISPLAY; EVINCE; EXHIBIT; EXPOSE; GUIDE; INDICATE; MATINEE; MUSICAL; PARADE; PRESENT; REPRESENT; REVEAL; REVUE; RODEO; SCREEN; SPECTACLE; TURN; WEAR; *see* EXHIBITION; can act as the joining word between the anagram letters and its definition; run indicator; can indicate the name of a well-known musical such as CATS, GREASE, HAIR, EVITA

show amazement GASP

show approval CHEER; CLAP; NOD

show boredom YAWN

show business STAGE

show concern CARE

show contempt SNEER

show disapproval audibly BOO

show distress CRY

show endurance LAST

show familiarity with KNOW

show fondness DOTE; LOVE

show friendliness BEAM; SMILE

show obeisance BOW; KNEEL

show of *see* EXPRESSION OF

show off FLAUNT; POSE; STRUT

show-off POSER; can indicate something to do with a peacock

show OK TICK

show pleasure SMILE

show prominently SPLASH

show resentment BRIDLE

show respect/reverence BOW

show sadness SIGH; ■ CRY; WEEP

show sorrow CRY

show surprise START

show tiredness FLAG

show the way LEAD

show up COME; ■ ARRIVE; can indicate the reversal of a synonym for show (qv) such as

ATIVE (which is useful to construct RELATIVE for example)
showed BORE
showed the way LED
shower FALL; HAIL; PELT;
RAIN; SPLASH; WASH; ana-
gram indicator; note, the less
common different pronunciation
leads to the notion of exhibitor,
projectionist etc.
shower, brief SPAT
shower, cold HAIL
shower, make RAIN
showers anagram indicator
showing ON; anagram indicator
showing anger CROSS; MAD
shows run indicator
shows only partly run indicator
showy FLASHY; ■ GAUDY
shred CUT; MINCE; RIP; SCRAP;
TEAR; WISP; ■ PIECE;
SLIVER
shredded anagram indicator
shreds anagram indicator
shrew KATE
shrewd ARCH; CANNY; FLY
shrewdness SAVVY
shriek SCREAM
shrimps, some* POTTED ■
shrine ORACLE; TOMB; ■
TEMPLE
shrink FLINCH; ■ CONTRACT;
DECREASE; WINCE; can indicate something to do with psychiatrist
shrinking COY; TIMID; *see*
SHRINK
shrivelled up anagram indicator
shroud COVER; PALL
shrouded HID
shrub BOX; BROOM; ELDER;
SPURGE
shrunken TIGHT
shuck SHELL
shudder QUAKE; SHAKE (qv);
SHIVER
shuddering anagram indicator
shuffle GAIT; SHAMBLE; anagram indicator; [◊ CARDS,
DEAL]

shuffled, shuffles, shuffling anagram indicator; followed by a
word such as "in" can be a nesting indicator
shufti LOOK
shun AVOID; omission indicator
shunning omission indicator
shut CLOSE; LATCH; SLAM
shut-eye *see* SLEEP
shut up COOP; CLAM; FASTEN;
PEN; PENT; SH; ■ CORK;
GAG; QUIET(!); SILENCE(!);
see CLOSE
shutting CLOSING
shutter LID
shy CAST; COY; LEERY; LOB;
RECOIL; SHORT; RES;
THROW; ■ RESERVED
shy at first first letter to be omitted
shy away FLINCH
shy people MICE
shy person MOUSE
shyness RESERVE
Siamese currency, old TICAL
sibilant S
sibling BRO; BROTHER; SIS;
SISTER
siblings BROS
sic THUS
sick AILING; BAD; DOWN; ILL;
OFF; PEAKY; SEEDY; WEAK;
anagram indicator
sick, be AIL; RETCH
sick, no longer BETTER; WELL
sick of FO (i.e. "of" reversed)
sick person LEPER
sick, was AILED
sicken AIL
sickening DICKY
sickle CUTTER
sickly ILL; PALE; ■ DOUGHY;
anagram indicator; [◊ AIL]
sickly feeling BILE
sickly-looking PALE; SALLOW
side AIR; ALLY; BANK;
BORDER; CLUB; EDGE;
FACE; FACET; FLANK; L;
LEFT; PART; PARTY; PORT; R;
RIGHT; SLOPE; SPIN; TEAM;
VERGE; WALL; WING; ■
GROUP; also sides on a cricket

ground: OFF, ON, LEG, etc.; can indicate one of the points of the compass

side of first or last letter of ensuing word to be used

side of, be on the BACK

side, on the WITH

side, one IL; IR; L; R

side road TURNING

side-splitting a component to be nested between L and R (or R and L)

side-walk SIDLE; can indicate something to do with a marine crustacean as "Side-walk pedestrian" → CRAB

sides BORDERS; EDGES; LR; RL; SLOPES; WINGS; first and last letters indicator

sides, both LR; RL; first and last letters indicator

sides, changing within target word, R to replace L, or vice versa; or first and last letters to be interchanged

sides, round the LR or RL to be nested within a component

siding ALLYING; BRANCH

Sidney SID

siege, old can indicate something to do with the siege of Troy and its participants e.g. Achilles, Helen, Nestor, Paris, Priam

siesta NAP; SLEEP

sieve MESH; RIDDLE; SIFT; STRAIN

sift SIEVE; RIDDLE; WINNOW

sigh LONG

sigh of pleasure AH

sigh of relief AH; PHEW

sigh, painful GROAN

sigh, produce a HEAVE

sight CATCH; EYE; LOT; SEE; SEEING; SPOT; ■ ESPY; SPY; VIEW; [◊ EYE; OPTIC]

sight, keep out of HIDE

sighted SEEN

sightless BLIND

sign BADGE; CROSS; LION; MARK; MARKER; OMEN; PLUS; RAM; SHOW; TRACE; ■ CARET (printing); INDEX;

SYMBOL; TOKEN; TRACK; can indicate sign of the zodiac, e.g. ARIES, LEO, LIBRA, SCORPIO.

sign, computer SLASH

sign from heaven can indicate a sign of the zodiac e.g. LEO

sign, inn BUSH

sign of approval TICK

sign of doubt ER; UM

sign of embarrassment BLUSH; FLUSH

sign of fault CROSS; X

sign of hesitation UM; ER

sign of life ANKH

sign of nautical progress WAKE

signal BEAM; BECK; CUE; DASH; DOT; FLAG; KNELL; NOD; NOTE; PETER; WAVE; ■ FLASH; HERALD; HOOTER; RECEPTION; RING; STRIKING; WINK; anagram indicator; can indicate a traffic light, so AMBER, GREEN, RED

Signal Corps SC

signal, give CUE; FLAG; WAVE

signal silently NOD; WAVE

signal to stop RED

signalled RANG;

signet SEAL

significance POINT; ■ IMPORT; MEANING

significance, of little LIGHT; MINOR; SMALL; ■ SLEIGHT

significant GREAT; KEY; ■ TELLING

significant, be COUNT

signify MEAN; SAY; SPELL; *see* MEAN

Silas MARNER

silence GAG; HUSH; MUTE; SH; ■ MUZZLE; PEACE; QUIET; REPRESS

silence, call for SH

silence to speak PIECE

silenced MUTE

silencer GAG

silent DUMB; MUM; MUTE; TACIT

silent actor MIME

silent, be HUSH; *see* SILENCE

silent comic CHAPLIN
silent signal NOD; WINK
silicon CHIP
silk hat TOPPER
sill LEDGE; SHELF
silly BARMY; DAFT; S; SOFT; RASH; ■ DAFFY; INANE; *see* STUPID; anagram indicator; accompanied by a whimsy indicator can refer to something to do with a window (it has a sill!)
silly behaviour ANTIC; PRANK
silly person GOON; PRAT; TWIT; ■ GOOSE; TWERP; *see* FOOL
silo PIT
silver AG; SECOND
Silver can indicate something to do with Stevenson's character, e.g. cook, Long John, Treasure Island
silver medallist SECOND
similar AKIN; ALIKE; LIKE
similar, regard as EQUATE
similar things SUCH
simmer STEW
Simon SIMPLE
simple BARE; DAFT; EASY; HERB; MERE; PLAIN; PURE THICK; ■ ARTLESS; NAIF; NAIVE
simple character SIMON
simple-minded person *see* SIMPLETON
simple, not FANCY; HARD; STIFF
Simple Simon *see* SIMPLETON
simple thing CINCH
simpleton GULL; LOON; SAP; ■ NINNY; NOODLE; *see* FOOL
simplicity EASE
simply JUST; ONLY
simultaneously anagram indicator
simulate APE; FEIGN; SHAM
sin ANGER; ERR; ERROR; FALL; GREED; LAPSE; LUST; PRIDE; SLOTH; VICE; ■ ENVY; note that "sin" is an alternative spelling for the trigonometric function SINE
sin, almost a ER
Sinai* MOUNT
since AS; AGO; ■ BECAUSE

sincere FRANK (qv.); ■ EARNEST
sincerity TRUTH
sing CHANT; CROON; GRASS; NARK; TALK; TRILL; ■ CHIRP; PEACH; TROLL; VOICE; YODEL
sing loudly BELT
sing shrilly PIPE
sing (to sleep) LULL
singe BURN; CHAR; TOAST
singer ALTO; BING; BASS; BASSO; BIRD; BUFFO; CHER; DIVA; TREBLE; ■ CHANTER; MEZZO; TENOR; CROONER; can indicate a bird known for its singing e.g. BUNTING, FINCH, LARK, LINNET
singer briefly SOP
singers BASSI; CHOIR
singing CHORAL; VOCAL
singing, monastic CHANT
single I; LONE; MISS; ONE; ONLY; RUN; S; SOLE; UNIT; ■ BACHELOR; UNWED
single-channel MONO
single chap/person ONE
★ **single definition clue** such a clue has the appearance of a simple factual clue from a 'quicky' crossword but to justify its being in a cryptic puzzle it must embody some attempt at deception (such as "Gain from Labour" → EARN)
singlet VEST
singular I; ODD; ONE; RUM; S; ■ UNIQUE
singular claim IM (i.e. I'm)
singular garment DUD; TIGHT; TOG
sinister DARK; GRIM; LEFT; PORT; ■ EERIE
sinister, not/nothing RIGHT
sink DOWN; DROP; FALL; SAG; ■ BASIN; FOUNDER; LOWER; SCUPPER; STOOP
sink ball POT
sink deliberately SCUTTLE
sink into nesting indicator
sinner GLUTTON
Sioux BRAVE

sir KNIGHT; MASTER; MISTER

Sir Andrew AGUE (from Shake-speare)

Sir Thomas MORE

sire FATHER

siren HORN

sisal ROPE

sister NUN; SIB; SIS; SR; can sig-nal something to do with hospital e.g. WARD

sister, little SIS

sister, weird WITCH

sit BROOD; POSE; REST; STAY; ■ PERCH

sit back lazily BASK

sit holding one POISE

sit-in DEMO

site DIG; LOT; PLACE; PUT; SPOT; ■ GROUND; POSITION

site of castle MOTTE

siting PLACING; ■ LOCATION; nesting indicator

sitter CHAIR; DOLLY (i.e. easy catch in cricket); MODEL; POSER

sitting SESSION

sitting in nesting indicator

sitting room PARLOUR

situate POSITION

situated nesting indicator

situation BERTH; HOLE; JOB; LIE; PLACE; POST; SPOT; STATE; ■ LOCATION; POSITION; SCENE; TWIST; nesting indicator

situation, tricky CORNER; SPOT

six VI

six balls OVER (i.e. cricket)

six counties NI

six-footer can indicate an insect, commonly ant; can refer to po-etry i.e. hexameter

six hundred DC

six hundred, nearly DIC

six in the morning PRIME (i.e. second hour of prayer)

six nips GILL

six pupils VILL

sixpence TANNER

sixth VI

sixth sense ESP

66 ft CHAIN

60s teenager MOD

sixty LX

sixty minutes DEGREE; HOUR

size GLAZE; ■ GAUGE; LENGTH

sizzle BURN

skate FISH; GLIDE; RAY; SLIDE

skater [◊ RINK]

skating ONICE (i.e. on ice)

skating arena RINK

skating, not/no longer OFFICE (i.e. off ice)

skedaddle GO; SCRAM

skeleton FRAME

skeleton, part of BONE; RIB; SKULL; see BONE

sketch DRAFT; DRAW; LINE; PLAN; ROUGH; SKIT; ■ DRAWING; OUTLINE

sketch, producer of ARTIST; CRAYON

sketched DRAWN; DREW

skew SLANT

skewer SPIT

ski SLIDE; SLIP

skid SLIDE; SLIP

skies HEAVEN

skilful ABLE; APT; CANNY; DEFT; SLEIGHT; SLICK; ■ ADEPT

skilfully ABLY; WELL

skill ART; CRAFT; ■ ABILITY; FINESSE; MASTERY; TECHNIQUE

skill, basic R (i.e. as the three R's)

skill, demonstrating see SKILLED

skill, with see SKILLED

skilled ABLE; DEFT

skim GLIDE

skimmed first letter to be omitted

skimp STINT

skimping omission indicator

skin COAT; COVER; FELL; FLAY; FUR; HIDE; PEEL; RIND; ■ CUTIS; EPIDERMIS; FLESH

skin blemish WART

skin disease/disorder HIVES; RASH

skin, feature of PORE
skin, hard CORN
skin infection RASH
skin of your teeth JUST
skin opening PORE
skin treatment can indicate something to do with tanning, leather, tannery etc
skinflint MISER
skinhead S
skinned PEELED; first and last letters to be omitted
skinny GAUNT; MEAN; THIN (qv)
skinny person RAKE
skip CAPER; CUT; DANCE; HOP; JUMP; LEAP; MISS; OMIT; SPRING; anagram indicator; omission indicator
skipper CAPT; LAMB; can indicate something to do with butterfly
skipping anagram indicator; omission indicator
skirmish BRUSH
skirt MIDI; MINI; RIM; ■ DRESS; GEAR
skirts round nesting indicator
skittle PIN
skulk PROWL
skull HEAD; SCALP
sky AIR; BLUE; ■ HEAVEN
sky, canopy of DOME
sky-diver PARA
Skywalker's enemy VADER
slab TABLET
slack COAL; EVEN; IDLE; LOOSE
slack, having no TAUT; TIGHT
slacken EASE; REMIT
slackly anagram indicator
slackness SLOTH
slag WASTE
slam BANG; BEAT; HIT (qv)
slander MUD; SLUR; ■ DEFILE; MALIGN
slang ARGOT; CANT
slang, tasteless NAFF
slant ANGLE; SKEW; SPIN
slanting ANGLED
slap BEAT; HIT; SMACK; TAP

slapdash anagram indicator
slash CUT; PEE; SIGN (i.e. computer)
slat FLAY; ROOF; STAVE
slate PAN; ROAST; SCOLD; TILE
slaughtered KILLED; SLEW; anagram indicator
slaughterhouse SHAMBLES
Slav SERB
slave SERF
slaver SLOBBER; ■ DROOL; DRIBBLE
slay DO; KILL (qv)
sleazy bar DIVE
sledge HAMMER; LUGE
sleek SMOOTH; ■ GLOSSY
sleep DOSS; DOZE; FLOP; KIP; NAP; NOD; REST; ZZ; ■ SIESTA; SLUMBER; [◊ SNORE]
sleep, part of REM
sleep moment WINK
sleep, place for BED; COT; ROOST
sleep, somewhere to BED; COT; BUNK
sleep soundly SNORE
sleeper TIE; ■ DOZER; KIPPER; can indicate something to do with railway track, or earring
sleeping OUT; can indicate that a component is to be nested within BED or ABED (as "A king sleeping gets very hot" signals BAKED)
sleeping, stop AWAKE; WAKE
sleeve ARM; COVER
slender NARROW; SLIGHT; SLIM; SPARE; THIN
sleuth TEC; *see* DETECTIVE
slice CARVE; CUT (qv); PIECE
slice of run indicator
sliced anagram indicator
slick OILY; PAT
slide CHUTE; SLIP; SKID
sliding anagram indicator
slight CUT; PET; SCANT; SLUR; SMALL; SNUB; THIN; ■ FAINT; GENTLE; LITTLE; SLENDER; TENUOUS; *see* INSULT

slightly ABIT (i.e. a bit)

slim LEAN; SLENDER; SLIGHT (qv); THIN; TRIM; ▪ DIET; FAST; SLENDER

slim not FAT; HEAVY

slime MUD; ▪ GUCK

slimmed down can indicate first and last letters to be omitted

slimmer, get TAPER

sling CAST; DRINK; DUMP; HANG; PITCH; anagram indicator; *see* THROW

slip DRESS; DROP; ERR; ERROR; FALL; GALLEY (printing); GLIDE; LAPSE; NOD; SAG; SCAPE; SKID; SLIDE; STRIP; ▪ BLUNDER; BUNGLE; MOVE; SKI; anagram indicator

slip back RRE

slip into DON

slip up ERR; SIN; a synonym of "slip" to be reversed, hence RRE, NIS etc; *see* SLIP

slipped SLID

slipper MULE

slippery SHADY; anagram indicator; [◊ EEL]

slippery surface ICE

slipping LAX; ▪ ERRING; SKIDDING; SLIDING; anagram indicator

slips anagram indicator

slit in jacket VENT

slither SLIDE

sliver CHIP; SHRED; SLICE

slob LOUT; OAF

slobber SLAVER

sloe [◊ GIN]

slog CHORE; HIT (qv); LABOUR

slogan CHANT; MOTTO; OUT; ▪ ADAGE

slop SPILL

slope LEAN; LIST; RAKE; RAMP; RISE; TILT; ▪ ESCARP; INCLINE; PISTE

slope off GO; anagram of SLOPE

sloppily anagram indicator

sloppy REMISS; anagram indicator

sloshed anagram indicator; *see* DRUNK

sloshy MOIST

slot NICHE; GROOVE; RUT

slough BOG; SHED

slovenly anagram indicator

slovenly, girl SLUT; TART

slovenly person SLOB

slovenly, woman SLUT; TART

slow DULL; LARGO; LATE; LENTO; THICK; ▪ BRAKE; TARDY

slow ball LOB

slow down BRAKE; FLAG; ▪ DECELERATE

slow, go POTTER

slow movement/music/passage LARGO; LENTO

slow process anagram of SLOW

slowly LENTO; ▪ ADAGIO; can indicate something to do with speed, rate

slug BALL; DRINK; HIT; PEST; SHOT; TOT; ▪ BULLET

sluggish IDLE; SLOW; anagram indicator

slum area GHETTO

slumber *see* SLEEP

slump DROOP; DROP

slur BLAME; MUMBLE; SLIGHT; STAIN; TIE (mus,)

slurred anagram indicator

slut DRUDGE; TART

sly *see* CUNNING

Sly a character in *The Taming of the Shrew* so can indicate something to do with the play or its characters e.g. tinker

sly look PEEK

sly person WEASEL

smack BLOW; BOAT; CLIP; CUFF; KISS; SLAP; TANG; TAP; TASTE; ▪ SMELL; SWAT

small BABY; LIGHT; LITTLE; MICRO; MINI; SHORT; SLIGHT; WEE; ▪ DWARF; MINOR; TINY; TITCHY; abbreviation indicator

small amount BIT; CENT; CHIP; DAB; DRAM; DRIB; DROP; GRAM; OZ; PINT; TAD; WHIT

small amount of can indicate one or two letters from the succeeding word

small amounts can indicate that only the initial letters of associated words be used

small and sweet TWEE

small and weak PUNY

small beer HALF

small boy abbreviated form of boy's name e.g. ANDY *see* LITTLE BOY

small business BUS; CO

small car MINI

small change COIN; P; can indicate the subdivision of a currency (cent, penny, pence, sen, sou etc)

small change in Japan SEN

small charge BABY

small, comparatively MINOR; *see* SMALL

small distance INCH

small dwelling HO

small establishment COTTAGE

small flag JACK

small group CELL; DUO; TRIO

small insects THRIPS

small island I; IS; ISLE; KEY

small matter DETAIL

small-minded PETTY

small number N; NO; SOME; ■ COUPLE; PAIR; can indicate a low number, one, two etc

small one RUNT; TICH

small Parisian PETIT(E)

small part BIT; CAMEO; ORT; ■ PORTION; WALK-ON

small portion/quantity CL; GRAM; OUNCE; OZ; TASTE

small quantity of can indicate one or two letters from the succeeding word

small room CELL

small section DEPT

small thing ATOM

small, too SKIMPY

small unit MIL

small, very MINI; TEENY; TINY

small volume CC; CL; *see* VOLUME

smaller LESS; MINOR

smaller extent, to a LESS

smaller, make CUT; REDUCE

smaller quantity LESS

smallest LEAST

smallest part WHIT

smarm UNCTION

smart BRISK; CHIC; CLEVER; CUTE; FLY; NEAT; PACY; POSH; QUICK; STING; SWISH; TRIM; WISE; ■ ACHE; DAPPER; DRESSY; NATTY; NIFTY; SHARP; TRENDY

smart appearance DASH

smart guy ALEC

smart man SWELL

smart pace CLIP

smarten up GROOM; PRIMP; TIDY

smartly-dressed CHIPPER

smash BREAK; BUST; CRUSH; SHATTER; anagram indicator

smashed BUST; HIT; TIGHT; *see* DRUNK; anagram indicator

smasher DISH

smashing GRAND; GREAT; SUPER; anagram indicator

smear BLUR; DAUB; DEFAME; LIBEL; MARK; SLUR; SPLODGE; STAIN; TAINT; *see* TAINT

smeared anagram indicator

smell BO; HUM; NIFF; NOSE; ODOUR; PONG; REEK; SCENT; SMACK; STENCH; STINK; TANG; WHIFF

smell, bad/unpleasant BO; STENCH; *see* SMELL

smell, foul/strong PONG; REEK; *see* SMELL

smelling bad HIGH; RANK

smelly OLID

smelt STANK

smidgeon TRACE

smile BEAM; GRIN; LEER; [◊ CHEESE]

smile, silly (to make, give, put on) SIMPER

smirk LEER

smite *see* HIT

smithy FORGE

smitten anagram indicator

smoke CIG; CURE; DRAG; FAG; FUME; PIPE; ■ CIGAR; HAVANA; REEK; can indicate something to do with London;

can indicate something to do with a volcano

smoke, some CLOUD

smoker PUFFER; *see* SMOKE; can indicate a volcano

smokestack FUNNEL

smoking, some FUME

smoky atmosphere FUG

smooch NECK; SPOON

smooth BLAND; DRESS; EVEN; FLAT; IRON; LEVEL; PRESS; SAND; SATIN; SLEEK; SLICK; SLIPPY; SUAVE; ■ CHARM; GLABROUS; GLASSY; SHAVEN; LEGATO

smooth passage GLIDE

smoother FILE; IRON; PLANE; *see* SMOOTH and consider adding -ER to one of the synonyms there e.g. FLATTER

smoothie CHARMER

smoothing agent *see* SMOOTHER

smoothly LEGATO

smoothly, go GLIDE; SKATE; SLIDE; ■ FLOAT

smoothly, made to go OILED

smote HIT; STRUCK

smudge BLOT; BLUR

smug PI

smuggle RUN

smuggled RAN

smuggler RUNNER

smuggling nesting indicator

smut SOOT; SPECK

smut, free of CLEAN

smutty BLUE

snack BITE; CANAPE

snack bar CAFF; BUFFET

snack meal PIE

snacks EATS

snaffle BIT; PINCH; STEAL

snag BIND; BUG; CATCH; HITCH; RUB; TEAR

snagged CAUGHT; anagram indicator

snake ADDER; ASP; BOA; TWINE; WIND; ■ GARTER; HYDRA; MAMBA; MEANDER; RATTLER; VIPER

snap BARK; BITE; BREAK; NIP; NUT; PART; PHOTO; PIC; SHOT; SPELL (i.e. cold spell); STILL; TANG; anagram indicator

snapped BITE; BROKE; SHOT; anagram indicator

snapped by nesting indicator

snapper BITER; NIPPER

snappy CHIC; CROSS (qv); CURT; SHORT; TESTY

snare CATCH; GIN; NET; NOOSE; TRAP; ■ DRUM; SPRINGE (i.e. verb)

snare, use SPRINGE; *see* SNARE

snarl GROWL; RAVEL; TANGLE; ■ FOUL UP

snarl-up JAM

snarled anagram indicator

snatch GRAB; GRASP; NAB; REST; STEAL; WREST; ■ KIDNAP

snatched STOLE

snatching nesting indicator

sneak CREEP; GRASS; SIDLE; SLIP

sneezewort YARROW

snick CUT; EDGE; SNIP

sniffer HUNTER

snip CUT

snipe SHOOT

snippet SCRAP

snitch GRASS; PEACH; TELL

snooker can indicate something to do with cue, pot etc [◊ FRAME; POCKET]

snooker, one in RED (or any of the other coloured balls)

snooker, play at CUE

snooker sequence BREAK

snooker shot PLANT; POT

snooker, start playing BREAK

snooker, success in POT

snoop NOSE; PRY; SPY

snooze DOZE; NAP; REST; ZZ

snort DRINK (qv); TOT

snout HOOTER; NOSE

snow CRACK; FLAKE; S; [◊ NIVAL]

snow, covered in WHITE

snow-leopard OUNCE

snow, mass of DRIFT; NEVE

snow, soft SLEET; SLUSH

snow travel over MUSH

snowdrop although can refer to the flower, usually refers to avalanche

snowstorm anagram of SNOW

snub CUT; SLIGHT; ∎ REBUFF

snub-nose anagram of NOSE

snubbed CUT

snug COSY; TIGHT; WARM; ∎ COMPACT

snug retreat NEST

snuggle NESTLE

snuggle into nesting indicator

so AS; ERGO; HENCE; SIC; SUCH; THUS; TRUE; VERY

so-and-so BLIGHTER; BLOOMING

so badly OS

so backward OGRE

so be it AMEN

so-called QUASI; homophone indicator; can also indicate a nom-de-plume, one popular among compilers being ELIA (used by essayist Charles Lamb); also SAKI

so far AS

so it is written SIC

so long TATA (i.e. ta-ta); VALE

so-so FAIR

so to speak homophone indicator

so what? WELL

soak BATH; RET; SOP; SOT; STEEP; TAN; WET; ∎ DRENCH; MARINATE

soak up MOP

soak up sun BASK

soaked WET; see DRUNK

soaked, get RET

soaking BATH; WET; ∎ DRIPPING; SODDEN

soak, wanting to RET (archaic)

soap CLEANSE; can indicate something to do with a soap opera; [◊ BAR; OPERA]

soap, piece of BAR; CAKE; TABLET

soap, soft FLATTER

soapbox STUMP

soar FLY (qv); RISE; PLANE; TOWER

soaring reversal indicator; can indicate something to do with a bird known for soaring e.g. eagle

sob BLUB; CRY; GRASP; WEEP

sober TT; ∎ CHASTE; STAID

sober person TT

soccer* SPORT

soccer authorities, body FA

soccer clubs FA

soccer match, one point from DRAW

soccer official REF

social PARTY

social class (or division, group, order, position etc) CASTE; CLASS

social engagement DATE

social error GAFFE

social event BALL; BASH; DANCE; DO; ∎ RECEPTION; see PARTY

social function see SOCIAL EVENT

social gathering BALL; BEE; DANCE

social group BEE; CIRCLE; see GROUP

social occasion see SOCIAL EVENT

social organisation CLUB

social security DOLE; UB; ∎ BENEFIT; HANDOUT

social standing STATURE

social worker ANT; BEE; CARER

socialist LEFT; PINK; RED; ∎ MARX; see LEFT-WINGER

socialite SNOB

socially acceptable DONE; IN; U

socially unacceptable NONU (i.e. non-U); OUT

society CLUB; GROUP (qv); S; TRIAD; ∎ ELITE; can refer to something to do with creatures known for being social, for example: "Building society deposit" leading to ANTHILL

society girl DEB

society, member of FRIEND (i.e. Quaker)

sock BLOW; HIT; SMITE

socks HOSE

sod GROUND

soda MIXER

sodium NA

sofa BED; SEAT; ■ SETTEE

soft LIGHT; LIMP; P; S; ■ GENTLE; PLIANT; SOGGY; TENDER

soft-hearted P to be nested in centre of component

soften MELT

softly, not loudly P to replace F

software, transfer PORT

soggy SOFT

Soho club can indicate something to do with stripping

soil EARTH; GROUND; MARK; SPOT; ■ DIRT; HUMUS; LOAM

soil acidity PH

soil material MOR

soil, work the TILL

solar SUN

solar system body METEOR; PLANET; SUN; can call for the specific name of a planet

solder FUSE; JOIN

soldier ANT; GI; MAN; MERC; NCO; PARA; RM; SM; ■ GUNNER; LANCER; MARINE; NYM (Shakespearian character); ORDERLY; PONGO; PRIVATE; RANKER; REGULAR; TROOPER

soldier, captured POW

soldier, mounted KNIGHT

soldier, old VET

soldiers GIS; MEN; OR; RA; RE; REME; RO; SQUAD; TA; UNIT; ■ CORPS; REGIMENT; TROOP; can indicate something to do with toast (i.e. cut as "soldiers") and egg, egg-cup, soft-boil etc

soldiers, body/group of CORPS; COY; FORCE; SQUAD; UNIT; *see* REGIMENT, SOLDIERS

soldiers, some RESERVE; TA; *see* SOLDIERS

sole FISH; LONE; can indicate something to do with the foot; can indicate something to do with fish as "Sole trader?" → FISHMONGER

sole mate HEEL

sole part TREAD

solemn DEAD; EARNEST

solemn individual OWL

solemn pronouncement OATH

solicit TOUT; WOO; ■ PROPOSITION

solicitor BEGGAR; NP (i.e. Notary-Public); SOL; TOUT; ■ TRULL

solicitor, training as ARTICLED

solid CONE; CUBE; FAT; FIRM; HARD; LOYAL; STIFF

solid body LUMP

solid figure CONE; CUBE

solidarity UNION

solidified HARD; SET

solitary LONE; LONER; SOLE; ■ ROGUE (as with elephant)

solitary confinement, in a component to be nested within ALONE, LONE or SOLE

solitary type LONER; *see* RECLUSE

solo ALONE; LONE;

solo trip anag. of SOLO

solution KEY; LIGHT (i.e. crossword solution); SOL; WATER; anagram indicator (as "solution of code" → EDCO)

solve CRACK

solved anagram indicator

solvent ETHER; SOUND

solver YOU

solvers YE; YOU

sombre GRAVE; ■ STAID

some ANY; BIT; PART; PIECE; can indicate a word which means something less, e.g. NET; run indicator

some cabbage HEART

some cash SUM

some days WEEK

some French DE; DES

some, just ABIT; BIT

some music PIECE

some spirit DRAM; TOT
some time ago ONCE
some weeks usually indicates a specifically named month, often abbreviated; *see* MONTH
somebody ONE
somebody ferreting ROOTER
somehow anagram indicator
someone PERSON; VIP
someone drawing TOWER
someone escaping BOLTER
someone for fighting HAWK
someone in custody WARD
someone learning *see* LEARNER
someone other than me NOTI (i.e. not I)
someone to go out with DATE
Somerset town STREET
something IT
something added PS; RIDER
something afoot SHOE
something caught BUS
something, do ACT
something done ACT; DEED
something enjoyable GAS
something for nothing PRESENT
something for sale LOT
something good ASSET
something in the way *see* IMPEDIMENT
something missed LOSS
something of run indicator
something one can't do without MUST
something other than NOT
something placed BET
something popular HIT; ■ SUCCESS
something remarkable ONER; WONDER
something special PLUM
something that happens EVENT
something to discuss TOPIC
something to read *see* BOOK
something to wear HABIT; *see* CLOTHES, CLOTHING
somewhat ABIT (i.e. a bit); BIT; PRETTY; QUITE; RATHER; run indicator; can indicate the possi-

ble stretching of a point by the compiler, where the connection between concepts is slight
son BOY; ISSUE; LAD; S
song AIR; ARIA; CHANT; GLEE; LAY; LIED; ROUND; TRACK; TUNE; ■ ANTHEM; BALLAD; CANTO; CAROL; DITTY; MELODY; NUMBER; PSALM; SHANTY
song about it, make a a component to be nested within SING
song and dance FUSS
song, bird's TWEET
song, part of VERSE
song series CYCLE
songbook HYMNAL
songs CYCLE
songs, set of CYCLE
songster LARK; *see* BIRD, SINGER
songwriter BERLIN; LENNON
soon ANON; EARLY
soon, too EARLY
sooner RATHER
soothe EASE; ■ CALM; LULL
soothed EASED
soothing BALMY
soothing, something BALM
soothsayer SEER
sop BRIBE; BUNG; SOAK
soprano SOP
sorcerer MAGE
sorceress WITCH
sorcery MAGIC
sordid SEAMY
sore MAD; RED; ■ CHAP; CROSS; TENDER
sore, very RAW
sorrow MISERY; REGRET; WOE; ■ GRIEF; [◊ TEAR]
sorrow, show CRY; WEEP
sorry POOR; SAD; ■ OOPS; RUING; WRETCHED; anagram indicator
sorry, be RUE; ■ GRIEVE; LAMENT; MOURN
sorry to say, I'm ALAS
sort ALIGN; ARRANGE; CLASS; KIDNEY; KIND; ORDER; TYPE; ■ SPECIES; STAMP;

anagram indicator; can indicate a particular sort of person as "possessive sort" clues OWNER

sort of anagram indicator

sort out HANDLE; SOLVE; anagram of SORT e.g. ROST, ROTS

sorted/sorting out anagram indicator

sortie SALLY

sorts, out of ILL

sot DRUNK; LUSH; SOAK; TOPER

soufflé anagram indicator

soul, merry old COLE

soul, poor anagram of SOUL

Soule's advice some implication stemming from "Go West, young man" (from editorial by J. L. B. Soule in 1851 American newspaper)

soulless worker ROBOT

sound AUDIO; BANG; BLIP; CHORD; CLANG; CLASH; CLINK; DRONE; FIT; HALE; HUM; NOTE; PEEP; PING; PLUMB; PURR; RING; SAFE; SANE; TICK; TING; TONE; TRILL; WATER; WHINE; WISE; ■ INLET; NOISE; PLUMMET; PROBE; RATTLE; REPORT; RINGING; SOLID; SOLVENT; STRAIGHT; STRAIT (i.e. stretch of water); TICKING; TWANG; homophone indicator, as "sound sense" → CITE

sound as a bell *see* BELL SOUND

sound, beastly BRAY; GROWL; GRUNT; ■ OINK

sound dejected SIGH

sound disgusted UGH

sound exercise EWES; YEWS

sound happy PURR

sound, harsh CLANG

sound, high PING

sound, hollow BONG

sound horn TOOT

sound, little RUSTLE

sound loose RATTLE

sound murmurous HUM

sound of bell DING; PEAL; TING; TOLL

sound of bird CAW; CHEEP; PEEP; SQUAWK

sound of cat MEW; PURR

sound of it, by the homophone indicator

sound of pain GROAN

sound of pleasure AH

sound of glasses CLINK

sound of sheep BAA

sound of steam HISS

sound off RATE

sound pleased PURR

sound, producing SONIC

sound record LOGUE

sound, recurrent TICK

sound reproduction AUDIO; TAPE; ■ RECORD

sound sense CITE

sound, triumphant HA

sound unhappy CRY

sound unoriginal ECHO

sound vessel EARN

sound, vocal TONE

sounder PIG; SWINE

sounding homophone indicator

soundly homophone indicator

soundly disapprove BOO; HISS

soundproofing BAFFLE

sounds TONES; *see* SOUND; homophone indicator

sounds like homophone indicator

sounds, make ERNE (i.e. homophone of EARN)

soundtrack, on homophone indicator

soup BROTH; STOCK; ■ CHOWDER; STARTER

soup, kind of LEEK

sour DOUR; OFF; TART; ■ ACID; BITTER

source CAUSE; EGG; FOUNT; ORE; ROOT; WELL; ■ MINE; ORIGIN; PROVIDER; initial letter indicator; run indicator

source of run indicator; the initial letter of the word that immediately follows to be used (as "source of terror" cues T)

source of colour CRAYON

source of income LIVING; *see* JOB

source of inspiration MUSE

source of mineral MINE; PIT

source of power MAINS

source of song can indicate a bird e.g. LARK, TIT

source of spirits STILL

source of warning ALARM; BLEEPER; SIREN

source of water SPRING; TAP; WELL

sources of the initials of the words that follow to be used

South S; last letter indicator

South Africa SA; ZA

South African BOER; SA

South African group/organisation ANC

South African white BLANK

South America SA; SUS

South American SUS

South American city RIO

South Carolina SC

south of France SUD

south wind AUSTER

Southampton* PORT

souvenir RELIC

sovereign ER; GR; KING (qv); L (former gold pound coin); SULTAN; ■ CROWN; IMPERIAL; RULER (qv); *see* QUEEN

sovereign's advisers COURT

sovereignty RAJ

Soviet RED; RUSSIAN

Soviet police chief BERIA

sow SEED

sizzled DRUNK (qv)

SP ODDS

spa HYDRO; SPRING; WELL; ■ RESORT

space EM; EN; GAP; HOLE; PLACE; ROOM; VOID; ■ AREA; INTERVAL; LATITUDE

space, confined COOP

space creature ET

space, enclosed YARD; *see* ENCLOSURE

space for cargo HOLD

space module LEM

space, open FIELD; GLADE

space station EMIR

space, those in NASA

space, tiny EN

space traveller COMET; PLANET; ■ ASTEROID; *see* PLANET

space station MIR

space, vertical SHAFT

spacecraft LEM

spaced-out ROOMY

spaceman DARE (i.e. Dan); GORDON (i.e. Flash)

spacer WASHER

spaceship LANDER

spacious ROOMY

spade S; SHOVEL

spade's length SPIT

spade, small TROWEL

spadeful SPIT

spades S

Spain E

Spain, approbation in OLE

Spain, table in MESA

span BRIDGE; COVER; CROSS; REACH; TIME; ■ PERIOD; RANGE; STRETCH

spangle SEQUIN

Spaniard SENOR

spaniel COCKER; ■ CLUMBER; SPRINGER

Spanish SP

Spanish agreement SI

Spanish bar CANTINA

Spanish certainly SI

Spanish cheer OLE

Spanish coin, currency/old REAL

Spanish cry OLE

Spanish dish PAELLA

Spanish for POR

Spanish gent DON

Spanish girl INES

Spanish, hero CID

Spanish lady DONA

Spanish peasant PEON

Spanish port VIGO

Spanish river RIO

Spanish royal REAL

Spanish soldier, famous CID

Spanish, the EL; LAS; LOS

Spanish, what QUE

spanner BRIDGE; TOOL; WRENCH

spar BAR; BOON; BOX; ROD; SPRIT; YARD

spare BONY; EXTRA; GASH; GAUNT; LEAN; SAVE; SLENDER; THIN

sparing MEAN; SAVING

sparing, be SKIMP

spark FLASH

spark off LIGHT

sparked off LIT

sparkle GLISTEN; GLITTER

sparkler STAR; *see* GEM

sparklers can indicate something to do with stars or a constellation; *see* GEM

sparkling anagram indicator

sparse SCANT; THIN; SCANTY

Sparta, wife of king of LEDA

Spartan BASIC; HARSH; PLAIN; SEVERE

spasm FIT; TIC; TWITCH

spat GAITER; *see* QUARREL

spate FLOOD; RUSH

spawn SPAT

speak CHAT; GAS; ORATE; SAY; TALK; UTTER; ■ ADDRESS; ALLUDE; DRAWL; VOICE; homophone indicator

speak at length DWELL; ■ DRONE

speak haltingly STAMMER

speak harshly GRATE

speak honestly LEVEL

speak irritably SNAP

speak sharply SNAP

speak slowly DRAWL

speak tartly SNAP

speak tenderly COO

speak vehemently RANT

speak well of PRAISE

speaker ORATOR; ■ MOUTH; PHONE; SAYER; TRAP; [◊ DAIS]; homophone indicator

speaker, belonging to MY

speaker, for a homophone indicator

speaker, of MY; homophone indicator

speaker, supporter for DAIS

speaking DICTION; homophone indicator

speaking, loosely homophone indicator

speaking, manner (way) of ACCENT; DICTION; DRAWL; TWANG

speaks in French DIT

spear GAFF; PIKE; STAB; ■ IMPALE; LANCE; LEISTER (for salmon); SHOOT

spearhead LEAD

spec BRIEF

special EXTRA; RARE; SP; anagram indicator

special case anagram e.g. ACES, CEAS, SACE

special constable SC

special edition EXTRA

special force PARAS; SAS

special group ELITE

special information LORE

special offer(s) SALE

special troops PARAS

special word MANTRA

specially anagram indicator

specie BREED; KIND; TYPE

species KIND; SORT; SP; TYPE; ■ GENERA

specific CURE; LIMITED; ■ PARTICULAR

specified THAT as "the church specified" clues THATCH (i.e. THAT-CH)

specify DETAIL; NAME; PICK; SELECT; STATE

specimen SAMPLE; SORT; TASTE

specimens of run indicator

speck DOT; FLECK; MOTE; SMUT; SPOT

speck, dust MOTE

speckle STIPPLE

spectacle SHOW; SIGHT; ■ EPIC: SCENE

spectacles OO

spectators GATE; ■ AUDIENCE; CROWD; OBSERVERS; WATCHERS

spectators' area STAND

spectators, number of GATE
spectral EERIE
speculate BET; GUESS
speculator BETTER; BEAR; BULL; STAG
spectre GHOST
speculation FANCY; IDEA
sped RAN
speech ADDRESS; ARGOT; DICTION; LECTURE; ORAL; ORATION; SAY; TALK; ■ TONGUE; colloquialism indicator; homophone indicator (as "Churchill speech" can signal WHINNY or WINNI); can refer to a specific language
speech, by ORAL; VOCAL; homophone indicator
speech clarity DICTION
speech, emotional RANT; ■ TIRADE
speech, glib CANT; ■ PATTER; SPIEL
speech, impassioned/intemperate RANT
speech, long ORATION; SCREED
speech, make ORATE; SPEAK; TALK; VOICE
speech, making ORATING; TALKING; VOICING
speech, manner of DICTION
speech, part of NOUN; SOUND; VERB; WORD; ■ PHRASE
speech, peculiar ARGOT
speeches ORATORY
speechify ORATE
speechless MUTE
speechless with emotion, be CHOKE
speed BAT; BELT; CLIP; DART; DASH; DRUG; HASTE; HIE; KNOT; KNOTS; LICK; MPH; NIP; PACE; PAR; RATE; RUN; RUSH; TEMPO; ■ BOWL; CELERITY; TEMPI
speed, at APACE; PAST
speed, maximum C
speed, measure of KNOT; MPH
speed-merchant RACER
speed of engine, increase REV
speed of light C

speed, ship's KNOT(S)
speeding, one RACER
speedy FAST
spell BOUT; CHARM; FIT; HEX; MARK; SHIFT; SNAP; TERM; TIME; TURN; ■ CANTRIP; PERIOD; WHAMMY
spell, given another anagram indicator
spell in America usually refers to taking advantage of the different spelling in the U.S. (COLOR, LITER, ESTHETE etc.) to provide a component in building up an answer
spell of bowling OVER
spell of illness BOUT; TURN
spell of playing GAME; GIG; MATCH; SESSION; SET
spell, wild FLING
spellbound RAPT
spelling SP
spelling, aid to WAND
spells, short FITS
spelt out can indicate that THEN is to be inserted between two letters as "Capital A's spelt out" → ATHENS (i.e. a-then-s)
spend BLOW; PASS; USE
spend frivolously FRITTER
spend unwisely BLOW; BLUE
spender USER
spending, not SAVING
spent BLEW; BLOWN; GONE; PAST; USED; WEARY; ■ TIRED; anagram indicator
spent in in the sense of "used" can serve as a run indicator
spent recklessly BLEW
sphere BALL; FIELD; GLOBE; ORB; ■ ELEMENT; WORLD
spherical shape ORB
spice CHILLI; CLOVE; MACE
spicy HOT
spicy food CHILI
spider REST; SPINNER
spiel PATTER; PITCH
spies CIA
spigot TAP

spike BARB; LACE; NAIL; PIN; POINT; TINE; ■ IMPALE; PRONG

spill FALL; LIGHTER; TAPER; anagram indicator

spill the beans GRASS; SING; TELL; ■ RELATE

spillage anagram indicator

spilled, spilling, spilt anagram indicator

spilt SHED; anagram indicator, as "spilt oil" → OLI

spin CYCLE; DRIVE; GLOSS; HYPE; REEL; ROLL; SIDE; SLANT; TRIP; TURN; ■ BIAS; SWIRL; WHIRL; anagram indicator; [◊ DOCTOR; DRIER; TOP]

spin, exponent of TOP

spin, give a PLAY; *see* TURN

spin, in a anagram indicator; reversal indicator

spin-off anagram of SPIN

spine BACK; GUTS; THORN; ■ PRICKLE

spineless person WORM

spinner TOP; ■ GYROSCOPE; SPIDER

spinning anagram indicator

spinster MISS

spiralling anagram indicator

spire TOWER

spirit ANGEL; BOTTLE; CORE; DASH; DEMON; DEVIL; ELF; GHOST; GIN; GO; GUM; HEART; IMP; RUM; SCOTCH; SHADE; SHORT; SOUL; TONE; ■ ELAN; ELEMENTAL; ETHOS; GEIST; LIFE; MORALE; OUZO; PERI; SPECTRE; WRAITH; ZING; [◊ MEDIUM]; can have something to do with exorcism

spirit, foreign GEIST

spirit, some DRAM; TOT

spirit's strength PROOF

spirit, with RACY

spirit, with extra LACED

spirited GAME; RACY

spirited interpreter MEDIUM

spirited measure can indicate a measure of alcohol e.g. noggin; *see* DRINK

spiritless POOR

spirits ELVES; HUMOUR; MOOD; PECKER (i.e. mood); *see* SPIRIT

spirits, dose of PEG

spirits, measure of TOT

spirits, put ban on this usually refers to exorcism

spirits, raise ELATE

spiritual, sort of NEGRO

spiritualists' meeting SEANCE

spit RAIN; ROD; ■ BROACH; DIG (i.e. with reference to spade); DOUBLE

spite MALICE

spiteful CATTY; NASTY

spiteful person SHREW

spiteful woman CAT; SHREW

spiv TOUT

splash WET; anagram indicator; can indicate something to do with a headline

splash about anagram indicator

splashdown can indicate rain or cataract, waterfall etc

splashed around anagram indicator

splashes anagram indicator

splatter DASH; SPLODGE

splay SPREAD

splayed SPREAD; anagram indicator

spleen BILE; ■ VITRIOL

splendid BRAVE; FINE; GRAND; GREAT; SUPER; SUPERB; TOP

splice GRAFT

spliff JOINT; REEFER

splinter BREAK; SLICE; SLIVER

splinter-group SECT

splinters (in) anagram indicator

split BREACH; BREAK; CHAP; CLEAVE; CLEFT; CLOVE; CUT; FLED; GO; GONE; GULF; LEAVE; LEFT; PART; QUIT; RAN; REND; RENT; RIFT; RIP; RIVE; SNAP; TEAR; TORN; ■ BISECT; BURST; CLOVEN; INFORM; RIVEN; SCHISM; SHATTER; SUNDER;

with a capital letter, thereby denoting the Serbo-Croatian town, can indicate something to do with that country or its language; anagram indicator

Split PORT; *see* SPLIT

split into two HALVE; run indicator, where element crosses two words within the clue

split by nesting indicator

splits, one who RIVER; *see* SPLIT

splitting anagram indicator; nesting indicator; if applied to the letter W, it can indicate that W becomes VV

splitting hairs PARTING

splodge BLOT; BLOTCH; DAUB; SMEAR; ■ SPLATTER

splodges, leave SPLATTER

splosh SLOP

splutter CHOKE

Spock, Mr ALIEN

spoil DISH; HURT; IMPAIR; MAR; MUFF; RUIN; SACK

spoiled MARRED; OFF; anagram indicator

spoiler FLAP

spoils BOOTY; LOOT; anagram indicator; *see* SPOIL

spoilt anagram indicator

spoke RUNG; SAID; ■ BAT; CHATTED; can indicate something to do with wheel

spoke at length DWELT

spoke of homophone indicator

spoke sharply SNAPPED

spoken ORAL; SAID; homophone indicator

spoken about a component to be nested within ORAL

spoken, having SAID

spokesman MOUTH

spokesperson VOICE

sponge BUM; CADGE; WIPER; ■ ALCOHOLIC; LOOFA

sponsor BACK; BACKER; ■ GODFATHER

spook anagram indicator; *see* GHOST

spool REEL; ROLL

spoon, use STIR

Spooner can indicate the initial letters of two words are to be transposed as in "Spooner's dog, lean for so long" which gives TOODLE-PIP!

spoor TRACK; TRAIL

sporran POKE

sport ANGLING; BRICK; CRICKET; FIVES; FOOTER; FUN; GAME; GOLF; PLAY; RACING; RACKETS; ROWING; RU; WEAR; ■ PLAYING; GAMES; MATE (i.e. friend); SHOW; anagram indicator; *see* GAME

sport, area of COURT; FIELD; PITCH

sported WORE; anagram indicator

sporting FAIR; GAME; anagram indicator

sporting arena RING

sporting encounter MEET

sporting etiquette, breach of FOUL

sports GAMES; *see* SPORT

sports administrators FA; LTA

sports arena GROUND

sports club BAT

sports contest EVENT

sports gear KIT; STRIP

sports car GT

sports group TEAM

sports meeting EVENT; MATCH

sportsman ANGLER; BLUE; DIVER; OAR; PRO; RIDER; ROWER; ■ ATHLETE; BATTER; PLAYER; RUNNER; SKIER

sportsmen EIGHT; SIDE; TEAM; *see* SPORTSMAN

sportswear KIT; SHORTS; STRIP; TOP

sporty vehicle QUAD

spot BIND; BIT; BLOT; DAB; DEFECT; DOT; DRIP; DROP; ESPY; EYE; FIX; FLAW; FLECK; MARK; MOTE; NOTE; PATCH; PIP (on playing card); PLACE; POCK; POINT; SEE; SIGHT; SITE; SOIL; SPECK; SPY; STAIN; ■ CORNER;

MACKLE; PIMPLE; SPLODGE; TARNISH; ZIT

spot, nasty WEN

spotless CLEAN; PURE; WHITE

spotlight BEAM; LASER

spots RASH; ■ ACNE; MEASLES

spots, marked with DAPPLE

spotted DAPPLED; MEASLY; SAW; SEEN

Spotted Dick PUD

spotted in run indicator

spotted, not CLEAN; PLAIN; ■ UNSTAINED; *see* PURE

spouse HUBBY; MATE; WIFE

spouse no longer EX

spout GUSH; JET; ORATE; TALK

sprain RICK

sprang LEAPT

sprang up ROSE

sprawled, sprawling anagram indicator

spray BUNCH; COAT; JET; ■ WATER

sprayed anagram indicator

spread AIR; BUTTER; COVER; FEAST; LAY; MARG; MARGE; MEAL; OPEN; PAGES; PASTE; PATE; RANCH; RANGE; SPAN; SPLAY; STREW; TED; WIDEN; ■ CONSERVE; DINNER; EMANATE; EXTEND; GROW; LAYER; anagram indicator; can indicate a specific conserve such as marmalade; can indicate something to do with the page aspect of printing as "Part of spread that's left" clues VERSO

spread out SPLAY; anagram indicator

spread over nesting indicator

spreads over anagram indicator

spreading anagram indicator

spree BINGE; FLING; JUNKET; REVEL; ROMP; anagram indicator

sprig BRANCH; SHOOT; STALK; YOUTH

spring BOUND; CAPER; COIL; FOUNT; HOP; ISSUE; JETE; JUMP; LEAP; LENT (i.e. time of the religious festival); MAY; SHOOT; SKIP; SPA; SPRIG; STEM; WELL; ■ BOUNCE; GEYSER; POUNCE; VERNAL; WATER

spring, early MARCH

spring from STEM

spring, of VERNAL

spring time MAY

spring up APS (i.e. rev. of "spa"); REAR

springs anagram indicator

springtime MAY

sprinkle HOSE; PEPPER; SPLATTER; SPRAY; anagram indicator

sprinkled anagram indicator

sprinkling SHOWER

sprint DASH; RACE; RUN

sprit SPAR

sprite ELF; IMP; PUCK

spruce NEAT; SMART; TIDY; TREE; TRIM; ■ NATTY; SMARTEN

spry BRISK; NIMBLE

spun anagram indicator

spur DRIVE; EGG; HEEL; PRICK; RIDGE; URGE; ■ BRANCH; GOAD; MOTIVE; POINT; PRESS

spurious BAD; FALSE; anagram indicator

spurn REJECT; REPULSE

spurt RUSH

spy AGENT; BOND; MOLE; PEEK; PLANT; SCOUT; SEE; SIGHT; SPOT; ■ BLUNT; INFORMER

spy, American SPOOK

spy chief M

spy on STALK

spy organisation CIA

spy, police NARK

spymaster M; ■ BERIA

squabble SPAT; WRANGLE; *see* ROW; ■ BICKER; SETTO (i.e. set-to)

squad CREW; FLEET; SIDE; TEAM; ■ ARMADA; FORCE

squadron WING

squadron leader S

squalid SEEDY; TACKY; ■ SLUMMY

squalid area SLUM

squalid house SLUM

squalid surroundings can indicate a component is to be nested within SEEDY, as "Quick parking in squalid surroundings" → SPEEDY

squall GUST

squander BLOW; BLUE; WASTE

squandered BLEW; BLOWN anagram indicator

square EVEN; PAY; QUAD; SETTLE; S; STRAIGHT; T; TRUE; can indicate any mathematical square, and so FOUR, NINE etc

square-ended T to be placed at the end of a component

square in Italy PIAZZA

squash CRAMP; CRUSH; DRINK; ■ MARROW; PRESS; SQUEEZE

squashed PENT; anagram indicator

squashy SOFT

squat CROUCH; DUMPY; SIT

squatting nesting indicator

squeal NARK; SHOP

squeak PEEP

squeeze HUG; NIP; PRESS; WRING; ■ EMBRACE; EXACT; SQUASH; [◊ TRIGGER; VICE]

squeeze out EXPRESS; OUT to be nested within one or more components

squeezer MANGLE

squeezing nesting indicator

squiffy anagram indicator

squint CAST

squire PAGE

squirm WRITHE; ■ WRIGGLE

squirming anagram indicator

squirrel's home DREY

stab CRACK; GO; JAB; SHOT; SPEAR; STICK; TURN; ■ GUESS; POKE; WOUND

stab, to nesting indicator

stabilise PEG

stable FAST; FIRM; HOUSE (i.e. as a verb}; STALL; STATIC; ■ SOUND; STEADY; STRING (i.e. horses); SURE

stable worker GROOM

stableman GROOM

stables MEWS

stack HEAP; LOT; PILE; POT; RAFT; RICK

stacked up reversal indicator

stadium GROUND; ■ ARENA

staff BAR; CARE; CLUB; CREW; CROOK; HANDS; MACE; MAN; MAST; MEN; MINIM; PIKE; POLE; ROD; STICK; SHARP; TEAM; ■ CROSIER; can indicate something to do with bread (i.e. the staff of life); can indicate something to do with musical notation

staff officer SO

stag DEER; HART

stag's cry BELL

stage LEG; LEVEL; MOUNT; PHASE; PUPA; STAND; STEP; TIER; ■ APRON; COACH; MOMENT; PERIOD; PODIUM; POINT; PRESENT

stage appearance DEBUT; ■ ENTRANCE

stage, come onto the ENTER

stage direction ENTER; EXIT

stage of journey HOP; LEG

stage production DRAMA; MOUNT; PLAY; *see* MUSICAL

stage profession ACTING

stage, take the ACT

stage, used to be on ACTED; DIDACT (i.e. did act)

staged, being ON

stagger REEL; ROCK; ROLL; SHOCK; ■ AMAZE; LURCH; TOTTER

staggering anagram indicator

staggering, is REELS; ROCKS; ROLLS; SHOCKS

stagnant STANDING

staid QUIET; SOBER

stain BLOT; MAR; MARK; SHAME; SLUR; SPOT; TAINT; ■ DYE; BLACKEN; SULLY; *see* TAINT

stainer DYER

staircase component
LANDING; NEWEL; RISER;
STEP; TREAD

stairs FLIGHT

stairs, part of *see* STAIRCASE
COMPONENT

stake ANTE; BET; CHIP; PALE;
PILE; POST; ■ LAG; STAVE; [◊
POT]

stakes POOL

staked ON

stale FLAT; MUSTY; OFF; OLD;
TIRED; ■ MOULDY

stale, become DATE

stalk BRANCH; DOG; STEM;
TAIL

stall BOOTH; SEAT; SHY;
STABLE; STAND; STOP; ■
COVER; DELAY; TARRY

stalls PIT

stamen, part of ANTHER

stammering the first letter of word
to be repeated

stamp COIN; DIE; FRANK;
KIND; MARK; SEAL; TREAD;
■ IMPRINT; SORT

stamp, special CACHET

stamped TROD

stamped on anagram indicator

stampede RUSH; ■ CAREER

stampeded/ing anagram indicator

stance POSE; POSITION; STAND

stance, took a POSED

stand BEAR; BOOTH; BROOK;
EASEL; GANTRY; HACK;
LAST (i.e. cobbler's); PLACE;
POSE; POSITION; RISE; SET;
STAGE; STALL; STANCE;
TAKE; TEE; TREAT; WEAR; ■
RELY; reversal indicator; in the
sense of a stand of trees can de-
note a specific tree in the plural
e.g. OAKS

stand, can't HATE

stand, did not SAT

stand for BROOK; TAKE; ■
REPRESENT

stand high TOWER

stand-in PROXY; RELIEF; SUB;
TEMP; VICE

stand on hind legs REAR

stand, one-night GIG

stand up WASH (i.e. is not supported by the evidence)

stand up to FIGHT

standard ENSIGN; FLAG;
FORM; JACK; NORM; PAR;
STOCK; ■ EAGLE; NORMAL;
ONPAR (i.e. on par);

standard issue PARSON (i.e. par
son)

standards CODE; MORALS

standing NAME; PLACE; RANK;
RATE; REP; STATION; UP; ■
ERECT; POSITION;
STAGNANT; STATIC; STATUS;
UPRIGHT; reversal indicator;
can indicate something to do with
standing for election (or in U.S.
"running for election") to be
member, MP, delegate, representative etc

standing out PROUD

standing up ERECT; UPRIGHT;
reversal indicator

standstill OMPH (i.e. 0 mph)

stank SMELT

Stanley STAN

stannic TIN

staple CHIEF; CLIP; MAIN;
PRIME; RICE; ■ BASIC

star ACE; LEAD; NAME; NOVA;
PAPER; PIP; SUN; TOP; ■
CELEBRITY; DWARF;
LEADING; LION; MAIN;
MAJOR; POLARIS; VEGA

star group ARIES; BEAR; LEO;
PLOUGH; VIRGO

star, Hollywood COOPER;
GABLE

star player ACE

star, tennis SEED

starchy FORMAL; STIFF

stare GAPE; GAWP; GAZE;
GLOWER; LEER; LOOK;
OGLE

stark BALD; CLEAR; GRIM;
PLAIN; ■ BLUNT

starkers NAKED (qv)

strarry ASTRAL

stars LYRA; ORION; PLOUGH;
VIRGO; *see* STAR GROUP

start BEGIN; DAWN; ENTER;
FLINCH; FOUND; GO; INTRO;

JUMP; LEAD; OFF; ONSET; OPEN; RISE; SHY; TRIGGER; ■ ACTIVATE; AWAY (as in 'the away'); FIRST; INSTITUTE; LAUNCH; OFF; PROCEED; RECOIL; ROUSE; initial letter indicator

start a game SERVE

start filming F; ROLL; SHOOT

start, from the initial letter(s) to be used

start of O; initial letter indicator

start of play ACTI (i.e. ACT I); P

start of puzzle ONE (i.e. first clue, one across); P

start of week MON; W

start off O; initial letter indicator; initial letter to be omitted, as "start off quick" → RISK; *see* START

started off badly can indicate an anagram of the first few letters of a word

start operation LAUNCH; O; ROLL

start to finish AZ; first letter to go to the end of a word; first and last letters of a word to be transposed

start young Y

started BEGAN; SHIED

started, just OFF

starter COURSE; ENTRE; ■ SOUP; initial letter indicator

starter, we hear GO

starter, without a omission indicator for an initial letter

starters can indicate the initial letters of associated words or the first two or three letters of one word

starting NASCENT; initial letter indicator (as "starting soon" → S); *see* START

starting late L; first letter to be omitted

startle SCARE; SHOCK

starts off O; *see* START

starts to turn first letters of word to be reversed, as "Starts to turn on dubious type of power supply" converts UNCLEAR (dubious) to NUCLEAR

stash STOW

state AVER; COMA; FORM; LAND; LIMBO; MESS; MOOD; NAME; NATION; REALM; SAY; ■ CONDITION; COUNTRY; ENOUNCE; EXPRESS; LATHER; REPORT; a national state in its full form e.g. GOA, OMAN; or abbreviation e.g. UK, US; an abbreviation for a state within a country, usually American, *see* AMERICAN STATE; note than an eastern state can refer to one on the eastern side of the U.S. as well as an eastern country; can indicate an abstract word ending in -SHIP (friendship, hardship etc)

state, Atlantic RI

state benefit DOLE

state briefly can indicate the standard abbreviation for an American state (qv)

state, French ETAT

state, German REICH

state, Mid-Western ILL

state of mind MOOD

state, southern GA; LA; *see* AMERICAN STATE

stated ORAL; SAID; homophone indicator (as "stated why" → Y)

stated, as homophone indicator (example: "I, as stated" → EYE)

stately IMPOSING

stately home PALACE; PILE

statement COMMENT; REPORT; STORY; ■ AVOWAL; BILL; PROFESSION; RELATION; REMARK; can indicate a word beginning with IM, as "Brusque statement of case" → IMPATIENT

statement, inaccurate LIE

statement, legal PLAINT

statement, make a AVER

statement of faith CREED

statement of intent WILL

States US

statesman HOME (i.e. former prime minister); can indicate the term describing a person from a specific country (usually

AMERICAN); or a man from a specific American state e.g. TEXAN

statesman, former HOME; NORTH; ■ BURKE

statesman, leading PM

statesman, old *see* STATESMAN, FORMER

statesman, old Roman CATO

static DEAD; STABLE; STANDING; STILL

station BASE; FORT; PLACE; PORT; RANK; STOP; ■ DEPOT; LEVEL; POSITION; STANDING; can indicate something to do with police; [◊ TRAIN]

station, Parisian GARE

stationery item INK; PEN; ■ ERASER

statistic FIGURE

statistics DATA; TABLE

statue FIGURE; IDOL

stature HEIGHT

status RANK; ■ POSITION; *see* STATION; [◊ QUO]

status, of BIG

statute ACT; LAW; ORDER

staunch CHECK; FIRM; STEM; STOP; TRUE; ■ RELIABLE; STOUT

stave LAG; STAKE

stay ABIDE; BIDE; BOARD; BRACE; CHECK; DEFER; DWELL; LAST; LINGER; LODGE; PROP; REST; ROPE; SIT; STICK; TARRY; TIE; ■ ANCHOR; CORSET; HOLD; REMAIN; STRUT; WAIT

stay awhile CAMP; LINGER; *see* STAY

stay home DWELL; RESIDE

stay behind LINGER

stay, decide to SETTLE

stay, not LEAVE

stay put WAIT

stay put, told to WEIGHT

stay temporarily CAMP; LODGE

stay up STAND

stead PLACE

steady FIRM; FIXED; STABLE; STAID

steadying influence LEG; PROP

steak JOINT; MEAT; RUMP

steak, stewing SHIN

steal LIFT; LOOT; NICK; PALM; PINCH; POACH; POCKET; ROB; RUSTLE; SIDLE; SWIPE; WHIP; ■ BAG; SCRUMP; SNAFFLE

steal away ELOPE

steal food POACH

steal from orchard SCRUMP

stealing THEFT; THIEVERY

stealthily, move EDGE; INCH

steam MIST; STEW; ■ CHUFF; FUME; [◊ POWER]

steamer BOILER; PACKET; SS; TRAMP; ■ KETTLE

steamy HOT

steel SWORD

steep BATHE; HIGH; RET; SHEER; SOAK

steepness of roof PITCH

steeple SPIRE

steer BULL; CON; COW; DRIVE; LEAD; OX; ■ COX; DIRECT; PILOT; STOT; TURN

steerer COX; DRIVER

steering apparatus/ device HELM; RUDDER; ■ TILLER; WHEEL

steering station HELM

stein MUG

stella STAR

stellar ASTRAL; STARRY

stem BOUGH; BOW; CHECK; PROW; SHOOT; STALK; STAUNCH; STOP; ■ LINE; SPRING

stem, flexible BINE

stem of plant CANE

stemmed by run indicator

stench BO; NIFF; PONG; REEK

step PACE; PAS; RUNG; STAGE; STAIR; TREAD; WALK; ■ ACTION; DEGREE; STRIDE; [◊ NOSING]

step back SAP

step on spiral staircase WINDER

step, out of anagram indicator

steppe PLAIN

stepped TROD

steps FLIGHT; DANCE; STILE; or can indicate a specific dance

steps, moveable RAMP

steps, take DANCE; TRAMPLE; TREAD; *see* WALK

stern AFT; BACK; DOUR; GRAVE; GRIM; HARD; HARSH; HIND; REAR; SEVERE; STRICT; ■ TRANSOM

stern, towards AFT

steroid DRUG

stew BROOD; COOK; HOLE; JAM; MESS; OLIO; SIMMER; STEAM; ■ CORNER; HOTPOT; LATHER; MUDDLE; PICKLE; anagram indicator

steward REEVE; WAITER

stewed PICKLED; anagram indicator

stick BAT; CANE; CLEAVE; CLING; CLUB; CUE; FIX; GLUE; GUM; JAM; LANCE; LAST; LEVER; PASTE; PIN; POLE; ROD; STAB; STAFF; STAY; STRING; SWITCH; TWIG; WAND; WEAR; ■ AFFIX; BATON; CLUTCH; ENDURE; FLAK; PIERCE

stick closely CLING

stick, get some CHID

stick to CLING

sticker BUR; BURR; POSTER; ■ GLUE

sticky TACKY; TARRY

sticky stuff/substance GEL; GOO; GUM; JAM; LAC; PASTE; TAR; ■ GLUE; RESIN; TREACLE; WAX

stiff BODY; FIRM; HARD; PRIM; RIGID; can signify something to do with death or a mortuary e.g. CORONER; ■ CORPSE; STARCHY; UNBENDING

stiff with age RUSTY

stiffener STARCH

stiffness STARCH

stifle STUNT

stigma MARK; STAIN

still BUT; DEAD; EVEN; HUSH; SHOT (i.e. photograph); SNAP; YET; ■ CALM; CONSTANT; FRAME (i.e. in cinema film); INERT; RETORT (i.e. equipment); STATIC

still standing EXTANT

stilted WOODEN

stimulant UPPER

stimulate AROUSE; PROD; SPARK; SPUR; URGE; WHET; ■ INCITE; PIQUE; PUSH

stimulus CHEAT; PROD; SPUR; ■ FILLIP; TONIC

sting BITE; CHEAT; CON; PAIN; SCAM; SMART; ■ HURT; NETTLE; SWINDLE

stingy MEAN; TIGHT; *see* TIGHT-FISTED

stingy social worker BEE; WASP

stink BO; SMELL (qv); STENCH (qv)

stink, causing a OLID; ■ SMELLY

stinker CAD; RAT

stinking BAD; HIGH; RANK

stint SCANT; SCRIMP; SKIMP; TASK; TERM; note, can also refer to a wading bird

stipple DOT

stipulation IF; RIDER

stir ADO; BUDGE; BUSTLE; CAN; JUG; MIX; MOVE; ROUSE; ROUST; SHIFT; ■ FLURRY; RUFFLE; WHISK; *see* PRISON; anagram indicator

stir, create a anagram of STIR; *see* AGITATE, STIR

stir up anagram indicator

stirred MOVED; anagram indicator

stirring, stirring up anagram indicator

stitch PAIN; SEW; TACK; [◊ GARTER]

stitch up FRAME; SCREW; WES (rev)

stitches, series of SEAM

stoat ERMINE

stoat-like creature MINK

stock CATTLE; COWS; KEEP; HANDLE; KIN; RACE; RESERVE; STORE; STRAIN; USUAL; ■ BANK; COMMON; KEEP; SUPPLY; TRUNK;

SOUP; can indicate something to do with farm animals, sheep etc

stock identification BRAND

stock item LINE

stock of gun BUTT

stock, take RUSTLE

stock-take RUSTLE

stock-taker RUSTLER

stockholder BYRE; PEN; ■ CORRAL; RIFLEMAN

stocking nesting indicator; run indicator

stocking filler SANTA

stockings HOSE

stockings etc HOSIERY

stockman can indicate a worker ending in HERD, e.g. cowherd.

stockpile HOARD

stocks nesting indicator (as "stocks" nothing" → O to be nested within a component or word)

stocky STURDY

stole BOA; FUR; SCARF; TOOK; WRAP; ■ TIPPET

stolen HOT

stolen goods HAUL; SWAG

stomach BEAR; BELLY; FACE; GUT; STAND; POT; TUM; ■ MAWS

stomach ache COLIC

stomach as food TRIPE

stomach, interior of PIT

stomach pains COLIC

stomach-turning MUT (i.e. reversal of "tum")

stone AGATE; BLOCK; FLINT; GEM; HONE; JET; LOGAN; MARBLE; OPAL; PIP; PIT; ROCK; RUBY; SEED; ST; ■ JADE

stone, piece of SLAB

stone work STOP (i.e. ST-OP)

stonecrop ORPIN

stoned HIGH

stones HAIL; SCREE

stones, small GRIT

stone, semi-precious JADE

stood up anagram indicator

stool SEAT; ■ REST

stoop BEND; BOW; BUNG; DEIGN; LEAN; SINK

stop AVAST; BAN; BAR; BLACK; BLOCK; BRAKE; BREAK; CEASE; CLOSE; CURB; DAM; DETER; DIE; DOT; END; FIELD (cric.); FREEZE; HALT; PARK; PERIOD; PLUG; POINT; PORT (i.e. port of call); QUIT; SEAL; STALL; STAY; STEM; ■ ARREST; BUNG; CHECK; COMMA; DESIST; EMBARGO; PAUSE; PREVENT; REFRAIN; SCOTCH; STATION; STAUNCH; YIELD; WHOA

stop at sea AVAST

stop-cock TAP

stop eating FAST

stop flow DAM

stop from pay DOCK

stop, full PERIOD

stop in U.S. PERIOD

stop moving FREEZE

stop payment, to component to be nested within a synonym of "payment" e.g. RENT

stop to, put a CEASE; *see* STOP

stop up TAMP

stop without starting EASE (i.e. first letter omitted)

stopover BREAK; HALT; REST

stoppage BAN; BAR; END; BLOCK; STAND; STRIKE

stoppage, current DAM

stopped OFF; OVER; *see* END, FINISH, STOP

stopper BUNG; CORK; PLUG

stopping nesting indicator

stops can indicate something to do with organ, organist etc

storage compartment DRAWER

storage container HOLDER

storage facility BANK; BARN; SILO

storage pit SILO

storage structure RACK

store BARN; BIN; COOP (i.e. Co-op); DELI; FUND; HOARD; HOLD; KEEP; RACK; RESERVE; SAVE; SHOP; SILO; STASH; STOCK; ■ CACHE; DEPOT; PANTRY; SHED

store carefully CONSERVE
store, is in AWAITS
stored in run indicator
storehouse BARN; DEPOT; *see* STORE
storey FLOOR; LAYER; LEVEL
stories ANA; FICTION; LIES; LORE; note, can refer to the floors of a building
stories, collection of ANA
storm GALE; HAIL; RAGE; RAID; RAIN; RANT; RAVE; anagram indicator
storm, affected by anagram indicator
storm, centre of EYE; O
stormy anagram indicator
story ACCOUNT; CONTE (Fr.); DOPE; EPIC; FABLE; FICTION; LIE; PLOT; SAGA; SCOOP; TALE; YARN; ■ MYTH; PARABLE; RELATION; note, can also refer to the floor of a building
story element PLOT; STRAND
story-line PLOT
story, main LEAD
story, short last letter to be eliminated from STORY or a synonym, hence STOR, TAL, YAR etc, *see* STORY
story-teller LIAR
storybook TALENT (i.e. tale + NT)
storyteller GRIMM
storytelling FICTION; LIES
stout ALE; AMPLE; FAT; PLUMP; PORTER; PORTLY; ■ ROBUST; STAUNCH
stove AGA; RANGE; OVEN; ■ HEATER
stow CRAM; PACK; STASH; STORE ■ LODGE
stowage, provides *see* CONTAINER
straight DIRECT; EVEN; FAIR; FRANK; JUST; NEAT; SQUARE; ■ HONEST; PROPER; SOUND; TRUE
straight, get ALIGN
straight-laced PRIM
straight man FEED

straight, not CURLY
straight, not going LIST
straight, put ALIGN; CORRECT; REPAIR; RIGHTEN
straight up SHEER
straighten ALIGN; DRESS; ORDER
straighten the line DRESS
straightened out anagram indicator
straightforward FRANK
strain AIR; BREED; DITTY; FRAY; RACE; RICK; SIFT; SONG; STOCK; STRESS; TAX; TEST; TUNE; ■ FILTER; FORCE; RIDDLE; SIEVE; STREAK; TAXING; TENSION; TROUBLE
strain, severe ORDEAL; TEST
strain, under *see* STRAINED
strained TAUT; TENSE
strained, become FRAY
strained food PUREE
strait SOLENT; SOUND; ST
strait-laced *see* STRAIGHT-LACED
straits *see* SPOT, TROUBLE; can refer to particular straits e.g. Gibraltar, Hellespont
strand LOCK; PLY; THREAD; TRESS; MAROON; ■ BEACH; GROUND; note, can refer to the shoreline e.g. BEACH
stranded AGROUND; LEFT; WISPY
strange ODD; RUM; WEIRD; ■ ALIEN; ATYPICAL; NEW; QUAINT; anagram indicator; can indicate something to do with the paranormal, e.g. ESP, telepathy
strange thing NIGHT
strangely anagram indicator
stranger ALIEN; ODDER; anagram indicator
strangle CHOKE
strangled by nesting indicator
strap BEAT; BIND; THONG; TIE; ■ JESS; REIN
strapping TALL
stratagem DODGE; PLAN; PLOY; RUSE; TRICK; WILE

strategy PLAN; ■ GAME PLAN; TACTIC

Stratford, role at indicates a Shakespearian character

stratum LAYER

straw THATCH; [◊ CAMEL; LAST]

stray DRIFT; ERR (qv); GAMIN; ■ DIGRESS; WANDER (qv); anagram indicator

straying ROVING; anagram indicator

streak BAND; BAR; FLASH; LINE; RUN; STRIPE; WISP

streaked FLEW

streaker NUDE

stream BECK; BROOK; BURN; CREEK; FILE; FLOW; POUR; RILL; RIVER; SPOUT; TRICKLE; can indicate some aspect of water; can indicate a small river e.g. CAM; also can refer to a class at school

stream of water JET; *see* STREAM

streamer FLAG; RIBBON

street AVE; CLOSE; CRESCENT; GATE; MEWS; ROAD; ROW; ST; WAY

street, acceptability on CRED

street, French RUE

street-guide (-map) AZ

street in Rome VIA

street, narrow ALLEY

streetcar TRAM; ■ DESIRE

streetwise HIP

strength BRAWN; FORCE; MIGHT; POWER; PROOF (drink)

strength, having ABLE

strengthen CLAMP; PROP; TEMPER; ■ BUTTRESS

strenuous HARD

strenuously HARD; anagram indicator

stress ACCENT; STRAIN; TAX; ■ ICTUS (prosody); TENSION; UNDERLINE

stress, absence of CALM; ■ ATONY

stressed TAUT

stretch CRANE; DRAG; REACH; SPAN; STRAIN; TENSE; ■ EXPANSE; EXTEND; LENGTH

stretch in run indicator

stretch of run indicator

stretch of countryside PLAIN

stretch of river REACH

stretch, short YARD; YD

stretch of water RIVER; SEA

stretched TENSE; TAUT; TIGHT; anagram indicator

stretcher BRICK; LITTER

strewn anagram indicator

stricken AILING; ILL; anagram indicator

strict HARD; HEAVY; STERN; ■ HARSH; PRECISE; RIGID

strict, be less RELENT

stride LOPE; MARCH; PACE; STEP; WALK

strike BANG; BASH; BAT; BEAT; BUMP; BUTT; CHOP; CLAP; CLIP; CLOCK; CLUB; CRACK; CUFF; DELETE; HIT; KNAP; KNOCK; LAM; LASH; LUNGE; PLUG; RAID; RAM; RAP; REACH; RING; SLAM; SLUG; SMACK; SPEAR; SWAT; TAP; WHACK; ■ ACTION; ATTACK; BELT; BUFFET; CHIME; CLOBBER; CLOUT; HAMMER; POUND; PUNCH; [◊ GOLD; OIL]; anagram indicator; can indicate something to do with matches

strike-breaker SCAB

strike, non-violent TAP

strike, on OUT

strike out ERASE; DELETE

strike repeatedly BATTER

striker BAT; CANE; FIST; ■ BATTER; FORWARD; HAMMER; MATCH; PLAYER; RAPPER; VESTA; can indicate a venomous snake

striking OUT; SIGNAL; can indicate something to do with matches

striking, not BLACK

Strindberg AUGUST

string CORD; LACE; LINE; ROW; STICK; TIE; TWINE; designation of string-note on instrument, B, G etc see NOTE, KEY; [◊ PLUCK]

string-player BASSIST
stringent STRICT
stringy TOUGH
strip BAND; BARE; FLAY; LATH; PEEL; RIDGE; RIG; SASH; SLIP; STAVE; TAB; TAPE; TEAR; THONG; WEAR (as in football strip); ■ DENUDE; DIVEST; PLASTER; RUNWAY; WICK; [◊ TEASE]
strip in the kitchen can indicate noodle, spaghetti etc
strip lighting NEON
strip of wood LATH
strip off PEEL
stripe BAND; BAR; BLOW; STREAK
stripling SPEAR
stripped first and last letters to be omitted
stripped of its borders first and last letters to be omitted, as "Spain stripped of its borders" → PAI
stripped off omission indicator
stripper TURPS
stripping BARING
stroke BLOW; CRAWL; DRIVE; FIT; HOOK; LASH; LINE; LOB; OAR; PAT; TOLL; ■ CARESS; FONDLE; MASSE (billiards); ROWER
stroke in golf PUT
stroke of luck FLUKE
stroke rating PAR
strokes RALLY; see STROKE
strokes, series of RALLY
stroll AMBLE; TODDLE; ■ SAUNTER
Stromboli can indicate a word beginning with HOT e.g. hot-headed
strong BEEFY; F; FIRM; HARDY; MANLY; STR; ■ DOUBLE (as in drink); POTENT; ROBUST
strong ale PORTER
strong chap/man HEMAN (i.e. he-man); TITAN
strong effect IMPACT

strong effect, have IMPRESS
strong player SEED
strong point FORTE ■ MERIT; PLUS
strongbox COFFER; SAFE
stronghold FORT; KEEP; ■ CASTLE
strongly-built STOCKY
strongly flavoured RICH
strongly-made ROBUST
strove PLIED; TOILED
struck HIT (qv); SMIT; SMITTEN; SMOTE; TAPPED; see STRIKE; anagram indicator
structure anagram indicator
structure, tall TOWER
structured anagram indicator
struggle FIGHT; FRAY; STRIVE; VIE; WAR; ■ BATTLE; CONTEND; CONTEST; RESIST; SCRUM; STRAIN; anagram indicator
struggle for breath GASP; PANT
struggled FOUGHT; STROVE; VIED
struggling anagram indicator
strumpet BAWD; see WOMAN, VULGAR
strut BRACE; MARCH; STAY
stubborn creature MULE
stuck FIXED; JAMMED; LOCKED; see RIGID
stuck, get JAM
stuck into nesting indicator
stud BOLT; BOSS; FARM; POST; RIVET; STABLE; can refer to a breeding horse
student L; MEDIC; READER; ■ PUPIL; SCHOLAR; TUTEE
student body NUS
student, diligent SWOT
student festival/fundraiser RAG
student society, member of FRAT
student, successful BA
students NUS; [◊ RAG]
students, first year FRESHMEN
students' fun RAG
students, group of YEAR
students, lot of STREAM
studentship PLACE

studied READ; runs indicator
studies ARTS; CONS; READS; *see* STUDY
study CON; CAN (var. of con); CRAM; DEN; DO; EYE; MULL; PORE; READ; ROOM; SCAN; SWOT; WORK; ■ ETUDE; PERUSE; anagram indicator; [◊ DEGREE]
study, American MATH
study hard BONE; CRAM; SWOT
study period CLASS; LESSON; TERM
study programme COURSE
stumble FALL; TRIP
stuff CRAM; GORGE; JAM; MATTER; PACK; PIG; RAM; REP; can refer to a specific fabric (qv), material (qv) etc
stuff, cheap TAT
stuff, delicate LACE
stuff, used to nesting indicator; run indicator
stuffed with nesting indicator
stuffiness FUG
stuffy CLOSE; DULL
stumble TRIP
stumbling anagram indicator
stump BOWL; WICKET; ■ TRUNK
stumped ST
stumpy SHORT
stun KO; SHOCK
stunner DISH; KO; PEACH
stunt ACT; CRAMP; DEED; DEFORM; FEAT; STIFLE; TRICK; ■ ESCAPADE; EXPLOIT
stupefy NUMB
stupefied PUNCHY
stupefied, more NUMBER
stupid CRASS; DENSE; DIM; DULL; DUMB; NUTS; SILLY; THICK; LOOPY; ■ IDIOTIC; INANE; INSANE; POINTLESS; anagram indicator
stupid person ASS; CLOT; DOLT; DRIP; DUNCE; MUG; MUTT; OAF; PRAT; TWIT; ■ BERK; JERK; PUDDING
stupid talk ROT; *see* RUBBISH

stupidly anagram indicator
stupor, in a state of OUT
sturdy FIRM; HARDY; SOLID; STABLE; STOCKY
stutter STAMMER; *see* STUTTERING; letter to be repeated
stuttered opening a word given the appearance of a stutter can be an attempt to disguise the simple use of a letter, as "It is a f-feat to tell the truth" → FACT (i.e. F-ACT). But it can get more complicated. Consider "Have recourse to a r-ring" (6). Here we are required to think of a word meaning "ring" such that when we repeat its opening letter (as in a stutter) we arrive at a word meaning "Have recourse (to)". This is satisfied by APPEAL (i.e. A-P-PEAL)
stuttering a letter to be repeated, usually the first, as in "A habit of stuttering, get one inured to" → ACCUSTOM where the first letter of "custom" is repeated
sty PEN
style CUT; DASH; FLAIR; GRAVER; MANNER; METHOD; MODE; NAME; TAG; TERM; TITLE; TON; TONE; WAY; ■ ALA (i.e. "a la" as in "Northern-style fellow" → ALAN); ATTIC; DESIGN; ELAN; GENRE; PANACHE; TOUCH; TREND; anagram indicator; can require a specific name, as "Style of house" calls for TUDOR
style, Classical ATTIC; DORIC; IONIC
style, in HIP
style of, in the anagram indicator
style, with *see* STYLISH
styled anagram indicator
stylish CHIC; CLASSY; FLASH; HIP; IN; SMART; SWISH; U; ■ GOOD; POSH
stylishness CHIC; FLAIR
stylite [◊ PILLAR; POLE]
suave SMOOTH

sub ADVANCE; [◊ BELOW; UNDER]
subdivide QUARTER
subdivision DEPT; PART
sub-machine gun UZI
subdue COW; MUTE; QUELL; TAME; ■ QUENCH
subdued LOW; QUIET
subject ISSUE; MATTER; THEME; TOPIC; ■ NATIONAL
subject matter CONTENT
subject of/on the ABOUT; RE; *see* CONCERNING
subject, school RE
subject to LIABLE; ST; UNDER
subject to investigation CASE
subjected to UNDER
subjective CASE
sublime LOFTY; ■ AUGUST; PERFECT
submarine FISH; ■ U-BOAT
submariner NEMO
submerge SINK; nesting indicator
submerged UNDER
submission ENTRY
submission, make a *see* SUBMIT
submissive GENTLE; MEEK
submit CEDE; DEFER; ENTER; RESIGN; TABLE; YIELD
submit to ENDURE
subordinate BELOW; LOWER; SIDE (as a side issue); UNDER; ■ JUNIOR; SECOND; can indicate that one element should follow another
subordinate situation MINOR
subscribe SIGN
subscription SUB; can indicate something added to the foot of text e.g. signature
subsequent AFTER; LATER; NEXT; SECOND; can indicate one element should follow another; can indicate a word beginning with RE
subsequently AFTER; LATER; NEXT; THEN; ■ SINCE; can indicate one element should follow another
subservience, show BOW
subservient UNDER

subside DIE; ■ ABATE
subsidiary route BROAD (i.e. B-road)
subsidence SAG
subsidy GRANT
substance CONTENT; GIST; MATTER; MIST; *see* POINT
substandard POOR
substantial BIG; FAT; HIGH; MAIN; REAL; ■ TIDY, as in a tidy sum
substitute LOCUM; RESERVE; SUB; SWITCH; ■ ERSATZ; PROXY; STANDIN; anagram indicator; can indicate that one letter has to be changed for another
subterfuge RUSE; TRICK; ■ DODGE; DECEPTION
subtle NICE; SOFT ■ DRY (as in humour); anagram indicator
subtle emanation AURA
subtly anagram indicator
subtract DEDUCT
suburb KEW
succeed ENSUE; FOLLOW; PASS; WIN; ■ PROSPER; REPLACE
succeed, didn't FAILED; LOST
succeed, do not FAIL
succeed in examination PASS
succeed, one about to HEIR
succeeded S; WON
succeeded, not having LOST; S to be omitted
succeeded in DID
success COUP; GO; HIT; UP; WIN; WINNER; ■ GAIN; VICTORY
success, achieve ARRIVE; WIN
success, exam PASS
success in snooker POT
success in theatre HIT; RUN
success, period of BOOM; UP
successful GOING; MADE
successful action COUP; WIN
successful, are/be WIN; WORK
successful, likely to be ON
successful record HIT
successful, was WON; ■ PASSED
successfully WELL

succession LINE; ■ SEQUENCE

successor HEIR; can indicate a word that often follows another (for example, as "Ben's successor" clues NEVIS)

succinct PITHY; SHORT; ■ CURT; TERSE

succour AID; HELP (qv); RELIEF

succulent AGAVE; SWEET

succumb FALL

such SO; THOSE; THUS

such French TEL

sucker DUPE; GULL; SAP; SHOOT; STRAW; SWEET; ■ DUMMY; LOLLIPOP; *see* FOOL

sudden NEW; RAPID; SNAP

sudden blow SQUALL

sudden influx SURGE

sudden move LUNGE

suddenly put down PLONK

suds FROTH

sue BEG; CHARGE; PLEAD

suede KID

suffer ACHE; AIL; BEAR; DIE; HAVE; STAND

suffer on stage DIE

suffered LET; anagram indicator

sufferer JOB

suffering ACHING; HELL; NEEDY; PAIN; ■ ACHE; HURT; anagram indicator

suffering cut last letter to be omitted

suffering injury anagram indicator

suffering, man JOB

suffering, source of SCOURGE

suffers anagram indicator

sufficient AMPLE; FULL; PAT

sufficient, are RUNTO (i.e. run to)

sufficient, barely SCANT

sufficient, were RANTO (i.e. ran to)

Suffolk can indicate something to do with sheep (e.g. ram, lamb)

suffrage VOTE

sugar BEAT; CANE; CASTER

sugar-coated ICED

sugar crop CANE

sugar preparation ICING

sugary SWEET

suggest HINT; IMPLY; POSE; RAISE; ■ POSIT

suggestion CLUE; HINT; IDEA; SMACK; TRACE; TIP; ■ IMPLICATION; INNUENDO; THOUGHT

suggestion of initial letter indicator

suggestive RACY

suggestive gesture WINK

suggestive question, put LEAD

suit ACTION; BEFIT; CASE; DO; ETON; FIT; FLATTER; KIT; MATCH; PLEA; PLEASE; TRUMPS; ■ BECOME; CLOTHING; PETITION; UNIFORM; can refer to a card suit CLUB, DIAMOND, HEART, SPADE (singular or plural); can indicate something to do with courtship e.g. beau, valentine; [◊ CLOTH; LOUNGE; TAILOR]

suit, more powerful TRUMP

suit, not follow REVOKE

suit, old type of ZOOT

suitable APT; DUE; FIT; ON; PAT; ■ APPROPRIATE; CONVENIENT; FITTING; MEET; PROPER

suitable, made anagram indicator

suitable, more APTER; FITTER

suitable place NICHE

suitable to FOR

suitably WELL

suited FOR

suited, not CASUAL

suitor RIVAL; SWAIN

sulk BROOD; PET; POUT

sulky, look POUT

sullen DOUR; MOODY

sullen, look POUT

sullied anagram indicator

sulphur S

sultanate OMAN

sultry HOT

sum ADD; BID; COUNT; TOTAL; ■ AMOUNT; FIGURE

sum, big POT

sum owed DEBIT; DEBT; [◊ IOU]

sum up MUS

summarise PRECIS

summary DIGEST; PRECIS; RESUME; REVIEW

summary, short SUM; *see* SUMMARY

summate ADD

summer ADDER; SEASON; TIME; can indicate something to do with accountancy, calculation, adding machine, etc

summer in France/Provence ETE

summer on the Continent ETE

summerhouse GAZEBO

summertime JUL; JUN; AUG

summit APEX; CAP; HEIGHT; PEAK; TIP; TOP; ■ ACME

summon BRING; CALL; CITE; GONG; PAGE; ■ CONVENE; EVOKE

summon loudly GONG

summon up BRING; CALL; in a DC can signify a rev. e.g. ETIC, LLAC

summonsed SUED; ■ PAGED

Sumo BASHO

sumptuous LAVISH; LUSH; RICH; ■ PALATIAL

sun BASK; RA; S; SOL; STAR ■ SETTER; TANNER

Sun PAPER

sun-burn TAN

sun god RA

sun hat TOPI

sun, lie in the *see* SUNBATHE

sun out UNS

sun-rise NUS

sun-set anagram of SUN

sunbathe BASK; TAN

sunblind AWNING

sunburn TAN

sunburnt BROWN; RED; ■ PEELING; TANNED

Sunday S; SUN; WHIT

Sunday dinner, traditional ROAST

Sunday School SS

sunder CLEAVE; PART

sundial TIMER

sundry DIVERS

sunk DOWN; GONE; nesting indicator

sunk in, to be nesting indicator

sunny BRIGHT

sunrise DAWN; NUS; RA; [◊ EAST]

sunscreen VISOR

sunshine, little RAY

Suomi FINNISH

sup DRINK; EAT

super ACE; FAB; GRAND; MEGA

supercilious SNIFFY

superficial SHALLOW; ■ FACILE

superficial brilliance GLOSS

superficially initial letter(s) indicator

superfluity GLUT

superfluous EXTRA; OVER; ■ TOO

superintend DIRECT: RUN

superior A; ABOVE; ARCH; BEST; BETTER; CINC (i.e. C-in-C); ELDER; FINER; HIGH; OVER; PRIOR; TOP; U; UP; UPPER; ■ HIGHER; PLUM; *see* CHIEF; can indicate that one component should precede another; with capital letter can refer to the lake of the same name; reversal indicator

superior position TOP; can refer to something that is physically high (crow's nest or maintop on a ship for example)

superior, sound HIRE

superior type GENT

superlatively can indicate a superlative adjective (i.e. ending in EST)

Superman HERO

Superman's girlfriend LOIS

supernatural being ELEMENTAL; *see* GOD

supernatural creature TROLL

superpower US

superstar IDOL

supervise DIRECT; RUN

supervised by UNDER

supervising OVER

supine PRONE

supper EATER

supplant OUST

supple LITHE; anagram indicator

supplement ADD; BACK; EKE; ■ ADDITION; ADDITIVE; INSERT; EXTRA

supplemental EXTRA

supplicate PRAY

supplication PLEA; PRAYER; ■ ORISON; ROGATION

supplied FED; GAVE; IN; ■ GIVEN

supplier CO; SOURCE

supplier, nautical CHANDLER

suppliers anagram indicator

supplies KIT

supply CATER; ENDUE; EQUIP; FEED; FILL; FIND; PIPE; STOCKING; RATION; STOCK; ■ AMOUNT; FUND; HOARD; PROVIDE; PROVISION; anagram indicator; note this has two pronunciations and therefore two meanings, one to do with "stock" and the other meaning "lithely"

supply food CATER

supply of drink WELL

supply, in short LOW

supply, shared POOL

supply ship TENDER

supply with capital BACK; FUND

supplying, keep PLY

support AID; ARCH; BACK; BASE; BEAM; BEAR; BRA; BRACE; EASEL; FAVOUR; FOOT; FUND; GUY; HAND; LEG; PIER; POST; PROP; RACK; RAIL; REST; ROCK; ROOST; RUNG; SIDE; SHORE; SLING; SPINE; STAGE; STAY; STEM; STICK (as in candle-stick); STRUT; TEE; TRAY; WALL; ■ ARMREST; ASSIST; BACKING; BOLSTER; BRACING; COLUMN; ENDORSE: GANTRY; HELP; MAINTAIN; SECOND; SLEEPER; SPONSOR; SUSTAIN; TRESTLE; TRUSS; can indicate one element is to follow another; can indicate that an element is to be placed at the end

support for education GRANT

support of, in FOR; PRO

support, give AID; BRACE; ■ HELP

support, providing BRACING

support, show ROOT

support, strong ROCK

support structure ARCH

support, without ALONE

supported by ON; in a Down clue can indicate that the word or component following is to be placed at the end

supporter AID; ALLY; ANGEL; BRA; BRACE; BRACKET; BUFF; EASEL; FAN; FRIEND; HORSE; LEG; POST; RAFTER; REST (as in headrest); STAY; STRAP; TEE; ■ ADHERENT; STADDLE' TABLE; TRAY

supporter, new CONVERT

supporter of art EASEL

supporters, royal COURT

supporting, supportive FOR; ON; PRO; can indicate that one component comes behind another

supports can mean the preceding component comes second to the one that follows in the clue

suppose GUESS; OPINE; PRESUME

supreme ARCH; BEST; FIRST; MAIN; TOP

supreme commander CINC (i.e. C-in-C)

supreme happiness HEAVEN

supreme quality TOPS; *see* BEST

supremo BOSS; *see* CHIEF

suppress CHOKE; nesting indicator, as "to suppress" implies a component is to be "suppressed" by others

suppressed nesting indicator

sure CLEAR; BOUND; FIXED; SAFE; STABLE; YES; ■ CONFIDENT; POSITIVE

sure, be BET

sure-fire CERT

sure, for a poet it's TWILL

sure, make CLINCH

sure thing CERT

surely REALLY; ■ CERTES

surety PAWN
surf WAVES
surface COAT; COVER; RISE; TABLE; TOP; initial letter indicator; reversal indicator
surface, flat TABLE
surface, on the OUTSIDE
surfaces reversal indicator
surfacing COAT; RISING; reversal indicator
surfacing material MACADAM
surfeit CLOY; GLUT
surfeited BLASE
surge FLOOD; FLOW; PRESS; RUSH; SWELL; WELL
surgeon BS; LISTER; VET
surgeon, type of ENT
surgery OP; OPS; anagram indicator
surgery, result of SCAR
surgical instrument LANCET; PROBE
surgical procedure OP
surly GRUFF; ■ CRABBED; GRUMPY
surpass CAP; TOP
surplus EXTRA; OVER
surplus, without LEAN; SPARE
surprise AMAZE; START; STARTLE; STUN; ■ ASTONISH; TWIST; WONDER
surprise, by ABACK
surprise, cry/expression of BOY; COR; GEE; GOD; HA; MY; OH; OO
surprisingly anagram indicator
surrealist DALI
surrender CEDE; FALL; FORGO; GIVE; YIELD; ■ GIVING; RENOUNCE; omission indicator
surrender a A to be omitted
surreptitious movement STEALTH
surround RING
surrounded AMID
surrounding(s) nesting indicator
Surrey SY
Surrey location ESHER
survey EYE; POLL; SCAN; SEE; VIEW; ■ BROWSE; CENSUS; REVIEW; WATCH

surveyor EYE; can refer to a particular mountain
survive LAST; LIVE; ■ ENDURE; EXIST; WEATHER
survive, likely to FIT
survive about DEVIL (i.e. rev.)
suspect FISHY; IFFY; anagram indicator
suspected anagram indicator
suspend DANGLE; HANG; HOVER; STRING
suspended HUNG; SLUNG; STRUNG; ■ DANGLED; ONICE (i.e. on ice)
suspended, be HANG
suspense, be in HANG; HOVER
suspense, in ONICE (i.e. on ice)
suspension STAY
suspicion HINT; SUS; TRACE
suspicion, with anagram indicator
suspicious FISHY; WARY
Sussex can refer to a breed of cow as well as the county
Sussex town RYE
sustain AFFORD; *see* SUPPORT
sustained BORE; LONG
sustenance, take DINE; EAT; FEED
sustenance, provided FED
swab MOB
swag LOOT; PLUNDER
swagger BLUSTER; PRANCE; STRUT; SWANK
Swahili* BANTU
swallow DOWN; EAT; GULP; SIP; SWIG; TAKE; ■ MARTIN; nesting indicator
swallow, prepare to CHEW
swallowed ATE; EATEN; *see* EAT, SWALLOW; nesting indicator
swallowed by nesting indicator
swallowed, things FOOD
swallowing DOWNING; EATING; nesting indicator
swamp BOG; DROWN; ENGULF; MARSH
swan COB; PEN
Swan of Avon BARD; BILL; WILL; usually indicates something to do with Shakespeare

swanning about anagram indicator

swap DEAL; CHANGE; TRADE; ■ EXCHANGE; can indicate letters or components are to be changed over

swapped can indicate letters or components are to be changed over

sward GRASS; TURF

swarm ABOUND; HORDE; anagram indicator

swarming anagram indicator

swat KILL; SMACK; STRIKE; anagram indicator; *see* HIT

swatch SAMPLE

sway HEEL; REIGN; ROCK; SWING; TOTTER

swaying anagram indicator

swear BLAST; CURSE; CUSS; VOW; ■ ABUSE; ATTEST

swear-word OATH

swearing ABUSING

swearword CUSS

sweat LATHER; SPOT; STEW

sweater KNIT; POLO

Swede SVEN

Sweden S

Swedish chap LARS

Swedish product VOLVO

sweep BRUSH; CLEAN; OAR; RANGE

sweep away anagram indicator

sweeper BACK; BROOM; BRUSH

sweeping HUGE; VAST

sweet AFTERS; CANDY; CHOC; COMFIT; CUTE; DROP; GUM; HONEY; ICE; KISS; LOLLY; MINT; PUD; ROCK; TART; ■ LIQUORICE; MOUSSE; PRETTY; PUDDING; WINNING; can indicate something to do with revenge; *see* DESSERT

sweet, cold ICE

sweet course PUD; TART

sweet, not BITTER; DRY; TART

sweet, not so DRIER

sweet sauce TOPPING

sweet, sentimentally TWEE

sweet souvenir ROCK

sweet stick ROCK

sweetener BRIBE; BUNG

sweeter, become MELLOW

sweetheart E; FLAME; LOVE; LOVER; PET; ■ DONA; SUGAR

sweetheart, former/old LEMAN

sweetie DEAR; FRUIT; LOVE

sweetness HONEY

sweets AFTERS; ICES; TUCK; *see* SWEET

swell BLOAT; FOP; NOB; PAD; RISE; ROLL; ROLLER; SEA; SURGE; TOFF; ■ ENLARGE; EXPAND; HEAVE

swelling BOIL; BUNION; LUMP; NODE; TUBER

sweltering TROPICAL (qv)

swerve YAW; ■ DEFLECT; WARP

swift BIRD; FAST; FLEET; NIPPY; QUICK

Swift can indicate something from the writings of Dean Swift e.g. Gulliver, Lilliput, yahoo

Swift alias for Esther STELLA

swilling anagram indicator

swim BATHE; CRAWL; DIP

swim, quick DIP

swimmer LEANDER (myth.); can indicate a fish or other aquatic animal e.g. OTTER *see* FISH

swimmer's assistant FIN

swimmer, young ELVER

swimmers, group of SCHOOL

swimmers, like GILLED

swimmers, lots of SCHOOL(S)

swimming anagram indicator

swimming pool LIDO

swimming-stroke BREAST; CRAWL

swindle CHEAT; CLIP; CON; DO; GYP; RAMP; RICK; ROB; ROOK; SCAM (qv); SKIN; STING; ■ DOCTOR; FIDDLE; FLEECE; FRAUD; NOBBLE

swindled BITTEN; DID; DONE; HAD; STUNG; ■ CHEATED; CONNED; STUNG

swindler CON: CROOK; FRAUD; KNAVE; ROGUE; ROOK; SHARK; SHARP

swine BOAR; CAD; HEEL; HOG; PIG; RAT; ■ SOUNDER

swine's food SWILL

swing GO; HANG; LILT; LURCH; SLEW; SWAY

swing wildly FLAIL

swingeing SEVERE

swinger can refer to a hangman, particularly an infamous one (as "old swinger" → JACK KETCH)

swinging HIP; SWAYING; anagram indicator

swings and roundabouts FAIR

swipe BELT; HIT; LIFT; NICK; PINCH; STEAL

swipes BEER

swirl EDDY; SPIN; anagram indicator

swirled EDDIED

swirling anagram indicator

swish CHIC; SMART; anagram indicator

Swiss capital BERN

Swiss hero TELL

Swiss mountain RIGI

Swiss subdivision CANTON

Swiss toboggan LUGE

switch BEAT; CANE; HAIR; LASH; ROD; SHOOT; STICK; TRESS; TURN; TWIG; ■ CHANGE; TOGGLE; anagram indicator; reversal indicator; can indicate that a letter has to be moved, the role it performs in "End, switch south for wood" to change LAST to the answer SLAT

switch on START; can indicate an anagram which includes ON

switched, switching anagram indicator; reversal indicator

switches, subject to extreme first and last letters to be interchanged

Switzerland CH

swivel SWING

swivel camera PAN

swivelling, swivels reverse indicator

swoon FAINT

swoop RAID

sword BLADE; EPEE; FOIL; SABRE; STEEL

sword-fighter FENCER

sword, use FENCE

swore VOWED

swot CRAM

sycophant TOADY

Sybil's husband BASIL

Sykes BILL

symbol BADGE; CROWN; FLAG; LETTER; LION; LOGO; MACE; ORB; SIGN; STAR; TOKEN; TOTEM

symbol of innocence LAMB

symbol of nationhood FLAG

symbol of office BADGE; CROWN; MACE; ROBE

symbol of life ANKH

symbol of rank STAR

symmetry ORDER

sympathetic gesture HUG

sympathetic word THERE

sympathy, expression of THERE

symphony FIFTH

syncopated music RAG

syncopating anagram indicator

syndicate GROUP; RING; ■ ALLIANCE

★ **synonym** a word that has the same or similar meaning to another, say "match" and "game". However crafty compilers will often choose pairs which are synonymous only in very particular settings. For example "tall" and "high" may be obvious synonyms when applied to a building where both have their more common meanings. But could "tall" be synonymous with "weak"? Well yes, in the instance where it is applied to a flimsy excuse, which may be called a "tall story" or a "weak story". So be on the look-out for such distant synonyms.

synthesise anagram indicator

synthetic, synthesized anagram indicator

syringe HYPO

system BODY; FORM; GROUP; METHOD; NET; ORDER; SET; WAY

system of belief CREED

Tt

T-junction T; can indicate something to do with hyphen

T-shirt TOP; can indicate something to do with hyphen

T, we hear TEA; TEE

tab BILL; FLAP; ■ LABEL; STRIP; TAG

tabby CAT

table BOARD; CHART; CLASS; DESK; FARE; LIST; MENU; ROLL; ROTA; ■ COUNTER; ROSTER; [◊ EAT; EATING]

table mat DOILY

tableau SCENE

tables NEST

tablet PILL; SLAB; ■ PLAQUE

tabloid MIRROR; SUN

tache CLASP

tacit agreement NOD

tack FOOD; HOOK; NAIL; PIN; ROPE; SEW; SHEER; STUD; VEER; WIRE; ■ BASTE; BUCKLE; COURSE; STITCH; can indicate something to do with saddlery

tack, some BIT; GIRTH; SADDLE

tackle FACE; GEAR; HANDLE; HARNESS; KIT; TRY; ■ BURTON

tacky CHEESY; GUMMY; STICKY; anagram indicator; can indicate something to do with nails

tacky, something GUM

tactic PLOY; ■ FINESSE

tactless, be OFFEND

tactless remark GAFFE

tad BIT

tag BADGE; LABEL; NAME; TAB; ■ AGLET

tail BACK; BRUSH; CHASE; DOCK; DOG; END; SCUT; STERN; ■ PURSUE; can indicate that the end of a word (maybe several letters but usually the last letter only) is to be used or omitted

tail, fox-hound's STERN

tail, lacking last letter to be omitted

tail, moving last letter to be omitted and re-inserted earlier in the word

tail of dart FLIGHT

tail off TAPER; last letter to be omitted

tail-piece CODA; PS; RIDER

tail snapped last letter to be omitted

tail, turning last two letters to be interchanged

tailless last letter to be omitted as "tailless rabbit" → TAL (i.e. less last letter from "talk")

tailor FIT; STYLE; ■ ADAPT; GEAR; anagram indicator

tails ENDS; *see* TAIL; [◊ HEADS]

taint BRAND; DEFILE; MAR; STAIN; *see* SMEAR

tainted anagram indicator

take BAG; CHARM; CUT; DRAW; EAT; FILCH; GRAB; GRASP; HACK; HAVE; HOOK; NET; NICK; RIDE; SEIZE; STEAL; TRAP; USE; WIN; ■ CATCH; WREST; *see* OPINION; as an instruction can cue DO

take a little SAMPLE; TASTE

take aback START

take action ACT; SUE

take advantage of ABUSE; USE

take another course TACK

take away MINUS; REMOVE

take back RESUME; ■ RECLAIM; can indicator the reverse of a synonym for "take", hence GAB, TEN, *see* TAKE

take by surprise AMBUSH

take care of GUARD; MIND; TEND

take catch LAND

take courses DINE; EAT

take, don't LEAVE

take exam SIT

take five BREAK; REST

take food EAT

take full account of APPRECIATE

take heed of NOTE; ■ NOTICE (qv)

take hold GRASP; GRIP

take home EARN; NET (as in take home pay)

take in CHEAT; CON; DUPE; EAT; GULL; REEF; ■ AGIST; EMBRACE; INHALE; *see* DECEIVE

take it easy REST

take journey RIDE

take meeting CHAIR; PRESIDE

take off APE; COPY; DOCK; DROP; FLY; JUMP; SHED; SKIT; STRIP; ■ IMITATE; REMOVE

take off, don't allow to GROUND

take-off, emergency SCRAMBLE

take-off, move before TAXI

take on FACE; HIRE; PLAY; ■ SHOULDER

take out DATE; DELETE; DRAW; KILL; SLAY; ■ DELETE; EXTRACT; OMIT; REMOVE

take over anagram of TAKE; a synonym of "take" to be reversed leading to WARD, TEN etc

take part ENTER; SIDE

take pictures SNAP

take place as shorthand for "take the place of" can signify substitute, relieve etc

take pleasure WALLOW

take position STAND

take responsibility CARRY

take steps DANCE

take stock RUSTLE

take time off BREAK; IDLE; LAZE; REST; T to be omitted

take to task RATE

take to the air FLY (qv)

take to the cleaners CHEAT (qv)

take turns STROLL; WALK

take up a synonym for "take" to be reversed e.g. BARG

taken GOT; ■ CHARMED; STOLEN

taken advantage of USED

taken apart anagram indicator

taken by run indicator

taken in EATEN; nesting indicator

taken in hand LED

taken in, that can be EDIBLE

takes nesting indicator

takes off APES; SKATE (anag.)

takes on ON to be nested within a word or component

taken outside nesting indicator

taking CUTE; anagram indicator

taking a spin anagram indicator

taking foot off FT to be omitted

taking half a day off omission of SUN, MON etc

taking off FLYING; SKIT

taking in nesting indicator

taking place ON

taking regularly, is ISON (i.e. is on)

taking time T to be included (usually at end)

taking time off T, or some synonym for time (qv), to be omitted

tale FABLE; LIE; MYTH; SAGA; STORY; YARN; ■ CONTE

tale-teller, Shakespearian ELIA

talent ART; FLAIR; SKILL; T; ■ ABILITY; BENT; GIFT; KNACK

talent, showing ABLE (qv)

talent, with some WELL; *see* ABLE

talented ABLE (qv); GOOD

tales, told SANG

talisman CHARM

talk BABBLE; BAITER; CHAT; GAB; GAS; JAW; LINGO; ORATE; PATTER; PRATE; RABBIT; RAP; RATTLE; SPEAK; ■ CHATTER; DISCOURSE; EXPRESS; GABBLE; NATTER; PARLEY; PRATTLE; SPEECH; SPOUT;

YABBER; YAMMER; homophone indicator; can indicate a particular language, either national or jargon e.g. legalese

talk about homophone indicator as "talk about a queue" → ALIGN; a synonym for "talk" to be reversed (e.g. BAG); a component to be nested within a synonym for "talk" (as "I talk about" → PIRATE)

talk affectedly MINCE

talk big BOAST; CROW

talk boringly DRONE

talk, empty GAS; WIND; *see* RUBBISH

talk endlessly PRATE; SPEA (i.e. "speak" minus last letter); TAL (i.e. "talk" minus last letter)

talk foolishly PRATE

talk, glib CANT; PATTER; PITCH; SPIEL

talk, idle CHATTER; GAS; ■ INFORMAL

talk idly CHATTER; GAS; NATTER; PRATE; PRATTLE

talk incoherently RAMBLE

talk, insincere CANT

talk madly RAVE

talk rubbish JABBER; PRATE; PRATTLE; SPOUT; WAFFLE

talk, sales PITCH

talk softly PANT ■ WHISPER

talk wildly RANT; RAVE

talked big CREW

talked of homophone indicator

talkies, in the homophone indicator

talking ORAL; homophone indicator, as "Politician's talking horse" → MAYOR

talks, in homophone indicator

tall BIG; HIGH; LOFTY; LONG; ■ LANKY; STRAPPING

tall structure TOWER

tallow FAT

tally LABEL; MATCH

talon CLAW; RAPTOR

tam CAP; HAT

tame FLAT; MASTER; TRAIN

tamp PACK

tamper FIDDLE

tamper with FIX; RIG

tampered with anagram indicator

Tamworth PIG

Tamworth residence STY

tan BAKE; BEAT; BROWN; THRASH; ■ BRONZE; SOAK; WALLOP

tang BITE; SMACK; ■ SAVOUR

tangible REAL

tangle KNOT; MESS; RAVEL; anagram indicator; can refer to seaweed (e.g. oarweed, oreweed)

tangle with two or more words to be used in anagram

tangled anagram indicator

tank VAT

tank, type of SEPTIC

tankard POT

tanker OILER; OILSS (i.e. oil SS)

tanks ARMOURY

tanned BROWN; BURNT; RUDDY; anagram indicator

tanned, excessively BURNT

tanner SUN

tantalise TEASE

tantalum TA

tantrum FIT; PET; *see* TEMPER

tap BUG; C; COLD; H; HOT; PAT; ■ KNOCK

tape BIND; RECORD; STRAP; STRIP

tape, decorative BRAID

tape recorder STEREO

taped BOUND

taper LIGHT; NARROW

tapering utensil FUNNEL

tapestry ARRAS

taps, a couple of ACH; CH

tar AB; PAY (with regard to a boat); PITCH; TAR; *see* SAILOR

tardy LATE; SLOW

target AIM; BULL; END; GAME (as in "fair game"); GOAL; HOME; INNER; MARK; OUTER; TEE

target area RANGE

target, part of BULL; INNER; OUTER

targeted child IT (i.e. in game of tag)

targets BUTTS

tariff LIST

Tarka OTTER

tarn LAKE

tarnish STAIN (qv)

Tarot suit SWORDS

tarred PITCHED

tarry LINGER; STALL; STAY; STICKY; WAIT; ■ DELAY

tart ACID; FLAN; HARLOT; PIE; SHARP; SWEET; SOUR ■ SLUT; TORTE

tartan PLAID

Tarter ruler KHAN

tartar sauce [◊ CAPER (*ingredient*)]

task CHORE; TASK; ■ MISSION; PROJECT; ROLE; *see* JOB

task not done OMISSION

task, tiring FAG

task, wearisome CHORE; FAG

taste DROP; FLAVOUR; LICK; NIP; SAMPLE; SIP; SMACK; TANG; TRY

taste in music EAR

taste, with CHIC; ■ SAPID; SEASONED

tasteless BLAND; TACKY; ■ GARISH; WATERY

tasteless material TACK

Tatar wagon ARBA

tatter RAG

tattered anagram indicator

tattle PRATE

tatty FRAYED; SCRUFFY; anagram indicator

tatty work LACE

Tatum ART

taunt DIG; JEST; MOCK; RIB; SCOFF; TEASE; TWIT; WIG; ■ DERIDE; JEER

taut TENSE

taut, not LOOSE; SLACK

tautological, tautology can indicate that a word (or its synonym) is to be repeated to give solutions such as THAT'S THAT, TUT-TUT, HOT-SHOT

tavern BAR; INN; PUB

tawdry GAUDY

tawdry stuff TAT

tax CESS; CUSTOM; DRAIN; DUTY; PAYE; RATE; RATES; SCOT; STRAIN; STRESS; TEST; TITHE; TOLL; VAT; ■ EXCISE; LEVY; STRETCH

tax, commodity EXCISE

tax returns TAV

tax, sort of POLL

taxation RATES

taxi CAB; can indicate something to do with aircraft taking off; [◊ RANK, RUNWAY; STAND]

taxi-driver CABBY

taxi, where you'll find STAND

taxidermist SKINNER

taxing IMPOSING; STRAIN

tea CHA; CHAR; MEAL; ■ CHINA; GREEN; NETTLE; ROSIE

tea-break anagram of TEA; TEA (or CHA) to be nested

tea-dance anagram of TEA

tea-party, one at the HATTER

tea-maker URN

tea-time treat SCONE

teach TRAIN; ■ GUIDE; *see* TRAIN

teach, easy to CLEVER

teacher BEAK; DON; HEAD; MASTER; MISS; PROF; RABBI; SIR; TUTOR; ■ COACH; GURU; MENTOR; MISTRESS

teacher, female MISS

teacher, job for a CHAIR

teacher, leading HEAD

teacher, old USHER

teacher, top HEAD; T

teachers NUT; STAFF; *see* TEACHER

teaching CLASS; LESSON; RI; ■ COURSE; TUITION

teaching qualification BED

teaching union NUT

teacup [◊ BREW; LEAVES; STORM]

team BAND; CREW; GROUP; PANEL; SIDE; SQUAD; STAFF; XI; ■ COLOUR; GANG; SECTION; *see* TEAM, FOOTBALL

team, football FOREST; ORIENT; VILLA

team leader T

team, less than a full TEN

team, put out a PLAY

team up with JOIN; ■ CONJOIN

teamaker URN

teamed up ALLIED

teamster DRIVER

tear DROP; GASH; REND; RENT; RIP; RIVE; RUN; SNAG; SPEED; ■ BOLT

tear-jerker MACE; ■ ONION

tear off CAREER

tearful WATERY

tears anagram indicator

tears, affected by MOIST

tease BAIT; GUY; KID; RAG; RIB; TWIT; ■ CHAFF; SPLIT; [◊ STRIP]; sounding like T's this word can, with a homophone indicator, refer to TT as in "We hear torment in the account – but that's just idle talk" → TATTLE (i.e. TA-TT-LE)

teased RAGGED

teashop CAFE

teasing ARCH; RIBBING

teatime FOUR; IV

technique ART; MODE; STYLE; TOUCH; TRICK; WAY;

technology IT

technology institute MIT

teddy bear TOY

tedious DRY; DULL; FLAT; LONG; ■ BORING; DRAGGING; WEARING; VAPID

tedious, be BORE; DRAG; WEAR

tedious, become PALL

tedious procedure CHORE; RUT

tedious speech SCREED

tedious task, work BIND; CHORE; DRUDGE; FAG; GRIND; STRAIN; SWEAT; TOIL; ■ DRUDGERY; LABOUR

tedious to hear, was BOARD

tedious type BORE

tee PEG; T; STAND

tee, hit off the DRIVE

teem ABOUND

teenage rebel TED

teenager MOD; ROCKER; TED; YOUTH

teenager once (1960s) MOD; *see* TEENAGER

teeter YAW

teetering anagram indicator

teeth FORCE; POWER; SET

teeth, bare GRIN

teeth, preparation for PASTE

teeth, use your BITE; CHAMP; CHEW

teeth, used BIT

teetotal DRY; TT

tele FAR; *see* TELEVISION, TV

telegram CABLE; WIRE

telepathy ESP

telephone CALL; RING; TEL

telephone usage CALLING; RINGING

telephone, use CALL; RING

television BOX; CABLE; SET; TELLY; TUBE; TV; ■ DIGITAL; SCREEN; *see* TV *and the entries below under* TELEVISION

television regulator ITC

television supplier BBC; CABLE; SKY

tell ORDER; SAY; ■ COUNT; GRASS; INFORM; RECOUNT; RELATE; REPORT; RETAIL; SNITCH

Tell ARCHER; SWISS

tell-off RATE; SCOLD (qv)

tell one to DIRECT; ORDER

tell tales LIE; WRITE

tell the tale LIE

Tell, William ARCHER; SWISS

telling RELATION; homophone indicator

telling all FRANK

telltale SNEAK

telly BOX; *see* TELEVISION, TV

temerity FRONT

temper ANGER; BATE; HUFF; INURE; IRISH; MOOD; PET; RAGE; SEASON; TONE; TUNE; ■ DANDER

temper, bad SPLEEN

temper, hit by someone in a ROOF

temper, in bad CRABBY

temper, display of PADDY; RAGE

temper, public display of SCENE

temperament BLOOD; MOOD

temperamental MOODY

temperature C; F; T; ■ HEAT

temperature having changed interchange letters H and C

temperature, running a high HOT

tempest STORM

tempestuous WINDY; anagram indicator

tempestuous character PROSPERO

temple FANE; can indicate something to do with the forehead; ■ CHURCH; SHRINE

tempo PACE; RATE; TIME

temporary ACTING; ■ LOCUM; PASSING

temporary accommodation CAMP; TENT; ■ LODGING

temporary cover TENT

temporary provision LOAN

temporary settlement CAMP

temporary shelter BOOTH; TENT

temporary worker TEMP; ■ LOCUM; TRANSIENT

temporise STALL

tempt DRAW; EGG; LURE; ■ SEDUCE

temptation LURE

tempting item APPLE

temptress SIREN

ten X; ■ IO

ten cents DIME

$10 TEND (i.e. ten D)

ten-dollar coin EAGLE

ten in Roman numerals CROSS; X

ten percent TITHE; ■ DECI

ten, under IX; NINE

ten years DECADE; can indicate a specific decade (e.g. EIGHTIES

which can be used to build up WEIGHTIEST)

tenancy LEASE

tenancy, arrange LEASE; LET

tenant LEASER

tenant's agreement LEASE

tenant, time as LEASE; LET

tend CARE; LEAN; MIND; NURSE; SERVE ■ KNACK

tendency BENT; DRIFT; LEANING; TREND; VEIN

tendency, natural STRAIN

tender BID; OFFER; PUT; READY; SORE; SOFT; TRUCK; ■ DOUGH; NURSE; QUEASY; in the sense of "one who tends" can indicate a shepherd, swineherd etc; can refer to money, *see* CASH, MONEY, CURRENCY; can indicate something to do with a railway

tender skin CORN

tending PRONE

tending to leave out OMISSIVE

tendon SINEW

tenet BELIEF

tenfold, increased L to be changed to D

tenner NOTE

tennis GAME; SPORT; [◊ COURT; LAWN; SERVE; SET]

tennis champ BORG

tennis decision LET; NET; OUT

tennis facility COURT

tennis fixture NET

tennis, form of REALM

tennis, game(s) of SET; SETS; ■ DOUBLES

tennis player SERVER

tennis serve ACE

tennis, some SET; SETS

tennis star SEED

tennis, start game of SERVE

Tennyson poem MAUD

tenor COURSE; SINGER; TONE; ■ CARUSO; THEME

tense BRACE; DRAWN; PAST; T; TAUT; TIGHT; ■ FUTURE; PERFECT

tense situation DRAMA

tension STRAIN; STRESS

tension, create TIGHTEN
tent-site CAMP
tenth TITHE
tenuous SLIGHT
tepid COOL
tequila, source of AGAVE; T
term CALL; CLASS; LENT;
  NAME; SPELL; TIME; WORD;
  ■ HILARY (university term);
  SEASON; SESSION
termagant SCOLD
terminal END; FINAL; ■ DEPOT;
  STATION; WATERLOO; last letter indicator
terminate END
terminated ENDED; OFF
termination last letter indicator
terminology USAGE
terminology, specialised
  JARGON; SLANG
terminus END
termite ANT
terms RATE
terms of reference BRIEF;
  REMIT
terms, on good IN
terms with, come to FACE
terrace ROW; SHELF; TER; TIER
terrain GROUND; LAND
terrible AWFUL; anagram indicator
terrible place/situation HELL
terribly VERY; anagram indicator
Terriers TA
terrific FAB; MEGA
terrify SCARE
terrine PATE
territorial detachment ISLE
territory PATCH; TER; ■ AREA;
  DOMAIN; FIELD; TRACT; *see*
  REGION
terror AWE; BRAT; DREAD;
  FEAR; FRIGHT; IMP; SCARE
terror, little BRAT; IMP
terrorist group CELL
terrorists IRA
terse BRIEF; CURT; PITHY;
  SHORT
test CHECK; EXAM; MATCH;
  MOT; ORAL; ORDEAL;
  PROBE; RUN; SAMPLE;

SCAN; SOUND; TASTE; TAX;
  TRIAL; TRY; VET; ■
  EXAMINATION; *see* TEST
Test RIVER; can indicate something to do with cricket; [◊ CAP]
test centre ES; LORDS
test piece SAMPLE
test, pre-exam MOCK
test situation OVAL
Testament NT; OT; VERSE
tested PROVEN; *see* TEST
testify SWEAR; ■ ATTEST;
  DEPOSE
testimonial TRIBUTE
testy CROSS
tetchy LIVERY
tether CHAIN; ROPE; TIE; ■
  HITCH; MOOR
Texas TX
text COPY; MS; PROSE; SCRIPT;
  VERSE; WORDS; WORK
text, piece of EXCERPT; PARA
text, some PARA
textbook READER
textile JUTE; SERGE; *see*
  FABRIC
textile, instrument CARD;
  LOOM
textile machinery LOOM
textile worker DYER
Thailand SIAM; T
thane ROSS; ■ BANQUO
thank TIP
Thank God DG
thank you, thanks TA
thanks TA; TAS
thanks French MERCI
thanks, returning AT
thanks to many TAC
that WHO; YON; YONDER
that chap/fellow/man HIM
that hurts OUCH; OW
that in France/Paris QUE
that is IB; ID (i.e. idem); IDEST;
  SC
that is between the sides LIER
  (L-ie-R); RIEL (R-ie-L)
that is to say *see* THAT IS
that old YON
that place THERE
that's IE

that's remarkable MY(!)
that's right IER
that's so ERGO
that woman HER
thatch HAIR; ROOF
thatching stalk REED
Thatcherite DRY (i.e. as opposed
  to a "wet")
thatching REED
thaw MELT
the beware that the innocent article
  "the" can itself be part of an anagram or the solution, as "Lifting
  the feet" → THEFT
the boundaries TE
the continental see THE
  FOREIGN
the empty TE
the European see THE FOREIGN
the first T
the foreign DER; DIE; EL; IL;
  LA; LAS; LE; LES; LOS
the foreign couple can indicate a
  combination of two foreign articles (see THE FOREIGN) in
  combination as "The foreign couple are a plant" → ELDER
the French LA; LE; LES
the German DER; DIE
the Italian IL
the northern T
the old YE
the Parisienne style see THE
  FRENCH
the short TH
the Spanish EL; LAS; LOS
the top T
the wild anagram of THE
theatre ARENA; HALL; LYRIC;
  REP; SHOW; STAGE; ■
  ODEON; OLIVIER; note, theatre
  can mean an operating theatre
theatre, accommodation in BOX
theatre audience HOUSE
theatre company REP
theatre, foreign NOH
theatre of war FRONT
theatre outside West End
  FRINGE

theatre, part of APRON;
  CIRCLE; PIT; STAGE; STALLS;
  WINGS
theatre seats CIRCLE; STALLS
theatrical CAMP; SHOWY; [◊
  SHOW]; can indicate something
  to do with an operating theatre
theatrical group CAST; EQUITY;
  PLAYERS
theatrical part ROLE; see
  THEATRE, PART OF
theatrical show PLAY
theatrical work ACTING
theft CRIME; ■ PIRACY; STEAL;
  STEALING
them EM; REST
them informally EM
theme IDEA; MATTER; TOPIC; ■
  SUBJECT
then AND; LATER
theologian DD
theology RE
theory IDEA; ISM; ■ GUESS;
  NOTION
these days AD; LATELY; NOW;
  PRESENT
therapy CURE; ECT
there, be ATTEND
there, not HERE
there, over YONDER
therefore ERGO; SO; THUS
therein run indicator
thermal rating TOG
these days AD; NOW
these in Paris CES
thesis PAPER; TRACT
thespian ACTOR
they PRONOUN
they emptied TY
they say homophone indicator
thick DENSE; DIM; DUMB; FAT;
  SLOW; ■ CREAMY; SIMPLE
thick coat, put on PLASTER(ED)
thick, lay on SMEAR
thick mixture PASTE ; see
  STICKY STUFF
thicket BRAKE; COPSE; GROVE
thickset BEEFY; STOCKY;
  STUBBY
thief CROOK; KNAVE; LIFTER
thief, behave like a see STEAL

thieve NICK; ROB; STEAL; WHIP

thievery STEALING

thigh HAM

thighbone FEMUR

thin BONY; FINE; LAME; LEAN; LIGHT; RARE; SHEER; SLIGHT; SLIM; SPARE; WEAK; ■ GAUNT; NARROW; REEDY; SCRAGGY; SLENDER; SPARSE; WEEDY

thin edge WEDGE

thin, unhealthily GAUNT

thing ARTICLE; IT; OBJECT; ■ DEVICE; can indicate an obsession, enthusiasm or mania as "A thing for lighting fires?" → PYROMANIA

thing accomplished ACTION; DEED; FETE

thing, beautiful GEM

thing, delightful GAS

thing done ACTION; DEED

thing, funny HOOT; NIGHT (anagram)

thing mended NIGHT (anagram)

thing wanted/wanting LACK

things philosophically ENTIA (metaphysical)

things worn WEAR

think DEEM; DREAM; FEEL; HOLD; MULL; MUSE; OPINE; PONDER; REASON; ■ GUESS; IMAGINE; MEDITATE; PRESUME; REFLECT; WONDER

think fit DEIGN

think highly of RATE; *see* ESTEEM

think it funny GRIN; ■ LAUGH; SMILE

think logically REASON

think out REASON

think wildly DREAM

thinker BRAIN; MUSER

thinking MIND; PENSIVE; THOUGHT

thinking, way of SCHOOL

thinner LEANER; SOLVENT

third-born R

third-born child RSON (i.e. R-son)

third-class A; B; POOR

third degree G; GRILL

third of third letter of succeeding word

third power CUBE

third-rate C; POOR; T

thirst CRAVING; ITCH

thirsty DRY

13th of month, Roman IDES

thirty days can indicate a month of thirty days (usually abbreviated form) namely APR, JUNE, SEPT, NOV

thirty-one days can indicate a month of thirty-one days (usually abbreviated form) namely JAN, MAR, MAY, JUL, AUG, OCT, DEC

thirty seconds MIN

this classical HIC

this compiler ME

this country GB; UK

this French CE

this Latin HIC

this month INST

this old HIC

this person ME

this place HERE

this point, at HERE

this state UK

this writer ME

this writer's MINE

Thomas can indicate something to do with doubt, doubting, doubtful

thong STRAP; TAW; TAWS

thorax CHEST

thorn PRICKLE; SPINE

thorough EXACT; EXACTING; SEARCHING

thoroughbred, not CROSS

thoroughfare LANE; RD; ROAD; ST; ■ ROUTE

thoroughly FULLY; WELL

those EM (i.e. 'em); THEM; THEY

those lacking socks T

those left REST

those on the outside TE

those people *see* THOSE

those people, of THEIR

those running FIELD

though IF; THO

thought BELIEF; IDEA; MUSED; NOTION; ■ TRIFLE; can indicate something to do with ESP, telepathy

thought, lost in RAPT

thoughtful KIND; ■ MUSING; PENSIVE

thousand GRAND; K; M; ■ DD (i.e. 2 x 500)

thousand in two instalments DD

thousand pounds GRAND; K; MONKEY

thousand, two MM

thousandth THOU

thrall SLAVERY

thrash BEAT; BEST; FLOG; LAM; TAN; WHIP; ■ BASTE; LEATHER; PARTY; SLIPPER; TOWEL; TROUNCE; WRITHE

thrashed BEAT

thrashing BEATING; DOING

thread CORD; FLOSS; LACE; PLY; REEVE; STRAND; TWINE; YARN; ■ LISLE; WIRE

thread, lose RAMBLE

threat PERIL; RISK; ■ DANGER; MENACE

threat to crops LOCUST

threat to king CHECK

threaten LOOM; ■ IMPERIL; MENACE; PORTEND

threaten to go out GUTTER

threatening BLACK; DIRE; ■ CREEPY

threats, use HECTOR

three PRIME; TRE; TRI; TRIO

three consecutive letters DEF; NOP

three couples, pairs VI

three feet YARD

three-foot YARD

three months FALL; QUARTER; SEASON

three notes DEF

three-quarters some combination of three letters to be taken from N, S, E, W

three times TER; ■ THRICE; TREBLE; TRIPLE

threewheeler TRIKE

thresh BEAT

threshold of first letter indicator

threshing anagram indicator

threw CAST; FLUNG

threw off anagram of THREW

threw out anagram indicator; anagram of THREW

thrice TER (Lat.)

thrifty CANNY

thrifty buy SNIP

thrill KICK; ■ BUZZ; TINGLE

thrilled anagram indicator

thriller GRIPPER

thrive BLOOM

throat CRAW; GORGE

throaty HUSKY

throat irritation FROG

throaty sound COUGH

throat trouble CROUP

throb BEAT; PULSE

throne LOO; SEAT

throne, on the REGNANT

throng ABOUND; HORDE; *see* CROWD

throttle CHOKE; PEDAL

throttling nesting indicator

through BY; OVER; PER; VIA; nesting indicator

throughout DURING

throw BUCK; CAST; FLING; HEAVE; HURL; LOB; PELT; PITCH; SHY; SLING; SPIT; TOSS; anagram indicator

throw around WORTH

throw away BIN; WASTE; *see* DISPENSE WITH

throw (dice) ROLL

throw off balance ROCK

throw out DUMP (qv); EJECT; EMIT; EVICT; REJECT; a component to be nested within SHY

throw out of country DEPORT

throwing anagram indicator

thrown CAST; FLUNG; anagram indicator

thrown about anagram indicator

thrown out EJECTED; anagram indicator; *see* DUMP

thrown out of omission indicator

thrown outside component(s) to be nested within CAST

thrown up reversal indicator

thrust DRIVE; LUNGE; POINT; PUSH; TILT; ■ FORCE; IMPULSE

thug GOON; HEAVY; ROUGH; TOUGH

thumbed READ (as in "well thumbed" giving "much read")

thump BANG; BEAT; BLOW; HIT; POUND; WHOP; ■ CLOBBER

thunder CLAP

Thunderer THOR; TIMES

thundering, thunderous LOUD

thurible CENSER

Thursday TH; via the nursery rhyme can indicate "having far to go"

thus ERGO; SIC; SO; with a particular form of wording can indicate AS e.g. "thus primed" gives ASSET (i.e. as set); anagram indicator

thus, Latin HOC

thwart BALK; CHECK; DASH; FOIL; SEAT

Tibet, native of YAK

Tibetan wild man YETI

tick BEAT; FLASH; MARK; MO; SEC; ■ CREDIT; SECOND

ticker CLOCK; HEART; HUNTER; WATCH

ticket CARD; FINE; LABEL; PASS; TAG; TOKEN ■ RETURN; SINGLE; [◊ FARE]

ticket, meal LV

ticket price FARE

ticket seller/supplier TOUT

tickle AMUSE; DELIGHT; DIVERT; [◊ LAUGH]

tidal area SALTING(S)

tidal flood *see* TIDAL WAVE

tidal flow RIP

tidal wave BORE; EAGRE

Tiddles CAT (qv)

tiddly MERRY; *see* DRUNK

tide DRIFT; RIP; TREND; ■ CURRENT

tide, part of WAVE

tidy CLEAN; COVER; HOE; NEAT; SEA; TRIM; ■ CLEAR; anagram indicator

tidy garden HOE; WEED

tie BAND; BIND; BOND; DRAW; EQUAL; FIX; KNOT; LACE; LASH; LINK; MATCH; TETHER; ■ CHAIN; COPULA; SLEEPER

tie-breaker anagram of TIE

tie up BIND; FIX; MOOR; STAKE; ■ HITCH; TETHER; TRUSS

tied BOUND; DREW; ■ MOORED

tied up BOUND; HITCHED; ■ DECAL i.e. "reverse of "laced"; anagram indicator

tier BAND; BANK; LEVEL; RANK; ROW

tiff BRUSH; PET; ROW; SPAT

tiger CAT; ■ STRIPED; STRIPES

tigerish Khan SHERE

tight CLOSE; DRUNK (qv); FIRM; MEAN; NEAR; PROOF (as in watertight/proof); SMASHED; SNUG; STINGY; TENSES; ■ SECURE; anagram indicator; [◊ VICE]

tight-fisted MEAN; NEAR; STINGY; can indicate something to do with being tense

tight grip TRACTION

tight, not FREE; LOOSE; ■ POROUS

tight spot FIX; HOLE; SCRAPE; *see* DIFFICULTY

tile BOWLER ■ SHINGLE

tile mortar GROUT

tiler ROOFER

tiling, finish GROUT

till DIG; PLOUGH

till tender CASHIER

tiller PEASANT; RUDDER; SHOOT

tilt LEAN; LIST

timber ASH; BOARD; BEAM; FIR; LOG; PINE; PLANK; TEAK; TREE; WOOD; ■ EBONY; can refer to specific wood or tree, *see* TREE, WOOD

timbre TONE

time gone PAST

time on earth LIFE

time AGE; AM; BIRD; CLOCK; DATE; DAY; ENEMY; EON; ERA; EVE; HOUR; MIN; MO; NOON; NOW; PERIOD; PM; SEASON; SEC; SHIFT; SPAN; SPELL; T; TEMPO; TERM; THEN; TICK; YEAR; ■ AEON; DECADE; DURATION; SENTENCE; TIDE; can indicate something to do with prison term

time after that SINCE

time after time MINT; MOT; OFT; TT

time, ahead of EARLY

time, almost NIGHT (i.e. NIGH + T)

time and time again *see* TIME AFTER TIME

time, appointed DATE

time, astronomical EPACT

time, at that THEN

time, before EARLY; EVE

time being NONCE; PRESENT; ■ DURATION

time-consuming FIDDLING

time, doing INSIDE

time for a A to be replaced by T

time for bed NIGHT

time for cutting down on food FAST; LENT

time for, leaving T to be omitted

time, good BALL; FUN

time, has no T to be omitted

time in prison STRETCH

time in Rome IDES

time, little MIN; MO; SEC; T; TICK; ■ SECOND; TRICE; *see* TIME

time, long YONKS; *see* TIME

time, make full use of SPAN

time of one's life AGE

time of our lives, the AD; AGE

time, of past OLDEN

time off REST; T to be omitted

time on earth LIFE

time, our AD

time, passing of indicates that T is to be omitted from associated word

time, precise INSTANT

time-reporter *see* TIMEKEEPER

time-serve TRIM

time, short JIFFY; SECOND; T; can indicate an abbreviation of a unit of time hence SEC, MIN, YR etc, *see* TIME, LITTLE

time, short of T to be omitted

time, sound TICK

time wasted, wasting T to be omitted

timekeeper CLOCK; WATCH

timekeeping a component to be nested within TIME (or a synonym – *see* TIME)

timeless indicator for the omission of a synonym for "time" e.g. T, AGE, ERA, *see* TIME

timelessly T (or a synonym for time e.g. AGE) to be omitted

timepiece CLOCK; HUNTER; WATCH

times CROSS; X

Times DAILY; PAPER; *see* TIMES *above*

times, at all EVER

times, behind the DATED; RUSTY

times by itself SQUARE

times gone by AGO

times, old BC

times, the AGE

timid SHY

timid character MOUSE

timid person HEN; MOUSE

timid thing FAWN; MOUSE

timing device apart from the obvious such as clock and chronometer, can also refer to HAND

tin CAN; SN; ■ MONEY; PRESERVE

tin-opener T

tin-plated component to be nested within SN as "Tin-plated uranium" gives SUN

tincture GULES

tine POINT; PRONG; SPIKE

tinge DASH; TRACE

tingle THRILL

tinker SLY (i.e. Shakespearian character); ■ FIDDLE; POTTER

Tinkerbell FAIRY

tint DYE; SHADE; ■ COLOUR

tinware TOLE

tiny BABY; SMALL; WEE; ■ INFANT; MINUTE; MICRO; TITCHY; with a capital letter can refer to Tiny Tim, the Dickens character

tiny amount ATOM; BIT; DOT; DROP; MIL; SPLASH; WHIT

tiny distance MIL

tiny piece/thing ATOM

tip BANK; CUE; CLUE; END; FIRST; HEAD; HINT; LEAN; LIST; PEAK; POINT; TOE; ■ CAP; DUMP; NAP; NIB; POUR; PRESENT; UP-END; initial letter indicator; reversal indicator

tip-off initial letter to be omitted; anagram of TIP (e.g. PIT)

tip-top AI

tipple DRAM; RUM; SHOT; TOT

tipster TOUT

tipster's choice NAP

tipsy HIGH; TIGHT; anagram indicator

tiptop SPIRE

tirade RANT

tire FLAG; WEAR; ■ BORE; DROOP; WEARY

tired DEAD; DRAWN; SPENT; STALE; TRITE; WEARY

tiredness FLAG

tiresome TRYING

tiresome person BORE; PEST; PILL

tiresome work BORE; CHORE; FAG

tissue FLESH; PAPER ■ FABRIC; SINEW

titchy TINY; *see* SMALL

tithe CHARGE; FRACTION; TAX

titian RED

titivate PRIMP

title CLAIM; COUNT; DEED; DOM; EARL; HANDLE; HEAD; LORD; MISTER; MR; NAME; PASHA; SIR; SIRE; RIGHT; ■ ADDRESS; CALL; HEADING

title, have OWN

title holder CHAMP

title, seek to maintain DEFEND

title, short HON

title, without ANON

titled lady DAME

titled man SIR; *see* TITLE

titled person EARL; *see* NOBLE

Titus TIT

tizz, in a anagram indicator

TNT, use BLAST

to and fro can indicate the answer is a palindrome

to back OT

to be (with some indication of French) ETRE

to boot TOO

to-do FUSS; SPLASH

to east TOE

to get back OT

to give can indicate that the definition follows

to north TON

to notice TOAD (i.e. to ad)

to the French A; ALA; AU; AUX

to west TOW

to wit VIZ

toady CREEP

toast BREAD; BROWN; CHEER; CHEERS; GRILL; PRAISE; SINGE; WARM; ■ HEALTH; PLEDGE; SKOL

toast, half of CHIN (i.e. from chin-chin)

toaster GRILL

tobacco SNUFF

toboggan, Swiss LUGE

tod FOX

today AD; NOW; ■ OURAGE (i.e. our age); when the crossword is in a daily newspaper, can indicate the day of publication, either full or abbreviated

toddle AMBLE; STROLL

toe TIP

toff DANDY; GENT; NOB; SWELL

toffee SWEET

together anagram indicator

toggle SWITCH

toil NET; PLY; WORK; *see* WORK

toilet CAN; GENTS; HEAD; HEADS; JOHN; LOO; ■ BOG; LAV; PRIVY; WC

token COUNTER; DISC; SIGN; TICKET; ■ EARNEST; HOLLOW (as in a token gesture); VOUCHER

token of love RING

told BADE; ■ ORDERED; RELATED; homophone indicator

told, be HEAR

told off CHID; an anagram of TOLD e.g. DOLT, OLD-T

told tales SANG

Toledo SWORD

tolerance GIVE; PLAY

tolerate ABIDE; BEAR; HACK; STAND; STICK; WEAR

tolerated LET; STOOD

toleration LATITUDE

toll COST; DUTY; FEE; PRICE RING; STROKE; TAX; ■ CHARGE; CHIME

tolled RANG; RUNG

Tolstoy COUNT; LEO

Tom CAT; MOGGY; PUSS; PUSSY; THOS; THUMB; ■ HECAT (i.e. he-cat); SAWYER

Tom Cobbleigh* UNCLE

Tom Hanks'character GUMP

Tom, young KITTEN; KITTY

tomb GRAVE; ■ CIST; SHRINE

tome BOOK

Tommies see SOLDIERS

Tommy see SOLDIER

ton T

tone SOUND; NOTE; PITCH; ■ ACCENT; BLACK; TENOR; see COLOUR

tone down TEMPER

Tongan can indicate something to do with being friendly (i.e. from Friendly Islands)

tongue FLAP; LINGO; SPIT; ■ CLAPPER; SPEECH; can indicate a specific language, FRENCH, etc; [◊ LICK; LINGUIST]

tonic SHOT

tons T

too ABOVE; ALSO; DITTO; OVER; can indicate a verb beginning with OVER or UNDER

too-clever FLIP

too far OVER

too little UNDER

too many OVER; can indicate a word beginning with OVER

too much EXTRA; GLUT; OTT; OVER; ■ EXCESS

too much for a Frenchman TROP

too short ALS; TO

too soon EARLY

took STOLE

took action DID; SUED

took a lift RODE

took chair SAT

took charge, took the lead HEADED; LED

took cover HID

took exam SAT

took food ATE

took in ATE

took off APED; SHED

took part ACTED; PLAYED; SIDED

took precedence LED

took refuge HID

tool AGENT; AWL; AXE; BRACE; BIT; CLAMP; FILE; FORK; GAT; HOE; JIG; LATHE; PICK; PLANE; RAKE; RASP; SAW; ■ HAMMER; HATCHET; SHOVEL; SPADE; SPANNER; TROWEL; WRENCH; see IMPLEMENT, INSTRUMENT

tool, inscribing GRAVER

tools, set of KIT

tooth FANG; MOLAR; TUSK

tooth, cut a FAN; TUS

tooth decay CARIES

tooth, poisonous FANG

tootle TRIP

top AI; APEX; ARCH; BEAT; BEST; CAP; COVER; FIRST; HEAD; HIGH; LID; PEAK; ROOF; SHELF; STAR; TOR; ■ ACME; BEHEAD; BETTER; BLOUSE; CHIEF; CRACK; CROWN; COPING; JUMPER;

LEADING; LIMIT; REVOLVER; SHIRT; SPINNER; TURNER; UPPER; initial letter indicator; can indicate something to do with head, *see* HEAD, TOP OF; first letter to be omitted (i.e. as in "to top" i.e. decapitate); [◊ ACE; UP]

top among first letters of the words that follows to be used

top and bottom of first and last letter indicator

top award A; GOLD

top bananas OPT

top car C; GT

top class AI; C; SUPER; SUPERB; U; ■ CAPITAL

top commander C; CINC (i.e. C-in-C)

top decoration D; can refer to some headgear, especially a decorative one e.g. CROWN, TIARA

top dog D

top drawer D; GENTRY; U

top gear G; HAT

top golfer G; PRO

top grade A; ALPHA

top-heavy H

top honour ACE; H

top light RED

top man BOSS; CAPT; CHIEF; HEAD; KING; LEADER; M; OC

top management BOARD; M

top mark A; M

top marks can indicate high-ranking grade consisting of letters A,B,C

top of initial letter indicator

top of car C; ROOF

top of house ROOF

top, on OVER; UP; first letter(s) indicator; can indicate a component is to be placed at the beginning of the answer;

top, over the OTT

top pair first two letters

top performance RECORD

top performer STAR

top person ACE; P; QUEEN; ROYAL; *see* TOP MAN

top player ACE; P; SEED; STAR

top position PEAK; *see* TOP

top quality AI; Q; *see* TOP

top removed first letter to be omitted

top room ATTIC; R

top secret S

top, the T

tope DRINK

toper DRUNK; LUSH; SOAK; SOT

topic ISSUE; SUBJECT; THEME

topical IN; LOCAL

topless first letter to be omitted

topped first letter to be omitted

topped and tailed first letter and last letter to be omitted

topping BRILL; ICING; SHELF; first letter to be omitted; can refer to some kind of hat

topping wear HAT (qv)

topping, with ICED; fist letter to be omitted

topple TIP; UPEND

toppled anagram indicator

tor HILL; PEAK; RISE; ROCK

torch LIGHT

tore RIPPED

Tories RIGHT

torment HELL; NAG; RAG; ■ HAUNT

torment, in anagram indicator

tormented anagram indicator

torn RENT; SPLIT; anagram indicator; ■ RAGGED; RIPPED

torn apart RIVEN

torn off anagram of TORN

torn up anagram indicator

tornado SQUALL

torpedo RUIN

torpid NUMB

torque FORCE

torrent STREAM

torrential anagram indicator

torrid anagram indicator

torso TRUNK

tortilla dish TACO

tortuous anagram indicator

torture BOOT; RACK; anagram indicator

torture, instrument of RACK

tortured anagram indicator

Tory BLUE; CON; RIGHT

Tory leader T

Tory left T; WET

toss FLING; FLIP; LOB; ROLL; SHY; SLING; SPIN; ■ HURL; THROW

toss into the air LOFT

toss, outcome of HEADS; TAILS

tossed FLUNG; SPUR; anagram indicator

tossing SPINNING; anagram indicator

tossing and turning AWAKE; anagram indicator

tot ADD; DRAM; KID; NIP; SHOT; SLUG; SUM; ■ FINGER; MITE; NIPPER; TIPPLE

tot up ADD

total ADD; ALL; LOT; SUM; UTTER; WHOLE

totally different anagram indicator

total disaster anagram of TOTAL

total, one finding SUMMER

tote BEAR; CARRY

toting anagram indicator; nesting indicator

totter QUIVER; ROCK; REEL; SHAKE; SWAY; ■ QUIVER; STAGGER

touch ABUT; DAB; DASH; FEEL; KISS; MEET; MOVE; PAT; STYLE; TINGE; TRACE; ■ CADGE; CONTACT; SENSE

touch, barely GRAZE

touch-down ALIGHT; LAND; LIGHT

touch, in can indicate something to do with field game e.g. linesman

touch, light TAP

touch lightly BRUSH; KISS

touch of initial letter indicator

touch regularly SPONGE

touch, soft PAT

touchdown TRY

touched FELT; LOCO; MAD (qv); MET

touched down ALIT

touching RE; ■ TANGENT

touchy CROSS; TESTY

tough FIRM; HARD; HOOD (i.e. gangster); STERN; STRICT; ■ DEMANDING; LEATHERY; STRINGY

tough Cockney ARD (i.e. 'ard)

tough exterior SHELL

tough guy HEMAN; RAMBO

toughen by heat ANNEAL

toughness STEEL

toupee RUG; WIG

toupee, wearing a RUGGED

tour TRIP; ■ TRAVEL; anagram indicator, as "Paris tour" suggests an anag. of PARIS; nesting indicator

tour of duty STINT

tour, on anagram indicator

toured WENT; anagram indicator

touring anagram or nesting indicator

tourist attraction DOME; SIGHT

tourist, visit as a DO

tournament JOUST

tournaments LISTS; [◊ JOUST]

tourney, take part in JOUST

tout BARKER; HAWK; PEDDLE; ■ ALL

tow DRAG; DRAW; HAUL; PULL

tow-line DRAWL

towards AT; BOUND

towards me HITHER

towel CLOTH

tower BABEL; KEEP; LOOM; PEEL; PILE; SPIRE; STACK; TUG; ■ BROCH; REAR; SOAR; TURRET; note, the less common pronunciation of "tower" which can indicate TUGBOAT etc; [◊ IVORY]

town BARROW; BATH; BURY; CITY; CREWE; DEAL; DISS; HOVE; IVER; LEEK; LOOE; PLACE; SALE; SLOUGH; STAINES; STREET; TRING; WARE

town, big CITY

town centre OW

town, Herts TRING; WARE

town in East Anglia DISS

town in France LENS; *see* TOWN

town, Irish *see* IRISH TOWN

town, large CITY
town, Middlesex PINNER
town, one driven out of CTY
town, part of QUARTER; SECTION
town, Scottish PERTH
town, to UP
town, US MOBILE
townee, townsman CIT (slang)
toxic substance VENIN; ■ POISON
toxophilite ARCHER; TELL
toy BIT; DALLY; DOLL; HOOP; MODEL; PLAY; RATTLE; TEDDY; TOP; TRIFLE
toy explosive CAP
toying anagram indicator
trace DRAW; FIND; HINT; SIGN; SNIFF; TINGE; TRACK; ■ FOLLOW; RECORD; WHIFF
tracery PATTERN; ■ FILIGREE
traces of first letter indicator
track COURSE; DOG; FOLLOW; LANE; LINE; PATH; RAIL; ROUTE; ROW; RUT; SCENT; SIGN; SPOOR; STALK; TAIL; TRACE; TRACE; TRAIL; WAY; can indicate the name of a specific racecourse
track event RACE; RUN
tracked vehicle TANK
tracking device TAG
tracks RY
tract PLOT; SPREAD; ■ AREA; REGION; RESERVE
trade ART; BARTER; CRAFT; DEAL; LINE; MARKET; RUT; SELL; SWAP; SWOP; TRAFFIC; TRUCK; ■ EXCHANGE; *see* BUSINESS
trade* WIND
trade association EFTA
trade-centre MALL; MART
trade, disparity in GAP
trade fair EXPO
trade-mark BRAND; LOGO
trade, moneyless BARTER
trade-name BRAND
trade, practise a PLY
trade route CANAL
trade show FAIR

trade union NUM; TU; anagram of TRADE
trade unionist BROTHER
traded DEALT; SOLD
trademark BRAND; LOGO
trader SHIP; SS; ■ DEALER; MONGER; SELLER; can indicate some kind of shopkeeper
traders' gathering FAIR
tradesman BAKER; SELLER
tradesman's assistant MATE
tradesman's entrance T
tradesmen BAKER; MONGER; PLUMBER
trading floor PIT
trading place MALL; MART
trading station FORT
tradition LORE
tradition, following SQUARE
traditional OLD; TRAD
traditional ale, source of WOOD
traduced anagram indicator
traffic CARS; DEAL; TRADE; TRUCK; *see* TRADE
traffic controller LIGHT
traffic marker CONE
traffic problem JAM
tragedy DRAMA
tragic heroine MIMI
tragic subject LEAR
tragically anagram indicator
trail DOG; DRAG; DRAW; LAG; PATH; PLOD; PULL; ROUTE; SCENT; SIGN; SPOOR; STALK; TRACK; WAY; ■ FOLLOW; RETINUE
train AIM; COACH; DRILL; EL (U.S.); POINT; RAIL; REAR; RY; SCHOOL; TAME; TEACH; ■ CONDITION; ENGINE; EXERCISE; GUIDE; INURE; TUBE; anagram indicator; [◊ STATION; TRACK]
train-bearer LINE; TRACK
train, go like a CHUFF
train, on ABOARD
train park SIDING
train staff GUARD
trained TAME; TAUGHT; ■ PROFESSIONAL; anagram indicator

trainee CADET; INTERN; L; LEARNER; can refer to a passenger on a railway
trainee officers OTC
trainer COACH; SHOE
training COURSE; DRILL; PE; PT; anagram indicator; note, "training" can refer to journeying by train
training, piece of COURSE
trains RAIL; RY
trains briefly RY
traipse TRAIL; TRAMP; ■ TRUDGE
traitor CAD; RAT; WEASEL; ■ JUDAS; [◊ TREASON]
traitorous type *see* TRAITOR
trajectory, ball with a high LOB
tram CAR
trammel NET; SHACKLE
tramp BUM; DOSSER; HOBO; PAD; PLOD; TREAD; WALK; ■ TREK; VAGRANT
tramp, American BUM; HOBO
trample CRUSH; TREAD
tranquil QUIET; ■ PACIFIC
tranquiliser DOWNER
tranquility CALM; PEACE
transaction DEAL; SALE; TRADE
transcript COPY
transfer DECAL; PASS; ■ ATTORN (leg.); FERRY
transfer payment REMIT
transferred anagram indicator
transfiguration, transfigured anagram indicator
transfix PIN
transfixed, person STARER
transfixing nesting indicator
transform ALTER; *see* CHANGE
transformed, transforming anagram indicator
transgress ERR; SIN
transgression SIN; ■ CRIME; OFFENCE
transgressor SINNER
translate RENDER; anagram indicator
translated anagram indicator
translates anagram indicator

translation CRIB; VERSION; anagram indicator
translation, illicit CRIB
translation, provide a GLOSS
translator TR
transmission, means of GEAR; GEARING
transmit PIPE; RELAY; SEND
transmitted SENT
transmitted message CABLE; WIRE
transmitter SENDER; ■ MAST; RADIO
transom STERN
transparent CLEAR; GLASSY; SHEER; ■ LIMPID; *see* CLEAR
transplant GRAFT; RESET
transplanted anagram indicator
transport BEAR; BOAT; BUS; CAR; CARRY; CART; CHAIR; DELIGHT; ELATE; HAUL; RY; SEND; SHIP; TAKE; TAXI; TRAIN; TRAM; TRUCK; TUBE; WAIN; ■ CYCLE; ELATION; ENCHANT; ENTRANCE; GHARRY; JOY; SLEDGE; SLEIGH; WAGON; anagram indicator; *see* VEHICLE
transport, free LIFT
transport, intercontinental LINER
transport, provision for CRATE
transport, public BUS; COACH; LINER; TRAIN; TRAM; RY
transport, sea *see* BOAT
transport system RY
transport system, old BR
transport, Wild West STAGE
transport, winter SLEIGH
transported BORNE; CARTED; RAPT; SENT; anagram indicator
transported, was RODE
transporter *see* VEHICLE
transporting BEARING; anagram indicator; nesting indicator
transposed anagram indicator
transvestite apparel DRAG
trap CATCH; FLY; GIN; NET; WEB; ■ BOOBY; CORNER; GOB; HATCH; NOOSE; PIT; SNARE; SPRINGE (type of

trap); can refer to some type of carriage

trap in stream WEIR

trapped CAUGHT; NETTED; nesting indicator

trapped by nesting indicator

trapper HUNTER

trapping nesting indicator

traps DRUM

trash BIN; DRECK; ROT; *see* RUBBISH

trashed anagram indicator

trauma SHOCK; anagram indicator

traumatic, be HARROW

travail WORK

travel FARE; GO; RANGE; RIDE; ROVE; ROW; TOUR; WALK; WEND; anagram indicator; [◊ MOTION]

travel document PASS; VISA

travel fast RUSH; SPEED

travel, free HITCH; LIFT

travel guide NAP

travel regularly PLY

travelled RODE; WENT; anagram indicator

travelled round nesting indicator

travelled on the Underground TUBED

traveller FARER; HOBO; POLO; REP; ROM; ROVER; TRAMP; TRIPPER; ■ ROMANY

travellers ROMA

travelling anagram indicator

travelling from East to West reversal indicator

travelling in search of adventure ERRANT

travelling not so fast SLOWING

travelling through VIA

Travels the capital initial can indicate the reference is to "Gulliver's Travels", its author (SWIFT) or its characters (e.g. YAHOO)

travels regularly, one who PLIER

traverse CROSS

traverse freely RANGE

traversed by run indicator

travestied anagram indicator

travesty FARCE; PARODY

tray SALVER; WAITER

treacherous FALSE

treacherous daughter REGAN

treacherous person/type RAT; RATTER; WEASEL

treachery TREASON

tread GRIP; PACE; PAD; STEP; TRAMP; TRAMPLE

treadle LEVER

treason CRIME; SEDITION

treason, man found guilty of MORE

treasure GEM; VALUE; ■ HOARD

treasurer TR

treat CURE; DEAL; DRESS; STAND; USE; ■ DELIGHT; DOSE; ENTERTAIN; HANDLE

treat roughly MAUL

treated anagram indicator

treatise PAPER; TRACT

treatment CURE; DEAL; DOSE; ECT; USE; anagram indicator

treatment for an anagram of the word that follows is required

treaty PACT; PEACE; ■ CONTRACT; DEAL

treble BET; RING (darts); SINGER

tree ACER; APPLE; ASH; ALDER; BAY; BEECH; BIRCH; BOX; CROSS; ELDER; ELM; FIG; FIR; GUM; HOLLY; LARCH; LIME; OAK; ORANGE; PALM; PEAR; PINE; PLANE; POPLAR; SORB; TEAK; WILLOW; YEW; ■ ABELE; ABIE; ALMOND; BALSA; EBONY; OSIER; PLUM; QUINCE; SERVICE; SHEA; SPRUCE; SUMAC; ULE; can indicate something to do with ancestors, lineage, family tree, heir, etc; [◊ BARK; BRANCH; STUMP; TRUNK]

tree, evergreen LARCH

tree plantation FOREST; WOOD

tree, pollarded first letter to be omitted from a tree (in this way BEACH leads to EACH, for example)

tree potential ACORN
tree-top accommodation NEST
tree trunk BOLE; STOCK
treeless area CLEARING
trees CLUMP; COPSE; FOREST; GROVE; STAND; WOOD
trees, groups (etc) of *see* TREES
trek TRAMP
trek leader MOSES; T
tremble SHAKE; SHIVER; ■ DITHER; QUAKE; QUAVER; QUIVER
trembling anagram indicator
tremor SHAKE
tremulous anagram indicator
trench DITCH; PIT; SAP; ■ FOSSE
trenchant CUTTING
trencherman EATER; [◊ DIG]
trend TIDE; ■ COURSE; DRIFT; STYLE; VOGUE
trend-setting *see* TRENDY
trendy COOL; HIP; HEP; IN; SMART
trendy, not OUT
trendy-sounding place INN
trepidation AWE
trespass SIN
tress LOCK
trial ACTION; CASE; CROSS; GO; TEST; TRY; WOE; ■ HEARING; ORDEAL
trial, appearing for UP
trial examination MOCK
trial, on UP
trial run REHEARSAL
trial, send back to await REMAND
tribe CLAN; GAD; GROUP; LEVI; RACE; SEPT
tribe, ancient GAD
tribesman ANGLE; GOTH; IBO; JUTE; LEVI
tribunal COURT; HEARING; ROTA
tribute PRAISE
tribute to, pay PRAISE
trice MO; SEC; ■ INSTANT; SHAKE
trick CATCH; CHEAT; CON; DO; DIDO (U.S.); FEAT; FLANKER;

FOX; GUY; HOAX; JAPE; JOKE; KID; PLANT; PLOY; PRANK; RIG; RUSE; SCAM; STUNT; ■ DECEPTION; DODGE; ENTRAP; KNACK; anagram indicator
trick, do the WORK
tricked DONE; anagram indicator
trickle DRIP; SEEP; STREAM
tricks can indicate something to do with taking tricks at cards e.g. slam
tricky DICEY; SLY; anagram indicator
tricky situation HOLE; PICKLE; SCRAPE; *see* DIFFICULTY
tricorn HAT
tried hard STROVE
tried to listen HERD (i.e. hom.)
tried to move TIRED
trifle DALLY; PLAY; SPORT; TOY; ■ DESSERT; THOUGHT
trifled with anagram indicator
trifling LIGHT; PETTY; SLIGHT; ■ MINOR; PLAYING
trifling item TOY
trig (trigonometric) function COS; COSINE; SINE; TAN
trilby HAT
trill QUAVER; SING; TRA; WARBLE
trim BOB; CROP; CUT; DOCK; LOP; NEAT; ORDER; PARE; PRUNE; SLIM; SMART; ■ BORDER; TIDY
trim horns POLL
trimmed first or last letter (or both) to be omitted
trio THREE
trio, undistinguished can indicate something to do with Tom, Dick and Harry
trip CATCH; CRUISE; DANCE; DRIVE; FALL; FLIGHT; RIDE; ROW; RUN; SLIP; SPIN; STUMBLE; TOUR; ■ JOURNEY; OUTING; TOOTLE; VISIT; anagram indicator
trip, French TOUR
trip, on a HIGH; anagram indicator
trip, plane FLIGHT
trip, short SPIN

tripe ROT
trite BANAL; CORNY
trite jokes CORN
trite quotation TAG
triteness BATHOS
triumph WIN
triumph, expression of AHA; HA
triumphant cry CROW
triumphant, look GLOAT
triumphant, was WON
trivia DETAILS
trivial LIGHT; LITTLE; ■ FIDDLING; PETTY; SMALL
triviality DETAIL
Trojan PARIS
Trojan war champion AJAX
troll ELF
trolley BASKET; CART
trollop DOXY; DRAB; SLUT
troop FLOCK; GROUP; UNIT
troop, member of GUIDE
troops MEN; RA; RE; SAS; ■ MILITIA; REGIMENT
troops, crack SAS
troops at sea RM
troops, shock COMMANDO
trophy AWARD; CUP; PALM; POT; SCALP; URN
tropical HOT; STEAMY
trot JOG; PACE; RIDE; RUN
troth PLEDGE; TRUST
Trotsky LEON
trouble ADO; AIL; BANE; BOTHER; BUG; CARE; DOG; EAT; FUSS; ILL; IRK; JAM; NAG; PAIN; PEST; PLIGHT; SCRAPE; SPOT; STINK; STRAIN; TRIAL; WAR; WOE; ■ ACHE; AGGRO; CROSS; MIRE; TO-DO; VEX; WORRY; reversal indicator; anagram indicator; can indicate a specific illness
trouble afoot BUNION; CORN
trouble reported ALE
trouble with letters STUTTER; anagram indicator
trouble, in anagram indicator
troubled ATE; anagram indicator
troubled start T

troubled start, a AT
troublemaker IMP; PEST
troubles ILL
troublesome THORNY; ■ IMPISH; anagram indicator
troubling, was ATE
trough CHUTE; MANGER; ■ LAUNDER
trounce DEFEAT; THRASH; *see* BEAT
trounced BEAT; BEATEN; anagram indicator; *see* BEAT
trouncing BEATING; anagram indicator; *see* BEAT
trousers BAGS; PANTS; TREWS; ■ JEANS
trousers, bell-bottomed FLARES
trout, try to catch TICKLE
trowel SCOOP
truant MITCH
truck LORRY; TENDER; TRADE
truculent anagram indicator
trudge PLOD
true LOYAL; REAL; RIGHT; SO; VERY; ■ SQUARE; [◊ BLUE]
true, not BENT
true, possibly anagram of TRUE
true statement FACT
truism MAXIM
truly CERTES; REALLY; WELL
truly, yours ME
trump BEAT; BLAST; RUFF; WINNER
trumpet BUGLE; LUR
trumpeter can indicate something to do with an elephant
truncated AXED; CHOPPED; CUT (qv); omission indicator
trundle ROLL
trunk BOLE; LOG; STOCK; STUMP; TORSO
trussed BOUND
trust CREDIT; FAITH; FUND; ■ RELY; TROTH; [◊ UNIT]
trust, one we can't LIAR
trustee TR
trustworthy HONEST
truth FACT; ■ REALITY; VERITY
truth, old SOOTH
truthful HONEST

try CRACK; DO; GO; HEAR; OFFER; SAMPLE; SHOT; STAB; TACKLE; TASTE; TAX; TEST; ■ AIM; ESSAY; STRIVE

try hard STRAIN; STRIVE

try-on CON

try out TEST; anagram of TRY; *see* TRY

try to catch out FIELD

try to eat BITE

try to find LOOK; SEARCH; SEEK

try to find out PRY; SPOON; ■ FERRET

try to get SEEK

try to get money TOUCH

try to win COURT; WOO

trying person JUDGE; JUROR

trying situation COURT

trying to get AFTER

tsar IVAN; PETER

TT with a homophone indicator can call for TEASE

TT races, about SCATTER

tub BATH; BOAT

tubby FAT

tube ARTERY; DUCT; PIPE; VEIN; ■ DIODE

Tube TRAIN

tuber SPUD; YAM

tuck DART; EATS; FOLD; FOOD; GRUB; PLEAT

Tuck FRIAR

tuck in EAT

Tucker's companion BIB

tucked in ATE

tucking in/into nesting indicator

Tudor HOUSE

Tuesday via the nursery rhyme can indicate GRACE

tuft BOBBLE

tug BOAT; LUG; PULL; TOW; YANK; ■ JERK; TOWER

tugboat TOWER

tuition TEACHING

tumble FALL; anagram indicator

tumbled FELL; TRIPPED; anagram indicator; *see* FALL

tumbler GLASS

tumbling anagram indicator

tummy ache/pain GRIPE

tumulus MOUND

tumult RIOT

tumult, in anagram indicator

tun CASK

tundra PLAIN

tune AIR; ARIA; KEY; MARCH; NUMBER; PORT (Gael.); SONG; STRAIN

tune, in ONKEY (i.e. on key)

tune, jolly RANT

tungsten W

tuning fork PIN

tunnel BORE; DIG; HOLE; MINE; ■ BURROW

tunneller MOLE; WORM

tup RAM

tuppence, tuppenny PP

turbulent anagram indicator

turf GRASS; LAW; SOD; SWARD

turf accountant BOOKIE; ■ BET; BOOK

turkey FLOP

Turkey TR

Turkish bath HAMMAM

Turkish chief/commander/leader AGA; AGHA

Turkish governor BEY

turmoil DUST (slang); HELL; ■ COMMOTION; DISQUIET; MESS; STEW; anagram indicator

turmoil, in anagram indicator

turmoil, place of HELL

turn ACT; BEND; CRACK; FIT; GO; HEEL; HINGE; LUFF; PIVOT; ROLL; ROUND; SCREW; SHIFT; SHOCK; SHOT; SHOW; SOUR; SPELL; SPIN; TED; TWIST; U; WHEEL; WIND; ■ ANTE; CHANGE; CORNER; CYCLE; GYRATE; REVOLVE; ROTATE; STEER; anagram indicator; reversal indicator;

turn aside AVERT

turn away AVERT; DIVERT

turn back reverse indicator

turn down REFUSE

turn fast SPIN

turn grey AGE

turn in NI; RETIRE; a synonym (e.g. SPIN) to be nested

turn informer SING; *see* INFORM

turn inside out EVERT

turn into TION (i.e. anagram, very useful to form the end of a word)

turn key LOCK

turn off DETER; DIVERT

turn out COME; DRESS; MAKE; ■ PRODUCE; PROVIDE; anagram indicator

turn over FLIP; PTO; REVO (i.e. reverse of "over"); ROLL; TIF (i.e. reverse of "fit") ; TO; ■ RESIGN; YIELD; reversal indicator

turn over a new leaf PTO

turn tail FLEE; RUN; the last two letters of a word to be interchanged

turn, take a STROLL; anagram indicator

turn up COCK; COME; FOLD; OG (i.e. reverse of GO in a DC); SHOW; PU (i.e. reverse of "up"); ■ APPEAR; ARRIVE; ATTEND

turn-up anagram indicator; *see* TURN UP

turncoat RAT; anagram of COAT e.g. CATO

turned OFF; SPUN; anagram indicator; reversal indicator

turned aside WRY

turned back reversal indicator

turned green ENGER

turned into TION; anagram indicator

turned out CAME; SHOWED; anagram indicator, usually of the preceding word(s); anagram of OUT

turned over reversal indicator; anagram indicator

turned up CAME; FFO (i.e. "off", in the sense of "turned sour", reversed); PU (i.e. reverse of "up"); SHOWED

tuned up alone OLOS

turner SPIT; LATHE; TOP; ■ DOORKNOB; HANDLE

Turner can indicate something to do with the artist (e.g. painting,

oils) or one of his works (*The Fighting Temeraire*, etc); if the word is at the beginning of the clue its capital letter may be a diversion and it is being used in its general sense, *see* TURNER *above*

turning BEND; CORNER; SOURING; reversal indicator; anagram indicator

turning device LATHE; WINCH

turning out anagram indicator

turning over anagram indicator; reversal indicator

turning over, is SI

turning-point AXIS

turning red DER

turning tail *see* TURNTAIL

turnip NEEP

turnout CROWD; GATE

turnover YIELD; reversal indicator; *see* TURN OVER

turns anagram indicator

turns out to be anagram indicator

turns over STIF (i.e. reverse of "fits")

turns tails last two letters to be transposed

turns, take STROLL; WALK

turns up PU (i.e. reverse of UP); reversal indicator; in a DC can indicate that a synonym of "turns" is reversed, hence SOG

turret TOWER

Tuscan banker PO

tussle FIGHT

tutor COACH; DON; TEACH; TRAIN; ■ SCHOOL; TRAINER; *see* TEACH, TRAIN

TV TELLY; *see* TELEVISION

TV channel SKY

TV channels MEDIA

TV doctor WHO

TV programme usually refers to a programme type, commonly CHAT SHOW, SITCOM or SOAP OPERA

TV puppet SOOTY

TV serial SOAP

TV show PROG; *see* TV PROGRAMME

TV relay OB

TV trophy EMMY

twang PLUCK; [◊ ACCENT; BROGUE]

Tweed* CLOTH; FABRIC; RIVER

twelfth man RESERVE

twelve NOON; ■ DOZEN; JURY; XII

twelve dozen GROSS

twelve short DOZE; NOO (i.e. last letter omitted from "noon")

twelvemonth, every YEARLY

twenties DECADE; SCORES

twenty-eight/nine days FEB

twenty-five pounds PONY

twenty-five (or 25) sheets of paper QUIRE

twenty-four hours DAY; can indicate a specific day of the week, more commonly in abbreviated form e.g. SUN, SAT, MON etc

Twenty-Six (or 26) , Number Z

twenty-two (or 22) CATCH

twerp DOPE; see FOOL

Twickenham game RU

twig BRANCH; GET; SEE; SHOOT; STICK; ■ RUMBLE; WICKER; WITHE

twilight DUSK; ■ GLOAMING

twin DOUBLE; REMUS

twine COIL; STRING; THREAD; WIND; anagram indicator

twinge ACHE

twining anagram indicator

twinkler STAR

twinklers can indicate a galaxy, constellation, astrological house

twinkling TRICE; ■ INSTANT; anagram indicator

twins LIBRA; PAIR; SIGN

twirl SPIN

twirling anagram indicator

twist COIL; SCREW; SNAKE; SPIN; TURN; WARP; WIND; WRING; WRITHE

twist in the tail last two letters to be transposed

twisted WOUND; WRUNG; WRY; anagram indicator

twisted ankle SPRAIN

twisted back reversal indicator

twisted round anagram indicator, nesting indicator; reversal indicator

twister SCREW

twisting TORTUOUS; anagram indicator

twists anagram indicator; see COIL

twit ASS; DUNCE; GIT; PUDDING; TAUNT; TEASE; see FOOL

twitch JERK; PLUCK; TIC; anagram indicator

twitched anagram indicator

twitching TIC; anagram indicator

twitter TWEET

two BI; BOTH; BRACE; COUPLE; DUET; DUO; II; PAIR; ■ DUAL; PRIME (i.e. a prime number); TWAIN; [◊ SECOND]

two couples FOUR; IV

two-dimensional FLAT

two front teeth TE

252d GUINEA

two of us, being Cockney MEANDER (i.e. me and 'er)

two pints QUART

two-sided LR; RL

two, the BOTH

two thousand MM

2001 MMI

2240 pounds TON

two times TWICE

two-under score EAGLE

two-way can indicate a palindrome, as "Two-way action" → DEED

two-ways a pair of compass points e.g. SW

two-wheeler CYCLE

twofold DUAL

twosome PAIR; PAIRING

tycoon BARON; MAGNATE

Tyneside NE

type BREED; CLASS; ELITE; FACE; FONT; FOUNT; ILK; KIND; MAKE; SORT; KIND; MODEL; PICA; PRINT; ROMAN (i.e. printing); STYLE; ■ FORM; ITALIC; can refer to printer's type; can refer to a particular type of person as "possessive type" clues OWNER

type, mixed up PI; PIE

type of anagram indicator
type of wood *see* WOOD, TREE
type, put in SET
type, set of FOUNT
typesize ELITE; POINT
typical COMMON; ECHT; NORM; PAR; *see* NORM; can also indicate RIGHT as "Typical writer" clues RIGHT-HANDER
typically can indicate that a group term is required as "panthers typically" requires CATS; can indicate something to do with printing type as "Typically leaning to the right" clues ITALIC
typist TEMP
typo ERROR
tyrant AMIN; IVAN; ■ BULLY; DESPOT; NERO; TSAR
tyre RADIAL; SPARE; ■ RETREAD
tyre's grip TREAD

Uu

U-boat SUB; can indicate something to do with hyphen
U-turn BEND; ■ REVERSAL; can indicate something to do with hyphen; reversal indicator
ugly PLAIN; ■ FRIGHTFUL; anagram indicator
UK citizen BRIT
Ulster NI; note, can also refer to a coat
Ulster city DERRY
ultimate ALL; END; LAST; NET; last letter indicator as "ultimate downfall" → L
ultimate, in the the last letter of the word that follows to be used
ultimately LAST; ULT; ■ AT LAST; last letter indicator
ultimatum DEMAND
ultraviolet UV
um ER
umber BROWN

Umberto ECO
umbrage, take RESENT
umbrella COVER; [◊ RIBS]
umpire JUDGE; REF
un- can indicate a word ending in LESS; can indicate a word beginning with NO (as "Is common-sense un-American?" → NOUS)
UN body WHO
UN health agency WHO
unable to, are (am, is) CANT
unable to move STUCK
unable to supply OUT
unacceptable OFF; OUT; ■ NOTON (i.e. not on)
unaccompanied ALONE; BARE; LONE
unaccompanied (flight) SOLO
unaccountably anagram indicator
unadorned BALD; BARE; PLAIN
unadulterated NEAT; SHEER
unadventurous SAFE
unaffected by setback palindrome indicator (qv)
unaided ALONE
unambiguous DIRECT; PLAIN
unaspirated initial H to be omitted
unaspirated girl/lady/woman ER
unassertive type MOUSE; WIMP
unassuming MEEK; SHY; ■ HUMBLE; MODEST
unattached FREE; LOOSE; SINGLE
unattainable IDEAL
unattended LONE
unattracted (to) OFF
unavailable OFF; OUT; omission indicator
unbeaten BEST
unbelievable TALL; anagram indicator
unbending RIGID; STIFF; *see* FIRM
unbiased FAIR; JUST
unblock FREE
unbound FREE
unbridled FREE; anagram indicator
unbusy DEAD
uncanny ODD; WEIRD

unceasingly last letter to be omitted

uncertain IFFY

uncertainty, show WAVER

unceremoniously anagram indicator

uncertain IFFY; anagram indicator; *see* HESITATION

uncertainly anagram indicator

uncertainty DOUBT; IF; RISK

unchanged FREE

unchanging SET

uncharacteristic STRANGE; ■ ATYPICAL

uncharged FREE

uncivil RUDE; SHORT

uncivilised RUDE; WILD

uncle BOB; SAM; can indicate something to do with a pawnshop

uncle, give to/leave with HOCK; PAWN; POP

uncle, your BOB

uncle's pledge HOCK

unclear DIM; FOGGY; VAGUE

unclosed last letter of associated word to be omitted

unclothed BARE; NAKED; NUDE

unclothed, go STREAK

unclothed, practice of going NATURISM; ■ STREAKING

unclouded CLEAR

uncomfortable place HOLE

uncomfortably anagram indicator

uncommon RARE; ROYAL; ■ NOTABLE; anagram indicator

uncommonly anagram indicator

uncommunicative RESERVED; *see* SHY

uncomplicated PLAIN; SIMPLE; anagram indicator

uncompromising HARD; ■ CUT-THROAT; *see* FIRM

unconcealed OPEN; OUT; OVERT

unconcerned CALM; COOL; PLACID

unconcluded last letter to be omitted

unconfined FREE; LOOSE

unconscious ID; OUT; UNDER

unconscious at first solution to begin with OUT or UNDER

unconscious, knock/render STUN

uncontrollable anagram indicator

uncontrollably anagram indicator

unconventional RUM; anagram indicator

unconventionally anagram indicator

unconvincing LAME; THIN

uncooked RAW

uncouple anagram indicator

uncouth COARSE; anagram indicator

uncouth person BEAR; LOUT; OAF

uncover BARE; OUT; REVEAL; SKIN; STRIP

uncovered BARE; NUDE; first and last letters to be omitted

unction CHARM; GRACE; ■ ANOINTING

unctuous SOAPY

uncultivated CRUDE; FALLOW; RUDE

uncultivated area MOOR

uncut ROUGH

undecided, be HOVER

undefined number N; SOME; X

undemanding CUSHY; EASY; LIGHT

undemonstrative COLD; ICY

under DOWN; LOW; OUT; SHORT; SUB; BELOW; NEATH; ■ BENEATH; LOWER; can indicate something to do with anaesthetics

under attack IN CHECK

under back BUS (i.e. rev)

under canvas INTENT

under cover HIDDEN; UC; ■ INTENT; TENTED; a component to follow a synonym for "cover" such e.g. LID as in "Pool has nothing under cover" → LIDO; nesting indicator

under-eighteen MINOR

under-eleven TEN

under stress anagram indicator

under-tens NINES

under way AFOOT

under wraps SECRET
undercooked RARE
undercover *see* UNDER COVER
undercover operation STING
undercut SAP
underdone RAW; RED
underdressed BARE
undergarment *see* UNDERWEAR
undergo SUFFER
underground anagram of UNDER; with or without a capital initial it can indicate TUBE, METRO etc
Underground TUBE
underground chamber CAVE; CELLAR; CRYPT; VAULT
underground church CRYPT
underground river LETHE
underground room *see* UNDERGROUND CHAMBER
underground staff NUM; MINERS
underground takeaway service SEWER
underground toiler MINER
underground tunnel DRAIN
underground worker MINER
underhand SECRET
underhandedness STEALTH
underline STRESS
underling MINION
undermine SAP
undermined SAPPED; anagram indicator
underneath BELOW; in a Down clue can indicate that a component is to be at the end of the solution
underscore can indicate a number characterised by being below twenty e.g. TEENAGER
undersea can indicate that some component is to follow SEA or a synonym e.g. MAIN, MED
underside SOLE
undersized pig RUNT
understand DIG; FOLLOW; GATHER; GET; GRASP; KEN; KNOW; READ; SEE; TAKE; TWIG ■ APPRECIATE; DIGEST; REALISE; SENSE

understand when spoken NO
understanding CATCH; DEAL; GRASP; INSIGHT; KEN; TREATY; ■ GRASPING; LIGHTS (i.e. according to one's lights); SAVVY; SENSE; *see* INTERPRETATION
understanding, on PROVIDED
understands can indicate a word/component goes at the end (i.e. stands under)
understood GOT; READ; SAW; ■ ROGER; SEEN; TACIT
undertaking TASK; VOW; ■ MISSION; VENTURE
underwear BRA; BRAS; PANTS; SHOE; SLIP; SLIPS; STAYS; VEST; ■ BASQUE; SLIPPER; SMALLS; TEDDY; UNDIES
underweight LIGHT
underworld DIS; HADES; HELL; can indicate something to do with "Down Under" and Australia
underworld boss DIS
undesirable person LOUT; OAF
undeveloped RAW
undiluted NEAT
undisciplined anagram indicator
undisguised BALD; OPEN
undisturbed CALM; SERENE
undo OPEN; RUIN; ■ DEFEAT
undoing anagram indicator, as "his undoing" → ISH
undone anagram indicator
undreamed-of REAL
undress STRIP
undressed first and last letter to be omitted as "swimmer feels undressed" clues EEL
undulate RIPPLE
undulating WAVY; anagram indicator
unduly TOO
unease, feelings of QUALMS
uneasily anagram indicator
uneasy TENSE; ■ UPTIGHT; anagram indicator
unelected OUT
unemotional COLD; COOL; STOLID
unemployed FREE; IDLE
unemployed, was IDLED

unemployment benefit DOLE; UB

unending last letter to be omitted

unenlightened DARK

unenthusiastic COLD; COOL; LAME

uneven BUMPY; ODD; ■ SCRATCHY

uneven, make RUFFLE

unexpected SNAP; SUDDEN; anagram indicator

unexpected development TWIST

unexpected windfall MANNA

unexpectedly anagram indicator

unexploited VIRGIN

unfairly anagram indicator

unfamiliar NEW; RARE; ■ ALIEN; STRANGE; anagram indicator

unfashionable OUT

unfasten OPEN

unfavourable ADVERSE

unfed can indicate that O is to be nested within a component (i.e. figuratively "empty") as "unfed pet" signals COAT

unfeeling COLD; NUMB

unfilled VOID

unfinished omission indicator, usually of last letter

unfit ILL; SICK

unfit for service US (i.e. colloquialism for 'useless)

unflustered COOL

unfolded anagram indicator

unfolded, what's MAP

unforthcoming SHY; ■ RESERVED

unfortunate ILL; POOR; SAD; UNLUCKY

unfortunately ALACK; ALAS; ILL; anagram indicator

unfriendly COLD; CHILLY; FROSTY; STERN

unfurled anagram indicator

unfurnished BARE

ungenerous MEAN; TIGHT; ■ SELFISH

ungentlemanly, one who's CAD (qv); ROTTER

ungulate CAMEL

unhappily anagram indicator

unhappiness DISTRESS

unhappy BLUE; DOWN; GLUM; SAD; SOMBRE; anagram indicator

unhappy, sound SIGH

unharmed OK; WHOLE; ■ INTACT; see FINE

unhealthy AILING; ILL; PASTY; SICK

unhesitatingly ER, UM or UR to be omitted

unhurried PATIENT; see SLOW

unhygienic creature FLY

unidentified SOME

unidentified writer ANON

uniform DRESS; EQUAL; EVEN; FLAT; LEVEL; SAME; SUIT; U; ■ EQUABLE; LIVERY; REGULAR; STRAIGHT

uniform, part of BERET

unimagined REAL

unimportant PETTY; SMALL; ■ TRIVIAL

unimportant member COG

unimpressive PALE; WEAK

uninhibited FREE

uninjured see UNHARMED

uninspired STALE

unintelligent DIM; THICK (qv)

uninteresting ARID; DRY; see BORING

uninteresting person BORE; BORER

uninvited, come/go CRASH

union BOND; EU; LOCK; MATCH; NUM; TU; U; ■ CONCERT; EQUITY; JUNCTION; FEDERATION; LEAGUE; MARRIAGE; MERGER; WEDDING; can signal something to do with marriage or wedding; can indicate something to do with rugby

union cheater is likely to refer to adulterer, adultery etc

union fellow BROTHER

Union Jack* FLAG

union leader U

union, make a see UNITE

union man PICKET

union member BROTHER; can indicate husband, wife, bride or groom

union members TU

union, old NUM; NUR

union, teaching NUT

Unionist politician UMP

unique ALONE; LONE; ONE; ONLY; SINGLE; SOLE

uniquely ONCE

unit I; ONE; PART; SQUAD; WATT; *see* MEASURE; [◊ TRUST]

unit, Morse DASH; DOT

unit of speed KNOT

unit of weight K; KILO; L; LB; OZ; SI; TON

unit, sound BEL

unite ALLY; BOND; JOIN; KNIT; LINK; TIE.; WED; WELD; ■ FEDERATE; MARRY; MERGE

united ONE; U; UTD; WED; can indicate something to do with Siamese twins

United Nations UN; WORLD

United player RED

universal U

universe ALL; COSMOS

university ASTON; BATH; KEELE; LSE; MIT; OU; OXFORD; READING; U; UNI; YALE; [◊ COURSE; DEGREE; UP]

university, at UP

university course PPE

university course, take a READ

university crew ISIS

university entrance U

university exams GREATS

university, in READING; UP

university man BA; DON

university, member of DON; PROF; ■ DEAN; PROCTOR

university official DEAN

university period TERM

university place CAMPUS

university position CHAIR

university sportsman BLUE

university student SIZAR; SIZER

university type BLUE

unjustified anagram indicator

unkempt RAGGED; SHAGGY

unkind ILL

unkind act CUT

unknown ANON; BLIND; X; Y; Z; ■ STRANGER

unknown amount X; Y; Z

unknown author ANON

unknown, previously NEW; NOVEL

unknown quantity X; Y; Z

unknown sound EX; WHI (for example to construct WHILE); WHY

unladen O (i.e. nothing) to be nested within a component

unlicensed driver L

unlike OTHER; opposite indicator

unlikely anagram indicator

unlikely to fail GOOD; SAFE; SECURE; SURE

unlimited FREE; first and last letters to be omitted (as "unlimited budget" → UDGE)

unlit DARK

unload DROP; ■ DELIVER

unlocked OPEN

unloved O to be omitted as "unloved dog" → DG

unlucky EVIL

unmanageable anagram indicator

unmannerly COARSE; RUDE

unmarried FREE; SINGLE; M to be omitted from associated word as "Unmarried girl said to be accomplished" clues ABLE (i.e. M from MABLE)

unmarried lady MISS; SPINSTER

unmatched ODD

unmoved FIRM; STABLE; STILL

unnamed N to be omitted from a word

unnatural growth WIG

unnecessary EXTRA; ■ NEEDLESS; SURPLUS

unnerve SPOOK

unoccupied FREE

unofficial PRIVATE

unofficially anagram indicator

unopened indicator that initial letter should be omitted

unoriginal OLD; STALE
unorthodox anagram indicator
unpaid FREE; LAY; ■ AMATEUR
unpainted BARE; PLAIN
unpalatable BITTER
unperceptive BLIND; can call for a term ending in -eyed (bleary-eyed etc)
unplanned anagram indicator
unpleasant AWFUL; FOUL; HAIRY; ICKY; ILL; NASTY; RANK; ROUGH; RUDE
unpleasant character/person BOUNDER; CAD; CRUD; HOUND; RAT
unpleasant experience, very HELL
unpleasant smell BO
unpleasant woman TROUT; WITCH
unpopular OUT
unpopular name MUD
unpractised GREEN; RUSTY
unpredictable SCATTY
unpredictably anagram indicator
unprepared RASH
unpretentious HUMBLE (qv)
unproductive DRY; LEAN; POOR; ■ BARREN
unprotected OPEN; first and last letters to be omitted
unpunctual LATE; ■ IRREGULAR
unqualified DEAD; LAY; SHEER; UTTER; ■ THOROUGH
unqualified person L
unravelled, unravelling anagram indicator
unreasonable MAD; TALL; anagram indicator
unreasonable charge, make EXACT
unreasonably anagram indicator
unrecorded LIVE; ■ TACIT
unrefined CRUDE; ROUGH; RAW; ■ COARSE
unrelaxed TAUT; TENSE; ■ STRAINED
unreliable DODGY; GAMMY; IFFY; anagram indicator
unreliably anagram indicator

unresolved LOOSE
unrest anagram indicator; ■ DISQUIET
unrestrained FREE; LOOSE; OPEN; WILD; anagram indicator
unrestricted FREE; LOOSE
unruffled EVEN; ■ SMOOTH
unruly anagram indicator
unruly child BRAT
unruly crowd MOB
unruly youngster/youth BRAT; TED
unsatisfactory BAD; OFF; POOR
unsavoury OFF
unscrupulous operator SPIV; *see* CRIMINAL, TRAITOR
unseasoned RAW
unseated U; anagram indicator
unseeing BLIND
unseemly SEEDY
unserviceable US (i.e. colloquialism for 'useless')
unsettled OWING; ■ OUTSTANDING; anagram indicator
unskilful player HAM
unskilled GREEN; RAW
unsmiling STERN
unsociable type LONER
unsophisticated CRUDE; ■ NAVE
unspeaking MUTE
unspecified amount SOME; X; Y
unspoken DUMB; TACIT; ■ IMPLICIT
unstable MAD; anagram indicator
unsteadily anagram indicator
unsteady, be LURCH; *see* STAGGER
unsteady gait ROLL
unstuck anagram indicator
unsuitable INAPT
unsullied CHASTE
unsympathetic HARD
untamed WILD
untanned PALE
untidiness MESS
untidy SLOPPY; anagram indicator
untidy home/place TIP
untidy person SCRUFF
untie LOOSE

until TILL

untold COUNTLESS

untouched VIRGINAL

untrendy OUT

untrue FALSE

untrue, was LIED

untrustworthy type BOUNDER; *see* ROGUE

untruth FIB; LIE; TALE

untruth, tell LIE

untypical *see* ODD

unusual EXTRA; NOVEL; ODD; OUTRE; RARE; RUM; SPECIAL; STRANGE; ■ QUAINT; SCARCE; anagram indicator

unusual item anagram of ITEM

unusual name anagram of NAME

unusually EXTRA; anagram indicator

unusually reared can refer to a Manx cat, or cat o'nine tails

unused GREEN; MINT; NEW; RAW; UN (i.e. "un" to be used)

unwanted fat FLAB

unwavering CONSTANT

unwelcome visitors LICE

unwelcoming FROSTY; ICY

unwell AILING; ILL; OFF; SICK

unwell, become AIL

unwell, was AILED

unwieldy anagram indicator

unwilling AVERSE; LOTH; SHY; can indicate the circumstances of being intestate

unwise RASH; ■ IMPRUDENT

unwisely anagram indicator

unworthy CHEAP; LOW; *see* LOW

unwound EASED; anagram indicator

unwritten ORAL

unyielding FIRM; HARD; SOLID; ■ IRON

up FAR; HIGH; OVER; RAISED; RIDING; RISE; RISEN; STAND; ■ ASTRIDE; STANDING; anagram indicator; reversal indicator in a DC; can indicate something to do with flying, pilot, trapeze artiste; in a down clue can indicate that the

last mentioned component is to be placed at the beginning

up and about ASTIR

up and down when in a DC can indicate the answer is a palindrome as "deck going up and down" → POOP

up and down, going *see* UP AND DOWN

up-country the name of a country to be reversed (thus EIRE → ERIE)

up-market TRAM (think about it)

up, one who's RIDER

up-stream reversal of a synonym, as FLOW → WOLF

up to TILL; ■ AFTER (as in "What's he up to?")

up-to-date HIP; LATE; MODERN; NEW; RECENT; ■ ABREAST; CURRENT

up the creek anagram indicator

up the Swanee anagram indicator

up to the time UNTIL

upbeat MAL (i.e. LAM reversed)

upbraid RATE

upfront AHEAD; OPEN; OVERT; first letter indicator

upheaval anagram indicator; reverse indicator in a DC

uphill reversal indicator

upholding reversal indicator

upland DOWN

upland area *see* UPLANDS

uplands MOOR

uplifted reversal indicator

uplifting reversal indicator

upon ATOP; NO (i.e. reverse of "on")

upper HIGH; LOFTY; TOP

upper chamber ATTIC

upper-class A; POSH; U

upper class chap/type TOFF

upper-class girl DEB

upper classes AB; ABS; ■ NOBS; TOFFS

upper crust PEERS; SIAL (geol.)

upper house SENATE

upper leg THIGH

uppers, on BROKE; SKINT

upping reversal indicator

upright ERECT; POST; MORAL; STANDING; STRAIGHT; TR (i.e. reversal of RT); WORTHY

uprising REVOLT; reversal indicator

uprising, small MOLEHILL

uproar CRY; DIN; NOISE; RACKET; RIOT; RUCTION

uprooted anagram indicator

ups and downs, have PITCH

upset CROSS; RATTLE; RILE; SAD; SPILL; TES (i.e. reverse of "set"); ■ INVERT; NETTLE; REVERSE; reversal indicator (as "a bit upset" → TRO or TRAP); anagram indicator; *see* ANNOY

upset about ER (i.e. reversal of RE)

upset, be CRY; WEEP

upset tummy BUG

upsetting anagram indicator; reverse indicator

upside-down anagram indicator; reversal indicator; ■ ONHEAD

upstanding ERECT

upsurge RISE; RISING; reversal indicator

upturn PU; RECOVERY

upturned PU (i.e. reverse of "up"); reversal indicator (as "upturned nose" → ESON)

upward DRAW (in a DC); reversal indicator;

upward progress RISE; can indicate that a synonym of "progress" is to be reversed, hence OG

upwards reversal indicator

uranium U

urchin ARAB; GAMIN

urge DRIVE; EGG; GOAD; HIE; ITCH; PRESS; PROD; YEN

urgent PRESSING

urgent message SOS

Uriah HEEP

Uriah Heep, like UMBLE

urn POT

Uruguay U

us WE

US STATES; can indicate American spelling; also beware that it can indicate a word or usage which is peculiar to the U.S. and not else-where (for example, "specialist in US court" → ALIENIST)

US agent FED; ■ REALTOR

US agents CIA; GMEN

us, all of WE

US car DODGE

US chap BO

US city LA; EC; GARY; NY; RENO; ■ SEATTLE; WACO

US college MIT

US company INC

US conflict NAM

US explorers NASA

US friend BUD

US intelligence CIA

US industrialist FORD

US institute MIT

US investigator GMAN

US investigators CIA; GMEN

US lawyer DA

US mag LIFE; TIME

US mail ARMOR

US novelist COOPER

us, of OUR

US official DA

US petrol GAS

US politician DEM

US president ABE; BUSH; CARTER; FORD; GRANT; NIXON

US quarters CASH

US railroad EL

US seaman GOB

US soldier, old VET

US sports stadium BOWL

US statesman DULLES

US student COED; MAJOR

US tool AX

US town BURG

US volume LITER

usage CUSTOM; HABIT; anagram indicator

use APPLY; AVAIL; DO; WEAR; ■ EMPLOY; FUNCTION; anagram indicator; sounding like U's this word can, with a homophone indicator, call for UU

use different anagram of USE e.g. SUE

use, do not OMIT; SPARE

use force PRESS

use less HUSBAND
use of drugs TRIP
use, to be of AVAIL; SERVE
use wrong words LIE.
use wrongly SUE (anagram of "use")
used OLD; anagram indicator
used as leader the preceding word or component to be placed at the front of the solution
used by run indicator
used for the previous word(s) to be used as an anagram for what follows
used, something TOOL
used to be WAS; WERE
used to court DATED; WOOED
used to have HAD
used up anagram or reversal indicator
useful BOOT; HANDY
useful quality ASSET
useful, something ASSET
useless DUD; DUFF; IDLE; OFF; TRASHY; US; VAIN
useless article LEMON
useless lot SHOWER
useless person DRIP; LEMON
useless thing ASSET
user SPENDER
usher GUIDE; LEAD; PILOT; SHOW; STEER
usher in nesting indicator
using PER; WITH; run indicator
usual PAR; ■ GENERAL; NORMAL
usual behaviour HABIT; CUSTOM; FORM
usual, not the anagram indicator
usurping replacement indicator, as in "Route: man usurping brave city-dweller" → ROMAN
Utah UT
utensil FORK; SPOON
utilise USE
utilised USED; anagram indicator
utmost, do one's STRAIN; STRIVE
utter ISSUE; SAY; SPEAK; STATE; TALK; TOTAL; VOICE; ■ ARRANT; COMPLETE; ho-

mophone indicator; can indicate the first and last letter of a word
utterly PLUMB; homophone indicator, as "utterly enthusiastic bore" → EAGRE
UU with a homophone indicator can call for USE

Vv

vacant BARE; BLANK; FREE; HOLLOW; VAIN; can indicate that all but the first and last letters are to be omitted as "vacant possession" clues PN
vacate omission indicator, as "Cleaner seat I vacate" → CHAR
vacated all but the first and last letters to be omitted as "vacated house" clues HE; see VACANT
vacation REST; VAC
vacillate HOVER; WAVER; ■ TEETER
vacillating anagram indicator
vacuous middle letters of associated word to be omitted
vacuum VOID
vagrant HOBO; TRAMP; anagram indicator
vague DIM; FAINT; ■ HAZY; INDISTINCT; anagram indicator;
vaguely IDLY; anagram indicator
vain IDLE; ■ USELESS
vain display POMP
vainly, acting FUTILITY
vale GLEN; can indicate some form of goodbye (adieu, cheerio, ciao, farewell, so long etc)
valet MAN; ■ LACKEY; see SERVANT
valiant BOLD; BRAVE; DOUGHTY
valid RIGHT
valid, no longer UP
valise CASE

valley COMBE; DALE; DENE; DELL; DINGLE; DIP; GLADE; GLEN; GORGE; GULLY; VALE; ■ COOMB; RIA; TEMPE

valley, middle of COMB

valour BRAVERY; COURAGE

valuable ASSET

valuable card TRUMP

valuable possession ASSET

valuable, something ASSET

valuables TROVE; ■ TREASURE

valuable, hidden TROVE

value COST; PRICE; RATE; ■ AMOUNT; PRIZE; RESPECT; SET; WORTH

value, of little BASE; CHEAP

valueless thing FIG

vamoose SCARPER

vamp FLIRT

van FORE; FRONT; LEAD; ■ CAMPER; HEAD

van, in the LEADS; LED; can indicate component to be placed at the beginning

vandalised anagram indicator

vanish END; GO

vanished GONE

vanishing omission indicator

vapid BORING; DULL; FLAT; *see* TEDIOUS

vaporizer MISTER

vapour FOG; MIST; STEAM

vapours FUMES

variable X; Y

variation CHANGE; ■ TYPE; anagram indicator

varied anagram indicator

variegated anagram indicator

varies anagram indicator

variety KIND; MAKE; RANGE; SORT; TYPE; anagram indicator

variety available RANGE

variety, bit of ACT; TURN

various DIVERS; DIVERSE; SUNDRY; anagram indicator

varnish COAT; GLOSS; can indicate something to do with finger-nail

vary CHANGE; WAVER

vase POT; URN

vase, Chinese MING

vassal SLAVE

vast GREAT; HUGE; SEA; ■ SWEEPING

vast expanse SEA; SPACE

vat TANK

Vat man COOPER

Vatican edict BULL

vault ARCH; CLEAR; CRYPT; JUMP; LEAP; SKY; anagram indicator

veer TACK

vegetable BEAN; BEET; CHARD; PEA; LEEK; PLANT; SPROUT; SPUD; ■ MARROW; NEEP; ONION; SQUASH; SWEDE

vegetable, inedible part of CHOKE

vegetables CHIPS; PEAS; sounding like P's this word can, with a homophone indicator, call for PP

vegetarian food PULSE

vegetation SCRUB; SEDGE

vehicle AGENT; BIKE; BRAKE; BUS; CAB; CAR; CART; COACH; DRAY; FLOAT; GIG; LIMO; MINI; ROLLS; SLED; SLEDGE; STAGE; TANK; TRAIN; TRAM; TRAP; TRIKE; TRUCK; VAN; ■ CAMPER; CHANNEL; SCOOTER; SLEIGH; TRACTOR

vehicle, electric FLOAT

vehicle, leave PARK

vehicle, old CRATE

vehicle, public UTE; *see* VEHICLE

vehicle, slow-moving HEARSE

vehicle, sort of TURBO; *see* VEHICLE

vehicle, specialist HEARSE; *see* VEHICLE

veil COVER; NET; SCREEN

vein LODE; MOOD; [◊ ORE]

velocity SPEED; V

velocity of light C

vend SELL

vendor SELLER

veneer FACE

venerable churchman BEDE

Venetian BLIND

Venetian merchant POLO
Venetian lawman DOGE
vengeance ATE (i.e. goddess)
venison, source of DEER
venison supplier DEER
venom MALICE; SPITE; STING
venomous indicative of a snake, scorpion etc.
venomous creature RATTLER
vent FLUE; GAP; SLIT
ventilate AIR
ventilated AIRED; AIRY
ventriloquist [◊ DUMMY]
venture BET; CHANCE; DARE; GAMBLE; PRESUME; RISK; STAKE; TRY
venture, commercial SPEC
venue FAIR; PLACE; SITE; SPOT
venue, sporting ARENA; FIELD; GROUND; RING
Venus de Milo can indicate something to do with the Louvre or lack of arms
veracity TRUTH
verb WORD
verbal, verbally can signal a colloquialism such as a slang term; homophone indicator
verbal thrust DIG
verbose WINDY
verdant GREEN; LUSH
Verdi opera AIDA
Verdi production AIDA
verge BRIM; BORDER; EDGE; HEM; LIP; SIDE; TEND
verify CHECK; TEST; ■ CONFIRM
verily YEA
verisimilitude REALISM; TRUTH
verity TRUTH
vermin LOUSE; RAT; RATS; MICE; ■ MOUSE
verminous RATTY
vermouth IT; ITALIAN
vernacular CANT; SLANG
Verne JULES; [◊ EIGHTY; WORLD]
Veronica can indicate something to do with speedwell
versatile anagram indicator

verse CANTO; DITTY; EPIC; LINES; LYRIC; ODE; POEM; STAVE; TEXT; V; ■ JINGLE; TENSON; [◊ FEET]
verse competition TENSON
verse once RIME
verse, piece of LINE
versed, well UP
verses, pieces of FEET
version EDITION; FORM; KIND; SORT; TYPE; anagram indicator as "screen version" can call for an anagram of SCREEN
vertebra AXIS
vertical PLUMB
vertical aspect FACE
vertiginous STEEP
very JOLLY; REAL; SO; TOO; V; WELL; ■ AWFUL; AWFULLY; MIGHTY; TRUE
very bad CHRONIC; DIRE
very big OS
very briefly FUL
very cold ICY
very distant FAR; ■ REMOTE
very fast PRESTO
very fat OS
very fit AI
very fine AI
very French TRES
very good ACE; AI; BOFFO (U.S.); CLASS; CLASSI (i.e. class 1); FINE; OK; PI; PLUM; RIGHT; SO; STAR
very good guide SAINT
very good, not omission of PI
very good thing TOPS
very good person BRICK; GEM; SAINT
very heartless VY
very, in America REAL
very interested in INTO
very keen MAD; ■ INTO
very large OS
very little DROP; GRAIN; LEAST; WHIT
very long time AGES
very loud FF
very many MASSES; ■ UNTOLD; *see* LOTS, MANY
very much FAR; SO

very musical ASSAI; MOLTO
very nearly ALMOST; VER
very old SORE
very ordinary VO
very precise NICE
very quiet/quietly PP
very recently JUST
very same SPIT
very small MINI; SLIGHT; TEENY; V; WEE
very small one TICH
very soft PP
very special RARE
very steep SHEER
vessel ARK; BARK; BATH; BIN; BOAT; BOTTLE; BOWL; BRIG; CAN; CRAFT; CROCK; CRUSE; CUP; EWER; FONT; FLUTE; GLASS; JAR; KETCH; KETTLE; LAUNCH; LINER; MY (i.e. motor yacht); OILER; PAIL; PAN; POT; RAFT; SCOW; SHE; SHIP; SLOOP; SS; SUB; TIN; TUN; URN, VASE; VAT; VEIN; WOK; YAWL; ■ BARQUE; BASIN; BEAKER; CHURN; CUTTER; DINGHY; SCHOONER; STEAMER; WHERRY; *see* BOAT, CONTAINER, SHIP
vessel, American US; USS
vessel, Chinese WOK
vessel, cooking PAN; POT
vessel, on a component to be nested within SS
vessel, powered SS; MY
vest SINGLET
vestibule HALL
vestige EMBER
vestment ALB; COPE; ROBE; STOLE
vet CHECK; OK; ■ SCREEN; SURGEON
vetch ERS; FODDER
veteran OLD; OLDIE
veto BAN; BAR; BLACK; NO
veto by France NON
vex GALL; IRK; NAG; RILE; SORE
vexation ANGER; GALL; HUMP
via BY; THROUGH; WAY
viaduct BRIDGE

vibrate ROCK
vibration PULSE
vicar CURATE; REV; [◊ BRAY]
vicar's home BRAY; MANSE
vicarage VIC
vice CLAMP; GRIP; PORN; SIN; ■ FAILING; GRIPPER
Vichy water EAU
vicinity CLOSE; NEAR; NIGH
vicinity, in the ABOUT
vicious HARD; ■ LETHAL; *see* CRUEL; anagram indicator
viciously anagram indicator
vicissitude CROSS
victim ABEL; BUTT; PREY; GAME; ■ QUARRY; SUCKER
victim of con PIGEON
victim of fratricide ABEL
victim of disease LEPER
victimise FRAME
victor CHAMP; WINNER
Victoria PLUM; V; VIC; VR; can indicate something to do with the railway station; can indicate something to do with Australia
Victorian OLD; can indicate something Australian (via state of Victoria)
victory MATE; V; VE (i.e. VE Day); WIN; ■ TRIUMPH
victory, day of VE
victory, easy ROMP
victory, gain a WIN
victory, gained a WON
victory in Europe VE
victory, sign of V
video TAPE; ■ RECORDER
vie CONTEND
view ANGLE; EYE; FACET; GAZE; PEER; PEEK; SCAN; SCENE; SEE; SIGHT; SLANT TAKE; ■ ATTITUDE; OPINION; PROSPECT; REGARD; STANCE; VISTA; WATCH
view, had in SAW
view, have OPINE
viewed SAW
viewed from starboard reversal indicator
viewer EYE; OPTIC

viewpoint ANGLE; SLANT; ■ OPINION; PROSPECT; STANCE; *see* VIEW

vigil WATCH

vigilant AWAKE; AWARE

vigorous HEARTY; LUSTY; RACY; WELL

vigorous activity GO; *see* VIGOUR

vigorously anagram indicator

vigour DASH; GO; GUSTO; DRIVE; FIRE; HEART; PEP; SAP; STEAM; *see* VITALITY

Viking leader ROLLO; V

vile BASE

village, small VIL

villain CAD; CHEAT; CROOK; HEAVY; ROGUE; ■ BADDY; BANDIT; BRAVO; THUG

villainous BAD; EVIL; SINISTER

villainy EVIL

vindicate CLEAR

vinegary SOUR

vineyard CRU

vintage AGE; CROP; OLD; YEAR

Viola TWIN

violated anagram indicator

violence FORCE

violent RABID; SAVAGE; STORMY; TOUGH; anagram indicator

violent person BRUTE; ROUGH

violently anagram indicator

Violet VI

Violet's VIS (i.e. Vi's)

violin BOW

violin part BRIDGE; NECK

violin's accompaniment BOW

violinist BOW; STERN

VIP CELEB; NIB; NOB; SWELL

viral infection COLD; FLU

virgin NEW; ■ GREEN; RAW

Virginia VA; can indicate something to do with tobacco

Virgo SIGN

virile MACHO

virile types HEMEN (i.e. he-men)

virtually all but the last letter of a word to be used

virtually everything AL

virtually immobile STUCK

virtue HOPE

virtue of being, by QUA

virtuous CHASTE; GOOD; JUST; PI; MORAL

virtuoso ACE; EXPERT; PRO

virtuous person ST

virus BUG; FLU

virus, deadly EBOLA

visa PASS

viscosity, measure of STOKE

viscous liquid OIL

visibility, an aid to LIGHT (qv); LIGHTING

visible OUT

visible, barely DIM

visible in run indicator

vision DREAM; IDEA; SIGHT

vision, have a DREAM

visionary EYE; PROPHET; SEER

visit CALL; HAUNT; SEE; STAY; TRIP; nesting indicator

visited SAW

visiting IN; nesting indicator as "Judge visiting fine islands" clues FIJI

visitor CALLER; GUEST; ■ STRANGER

visitor from outer space ET

visitors, unwelcome LICE

visor MASK; PEAK

vista VIEW

vital KEY; LIVE; can refer to some vital function or part of the body, organ etc.

vital energy *see* LIFE FORCE

vital fluid BLOOD

vital fluid, lost BLED

vital part ORGAN

vitality GO; VIM; SAP; ZEST; ZING; *see* VIGOUR

vitamin STEROID; also the letters A, C etc

vitiate FLAW

vivacity BRIO; GO

vivid BRIGHT; GRAPHIC

Vivien LEIGH

vocal LOUD; ORAL; homophone indicator as "vocal ensemble" → QUIRE

vocal exercise SCALE

vocal expression TONE; homophone indicator

vocal item SONG

vocal piece CANTO; CHANT; SONG; *see* SONG

vocal style DICTION; ■ ACCENT; BROGUE; INFLECTION

vocalise SING

vocalised homophone indicator

vocalist SINGER

vocally homophone indicator

vocation CALL; CALLING; *see* JOB

vociferous homophone indicator

vogue FAD; RAGE; TREND

voguish IN

voice AIR; ALTO; BASS; EMIT; PART; PASSIVE; SAY; SING; SINGER; SPEAK; TENOR; TONE; UTTER

voice, given homophone indicator

voiced homophone indicator

voiced disapproval TUT

voices homophone indicator

void BLANK; EMPTY; NULL; SPACE

void in, a NO

void of omission indicator

volatile anagram indicator

volatile liquid ETHER

volcano ETNA

volcanic anagram indicator

volley BURST; FIRE; SALVO

Voltaire's work CANDIDE

volte-face a synonym of "face" to be reversed e.g. GUM

volume AMOUNT; BOOK; BULK; CC; CL; GAL; MASS; QUART; SIZE; SPACE; TOMB; V; VOL; ■ BODY; PUBLICATION; STERE; can indicate a volume level in music e.g. piano, forte

volume, American LITER

volume, negligible CC

voluntary FREE; ■ OPTIONAL

voluntary basis, on a FREE

volunteer OFFER; ■ IRREGULAR; TENDER

volunteer force TA

volunteers TA

volunteers in school PTA

vomit CAT; SPEW

vote AY; AYE; CROSS; ELECT; NAY; NO; POLL; X; YES; ■ SELECT

vote against NAY; NO

vote cast VETO (i.e. an anagram)

vote, consenting/for/in favour AY; AYE; YES; ■ NOD; TICK

vote of approval AY; AYE; NOD; YES

votes against NOES

votes cast BALLOT

voting, change in SWING

voting method PR

voting no ANTI

voting scheme/system PR

voucher CHIT; TICKET; TOKEN; ■ COUPON

vow OATH; SWEAR; WORD

vowed SWORE

voyage SAIL; TRIP; ■ CRUISE; TRAVEL; anagram indicator

voyager *see* SAILOR

vulgar BASE; CHEAP; CRASS; FLASHY; GROSS; LOUD; LOW; RUDE; TACKY; ■ COMMON; NON-U; colloquialism indicator; can indicate the omission of an initial H

vulgar, not PURE

vulgar people, those EM (i.e. 'em)

vulnerable OPEN; ■ EXPOSED; anagram indicator

Ww

wacky anagram indicator

wad BUN; PAD; ROLL

wade FORD; PADDLE

waffle CAKE; PRATTLE; ■ RABBIT

wag CARD; COMIC; JOKER; WAVE; WIT

wage PAY; SCREW; ■ INCOME

wage deduction NI
wage increase RAISE; RISE
wager BET; PUNT
wagered, amount STAKE
wages HIRE; ■ GUERDON; *see* WAGE
wagging anagram indicator
Wagner's operas RING
wagon CART; DRAY; VAN; WAIN; ■ HOPPER
wagon, be on ABSTAIN
wagon, man on the TT
wagon, on the DRY; SOBER; TT
wail BAWL; HOWL; KEEN; YAMMER
wailer KEENER
wain CART
waist can indicate middle letters
waistcoat, American VEST
wait BIDE; HOVER; STAY; TARRY; ■ ATTEND; LINGER; PAUSE; SERVE
wait outside component(s) to be nested within BIDE
wait, prepared to PATIENT
waiter TRAY; ■ STEWARD
waiters can indicate something to do with a queue (Example: "Tip the waiters, say" leading to CUE)
wake ROUSE; WASH
wake, hold MOURN
wake up ROUSE
waking UP
walk AMBLE; GAIT; MALL; MARCH; PACE; PAD; PLOD; PROM; REEL; STEP; TRAMP; TREAD; ■ RAMBLE; STRIDE; STROLL; TURN; WADDLE; [◊ FOOT]
walk (about) GAD
walk affectedly MINCE
walk briskly STRIDE
walk clumsily LUMBER
walk, covered STOA
walk, difficult LIMP
walk gently AMBLE
walk, go for a RAMBLE
walk, graceless WADDLE
walk haughtily STALK; STRUT
walk heavily RAMBLE; TRAMP

walk hesitatingly HALT; LIMP; REEL; STAGGER
walk lamely HOBBLE; LIMP
walk, long TRAMP
walk-out STRIKE
walk out on LEAVE; STRAND
walk proudly STRUT
walk quietly SNEAK
walk round ECAP (i.e. rev.)
walk, short STEP; can refer to any synonym for "walk" having its last letter omitted – *see* WALK
walk slowly AMBLE; CRAWL
walk unevenly WADDLE
walk unsteadily TODDLE
walk wearily PLOD; TRAMP
walked TROD; ■ TRODDEN; *see* WALK
walked off QUIT; LEFT
walked purposefully STRODE
walker LEG; ■ TRAMP
walkers reported FEAT
walking stick STAFF
walkway RAMP
wall DYKE; ■ BARRIER
wall fitting TILE
wall, part of, under roof GABLE
wall, put top on COPE
Wallace [◊ SANDERS]
wallet CASE
wallop ALE; BEAT; BEER; BLOW; HIT (qv); SLAP; TAN; THUMP
wallpaper, sort of FLOCK
Walpole WHIG
walrus MORSE; TACHE (i.e. moustache)
Walter MITTY; SCOTT
wan FAINT; PALE
wand STICK
wander ERR; DRIFT; GAD; RANGE; ROAM; ROVE; STRAY; ■ AMBLE; MEANDER; RAMBLE
wander aimlessly MOON
wander idly MOON
wanderer ROVER
wandering ASTRAY; ERRANT; MAD; ■ SHORTFALL; anagram indicator

wandering around anagram indicator

wane DECREASE; *see* DECLINE

want COVET; DEARTH; DESIRE; LACK; LONG; NEED; WISH

want, badly LONG

want to change anagram of WANT

wanted, exactly what's IT

wanting omission indicator

wanton TROLLOP; anagram indicator

wantonly anagram indicator

war FIGHT; SCRAP; ■ BATTLE; CONFLICT; FIGHTING

War Department MOD

war, end of PEACE; R

war, god/personification of ARES; MARS

war hero ACE; BADER

War Ministry MOD

war, outbreak of W

war paint usually indicates something to do with make-up and cosmetics

war, place of FRONT

war, prepare for ARM

war, proponent of HAWK

war-time hero, pilot *see* WAR HERO

war vessel SUB

warble QUAVER; TRILL

warbler SEDGE

ward CHARGE; PARRY; ROOM; ■ MINOR

ward off FEND; PARRY; ■ AVERT

warden RANGER

warder GUARD; SCREW

wardrobe GARB; *see* CLOTHING, GARMENT

warehouse DEPOT; STORE; ■ GODOWN (Eastern)

warfare ACTION

warhorse CHARGER

warm AIR; CLOSE; COSY; FAIR; HEARTY; HEAT; HOT; NEAR (i.e. clue in guessing game); SNUG; TOAST

warm covering FUR

warm, seriously BAKE

warm up HEAT

warmonger HAWK

warmth GLOW; HEAT; SUN

warmth, source of COAL; FIRE; SUN

warn BEEP; TELL; ■ CAUTION; TOOT

warning ALARM; AMBER; CAVE; FORE; HOOT; HOOTER; HOOTING; HORN; MIND; OMEN; SIREN; STEADY; ■ ALERT; CAUTION; CAVEAT; TELLING; THREAT

warning, give BEEP; HOOT; TOOT

warning light AMBER; BEACON

warning, player's FORE

warning signal BEEP; HOOTER; ■ SIREN

warp BEND; BUCKLE; TWIST

warped, warps anagram indicator

warplane FIGHTER; ZERO

warrant EARN; PLEDGE; PROOF; WRIT; ■ DESERVE

warrant-officer SM

warren MAZE

warring anagram indicator

warrior BRAVE; KNIGHT; ■ FIGHTER; *see* SOLDIER

warrior, great HERO

warriors IMPI

wars, in the anagram indicator

warship RAM; SUB; ■ CRUISER

warship, ancient RAM

warships NAVY

warmth, feeling of GLOW

wartime FIELD (as in field action denoting a battle)

wartime bomb VI

wartime leader DUCE; TITO

Warwick EARL

wary CHARY

was EX; LIVED

was carried RODE

was first LED

was informed HEARD; TOLD

was MP SAT

was obliged HAD

was quick RAN; SPED

wash BATHE; CLEAN; FLUSH; LAVE; MOP; RINSE; SCRUB; WAKE; ■ LAUNDER

wash and iron LAUNDER

wash gently LAP

washed out PALE; WAN

washer O

washing agent SOAP

Washington WA

Washington area DC

wasn't feeling well AILED

wasp, large HORNET

wastage LOSS

waste BLUE (spend extravagantly); GASH; KILL; LOSE; REFUSE; SCRAP; SLAG; WITHER; ■ DESERT; DREGS

waste away ATROPHY

waste disposal anagram of WASTE

waste, lay RAVAGE

waste material LITTER; *see* RUBBISH

waste product ASH; SLAG

waste receptacle BIN

waste time DALLY; IDLE; TRIFLE

wasted anagram indicator; omission indicator e.g. "with nothing wasted" instructs that O be omitted

wasteful of the word which follows to be omitted

wasting LOSING; ■ DECAY; anagram indicator; omission indicator as "time wasting" requires T to be omitted

wasting time IDLING; ■ TRIFLING; T to be omitted

watch EYE; GUARD; HUNTER; LO; REGARD; SCAN; SEE; SHIFT; TICKER; TIMER; VIEW; VIGIL; WAKE; [◊ TIME]

watch open-mouthed GAPE; GAWP

watch out CAVE (Latin); MIND

watch over GUARD; REMIT (i.e. reversal of "timer")

watched EYED; SAW; SEEN; *see* SEE

watcher EYE

watchword MOTTO

water AQUA; BROOK; BURN; CHANNEL; LAKE; MAIN; MED; MERE; OUSE; POND; POOL; RAIN; REACH; RILL; RIVER; SEA; SOUND; SPRING; STREAM; TARN; TIDE; URE; URINE; ■ ADAM'S ALE; CANAL; DILUTE; OCEAN; SPRAY; SPRING; can indicate a specific river, sea or ocean, *see* RIVER, SEA; [◊ LAVENDER]

water-basin LAVER

water, behave like FLOW

water bird SWAN

water channel GUTTER

water control TAP

water course STREAM

water, deep TROUBLE

water, dabble in PADDLE

water, drops of RAIN

water escaping LEAK

water excess FLOOD

water, foreign EAU

water, go through ROW; SWIM

water-heater BOILER

water, in deep anagram indicator

water, lacking NEAT; *see* WATER, OUT OF

water, let in LEAK

water, means of piping MAINS

water, much SEA

water, not a lot of DROP

water on, pour DOUSE

water, out of/short of ARID; DRY; ■ PARCHED

water, quantity of POOL; SEA; *see* WATER

water, running RILL; *see* RIVER

water, salt SOLENT; *see* SEA

water-shaft WELL

water, shallow FORD

water-ski SURF

water, small amount of DROP

water, source of WELL

water, splash in WALLOW

water, still POOL; POND

water, stretch of CHANNEL

water supply SPA; SPRING; WELL

water, take to SWIM

water, without ARID; DRY; NEAT

watercourse DYKE; ■ CANAL; RIVER

watered, being can indicate a component is to be nested within a form of water e.g. rain, as in "After square being watered, German will provide level" → RATING

waterfowl SWAN; *see* BIRD

watering-hole/place BAR; RESORT; SPA; *see* TAVERN

waterlogged area SWAMP

Waterloo ROUT; can indicate something to do with the battle or the railway station

waterproof MAC

waters SWELL; SEAS

waterside BANK; BEACH; SHORE

waterway CANAL; RIVER; can indicate a specific river, *see* RIVER

watery SEROUS

watery monster HYDRA

watts W

Waugh novel SCOOP

wave BAND (i.e. radio); BECK; BORE; FLAG; GREET; SIGN; WAG; WASH; ■ BILLOW; BREAKER; EAGRE; RIPPLE; ROLLER; anagram indicator, as "crime wave" → MERCI; *see* WAVES

wave top CREST

waver HOVER; ROCK; VARY; anagram indicator

wavering anagram indicator

wavering sound TRILL

waves SEA; SURF; ■ CREST; anagram indicator; can indicate something to do with hair or hairdressing; also *see* WAVE

waves, breaking SURF

waves, in anagram indicator

waves, make SPLASH; SURF

waving anagram indicator

wax GROW; IRE; RISE

waxy stuff RESIN

way AISLE; AVE; DOOR; E; GATE; HOW; LANE; M (i.e. motorway); MALL; MODE; N; PASS; PATH; RD; ROAD; ROUTE; S; ST; TRACK; TRAIL; VIA; W; WALK; WISE; ■ ALLEY; CIRCUIT; COURSE; METHOD; [◊ LINE]

way back can indicate the reversal of a "way", so Rd becomes DR, door becomes ROOD, St becomes TS and so on

way back, on the reversal indicator

way before ST to be placed at the beginning

way, by the can indicate something to do with street furniture, kerb, pavement, sidewalk, etc

way for the French (of the French) *see* WAY, THE FRENCH

way in ENTRY; can indicate that WAY or a synonym (e.g. RD, ST) is to be nested

way, in a anagram indicator

way in France/Paris *see* WAY, THE FRENCH

way, long FAR

way, make WEND; *see* TRAVEL

way of doing things HOW

way of looking ANGLE

way of speaking DICTION

way of working MO

way off FAR

way, old WISE

way, old-fashioned WISE

way out AFAR; DOOR; EGRESS; EXIT; OTT; YAW (i.e. anag.); can indicate a body in space as "Radio set retuned to way out rock" → ASTEROID

way out, on the LEAVING

way, show the LEAD; USHER

way, shown the LED

way, the ALA (i.e. a la)

way, the French RUE; ■ CHEMIN

way things are, the ASIS (i.e. as is)

way, this SO

way though mountains COL; PASS

way to can indicate a verb beginning with BY

way to, the anagram indicator

way up ASCENT; a synonym of "way" (e.g. lane, St) to be re-versed

wayside, the followed by ? can call for DITCH

wayward anagram indicator

we PRONOUN

we'd heard WEED

we had WED

we have, that OUR

we hear homophone indicator

we object US

we objectively US

we're told homophone indicator

we see run indicator

weak FAINT; FEEBLE; FRAIL; LAME; LAX; LIGHT; POOR; PUNY; SLIGHT; THIN; W; ■ MEAGRE

weak, become FADE; ROT

weak person SOP; WEED

weaken AIL; SAP; SHAKE

weakling RUNT

weakness FAILING; LAPSE; VICE; ■ FAULT; can indicate something to do with Achilles' heel

wealth GOLD; MEANS; MONEY; RICHES

wealth, source of MINE

wealthy RICH; ROLLING

wealthy man DIVES

wealthy person NOB

weapon ARM; ARROW; AXE; BILL; BOMB; BOW; DART; GUN; LANCE; PIKE; RIFLE; SPEAR; SWORD ■ DAGGER; EPEE; FLAIL; LUGER; MAUSER; NUKE

weapon in US AX

weapon, jousting LANCE

weapon, sawn-off GU (i.e. last letter omitted from GUN)

weapon store ARMOURY; ■ ARSENAL

weaponry ARMS

weapons, position of PORT

weapons, provided with ARMED

weapons, supply ARM

wear DRESS; GRATE; LAST; SPORT; STAND; STICK; USE; ■ GARB; SHOW; can indicate a specific garment e.g. skirt

Wear* RIVER

wear away ABRADE; ERODE

wear down ERODE; TIRE

wear out TIRE

wearing CLAD; IN; ON; nesting indicator; run indicator

wearing glasses OO to be nested

weary FLAG; SPENT; TIRE; TIRED

weary, get FLAG; TIRE

weasel words SPIN

weaselly type STOAT

weather CLIME

weather, bad FOG; RAIN; SNOW; STORM

weather, dire HAIL

weather feature HIGH; WIND

weather forecasters MET

weather, indication of COCK, GLASS, VANE

weather instrument GLASS

weather the storm COPE

weather, under the ILL; PEAKY; SEEDY; see ILL, SICK

weather, wet RAIN

weathercock VANE

weave WIND

weaver BOTTOM; [◊ LOOM]

weaving anagram indicator

weaving machine LOOM

web TRAP; ■ MAZE

web designer SPIDER

web, use SURF

wed HITCH; MARRIED; MARRY; MATE; SPLICE

wed, get MARRY; MATE

wedding HITCH; UNION

wedding, before the NEE

wedding, person at BRIDE; GROOM; USHER

wedding present TOASTER

wedding response IDO

wedge CHOCK; SCOTCH; ■ PIECE

Wednesday can indicate WOE (via the nursery rhyme)

wee see SMALL, TINY

wee drink DRAM; TOT
weed DOCK; DOPE; GRASS;
HOE; POT; TARE; ■ DAISY;
NETTLE; VETCH; can indicate
a cigarette e.g. fag; or a weak or
thin person e.g. ECTOMORPH
weeds, get rid of HOE
weedy THIN; can indicate something to do with smoking
week WK
weekend K
weekend, part of SAT; SUN
weekly COMIC
weeks can indicate the name of a
month e.g. MAY or an abbrev.
(JAN etc)
weep CRY; REGRET; SOB; ■
LAMENT
weft WOOF
weigh PONDER
weighing device SCALE
weight CT; GRAM; KG; LB;
LOAD; MASS; OUNCE; OZ;
PLUMB; POUND; ST; STONE;
TON, TONNE; ■ DENIER;
GRAMME; MATTER
weight-lifter CRANE; HOIST;
JACK; ■ WINCH
weight, little can indicate either a
weight of relatively small volume
(e.g. OUNCE) or the abbreviated
form of any weight (e.g. L, OZ)
weight-loss plan DIET
weight, of little LIGHT
weight, reduced OZ; ST
weighty HEAVY; THICK
weighty, not LIGHT
weir DAM
weird CREEPY; EERIE; FEY;
ODD; RUM; STRANGE; ana-
gram indicator
welcome AVE; GREET; HELLO;
HI; ■ ACCLAIM; EMBRACE;
SALUTE; nesting indicator
welcoming PLEASANT; ■
CORDIAL
weld BOND; FUSE; JOIN
welfare money DOLE
well ABLY; BORE; FINE; FIT;
HALE; MY (excl.); OK; PIT;
RISE; SO (as in "So?"); SPA;
SPRING; SURGE; ■ AMPLY;

ARTESIAN; GUSHER;
HEALTHY; RESERVOIR;
SOURCE; [◊ OIL; STAIR;
WATER]
well-armed can refer to an octopus
well-being HEALTH
well-connected TIED; [◊
CHAIN]; a synonym of "well"
(qv) to be added
well content OIL; WATER
well-cooked DONE
well-cooked, far from RARE
well-defined CLEAR
well, didn't feel AILED
well done in Spain OLE
well down LOW
well-dressed anagram indicator
well-dressed person DANDY;
TOFF
well-earned DUE
well-endowed FLUSH; RICH;
ROLLING
well-established FAST; FIRM;
SET; SOLID
well, go PROSPER
well-groomed NEAT; SLEEK
well in France BIEN
well in Greek EU
well-informed ABREAST; UP;
UPIN (i.e. up in)
well-kept TRIM
well-made anagram indicator
well-mannered GOOD; ■
POLITE
well, not ROUGH; SICK; anagram
indicator; *see* SICK
well, not feeling ROUGH; SICK;
see SICK
well off RICH
well-ordered NEAT; SNUG
well-organised TOGETHER; anagram indicator
well-paid job EARNER
well qualified persons MAS
well-read LEARNED; LITERATE
well regarded in Rome BENE
well-supplied RICH
well-turned out SMART
well-turned anagram indicator
well-ventilated AIRY
well versed UP

Weller Senior TONY

Wellington BOOT; can refer to the general, or something to do specifically with New Zealand e.g. kiwi

Welsh W

Welsh county GLAM

Welsh, dear to BACH

Welsh port BARRY

Welsh river TAFF

Welshman DAI; EVAN

welt HIT; MARK; WEAL; *see* HIT

went LEFT; WENDED

went ahead, first LED

went down in the U.S. DOVE

went fast RAN

went off anagram indicator; particularly can call for an anagram of WENT

went quickly RACED; RAN

went to court SUED

went up reversal indicator

Wessex girl TESS

west POINT; W; reversal indicator

West MAE

West Country area DORSET

West End T

west-facing reversal indicator

west, heading W; reversal indicator

West Indian WI

West Indian captain, former VIV

West Indian dance LIMBO

West Indian music REGGAE

West Indies WI

west of can indicate that the initial letter of the ensuing word is to be used

West, out W to be omitted

western W

Western actor WAYNE

western half of can indicate that the first half of the ensuing word is to be used

Western show RODEO

western state can refer to a western state of the U.S. (e.g. CAL) as well as a western country

Westminster CITY; SWI; can indicate something to do with Parliament; [◊ ABBEY]

westward reversal indicator in an AC

wet DAMP; DOUSE; MOIST; RAIN; RAINY; RET; SODDEN; TACKY; WIMP; ■ DEWY; SLOPPY; SPLASH

wet behind the ears CALLOW; GREEN

wet conditions MUD

wet land BOG

wet patch CARR

wet sand, soil MUD

wet season RAINS

wet thoroughly DOUSE; SOUSE

wet through STEEP

wet weather RAIN

whack CUT; HIT; SHARE; *see* STRIKE

whacked HIT; TIRED; anagram indicator; *see* STRIKE

whacking VERY; anagram indicator

whale ORCA; ■ KILLER; [◊ SPOUT]

whale, small MINKY

whaler AHAB

whales POD

wham BANG

whammy SPELL

wharf DOCK; PIER; QUAY

what EH; SOME (as used in the exclamation "What cheek!")

what did you say? EH

what French QUE; QUOI

what horror! UGH

what is essential to run indicator

what might make anagram indicator

what Parisian QUE; QUOI

what's funny? anagram indicator

what's left *see* RESIDUE

what's needed IT

what should not be said DIE

what Spanish QUE

what you cook STEW

wheat CROP; GRAIN; SPELT; ■ EMMER; GRASS

wheat, ground FLOUR

wheedle CADGE
wheel CASTER; CASTOR; EDDY; ROLL; TURN; ▪ ROWEL; reverse indicator as "cart-wheel" denotes that CART is to be reversed; anagram indicator; [◊ HUB; RIM; SPAN; SPIN; SPOKE]
wheel, be at the DRIVE
wheel, part of HUB; RIM; TREAD
wheel, work at SPIN
wheeling anagram indicator; reverse indicator
wheels anagram indicator
wheels, be on ROLL
wheels, set of BOGIE
wheeze IDEA
whelp CUB; PUP
when AS; ▪ TIME
when French QUAND
when held up SA
when retired a component to be nested within BED as "toast, say, when retired" → BUTTERED
when spoken AZ
whenever IF; ONCE
where run indicator
where French OU
where in France OU
where one lives LODGING; *see* HOME
where to see can indicate a word beginning with IN, ON, OVER etc
where you'll find can indicate a word beginning with IN or ON followed by a location
whet HONE
which THAT
which Parisian QUE
which person WHO
whichever ANY
whichever way you look at it palindrome indicator, as "a mistake whichever way you look at it" → BOOB
whiff TRACE
Whig NOTORY (i.e. "no Tory")
while AS; TIME; ▪ STRETCH; WHEN; YET

while away PASS
while, in a little SOON
whim CRAZE; FAD; ▪ IMPULSE
whimper CRY; ▪ GRIZZLE; PULE
whimsical QUAINT
whine BEEF; CARP; ▪ SNIVEL
whinge GROUSE
whinny NEIGH
whip CAT; CRACK; CROP; LASH; STEAL; SWITCH; ▪ DASH; KNOUT; LEATHER; SCOURGE; TROUNCE; *see* BEAT
whip off DASH
whip, part of THONG
whip-round TAC
whip up TAC
whirl EDDY; GO; SPIN; TURN
whirl, in a anagram indicator; reversal indicator
whirlpool EDDY
whisk STIR; anagram indicator
whisker HAIR
whisky BLEND; DRAM; GRAIN; HOOCH; MALT; RYE; SCOTCH; TOT; ▪ DOUBLE; PEG; SPIRIT
whispered LOW
whispered comment ASIDE
whistle BLOW; can indicate something to do with a referee
whistler REF; ▪ KETTLE
white BLEACH; GLAIR; LILY; MILK; PURE; WINE
white, become BLEACH
white, go PALE
White House trainee INTERN
white, make BLEACH
white, South African BLANK
white, Spanish BLANCA
white stuff FLOUR
white trousers DUCKS
whiten BLEACH
whitish PALE
Who can refer to the TV doctor, Dalek etc
who heard HOO
who in France QUI
who travelled HOW

whole ALL; LOT; SUM; TOTAL;
■ COMPLETE; ENTIRE;
HEALTHY; MASS

whole country, applying to
NATIONAL

whole lot *see* WHOLE

whole lot, reportedly AWL; ORL

whole, not PART

wholly ALL; QUITE

whoopee, make ROISTER

whop THUMP

whopper FIB; LIE

whose lacking socks W

why REASON; can indicate a word
or phrase beginning with TO effectively constructing an answer
to a question. Example: "Why
Orpheus went to Hades for
Eurydice without a break?" →
TOGETHER (i.e. to get her!)

why I hear/say Y

why it's said Y

WI can indicate something to do
with West Indies or Women's Institute e.g. jam.

wick TAPER

wicked BAD; EVIL; ■ HEINOUS;
SINFUL; SINNING; VILE;
WRONG; anagram indicator;
also an old standby to indicate
something to do with a candle (a
candle is wicked (!) i.e. has a
wick)

wicked, be SIN

wicked behaviour SIN

wicked deed CRIME ; SIN

wicked person DEMON

wicked thing SIN

wickedness EVIL; SIN; VICE

wicker OSIER; TWIG

wicket DOOR; GATE; STUMP; W

wicket, at the BAT; BATTING

wicket cross-piece BAIL

wicket, part of BAIL; STUMP

wicket, time at INNINGS

wide BROAD, EXTRA; V

wide and flat SPLAYED

wide and flat, put SPLAY

wide-awake ALERT; FLY

wide berth, give W to be nested
within a component

wide boy SPIV

wide-eyed NAIVE

widen FLARE; REAM

widespread MASS; RIFE; ■
GENERAL

widow RELICT; can indicate
something to do with a mite, i.e.
the widow's mite in the Bible
story

width BEAM

wielded anagram indicator

wife BRIDE; DUTCH; FRAU;
KATE; MATE; MRS; RIB; W; ■
MISSUS; MRS; SPOUSE

wife-batterer PUNCH

wife, new BRIDE

wife no longer EX

wife, old EX

wife, sixth PARR

wig RUG; can indicate something
to do with reprimanding, berate,
carpet etc

wiggle, to ROCK; anagram indicator

wild CROSS; FAST; FERAL;
MAD; STORMY; ■ FRANTIC;
RABID; anagram indicator

wild animals GAME

wild birds GAME

wild card JOKER

wild celebration RAVE

wild enthusiasm RAVING

wild, go RAVE

wild, less TAMER

wild, not TAME

wild open country BUSH

wild parts anagram indicator as
"wild parts of Bosnia" →
BONSAI

wild party ORGY; RAVE

wild, the anagram of THE

Wild West STEW (anag.)

Wild West city DODGE

wild youth BLOOD

wildcat anagram of CAT; *see* CAT

wildebeest GNU

wildlife DEER

wildly anagram indicator

wile PLOY

will LEAVE; LL (i.e. 'll, shortening
of "will" in speech); SHALL;

WISH; ■ DESIRE;
TESTAMENT; can indicate
something to do with inheritance

Will can refer to Shakespeare; or
William I and so indicate some-
thing to do with the Norman
Conquest; ■ BILL; BILLY

will emphatically SHALL

will, he HELL

will, I ILL

will, in short LL

will, left in BEQUEST

will possibly MAY

will power can refer to the administration of a will (e.g. executor
or executrix)

will, with a TESTATE

William BILL; BILLY; TELL;
WILL; can indicate something to
do with the Norman Conquest, or
orange i.e. William of Orange

William in Scotland FORT

William's home ORANGE

willing ABLE; GAME; KEEN;
ON; READY; can indicate something with a will as a legal document (e, heir, legatee); *see* WILL

willing participant SPORT

willing to participate ON

willingly LIEF; can indicate something to do with inheritance, heir
etc

willingness, show OFFER

willow BAT; OSIER

willy-nilly anagram indicator

wilt DIE; DROOP; FLAG; PINE;
WITHER

wily CRAFTY; anagram indicator

Wimbledon game TENNIS

wimp DRIP; WEED; WET

wimpish WEEDY; WET

win BEAT; EARN; GAIN; GET;
LAND; MATE; NET; TAKE

win attempt to COURT; WOO

win easily THRASH

win once more REGAIN

win, try to WOO

wince FLINCH; SHRINK

winch CRANK

Winchester RIFLE; SCHOOL

wind AIR; BLAST; BLOW; COIL;
GALE; GUST; LOOP; PUFF;
RACK; REEL; ROLL; TURN;
TWINE; WEAVE; ■ AUSTER;
CHINOOK; COLIC; CURL;
DRAUGHT; EASTERLY;
SNAKE; TWIST; anagram indi-
cator; can refer to the wind in-
struments of the orchestra e.g.
flute, oboe; can indicate a spe-
cific wind e.g. north-easter, si-
rocco

***Wind in the Willows* motorist**
TOAD

wind, indicator of COCK; SOCK;
VANE

wind instrument FLUTE;
RECORDER; *see* MUSICAL
INSTRUMENT

wind, south AUSTER

wind up CLOSE; END; ROLL;
can indicate that WIND or a synonym of "wind" is to be reversed
e.g. ELAG

wind up, put FRIGHTEN; SCARE

winded AIR to nested within com-
ponent(s)

winder CLOCK; REEL

winding device REEL

windlass WINCH

window BAY; GLASS; LANCET;
LIGHT; ORIEL; PANE; SASH

window cleaner WIPER

window frame SASH

window, grated GRILLE

window opening LANCET

window, type of SASH

winds anagram indicator

Windsor CHAIR; KNOT; SOUP;
can indicate something to do with
the Royal family, or something to
do with a neck-tie

Windsor mistress PAGE (Shakespearean character)

Windsor, women in WIVES

wine ASTI; CRU; HOCK;
PLONK; PORT; RED; ROSE;
SACK; SAKE; TENT; VIN;
WHITE; ■ CLARET; MEDOC;
PINOT; SOAVE; TOKAY; [◊
BODY; CASK; PEG]

wine and dine FETE

wine collection CELLAR
wine, German HOCK; VEIN
wine, like some DRY
wine maker TREADER
wine, new MUST
wine, quantity of TUN
wine region LOIRE
wine store BIN; CELLAR
wine, source of GRAPE
wine, white HOCK
wing ARM; FLANK; FLAP; FLIGHT; FLY; LIMB; SIDE; ■ PINION; WOUND; [◊ ALAR]
winged ALIATE
winger can refer to a bird, flying insect, plane or footballer
wings LR; RL; indicator of first and last letters; can indicate something to do with offstage in the theatre
wings off first and last letters to be omitted
wings on can indicate two components are to be added to the beginning and end as "Registered space with men on wings" → PATENTED (i.e. PAT -EN-TED)
winner ACE; BEST; CHAMP; GOLD; HIT; NAP; TOP; TRUMP; ■ CHAMPION; VICTOR; can indicate something which is a winner in particular circumstances e.g. ace in cards, bull in darts
winning AHEAD; SWEET; TOP; TRUMP; UP; ■ EARNING; LEADING; nesting indicator, as "Gamble, winning a pound" → BEAT
winnings GAIN(S)
wino ALKY
winter abroad HIVER
winter sports, indulge in SKI
winter sportsman SKIER
winter transport SLED
Winter festival NOEL
wintry COLD
wipe RUB
wiped out anagram indicator
wiper CLOTH; RAG; SPONGE; TOWEL; ■ BATH TOWEL

wire CABLE; THREAD; can refer to electrical plug leads e.g. live, neutral, earth
wireless receiver SET
wisdom DEPTH; INSIGHT; LORE; SENSE
wisdom, lacking GREEN; NAIVE
wise SAGE; SOUND; WAY; ■ LEARNED
wise group MAGI
wise man MAGE; SAGE; ■ SOLON
wise men MAGI
wise men, say TRIO
wise old man NESTOR
wise, someone who is *see* WISE MAN
wise sounding YY (i.e. hom.)
wise words SAW
wisecrack BARB
wised-up SAGE
wisest BEST
wish DESIRE; WANT; WILL
wish, nagging ITCH
wish it hadn't happened RUE
wish you still had MISS
wishing well KIND
wisp PLUME; SHRED
wispy SCRAPPY
wit BRAINS; CARD; JOKER; PUN; WAG; ■ ESPRIT; NOUS; SALT; SENSE
wit's end, at T
wit, to VIZ
witch HAG; ■ CHARMER; ENDOR; HEX; SYBIL
witch's place ENDOR
witchcraft apart from indicating sorcery this is an old standby for BROOMSTICK(!)
witches COVEN
with AND; BY; CON; CUM; HAVING; IN; W; run indicator; note, "with" is an alternative spelling of withe (qv)
with a crick anagram indicator
with a lot of effort HARD
with everything WALL
with German MIT
with gifts ABLE
with it COOL; HIP; TRENDY

with Italian CON
with no authority NOOK
with no brains *see* FOOLISH
with no leader ITH (i.e. first letter omitted); can indicate that the first letter of the associated word is to be omitted
with no love O to be omitted
with no points can indicate that letters representing the points of the compasses (N, S, E, W) are to be omitted; an interesting variant is where NOSE (i.e. no SE!) is to be added to a word or component
with no sides first and last letters of a word to be omitted; or R and L to be omitted
with nothing on O to be added to the end of a component
with regard to *see* CONCERNING
withdraw BACK; YIELD; ■ LEAVE; RECANT; RECEDE; RETREAT; SCRATCH; SECEDE; SHRINK
withdrawal omission indicator (as "withdrawal of US" cues US to be omitted)
withdrawing reversal indicator; omission indicator
withdrawn COY; OFF; SHY; omission indicator; run indicator
withdrew LEFT
withe TWIG
wither DIE; WASTE; WILT; ■ FADE
withered DEAD; SEAR
withering DYING
withhold omission indicator
within IN; ■ INTO; nesting indicator; run indicator, as "from within" → RO
within confines of can signify use of first and last letters only
within the law LEGAL; LICIT
without EX; FREE; LESS; OUT OF; WO; nesting indicator, for example where OM is required to be nested in "the man is without honour" → HOME; can indicate NO is to be followed by another component, as "without identifi-

cation" clues NOID (i.e. no ID) for instance in building up PARANOID; can indicate an adjective beginning with UN- or ending in -LESS; omission indicator;
without any ANY to be omitted; ANY to be nested within a component
without authority NOOK
without, be LACK; NEED
without borders/verges first and last letters to be omitted
without charge/cost/rental FREE
without defeat DRAW
without delay NOW
without doubt CERTAIN; SURE
without drink TT
without exception ALL
without fencing OPEN
without flaws CLEAN
without help ALONE; AID to be omitted; AID to be nested within a component; a component to be nested within AID
without liquid DRY
without limit ALL
without love O to be omitted
without notice either AD to be omitted, or nested within a component
without payment FREE
without prejudice OPEN
without purpose IDLE; IDLY
without question either Q or QU to be omitted, or nested within a component
without shelter OUT
without speaking TACIT
without water ARID; DRY; NEAT
witness SEE; SEER; ■ ATTEST; DEPOSE
witnessed SAW
witnessed by nesting indicator; run indicator
witticism JEST; MOT; PUN; QUIP
witty DROLL; FUNNY
witty remark SALLY
witty saying MOT; *see* WITTICISM

wizard MAGE; ■ MERLIN; WARLOCK

wizard-place OZ

wizard, would-be POTTER

wizard, young POTTER

wizards MAGI

wobble REEL; ROCK; ■ TEETER; TOTTER; TREMBLE; anagram indicator

wobbling anagram indicator

wobbly anagram indicator; ■ TOTTERY

woe DOLE; can indicate something to do with Wednesday (e.g. WED) as in "Wednesday's child"

Woe is me! ALAS

wold DOWN

wolf EAT; GORGE; ROMEO; SCOFF

wolves PACK

woman DAME; DISH; DOLL; GAL; HEN; HER; LADY; LASS; MAID; MISS; MS; WENCH; often calls for a female proper name – see WOMAN'S NAME; *also see* GIRL

woman, beautiful BELLE; HELEN; VENUS

woman, common ER

woman, disreputable JADE; TRULL

woman, dowdy FRUMP

woman, enchanting CIRCE; WITCH

woman, evil WITCH

woman, for a HERS

woman, formidable/monstrous OGRESS; ■ GORGON; DRAGON

woman had SHED (i.e. she'd)

woman, harassing NAG

woman, honoured DAME; LADY

woman, horrible old/ugly/unpleasant HAG; TROUT

woman hunting DIANA

woman in order NUN

woman, initially EVE; W; ■ SPARE RIB

woman, intimidating DRAGON

woman, little JO (i.e. from book); can indicate the diminutive of a woman's name – see WOMAN

woman, loose see WOMAN, VULGAR

woman, malicious CAT

woman, monstrous DRAGON

woman, of HERS

woman, old CRONE; GRAN; HAG; TROUT; ■ GRANDMA; GRANNY; can call for a woman's name preceded by O (as "Write old woman a letter?" → OMEGA)

woman, OT RIB

woman, promiscuous TRAMP

woman's HER

woman's name ADA; AMY; ANNA; ANNE; ANNIE; AVA; BELLE; BETH; CATH; CLARE; CON; CORA; DAWN; DEB; DEE; DI; DOLL; DORA; DOT; ELLA; ENA; ENID; EVA; EVE; FAITH; FLO; FRAN; GINA; GRACE; HONOR; IDA; INA; IVY; JAN; JO; JOY; KATE; KAY; LORNA; LOU; MABLE; MAE; MAI; MAY; MEG; MO; MOLL; NAN; NELL; NINA; NORMA; PAM; PAT; PEARL; PEG; RITA; ROMA; ROSA; ROSE; RUTH; SAL; SALLY; SHE; STELLA; SU; SUE; TINA; TRU; UNA; VAL; VERA; VI; VIV; ■ ABBY; AGNES; ANGIE; BERTHA; BLANCHE; CAROL; CARRIE; CATHY; CHERIE; CHLOE; DAISY; DIANA; ELAINE; EMMA; ETHEL; HESTER; IRENE; IRMA; ISLA; JOAN; KITTY; LANA; LILY; LISA; LULU; MARIE; MARY; MAUD; MIA; MILLIE; MIMI; MOLLIE; MOLLY; NANCY; NICKY; NORA; PENNY; POLLY; SOPHY; TESS; TARA; TESSA; THEA; ZARA; *see* GIRL

woman, sad WIDOW

woman, seductive VAMP

woman, spiteful CAT

woman, that HER

woman, that Cockney ER
woman told to get gun ANNIE
woman, ugly HAG; TROUT; ■ GORGON
woman, unpleasant WITCH
woman, vulgar BAWD; HUSSY; PRO; TART; TIT; ■ STRUMPET
woman, wicked OGRESS; WITCH
woman, young CHICK; GAL; GIRL; MAID; MISS
womaniser RAKE; ROUE
women HENS; WENCHES
women, excluding STAG
women, group of WI
women only NOMEN (i.e. no men)
women's organisation WI
women's quarters HAREM
women who used to serve ATS
won EARNED; TOOK
won over NOW (or some anag. of WON)
won't start first letter to be omitted
wonder AWE; GAPE; MARVEL
wonder, cause AMAZE
wonder, expression of COR; LOR
wonderful ACE; AI; SUPER; WIZARD
wonderful place HEAVEN
wonky anagram indicator
wont CUSTOM; HABIT
woo COURT; SPOON; TEMPT
wood ARDEN; ASH; BEAM; BEECH; BOWL; BOX; BRANCH; COPSE; DEAL; EBONY; ELM; FIR; GROVE; LOG; LATH; PINE; SHAW (thicket); SLAT; TEAK; ■ CLUB; FOREST; LUMBER; HURST; SANDAL; TIMBER; TINDER; see TREE
wood, a lot of FOREST
wood, block of LOG
wood, hard TEAK
wood, large piece of PLANK
wood, pale ASH
wood, piece of BOARD; BOUGH; BRANCH; LATH;

PANEL; PLANK; SLAT; SLIVER; STICK; TWIG
wooded area WEALD
wooden LOG
woodman can indicate something to do with carpenter, forester, logger, lumberjack etc
woodwork JOINERY
woof WEFT
wooden STOLID; TREEN
wool DOWN; FLEECE; FUR; HAIR; HANK; KEMP; YARN; ■ ANGORA; STAPLE
wool-producer see SHEEP
woollen garment KNIT
woolly EWE; VAGUE; ■ CARDI; CARDY; see SHEEP
woolly jumper EWE; LAMB; RAM; SHEEP; TUP
Wooster VALET
Worcester can refer to race course, sauce, cathedral, apple (pearmain), porcelain
word MOT; NAME; NEWS; NOUN; OATH; PLEDGE; TERM; VERB
word, last AMEN
word of agreement YES; see AGREEMENT
word of comfort THERE
word of mouth, by ORAL
words PROSE; TEXT; VERSE; ■ SENTENCE
words added PS
words, few CHAT; LINE; NOTE; ■ PHRASE; SENTENCE
words, group of SPEECH; TALK; ■ CLAUSE; PHRASE; SENTENCE; POEM; VERSE
words, high-blown RANT
words, in other SC
words in print BOOK; TEXT
words of wisdom PROVERB; see SAW
words, original TEXT
words, play with PUN
words, to have SPEAK
words, use wrong LIE
wordy TALKING
wore SPORTED

work ACT; ART; BOOK; CHORE; CRAFT; DO; ERG; GO; GRAFT; GRIND; JOB; LINE; OIL (i.e. art); OP; OPERA; OPUS; PLAY; PLY; SERVE; SLAVE; STUDY; TASK; TILL; TOIL; TRACT; ■ CAREER; FUNCTION; HARNESS; KNEAD; LOAD; OEUVRE; OPERATE; POINT (as to work/point in one direction); STRIVE; TEXT; THESIS; anagram indicator; [◊ HORSE]

work, amount of ERG

work, at EARNING; ON; OUT

work, bit of ERG

work, body of CORPUS

work both ways POOP (i.e. PO + OP; similarly OPPO)

work diligently PLY

work effectively FUNCTION; GEL

work excessively SLAVE

work for SERVE

work for a time TEMP

work, hard CHORE; FAG; GRAFT; GRIND; SLAVE; ■ APPLY

work in a shop SELL

work in America LABOR

work in restaurant WAIT

work, lacking IDLE

work, not IDLE; LAZE; REST

work, not at OFF

work of art BUST; MURAL; OIL; STATUE; ■ PAINTING; PIECE

work on newspaper EDIT

work out PE; PT; SOLVE; SORT; SUS; ■ FIGURE; RUMBLE; SETTLE; anagram indicator

work, out of IDLE; OP to be omitted

work, place of see WORKROOM

work, refuse to STRIKE

work, refusing to OUT

work regularly PLY

work-related talk SHOP

work, religious AV; BIBLE; NT; OT; TRACT

work schedule ROTA

work, some ERG

work steadily PEG; PLY; PLOD

work time SHIFT

work, tiresome CHORE; see WORK, HARD

work unit ERG

work, very little STROKE

work, without IDLE

worked DID; PLIED; ■ STROVE; TOILED; anagram indicator as "worked together" suggests an anagram of TOGETHER

worked out CRACKED; SOLVED; anagram indicator

worked steadily PLIED

worker ANT; BEE; HAND; MAN; TEMP; ■ ARTISAN; MASON; MINER; POTTER; RIGGER; SMITH; TOILER

worker, hard BEE

worker on land PEASANT; SERF; ■ FARMER

worker, paid PRO

worker, short-term TEMP

worker, unpaid SLAVE

workers CREW; GANG; GUILD; MEN; SHIFT; STAFF; TU; UNION; ■ PEASANTRY

workers, group of GANG; SHIFT; see WORKERS

workers' organization see WORKERS

workforce STAFF; see WORKERS

working ACTIVE; AT (i.e. at it); ON; USING; anagram indicator

working behind counter BARON (i.e. BAR-ON)

working hard ATIT (i.e. at it); TOILING

working, not DOWN; OFF; OUT; ■ DEAD; DUD

working on AT

working out a component to be nested within an anagram

working time SHIFT; STINT

workings of an anagram to be made of the words that follow

workplace FORGE; SHOP; STUDIO; PLANT; ■ FACTORY; OPPOSITION (i.e. op + position)

workroom DEN; LAB; OFFICE; STUDIO; STUDY

workshop see WORKROOM

works OPS; MILL; PLANT; PLIES; ■ FACTORY; FORGE; OEUVRE; OPERA; anagram indicator

world EARTH; PLANET; can indicate the name of a planet

world, all corners of the NEWS

world, our part of WEST

worm GRUB; ■ TAGTAIL

worm, sort of LOB

Worms DIET

worn OLD; ON; ■ FRAYED; anagram indicator

worn by nesting indicator

worn-out DONE; OVER; STALE; STOCK; TIRED; TRITE

worn track RUT

worried ATE; CARED; anagram indicator

worried, be *see* WORRY

worried look FROWN

worries STRESS; *see* WORRY

worry AIL; BROOD; CARE; DOG; EAT; FEAR; FRET; FUSS; NAG; QUAIL; STEW; STRESS; ■ CONCERN; GNAW; HARRY; TROUBLE

worry over can indicate a synonym of "worry" to be reversed, hence GAN, GOD, LIA

worrying OMINOUS; anagram indicator

worrying, is EATS

worrying, one HARRIER

worse VILER; ■ DIRER

worse luck ALAS

worse off SWORE

worship ADORE; DEIFY; LOVE; PRAISE; REVERE

worship, place of CHAPEL; ■ CHURCH; MOSQUE; SHRINE; TEMPLE

worshipper FAN; VOTARY

worshippers, group of CHURCH; CULT; FLOCK; SECT

worst BEST

worst situation PITS

worsted SERGE

worth MERIT; RATE; RATING; ■ VALUE

worthless BASE; IDLE; POXY; TRASHY; ■ FUTILE; SILLY

worthless thing VANITY

worthy GOOD; ■ UPRIGHT

worth, be DESERVE; *see* MERIT

Wotan ODIN

would, I ID

would say, some can indicate a homophone for a "piece of wood", hence BORED (board), PLANCK (plank)

wound CUT; GASH; LESION; MAIM; SCAR; SORE; STAB; STING; WING; ■ SNAKED; REELED

wound, effect of SCAR

wound, sign of skin SCAB

wound, sort of FLESH

wounded BLED; CUT; HURT; ■ BITTEN; anagram indicator

wounded, was BLED

woven anagram indicator

woven material braid; *see* FABRIC

wow AMAZE

wow! BOY; COR; MAN (i.e. "Man!")

wrap COVER; SCARF; SHAWL; STOLE

wrap up BIND; SWADDLE

wrapped around/round anagram or nesting indicator

wrapper COVER (qv); HIDE; PACKET; SKIN; *see* WRAP

wrapping COVER; TISSUE; nesting indicator; ■ CLOAK; SEGUM

wrapping paper TISSUE

wrath ANGER; FURY; IRE; RAGE

wreath LEI

wreathe COIL; CURL; WIND

wreck RUIN; UNDO; ■ FOUNDER; anagram indicator

wreckage RUIN

wrecked SORRY; anagram indicator

wrench RICK; SPRAIN; STAIN; WRICK; ■ SPANNER; TWIST; YANK

wrest PULL; TAKE; ■ FORCE

wrestler's hold CHANCERY

wrestling SUMO; anagram indicator

wrestling event BASHO

wrestling manoeuvre THROW

wretch CUR; DOG

wretched ABJECT; BAD; BALLY; ILL; POOR; SORRY; anagram indicator

wretched fellow CUR; DOG; RAT

wretchedly anagram indicator

wriggle TWIST; anagram indicator

wriggles, wriggling anagram indicator

wring TWIST; ■ EXTORT

wringer MANGLE

wrinkle CREASE; KNIT; LINE; RUT; ■ CRUMPLE; PUCKER

wrinkle forehead FROWN

wrinkled LINED; SEAR; anagram indicator

writ anagram indicator

write JOT; NOTE; PEN; POST; SPELL; ■ AUTHOR; INDITE

write about NEP (rev.)

write back RESPOND; *see* WRITE-UP

write down LIST; *see* WRITE

write in ENTER

write in capitals PRINT

write-off TOTAL

write-up reversal indicator; can indicate the reversal of a synonym e.g. NEP

writer AUTHOR; FORD; GREENE; MAILER; ME; NIB; PEN; POE; POET; QUILL; READE; SAYERS; TRAVERS; WELLS; WILDE; WOOLF ■ BARRIE; BIRO; BROWNING; CHANDLER; DAHL; DICKENS; EVELYN; FLEMING; GIBBON; ROMANCER; SAKI; SCRIBE; STEIN; *see* AUTHOR, NOVELIST, POET; can indicate a writing instrument e.g. pen, pencil, crayon, nib, biro

writer, children's RANSOME

writer, controversial MARX

writer, French GIDE

writer, Irish SHAW; STERNE; WILDE

writer, medieval ROMANCER

writer, old QUILL

writer, poor HACK

writer's MINE; MY

writer's complaint BLOCK; CRAMP

writer's material INK; PAPER

writer, this I; ME

writer, thriller AMBLER

writer, woman SAND; *see* WRITER

writer, uninspired HACK

writhe TURN; TWIST; ■ THRASH

writhing anagram indicator

writing COPY; HAND; MS; PROSE; R (as in three R's); SCRIPT; TEXT; ■ LINES; ESSAY

writing, bit of (piece of etc) CHAPTER; LINE; NOTE; ODE; PARA; PLAY; POEM; TRACT; VERSE; ■ ARTICLE; SENTENCE

writing, in DOWN

writing materials INK; PAPER; PENS

writing, put in PEN

writing, short piece of CHAP; NOTE; PARA

writing style, relating to CURSIVE

writings MSS

written after letter PS

written communication LETTER; NOTE

written out anagram indicator; omission indicator

written work MS; TRACT

wrong AMISS; ASTRAY; CRIME (qv); EVIL; ILL; OFF; OUT; SIN; TORT; VICE; X (i.e. teacher's mark); ■ ASKEW; AWRY; anagram indicator, for example "the wrong time" → EMIT

wrong, do SIN

wrong done anagram of DONE

wrong-doing SIN

wrong, go ERR; FALL; TRIP

wrong, going anagram indicator
wrong side of, get on CROSS
wrong, something HITCH
wrong time, at the EARLY; LATE
wrong turning a synonym of "wrong" to be reversed, hence LOVE, NIS, TROT
wrong way anagram indicator
wrong way, going the can indicate something to do with anticlockwise
wrong, we hear SYN
wrong, went ERRED
wrong words, use LIE
wrongdoer SINNER; anagram of DOER
wrongdoer briefly CRIM
wrongdoing CRIME; ERROR; EVIL; SIN
wrongly ILL; anagram indicator, as "wrongly set" → EST
wrongly positioned anagram indicator
wrote about TOWER (i.e. anag.)
wrought anagram indicator
wrought iron an anagram of IRON
wry DROLL

XxYyZz

X CHI; CROSS; TEN; ■ KISS; can indicate something to do with voting (e.g. in making an X)
Xhosa* BANTU
XX SCORE; ■ TENS; TWENTY
yachting SAILING
yahoo BOOR; LOUT
Yale can indicate something to do with key, lock
yank DRAG; HEAVE; JERK; PULL; TUG; ■ WRENCH
Yank GI; TUG
Yankee BET; Y
yap BARK
yard PATIO; QUAD; SPAR; YD; ■ GARDEN
yardmen CID

yarn LISLE; STORY; TALE; THREAD; WOOL; ■ CREWEL
yarn, tell the SPIN
yawn GAPE
year ANNO; ANNUM; DATE; Y; note that when age is expressed as "in the xth year", it signifies the *previous* year, for example, "in the fifth year" signifies the number FOUR
year away, a Y (or AY) to be omitted
year, early in the JAN; FEB; MAR; MARCH
year-end DEC; R
year, every ANNUAL
year's opening JAN; Y; ■ SPRING
yearbook can indicate something to do with Orwell's novel *1984*
yearly PA
yearly publication ANNUAL
yearn ACHE; HANKER; ITCH; LONG; WAIT
yearn poetically SUSPIRE
years AGE; DECADE; TIME
years in prison TIME; ■ BIRD; STRETCH; SENTENCE; TERM
years, many AGE; DECADE; EON; ERA
yell SCREAM; SHOUT; ■ SCREECH
yellow AMBER; CRAVEN; CREAM; GOLD; GOLDEN; OR; SALLOW; STRAW; ■ CHICKEN; OCHRE; YOLK; can indicate something to do with cowardly, spineless etc
yellow, deep AMBER
yellow, pale STRAW
yellowish AMBER; GOLDEN SALLOW
yellowish-brown AMBER; TAN
yelp SCREAM
yen ITCH; NEED; URGE; WAIT; Y; ■ YEARNING
yes AY; AYE; OK; RIGHT; Y; YEA; YEP; YUP
yes-man ROGER
yesteryear PAST
yet EVEN; STILL; THO
yet goes astray anagram of YET

yet to be dealt with LEFT; OVER

yet to be decided MOOT; OPEN

yet to be paid OWING

yield BEAR; CEDE; CROP; DEFER; GIVE; GRANT; RENDER; STOP; ■ AFFORD; CAPITULATE; RETURN; anagram indicator

yielded BORE; *see* YIELD

yielding SUPPLE; anagram indicator; *see* YIELD

Yippee! BOY

yob TED; LOUT; OIK

yoke BOND; FRAME; INSPAN; JOIN; ■ COUPLE

yokel HICK; RUSTIC

yolk YELLOW

yon THAT

york BOWL

Yorick JESTER

York HOUSE; ■ EBOR (Roman name for the city)

yorker BALL; TICE

Yorkshire NORTH; can indicate RIDING

Yorkshire river URE

Yorkshire town SETTLE

Yorkshireman TIKE; TYKE

you ONE; THOU; Y; YE; ■ READER; SOLVER

you and I US; WE

you and me US

you are said UR

you, belonging to THY; YOURS

you declared U

you, for example PRONOUN

you heard *see* YOU SAID

you, in France TU

you old, once THEE; THOU; YE

you or I PRONOUN

you reportedly *see* YOU SAID

you said/say EU; U; YEW; YU

you soundly *see* YOU SAID

young BROOD; EARLY; FRY; ISSUE; LITTER; SPAWN; Y; ■ BABY; CHILD; INFANT; can indicate a low cardinal number reflecting tender years such as TEN in "A little young to have been infected" which leads to BITTEN

(i.e. bit ten); *see* YOUNG ANIMAL, YOUNGSTER

young animal/creature CHICK; COLT; CUB; KID; KIT; LAMB; PUP

young animals LITTER

young chap, dashing BLADE

young chap SON

young cricketer/footballer, etc COLT

young fellow BOY; LAD; PUP; SPRIG

young girl DEB

young lad SHAVER; ■ BOY; YOUTH

young lady MISS; *see* YOUNG WOMAN

young lover SWAIN

young man BEAU; LAD; MASTER; SPRIG

young man, aristocratic BUCK

young man, arrogant PUP

young man, wild TED

young, no longer AGED; OLD

young player COLT

young, produce BREED; SPAWN

young reporter CUB

young thing LAMB; *see* YOUNG ANIMAL

young woman CHICK; GAL; LASS; MAID; MISS; ■ GIRL

young woman, attractive CUTIE

younger member SCION; SPRIG

youngster BOY; CHILD; COLT; CUB; KID; LAD; LAMB; MINOR; NIPPER; PUP; SHAVER; *see* YOUNG ANIMAL

youngster, conceited PUP

youngster, impudent BRAT; IMP

youngster, Scottish WEAN

youngster, unruly BRAT; IMP

youngsters BROOD; ISSUE; LITTER; ■ OFFSPRING; *see* YOUNGSTER

your THY; YR

your and my OUR

your first Y

your old/old form/old-fashioned THY

yours THINE

yours and mine OURS
yours truly I; ME; SETTER
yours truly, owned by MINE
yours truly, say EYE
youth BOY; KID; LAD; SPEAR; SPRIG; *see* YOUNG MAN
youth, boisterous TED
youth, 1950's TED
youth-leader Y
youth, wild BLOOD
youthful VERNAL; YOUNG
youthful beauty HEBE
yuk UGH
YY with a homophone indicator can call for WISE
zany JESTER; anagram indicator; *see* CRAZY
zapped HIT; anagram indicator
zeal ARDOUR
zealot FAN
zealous EAGER; KEEN

Zeno can indicate something to do with philosophy, stoic, stoa
zero DUCK; O; LOVE; NIL; NOUGHT; RING; ROUND
zero score DUCK
zest GUSTO; TANG
Zeus's wife HERA
zigzag TACK
zigzag edge, cut with PINK
zilch *see* NOTHING
zinc ZN
zing GO; SPIRIT; ■ OOMPH
zip RUSH
zit SPOT
Zola can indicate something to do with Zola's book *J'accuse*
Zola's coquette/heroine NANA
zone AREA; PLACE; SECTOR
zoological group GENUS
zoom SOAR
Zoroastrian PARSI
Zulu warriors IMPI